HERESIES

HERESIES

*Heresy And
Orthodoxy
In The History
Of The Church*

Harold O. J. Brown

HENDRICKSON PUBLISHERS

Hendrickson Publishers, Inc.
P.O. Box 3473
Peabody, Massachusetts 01961-3473

Printed in the United States of America
ISBN 1-56563-365-2

Hendrickson Publishers' edition reprinted by arrangement with Baker Book
House Company.

Fourth Printing—February 2003

ACKNOWLEDGMENTS

It is not surprising that a work of this size could hardly have been written without the help, encouragement, and interaction of many people. To several, special words of acknowledgment are due. Perhaps it is best to begin in something like chronological order. Georges Florovsky and George Williams at Harvard gave me an appreciation of true catholicity and the continuity of the orthodox faith. Alexander Liepa and Robert T. Heller, editors at Doubleday, stimulated, encouraged, and supported, waiting long for the final result; more recently, Theresa D'Orsogna has taken upon herself the task of putting this mass of material into presentable form. Trinity Evangelical Divinity School graciously accorded me a one year's leave; the Association of Theological Schools in the United States and Canada and the Light of Life Foundation of Gladwyn, Pennsylvania, provided grants making it possible to travel to Basel, Switzerland, for that leave; while the Texas Policy Institute commissioned work that helped our family to get through a year without regular salary. The most continual and substantial support and encouragement came from Ernst and Greta Ganz of Zurich, to whom this work is dedicated.

My parents-in-law, Edward and Winifred Hancox, Edward and Elizabeth Hughes, C. Everett Koop, Surgeon General, and Howard Philips provided encouragement and support at critical times, as did Harold and Lynne Schweizer, Dieter and Irene Bode, and Frido and Christel Schrader. Attorney Jean Jene, Oberkreisdirektor Rudolf Pezely, and Stadtoberinspektor Kurt Doll assisted with the formalities that enabled an American to live in West Germany and commute daily to the University Library at Basel, Switzerland, where Moritz Hagmann and Herbert Sutter offered patient help. Hospitality for the work of writing and revision was offered by the Janz Team, a German-Canadian missionary society, and by the Reformed Church of Klosters, Switzerland.

Several present and former students at Trinity have worked on the project, among them C. Eric Morgenthaler, Paul F. Luedtke, and Joseph Mok. My secretary, Marty Irwin, put colleagues' work aside to help meet the final deadlines. By far the most substantial and constant assistance came from my teaching assistant, Kurt A. Richardson, who accompanied me to Basel and who has had a part in every aspect of the writing.

My children, Cynthia and Peter, bore with patience the uprooting and indignity of starting new schools in an unknown language in order to permit our stay in Lörrach. Most of all I am grateful to my wife Grace, who not only gave up her own leadership role in the Bible Study Fellowship to travel to a small town in Germany, but who discussed, criticized, expanded, and repeatedly typed most of the manuscript. All of those named, in varying degrees, have contributed to this work, but the errors, omissions, and infelicities that remain are my own responsibility.

CONTENTS

4

STRUCTURE AND VARIATION 38

5

BEFORE THE NEW TESTAMENT   70

6

THE APOLOGISTS   76

7

MONARCHIANISM 95

8

THE GREAT ALTERNATIVE: ARIANISM   104

9

THE DOCTRINE OF THE TRINITY   145

14

THE NEW CHURCH AND THE OLD HERESY: SCHOLASTICISM, THE CRUSADES, AND DUALISM   239

15

THE PIOUS HERETICS   280

16

THE PROTESTANT REFORMATION 296

19

THE HERESY OF ENLIGHTENMENT   395

20

THE ORTHODOXY OF REVIVAL: A REVIVAL OF ORTHODOXY? 416

21

THE RESURGENCE AND RELAPSE OF ORTHODOXY 430

EPILOGUE: SIGNS OF HIS COMING? 447

FOREWORD

Hilary of Poitiers (d. ca. 367), called the "Athanasius of the West," in his *On the Trinity*, II, 3, wrote: "Heresy lies in the sense assigned, not in the word written [*in Scriptura*]; and the guilt [*crimen*] is that of the expositor, not of the text." Hilary was renowned for his irenicism during a century of fierce controversy about the doctrine of the Trinity and at the beginning of what would be four centuries of christological debate, ending in the seventh ecumenical council of II Nicaea, 787—the last for the Orthodox Church. Professor Brown is, to be sure, primarily concerned about the normative role of the fourth ecumenical council, that of Chalcedon, 451, which summarized and proclaimed the doctrine of the Trinity as clarified by the two earlier ecumenical councils of I Nicaea, 325, and I Constantinople, 381, and on its own climaxed a century and a half of christological debate with its own great definition of Jesus Christ as one Person in two natures, as fully God and fully man. Hilary was a Latin Father whose name suggests jovial good cheer. Professor Brown is serious and, as he comes to the end of his volume, he is even somewhat alarmed and surely theologically anxious; but as a historian of Christian thought from the doctrinal points of concern most distinctively Christian, namely, those about the Holy Trinity and Jesus Christ, also most closely interconnected, he surely displays a certain Christian jocundity and even scholarly happiness as he, with the mastery of a vast range of material, holds up the mirror of successive heresy to truth. But for him revealed truth is itself dynamic and contextual.

Alert to the most recent findings of biblical scholarship, the author understands even better than Hilary of Poitiers and the other Church Fathers or than the classical Protestant Reformers that the abiding truth, "the faith once delivered to the saints" (Jude v. 3), was set against heresies represented by premature hardening and partializing of the plenitude of the Christ Event even in the earliest Christian communities themselves; that these congregations refracted the truth in the extant canonical writings but only insofar as the saving faith and the revealed truth were explicated from their canonical collectivity. Thus Professor Brown recognizes that the clear truth of and about Jesus Christ and the only begotten Son among the Three Persons of the Trinity was gained only after centuries of theological debate and conciliar clarification and definition. With Hilary, Professor Brown has no difficulty in recognizing the positive role of all premature and partial formulations, heresies, in obliging the Church catholic and evangelical to become as clear as it finally did at Chalcedon, renewing this faith in fresh formulations at various subsequent critical moments in Church history.

He regards heresy of either type, premature or of undue concentration on a special aspect of faith, as a succession of formulations that, though causing temporary confusion and even schism, have served the theologians of the Church catholic down through the centuries in clarifying the faith without the loss of the plenitude of Christ. He would, of course, deplore any past mistreatment of heretics, many of whom, he acknowledges, were personally courageous and often theologically creative, too often mercilessly maligned for many spurious reasons by the eventually victorious orthodox. The author would again agree with Hilary of Poitiers that "the errors of heretics . . . force us to deal with unlawful matters, to scale the perilous heights, to speak unutterable words, to trespass on forbidden ground," compelling "us *to err* in daring to embody in human terms truths which ought to be hidden in the silent veneration of the heart" (*On the Trinity* 2.2).

When the author comes to the century existentially the most congenial to him, that of the Reformation, he is quite forthright in showing how Martin Luther himself almost erred, verging on the ancient heresy of Monophysitism (the doctrine of a single nature) condemned by Chalcedon, all in his effort to insist on precisely the *divine* humanity of Jesus Christ even in diapers and tended by the Virgin Mary; how Ulrich Zwingli and John Calvin in their turn came perilously close to the other, the counterpart heresy of antiquity, Nestorianism, in dividing the divine and the human in Jesus Christ with special reference to the crucifixion and the eucharist.

Going far beyond what the author himself describes as a book somewhere between the record of "a personal quest" and "a journalistic account," he in fact shares with readers even well versed in Christian thought a great deal that is often marginalized or wholly neglected in large works on the subject, as for example, in his treatment of Christology of the magisterial treatises of Lutheran Orthodoxy into the seventeenth century. In comparable coverages the author also accords much more space than is ordinarily the case to the Anabaptists (Mennonites) and other radicals usually bypassed in disdain or scorn. Instead, he treats them, too, with compassion and understanding, pointing to the inadequacies of their solutions to real problems, when once again in the sixteenth century everything on principle revolved for non-Catholics on Scripture alone and when, therefore, many of "the wrong turnings, deceptions, and disappointments" of ancient heretics were tried out by a belated generation of earnest seekers in the environment of "the return to the sources," i. e., for Christians, to Scripture. Judgment is seldom passed directly on anyone. The inadequacy of the solutions is simply made clear by the author against the Chalcedonian norm.

The reader of his book should know, therefore, that by concentrating on the two distinctive truths of Christianity as distinguished from the prophetic monotheism from which it sprang, Professor Brown is able to give one the sense of the whole of Christian thought while seeming to deal with successive heresies. There is a certain happy genius in the conceptualization, a lightheartedness that leaves the participant in the grand tour of the Christian centuries with something far more tangible than a jumble of names and places confusedly superimposed upon what would have otherwise been an overtaxed memory. No, the traveler ends his journey with many a vivid mental snapshot that will not fade—of persons, events, and theological traceries of considerable complexity. The specialist in any given period or place might have pedantically insisted on more precision in some of the details, but that would be largely because he was the vested custodian of that particular site. Brown has miles to cover and many flight schedules to juggle and coordinate. And his is not the set speech of an instructed guide. At many points the specialist will see things he himself had not noticed before in his own site.

Heresies is the work of an irenic Evangelical scholar who deplores the cruel treatment meted out to past heretics and heresiarchs with torture, fire, and sword but who also strongly deplores heresy and the facile toleration of it and the failure on the part of mainstream Protestantism and other groupings to recognize that in updating the creeds under various pressures, including the women's liberation movement, to eliminate the gender terminology in Triadology, Christology, and elsewhere, they could unwittingly forfeit the essence of the faith as a system of coherent beliefs, which was cast in language once acceptable to women as well as men in a less sensitized age.

While respecting as unchanged the covenant of God with the Jews, Professor Brown feels that the covenant with the Gentiles with, in, and through Christ is today in jeopardy in wide and disparate sectors of Christianity, not excluding those that are exclusively scriptural and professedly evangelical. Indeed, he cautiously suggests that "the times of the Gentiles" (Luke 21:24), between 451 and 1951, may be approximately fulfilled, a generous thousand years and five centuries expired (cf. Rev. 20:7). The author attaches importance to the Israeli recovery of Jerusalem in 1967, two years after Vatican II (1962–65), which according to him yielded too much to liberal Protestant thought and its Catholic analogues in Teilhard de Chardin and the New Theology, leading the Catholic Church itself to the reductionist Christology of Edward Schillebeeckx, simplified though it may be for the purpose of a more effective apologetic offensive against secularism.

The author at the end is both hopeful and admonitory. He never wavers in his own steadfastness and sustained Christian joy and humorous strictures on his own most dire predictions. He is willing to engage in dialogue with any who postulate an eternal truth accessible to enlightened reason and who, further, espouse revealed truth and remain humble, "as they dare to embody it" in twentieth-century terms, to paraphrase Hilary of Poitiers, and thus *to err* in the quest for updated formulations true to the faith once for all delivered to the saints; but his pen blackens acidulously as he refers to those today in high places in the Christian establishment wherever in the world who do not even try to understand what even heretics were prepared in some cases to die for: the awareness of an objective truth in faith and morals.

George H. Williams
Hollis Professor of Divinity Emeritus
Harvard University
February 1983

INTRODUCTION

How did *Heresies* come to be written? Formally, it is the story of how succeeding generations of Christians through almost twenty centuries have tried to understand, trust, and obey Jesus Christ. The history of Christian theology is in large part a history of heresies because Jesus and the claims he made, as well as the claims his disciples made about him, seemed to be incredible. The religious orthodoxy of his own day and nation found his claims blasphemous, and had him put to death for making them. His followers, instead of abandoning them, proclaimed that he had risen from the dead and was thus demonstrated beyond all doubt to be "the Son of God with power" by his resurrection from the dead (Rom. 1:4). The Risen Christ commanded them to "teach all nations" (Matt. 28:19).

The Christ proclaimed by the first Christians was so attractive and so compelling that a large part of the human race has come to own him as Lord and Saviour and confess him to be of the same nature as God the Father. This confession was formally adopted for the first time in the year 325, at the Council of Nicaea, but something very much like it was already being taught in the second century of Christianity. Alongside those who accepted the doctrine of Nicaea as the truth about Jesus Christ, there were and still are tens, even hundreds, of millions of others unwilling to accept such a definition, but equally unwilling to abandon Christ. To the extent that they formulated different doctrines and expressed them openly, these millions became the great heretics of Christian history.

During his ministry on earth, Jesus told his disciples, "I am the way, the truth, and the life: no man cometh unto the Father, but by me" (John 14:6). But precisely who and what was he, and is he? His disciples, including even some of those who knew him best, have said many different things about him. They have insisted that it is necessary to belong to Christ in order to have eternal life, and often that it is necessary to know and believe the right things about him in order to belong to him. If Jesus Christ were a trivial figure on the margin of world history, the fact that his would-be followers and imitators give different accounts of him might be interesting, but it would hardly be something to fight and die about.

Jesus Christ is not a marginal figure. The fact that his birth divides history into the years B.C. and A.D. is not merely an accident of Western chronography: it is symbolic evidence of the decisive impact this one man has had on history. Most of those making claims anything like that of Jesus, to be the only way to God, have been shouldered aside and now lie in the dustbin of history. This has not happened with Jesus, and it does not seem likely that it is going to happen in the foreseeable future. The question that he put to his disciples, "Whom say ye that I am?" (Mark 8:29), will be asked of most of the earth's people once, twice, or many times during their lives. And there will be, as there have been, a confusing variety of answers.

Those who want to know who Jesus is and what he should mean to them may turn to the Scripture. If they do so, they do well, for as Jesus himself said, it is the writings of Scripture that testify of him (John 5:39). Alas, despite the confident Reformation assertions that Scripture itself is both sufficient and clear, it is not always easy to grasp the meaning of what it testifies about Jesus. And so, through the centuries, inquirers have asked his followers what these texts may mean, what they are to believe about Jesus if they want to belong to him. The answers have been—and still are—varied, so varied that countless men and women of good intentions have simply thrown up their hands and given up the effort to understand. But others—a greater number, perhaps, from among those who have heard the Gospel story—find it impossible to abandon Jesus to the scrap heap of the theologians or to the dustbin of history, and keep on trying to find the true original in the midst of a labyrinth of images.

Heresies is thus, formally speaking, the story of the church's quest, of many wrong turnings, deceptions, and disappointments, and perhaps—as we hope—of discovery as well. But on a different level, it is more than just the story of the church. It is also the story of countless people who have wanted to find and follow Christ, and who have sought him in the lecture halls and sanctuaries, in the textbooks and the tracts of a church that has talked and written more than any other institution in human history. It is in fact in a real way my own story, for together with my sisters I grew up in a confessionally mixed family, where Christ seemed important enough for the parents to send their children to church and religious instruction, but not enough for the parents to accompany them. In church and school I heard enough of the claims of Christ to realize that if they were true, there could be nothing more important for any human being than knowing him, and knowing him rightly—and that if they were false, he deserved to be ignored and consigned to oblivion. By chance or by Providence, in college courses I was assigned to read several of the great documents of the Reformation era. Thus I learned that there were thinkers of great force and compelling power who believed some very clear and definite things about Christ, and who disagreed among themselves about what they believed. I began a kind of a search for the age and the circumstances when the church was still pure and its image of Christ clear and undistorted.

In the initial stages, this search was a terrible thing, for the pure church and clear doctrine seemed to become increasingly elusive. In the earliest centuries, the age of the martyrs, when men and women had to be prepared to die for what they believed about Jesus Christ, wrangling theologians, denouncing one another as false believers and heretics, were sometimes thrown by the indiscriminate Romans to the same lions. Even the very earliest congregations were threatened by vain philosophy, human tradition, and cunningly devised myths (Col. 2:8; 2 Pet. 1:16)—a discouraging situation. Yet in the midst of the confusion, a certain clarity began to emerge. At the very least, it soon became evident that Jesus Christ had to have been a real figure of compelling authority for generations of saints and sinners, scholars and simpletons, to be willing to quarrel and die for him. With further study, it became apparent that men and women as different as the lawyer Tertullian and the Empress-Mother Helena, the scholarly Origen and the diplomatic Catherine of Siena, the elegant Anselm, stolid Aquinas, bellicose Luther, and austere Calvin, and also the industrious Spener, tender Zinzendorf, and energetic John Wesley, knew far too much the same Jesus Christ for him to be a counterfeit fashioned from scholars' theses or debaters' points. Out of the confusion, in fact, there emerged a figure of Jesus Christ substantial, compelling, and believable; indeed, not only believable, but sufficiently clear and coherent so that one can truly say, believed by Christians through the centuries.

In human terms, I owe my own vision of this figure to countless Christians through the centuries, both to those who have seen clearly, and to some of those who by deforming the picture forced me to look elsewhere and to seek greater clarity. Most of them will appear in the pages of this book. Among those I have known and learned from in person, not merely from the printed page, there are many to whom I am indebted, and two of whom I cannot fail to name in a book that deals with the history of Christ's people: two teachers at Harvard, the late Georges Florovsky and George Hunston Williams.

From the brief list of saints and scholars whose vision of Christ I have caught and seek to share, it is apparent that denominational labels are not decisive: a line can be followed from early Christianity through medieval Catholicism and Eastern Orthodoxy into the Reformation, Pietism, and beyond. Those of Roman Catholic heritage will be quick to note that this Protestant claims many Catholics, through the centuries, as his teachers and models. Yet it cannot escape their notice that after the Protestant Reformation, or more particularly, the Catholic Counter-Reformation, Roman Catholicism ceases to play a significant role in our story. This is in part due to the good sense that Catholicism long had in avoiding those particular heresies that are our chief concern: heresies affecting our image of Christ. Additionally, it is partly due to the fact that for me, as a Protestant today, in the midst of a theological pandemonium unparalleled in our history, it is important to show that in Protestantism, for all its contemporary confusion, there is a direct tie to "the faith which was once delivered unto the saints."

Scholars, and among them my cherished mentor George Williams, will not fail to observe that this work, despite its conception in the greatest library of our nation's oldest university, is more story than history, more journalistic than scholarly. That is not necessarily bad, for its author is—or was—a journalist, and the Christ of whom we write should be our daily news, however much he has shaped our past history. There would be no point in trying to discern him in the past if we could not also hope to behold him in the future, on that Day when he comes, with glory, to judge the quick and the dead.

Deerfield, Illinois
Feast of the Manifestation of Christ to the Gentiles,
January 6, 1983

1

THE TWIST OF HERESY

Corruptio optimi pessimum est.

Latin proverb.

What is a heretic? The Greek word from which the English terms "heresy" and "heretic" are derived simply means an "act of choice" or an "attachment." For a time, *hairesis* merely meant "party" (from "part") or "sect" (from the Latin verb "to cut") and did not imply any disparagement. At an early date in the history of Christianity heresy became almost the worst offense in which a Christian could become involved; in the Middle Ages, heresy became a capital crime. In our own day many familiar words have somehow "changed signs." Words with positive value have become negative, and vice versa. Thus to call someone "virtuous" is almost to disparage him, while to say that he is a "real sinner" often counts as a compliment. Something similar has happened with the terms "orthodoxy" and "heresy." "Orthodoxy" is derived from two Greek words meaning "right" and "honor." Orthodox faith and orthodox doctrines are those that honor God rightly, something that ought to be desirable and good. In Christian usage, the term "heresy" refers to a false doctrine, i.e. one that is simply not true and that is, in addition, so important that those who believe it, whom the church calls heretics, must be considered to have abandoned the faith. Nevertheless, in modern parlance, to call an individual or an idea orthodox is frequently to suggest that although it may be correct, it is probably dull and stultifying. A heresy, by contrast, is almost certain to be more interesting, and to call oneself a heretic is a kind of boast. The late Episcopal bishop James Pike, when under fire for his strange ideas, wrote a self-defense entitled *If This Be Heresy*. Princeton Professor Walter Kaufmann, one of the most brilliant intellectuals of our day, calls his personal manifesto *The Faith of a Heretic*.

One must give Bishop Pike credit for frankness. Even though he considered it a point of honor rather than of shame, he was quite correct in identifying his peculiar variety of Christianity as heresy. Professor Kaufmann, on the other hand, is not really entitled to call himself a heretic, for his "faith" is atheism, too far removed from both Judaism and Christianity to be considered a deviation, even an extreme one, from either. In order to have heresy, to be a heretic, it is necessary that there be an orthodoxy against which to react. In religious matters, to have an orthodoxy demands a reliable source of religious knowledge upon which to build it; in other words, it demands a reliable divine revelation, a Word of God. It is thus no accident that the term "heresy" is far more relevant to the religions of revelation than to others, specifically, to Judaism, Christianity, and Islam.

In principle, each of the three great "religions of the Book," Judaism, Christianity, and Islam, has a definite revelation that permits it to classify certain doctrines and ideas as true or orthodox and others as false or heretical. In practice, however, Christianity is considerably more characterized by heresies and more preoccupied with suppressing them than either Judaism or Islam. The reason lies in the fact that Christianity has produced the institution of the church. Christians believe that the church is not merely an assembly, an association, or a fellowship, but the very body of Christ. The church is not merely the product of faith, but it is to a degree an article of faith. In some sense, all Christians believe that it is necessary to be part of the church in order to be saved. (The church is often defined in spiritual rather than organizational terms, and one may become part of it simply by believing in Christ, without having to join any institution or fellowship.) Traditionally, the church has often been symbolized by an ark; those who board the ark will survive the deluge. Heresy not merely undermines one's intellectual understanding of Christian doctrine, but threatens to sink the ark, and thus to make salvation impossible for everyone, not merely for the individual heretic.

1. A DEFINITION OF HERESY

The word "heresy," as we have noted, is the English version of the Greek noun *hairesis,* originally meaning nothing more insidious than "party." It is used in this neutral sense in Acts 5:17, 15:5, and 26:5. Early in the history of the first Christians, however, "heresy" came to be used to mean a separation or split resulting from a false faith (1 Cor. 11:19; Gal. 5:20). It designated either a doctrine or the party holding the doctrine, a doctrine that was sufficiently intolerable to destroy the unity of the Christian church. In the early church, heresy did not refer to simply any doctrinal disagreement, but to something that seemed to undercut the very basis for Christian existence. Practically speaking, heresy involved the doctrine of

God and the doctrine of Christ—later called "special theology" and "Christology."

Corruptio optimi pessimum est, says the proverb: "the corruption of the best is the worst." The early Christians felt a measure of tolerance for the pagans, even though they were persecuted by them, for the pagans were ignorant. "This ignorance," Paul told the Athenians, "God winked at" (Acts 17:30). But Paul did not wink at him who brought "any other Gospel" within the context of the Christian community. "Let him be accursed," he told the Galatian church (Gal. 1:8). Honorable enemies are regarded with less hostility than the traitor from within one's own camp. The Christian life is often presented as spiritual warfare; if the pagans are the enemies, the heretics are the traitors.

It is often difficult for people today to understand the ferocious hostility heresy and heretics so often aroused in Christians. Perhaps it can best be understood in the light of the persecution and martyrdom that characterized the first three centuries of Christianity. Other great religions have encountered hostility, but more often than not they were sovereign within their own sphere during their formative years. If we date the beginnings of Jewish religion, properly so-called, from the Exodus and the conquest of the Holy Land, then we must say that while the Hebrews had to fight foreign enemies, within their own communities they were sovereign. The followers of Mohammed had to contend with some hostility at first, but within a few years they embarked on a fantastic career of conquest that made them the masters everywhere they went. Christianity was persecuted for two and one half centuries before the Emperor Constantine the Great established toleration in 313 (the Edict, or Constitution, of Milan). During those centuries, Christians were always faced with the possibility, sometimes the probability, of having to die for what they believed. Those within their own camp who wanted to question or change the faith were more dangerous than the persecutors. The persecutors could—and frequently did—put Christians to death, but they could not deprive them of eternal life, nor of the confidence they had in eternal life. This heretics threatened to do, and therefore they were regarded with the utmost loathing.

When we behold a Byzantine emperor, such as Alexius I, putting a Bogomil heretic to death, or English clergy decreeing the burning of Joan of Arc, we find it almost impossible to imagine how sane persons could have interpreted the Gospel of Jesus Christ in such a way that they felt that such things were not merely permitted but were required. Indeed, it is impossible to excuse, in this age or any other, the idea that people ought to be burned at the stake for their ideas. Nevertheless, in a century in which millions have been gassed for their racial affiliation (by Nazi Germany), or roasted to death for residing in an enemy metropolis (by the United States and Great Britain), condemned to death by overwork and exposure in arctic conditions (by the Soviet Union), or murdered in cowardly ambushes to draw attention to alleged political wrongs (by terrorists in several nations), we ought to be restrained in condemning those who put individuals to death because they sincerely believed that they were threatening the eternal salvation of millions. Without in any way exculpating or excusing those Christians in power who persecuted, imprisoned, and executed others who disagreed with them, we ought to make the effort to understand them, for even their cruelty can teach us something that is very important in our own day, when tolerance so often means indifference to truth, justice, and morality: just as there are doctrines that are true, and that can bring salvation, there are those that are false, so false that they can spell eternal damnation for those who have the misfortune to become entrapped by them.

2. THE POSITIVE SIDE OF HERESY

Although it is important to sense the horribly negative power of heresy, as the early and medieval Christians understood it, it is also important to understand its positive side. Since the early modern era, a number of historians and theologians have tried to demonstrate that the heretics—the innovators, the nonconformists, the protesters—were the truest and best imitators of Christ, no matter how far removed their doctrines might be from what he did and taught. It is this heritage that an atheist such as Walter Kaufmann seeks to claim by calling himself a heretic. It is not necessary to think that heretics are the truest Christians, or the best followers of Christ. Indeed, we should not, for to do so would be false. What we can and should do, however, is to note what orthodoxy owes to heresy: in a sense, it owes its very existence.

Heresy, as we said earlier, presupposes orthodoxy. And, curiously enough, it is heresy that offers us some of the best evidence for orthodoxy, for while heresy is often very explicit in the first centuries of Christianity, orthodoxy is often only implicit. If we hope, today, that the orthodoxy we believe is the "faith once delivered to the saints" (Jude v. 3), then it is necessary to assume that it is older than heresy. But heresy appears on the historical record earlier, and is better documented, than what most of the church came to call orthodoxy. How then can heresy be younger, orthodoxy more original? The answer is that orthodoxy was there from the beginning, and heresy reflected it. Sometimes one catches a glimpse of another person or object in a mirror or a lake before seeing the original. But the original preceded the reflection, and our perception of it. The same, we would argue, is true of orthodoxy—the original—and heresy—the reflection. The heresy we frequently see first, but orthodoxy preceded it.

Christianity is a traditional religion in a very important sense—not merely that old customs are perpetuated for centuries, something that happens in many if not all religions. In Christianity, the process of tradition is very important. The Latin word *traditio,* which is related to "trade," refers to a process of transmission, literally, to the handing over of things. The first and most important things Christians handed over, handed down from one generation to the next, were the Scriptures themselves. Secondarily, and hardly less important, was the traditional understanding and interpretation of what those laconic and sometimes mysterious Scripture passages meant. What we now call orthodoxy is a *traditional* understanding. Is it the correct one? The fact that heresy *preceded* orthodoxy, and appears to have been suppressed and supplanted by it, would seem to suggest the contrary.

There is one very good argument that the story of heresy provides to persuade us that it itself is secondary, a reaction to orthodoxy, and not the other way around. It is impossible to document what we now call orthodoxy in the first two centuries of Christianity; heresy often appears more prominently, so much so that orthodoxy looks like a reaction to it. But we can document orthodoxy for all the centuries since then—in other words, for close to seventeen centuries of the church's existence. And we discover that orthodoxy, which has become and been an identifiable constant for so long, continues to evoke the same reaction. Century after century, man's religious imagination leads him to re-create ancient heresies in reaction to the same orthodoxy, which has now been constant for so long. Were the very first heresies, which we glimpse *before* we glimpse orthodoxy, also reactions? If they were, then it can reasonably be argued that the story of Christian theology is the story of truth. If not, it would be necessary to concede that the history of orthodoxy is the history of a usurpation—as indeed many eminent scholars have argued and still argue. It is not necessary to make this concession, and the history of orthodoxy is the history of truth. It is this that our story of heresy shows.

2

WHY HERESIES?

Error, indeed, is never set forth in its naked deformity, lest, being thus exposed, it should at once be detected. But it is craftily decked out in an attractive dress, so as, by its outward form, to make it appear to the inexperienced (ridiculous as the expression may seem) more true than truth itself.

Irenaeus Against Heresies 1.2

The Christian religion has produced more heresies than any other religion, and the heresies it produces are more tenacious than those of any other religion. In fact, it sometimes seems as though the most vigorous, committed, and rapidly multiplying Christians in any age are those we like to call heretics. Why is Christianity so productive of divisive opinions, held with great conviction, that lead to splits in the church and charges and counter-charges of heresy? The reason is simple: Christianity consists of a message that claims to be absolutely true and that is at the same time deeply and perplexingly mysterious.

From the very beginning, Christianity has taught that salvation and eternal life come by faith, and that faith consists in believing certain things about one historic individual, Jesus of Nazareth, called the Christ. The details of the message about his life, death, resurrection, and impending return and what each means are of life-and-death importance to the individual Christian. For one person to challenge the basic understanding of another was not merely to question his private opinion, but to jeopardize his eternal salvation.

The New Testament message concerning Jesus Christ and the early church proclamation based on it were surprisingly brief. It is often summed up in the phrase "Jesus is Lord." This brief sentence is a slogan, a watch-word, and it was one for which countless Christians were willing to lay down their lives. But apart from an adequate context, it is meaningless. It does not explain anything. Who is this Jesus? What kind of a being is he? Or is he a personal being at all, and not an idea or a symbol? What is meant by the word "Lord"? God? One God among many, or the One God himself?

Christian doctrine is the attempt to spell out the significant concepts of the Gospel and place them in relationship to the individual and the world. The most familiar Christian doctrinal statement, the Apostles' Creed, begins with the words, "I believe in God, the Father Almighty, Maker of heaven and earth." The specific statements about Jesus Christ that will follow are placed in the specific context of God, the Father and Maker of all. But the Apostles' Creed does not explain: it merely defines. Jesus is the Father's "only Son, our Lord, begotten of the Holy Spirit, conceived by the Virgin Mary . . ." What does it mean to say that a man born of woman is the Son of God? The Nicene Creed (325) attempts to explain it, and tells us that Jesus Christ is "of one substance with the Father." But then what was his relationship to mankind? That the Chalcedonian Creed (451) defines, "of one substance with us, according to the humanity, in all things like us, saving sin."

Between the death and resurrection of Christ and the Council of Chalcedon in 451, over four centuries had passed. It took four centuries for most Christians to arrive at a statement (not an explanation) of the relationship between God and man in Jesus Christ. Prior to 451, and even afterward, alternative statements and explanations were put forward. If they did not correspond with what was said at Chalcedon, or went beyond it, they were deemed heretical. The Bible alone, which is our source of knowledge about Christ, did not prevent some Christians from calling Jesus the adopted Son of God. This the Apostles' Creed outlawed by calling him "only begotten," but it did not say when he was begotten, nor that he is eternal. The Nicene Creed affirms that he was begotten "before all words," and, in its earliest version, condemns all who say that the Father ever existed alone, apart from his only begotten Son. But if the Son too is eternal, to what extent can he be truly man, as human beings are not eternal? Do Christians believe that he was merely posing as human, "dressed up like a man," as Bishop John A. T. Robinson flippantly put it? Chalcedon tells us that Jesus Christ is every bit as human as we are, and then in effect tells us to believe it and confess it, but to stop trying to explain it or make it understandable.

If the early Christians had not tried to explain the mystery of Jesus Christ, perhaps there would have been no Christological heresies and no need for the Chalcedonian Creed. If later Christians had heeded Chalcedon and not gone on trying to explain him, there would have been no Christological heresies after Chalcedon. As a matter of fact, Chalcedon inaugurated a millennium of comparative unity among Christians concerning the person and natures of Christ. It was successful partly because it really did express the consensus of most Christians, but also because large numbers of those who were not satisfied with it lived in territories that were shortly to be lost to Islam and thus removed from the jurisdiction of the catholic church and the Roman emperors who enforced its doctrines.

After Chalcedon, the Christian faith enjoyed a millennium of relative doctrinal stability—at least by comparison with what had gone before and with what would follow Martin Luther's Reformation, begun in 1517. For a thousand years, the faith the early church fought so hard to express and define came to be taken rather for granted, and the challenges of the Christian life were seen more in the area of obedience. Monasticism and the Crusades were two of the ways in which medieval Christians sought to assure themselves of their salvation.

Luther told Christians that such things were at best superfluous, at worst positively detrimental to one's salvation. He proclaimed "justification by faith alone." The emphasis on faith brought a new insistence on knowing the precise content of faith, and both the Reformation and the Roman Catholicism that opposed it were pushed to spell it out in great detail in what has come to be called the Age of Orthodoxy. Luther, Zwingli, Calvin, and the other major Reformers all agreed with their Roman Catholic opponents in accepting the Christology of Chalcedon, then over one thousand years old. But the intellectual liberation and religious questing the sixteenth century unleashed brought, once again, the desire to understand and explain the mystery of Jesus Christ. For many—not the majority, but a significant number—the explanations of Nicaea and Chalcedon were neither binding nor satisfactory. Once again, the old issues were raised. In the sixteenth century, many if not all of the ancient Christological heresies were revived, and many if by no means all of their exponents paid for their convictions with their lives. Persecution of religious dissenters ceased relatively quickly among Protestants, and somewhat later among Roman Catholics, but for another three centuries after the beginning of the Reformation the doctrines of Chalcedon continued to be the touchstone of Christological orthodoxy. Today heresy and orthodoxy have changed roles. It is fashionable, not dangerous, to be a heretic, and dull if not unsafe to be orthodox.

From the perspective of the late twentieth century it is hard to grasp how important heresy and orthodoxy were to Christianity for fifteen hundred years—from Constantine to Napoleon. But for a millennium and a half the battle to preserve orthodoxy and suppress heresy was taken by almost all Christians to be a holy and necessary task. It was the task of preserving the "faith once delivered to the saints" (Jude v. 3).

Was there actually such a "faith once delivered"? Most of Christendom, and all of Christian orthodoxy, assumes that there was, and that this faith still exists today. The modern church, especially since the introduction of the historical method in theology in the nineteenth century, assumes the contrary. It has more or less given up the idea that there ever was a well-defined, original, internally consistent "old-time religion." The fifth-century church father Vincent of Lérins called on Christians to believe all that has been believed *ubique, semper, et ab omnibus,* i.e. "everywhere, always, and by everyone." Orthodoxy is supposed to be the traditional, timeless faith of the whole church, while heresy is the error of a faction.

The difficulty with St. Vincent's doctrine, as with Jude's slogan concerning the "faith once delivered," is that there is hardly a single doctrine that has not been denied somewhere, at some time, by someone claiming to be Christian. In retrospect, what we now call orthodoxy was sometimes apparently the faith of only a tiny minority. In the middle of the fourth century, it was "Athanasius against the world," as Vincent was fully aware.

Those who accept the Bible as "the only perfect rule of faith and practice" cannot fail to be perplexed as they observe that the Bible can be interpreted in bewilderingly different ways, despite the Reformers' principle of the *claritas Scripturae,* the "clarity (perspicuity) of Scripture." And those who would find a guide or norm in the universal tradition of the church, adhering to the rule of St. Vincent, must acknowledge that it is often hard to find any specific doctrine that fulfills his rule.

Nevertheless, the conviction of the Christian church through the ages is that there really was and is a "faith once delivered to the saints." The testimony of Scripture, while not unambiguously clear or totally free of apparent discrepancies, has been clear enough to create a recognizable body of faith. The voice of the church, despite all the quarreling and occasionally violent conflicts, does have a certain unity, especially when heard from a distance, away from the scene of petty bickering and squabbling, and when carefully followed through the centuries.

No religion has emphasized faith and the necessity of holding right doctrine more than Christianity, and no religion has been more productive of doctrinal controversies and heretical opinions. Paradoxically, salvation for the Christian depends on orthodoxy, yet orthodoxy is difficult to identify. The continuity of the church—which Jesus promised would endure until his return—depends on a continuity of the "faith once delivered," yet a cursory look at church history reveals more confusion and controversy than continuity.

Nevertheless, in the very confusion there are elements that reveal an inner continuity. Theology, we admit, is to a large extent a reaction against heresy. But heresy, we claim, is to a large attempt a response to truth. It is a response to truths imperfectly understood, taken out of context, or perceived as inadequate or unsatisfying. Nevertheless, the existence of heresy in Christianity presupposes the existence of a truth to which the heretics were responding, and which they sought to explain or to understand better than they perceived the more conventionally orthodox to be doing it. Thus in a sense, even when it advances to the point of denying certain fundamental assumptions of orthodoxy, heresy gives evidence for the fact that those assumptions existed, and that they were held to be fundamental.

A still more striking indication of the fact that the doctrines of historic Christianity are based on realities and are not merely intellectual theories is offered by the persistence and recurrence of major heresies. Over and over again, in widely separated cultures, in different centuries, the same basic misunderstandings and misinterpretations of the person and work of Christ and his message reappear. The persistence of the same stimulus, so to speak, repeatedly produces the same or similar reactions. The doctrine of the holy Trinity is a difficult and highly controverted one. The fact that the same objections can be raised to it in the fourth, sixteenth, and nineteenth centuries shows that despite its complexity and difficulty, it has persisted among Christians through all those centuries. The fact that it has thus persisted and endured, despite its evident difficulty, may be offered as evidence of the claim that it is the proper and necessary interpretation of the Bible's testimony to God, and is indeed essential and integral to the Christian faith.

Orthodoxy historically has defined itself later than heresy, and often only in response to the propositions put forward by well-meaning heretics, but rejected by the community of faith. Indeed, Christianity as a whole has always defined itself by contrast with something older: first by contrast with the Judaism out of which it emerged, then by contrast with the pagan culture and religion of the society that surrounded it.

1. PERSPECTIVES JEWISH AND PAGAN

Jesus was a Palestinian Jew; most of his early followers were Jews, and for a number of years the civil authorities and the surrounding secular world looked on Christianity as a variety of Judaism. Indeed, for at least thirty or forty years, until the conquest of Jerusalem by the Romans in A.D. 70, most Christians in Palestine appear to have considered themselves Jews—more knowledgeable Jews, fulfilled Jews, obedient Jews, but Jews nonetheless. But the very nature of the Christians' claims—that Jesus was the expected Messiah, and that their understanding was fuller and more complete, while that of the unconverted Jewish majority was inadequate, obsolete, and willfully blind—naturally set them off against the unconvinced, traditional Jews around them.

Before the breach between Christianity and Judaism was complete, indeed, before all the books of the New Testament itself were written, and long before anyone began to write works of what we now call theology, Christianity had begun to attract pagans as well as Jews. Judaism gave to Christianity its fundamental conviction that the eternal, omnipresent, changeless God works in time and space, in the particular circumstances and conditions of human history. The Apostles' Creed tells us that Jesus Christ suffered and died "under Pontius Pilate," a rather mediocre, middle-level Roman bureaucrat. The reference is Roman, but the idea is Jewish: that the Word of God is not an ineffable, timeless, spaceless Principle, but lived in human flesh and blood at a particular time, in a particular place, and under a rather undistinguished Roman governor.

But time passes, and even the most overwhelming of historical personalities and events are obscured and fade from human memory. The Jewish religion was decisively shaped by Moses, and took its origin in the tremendous event of the Exodus from Egypt. Judaism, more than any other great religion, is characterized by the Law, and the Jewish Law specifically hearkens back to the liberation of the Hebrews from Egypt: "I am the Lord thy God, which have brought thee out of the land of Egypt . . ." (Exod. 20:2). These words, this reference to an epoch-making historical event, introduce the Ten Commandments. Passover, one of the two greatest feasts of the Jewish calendar, involves the effort to embed the memory of the Exodus and its importance in the mind of every Jewish child by the family observance of the Passover meal.

But other things have happened to the Jewish people that have caused the present awareness of that historic event, no more than three millennia in the past, to fade. There was captivity in Babylon, then return from Exile. There was oppression under various rulers, then a brief time of national renewal under the Maccabees. There was submission to Rome, revolt, and the virtual wiping out of Palestinian Judaism in the Jewish Wars of A.D. 66–70. During the twentieth century, there was the incredible Nazi persecution of the Jews, culminating in the Holocaust during World War II, which wiped out at least one third of the Jewish population of the world. Following World War II, the state of Israel was established, restoring national sovereignty to the Jews for the first time in two thousand years. All of these historical events, and especially the Holocaust, entered into the historical awareness of the Jewish people and may tend to displace the historical memory of the Exodus, despite the fact that the spiritual importance of Moses and the Law remains paramount.

Christianity, like Judaism, is based on an event, or a series of events, i.e. on the historic person and work of Jesus of Nazareth, the Christ. But the person and work of Jesus—his ministry, his death, and his resurrection—were experienced by relatively few people. Most of those who came to believe in him only heard of him and his work, or, after the Scripture became available, read of them. The basis for remembering the work of Christ as a foundational historic event surpassing that of the Exodus was narrow. The Exodus was experienced by all of the Hebrews alive at the time, and had direct repercussions for Egypt as well as for other Near Eastern nations. The events of the life, death, and resurrection of Christ, witnessed by only a few people, were immediately contested by the civil and religious authorities.

In addition to the fact that the Christ-event, as history, was directly experienced by only a few people, the Gentiles to whom it was soon to be proclaimed were not, like the Jews, used to basing their religious life on individual historical events. Not only the intellectuals but even the common people of the Hellenistic world tended to think in terms of universals, rather than of individuals and events. When Paul presented the concept of a Mediator between God and men, that was something they could easily grasp. It seemed self-evident that there necessarily has to be a Mediator between the infinite, ineffable, unknowable, transcendent One, and the world of particularity and diversity. But when Paul named the Mediator, "the man Christ Jesus" (1 Tim. 2:5), thus tying the principle to a particular, historic individual, a problem immediately arose. For the religious consciousness of the Gentile Christian to be centered on the single, historic, individual figure of the past, even the recent past, Jesus of Nazareth, an adequate explanation and interpretation of his relationship to the transcendent One was needed—not merely a statement of his place in the historic promises made to Israel.

Gentile Christians were far less able than Christians of Jewish background to believe in the transcendent, cosmic importance of a man and his personal history. Often they could be attracted and even won by the example of other Christians, by their compassion, their mutual love, and the courageous way they witnessed to Christ, even to the point of martyrdom. But in order to be firmly established in the new faith, and to be able to grow in it and communicate it with others, they had to be able to place it in the context of philosophical ideas. These things had to be thought through and explained to them, and to the extent that the most firmly established Christians were slow to do so, others took up the task.

The impact Christ and his followers made on the ancient world was so immense that it simply could not be ignored. Roman officialdom reacted with persecutions, at first sporadic, then more systematic, until it finally admitted defeat and the state was Christianized. Many Gentiles were converted, and even more, including philosophers and religious thinkers, were impressed. Unwilling to accept Christ as their Lord, they nevertheless sought to find a place for him in the religious and metaphysical views they already held.

2. THE IMPORTANCE OF
THE PERSON OF JESUS CHRIST

Christianity takes its name from its founder, or rather from what he was called, the Christ. Buddhism is also named for its founder, and non-Moslems often call Islam Mohammedanism. But while Buddhism and Islam are based primarily on the *teaching* of the Buddha and Mohammed, respectively, Christianity is based primarily on the *person* of Christ. The Christian faith is not belief in his teaching, but in what is taught about him. The appeal of Protestant liberals to "believe as Jesus believed," rather than to believe in Jesus, is a dramatic transformation of the fundamental nature of Christianity.

a. Vis-à-vis Judaism

The church is the daughter of the synagogue and as such has much in common with her mother. But the church is also the bride of Christ, and as such is dramatically different from the synagogue. Through the centuries of Christian history, Christians have vacillated between two extremes in their attitude toward the elder religion and its adherents. At the one extreme there has been a religious and racial anti-Semitism that excoriated and persecuted Jews as Christ-killers. This extreme is found particularly often, if not only, in the established churches, Roman Catholicism, Eastern Orthodoxy, and various forms of established Protestantism. At the other extreme there is a kind of naive philo-Semitism that views all Jews—often to their exasperation—as God's chosen ones, destined to be converted to Christ and saved, regardless of their own opinions. The state of Israel is seen as the fulfillment of messianic prophecy as Christians interpret it. This extreme, less common than the other, is frequently found among enthusiastic Protestant fundamentalists of a revivalistic or Pietistic inclination.

To what extent is Christianity a radical break with Judaism, implying its inadequacy and obsolescence? To what extent is it a continuation, a preliminary fulfillment awaiting the conversion of the Jews for its own consummation? Christian orthodoxy has frequently been intolerant of the Jews, despite formal professions of respect for them as God's chosen people. Liberal Christianity, in its various forms, generally professes tolerance, sometimes even exalting Judaism above Christian orthodoxy, as Gotthold Lessing did in his Enlightenment drama *Nathan the Wise*. On the other hand, in our own day it is the most orthodox of Protestants who woo the Jewish people—both by active evangelism, which most Jews resent, and by militant support for the state of Israel, which is more readily welcomed by Jews even when its theological motivation is not appreciated. Among Protestant intellectuals, anti-Semitism has made inroads in part due to the impact of liberal biblical criticism on the Genesis account that makes Adam and Eve the first parents of all mankind while giving to the Jews a special place in the plan of God. Disposing of Genesis as a Jewish "myth" made it possible for nineteenth-century Germans—and for others as well—to exalt their own race and culture and denigrate that of the "fossilized" Jews.[1] On the whole, contemporary Jewish people are wary of conservative Protestants and try to discourage their efforts at Jewish evangelism; they assume that the liberal Protestants are their natural allies. This alliance has arisen, for example, in movements favoring civil liberty, and only a few Jews have become alert to the fact that liberal Protestantism is naturally hostile to racial, religious, and cultural particularism, and hence implicitly to the distinctiveness of Judaism and Jewish culture.

Early in the Reformation, Martin Luther expressed great sympathy for the Jews, defending them against the prejudice with which Catholicism often treated them. When he discovered that most Jews were no more receptive to his reinterpretation of the Gospel message concerning Jesus the Messiah than they had been to Catholic sacerdotalism, Luther reacted passionately. Shortly before the end of his life he published two viciously anti-Jewish tracts, one entitled *Concerning the Jews and Their Lies* (1542, four years before his death early in 1546). The anti-Semitic outbursts of Luther's declining years have been bitterly resented by Jews for centuries, and have furnished the pretext for anti-Semitism within the context of Lutheranism as well as for an abiding Jewish suspiciousness of the Lutheran movement. Luther's first enthusiasm about winning the Jews to the Gospel and his subsequent hostility contrast with the tolerant acceptance and even praise of Lessing's *Nathan the Wise*. Unfortunately, many liberal Protestant circles that at first proclaimed tolerance and sought the full integration of the Jews into modern society ultimately reacted just as Luther did, turning against the Jews when they did not respond as expected to the overtures made to them.

b. The Contributions of Judaism to Christianity

The contributions of Judaism to Christianity are so manifold that it is impossible even to list them here. For our purposes it is enough to note that because Christianity grew out of Judaism, it was a second-generation religion and did not need to go through a stage of primitivism. Conservative Jews as well as Christians would deny that Judaism itself was ever primitive, inasmuch as they hold that it was divinely inspired from the very beginning. It is not necessary for us to argue that point here, as it is abundantly clear that Judaism was a higher religion at the time of Jesus. It was well thought out, intellectually developed, reflective, and coherent.[2]

Judaism was passionately monotheistic and believed in the personal nature of God. Consequently, early Christianity did not have to free itself either from polytheism, belief in many gods, or pantheism, the idea that God is impersonal, the All. From time to time during the history of the church, polytheistic tendencies emerge within Christianity, and pantheism is a recurring problem, but both of these tendencies would arise out of the encounter with paganism and Gentile culture, not from the Christian heritage itself. The Jewish people had already fought and won major spiritual and intellectual battles against the deeply rooted human religious impulses to polytheism and pantheism. The Christian church inherited the fruit of these victories and did not need to fight the battles again.

Because it came into the world as a "higher" rather than a "primitive" religion, Christianity inherited four fundamental concepts from Judaism: (1) monotheism; (2) the personhood of God; (3) the concept of verbal revelation; (4) the idea that God intervenes in real, space-time human history. The loss of any one of these destroys Christianity, just as historic Judaism is unthinkable without all of them.

Because of monotheism, Jesus neither presented himself nor was understood by his followers as another god alongside of the Father. Because the God of the Jews is personal, Jesus could enter into dialogue with the Father, not merely manifest or reflect him. Because God's revelation was in the form of words, not of inexpressible religious illumination, Jesus could repeat it, interpret it, and supplement it. It is this third point, of course, that brought him into conflict with contemporary Jewish religion, which considered the Word of God complete and already perfect and regarded any attempt at amplification as blasphemous. Because Judaism believed that God intervenes in history, for example, in liberating the Hebrews from slavery in Egypt and in giving them the Law at Sinai, it was possible for Jesus to present himself and his ministry as the action of God, not merely the activity of a man illuminated by the divine.

What distinguished Christianity from Judaism was not its general principles. They were compatible with Judaism, just as they were incompatible with pagan religion and Hellenistic culture (and indeed with the popular culture of the modern West). The conflict lay in the way Jesus and his disciples saw him and his ministry as the specific, divinely appointed fulfillment in space and time of those theological principles in which the devout Jews already believed. Thus, in the dramatic confrontation between Jesus and the High Priest Caiaphas during his trial, the high priest did not object to the principle of a coming judgment of the world. Pilate would have found it ridiculous, but not Caiaphas. What was intolerable for Caiaphas was that

Jesus presented *himself* as the Son of man who would come, in person and in great glory, to carry out that judgment (Mark 14:61–63).

The morality Jesus taught was quite compatible with traditional Jewish morality, even in its spiritual rigor. The rabbis of his day taught in the same way. But Jesus gave as the primary reason for observing the commandments not the historical reference to Moses and to God's deliverance of the Hebrews from Egypt (Exod. 20:2), but his disciples' relationship to himself: "If ye love me, keep my commandments" (John 14:15). Even those who were to come after him, who would not see him or know him in the flesh, were to be blessed by believing in him whom they did not see (John 20:29).

Christianity, like traditional Judaism, is characterized by its ethical rigor. In both of the great biblical religions, this ethical orientation is generally based on the doctrine of the Creation, on the conviction that the entire universe was made by the Word of God and that human beings, as rational creatures, accordingly ought to bring themselves into voluntary conformity with the will of God by obeying his Word. In both Judaism and Christianity, this general orientation is given a specific focus in history. The reason for obeying God is not a general, philosophical insight into the rightness of his commandments (although such an insight is not altogether discounted), but rather the moral obligation God's people bear because of something he has done for them in their own history. For the Jews, this great deed of God is epitomized in the release from Egypt, and thus God's deliverance from Pharaoh stands at the beginning of the Ten Commandments, the most fundamental expression of God's Law (Exod. 20:2). This was an epoch-making historical event, and part of the historical memory and family culture of the whole nation, reaffirmed every year at Passover. Although striking, the Exodus was a simple event, and easy to understand. Its implications are plain: because God delivered the Hebrews from their servitude in Egypt, they clearly have an obligation to render him a grateful obedience.

For the Christians, however, the moral obligation arises not out of a widely experienced historical event, the Exodus, but out of an event no one directly experienced, the resurrection of Jesus on Easter morning. And indeed it is not directly centered on the event of the resurrection, but on the person of the Risen One: "If ye love me, keep my commandments" (John 14:15). It was important for Christians not only to remember their history, as the Jews had to remember theirs, but to know precisely who and what Jesus was and is, in a degree to which Jews need not know Moses in order to know that they should follow Mosaic Law. Christology is essential to Christianity, whereas Judaism really does not have a "Moseology." It is this contrast that creates the tremendous importance of right doctrine about Christ. Judaism is equally historical but less dogmatic in its interest. Those who are by nature and temperament antidogmatic will always find Christianity uncongenial, for it cannot be what it must be without being deeply concerned with dogma.

c. Christianity Vis-à-vis Other Religions

Fundamentally, Christianity had less in common with the other major religions of the day than it did with Judaism. Because most pagan systems were less dogmatic and did not necessarily conflict with the claims of Jesus in principle, the nature of the clash between Christianity and pagan religion was different. Judaism was perfectly willing to admit, in principle, that the Messiah, who was to come in history, could come "under Pontius Pilate." It simply could not admit that that particular man, Jesus, in fact was the Messiah. Paganism readily accepted the idea of a Mediator, and could see human beings fulfilling such a role, but it had difficulty attributing so cosmic a task to a single man, or conceiving that it could have been carried out, once for all, in a particular historical setting, "under Pontius Pilate."

Contemporary Hellenistic religion and the culture it helped shape could be far more hedonistic and self-indulgent in practice than either Judaism or Christianity. (It should not be overlooked, of course, that the Hellenistic world also produced a number of extremely ascetic, world-denying religions.) Nevertheless, its mood was fundamentally pessimistic and negative. Its philosophers sought wisdom, but its prevailing attitude was the skepticism expressed in Pilate's question to Jesus "What is truth?" (John 18:38).

The Romans had dealt with Jews making messianic claims before Jesus, and it would deal with them again afterward. They could understand political rebels, even when they claimed to come with a mission from God. After all, the Emperor himself claimed to be divine, and most, if not all, monarchs of the Hellenistic era claimed a special relationship with God or the gods. Pilate could have understood a Jesus who claimed to be a king of this world, but not one who said, "I am . . . the truth" (John 14:6). Pilate and most of his contemporaries would have fully sympathized with the protest that Lessing would make seventeen centuries later: accidental truths of history cannot be the foundation for universal truths of reason.[3]

The Roman government had to misunderstand Jesus in order to deal with him: it in effect crucified him as a political rebel, even though Pilate admitted that the charge that he preached rebellion against Caesar was false. At first Rome regarded his followers, after his death and resurrection, as a troublesome faction among the Jews, but it soon came to look upon them as a distinct and problematic new religion. The Roman government had no difficulty accepting a new savior cult, provided that the cult in turn accom-

modated to the civil religion that venerated the Emperor and the Genius of
Rome. When Christianity refused to accommodate itself, it became a prohibited religion—a rare distinction in the pluralistic Roman world,. one
shared only by religions that promoted human sacrifice, such as that of the
Celtic Druids; and self-mutilation, such as the cult of the Great Mother.
Charges of moral depravity were raised against the early Christians, but they
were seldom taken seriously by the authorities and were not the reason for
the persecution of the church.

The evident reason for the long opposition of imperial Rome to Christianity was the conviction that it undermined the spiritual unity of its vast
and variegated dominions. Jesus indeed told his disciples to "render therefore unto Caesar the things which are Caesar's" (Matt. 22:21), but that
clearly presupposes that there are some things that are *not* Caesar's. Chief
among them was worship. Refusal to worship the Emperor even in the per-
functory way Roman laws required seemed to be a clear challenge to his
absolute sovereignty, the theory on which the peace and unity of the empire
were thought to depend. Because the empire was held to be the power that
guaranteed peace and well-being to mankind, failure to worship the Emperor
and the Genius of Rome was considered tantamount to hatred of the human
race. The ancient world perceived the Christians not merely as adherents of
a new religion, but as opponents of all religion, calling them atheists. This
gives some credence to the view of recent neoorthodoxy, namely, that
Christianity is not a religion at all.[4]

Contrasted with the many religions of personal salvation that vied with
one another in the Roman Empire, Christianity made an absolutistic claim:
it worshiped the only true God, it had access to the only true truth. What
was most obnoxious to ancient paganism was not the differentness of particular Christian doctrines and views, but the fact that Christianity asserted that
it alone was true and that all other religions were false and worse than
useless. Christianity finds it very difficult to tolerate religious pluralism, and
consequently a religiously pluralistic society finds it difficult to tolerate
Christianity, even though the principle of pluralism is that all diverse opinions ought to be tolerated.

d. Christianity Vis-à-vis
Ancient Humanism and Moral Philosophy

Just as Christian ethics closely resembled those of Judaism, differing
chiefly in the motivation behind them, so too they have parallels in the
natural law of Aristotle and Cicero as well as in the Stoic morality of Paul's
contemporary, the Stoic philosopher Seneca. In fact, the apparent similari-

ties between the ideas of Paul and those of Seneca led to the creation of a literary forgery, a fictitious correspondence between the two men.[5]

Christian morals differed from those of ancient pagan philosophy in their motivation and in their effectiveness. The goal of Aristotelian and Stoic morality was a worthy personal life, individual greatness of spirit. Such a goal can produce high standards of conduct, but only in those blessed with a certain nobility of character as their starting point. Christianity was both more and less pessimistic than the surrounding culture: more pessimistic with respect to the short run, more optimistic in the long run. Pagans—especially if they had no material worries, like the immensely wealthy Seneca—could idealize existence as days of wine and roses. Christians saw it through a veil of tears and blood. But beyond the roses, pagans knew, there was "one endless night that we must sleep."[6] No matter how pleasant and cultivated one's life, it must end. For the Christians, all this is "light affliction, which is but for a moment" (2 Cor. 4:17), for Christ is "the resurrection and the life" (John 11:25).

The noblest pagans could die heroically, stoically, tragically, but even simple Christians could and did die hopefully, confident that Jesus would reward them with "a far more exceeding and eternal weight of glory" (2 Cor. 4:17). Because they were prepared to die for their beliefs, and expected to rise again in Christ and reign with him in glory, and because they often had to die, it was very important to them to know precisely in whom they were believing (2 Tim. 1:12), who he was and is and what he can and will do. It was the constant threat and frequent reality of dying for the faith that made doctrine so important to the early church and caused heresy—false doctrine, which cost one's salvation—to appear so dreadful. The Apostle John promised believers, "We know we shall be like him [Jesus]" (1 John 3:2). For this reason it was very important to know what he was and is like.

3. THE IMPORTANCE OF DOCTRINE
AND DOCTRINAL PRECISION

For many religions, the cardinal test is right conduct or right observance; for Christianity it is right faith. Christianity is full of specific doctrines. While some seem evidently to be far more important than others, Christians have long been reluctant to admit that any of them are trivial. This is due in part to the conviction that all doctrine derives from God's infallible revelation. If it is not divinely revealed, it ought not to be doctrine at all; if it is divinely revealed, it can hardly be called trivial. For the early church, in theory at least, doctrines were not comments on faith or components of it. As Adolf von Harnack writes, "Dogma can be nothing other than the revealed faith itself.''[7] The great liberal church historian saw this as a problem for historical research conducted by Christians. Inasmuch as their individual salvation depends on holding faith, which involves receiving and believing Christian dogma, they find it very difficult to ask themselves how doctrine developed. If it developed historically, can it be what it must be in order to be a faith capable of saving us, the ''faith once delivered to the saints''?

It is a simple and undeniable historical fact that several major doctrines that now seem central to the Christian faith—such as the doctrine of the Trinity and the doctrine of the deity of Christ—were not present in a full and well-defined, generally accepted form until the fourth or fifth centuries. If they are essential today—as all of the orthodox creeds and confessions assert—it must be because they are true. If they are true, then they must always have been true; they cannot have become true in the fourth or fifth century. But if they are both true and essential, how can it be that the early church took centuries to formulate them?[8]

The answer, or at least the best attempt at an answer, lies of course in the assertion that they were *implicit* in Christian faith from the beginning, even though they did not become *explicit* until considerably later. As has already been suggested, one of the values of Christian heresy—which sometimes appears older than orthodoxy—is that it suggests that orthodox doctrine, against which it reacts, was present from a very early date, even though not expressly formulated. Sixteenth-century Socinianism, or unitarianism, was a reaction against the orthodox trinitarianism formulated by the church fathers and reaffirmed by the great Reformers. Fourth-century Arianism, which resembles it, appeared *before* the fathers formulated orthodoxy. Can it nevertheless also be a reaction against the orthodox doctrine of the Trinity, implicit in the faith of the early church although not yet explicit in its doctrine?

a. Faith as Doctrine and Faith as Trust

It is common to disparage any concept of faith that involves the ''mere'' acceptance of certain doctrines as true, and to contrast it unfavorably with faith as personal trust in Christ. Of course no martyr of the early church thought that he would be saved and attain eternal life because he held a certain set of propositions to be true. He believed that he would obtain eternal life because he trusted in Christ, not because he believed specific doctrines. But he did not make a dichotomy between faith as doctrine and faith as trust; part of trusting in Jesus Christ and his ability to "save to the uttermost" was the acceptance of certain propositions about the person and work of Christ. Trust in Christ, which is necessary for salvation, makes sense only in the context of certain doctrines, and what they tell us about him and his work.

b. The Importance of Creeds

Creeds played a prominent part in the daily worship and life of early Christians. To a degree that is hard for twentieth-century people to grasp, the early church believed that it was absolutely vital to know and accept some very specific statements about the nature and attributes of God and his Son Jesus Christ. It was so important that all Christians were required to repeat them frequently, to learn them by heart. The modern dichotomy between faith as trust and faith as acceptance of specific doctrines—usually coupled with a strong bias in favor of faith as "trust" without the need for "rigid doctrines"—would have been incomprehensible to the early Christians, who could trust Christ in the midst of persecution precisely because they were persuaded that certain very specific things about him are true. Some of these things—such as the Nicene doctrine of the consubstantiality of the Son with the Father (adopted in A.D. 325)—appear complex and mysterious. This fact should not cause us to fail to see how important they were to saving faith as the early church understood it.

4. HOW DOCTRINE CREATES THE CHURCH

Faith makes a Christian, but doctrine creates the church. It is possible for a church to endure long without a clear doctrinal base, or even in reaction to its earlier doctrinal base, but a church in our sense would not arise at all unless clear and significant doctrines were present. Contemporary Anglicanism, now famous for its doctrinal pluralism, could hardly have arisen on the basis of such a pluralism. In fact, it arose out of some very clear doctrinal convictions, for which several of its early bishops were prepared to give their lives. Many a modern denomination has been constituted on the basis of the compromising and blurring of formerly important doctrines; the United Presbyterian Church in the United States of America represents one such fusion, involving a considerable measure of doctrinal compromise and willingness to ignore disputed points. This quite new denomination has lost a sixth of its membership in recent years, despite the growth in America's population and the number of its professing Christians.

Although he may not think of it as "dogma" or refer to it as "doctrine," no one can be a Christian at all unless he accepts the truth of certain fundamental statements we usually call dogmas. Unless a religious community holds certain specific and well-defined teachings, it will gradually dissolve, and in any event cannot be considered a Christian community.

It is evident that within the broader Christian fellowship there is considerable disagreement concerning which dogmas are essential and must be believed. A certain level of disagreement is compatible with Christianity, and indeed has always existed, but beyond a certain point of disagreement, one can no longer speak of a community of faith. When the dogma in dispute is so important that it breaks up a community, it is a heresy. Those on our side, who reject it, thus "keep the faith," and are orthodox; the others are heretics.

The language of heresy and orthodoxy has been used frequently in the history of the church to justify intolerance, repression, even persecution. For this reason, it will always be somewhat distasteful to the contemporary mind, and flippant observations such as that in the preceding paragraph will be found to be in questionable taste. Nevertheless, with all possible tolerance of and respect for those who are attracted to what we call "heresy," it is important to recognize that the very life of Christianity in general as well as the salvation of individual Christians depends on at least a substantial measure of right doctrine, and where right doctrine exists, contrary views must be heresies.

SELECTED BIBLIOGRAPHY

Arnold, Gottfried. *Unparteiische Kirchen- und Ketzerhistorie: von Anfang des Neuen Testaments bis auf das Jahr Christi 1688.* vols. 1–4. Hildsheim: Georg Olms, 1967.

Bainton, Roland Herbert. *Concerning Heresies: A Collection of the Opinions of Learned Men Both Ancient and Modern.* New York: Columbia University Press, 1933.

Bardenhewer, Otto. *Patrology: The Lives and Works of the Fathers of the Church.* St. Louis: Herder, 1908.

Bauer, Walter. *Orthodoxy and Heresy in Earliest Christianity.* Philadelphia: Fortress Press, 1971.

Duchesne, Louis. *Early History of the Christian Church: From Its Foundation to the End of the Fifth Century.* London: John Murray, 1924.

Geffcken, Johannes. *The Last Days of Greco-Roman Paganism.* Translated by Sabine MacCormack. New York: North-Holland, 1978.

Jalland, T. G. *The Origin and Evolution of the Christian Church.* New York: Hutchinson, 1950.

Koijn, A. F. J., and G. J. Reinijk. *Patristic Evidence for Jewish-Christian Sects.* Leiden: Brill, 1973.

Lake, Kirsopp. *Landmarks in the History of Early Christianity*. London: Macmillan, 1920.

Lampe, G. W. H. *The Seal of the Spirit: A Study in the Doctrine of Baptism and Confirmation in the New Testament and the Fathers*. London: S.P.C.K., 1967.

Lebreton, Jules, et al. *The History of the Primitive Church*. New York: Macmillan, 1949.

Longenecker, Richard N. *The Christology of Early Jewish Christianity*. London: S.C.M., 1970.

Moule, C. F. D. *The Origin of Christology*. Cambridge: University Press, 1977.

Pelikan, Jaroslav. *Historical Theology: Continuity and Change in Christian Doctrine*. Washington, D.C.: Corpus, 1971.

Purinton, Carl Everett. *Christianity and Its Judaic Heritage*. New York: Ronald Press, 1961.

Sandmel, Samuel. *Judaism and Christian Beginnings*. New York: Oxford University Press, 1978.

Schoeps, Hans-Joachim. *Jewish Christianity*. Translated by Douglas R. A. Hare. Philadelphia: Fortress Press, 1969.

Spence-Jones, H. D. M. *The Early Christians in Rome*. New York: John Lane, 1911.

Svenster, Jan Nicolaas. *Paul and Seneca*. Leiden: Brill, 1961.

Winter, Eduard. *Ketzersgeschicksale, Christliche Denker aus neun Jahrhunderten*. Zurich: Benziger, 1980.

3

COMMON GROUND

Wherefore, forsaking the vanity of many, and their false doctrines, let us return to the Word which has been handed down to us from the beginning . . .

Polycarp, epistle 8

What is the starting point of the Christian faith and all the elaborate theology that has grown out of it? The New Testament, in one of its smallest books, speaks of the "faith once delivered to the saints" (Jude v. 3). Traditionally, Christians have accepted this image and have thought of their faith as a kind of fixed body of doctrine delivered in a single block to the first Christians. Some handed it down carefully and without alteration; these were the orthodox. Others changed it in various ways; these were the heretics. According to one legend, the Apostles convened and produced the Apostles' Creed as a group, each Apostle supplying a line or two.

Unfortunately, nothing like this happened. But if the story of the origin of the Apostles' Creed is legendary, does that mean that there was no common apostolic faith? The modern understanding of history tells us that ideas, like institutions, grow, develop, and change. We know that the institution of the papal hierarchy took centuries to develop. Is it possible that the faith was ever really "delivered" fully formed? If we were speaking merely of human wisdom, such a suggestion would be absurd. But the fundamental claim of Christianity is that it is revealed religion. Everything human has a history and is involved in development and change; the crucial question is whether the Christian faith is the result of an evolutionary process, or whether its substance was indeed "once delivered," so that its present form is merely an unfolding of that which was given to the saints.

For many centuries, the church held what we may call the naive view of the fixity of doctrine. It was taken for granted that the great ecumenical councils such as Nicaea (325), Constantinople (381), and Chalcedon (451),

which drew up the Nicene[1] and Chalcedonian creeds, were simply expressing what Christians had always believed. This view was taken over by the
major Protestant Reformers, especially by Luther's pupil and close associate
Philipp Melanchthon and by John Calvin. Although the Protestants affirmed
the doctrine known as *sola Scriptura* ("by Scripture alone," i.e. the conviction that the Bible is the only authoritative norm of faith), they accepted the
ecumenical creeds as authoritative formulations of what Scripture teaches.

During the Reformation era, however, suspicion of the creeds was also
expressed, and many Christians rejected them altogether: some, such as the
antitrinitarians and other radicals, because they did not believe what the
creeds say, others because they objected to any statements that were not
drawn directly from the Bible. On the whole, however, most major Christian denominations continued to accept the ecumenical creeds as well as
their own confessions as expressing the "faith once delivered," which they
assumed was always the faith of true Christians.

By the nineteenth century, however, the idea that development is fundamental to all life came to affect theology and doctrine. In biology, the old
idea of the fixity of species, based on the doctrine of direct divine Creation,
yielded to the concept of constant change through natural selection advocated by Charles Darwin. In the realm of ideas and institutions, Friedrich
Hegel's philosophy of history taught a process of constant change and development resulting from the interplay of thesis and antithesis to produce
synthesis.

Applied to the development of Christian doctrine, Hegel's idea of development inevitably wreaked havoc with the conviction that there was a
"faith once delivered." There was no need to introduce evidence to show
that the faith of Nicaea, for example, was an innovation grafted onto the
simpler faith of a more primitive early church. Development was assumed,
and it was taken for granted that the state of Christian doctrine, at any point
in its development, had to represent the synthesis of an earlier conflict between a thesis and its antithesis. Ferdinand Christian Baur (1792–1860) was
the first to adapt Hegel's dialectical method to the understanding of Christian
doctrine. He saw, even in the pages of the New Testament itself, a dialectical process in which a thesis, the Jewish Christianity of Peter, clashed with
its antithesis, the Gentile Christianity of Paul, to produce the synthesis we
know as early catholicism. Needless to say, such a view makes the specific
doctrines of the creeds, the standards by which Christians have measured
orthodoxy and heresy, nothing but the more or less fortuitous products of
historical development. Baur is considered the founder of what is called the
Tübingen school, a prominent expression of nineteenth-century liberal Protestantism; it actually should be called the second Tübingen school, as there
was also an earlier, more orthodox movement bearing that name.

At first, Baur's theories remained relatively unknown to the general churchgoing Christian public. Although the implications of his ideas were evident, Baur avoided direct confrontations with traditional believers and church authorities. A far greater upheaval was made by David Friedrich Strauss (1808–74), whose *Life of Jesus* (1835) portrayed Christ as a self-deceived leader who died with his work in ruins. It was his disciples who turned Christ into a cult figure. Strauss could not obtain a theological professorship because of the radicalism of his views, but he was an effective publicist and many others were attracted to his skeptical debunking of traditional doctrines.

Strauss challenged the historicity of many things Christians had always believed to be real historical events—Jesus' virgin birth, his miracles, his resurrection and ascension. Baur's view was far subtler and more sophisticated, and did not directly challenge the facts, but indicated that the doctrines derived from them had undergone a process of transformation that took them constantly further from their starting point in historical reality.

It is interesting to attempt to understand the motives of a tenured professor of theology, officially committed to the Lutheran confessions of faith, who thus explained away several of the most fundamental articles of that faith. Like many other theological radicals, Baur continued as an active churchman and certainly did not think of himself as undermining the Christian faith. He did, however, want to transform it from the acceptance of specific doctrines to the appreciation of a historical process, and in this he largely succeeded. Following Baur, most subsequent writers were less radical. They did not necessarily present early catholic doctrine as nothing but the synthetic result of a dialectical process. But after Baur it became more or less taken for granted in academic circles that theology has always been in process and that there never was a "faith once delivered." Prior to Baur, the prevailing view was that Christianity, whether it was true or false, was at least a relatively well-defined and fixed body of doctrine; after Baur, it was more often assumed that doctrine was constantly in the process of development and that "historic Christian orthodoxy," far from having been a constant for close to two thousand years, was only the theological fashion of a particular age.

In the modern conflict within Protestantism over the authority and infallibility of Scripture, for example, the "orthodox," or inerrantist, position is frequently denounced by its opponents as an innovation of nineteenth-century theologians and as not at all representative of the faith of the church through the ages. There is no question that the inerrantist position was thought through and skillfully expressed by the so-called Princeton school of American Presbyterian theology. Since Baur, it is foreign to the mentality of most religious thinkers to conceive that the nineteenth-century Princetonians could possibly have been expressing what Christians had believed for centuries. A product of the nineteenth century, by definition, virtually has to differ markedly from the thought of Luther and Calvin in the sixteenth, and of course also from that of the early church fathers.

1. THE REAL DEVELOPMENT

If there was a development in Christian consciousness and the formulation of Christian teaching—and of course there was—the most significant psychological transformation occurred at the very beginning of the church, in the first half of the first century. The very earliest disciples of Christ encountered him first of all as a man like themselves. Only gradually did they become aware of his extraordinary attributes and come to understand that he was claiming to be one with God the Father. The first Christians experienced Jesus as a man whom they slowly came to recognize as the Messiah, and ultimately acknowledged, in the words of doubting Thomas, as Lord and God (John 20:28). For them, the humanity of Jesus was self-evident; his deity was their confession of faith.

Following the passing of the first generation of believers, those who had known Jesus before his resurrection, later believers were almost invariably confronted first of all with his deity, and only slowly came to recognize that the Saviour was also fully human, just as we are. Because they heard him proclaimed as Lord and God, it was the news of his full humanity that was rather shocking and in a sense unexpected.

Since the establishment of Christianity as the official religion of the Roman Empire in the fourth century, it has become almost impossible for anyone within the orbit of Western civilization to encounter Jesus first as a man, and only subsequently to learn of his messianic claims and the doctrine of his deity. It is important to note that this transformation took place during the lifetime of the Apostles. Even Paul himself never knew Jesus after the flesh, as he puts it. He first encountered him in the claims—which he considered blasphemous—of his followers, who proclaimed him as the divine Son of God.

a. The First Heretics

From the second generation on, Christians and those to whom they witnessed no longer encountered Jesus as a man concerning whom they began to make greater and greater claims, but as a figure of compelling majesty and mystery with whom they sought to establish a personal relationship, based on faith, trust, and therefore understanding. In a sense, the first heretics were the more sophisticated and more intellectual Christians. Their faith immediately sought understanding. They were impatient with the hesitant, gradual attempts of those we now see as orthodox to come to terms with the mystery, intolerant of their greater willingness to concentrate on obedience, evangelism, and—of necessity—on preparing themselves for martyrdom.

Although the explanations proposed by the first heretics did not win acceptance from the church as a whole, they challenged it to produce better interpretations. From the perspective of many modern Christians—as well as of a certain kind of "fundamentalist" through the centuries—the early church fathers attempted too much, and produced an unnecessarily elaborate and complex theology. For many, the word "theology" itself is suspect, and the terms "dogma" and "doctrine" have something intrinsically unattractive about them. Nevertheless, the rise and proliferation of heresies in the period before doctrines were well formulated or theology created shows just how necessary doctrines and theology are. To the extent that doctrine is disdained and theological inquiry regarded as superfluous, even in our own day, old heresies reappear and new ones are created, even among those who think of themselves as orthodox and believe that they are firmly attached to the faith once delivered.

b. A Contrast Between
Orthodoxy and Heresy

In the preceding chapter, orthodoxy was characterized, perhaps a bit flippantly, as the doctrines we believe, heresy as what others believe. Clearly there is a measure of sense in this assertion, for presumably no one who claims to be a Christian will consciously hold something he knows to be a false doctrine, i.e. a heresy. Consequently, it is always those who disagree with one, who hold conflicting doctrines, who must be deemed heretical. In any treatment of the subject, no matter how balanced and objective it may seek to be, one cannot expect that the author will come to the conclusion that his own views are heretical. In other words, any discussion of the subject is naturally going to exhibit a certain degree of partiality and prior commitment, and the present inquiry can be no different.

Nevertheless, it may be possible even for a partisan of orthodoxy, as he understands it, to draw relevant contrasts between it and what he considers heresy. One such contrast has to do with the priority orthodoxy and heresy assign to truths of history on the one hand and to intellectual understanding on the other. Both orthodoxy and heresy are concerned about intellectual understanding as well as—almost always—about historical truth; both orthodoxy and most kinds of heresy engage in theological speculation, and neither is immune to letting such speculation run away with itself. In a general way, however, we can say that orthodoxy assigns the priority to history, heresy to understanding. Thus, in a general way, orthodoxy appeals to the less theological and more historical minds among the theologians, heresy to the more theological, more philosophical, and more imaginative. Of course there are philosophers and artists among the orthodox, and dull pedants among the heretics, but it seems fair to say that the heretics are frequently more imaginative, the orthodox more plodding.

At the same time, if theology is too pedestrian, if it never wrestles with conceptual problems at all, if it simply remains on the level of religious slogans and moral maxims, then it cannot attain to what we now call orthodoxy. From one perspective, orthodoxy is too dull, but from another—and this is the viewpoint of many who want to be sincere, devout, and pious "simple Christians"—orthodoxy is already too speculative, too complex, too elaborate. Orthodoxy is thus compelled to occupy a kind of intellectual middle ground; the challenge it faces is to occupy the middle without being mediocre, to make distinctions without being discriminatory, to define without becoming dull. That it has frequently been unequal to this challenge in the past is evident from the pages of church history, and many Christians can attest it from personal experience as well. Nevertheless, the challenge remains: it is implicit in Peter's admonition "Be ready always to give an answer to every man that asketh you a reason of the hope that is in you" (1 Pet. 3:15).

c. *"Fundamentalism" and Orthodoxy*

The term "fundamentals" became current in interconfessional theological controversies of the seventeenth century. "Fundamentalism" was coined in the context of the "Fundamentals Controversy" in American Protestantism at the beginning of the twentieth century, and it has become a term of abuse once again as applied to religious zealots of various kinds, such as the Ayatollah Khomeini and his followers in Iran. Traditional, orthodox Christians seldom want to be called fundamentalists, usually because of the unpleasant associations attached to the word. In fact, orthodox Protestants of necessity hold to the so-called fundamentals as set forth in the controversy, but not necessarily with the same priorities and intensity.

The major difference between Protestant orthodoxy and fundamentalist Protestantism lies in the fact that orthodoxy is doctrinally comprehensive, while fundamentalism is highly selective. Orthodoxy, with its creeds and confessions, presents a broad range of doctrines it considers vital, and integrates them into a dogmatic system. Fundamentalism is a derivative of orthodoxy; it selects a small number of doctrines as fundamental and fights for them: two important examples are the doctrine of biblical inerrancy and, for many fundamentalists, the doctrine of the premillennial return of Christ. Although these doctrines are part of the historic Christian tradition, by fighting selectively for them while virtually neglecting others, fundamentalism has become a very distinctive and somewhat one-sided branch of Protestant orthodoxy. In its preoccupation with a small number of doctrines, it resembles many of the classical heresies. Because of its combativeness, Protestant fundamentalism has succeeded in attracting the attention of the media and the general public, and by doing so has sometimes come to be mistaken for Protestant orthodoxy, of which it is only an important but somewhat unrepresentative part.

2. THE RESURRECTION AND THE INCARNATION

It is common to make a distinction between schools of thought that emphasize the *work* of Christ, particularly his crucifixion and resurrection, and those that emphasize his *person,* particularly his incarnation. Ideally, the doctrines of the person and work of Christ belong together; unless he is what Scripture and the creeds proclaim him to be, he could not have achieved the work ascribed to him. The work of Christ was done openly, on the stage of real human history, even though it attracted scant notice from the authorities and the general public of the Roman world at the time. The person, by contrast, was private. The incarnation also took place in human history, but the event itself—the birth of a child, a bit too soon after the wedding to be entirely correct—was not a public event, even in the sense of the public ministry, trial, and execution of Jesus some thirty years later.

It is again a touchstone in the distinction between orthodoxy and many heresies that orthodoxy begins with the work of Christ, with his crucifixion and particularly with his resurrection, and works back to the doctrine of the incarnation; heresy often begins with a conception of the nature of Christ and works forward to an interpretation of his work. If Christ truly rose from the dead, then, as Paul says (Rom. 1:4), he is demonstrated to be the Son of God. The orthodox doctrine of the deity of Christ ultimately derives from this conviction. On the other hand, if Christ is perceived first of all as the divine Son, it is natural to dispute the validity of the Gospel history that tells us that he was humiliated, crucified, and buried. Many heresies thus derive from the sincere attempt to do justice to the majesty of Christ as perceived by his followers, even though in so doing they lose contact with his actual human life and work in history.[2]

a. The Importance
of the Resurrection

Early Christian preaching proclaimed Jesus Christ: crucified, risen, ascended, and coming again. It proclaimed his resurrection as the guarantee and model for our own. His disciples were told that they must be prepared to suffer for him, but that they could be confident of rising and reigning with him. Paul said it very simply: "If Christ be not risen, then is our preaching vain, and your faith is also vain" (1 Cor. 15:14). For the first Christians, salvation was not something they had to earn; in fact, they could not earn it. It had already been purchased for them by the death and resurrection of Jesus Christ. Their entry into eternal life was assured by their identification with Christ through faith, baptism, and participation in the communion.

It is important to note the difference between the early Christian conception of eternal life and the widespread Hellenistic assumption of the immortality of the soul. Although the Bible speaks, like classical paganism, of man as having a soul as well as a body, it does not see him as consisting essentially of a soul imprisoned in a fleshly body, as Platonism and much Hellenistic spirituality did. It sees him as a unity of soul and body. The great creeds speak of the resurrection "of the body" (Apostles' Creed) or "of the dead" (Nicene Creed), not of the immortality of the soul. Because Christianity saw the human being as a soul-body unity, when it tried to understand the meaning of God becoming man in Christ, it ultimately had to acknowledge that Christ possesses a human soul as well as mere human flesh. Those from the Hellenistic world who did not recognize man as essentially a soul-body unity, but rather as a spirit temporarily embodied in flesh, found this interpretation of Jesus unattractive, and frequently diminished his full humanity, sometimes denying it altogether.

b. The Transmission of the Gospel

For the first Christians, the message of the resurrection was of vital importance, but the messengers who proclaimed it were also important. Judaism and Christianity both have a concept of election, or predestination: God has a chosen people, and his electing grace rests upon chosen individuals. One of the prime guarantees of the authenticity of the message of the resurrection was the authority and integrity of its messengers. The Apostles were chosen and called by Christ; their successors were also viewed as chosen representatives, called by God and also called and authenticated by the church. Often—very frequently indeed in the first two centuries—the chosen witnesses sealed their witness with martyrdom.

During the first two centuries of Christianity, there was a gradual shift from a situation in which the spiritual and personal integrity of the witnesses substantiated their message to one in which the authenticity of the message, its fidelity to Scripture, became a measure of the reliability of those claiming to be witnesses. Nevertheless, it was not until the Protestant Reformation (which followed shortly upon the invention of printing) that the Christian message and its associated doctrines came to the point where they could be largely transmitted in books and printed tracts, without necessarily having to be proclaimed and taught by a human agent.

For early Christianity, the human witness was very important. Willingness to endure martyrdom was one important authenticating element prior to the introduction of toleration by the Emperor Constantine. It was a necessary condition of being a reliable witness, but not a sufficient one, for the Romans made martyrs of heretics as well as of orthodox, and many heretics died for their faith as courageously as their more orthodox counterparts. A second authenticating element for witnesses was harmony with the unity of the church, but even this is not an altogether reliable guide to their orthodoxy. In the fourth century, the orthodox Athanasius seemed to stand virtually alone against a triumphant heresy, that of Arianism. In the sixteenth century, the Protestants were forced to argue that the greater part of the medieval church, which was united under the pope, had fallen into error, and that true apostolicity lies in harmony with the teachings of the Apostles, not in obedience to their supposed successors, the bishops.

For the early church, *tradition* was a very important concept, but its meaning was different in the first centuries. The concept of *paradosis,* or *traditio,* referred to the faithful handing over of the "faith once delivered." The primary part of this *traditio* being the Scripture itself, the act of tradition consisted primarily in faithfully handing it down from one generation to the next. This process of transmission was very important, and the act of transmitting or handing over was never separated from the actors—the bishops and presbyters and others involved in the ministry of the Word.

c. The Universality of the Gospel

Despite its emphasis on election or chosenness, Christianity differed strikingly from its Jewish parent in its universality. There is a measure of universality in the Old Testament, particularly in the Prophets, but essentially Judaism was perceived as the distinctive religion of a particular people. Judaism did make proselytes, but it did so on such a modest scale that it did not constitute a disruptive force in Roman society. The Roman government considered Judaism a *religio licita,* "lawful religion," even though Judaism, like Christianity, prohibited its followers from participating in Roman civil religion. Christianity, by contrast, was an actively proselytizing religion, rapidly won converts, and seemed to the Roman government to constitute an increasingly unpredictable and unstable element in Roman society.

The Jewishness of Jesus and the Jewish origins of Christianity were apparent. Both Jesus and the great Apostle to the Gentiles, Paul, made it plain that salvation is "of the Jews." But if Christ was to win the Hellenistic world—as he did—it had to be made plain to that world how a figure with such a distinctive and exclusively Jewish heritage could have a universal significance for all mankind. This many heretics attempted to do, and orthodox theology eventually succeeded in doing, by placing the person of Christ in the context not merely of Creation but of the inner life of the godhead itself.

d. The Rejection of National Israel

Although Jesus and his Apostles were Jews, only a minority of the Jewish people became Christians.[3] For centuries the Jewish people had derived comfort from the unconditional promises made to them in the Old Testament, including not only the coming of the Messiah but a restoration of their prosperity and power. For many Christians, these promises made to the Jewish people have never been abrogated, and the Jews still have a prominent place in God's plan for the future. The majority of Christians, however, came to resent Judaism for its ongoing rejection of Christ and to look on its continuing existence as a kind of affront to the church and its faith. The scriptural concepts of the New Israel, of spiritual Israel, were applied to the church, and the promises made to Israel were taken as referring to the people of the New Testament, the Christians.

It was against the background of these factors that early "catholic" theology developed: (1) the content of the Gospel, centered on the historic reality of the resurrection of Christ and the coming reality of personal resurrection; (2) the transmission of the Gospel, significantly entrusted to men trusted to be faithful to it; (3) the universality of the Gospel, extending to all nations; and, finally, (4) the implication of this universality in the displacement of old Israel from its privileged position as God's Chosen People.

3. THE BEGINNINGS OF "CATHOLIC" THEOLOGY

On first examination, early Christian theology seems to present us with a confusing babble of discordant voices. On closer inspection, however, we can recognize that despite all the discord, there is a remarkable unity. This unity is particularly striking in that it appeared at a time when Christianity was spreading rapidly, especially, if not exclusively, among the poorer and less educated classes, and when persecution or threat of persecution made communication difficult and an effective, centralized organization impossible.

a. Revival of Religious Interest

Traditional Roman religion was at a low point in the first century of the Christian Era; it could offer no serious resistance to the spread of the Gospel. From the reign of Antoninus Pius (ruled 138–61) onward, a significant revival of religious interest was apparent throughout the empire. To some extent this reawakening of interest facilitated the spread of the Gospel. A number of new religions were proclaimed, and the prevailing attitude of tolerance facilitated syncretism—the blending of religions or the practicing of more than one religion at a time. While Christianity is inimical to syncretism, the syncretistic trend did bring a tendency to consider God as one and each of the different religions a different way to approach him, reducing the tendency of the various religions to fight jealously for the honor of their particular divinities. Syncretism facilitated the spread of a kind of philosophical monotheism and thus made it easier for the Christians to proclaim one God, despite the nominal polytheism of the Hellenistic world.

Unlike several other religions of Near Eastern origin that were in competition with it, Christianity had a clear, understandable, and very recent historical foundation. This gave it an immediacy other religions of a more mystical and esoteric nature lacked.

b. The Importance of Societies

In addition to the philosophical-religious mood that opened the door to the influence of Christianity, another factor was the degree to which life in the ancient world depended on participation in what we may call societies for mutual benefit and protection. As noted by one of their early antagonists, Celsus, the first Christian congregations displayed a high standard of mutual support and benevolence. The social organization of the church was not an innovation in the ancient world; membership in something like a local Christian congregation was virtually a necessity for all but the wealthy.

c. The Revival of Interest in Morality

Although the later Roman Republic and the entire period of the Roman Empire are famed for licentiousness and immorality, by the time Christianity made its appearance, something of a reaction had set in, at least in theory. While the decline of traditional morality was apparent on every side, the intellectual leaders of the era increasingly opposed this trend. In the pagan world there was an increasing tendency to a dualistic approach to life, emphasizing the value of the individual soul, the need for individual asceticism, self-discipline, and a purified pattern of life. It was, however, only Christianity with its confidence in eternal life and its affirmation of the eternal significance of the "things done in his body" (2 Cor. 5:10) that provided the moral fervor necessary to produce the disciplined life of self-denial for which the philosophers were increasingly calling.

d. Roman Law

Every nation has laws, but two ancient peoples were peoples of the Law in a very special way: the Jewish and the Roman. For the Jews, the Law reveals the character and holiness of God and creates a holy people: it particularizes and separates. For the Romans, law is part of the divine order of nature and creates legitimacy: it universalizes, since in principle it is applicable to all peoples. Christianity took over the content of its law from Judaism, from the text of the Old Testament, but it took part of its understanding of the nature and function of law from Rome. Thus Christianity, by its historic development in the universal Roman Empire, has always sought to legislate not for itself or for the church alone, but for the world. Judaism may have confused religion with the Kingdom of Israel, but it never confused Israel with the other nations of the world. When Christianity first became deeply involved with the state, the state in question was not a national kingdom but the universal Roman Empire. Consequently, Christianity has identified itself with the world and its own laws with the laws of nature. Despite all of the problems and confusion such an identification has caused, it is in a way the inevitable consequence for a religious community that takes the First Article of its Nicene Creed seriously: "We believe in One God, the Father Almighty, Maker of heaven and earth and of all things, visible and invisible." If we are willing to accept the Hellenistic cast of Christian doctrine—in contradistinction to those who would confine Christianity to its Semitic origins—asserting that the Hellenistic culture was part of the situation "when the fulness of the time was come" (Gal. 4:4), then we must also acknowledge that Roman law with its claims to universality and its concept of legitimacy was also part of that culture and time.

Rome and its laws gave the early church two things: universality and the specifically Roman concept of the sacraments. Jewish religion has always known that the gods of the nations are idols, while the Lord made the heavens (Ps. 96:5). But Judaism has never sought to become a universe-wide institution to reflect the universal sovereignty of its God. From Hellenism Christianity derived the impulse to show that its doctrines can rule in the whole realm of the intellect, not merely in the life of devotion. And from Rome it derived the impulse to make its laws rule the life of the whole world, not merely of the congregation of believers. The concept of the sacraments, as it has come into the West through Latin-speaking Christianity, is legal rather than, or as well as, mystical, as it was in Greek thought. For the Greeks, the sacrament is *mysterion,* a "mystery," in which God declares and does something we can only sense and accept, but never comprehend. The Roman *sacramentum*—originally a military ceremony by which soldiers and officers bound themselves to one another and Rome—is not devoid of mystery, and also has the concept of legitimatizing and formalizing a permanent relationship.

The term "Roman" stands for two things in Christian history: for the old empire, which was pagan, and for the newer papacy, which early Protestants saw as corrupted by the older paganism. Protestantism has had a tendency to reject all that is Roman as wrong, an imposition on the religion of the Greek and Hebrew Scriptures. Contemporary Protestantism often goes further still, rejecting all that is Greek or Hellenistic and not Semitic as fraudulent. Yet Protestantism—both that of the Reformation and the liberal Protestantism of our era—is at least as marked by the Germanic world and its ways as Catholicism has been by the Roman; it is inconsistent for Protestants to shun the Emperor Constantine the Great and the religion he protected—and to some extent shaped in Rome—while extolling the Elector Frederick the Wise and the Lutheranism he nurtured in Wittenberg.

4. WHERE CHRISTIAN PROCLAMATION BEGAN

The earliest content of Christian proclamation reveals a pairing of two vital elements whose association, in a sense, virtually guarantees the subsequent development of Christian theology: (1) the confession of faith in the one, true God; and (2) the acknowledgment and confession of Jesus Christ as the Son of God, Lord, and Saviour. In addition to these two vital elements, we should mention: (3) the confession of the reality, presence, and ongoing work of the Holy Spirit in the life of believers; and (4) the burning conviction that the personal return of the Lord in glory was imminent. Point 1 gives us personal monotheism, which Christians shared with Jews but not with the philosophical monotheists of the Hellenistic world; 2 introduces in a dramatic way the concept of immanence and historicity to that of the transcendent, eternal God. Through giving the divine title Lord to a person other than the Father, it expresses the germ of the doctrine of the Trinity; 3

completes at least the outline of the doctrine of the Trinity and introduces legitimate aspects of mysticism and enthusiasm; and 4 gives a terrible relevance to human history and a wonderful urgency to evangelism, the proclamation of the Gospel of the kingdom of God.

SELECTED BIBLIOGRAPHY

Baus, Karl. "From the Apostolic Community to Constantine." In *Handbook of Church History*. Freiburg: Herder, 1965.

Burkill, T. Alec. *The Evolution of Christian Thought*. Ithaca: Cornell University Press, 1971.

Carpenter, J. Estlin. *Phases of Early Christianity*. New York and London: Putnam, 1916.

Corwin, Virginia. *St. Ignatius and Christianity in Antioch*. New Haven: Yale University Press, 1960.

Hess, Hamilton. *The Canons of the Council of Sardica A.D. 343: A Landmark in the Early Development of Canon Law*. Oxford: Clarendon, 1958.

King, N. Q. *The Emperor Theodosius and the Establishment of Christianity*. Philadelphia: Westminster, 1960.

Lecler, Joseph. *Toleration and the Reformation*. New York: Association Press, 1960.

Liguori, Alphonsus M. *The History of Heresies and Their Refutation; or the Triumph of the Church*. Translated by John T. Mullock. Dublin: James Duffy, 1847.

Pressense, Edmond de. *Heresy and Christian Doctrine*. London: Hodder & Stoughton, 1873.

Wessel, Leonard P. *G. E. Lessing's Theology—A Reinterpretation: A Study in the Problematic Nature of the Enlightenment*. The Hague: Mouton, 1977.

Wild, Robert. *The Treatment of the Jews in the Greek Christian Writers of the First Three Centuries*. Washington, D.C.: Catholic University Press, 1949.

4

STRUCTURE AND VARIATION

Everything flows.

Heraclitus

The Christian Gospel is essentially a very simple message, so simple that sophisticated hearers sometimes find it hard to take seriously. The Christian religion, by contrast, is extremely complex. It confronts us with a profusion of doctrines, practices, and institutions, often in conflict and sometimes apparently in direct contradiction with one another. Is there a unity to be found beneath all this diversity? Where does legitimate variation end and confusion begin? In contrast to the common Christian assumption that the Christian faith was once delivered, more or less intact, to the saints, nineteenth-century theologians, under the influence of F. C. Baur, contended that doctrine is and has always been an ongoing process of dialectical development. In these pages, we attempt to reaffirm the words of Jude's Epistle that speak of a faith once delivered. In order to do so, we must face the contention of Baur and those who agree with him that the faith is in constant flux and development.

It is apparent that not only the early church but the New Testament itself reflects doctrinal tensions. The Epistle to the Romans, for example, argues at length against works righteousness, and Galatians takes a stand against the influence of legalism in one early congregation. Colossians and 1 John appear to reflect a struggle against ideas that will later be known as gnostic and docetic. Both of these tendencies—to legalism on the one hand, to a kind of gnosis on the other—were definitely present in early Christianity and will recur at intervals throughout the history of the church. What is important to note is that while legalism and a kind of Gnosticism affected Christianity virtually from the beginning, they were not part of its heritage, but part of the human religious consciousness with which Christianity had to come to terms.

38

The tendency to see salvation as resulting from law-keeping, even when one believes in Christ, is called legalism or Judaizing. Carried to its ultimate conclusion, it suggests that human beings are able to merit salvation, and thus to remove the need for a vicarious or substitutionary atonement. In a Judaized Christianity, there is no need for a Son to act as Redeemer; hence the doctrines of the deity of Christ and the Trinity become superfluous.[1] The sixteenth-century Socinians, opposed to the doctrine of the Trinity and to the deity of Christ, proclaimed and practiced a high standard of personal morality, as was also to be the case with early nineteenth-century Unitarians in New England. The legalistic position, when allowed to develop, thus has serious Christological consequences.

The second fundamental human religious concept, which we call gnostic, involves an overvaluing of knowledge with respect to faith. The naive way to understand the Christian Gospel is to see it as a simple message, one that can be simply stated and relatively easily grasped, although it can be believed and accepted only by those who receive the gift of faith. For some of the more sophisticated, the idea of a message that cannot only be grasped but can even be preached by the simple is offensive; they feel that a proper religion must offer something more, an intellectual challenge that puts it beyond the reach of the simple. The gnostic position asserts that over and above the simple Gospel, which is all that ordinary spirits can understand, there is a secret, higher knowledge reserved for an elite. It is natural enough for people to ask more questions than the Gospel answers; the gnostic movement attempted to give the answers, and it did so by drawing on religious sources alien to Christianity and amalgamating them with elements of the Gospel faith.

Although legalism has theological implications, it was more of a practical than a theological problem for the early church. The gnostic movement, by contrast, produced one theological problem after another. It has seldom gone by that name since the early centuries, but Gnosticism has continued to reproduce itself within Christianity and reappears from time to time in new guises. (The movement called gnostic was a widespread religious phenomenon of the Hellenistic world at the beginning of the Christian Era. It influenced a number of religions. Its Christian manifestation is designated as "Gnosticism" in these pages, while the larger phenomenon is called the "gnostic movement.")

Gnosticism was a response to the widespread desire to understand the mystery of being: it offered detailed, secret knowledge of the whole order of reality, claiming to know and to be able to explain things of which ordinary, simple Christian faith was entirely ignorant. It divided mankind into various classes, and reserved its secret wisdom for those who were recognized as belonging to the highest, most spiritual class, a religious elite. Thus it naturally appealed to many who felt that they were above mingling with the common herd of ordinary Christians who were content with the simple Gospel.

Gnosticism and the gnostic movement generally are essentially dualistic. In other words, they view reality as a constant interplay between two fundamental principles, such as spirit and matter, soul and body, good and evil. Gnosticism denies the biblical doctrine of the Creation, because the fundamentally spiritual power, which we call God, cannot be the source of that which is radically opposed to it, the base material world.

Inasmuch as Christianity contains ideas and often uses language that sounds dualistic, it is important to note that it is not necessarily dualistic to speak of a conflict between flesh and spirit, but it is dualistic to think of that conflict as the ultimate and fundamental nature of reality. From a biblical perspective, man's conflict with God is not the result of man's fleshliness in contrast to God's spirituality. Man himself is partly spiritual, and it is his spirit, not his flesh alone, that rebels against God. In addition, the human spirit as well as human flesh is created by God. (A typical gnostic conception holds that the human spirit or soul emanated from the divine but has been imprisoned in a body of flesh, fabricated by an inferior sort of being known as the Demiurge.) Dualism has such a natural appeal as an explanation of the conflict between good and evil that it constantly crops up within Christianity, despite the fact that it is fundamentally incompatible with basic Christian views of God and the Creation.

Another fundamental religious or philosophical assumption, one that stands in radical contrast to dualism, is monism. Monism presupposes that all reality is ultimately one. All is derived from the Absolute, or God— necessarily conceived of as impersonal. The apparent diversity of the world, the apparent conflicts between good and evil, the apparent existence of separate, individual personalities, all of these things are either illusory or temporary manifestations that interfere with the ultimate return of all reality to the oneness from which it came. Monism is no more Christian than dualism, for while it denies the existence of a dualistic, evil principle opposed to the good God, it also conceives of God as impersonal and has no place for the Creation. What we call the world of reality is essentially unreal and illusory, or else part of the process by which the Absolute achieves self-realization. The religious form of monism is termed pantheism, the doctrine that God is all. It is currently reflected in a popular school of theology that has arisen within Christendom; called process theology or sometimes panentheism,[2] it is probably the most dangerous rival to orthodox theology within the general framework of Christian or religious thought today.

Both dualism and monism rest on fundamental assumptions about the nature of reality, assumptions that can neither be proved nor disproved on the basis of available evidence. In the one case, the assumption is that all reality consists of the interplay of two fundamentally opposing realities, such as spirit and matter; in the other, it is that all reality is essentially the working out of a single, spiritual principle. Biblical religion, including both Judaism and Christianity, resembles monism in that it sees a single spiritual power, God, as the Author of all reality, but differs significantly in that this power is personal and creates a real world that is totally distinct from God, not an emanation or manifestation of his being. It resembles dualism in that it admits that there is a fundamental dichotomy in the universe as it currently exists, but conflicts with it in that it sees this dichotomy, the contrast between the Creator and his Creation, not as an eternally existing condition, but as the result of the free decision of God to create. Biblical religion should thus be called neither dualistic nor monistic: it is more correctly called personal theism. Because the God of biblical religion is personal, he can and in fact does give us evidence of his reality by communicating with us through revelation.

The tendency to legalism within Christianity is inspired largely by a persistence of Jewish thinking and the Old Testament emphasis on obedience to the Law. In a sense it is a more natural element within Christianity than dualism, inasmuch as Christianity is directly descended from Judaism. It is tempting—but misleading—to see legalism as the Jewish element in Christianity, and dualism or Gnosticism the Gentile, Hellenistic contribution. Adolf von Harnack viewed Gnosticism as the attempted *secularization* of Christianity, in other words, as the attempt to integrate it into the contemporary, largely dualistic world of Hellenistic religion and philosophy. Christianity successfully resisted Gnosticism, and produced early catholic theology in the process. In Harnack's opinion, this early theology was itself a Hellenization, and thus a falsification, of the original, simpler Gospel message. One almost gains the impression that in his distaste for the development of early catholic theology, Harnack would have preferred the far more fanciful visions of Gnosticism.

If early Christian theology represented a Hellenization of theology in the effort to resist Gnosticism, then it would be necessary to say that although Gnosticism could not conquer Christianity, it forced it to destroy itself. If, however, early Christian theology represents a legitimate and necessary working out, in Hellenistic terms, of the authentic Gospel, then Gnosticism actually performed a service for the church, by compelling it to think the Gospel through and work out its implications.

Harnack's idea that Gnosticism involves the secularization of Christianity seems odd if we think of secularization as meaning bringing Christianity into conformity with the skeptical, materialistic outlook of our own day. Gnosticism is complex, credulous, and anything but materialistic. But if we recall that the word "secular" (from Latin *saeculum*, "age") refers to the spirit of the contemporaneous world—i.e. to the Hellenistic world in the case of Gnosticism—then his suggestion appears less strange. The terms "spiritual," "worldly," and "secular" are often ambivalent in modern usage. In the present work, an effort will be made to use them consistently, but the reader should be alert to the variations in meaning that accompany them throughout twenty centuries of Christian faith and thought.[3]

1. GNOSTICISM

Opinions differ as to which early Christian writer deserves to be called the first theologian. A claim may be made for the converted philosopher Justin Martyr (ca. 100–ca. 165), author of the celebrated *First Apology*, dealing with pagan arguments, and of the *Dialogue with Trypho the Jew*, dealing with Jewish ones. We shall choose the Greek-speaking Bishop of Lyons in southern Gaul, Irenaeus (ca. 125–ca. 202), author of a five-volume work, *Against Heresies*, written about 180–89. The full title is *The Unmasking and Refutation of Falsely So-Called Gnosis.*[4] Thus we see that one of the very earliest significant doctrinal works of Christianity was the direct result not of any desire to produce a comprehensive theology, but grew out of the necessity to deal with a dangerous and persistent heresy. The fact that *Against Heresies* is so comprehensive is due in no small measure to the fact that the heresy against which it speaks was not limited to a particular point or doctrine, but was an alternative vision of religious reality spanning a wide range of doctrines. Because of the importance of this work, it is possible to say that Gnosticism is in a sense the stepmother of systematic theology and that a heresy is the stepmother of orthodoxy.

a. The Spirit of Early Christianity

The first congregations were inspired in almost equal measure by the conviction that the Messiah had just come and by the eager expectation that he would speedily return in power and glory. The expectation of Christ's imminent return led to a short-lived experiment with community of goods, and then to a typical pattern of sharing and mutual support and concern. The loving and practical ways in which members of the early church supported one another caught the attention of pagans and was one of the reasons the church attracted so many converts despite the disapproval of the government and the ever-present threat of persecution.

Because the return of Christ was expected at virtually any moment, there was no tendency in the early congregations to develop a systematic structure of doctrines. The first Christian doctrinal handbook, *The Teaching of the Twelve Apostles*, or *Didache*, was written perhaps a century after

Christ.[5] The best-known Christian creed, which we call the Apostles' Creed, appears at about the same time as a confession spoken by new Christians at baptism; this early form is called the old Roman Creed or Symbol (the Greek term *symbolon,* Latin *symbolum,* is used as a synonym for our word "creed").

Apart from the *Didache,* which is rather brief and not very comprehensive, the first major treatments of Christian doctrine appeared as *apologies,* a distinctively literary form of the early church. The apology was a defense of the faith and conduct of Christians addressed to the outside world, usually to the government, sometimes—as in the case of Justin's *Dialogue with Trypho the Jew*—to the Jews. For the first two centuries or so, the early Christians were so persuaded that the knowledge that came from their faith was totally superior to the philosophy and mythology of the Hellenistic world that they made little or no attempt to compare the one to the other. John the Evangelist wrote, "Ye need not that any man teach you . . ." (1 John 2:27). Christian disdain for worldly wisdom was expressed by Tertullian of Carthage, a Roman jurist turned Christian (ca. 160–ca. 230): "What has Athens to do with Jerusalem, or the Stoa with the Porch of Solomon?"[6] Tertullian became one of the pioneers of Christian theology in Latin. In the latter part of his life, he found the church too lax, and went over to a heretical "reform" movement, Montanism.

Waiting for the Lord to return, the first Christians were reluctant to attempt to put their faith and convictions into a comprehensive form. While they tarried, others began to try to fit the overwhelming spiritual fact of Christ into a universal framework. The first and most dangerous of these attempts was made by the gnostics.

A number of theologians attach great importance to the delay of Christ's return for the development of Christian theology. Because Christ did not return when expected, an explanation had to be found, and this was the beginning of theology. There is a measure of truth in this position, although no orthodox Christian will accept the implication of some thinkers, such as theologians Martin Werner of Bern (1887–1964) and John A. T. Robinson of Cambridge (b. 1919), that Christ was deceived or deceived his followers about the imminence of his return. It is evident, however, that the long hesitation of early Christianity to produce a comprehensive theology made it possible for Gnosticism to present its synthesis between the Gospel of Christ and its own gnosis first. As a result, Christian theology had to be developed in reaction to Gnosticism, and this inevitably led the first theologians to choose their points of concentration in reaction to false doctrines, rather than in a fully logical and systematic exposition of the Gospel as proclaimed in the New Testament.[7]

So thoroughly did the early church fulfill its task of refuting Gnosticism that the works of the gnostics fell into oblivion, and their ideas were known for centuries primarily through the criticisms of the early church fathers, especially Irenaeus. As a result—because Irenaeus and others attacked the Christian wing of the broad gnostic movement—until recently it was thought that the whole movement was a phenomenon within the church. It was not recognized that the gnostic current affected the whole religious and intellectual culture of the ancient world, including Judaism and paganism as well as Christianity.

We now recognize that what we call Gnosticism—the Christian side of the movement—was only one aspect of an extremely broad philosophical-spiritual current that swept across the ancient world.[8] As a spiritual fashion, it may be likened to existentialism in the twentieth century; existentialism has inspired not only atheists and others who find religion absurd and who oppose Christianity; it has also been used within Christianity to develop a totally heretical understanding of Christ and the Gospel, especially by Rudolf Bultmann (1884–1976). In addition, it has profoundly influenced thinkers who stand far more solidly within the orthodox tradition, such as Jacques Maritain (1882–1973) and Nikolai Berdyaev (1874–1948). The principle of evolution is another example of a spiritual presupposition that comes from outside the Christian context and that has been used to oppose Christianity, but that also has been adapted within more or less traditional schemes of Christian thought.

The gnostic movement has two salient features that appeal to countless minds in every age, i.e. the claim to present a secret lore, explaining otherwise incomprehensible mysteries, and the assertion that its secrets are accessible only to the elite—thus by implication defining as elite all who take an active interest in them. As a result, gnostic ideas will frequently reappear on Christian soil, even in modern times. The "Christian Science" of Mary Baker Eddy (1821–1910) is a modern variety of Gnosticism. Indeed, political philosopher Eric Voegelin even calls Marxism a gnostic movement.[9]

Although Christianity has produced more than its share of scholars, pseudoscholars, and intellectual pedants and snobs, the Christian message offers no basis for the scholar or intellectual to think that his intellectual abilities and accomplishments qualify him as a member of a spiritual elite. In fact, even so gifted an intellectual as Paul himself warned against thinking that Christianity attracts many members of worldly elites (1 Cor. 1:26–27). Consequently, the tendency for intellectual Christians to glide over into one kind of Gnosticism or another, in which they think that intellectual attainments make them superior Christians, remains a perennial temptation.

b. Gnosticism Versus Particularity

Christianity has a universal appeal; in his Great Commission (Matt. 28:19–20), Jesus told his followers to make disciples of all nations. Nevertheless, Christianity is distinguished from the more speculative great religions such as Hinduism and Buddhism by its absolute dependence on the *historicity* and *particularity* of the Gospel. Jesus is indeed called the Logos ("Word") and the Mediator between God and man, but he is not seen as a cosmic or universal principle, but as a real flesh-and-blood human being, who suffered, died, and rose again under a real, historical, and trivial Roman official, Pontius Pilate. During the early twentieth century, attempts were made to deny the historicity of Jesus Christ, and to present him as the invention of his followers,[10] but there has never been an attempt to discredit the historicity of the unfortunate Pilate.

While Christians claim that a particular, historic figure, an "accident," so to speak, of history, is truth itself (John 14:6), many intellectuals in every age have firmly resisted the suggestion that spiritual and philosophical absolutes can be tied to something that just "happened" in history. Lessing, as noted earlier, expressed this objection well when he wrote, "Accidental truths of history cannot be the foundation for eternal truths of reason."[11]

To a large extent, the statements made in the Bible are historical in nature. It tells individuals what they must do to be saved, but it does not answer complex cosmological problems in any detail, other than to state the doctrine of the Creation as a historic event. This was very unsatisfying to countless inquiring minds. The sweeping panorama of the gnostics' visions was more fascinating and satisfying, rather like the modern book and television series by Carl Sagan, *Cosmos*—although both visions, that of the gnostics and of Sagan, are more imaginative than scientific.[12]

Educated, first-century Hellenistic Jews were embarrassed by what they considered the arbitrary, trivial, perhaps even barbarous aspects of their Old Testament revelation. Philo of Alexandria, a contemporary of Jesus and Paul and one of the greatest intellects of the ancient world, proposed to interpret revelation allegorically. This removed many of the difficulties, but of course deprived the Bible of one of its most characteristic features, namely, the fact that it is rooted in real space-and-time history. After a period of two centuries or so, many Christians followed the lead of Origen, also of Alexandria (ca. 185–ca. 254), in adopting the same allegorical method.

Because the biblical message does not tell us as much as inquiring minds often want to know, many who are attracted to it often add to it in imaginative ways,[13] as Origen pointed out in his response to a pagan critic, the philosopher Celsus:

> Because many people, and not only the working and servant classes, but also many from the educated classes of Greece, saw something worthy of honor in Christianity, it was inevitable that sects should arise. This was not simply out of pleasure in controversy and contradiction, but because many scholars sought to penetrate more deeply

into the truths of Christianity. Thus sects arose, taking their names
from men who indeed admired the basic nature of Christianity, but who
for many different reasons came to varying interpretations.[14]

In Alexandria, sophisticated, Hellenized Jews transformed their covenant faith into a kind of religious philosophy. Following their lead, many
Christians also resorted to the allegorical method, especially for the interpretation of the Old Testament. (An example of allegorical interpretation is
found in the New Testament itself, where Paul tells us that Hagar, Abraham's Gentile concubine, represents Mount Sinai and her son Ishmael the
old covenant, while freeborn Sarah and her son Isaac represent the new
[Gal. 4:22–31].) Where Hellenistic Jews generally sought to find a moral or
philosophical lesson in the Old Testament narrative, Christian allegorizers
looked for Christ or other elements of the New Testament.

2. THE NATURE OF GNOSTICISM

Gnosticism, as we call the Christian phase of the gnostic movement, is
extremely difficult to describe and categorize. First of all, it was part of a
large and complex religious and philosophical movement that swept through
the ancient Roman world. Secondly, at least some Christians used the term
"gnosis" for the Christian knowledge of God and called the mature Christian a "gnostic." Origen's teacher and predecessor as head of the catechetical school at Alexandria, Clement (d. ca. 215), is an example. Thirdly,
although Irenaeus and other Christians did all they could to disinfect Christianity totally and eliminate all traces of Gnosticism, it seems likely that it
must have left an impression. Franz Overbeck (1837–1905), a colleague and
friend of Friedrich Nietzsche (1844–1900) at Basel and a very hostile critic
of Christianity, claimed that Gnosticism in fact won a delayed victory and
that its ideas are reflected to a great extent in early catholicism.[15]

Adolf von Harnack compares the victory of orthodoxy theology over
Gnosticism to the restoration of monarchy by Napoleon after the French
Revolution—outwardly it was a restoration, but the radical ideas of the revolution were perpetuated under him. For Harnack, the early gnostics were
"nothing other than the theologians of first century Christianity. . . . Faith
in the Gospel was converted into a knowledge about God, nature, and history."[16] In other words, Harnack looks on Christian theology per se as a
Hellenization of the simple Gospel in the spirit of Gnosticism. From our
perspective, it would be more plausible to compare the philosophical and
religious speculation of Paul Tillich (1886–1965) or even the massive and
urbane learning of Harnack himself with Gnosticism.

In attempting to understand Gnosticism, it is necessary to consider both its general religious and philosophical stance and its specific relationship to the central doctrines of Christianity.

a. The Religious and Philosophical Stance of Gnosticism

On Christian soil, the gnostic impulse sought to preserve several Christian ideas and terms while giving up the specific dependence of Christianity on the history of the Jews and, in the New Testament, of Jesus and his disciples. The facts of biblical history were replaced with an elaborate gnosis about the origin and development of divine, spiritual beings—the so-called aeons—and ultimately of the material world.

Gnosticism did not find ready soil to work in the Jewish religious tradition, tied as firmly as it is to specific and very detailed events in the history of one small Semitic people. Christianity, however, was a rich source of ideas and terminology. The concepts of a Mediator, of the Logos, of fullness of the Spirit, or incarnation, regeneration, and salvation could all be detached from their historical roots in events in the life of Jesus and the first Christians and interpreted as universally valid philosophical and religious ideas. This was made easier by the fact that when the gnostic movement was having its maximum impact on Christianity—during the first half of the second century of the Christian Era—the writings of the New Testament had not yet been collected in a recognized canon and were not in circulation everywhere.

Gnosticism required something ordinary philosophy could not give it, namely, a knowledge superior to that of the schools and the philosophers. This religious dimension required revelation, and this is what Gnosticism borrowed or stole from Judaism via Christianity. Gnosticism presented itself as a supernaturally revealed, divinely guaranteed wisdom. The impact of Jesus Christ on those who knew him or heard about him spread the conviction that absolute, ultimate truth could be known and in fact had been revealed through an individual human being. Jesus called himself "the way, the truth, and the life" (John 14:6). This certainty the gnostics borrowed from the Christians; using it as a starting point, they erected on it an elaborate and fanciful structure of doctrines and ideas for which there was no guarantee other than their own imagination. This, indeed, many modern writers also do, and thus deserve to be compared to Gnosticism. Paul Tillich, for example, developed an elaborate religious philosophy using Christian terminology and supposedly taking its origin from the "New Being" in Christ, but preserving very few of the specific doctrines or historical facts of biblical Christianity. Among non-Christians, Karl Marx, Sigmund Freud, and quite recently Carl Sagan have created elaborate speculative philosophies that rival those of Gnosticism, ostensibly based on historical, psychological, or physical science, but evidently going far beyond the warrant of any scientific facts.

The gnostic movement and Christian Gnosticism present us with the first example of an effort that will be made over and over again in the history of civilization—the effort to adopt the figure of Christ and pay him honor, while freeing oneself of all ties both to that distinctive, peculiar, and somewhat exasperating people, the Jews, and to what seems like the tawdry history of a little-known rabbi and a motley band of undistinguished disciples in a corner of the mighty Roman Empire.

It is apparent that the New Testament itself makes much use of a number of concepts that were familiar elements of Hellenistic religious and philosophical thought in the first century. The idea of a Logos as Mediator between the Absolute and the world of multiplicity and the concept of God as light are two examples. Because of this it was common, especially during the nineteenth century, to think that even the New Testament itself, particularly the writings of John, had borrowed heavily from Hellenistic thought and had grafted its ideas onto the simple, Semitic message of Jesus. In this era, it was common to attribute a late, postapostolic date to the Gospel of John, a view that has been greatly revised by modern New Testament scholarship. In the twentieth century, particularly since the discovery of the Dead Sea Scrolls, it has become apparent that these ideas were not specifically Hellenistic, but were part of the Semitic intellectual and religious outlook as well. Consequently, their presence in the Gospel of John, for example, is no evidence for the claim either that John is a late, pseudonymous Gospel or that the Gospel borrows heavily from Hellenistic ideas.

What seems to be the case is that when the gnostic movement encountered Christianity, several of its major teachers adopted and adapted a number of basic New Testament ideas to their gnostic mentality and then sought to propagate the resulting synthesis among Christians and non-Christians alike. Because Christians naturally were interested in a fuller explanation of the mystery of the universe and existence than the simple Gospel offered, and because their own thinkers had not yet produced much in the way of a comprehensive theology, Gnosticism represented a real threat to Christianity. Orthodox writers found that they not only had to try to counter its false doctrines, but had to provide an alternative explanation for at least some of the cosmic mysteries with which it dealt—the origin of the universe, the origin and nature of evil, and the meaning of personal salvation. In any era in which Christian thinkers fail to do this, or do an inadequate job of it, Gnosticism will almost inevitably arise in some variety of reincarnation; the most dramatic example being Christian Science, which not merely offers a "gnosis" that it holds superior to the mere knowledge of the Bible, but revives a number of specifically gnostic ideas.

Gnosticism involved (1) a complicated cosmology based on ancient Near Eastern ideas, not biblical ones; (2) Hellenistic patterns of speculative thought; and (3) the acceptance of Jesus Christ as the Saviour of the world. It involved a speculative element, a religious-mystical element, and even a practical, ascetic element. Fundamentally, it "transformed all ethical problems into cosmological ones."[17] Its shift of ethical interest away from the sphere of personal conduct—where individuals had to decide whether or not to obey God—to the realm of the cosmological is paralleled by the tendency of many modern theologians to neglect the ethics of personal conduct and to treat all problems as political ones—over which the individual seldom has much influence.

In removing the accent from faith and placing it on a special kind of knowledge, Gnosticism was transforming the spirit of the Gospel as well as its content. An emphasis on knowledge as the means to salvation is inimical to the Gospel concept of receiving the kingdom like a little child (Matt. 18:3), and humility ceases to be a virtue. While many, if not all, of the gnostic schools did stress a high level of personal behavior, especially ascetic self-denial, the reason behind it was not a desire to obey God but the desire to keep the soul free for its spiritual quest by keeping bodily appetites under control.

b. The Clash with Christianity

Gnosticism clashed with biblical Christianity at many points, but two deserve special mention: the doctrine of Creation and the doctrine of Christ. Gnosticism totally denied the Creation. In the first place, the supreme Deity, as Gnosticism conceived it, was altogether too exalted to be capable of having anything to do with base matter; in consequence, an act of creation as such was impossible. The Bible also sees the world God has created as radically different from him. This difference, however, is not primarily that the world is evil, while God is good; in fact, biblical doctrine teaches that the world was created *good*, although it has been corrupted by the Fall of Man. For biblical thought, the world is radically distinct from God because he is the Creator, it is his creation. Gnosticism not only opposed the idea that God could have been involved in an act of creating a material world, but it also denied that the material world is meaningful in itself. There is no creation order, as Christian theology teaches. The material world, if not totally illusory, is meaningless, and no true wisdom can be gleaned by studying it. Presumably, if Gnosticism had triumphed, it could not have produced experimental natural science as Christianity did, for the simple reason that it looked on the material world as meaningless.

While Gnosticism repudiated Creation, it accepted Christ, although it gave him a drastically different interpretation from that of developing orthodox theology. Christianity might conceivably have accepted a gnostic Christology, for the Christ of orthodoxy also has a cosmic dimension. If it had done so, it would have lost its roots in history, for the Christ of Gnosticism was not the real, human Jesus of Nazareth and did not die under Pontius Pilate.

3. GNOSTIC CHRISTOLOGY

Gnostic motifs were already felt in Christian circles in the Age of the Apostles. Early church tradition attributes the rise of Gnosticism to Simon Magus, briefly mentioned in Acts 8:9–24. His attempt to purchase the gift of the Holy Spirit gives us the expression "simony" for the offense of buying and selling spiritual offices. According to the account in Acts, Simon repented. Later traditions tell us that he went to Rome, where he competed with the Apostle Peter and founded a gnostic sect. The second-century Christian writer Hegesippus, by contrast, tells that the gnostic movement preceded the ministry of Christ in Palestine. Gnosticism was a byproduct of "seven Jewish heresies," some of them involving gnostic currents.[18] The account of Hegesippus notes that the movement is older than Christianity, something many later writers failed to note.

The first two teachers to propagate gnostic ideas within Christian circles were Simon and his successor Menander. Unlike later and more famous representatives of Gnosticism, both Simon and Menander claimed divinity for themselves. According to Acts 8:9–11, Simon called himself the "great power of God." The Greek term he used, *dynamis,* was used by later, more orthodox theologians in reference to both the Son and the Holy Spirit. (From Simon's use of *dynamis* in reference to himself, it is evident that the term "power," in such a context, can be a person, not merely an impersonal force or influence. It is important to note this, for often the terms early Christianity applied to the Son and particularly to the Holy Spirit are suggestive of something impersonal rather than of a real Person in the sense of orthodox trinitarian teaching.) Justin Martyr also reports Simon's messianic claim.[19]

Simon's early Gnosticism was a strange blend of philosophy and self-worship. He met a certain Helena in a brothel in Tyre and discovered that she was a reincarnation of the primordial Ennoia ("Indwelling Mind"), the first conception of the spirit of God. As Ennoia she had generated angelic powers, some of which rebelled against God, captured her, and imprisoned her in a mortal body. Reincarnated many times, she was once Helen of Troy and, in Simon's day, a prostitute in Tyre, where he met her. She is the lost sheep of Jesus' parable (Matt. 18:10–14). To save her, the highest God himself appeared in Simon. Characteristically, Simon taught that the Old Testament was the revelation of malicious angels, and hence oppressive. To believe in him was to be free from its bondage.

Simon and his followers are charged by their Christian opponents with practicing magic and occult arts. This was natural enough; to the extent that they were impressed by his ability to work apparent miracles, the early Christians had no choice but to attribute them to the powers of evil. Many other gnostic figures were accused of necromancy, a not unlikely charge in view of their emphasis on their access to hidden, i.e. occult, knowledge and power.

Simon's system involved a number of points that will also characterize later heretical movements: (1) a syncretistic blending of biblical ideas with themes drawn from other, i.e. pagan, Near Eastern sources; (2) a dualistic interpretation of the material world as hopelessly estranged, by nature, from the purely spiritual Father;[20] (3) the teaching that a personal Saviour has appeared on earth; (4) a rejection of the Jewish Scriptures as fraudulent or malicious; (5) an interest not only in secret lore, but in magic and the occult.

The fact that Gnosticism, like certain later movements, ties rejection of the Hebrew Old Testament to fresh superstitions and an interest in the occult helps us to see the cardinal importance of the Old Testament for Christian orthodoxy. The major doctrines of Christianity are indeed drawn from the New Testament, and superficially it might appear as though the Old Testament is of interest chiefly as background. As a matter of fact, however, it is the Old Testament that guarantees the rootedness of Christ, his person, and his work in real history. Whenever the Old Testament is ignored or reduced to mere Jewish religious thought, Christians readily fall prey to various mythologies and occultism.[21] With the loss of confidence in the reliability of the Old Testament, brought about by, among other things, nineteenth-century liberal Bible criticism, some nominally Christian leaders developed an enthusiasm for pagan mythology. The Danish Lutheran N. F. S. Grundtvig (1783–1872) wanted to absorb heroic Norse mythology into Lutheranism.

Simon Magus appears to have reached Rome before people became fully conversant with Jesus' claim to be the Messiah and with the account of his death, resurrection, and ascension. Thus Simon could claim himself to be the Saviour, indeed, an incarnation of God himself. (After the Gospel story became common knowledge, later gnostic teachers would no longer claim to be the Christ, but only seek to work him into a suitable place in their speculative systems.) The extent that Jesus was presented as the Christ seemed an atrocity. Simon taught that his crucifixion and death had taken place in appearance only, just as Simon himself was God in reality and a man in appearance only. Gnosticism thus provides our introduction to what is known as "docetism" (from Greek *dokeo*, "to appear" or "seem"), the doctrine that tells us Christ only seemed to be a human being.

a. Docetism

The gnostic movement as a whole and even church-related Gnosticism are really too big and too foreign to the New Testament to be called heresies; they really represent an alternative religion. (The same indeed might be said, and is said, concerning liberalism, modernism, process theology, and other movements within Christianity; it needs to be taken as seriously there as in the present context. Neither German New Testament scholar Bultmann nor the Swiss Roman Catholic theologian Hans Küng put forward any such atrocious claims as those of Simon Magus, but it may well be the case that their Christologies are as fanciful as those of later representatives of Gnosticism.)

In producing docetism, Gnosticism presented us with the first heresy that can be clearly lodged *within* Christianity. Gnosticism was not a Christian movement, properly speaking, because apart from a limited number of shared ideas, its interests were quite different from those of biblical religion. The doctrine of Christ was a shared interest, however. Gnosticism produced docetism because it considered it intolerable to think that a pure spiritual being, Christ, could suffer as a man. Hence he must have been human in appearance only. This same thought occurred spontaneously in Christian circles. It is the reason why "Greeks" (some Gentile Christians, as well as non-Christian Gentiles) consider the doctrine of Christ crucified "foolishness" (1 Cor. 1:23).

Because docetism was the first of the Christian heresies, it naturally called forth the earliest formal Christian creed, that of Ignatius of Antioch. One of the early post–New Testament writers known as the Apostolic Fathers, Ignatius was martyred toward the end of the reign of the Emperor Trajan (ruled 98–117). Rather than seeking to escape this fate, he courted it, and admonished the Christians in Rome to do nothing to help him avoid it. In a few brief lines, the creed of Ignatius repeatedly emphasized that Jesus "truly, and not in appearance," did and experienced all that the New Testament ascribes to him, including truly, and not in appearance, being born, suffering, dying, and rising.[22] Inasmuch as Ignatius anticipated being put to death himself, truly, and not in appearance, his emphasis on the true resurrection of Jesus is entirely understandable.

The fact that docetism frequently recurs within Christendom illustrates the truth of Paul's statement that the preaching of the Cross is "folly to the Greeks." The folly lies in the idea, unpalatable to the philosophical and religious thought of Hellenism, that the divine can take on material substance and suffer the fate of material beings. A more modern version of the same prejudice is seen in the conviction of some theologians, such as Willi Marxsen, that Jesus could not actually have arisen bodily, but only seemed to his disciples to do so. Thus their proclamation is merely an interpretation of what Jesus meant to them, not a statement about what he really did.[23]

In the case of Simon Magus, it was necessary to explain the fact that he was still alive on earth after the supposed events of the crucifixion by saying that he was merely thought to have suffered, but did not actually do so.[24] A docetic view of Jesus Christ, which denies that he was truly a real, physical human being, is often accompanied by an interest in the occult, in which the "spiritual" activities of necromancy, words and magical gestures, produce a physical effect. Human beings seem to need to have some aspect of their lives in which the spiritual and the physical are seen as directly interrelated, and if this is not done in the historic person of Jesus Christ, as it is in orthodox Christianity, other substitutes will be sought, as in magical and occult practices. Despite the rise and apparent overwhelming dominance of the scientific world view in the second half of the twentieth century, there has been a wild proliferation of occult beliefs and practices, most pronounced in those areas where faith in the objective reality of Jesus Christ as the incarnate Son of God has declined.[25]

Simon, about whose life we know so little, appears to have been a kind of living preview of another major heresy of later years, one that will be known as modalism. He not only claimed to be the Saviour, in human form, but also the highest God, thus clearly expressing the idea that God and the Saviour (and Simon) are all one and the same Person, appearing and acting under different forms or modes of existence. Simon, in effect, was unwilling to share the highest divine honors he claimed for himself with any other, and thus claimed to be both Christ and the Father. The concept that divine honors can be shared among different Persons was an idea that had to be accepted in order for the doctrine of the Trinity to be formulated. We may dismiss Simon as an outrageous megalomaniac, but it is interesting to note that his concept of the unity of God was so strong that in making his outrageous claim to be divine, he refused to acknowledge the existence of any other person who could make a similar claim. This concern for the monarchy or unity of God, freed of blasphemous claims such as Simon's, will persist in Christian circles and will make it difficult to come to terms with the fact that the New Testament and the church make divine claims not for one only, the Father, but for two others as well, the Son and the Holy Spirit.

To return to Simon Magus and his claims, they did not prevent him from dying, as Ignatius would have said, truly, and not in appearance. His school was taken over by a certain Menander, who also claimed to be an incarnation, but only of the Saviour, not of the highest God. By saying that he was the incarnate Saviour, but not God, Menander made the Saviour, Christ, less than God. Simon had claimed to be both. For Simon, Father and Saviour were one Person; for Menander they were two, both divine, but not equally so.

To argue that the Saviour has only a partial deity is one plausible way of attempting to deal with the biblical statements that ascribe divine honors to Christ, without thereby creating two Gods. The Son, incarnate in Jesus, is in a sense divine, but does not possess full deity.[26] The views of Simon himself, by contrast, seem paradoxical, at times even incoherent, and as such resemble views of religious enthusiasts and charlatans found in every age. On the one hand, they engaged in occult practices and emphasized their ability to work wonders, and on the other they said that the most important thing was knowledge of them and faith in their divinity. On the one hand, they taught that every god should be honored, but on the other, they opposed the God of the Jews.[27]

If the Simon Magus of whom the legends and the early Fathers tell us is identical with the Simon whom Peter encountered in Acts, then it is possible that Paul's strictures in the Epistle to the Colossians are a reaction to Simon's specific errors. If that is the case, then we may say that rising heresies not only spurred the development of the formal creeds, but even helped to determine the contents of our New Testament, in that the Apostles were forced to write against them.

b. Inroads into Christianity

Although both Acts and later Christian traditions tell us that Simon clashed with the Apostle Peter, and although it appears that Simon wanted to align himself with Christianity—at least by purchasing a share of the Apostles' spiritual gifts—we cannot really reckon him to Christianity. His movement was virtually contemporary with the beginning of the Apostles' ministry and seems never to have been in any likelihood of merging with it. A different situation is represented by a man called Cerinthus of Ephesus, who is supposed to have clashed with the aged Apostle John.[28] In any event, the Gospel of John takes a position against views such as his. According to Irenaeus (although not according to any internal evidence in the Gospel itself), the Gospel of John presupposed the conflict with Cerinthus. Some later critics suggest that the striking references to the Logos, the beginning (*arche*), and the only begotten (*monogenes*) were added to the Prologue of

John 1 in direct reaction to the Gnosticism of Cerinthus. The Johannine writings in the New Testament include a number of themes that are categorically hostile to gnostic speculation, of which the most important is the affirmation that the Word *was made* flesh (1:14), an atrocity in gnostic eyes. It is at least conceivable that the author took special pains to preclude the possibility that certain current gnostic ideas could find their way into the faith of Christians. In light of the fact that John's Gospel presents a number of ideas that were very important to early gnostics, but in such a way that they oppose Gnosticism rather than support it, a few changes in the Gospel text would have made it a useful tool for gnostics. Gnostic Gospels were composed, but there was no significant meddling with the canonical text of John's Gospel, a fact that probably reflects the tremendous zeal with which the first Christians guarded the transmission of their holy Scriptures.

4. THE GNOSTIC CRISIS

The encounters between the Apostles and their successors on the one hand and the followers of Simon and Menander on the other were the prelude to the first full-fledged doctrinal challenge to confront Christianity. We may date this crisis in the half century between the time that the old Roman (Apostles') Creed began to come into use, around 125, and Irenaeus' composition of *Against Heresies* (180–89). The gnostic crisis cannot have burst upon the church prior to the introduction of the Roman creed, for if it had, the creed would surely have stressed that there is but one God, the Creator, who has made both the visible, material world as well as the invisible world of spirits. These affirmations are made in the Nicene Creed of 325.

Irenaeus wrote *Against Heresies* to refute Gnosticism, but the movement was already waning by the time he wrote. *Against Heresies* is an invaluable—and unusually amusing—document for our understanding both of early Christianity and the forces against which it had to contend. To the extent that gnostic influences can recur, it is because the church in other ages has some of the same characteristics that made Gnosticism a threat in the second century; for this reason, *Against Heresies* is worthwhile reading for Christians in every age.

There were three strains of religious life among the early Christians that proved receptive to Gnosticism: asceticism, charismatic tendencies, and a speculative, philosophical mood. Ascetically inclined Christians interpreted their obligations to the Law of Moses in terms of self-denial and resistance to all the appetites of the flesh. They naturally tended to dualism, with its doctrine that the flesh is evil. The charismatic element in the early church disliked congregational discipline and the restriction of the concept of revelation to the written Scripture, and hence was receptive to the suggestion that other revelations had been secretly transmitted by Jesus to the most spiritual of his followers. Those who were inclined to speculate on the relationship of the One to the many through the Logos found that orthodox Christianity did not give much scope to their fancies; Gnosticism offered far more. When the gnostic tendency that was so much a part of the intellectual world of Hellenism discovered that it could not successfully compete with Christianity, it in effect began to try to absorb it. The church historian Reinhold Seeberg puts it thus: "The success of Christ had tempted Simon to try to compete with him. This became less and less possible as time went on. It was impossible to impede the victorious advance of Christ, but if it was not possible against him, they could try it with him. Christ was irresistible in both West and East, but faith in the ancient wisdom of the East was also strong, together with the drive to solve all the puzzles of existence with sacred revelation. So this old Oriental syncretism placed itself in the 'service' of Christ."[29]

Christianity, like Judaism, has always resolutely opposed the blending of religions; it was not even willing to accommodate to the Judaism out of which it sprang. Referring to the "Judaizing" tendency to emphasize the keeping of the Law, Paul thundered at the Galatians: "But though we, or an angel from heaven, preach any other gospel . . . let him be accursed" (Gal. 1:8). How did Gnosticism, then, with its profoundly syncretistic character, succeed in becoming a threat? There are two reasons: first, neither the canonical New Testament nor any generally recognized creed was yet in common circulation when the menace of Gnosticism arose; second, there was little persecution under the "good emperors" of the first half of the second century, and people could dabble in Christianity with a measure of impunity. It was not so much that the Christians toyed with Gnosticism as that the Hellenistic world was trying to integrate Christ into its thinking without being profoundly changed by him, and proposed Gnosticism to the church as a means to this end. Jesus and his first disciples made such an overwhelming impact on the Mediterranean world that it could not be ignored, but his message was so contrary to Hellenistic culture that it could not simply be accepted, and so the effort was made to adapt it to the culture.

When Jesus said, "I am the light of the world" (John 8:12), he might have been portraying the impact his story was to make on Hellenistic civilization a century later. For second-century man, the cosmos was dark, cruel, bewildering, and essentially meaningless; history was nothing but a continual succession of purposeless cycles. Against this background, the story of Jesus, in the proclamation of his followers, flashed in brilliance with all the beauty of a supernatural love. The gnostics conceived of the universe as a great chain of brilliant worlds, peopled by angelic powers, suspended over a dark abyss of chaos, in which humanity languished. Humans had been plunged into that dark abyss without their will, and could not escape it unless a higher, heavenly spirit should descend to free them. What gnostic speculation postulated as necessary, the story of Jesus seemed to say had happened; indeed, it is easy to cast the story of Jesus in just such colorful imagery as the gnostics already used.

Ordinary Christians did not always recognize that while the historic reality of Jesus Christ was paramount for them, it was the imagery that appealed to the gnostics.[30] The non-Christian product of Hellenistic culture who found it difficult to accept the folly of the Cross when the Gospel was presented as the story of things happening on the earth under a very mortal Roman procurator could readily digest the Gospel if it was presented as the myth of a Saviour descending to save pure spirits imprisoned in vile bodies.

a. Brokers of Gnosticism

Two individuals, the Syrian Saturnilus, or Saturninus, and the Egyptian Basilides, active during the first quarter of the second century, adapted the idea of the Christ—not the history of the man Jesus—to the gnostic panorama of the universe. From John 1:18, Saturnilus took the assertion that the Father is unseen (and therefore unknown); he created a world of angels and archangels, principalities and powers (cf. Eph. 1:21, 6:12), seven of which made the world and man. Man was originally a creeping thing, until the supreme power breathed into some the "spark of life." Mankind is then divided into two races, a good, spiritual race, and an evil, earthy race (cf. the references to the children of light and the children of this world, e.g. Eph. 5:8). The Father sent his only begotten, the incorporeal Christ, to destroy the evil race and save those who have the spark of life; he was a man in appearance only. Salvation comes through belief in this gnostic Christ and an otherworldly, i.e. ascetic, pattern of life, including abstinence from marriage and procreation.[31] Belief in Christ is in effect the knowledge (gnosis) of all the complex relationships between the Father, the spiritual beings, and the world.

In the vision of reality developed by Saturnilus, three things stand out: (1) the notion of a descending chain of intermediate, more or less corruptible spiritual powers between the unknowable Father and the world; these are called "aeons," from a Greek word usually translated "ages," but here having the special meaning of a godlike spiritual entity. The God of the Jews and his angels are degenerate, base aeons, Christ a good one. (2) Superimposed on this chain is a dualism between the spiritual world and the material world; the spiritual entities, the aeons, may be good or evil, but the material world is the product of evil aeons and is itself evil. (3) The specifically gnostic concept of salvation involves the liberation of the embodied human spirits from their prisons of flesh and their return to the Father. This differs sharply from the New Testament concept, which involves the resurrection of the body as well as the survival of the soul.

The teaching of Saturnilus is subtler and less pretentious than that of Simon; he presented himself only as a teacher, not as the Christ. Saturnilus represented the ascetic stream in Gnosticism. A dualistic world view can lead to the condemnation of all fleshly self-indulgences, even the most necessary, such as eating and drinking, and to the desire to do as little as possible to fulfill bodily desires and appetites. It can also lead to the idea that inasmuch as the flesh is naturally evil, but has nothing whatsoever to do with the true life of the spirit, one can yield to all the lusts of the body without affecting the immaterial spirit at all. Most dualists, through the ages, have been ascetics, but the libertarian strain also reappears constantly alongside of the ascetic.

Following Saturnilus, Basilides appears, the first systematic "theologian" of Gnosticism. Basilides (d. ca. 140) antedates the first Greek-speaking Christian systematic theologian, Irenaeus (ca. 125–ca. 202), by half a century, and the first systematic theologian writing in Latin, Tertullian (ca. 160–ca. 230), by almost a century. Basilides attempted to answer the age-old question posed by the idea of the transcendence of God: if God is truly transcendent and totally above all material reality, how did the material world come into existence? What relationship can the absolutely pure, spiritual Father have with the corruptible world of material reality? Basilides taught that the Father himself had nothing to do with it. The Father is capable only of spiritual activity; by it Nous ("Mind") proceeds from him. This process is called emanation and has nothing in common with physical generation. From the Nous comes the Logos ("Word"). Gnosticism thus took over a fundamental biblical concept, but reduced it in stature from the absolute rank it holds in John 1 to that of a link in a descending sequence of aeons. From the highest aeons proceed Phronesis ("Prudence"), Sophia ("Wisdom"), and Dynamis ("Power"). Wisdom and Power are attracted to one another in a degrading passion; out of their desire proceed angelic beings, base by comparison with the first aeons. These angels create the first heaven; other angels arise from them and create a second, and so on until three hundred and sixty-five heavens have been created. The ruler of the angels who made the lowest heaven is the God of the Jews. Apparently the Jews and their God made enough of an impression on the gnostics so that they could not be overlooked and had to be assigned an important place. Although the heaven that rules our world is the lowest of three hundred and sixty-five, it is the one with which we have to deal, and consequently the God who rules it is extremely powerful in our own lives.

The God of the Jews produced the Law and sent the Prophets, who thus appear clothed with a measure of authority, but of a subordinate and malign kind. God the Father sent Christ, the firstborn aeon known as Nous (not Logos), to free the souls of the spiritual from the power of the base creative angels who hold them prisoner in vile physical bodies. According to Basilides, this Christ was a man only in appearance; Simon of Cyrene, whom the Romans pressed into service to help Jesus carry his Cross, was crucified in his place, while the Nous returned to the Father. Basilides held salvation to be a matter for the soul alone and, unlike Saturnilus, was not an ascetic, but a libertarian. Basilides cloaked his gnosis in secrecy, and engaged in magical arts, but what distinguished his view from those of mystery religions and various magical cults was its complexity and comprehensiveness: three hundred and sixty-five heavens through which the soul must ascend to reach the Father, aided by the appropriate magical incantations specified for each one.[32]

b. The Great Systematician

The system of Basilides was apparently too complex, for he was followed by a simplifier, Valentinus, active in Rome during the reign of Antoninus Pius (ruled 138–61). Valentinus presents what the church fathers took to be the classic expression of Gnosticism. He presents a more harmonious and less complex view of the aeons than Basilides. The Demiurge (artificer), who is the creator of the material world, was not a rebel against Autopator (Greek, "Self-Father"), but rather an image of him, drawn by the aeon Sophia. Like Basilides, Valentinus sought to overcome the dichotomy between the purely spiritual Autopator and the material world by interposing a descending series of gradually less spiritual and more material aeons, intending to show that in this way the spiritual primal Father has nothing to do with base material reality. Nevertheless, if one begins with the presupposition that the spiritual can have nothing to do with the material, it is difficult to see how increasing the number of intermediate beings really makes the leap from spirit to matter easier or more plausible. Irenaeus lampoons the system of Valentinus in a satire in which the utterly spiritual aeon, Only Begotten, produces another spiritual aeon, Utternothingness, which in turn produces an aeon called Gourd—palpable, edible, and utterly delicious. Gourd in turn produces Cucumber, and these four then generate all the other "delirious melons of Valentinus."[33]

According to Valentinus, Christ is the offspring of Sophia, the last of the thirty highest aeons who make up the pleroma, or fullness, of the aeons. He reveals the Father to those who have spiritual natures and leads them to salvation by a path of enlightenment. Christ was man in appearance only and of course neither ate nor drank. Although the gnostics emphasized the idea that man could attain necessary gnosis only through revelation, they accepted revelation as a principle only, and cut it off from the specific content of the Old and New Testaments. The gnostics wanted to make all of the highest impulses and thoughts of those who have spiritual natures revelation; in this, they anticipated eighteenth-century aesthetics and nineteenth-century philosophical idealists. "But this is precisely what destroys historical revelation," writes Seeberg, "for if all the thoughts of the human spirit are revelation, then there is no revelation, and if all religions are revelation, then it is impossible to speak of a special, revealed religion."[34]

Gnosticism places the source of evil in the order of nature, i.e. in the materiality of bodily existence, not in the moral order. When traditional Christianity speaks of a Fall, it means an act of willful rebellion; for Gnosticism, the Fall was an actual physical descent, so to speak, of sparks of spiritual light from the highest heaven into our lower world. The primary task of the heavenly Christ was to banish ignorance and death. Although Gnosticism used Christian terminology and many of its adherents remained within the church, the fact that for them Christ was only a lesser aeon and that they regarded themselves as worthy of salvation (because they were spiritual by nature) made them adopt a very supercilious attitude toward ordinary Christians.

Is salvation the result of trust and obedience, of voluntary submission to the lordship of Christ? Or is it the logical consequence of possessing a higher spiritual nature that enables one to understand gnostic revelation? Christianity affirmed the world as good, but saw as its primary task winning individuals to submission to Christ, "by whom all things were made" (Nicene Creed, based on John 1:4). Gnosticism renounced the world as evil, but saw as its primary task the sharing of the deepest secrets about the world, its origin and its true nature; this understanding would make man free. The difference between Gnosticism and Christianity is well illustrated by the contrast between the partial quotation from Jesus that adorns a gate into the Harvard Yard, and the full quotation. The Harvard gate reads, "Ye shall know the truth, and the truth shall make you free." The full quotation reads, "If ye continue in my word, then are ye my disciples indeed; and ye shall know the truth, and the truth shall make you free" (John 8:31–32).

5. ANOTHER POLE: MARCION

The church fathers paired Marcion with his contemporary Valentinus as the two worst gnostics. Like Valentinus and the other gnostic teachers, Marcion was strongly dualistic; like them, he disdained the God of the Jews and repudiated the Old Testament. But there was something quite distinct about Marcion, and he deserves separate consideration. From a practical perspective, Marcion possessed something none of the gnostic teachers seems to have shared: a high level of organizational ability. This gave to his distinctive doctrines a power others lacked. In addition, Marcion raised the dualism inherent in all Gnosticism to a high pitch and brought it to a climax in a marked contrast between the malign God of the Jews and the good Ultimate Father. This contrast was present in varying degrees among all the gnostics, none of whom held a high regard for the God of Abraham. But for them the God of Abraham, the Demiurge, was only a part of a great chain of spiritual powers; for Marcion, he was the real adversary. A major feature of Marcion's approach was the fact that he did not rely on gnostic speculation, but took his ideas directly from Paul, albeit via a one-sided interpretation.

The cardinal feature of Marcion's position is that in place of the concept of a fallen world (original sin) he substitutes the idea of an *alien God*. The creator of this world is alien to the true God and alien to spiritual man. He is the Yahweh of the Old Testament, a wild god, one who can rage, make mistakes, and repent, one who knows nothing of grace, but only strict justice. This God is responsible for the misery of man; and he gave us the Old Testament with all its features, including the Messiah. Christ himself is not the Messiah; he did not fulfill the predictions of the Old Testament, but came to save us from the God of wrath, in whose clutches we presently languish. Although Marcion relegated the God of the Old Testament to an inferior role, he did not consider his prophecies—in the Jewish Scriptures—to be false. Those who try to keep his Law in the present·age are good, but cannot be saved unless they are taken out of the domain of his Law through Christ, the manifestation of the unknown God of love. The Messiah promised by the God of the Jews is yet to come. In Marcion's eyes, then, the church of Christ is a means of freeing spiritual people from the ongoing course of worldly existence, dominated by the God of the Jews, by the Jews themselves, and by their God's promised Messiah. Marcion's idea that the church really is not part of world history appears again, centuries later, in a more orthodox form, in the view of J. N. Darby (1800–1882). Darby and the dispensationalists who follow him consider the church to be in a kind of parenthesis that really is not part of world history.

a. The First Great Heretic

Although we have named docetism as the first heresy, it was a widespread idea and not the product of any one teacher. We are limiting our concept of heresy to doctrines that deal directly with God (special theology) and Christ (Christology) and that diverge so sharply from traditional Chris-

tianity that they split the church. Great church-dividers—such as the patriarchs of Constantinople Photius in the ninth century and Michael Cerularius
in the eleventh, and their papal adversaries, or the great Protestant Reformers Luther and Calvin—are not necessarily heretics; not all great heretics
have in fact split the church: Friedrich Schleiermacher in the nineteenth century is a case in point. In Marcion, however, we have a man whose teaching
was radically at odds with orthodoxy and who succeeded in organizing a
rival church.

Gnosticism had taken a relatively simple religious message, that of the
Gospel, and rendered it incredibly complex. Marcion, by contrast, was a
simplifier: he seized on a single aspect of the New Testament, the conflict
between faith and law, and made it into a fundamental principle that domi-
nates everything. Both in his radical simplification and in his submission of
everything to one religious idea, Marcion is typical of most great heretics.
The Christian faith, although much simpler than the Gnosticism of Valentinus, is not totally simple. It does have mysteries, complexities, and apparent paradoxes or antinomies,[35] which no amount of theological inquiry or
philosophical speculation seems to be able to resolve fully.

From the perspective of our study, both Roman Catholicism and the
two major Protestant confessions, Lutheran and Reformed—as well as a
number of other Christian communions—are orthodox, in that they accept
the historic creeds that define orthodoxy. Nevertheless, the centrifugal tendencies that carried Gnosticism and Marcion beyond the limits of orthodoxy
did not disappear with them, but continue to exist within Christianity, sometimes producing again, after the passage of decades or centuries, new and
disruptive versions of old heresies. Even when the centrifugal tendencies do
not produce major doctrinal deviations or split the church, they may be
strong enough to affect the internal spiritual development of bodies that remain generally orthodox. Thus we may say that although early catholicism
overcame Gnosticism and rejected it, the gnostic love for complexity and
the desire to explain everything reappears in medieval and modern Roman
Catholicism, teaching—as the Reformers charged—"for doctrines the commandments of men," and "vainly puffed up by [his] fleshly mind" (Matt.
15:9–10; Col. 2:18). Luther and Calvin were reformers who wanted to bring
the church back to simple obedience to the Word of God in Scripture. They
did not follow Marcion in purging the Bible of everything except Paul and
a portion of Luke, but at times they did emphasize Paul and the contrast
between law and grace with a single-mindedness reminiscent of the ancient
heresiarch.[36]

Marcion, the first of the great heretics, was a contemporary of the gnostic teacher Valentinus in Rome; the date of his death is uncertain. He agreed
with Gnosticism in his categorical rejection of the Hebrew Scriptures as
valid divine revelation. Nevertheless, his attitude toward what he did con-

sider to be valid Scripture—the Gospel (most of Luke) and the Apostle (much of Paul)—was more like that of the Jews and the Christians toward their sacred texts than that of the gnostics. What he accepted as Scripture he took to be literally true and fully authoritative; of course he did so by first eliminating everything that seemed to him to be misguided or to affirm law instead of grace. (Fourteen centuries later, Martin Luther would again feel the tension between faith and works in Scripture, and would brand James "a right strawy epistle," but he did not amputate the canon.) Nevertheless, Marcion did have a Scripture principle; it was his emphasis on the authority of Scripture, combined with his very limited selection of texts as Scripture, that in effect forced Christians to draw up the first canon of the New Testament and thus to acknowledge the authority of texts Marcion did not accept.

Heresies such as Gnosticism do not create churches; what they produce are esoteric cliques within the church. Heretics such as Marcion have the personal energy and organizational talent necessary to set up a rival organization, which some church historians have dignified with the title of a reformed church. Was the accusation that Marcion had been excommunicated from a regular congregation for immorality true? We do not know, but if so, it would be one among many examples of a moral lapse leading to the founding of a rival doctrine or even a rival church. (The best-known example, of course, is the way King Henry VIII separated the Church of England from Roman Catholicism after Pope Leo X refused to annul Henry's marriage. Although the Church of England became thoroughly Protestant under Henry's successor, Edward VI, its somewhat inglorious beginning under Henry still causes Anglicans some embarrassment.)

b. Law and Gospel

Marcion faced the question of the relationship of the Gospel to the Jewish Law more forthrightly than anyone before him. He concluded that the Torah had been totally superseded by the Gospel. His detractors charged that he took this position because his own personal life was in gross violation of Old Testament standards of conduct. Whatever his reason, Marcion taught that the church as a whole was illegitimately mingling traditional Judaism with the radically new Gospel, and that he had restored the Gospel. He boasted of accomplishing precisely that which Tertullian would later accuse him of: "The separation of the Law and the Gospel is the fundamental work of Marcion."[37]

Orthodox Christianity has always lived in tension between the Law and the Gospel. Over thirteen centuries after Marcion, Martin Luther would once again emphasize the *discrimination of Law and Gospel,* and reaffirm that we are "justified by faith *alone,* apart from the works of the Law" (Rom.

3:28), adding the German word *allein* ("alone") in his translation of the Greek text. There is certainly a trace of Marcion in Luther's move, but unlike Marcion he possessed and treasured the entire canonical Scriptures. Consequently the separation between Law and Gospel in Lutheranism remains a *discriminatio* (distinction), not a radical separation. Marcion called for such a radical separation, but only a minority of Christians followed him.[38]

c. Christology

Marcion devised distinctive Christology to solve the problem of Law and Gospel. From Cerdo, a Syrian gnostic, Marcion adopted the idea that there are in fact two gods, the imperfect, wrathful war god of the Old Testament and the "unknown God," the spiritual Father who revealed himself in Jesus. Marcion did not adopt the elaborate aeons of Gnosticism, but only its dualistic distinction between the Creator, or Demiurge, and the true but unknown God, the Father. Because of his dualism, which viewed the material world and physical bodies as the handiwork of the Demiurge, Marcion denied that Christ ever was truly incarnate. Thus he too was a docetist.

Why is a docetic tendency so common in early Christianity? There is a simple reason: the claims the New Testament makes for Jesus Christ, and the impression he made on his followers, were so overwhelming that it was very difficult to conceive of him as really ever having been a man. The early Christians found it easier to accept Christ as God than to admit that, being God, he was also truly man. Marcion, the gnostics, and others as well resolved this problem simply by flatly denying that Jesus was truly human. Orthodoxy will ultimately strongly affirm his full humanity in credal statements, but even the orthodox will be troubled by a recurring tendency to see him as only divine, to the neglect of his humanity.

d. Marcion's Doctrine of God

For Christians, "special theology," or the doctrine of God, is primarily the doctrine of the Trinity. This could not yet have been true in the time of Marcion, for trinitarian language was only developed in the following century, first of all by Tertullian. Marcion taught the deity of Christ; how did he relate Christ to the Father, the supreme, good God? For Marcion, Christ—whom he often calls "the spirit of salvation"—is simply God himself. This is another reason why Marcion had to deny that Christ really suffered, for God cannot suffer and die. Marcion's successors so fully identified Christ with the Father that he appears to be merely a mode of the Father's existence, the position also taken by the Sabellians, or modalists, of the following century.

e. Eschatology

The first great heretic broke drastically with the faith of the early church in abandoning the doctrine of the imminent, personal return of Christ. Like the doctrines of the incarnation and the resurrection, the doctrine of the Second Coming places the spiritual and divine in direct, intimate contact with the human and fleshly. Marcion did not believe in a real incarnation, and consequently there was no logical place in his system for a real Second Coming. Although he stressed the goodness of the Father God, Marcion was not a universalist, but expected the majority of mankind to be lost. Although he denied the validity of the Old Testament and its Law, he was not an antinomian or a libertine, whatever he may have been before leaving the church. His foremost critic, Tertullian, acknowledged that Marcion was ''a most holy teacher,'' one who ''imposed sanctity on the flesh.''[39]

Marcion's categorical distinction between Law and Gospel has a more orthodox parallel not only in Lutheranism but in the nineteenth- and twentieth-century movement known as dispensationalism. Dispensationalism arrives at a similar distinction by a different route, i.e. not by denying the validity of the Old Testament and its Law, but by limiting it to an older dispensation intended only for the nation of Israel, and by seeing Christians as living in a completely different age and under a completely different dispensation, that of grace. Unlike Marcion, who rejected the Second Coming, and most Lutherans, who place it in a nonmillennial context, dispensationalism teaches that the Second Coming will initiate an earthly thousand-year reign of Christ, the millennium.

f. Marcion's Heritage

As the first great heretic, Marcion developed and perfected his heterodox system before orthodoxy had fully defined itself. Despite the fact that Marcion's views play havoc with the Old Testament, without which Christianity would be unthinkable, because he was a "Reformer," Marcion has enjoyed a certain vogue among later Protestant writers. Reinhold Seeberg (1859–1935), a slightly younger contemporary of Adolf von Harnack, considered himself very much a Lutheran. Luther, he believed, had rescued evangelical truth from the bondage to the legalism into which medieval Catholicism had plunged it. Unfortunately for Luther's reputation, Seeberg makes Marcion his model:

Marcion consciously sought to reform, but not for the sake of the [gnostic] superstitions of the educated, but in obedience to the Gospel. With unparalleled energy he dedicated his life to this task. Thus he is the first in the chain of Reformers, the last and greatest of which was

Luther. His appearance attests to us not only that legalistic Christianity had grown ever stronger in the church, but also that the Pauline tradition was still alive in her. Paul had to be discovered anew, but he could still be found.[40]

Seeberg believed that in the eighty years between Paul and Marcion Christianity had so deteriorated into legalism that a radically dualistic, anti-Jewish heresy such as Marcion's represented a necessary reformation. This clearly reveals his presumption that the "faith which was once delivered," if it ever actually existed, was in constant flux and never stable.

6. THE NEXT "REFORMER": MONTANUS

If it seems odd to hear Seeberg speak of Marcion as a "Reformer" before Christianity was a full century old, he is not the only recent or contemporary writer to hold that the church Jesus promised to build on the rock was soon in need of major improvements. The great church historian Karl Heussi speaks of our next major heresy, that of Montanus, as the "Montanist reformation."[41]

Like Marcion, Montanus was active under Antoninus Pius (ruled 138–61) and felt that the church was reverting to Judaism. Unlike Marcion, who took Paul as his point of departure, Montanus emphasized the writings of John. Marcion sought to undo what he felt was a pernicious legalism by teaching a radical dichotomy of Law and Grace. Montanus felt that the church—even after only a century of existence!—was falling back into worldliness, and tried to call it back to its first love by emphasizing the direct guidance of the Holy Spirit, whose spokesman he claimed to be. Marcion was in a sense a "fundamentalist," in that he believed that he was correctly interpreting an authoritative, written revelation; Montanus was a "charismatic," who maintained that he received direct revelation from the Holy Spirit. He considered himself the last great prophet, who would be immediately followed by the establishment of the heavenly Jerusalem.[42]

a. Beliefs of Montanism

The idea that the church needed a major reformation by the sixteenth century, or even by the thirteenth, is not strange, but that one was necessary within less than a century of the martyrdom of Peter and Paul, and while the whole church was still being recruited from people who were serious and committed enough to risk martyrdom themselves, seems astonishing.

Montanus believed that he had a special prophetic gift, which was shared by his two female disciples, Maximilla and Prisca. He quotes the

Spirit, supposedly speaking through him, "Behold, man is like a lyre and I fly over it like the plectrum."[43] Montanus' success in the early church clearly reveals that the first Christians were not convinced that revelation had ended with the close of what we now call the Age of the Apostles. If one reason for the definition of the canon of Scripture was to make certain that nothing was improperly excluded—as had been done by Marcion—a second reason was to set limits to the crucial concept of authoritative, verbal divine revelation, and to make certain that biblical revelation was not diluted by the addition of spurious private revelations. During the Reformation era, the major Protestant leaders, those whom we call the magisterial Reformers,[44] reemphasized their conviction that the canon of Scripture was closed and that direct revelation had ended with the Apocalypse of John in order to guard against the Roman Catholic practice of elevating tradition to the same level as scriptural revelation; from the nineteenth century onward, with the rise of Pentecostalism and its emphasis on direct revelation, the successors of the magisterial Reformers once again will begin to stress their belief that the wonder of direct inspiration ended with the Age of the Apostles.

Montanus' conviction that the end of the age was at hand led him to call on Christians to abstain from marriage, dissolve marriages already contracted, and gather in an appropriate place to await the descent of the heavenly city. The heavenly city did not descend when expected, and consequently Montanus and his followers had to come to terms with its delay, as the whole church had to learn to deal with the postponement of Christ's Second Coming. The concept of the Last Day was broadened into a concept of Last Days, during which Montanus called upon his followers to live a life of strict discipline and self-denial. The Montanists, in contrast to Marcion, were orthodox with respect to their doctrine of God—the doctrine of the Trinity had not yet been formulated—and merely wanted to intensify it by adding their new revelation. Because of this, the Montanists were able to win over the great Latin theologian Tertullian, who shaped some of the most important formulations of orthodox Christian doctrine.

b. Distinctives of Montanism

The comparison between Marcionism and Montanism is enlightening, because the varieties of deviation they represent will continue to reappear in the church through the centuries. Marcion represents a movement that so radically transformed the Christian doctrine of God and Christ that it can hardly be said to be Christian, but rather a different religion using some Christian concepts, such as the Jehovah's Witnesses. Montanism, by contrast, preserves most of the principles of orthodox theology, adding to them more recent, personal revelations of Montanus, the founder of the sect, and requiring a higher standard of asceticism than was usual in the rest of the church. A modern parallel appears to be offered by the Latter-Day Saints, or Mormons. The Mormons profess so much of what other Christians consider fundamental Christian doctrine that it is difficult to designate them as non-Christians. Nevertheless, the peculiarities of their doctrine of God in the last analysis place them even further from historic Christianity than the Montanists. Tertullian, who created important terms for the doctrines of the Trinity and original sin, became a Montanist; it is hard to think of him becoming a Mormon.

Montanism was not really very distinctive theologically. This fact, together with the asceticism and the willingness of its adherents to endure martyrdom, made the Montanists particularly difficult opponents for the rest of the church. It opposed and attacked Gnosticism just as orthodoxy did, but by creating a separate organization on different principles, Montanus posed a similar danger. The Montanist movement was defeated almost incidentally as a result of the measures the church took against Gnosticism and Marcionism, especially by the definition of the canon of Scripture, which closed the door to Montanus' new revelations.

Despite a few superficial similarities between the "Reformers" Marcion and Luther, and between the "rigorists" Montanus and Calvin, the two great Protestant Reformers remained solidly within the framework of orthodoxy in our sense. Perhaps this was because they had centuries of well-formed and relatively stable Christian theological tradition behind them, while Marcion and Montanus in a sense had to develop tradition for themselves. Certainly it is also due in large measure to the fact that the Reformers venerated the entire Bible, neither paring it down as Marcion did nor adding to it as did Montanus. To the extent that there are modern parallels to Marcion and Montanus, they lie beyond the borders of Christian orthodoxy.

SELECTED BIBLIOGRAPHY

Blackman, Edwin Cyril. *Marcion and His Influence*. London: S.P.C.K., 1948.

Bleeker, C. J. and Ugo Bianchi, eds. *Le origini dello gnosticismo: colloquio di Messina 13–18 aprile 1966*. Leiden: Brill, 1967.

Cadiou, René. *Origen: His Life at Alexandria*. Translated by John A. Southwell. St. Louis: Herder, 1944.

Ford, J. Massingberd. "Was Montanism a Jewish-Christian Heresy?" *Journal of Ecclesiastical History* 17 (October 1966): 145–58.

Grant, Robert M. "The Earliest Christian Gnosticism," *Church History* 22 (June 1953): 81–98.

————, ed. *Gnosticism: A Source Book of Heretical Writings from the Early Christian Period.* New York: Harper & Row, 1961.

Haardt, Robert. *Gnosis: Character and Testimony.* Leiden: Brill, 1971.

Lilla, Salvatore R. C. *Clement of Alexandria: A Study in Christian Platonism and Gnosticism.* Oxford: University Press, 1971.

Quispel, Gilles. *Gnostic Studies.* Istanbul: Nederlands Historisch-Archaeologisch Instituut in het Nabije Oosten, 1974.

Yamauchi, Edwin M. "Gnostic Ethics and Mandaean Origins." In *Harvard Theological Studies.* Vol. 24. Cambridge: Harvard University Press, 1970.

———— *Pre-Christian Gnosticism: A Survey of the Proposed Evidences.* London: Tyndale, 1973.

5

BEFORE THE
NEW TESTAMENT

For wherever it shall be manifest that the true Christian rule and faith shall be, there *will likewise be the true Scriptures and expositions thereof, and all the Christian traditions.*

Tertullian On the Prescription of Heretics *19*

Our consideration of the reformist efforts of Marcion and Montanus has brought us close to the end of the second century of the Christian Era. But what were they reforming? The church existed, real enough, and it had something like a generally accepted canon or standard of faith. But—as our discussion has indicated—in the second century these things were more implicit than explicit. Christianity did not work them out in detail and express them with clarity until after they had been challenged by dynamic leaders such as Marcion and Montanus. Paul wrote to Timothy reminding him that he had known "the Holy Scriptures" as a boy. But Paul's letter is itself part of *our* Holy Scriptures, and the canon of the New Testament was not to be acknowledged as completed for three more centuries, although the Muratorian Canon indicates that it was virtually complete by the end of the second century[1]—not long after Marcion.

The first officially recognized ecumenical creed dates from the Council of Nicaea in 325; the old Roman Creed, which we know as the Apostles' Creed, may have been in use two hundred years earlier, but only in certain localities, not throughout the whole church. Heresy appeared and was formulated before orthodoxy; by what standard could Christians judge and evaluate conflicting doctrines when no creed had yet been adopted? It is tempting to say, "by the Scripture." But the bulk of the New Testament was not even in existence when Paul wrote to Timothy.

Not only do the ecumenical creeds and the first major works of Christian theology owe their existence to the need to refute certain heresies, but the New Testament canon itself was established to counteract the views of Marcion's heresy, which accepted only a portion of it. How did Christianity, without creeds and without a canon of the New Testament, ever succeed in defending itself against the challenge of plausible heresies? Again, the naive assumption is that the New Testament books exercised their authority by virtue of their evident divine inspiration, long before the dimensions of the canon were officially defined. The challenge, presented in one of the pioneering works of what is called scientific criticism, is Johann Salomo Semler's contention that the present canon is arbitrary and represents the victory of the Roman see in the ecclesiastic politics of the early church.[2] In other words, the New Testament is not the source of orthodoxy but its product. How can it be our standard?

Did the Scripture produce the church, or the church the Scripture? Through the centuries of Christian history, the church had always accepted the Bible as infallible and binding, until the Reformation. Then the Reformers' Scripture principle, that belief was to be based on Scripture alone *(sola Scriptura),* challenged the authority of the Roman church to define faith and morals. Roman Catholics immediately began to claim that the New Testament derived its authority from the fact that the church had officially recognized it; the Protestants replied that the church was only acknowledging the authority inherent in the Scriptures in consequence of their divine inspiration.

The Protestant principle is appealing, and in a general way seems to describe what actually happened. The early church, in acknowledging certain books as divinely inspired Scripture, certainly was not under the illusion that it was thereby making them authoritative. Scripture was a given in the church, even before the full extent of the canon was determined and agreed upon. Nevertheless, the fact that the church took so long to come to a final conclusion about the contents of the canon does make one wonder what criteria were used to determine whether the texts were inspired, and why it took a number of centuries, in a few cases at least, to agree that certain books possess them.

It certainly is not true to suggest that the writings of the New Testament derived their authority from that of the ecclesiastical bodies that approved them, as though the authority of the church were primary and that of the Scripture secondary. On the other hand, the somewhat glib assumption of Protestant controversialists that the church was organized on the basis of the New Testament is also untenable. Sixteenth-century Protestants, convinced that the church needed to be reorganized according to New Testament principles, liked to suppose that they were only imitating the first Christians, who had also organized on the basis of Scripture, but a moment's reflection will reveal that this cannot be true. The church was organizing as the New Testament was being written, and to a considerable degree it was already organized by the time the Muratorian Canon was compiled. One can argue that the principles according to which the church was organized are those expounded in the New Testament, but hardly that the church derived them from the New Testament, which was not yet in existence. Nevertheless it is apparent that from the time it was in existence, it enjoyed an unquestioned authority in the church, an authority far superior to anything the church itself could have conferred.

1. RELATIVIZING THE IMPORTANCE OF SCRIPTURE

During the Reformation era, Roman Catholic traditionalism sought to combat the Protestant Scripture principle by insisting that there are *two* sources of authoritative divine revelation: Scripture and tradition. Scripture is only part of the whole. As serious as such a qualification is for the principle of *sola Scriptura,* even more serious was the nineteenth century's assumption that everything noble, elevated, and inspiring must therefore be "divinely" inspired and can be called "revelation." Sixteenth-century Roman Catholics claimed that their traditions were also revelation, alongside of Scripture, but they claimed for *both* an absolute authority Protestants would concede only to Scripture. Nineteenth-century Protestants—Adolf Harnack, for example—did not deny that the Scripture is inspired, but so loosened and generalized the concept of inspiration that it lost most of its authority. Late eighteenth- and early nineteenth-century movements such as classicism, idealism, and Romanticism saw poets, musicians, philosophers, and heroes as "inspired." Harnack read this mentality back into the early church, and thought that our present New Testament was only part of a much larger, loosely defined group of sacred writings. Accordingly, there is no particular reason to ascribe special authority to the New Testament.

Harnack quoted the *Didache,* or *The Teaching of the Twelve Apostles,* which had only recently been rediscovered, to bolster his contention that the early church had a very loose view of inspiration: "All that bears witness to the Lord comes by his Spirit."[3] Indeed, Paul says something similar: "No man can say that Jesus is the Lord, but by the Holy Ghost" (1 Cor. 12:3). Scripture itself Harnack saw as only the "residue" of a great body of revelation, much of which has been lost. But if all that is religious is somehow "inspired," then no particular inspired text, not even the New Testament, can have normative authority, since many ancient texts differ from and even conflict with one another, which Harnack knew far better than most. Admittedly, the early Christians had what might appear to us a loose usage of the word "holy." Many writings were called holy, just as their writers were, for the early Christians called all believers "saints," that is, holy. But just as they were able to make a categorical distinction between the Apostles and other holy men and women, so too they made a categorical distinction between the apostolic writings of the New Testament and the edifying works of other "holy men."

Contemporary Christians, both Protestants and Roman Catholics, generally take it for granted that the Bible can have at best a limited and relative authority in our day. It is not necessary to go into the reasoning behind this assumption, nor to discuss its wisdom, in order to recognize that we should not read it back into the first centuries of the church. The older Protestant attitude toward the Bible, indeed, the attitude of most Christians from the time a complete text was available, has been to look on it as a single book, almost as though it had been written at a single sitting and presented to the church in bound form by Jesus when he established it.

Christians have always known that the Bible as a whole and even the New Testament have a history; there was a time when the Revelation of John had not yet been written, then a long period during which it was only locally available, followed by an even longer period during which it was not universally accepted as canonical. Although they knew this, Christians tended to treat the Bible not merely as a harmonious, self-consistent unity, but really as a single document, a handbook of religious truth. When the science of biblical criticism began to concentrate on the process by which the text was formed, and illuminated the long decades at least several New Testament books required to secure general acceptance, the opposite misunderstanding began to spread: the New Testament was seen as an accumulation of miscellaneous writings and testimonies, often at variance with and at times even contradicting one another.

If we postulate that the New Testament is relatively late in origin and in general use among Christians, and even that it sometimes contradicts itself, then we will not expect to find in it the "faith once delivered." The creeds of the early church, as we know, are late in origin. Nevertheless, although the ecumenical creeds were very late, and even the New Testament itself was relatively late and was adopted in piecemeal fashion, it is possible to argue that both the creeds and the New Testament attest a faith that really was "once delivered." The fact that heresies continually arose, from the beginnings of Christianity, but were cast aside, leaving a solid nucleus of belief intact through the centuries, supports the contention that the nucleus was there and was solid from the beginning, even though the documents that define it, and that now serve us as our standards for comparison, are relatively late.

2. THE CLOSING OF THE
NEW TESTAMENT CANON

There were two challenges to the New Testament in its present form. The first, that of Marcion, would have excluded everything Jewish from Scripture, a process that in his hands left only bits of Luke (the "Gospel") and of Paul (the "Apostle"). The second challenge, that of Montanus, accepted the whole New Testament but added, as equally authoritative, the prophecies of Montanus and others to the body of divine revelation. Although Marcionites and Montanists have disappeared from the religious scene, contemporary Christianity is once again affected by what we may call minimalists and maximists with regard to revelation: the minimalists, like Marcion, would see little, if anything, as authoritative and would reduce Scripture to limited passages they have determined to be authentic. Modern minimalists, such as adherents of Rudolf Bultmann and his school of New Testament interpretation,[4] consider only a small part of the New Testament to be an authentic record of the actual words and deeds of Jesus. In addition, they allow themselves wide freedom in deciding how to apply even those passages they do not dispute. In this, they differ from Marcion, who at least attempted to follow, as rigorously as possible, those portions of Scripture he did accept. The modern religious scene on the fringes of Christianity also offers examples of "maximalists," who, like Marcion, add new revelation to the Bible. The Latter-Day Saints (Mormons), Christian Scientists, Jehovah's Witnesses, and certain others illustrate modern maximalism, and they go beyond Montanus in that their fresh revelations substantially modify the teaching of the Bible itself.

We may consider that the New Testament canon was effectively complete by A.D. 200, although a few books remained controversial until into the fourth century. The closing of the canon was of tremendous importance, because it meant that from then on theological disputes could no longer affect the source of doctrine, the text of Scripture itself. From this virtual closing of the New Testament canon in about 200, it will take two and one half more centuries for Christianity to reach agreement on two of its most fundamental doctrines: the doctrine of the Trinity and the doctrine of the one person and two natures of Christ.

Jude, in a little book that itself took some time to be accepted everywhere as part of Scripture, spoke of a faith once delivered to the saints. If it was really delivered, how and why did the early church take so long to understand it and define it as it did at Nicaea, Constantinople, and Chalcedon?

SELECTED BIBLIOGRAPHY

Chadwick, Henry. *The Circle and the Ellipse: Rival Concepts of Authority in the Early Church*. Oxford: Clarendon, 1959.

Florovsky, Georges. *Bible, Church, Tradition: An Eastern Orthodox View*. Belmont, Mass.: Nordland, 1972.

Robinson, John A. T. *Redating the New Testament*. Philadelphia: Westminster Press, 1976.

6

THE APOLOGISTS

In short, when God revealed the truth to man, He wished us only to know those things which it concerned man to know for the attainment of life; but as to the things which related to a profane and eager curiosity He was silent, that they might be secret. Why, then, do you inquire into things which you cannot know, and if you knew them you would not be happier? It is perfect wisdom in man, if he knows that there is but one God and that all things were made by Him.

Lactantius The Divine Precepts 2.9

When Sunday school children think of the early church, they are taught to think of martyrs. When theologians think of it, they learn to think of the apologists. During the first three centuries of the Christian Era, every Christian believer had to reckon with the possibility of being put to death for the faith. There is a link between the martyrs, who died for their faith, and the apologists, who tried to explain it (and many of whom also became martyrs themselves). The Roman authorities were on the whole not very happy about putting otherwise innocuous-seeming subjects to death for the sake of a religious belief in an age in which virtually every other religion was "licit" and tolerated. It was difficult for them to get good information, for the Christians had no constitution, no formal creeds, no generally accepted handbooks of doctrine. Some Christians began to feel that "good" emperors such as Antoninus Pius (ruled 138–61) and Marcus Aurelius (ruled 161–80) would approve of Christianity if they really understood it. A number of them took it upon themselves to explain and defend the faith to its persecutors: their writings are the great apologies of the early church. The apologists were not very successful in turning away the hostility of the government; it would take a direct vision imparted to Constantine, according to legend, before a crucial battle, to accomplish that. But they did something no Emperor could have done for them: they systematized the Christian faith and described the Christian life of those early centuries.

76

The first great apologist was Justin Martyr, a converted pagan philosopher. Justin (ca. 100–ca. 165) was killed under Marcus Aurelius. In addition to his great *First Apology*, he also wrote an evangelistic or apologetic appeal addressed to Jews, his *Dialogue with Trypho the Jew*. His disciple the Syrian Tatian, who combined the four Gospels into the *Diatessaron*, also wrote an important apology, as did Melito of Sardes, Theophilus of Antioch, and Athenagoras of Athens, all of whom died near the end of the second century.

Among the early apologists, the two greatest were Irenaeus of Lyons, the great adversary of the gnostics, and the Latin-speaking rhetor and attorney Tertullian of Carthage. Irenaeus and Tertullian were really productive theologians. Their apologies mark the emergence of Christianity as an intellectual force in the Hellenistic world. After having at first thought that the end of the world was imminent, Christianity began to try to come to terms with a culture that was old, proud, and rich, but also jaded, decadent, and cynical. The great apologies were the product of this necessity. Whenever the faith and morals of Christians clash with the values of the surrounding culture, apologies will continue to be needed.

The first apologists were the first interpreters of the Christian faith to the world; their predecessors had preached it and to some extent had explained it in the hope of winning converts; the aim of the apology was to win understanding. Because they were addressed to those who disliked or even despised Christianity, their authors put great effort into making them persuasive. It was essentially the apologists who created early catholic Christianity, which begins to take on clear shape during the reign of Marcus Aurelius. In a sense, it was the government's policy of persecution and repression that made the early church truly catholic and ecumenical. Because the persecution was empire-wide, the apologies were read all over the Roman Empire, as other theological texts probably would not have been. Thus the hostility of the government helped to popularize the first works of Christian theology. Long before Christianity was officially established, it had become an empire-wide institution.

Did the apologists succeed in their goal of changing the minds of emperors and government officials? There is no record that they did. What they did accomplish was to launch the intellectual discipline of theology, which eventually made Christianity the most thoroughly analyzed and academic of the world's great religions. Gnosticism, Marcionism, and Montanism soon made it apparent what would happen to Christianity if it had no generally accepted canons of Scripture and faith. Apologetics, now called the defense of the faith, began as the defense of the faithful.

As the Christian community began to express its beliefs more clearly and in greater detail, an orthodox faith, including sufficient, correct doctrine, came to be thought essential for personal salvation. Nineteenth-century liberalism criticized the development of standards of orthodoxy: "As faith became doctrine, the catholic church interposed itself between the individual and his salvation."[1] It is immediately apparent that subscription to a particular set of doctrines is not what Paul or the first Christians meant by the faith that justifies. Yet the faith of Paul was far more than a mere attitude of trust; it was a trust based on certain definite convictions. The challenge to orthodox theology was to state and define those convictions without doing so in such a dry, pedantic, and dull way that the trust aspect of faith would be lost.

Where there are fixed doctrinal standards, it is certainly possible for faith to degenerate into mere formalism. On the other hand, where there are no fixed, clearly acknowledged standards, the wildest and most fanciful notions can become mixed in with basic Christian doctrines and it becomes very hard to separate them. The experience of the early Christians before the creeds were formulated as well as that of modern Christians after the creeds have been relegated to oblivion show the same thing: where clear doctrinal norms do not exist, even Christians who intend to keep the faith can easily wander far from it and find themselves involved in some very remarkable errors. If we are not happy with heresy, then it will be necessary to accept a fairly substantial dose of doctrinal theology. Among the first Christians to provide the church with doctrine in sufficient strength were the two pioneers of theological literature in Greek and Latin respectively, Irenaeus and Tertullian.

1. THE GREAT APOLOGISTS: IRENAEUS AND TERTULLIAN

Irenaeus, a Greek-speaking Christian from Asia Minor, was active as bishop of Lyons in southern Gaul in the last third of the second century; he had sat under Polycarp of Smyrna, who was himself a disciple of the Apostle John, and thus represents a kind of personal link with the earliest days of the church. Tertullian, a layman, lived in Carthage, in North Africa (ca. 160–ca. 230), and is the first notable representative of Latin-speaking Christianity. Irenaeus is best known for his attacks on Gnosticism, and for many centuries his *Against Heresies* was the chief source for gnostic theologies; it is relatively reliable, despite its polemical intent. Tertullian wrote extensively against Marcion, but finished his career in the camp of the opposite heresy, that of Montanus. Tertullian is also the first Christian since Paul who wrote enough about himself to give us a good idea of his personality. Irenaeus contributed breadth to the nascent theology of the church; Tertullian, precision.

a. The Doctrine of God

The fundamental point of departure for both Gnosticism and Marcion's heresy was the denial that the true God is the Creator of the material universe. Irenaeus therefore begins his *magnum opus* with a declaration of faith in the *one* God, who is the Creator of both heaven and earth.[2] Irenaeus insists that there is one and only one God. Although he was forced to emphasize the oneness of God because of the conflict with Gnosticism and Marcionism, which asserted the contrary, Irenaeus thus also laid the groundwork for the expression of the distinctive Christian doctrine of the Trinity. Without a clear insistence on the oneness of God, to confess the deity of the Father, and of the Son, and of the Holy Spirit could easily have led to a kind of polytheism. Irenaeus warns against speculating about what happened before creation and about the way in which the Son was begotten.[3]

b. Anthropology

Traditionally the presentation of the doctrine of God is followed by anthropology, the doctrine of man—a logical preliminary to the presentation of the person of Christ, who is confessed to be God and man. Irenaeus held that man was created good, and became corrupt by the voluntary act of sinning, i.e. disobeying God. Man as created is both free and mortal: the soul is an immortal substance but lacks form unless it is embodied. Irenaeus sees the human race as united in Adam, the first man; through the sin of Adam, the whole human race has become sinful and the prey of death.[4] Although Irenaeus' doctrine of man is not highly developed, it does have important features: (1) man's predicament, to borrow the language of our own century, is not part of his nature; (2) it is a moral, not a physical defect; and (3) this is true even though the defect has now become hereditary. Tertullian introduced the first terminology for what we now call original sin: *vitium originis,* "vice (flaw) of origin," and *naevus peccati,* "birthmark of sin."[5] Tertullian and Irenaeus both taught that fallen man possesses part of the light of truth and freedom of the will.

c. Salvation and History

Gnosticism is essentially a religious philosophy; what is most important to it is understanding the relationships of the deity, the aeons, the worlds, and ourselves. It has a cosmic vision extending endlessly back before history. Irenaeus is not indifferent to the cosmic implications of Christian faith, but his interest is centered on the course of events in the real history of this world: God's dealing with man is conditioned not by cosmic processes involving the aeons of the pleroma, but by what man himself does in his human history. Irenaeus is thus a forerunner of both covenant theology and the concept of redemptive history *(Heilsgeschichte);* we already find mention of three covenants between God and man (Greek *diathekai,* Latin *foedera*), the first being the law of nature, the second the Decalogue, followed by the ceremonial law, and finally the third covenant in Christ. The first covenant was universal, the second particular, involving only the Jews; the third, again, is universal.[6]

d. Christology

The most characteristic feature of Irenaeus' theology is his Christology. He is the first Christian thinker to attempt to formulate the meaning of the person and work of Christ in a systematic way. As we look back on him, we see three important features of Irenaeus and his work: (1) he opposed Gnosticism in detail; (2) in so doing, he gave us an excellent early Christology; (3) he was a thoroughgoing biblicist, and as such the first great exponent of what we shall learn to call the Scripture principle in theology. He is "catholic" in the sense that he represents both the Johannine and the Pauline heritage, and a traditionalist where the interpretation of Scripture is concerned. Contrasted with other early church fathers—Clement of Alexandria, Tertullian, Origen, Cyprian, to name but four—Irenaeus is a remarkably solid, calm, and balanced advocate of biblical orthodoxy.

Irenaeus is probably best known to us for his attacks on Gnosticism, a mortal blow to that curious amalgam of religion and philosophy (although, as we shall see, the gnostic impulse emerges time and time again in the history of Christian thought). It was his opposition to Gnosticism that created in Irenaeus the distinctive combination of biblical authority and traditional interpretation with practical piety that is the hallmark of the early church. As long as tradition preserved the Scripture and contented itself primarily with explaining it, there was no need for the *sola Scriptura* of the Protestant Reformation. Even after medieval Catholicism had attributed to tradition and indeed to the pope himself the ability to make far-reaching doctrinal innovations and had thus stimulated the Reformers to a full-scale revolt against all tradition, early and later Protestants still continue to find in Irenaeus a kindred spirit.

Irenaeus' sole authority was Scripture: his polemic against the secret traditions of Gnosticism can readily be adapted by Protestant controversialists for use against the claims of Roman Catholics for the authority of Catholic tradition. For Irenaeus, Scripture had to be interpreted in accordance with tradition, for this is the only guarantee that one is really dealing properly with Scripture. Stressing the unity of the church's testimony, delivered through the bishops, Irenaeus effectively anticipated the maxim of Vincent of Lérins that we hold to that "which has been believed always, everywhere, and by all." The fact that Irenaeus could appeal to the harmony of the bishops as a touchstone for true doctrine indicates that there really must have been a widely perceived consensus of the church.[7] Although he did not formulate them in so many words, Irenaeus also anticipated the later concepts of the sufficiency and inerrancy of Scripture. The Bible does not give us all the information we might possibly wish to have, and it is not always easy to understand, but in its major points it is clear and tells us what we need to know.[8] The apostolic tradition, according to Irenaeus, leads us back to the presentation of those who wrote the Scriptures, the Apostles, whose testimony is totally free of all untruth.[9]

It is against the background of his assault on Gnosticism, his reliance on tradition, and the dominant place he assigned to Scripture that we should examine the Christology of Irenaeus. In so doing we shall discover that he had a well-developed understanding of the deity of Christ superimposed on a less fully articulated understanding of God.

Gnostics such as Valentinus proceeded from what they thought was a detailed and reliable gnosis of the "unknown God" (for which self-contradictory claim Irenaeus did not fail to ridicule them). This gnosis explained the innermost life of the deity, the pleroma, and the aeons before the world began. It then produced a Christologically defective, docetic view of the man who had lived among men and women as the Messiah. It claimed to know all about divine reality, but Gnosticism produced a doctrine of Christ that failed to deal with *his* reality, the fact that he really was born, suffered, died, and—according to the faith of Christians—rose again as a man, not a disembodied spirit or docetic phantom.

Irenaeus did not claim to know the inner nature of the godhead; instead, he dealt with the testimony of Scripture and the church concerning the person and work of Christ, and produced an impressive, consistent, believable Christology, one that stands up well against the most critical questioning of later ages. Where Irenaeus was not comprehensive was in the doctrine of God; his presentation of the Trinity remained rudimentary. The gnostics trivialized Christ by comparison with their fantastic pleroma of aeons. Irenaeus fully recognized him as a real man and at the same time confessed him to be God. If monotheism was to be preserved, this obviously called for an explanation of how Christ can be God and at the same time distinct from the Father, without implying two Gods. The full Christology of Irenaeus required the doctrine of the Trinity as the only alternative to ditheism or poly theism.

In contrast to the gnostics, as well as to Tertullian and Hippolytus (ca. 170–235)—both of whom eventually embroiled themselves in schismatic, if not heretical, activities—Irenaeus did not develop his Christology from general considerations concerning the nature of the Logos as the "one mediator between God and men" (1 Tim. 2:5). The idea of a Logos-Mediator between the One, transcendent, totally exalted, and often unknowable God dwelling in untroubled simplicity and unity and the contingent, transitory world of particularity and multiplicity was an old one; both Philo and the Stoics had worked on it. Tertullian and Hippolytus, like the apologists who preceded them, give the impression of beginning with a doctrine of the Logos, onto which the doctrine of the incarnation was superimposed. It is significant that Irenaeus, in combating Gnosticism with its pleroma of intermediary aeons between the unknown God and the world, went back to the Bible and the historic Person of Jesus. Whenever this is not done, Christianity runs the danger of becoming another religious philosophy. Christ becomes a key to understanding, but is no longer "the firstfruits of them that slept" (1 Cor. 15:20). Consequently, he cannot really be "the way, the truth, and the life" (John 14:6). Irenaeus did not try to evade the scandal of particularity that attaches to any effort to make an "accidental" historical event, even the event of Jesus Christ, part of eternal truth; by remaining in firm contact with the historic Jesus, Irenaeus offered an invaluable counterweight to the tendency of many Christians, even relatively orthodox ones, to see in Christ only the cosmic Mediator, not the human Jesus. When Irenaeus speaks of the Logos or of the Son of God, he almost invariably has Jesus Christ in mind.

Because of his fidelity to the historical Jesus, Irenaeus did not follow those earlier Christian thinkers who saw in Christ the Idea, the Creative Word, or the Reason (Nous) of God—all ideas that have something in common with Gnosticism. What is at stake will only become fully apparent two centuries later, when the discussion of the doctrine of the Trinity is in full swing, but even in Irenaeus, an important distinction is made. What is at stake is not the deity of the Son, i.e. of Christ, but his personhood, and this is what is not asserted by the use of terms such as "Idea," "Creative Word," Nous. Irenaeus also speaks of God himself as Logos,[10] but of course he cannot give up the term as a title for Christ, whom the Apostle John explicitly identifies as the Word made flesh (John 1:14).

e. Motifs in the Christology
of Irenaeus

Because Irenaeus was interested primarily in the saving work of Christ, not in relating him to cosmological speculation, his Christology, then, is first of all soteriology, i.e. the doctrine of what Christ has done to save mankind. This soteriology brings with it a high Christology. It is important to note the sequence: an understanding of the historic work of Christ leads to an understanding of his cosmic stature and ultimately of his deity. In the understanding of the work of Christ, Irenaeus repudiated Gnosticism with its spirit-flesh dualism. He then gave subsequent theology a basic motif: recapitulation. Salvation is a renewal and restoration of Creation, not its abrogation. Harnack offers an interesting comment: "Thus the Christology of Irenaeus in a certain sense occupies a middle position between that of the Valentinians and of Marcion on the one hand and the Logos-doctrine of the [earlier] apologists on the other: the apologists have a cosmological interest, Marcion soteriological only; Irenaeus has both a cosmological and a soteriological interest. The apologists based their speculation on the Old Testament, Marcion his on the New; Irenaeus relies on both the Old and the New."[11]

Irenaeus prudently refrained from trying to explain the deity of Christ and how it is related to the deity of the Father. In the second century the deity and personhood of Christ were not yet sufficiently well established to permit them to be taken for granted and a doctrine of the Trinity built on them. The concept of the Trinity was already implicitly present in the triadic formulas of the New Testament (e.g. Matt. 28:19), but it would not be stated, even in rudimentary form, until Tertullian coined it a generation after Irenaeus. Irenaeus' contribution to our understanding of the relationship of Christ to the godhead lies primarily in the things he rejected: Christ is not an emanation; the Logos did not emerge at a point in time.[12] The Logos is neither an attribute nor an expression of God, who is an utterly simple essence and does not change.[13] With these last assertions, Irenaeus sets a pattern for what has come to be called "classical theology," the doctrine that God possesses certain incommunicable attributes (incapable of being shared by creatures), specifically, infinity, eternity, and immutability. Irenaeus offers a number of statements that sound rather like later, more fully developed trinitarian presentations: the Logos has always existed as the One who reveals the Father,[14] and thereby is personally distinct from him, not a mode of the Father, to use later terminology. The Son is God by nature, true God.[15]

Irenaeus is a witness to the independent personhood of the Son. He did not deal with the later trends that would attempt to define the Son as nothing more than a manifestation of the one Person, the Father; according to Harnack, Irenaeus shows a "remarkable nonchalance" about demonstrating the unity of God in the light of the deity of the Son and the distinction between the Son and the Father.[16] Because Irenaeus was deeply interested in man as man—not as a spark of divinity entrapped in flesh—he was vitally interested in the incarnation and historicity of Christ, but not in the theological analysis subsequent generations would develop to explain how Christ can be God and distinct from the Father while God remains one, not two or three. He did not develop these ideas, and consequently Irenaeus is sometimes said to teach a primitive "economic trinitarianism." This means that he only deals with the deity of the Son and the Spirit in the context of their revelation and saving activity, i.e. in the context of the "economy" (plan) of salvation. He subordinates the Son to the Father in this economy, but does not hold that the Son is less than fully God.

f. Specific Features

Irenaeus' Christology depends on his view of man as created good, and fallen. At the time of his Fall, Adam was mankind, and in him the whole race fell. As all those who are united with Adam share in Adam's penalty, so all those of whom Christ is the head will share in the reward for his obedience. Irenaeus thus has a very realistic view of the unity of the human race and looks to a real incorporation of redeemed humanity in Christ. Christ has the task of "recapitulating" the Creation; the original, good Creation is not to be superseded, but restored. This idea that Christ recapitulates Creation might suggest universalism, i.e. the ultimate salvation of all, but Irenaeus did not fall into it. In order to be able to recapitulate, Jesus Christ had to possess the attributes of deity; in order to recover mankind, he had to be man. Irenaeus has bequeathed to us two crucial sentences: *Filius dei filius hominis factus*, "The Son of God [has] become a son of man," and *Jesus Christus vere homo, vere deus*, "Jesus Christ, true man and true God." Jesus Christ is "one and the same Jesus Christ, not a Jesus and a Christ, and not a merely temporary union between an aeon and a man, but one and the same, who created the world, was born, suffered, and has ascended."[17] Against the gnostics, Irenaeus affirmed that Christ is the incarnation of God, not of one of many aeons; against Marcion, that the world to which he came is his own, not alien to him. For Irenaeus, the redemptive work of Christ depends fully on the identity between his humanity and our humanity.[18] This is a high point of Christological clarity that will be attained again, but not surpassed, almost three centuries later at the Council of Chalcedon (451). These later developments only repeated the insight of Irenaeus in more definitive formulations. Tertullian expressed the idea that Jesus Christ possesses two natures, and in so doing laid the foundation for the formulation subsequently adopted at Chalcedon, but with respect to the concept, he is indebted to Irenaeus. Irenaeus did not face the question as to whether the incarnation involved a change in the nature of the Word as he became flesh. Tertullian denied any change, but spoke of a "union with" or "assumption of" the human nature by the Logos. Tertullian, like Irenaeus, insisted that what the Gospel tells us about the man Jesus must also be said of the Son as God. Thus he could speak of "God crucified," and even say, "God willed himself to be born." This second expression is doubly significant, because it affirms both that the One who was born is God, and also, incidentally, that we may speak of God, in the person of the Son, as becoming, not simply as absolute Being. Tertullian's language anticipates the explicit statements of Chalcedon. It reveals that what we shall come to know as Chalcedonian orthodoxy was already in evidence, at least by implication, as early as the beginning of the third century.

2. NEW DIRECTIONS: FROM THE UNKNOWN FATHER OF GNOSTICISM TO THE SUFFERING FATHER OF PATRIPASSIANISM

In the middle of the second century, both Gnosticism and Marcionism were teaching that the true Deity was an unknowable Father. The Father had nothing to do with the material world, which was the handiwork of degenerate aeons or of their agent, the Demiurge. The great opponents of these two movements, Irenaeus and Tertullian, took the opposite view of the Father. Far from being inaccessible and unknowable, God involved himself in the world not merely by creating it himself, but even more dramatically, by becoming incarnate in the man Jesus Christ. Some Christians interpreted the incarnation to mean that God the Father himself became man and suffered, a view known as *patripassianism* ("Father-suffering-ism"). It foreshadowed the modern heresy known as the "death of God" movement.[19] Patripassianism acknowledged that Christ is fully God, but it did not identify the Son as a separate Person, distinct from the Father. Indeed, neither the Greek term *hypostasis* nor the Latin word *persona* had yet taken on the meaning they came to assume during the struggle to conceptualize the mystery of the Trinity, namely, that of a distinct, enduring, indivisible consciousness.

The problem can be stated simply. The Scripture teaches, and Christians confess, that Jesus, the Son, is truly God. He possesses the attributes of deity and he does works that none but God can perform. The same statement can be made of the Holy Spirit, although there are fewer references to the Spirit as God than to the Son. At the same time, Christianity, in harmony with Judaism, insists that God is one. How is it possible to say that the Father is God and the Son is God, and indeed that the Holy Spirit too is God, denying that the Father *is* the Son or the Holy Spirit, and yet contend that there is only one God? A solution was proposed by Egypt's most celebrated theologian, Origen. Without the brilliant contribution of Origen, what we now call trinitarian orthodoxy would not have emerged. Unfortunately for the memory of this great Alexandrian, his imagination was so fertile and his speculation so elaborate that the Eastern Orthodox regard him not as a saint and Father of the church but as a great heretic. Origen, like Tertullian before him, made an invaluable contribution to the development of orthodox doctrine, but also produced so many unorthodox ideas that orthodox Christians are embarrassed by their debts to him, while great liberals, such as Harnack, embrace him.

a. The School of Alexandria

Even before the destruction of Jerusalem in A.D. 70, the Hellenistic metropolis of Alexandria had become the intellectual capital of Judaism. It was in Alexandria that the seventy scholars gathered to produce the Greek translation of the Hebrew Scriptures, the Septuagint Bible (traditionally abbreviated LXX). Alexandria was also the home of Philo, the Jewish scholar whose intellectual powers and productivity make him a fitting successor to the pagan Plato as well as a suitable forerunner of the Christian Origen. In the person of Origen (ca. 185–254), Christianity for the first time produced a mind capable of being ranked with the greatest thinkers and writers of antiquity.

To be a Christian in second-century Alexandria was to be confronted with high intellectual attainment among both pagans and Jews. It is not surprising that the city soon became the center of Christian scholarship as well: the first known Christian academy was there. Alexandria retained its influence well into the Chalcedonian era, ultimately fading from the center of the Christian stage only because of the Moslem conquest.

Before it became known for orthodox Christianity, Alexandria was the home of the celebrated gnostic heretic Valentinus. Valentinus adopted Philo's method of allegorical interpretation of Scripture to produce his fascinating, if incredible, theory of the universe. For a time, Valentinus and his followers coexisted with the orthodox Christians of Alexandria. The first really forceful reaction against Gnosticism came from the West.

Fanciful gnostic speculation and the allegorical method of interpreting Scripture were both familiar and popular in Alexandria. Alexandria's orthodox Christian thinkers were more inclined to speculative theology and less interested in the historical person of Jesus than those of any other important center of early Christian thought. Nevertheless, Alexandria also produced many champions of the doctrine of the full historicity and humanity of Christ, the most significant being the great Athanasius (ca. 293–373), the champion of the orthodox faith of Nicaea.

The catechetical school of Alexandria was established while Christianity was still a persecuted and clandestine faith. Its first leader, Pantaenus, is said to have left the school to take the Gospel to "India" (probably southern

Arabia) sometime after 190. The little-known Pantaenus was succeeded by Clement, known as Clement of Alexandria to distinguish him from Clement of Rome, called the first bishop of Rome after Peter. It was Clement of Alexandria, we recall, who confused the debate between Christian orthodoxy and Gnosticism by calling orthodoxy true gnosis and the mature Christian the true gnostic. Clement of Alexandria (ca. 150–ca. 215) is known as the first Christian to produce a systematic treatise on ethics, *The Tutor*. Like the gnostics he opposed, Clement distinguished the simple *pistis* ("faith") of the ordinary Christian from the gnosis of the well-instructed, mature believer, but unlike them he minimized the significance of the distinction and taught that simple faith was adequate for salvation, although a fuller gnosis was preferable. Although a bit later than Irenaeus, Clement represents a decline from his level. His ethical principles are admirable, but they owe as much to Stoicism as to the New Testament. His doctrine is more speculative, less biblical, and less mature than that of Irenaeus.

Among his apparent shortcomings, Clement does not appear to be aware of the full canon of the New Testament, nor to be particularly interested in the rule of faith, i.e. the early form of the Christian creed. Unlike Irenaeus, who detested it, Clement refers to secret tradition, and his affinities to Gnosticism seem to go beyond mere borrowing of gnostic terms. He is chiefly remembered as a teacher of ethics. Thanks to Clement, Christian doctrinal theology did not come into the world alone, but was accompanied by a well-developed system of ethics. From Clement's day onward, "moral theology" (ethics) has gone hand in hand with "dogmatic theology" (doctrine), and virtually every great flowering of Christian theology has given attention to ethics as well as to doctrine. (The first break in his alliance will not appear until the modern, or second, Pietist movement in the nineteenth century.)

Clement was a teacher and an ethicist, but contributed little to the development of doctrine. By contrast, his pupil and successor Origen contributed more than anyone before him and more than all but a very few of those who have followed him. Undoubtedly one of the most brilliant Christian thinkers of all time, Origen was of a fervent nature. As a young man, he took Christ's reference to some who have made themselves eunuchs for the sake of the kingdom of heaven (Matt. 19:12) as a command and emasculated himself. Consequently, he could never be ordained a priest.[20] Already a teacher at Clement's school at eighteen, Origen attended the lectures of the celebrated founder of Neoplatonism, Ammonius Saccas (d. ca. 242). Neoplatonism stressed a dualistic distinction between body and soul, and this dualism marks Origen's thought as well.

Origen is one of the most productive as well as imaginative intellectual figures in the history of Christianity; only a few, such as Augustine, John

Chrysostom, Thomas Aquinas, Martin Luther, John Calvin, and Karl Barth, can be compared to him. Origen may be called the founder of Christian scholarship; even though Irenaeus, Clement, and Tertullian each preceded him in important respects, it required a man of Origen's universal competence and tremendous productive capacity to assemble the necessary elements and construct for theology a sound scientific foundation. He is noted in three areas: (1) he was the first real Christian Bible scholar, producing both textual and exegetical studies and extensive commentaries; (2) in *De principiis* (Fundamentals) he has given us the first comprehensive work of dogmatics; (3) in *Against Celsus,* he concludes the great series of early Christian apologetics.

Origen had something to say about virtually every aspect of Christian faith; what particularly interests us is his Christology and the doctrine of God related to it. Like Tertullian, who contributed several valuable themes to orthodoxy but died as a Montanist, Origen gave vital help in establishing the orthodox doctrine of the Trinity, but himself had problems with eccentric ideas. Three centuries after his martyr's death, Origen was to be posthumously condemned as a heretic by the Fifth Ecumenical Council (553). It is ironic that orthodoxy ultimately condemned him, for it is to Origen that orthodoxy owes the key to its understanding of the Trinity as three persons but one God, without which orthodoxy would not exist.

b. The Trinity

A detailed discussion of this central doctrine does not belong in the age of Origen, i.e. the first half of the third century, for the doctrine was not adequately formulated until the decades following the Council of Nicaea (325). However, because of the importance of Origen's contribution, it is necessary to outline one of its central features here.

In pre-Christian Judaism, the expression "Son of God," like "Messiah" or "Christ," did not imply deity. A man's son is human like his father, but a "Son of God," in Jewish usage, is simply a man or an angel who fully does the will of God. A "Son of God" is, of course, distinct from God, and the word "Son" suggests both a later origin and a lesser dignity. When Christians took up the term for their own purposes, they went beyond the Jewish usage and understood it to imply a relationship by nature, not merely by personal obedience; but for the early Christians, the term continued to suggest subordination. To the extent that the Son is conceived as subordinate to the Father in his duties but not in his nature, this idea is called economic subordination ("economic," in this sense, referring to the organization of the family). For many early Christians, however, the concept of subordination implicit in the term "Son" meant inferiority of nature and succession in time as well as a subordination in duty. A Son simply had to come "after" his Father, even if both Son and Father were in existence before all of creation. To say that the Father begets the Son—as Scripture does—implies that the Father preceded the Son, and thus that there was a time, or at least an interval, when there was not yet a Son. In that case, the Son could not be fully God, for God has no beginning.

It was Origen who proposed to explain how the Son can truly be a Son and yet not have a beginning. The terminology of "Father" and "Son" refers to a relationship that is eternal, not to an act in time. The Father eternally begets the Son, and is never without him. This proposal does not explain the Trinity, but it does permit us to conceive of the Son as eternal and thus as fully God. Later theological language will express the mystery of the Trinity by saying that God subsists in the three Persons, the Father, the Son, and the Holy Spirit. By introducing a rare term, "subsist," theology seeks to show that the Trinity is not to be demystified by resorting to inapplicable comparisons. If one were to say, for example, that God *consists of* the Father, the Son, and the Holy Spirit, this might appear to suggest that God has three parts. By teaching that the Father eternally begets the Son, and that the Son, eternally begotten before all time, is thus effectively co-eternal with the Father, Origen prepared the way for our present understanding: God does not consist of parts, but subsists in Persons. These Persons are distinguished from one another by means of a relationship—in the case of the Father and the Son, by begetting and being begotten—but not by succession in time.

To countless Christians and non-Christians, attempts to make precise distinctions—such as Origen's and ours—seem pedantic, if not altogether meaningless. It is important to recognize that the terminology was not developed idly, but because it was urgently needed to clarify concepts such as the death of Christ, even though neither it nor any other intellectual tool can explain them. Inasmuch as the deity of Christ and the doctrine of the Trinity are embedded in the New Testament, although not explicitly formulated there, we must make the effort of wrestling with difficult terminology if we are not to fall an easy prey to misunderstanding or to actual heresy.

Origen called Christ the Word, the Wisdom, the Justice, and the Truth of God, which makes Christ sound a bit like an attribute. But at the same time, Origen asserts that it is Christ who creates, or through whom all things are created. Of crucial importance to Origen's insight is the awareness that the Logos is a Person. It is the conviction that the Logos is a Person, and not merely an influence, attribute, or manifestation of God the Father, that distinguishes the Christian doctrine of the Son of God from philosophical speculation about God's Logos as the intermediary between God and the world. Admittedly, Origen frequently uses language that resembles that of pagan Logos-speculation. He says that the Son proceeds from the Father in a spiritual manner, "as the will proceeds from the mind."[21] This might appear to imply that Origen looks on the Son as an impersonal influence, but he rules out this interpretation by insisting that the Logos became incarnate in real history, revealing himself as genuinely personal.

It is impossible to think of a mind that is devoid of thought or will: this may help us to understand that the Father never exists without his Word or before him. To say that the Father and the Son are coeternal seems odd in view of the ordinary meaning of the terms "father" and "son," according to which the father is always elder than the son. Origen argues that inasmuch as the Father by his very nature is eternal, all that he is and does he is and does from eternity.[22] In consequence, he eternally begets the Son and is the Father from eternity. From one perspective, it may be easier to understand this concept if we see that giving different names to the Father and the Son, although both are God, serves primarily to make it clear that they are distinct and individual Persons.

One of the problems with Origen's approach lies in the fact that he also taught the preexistence of individual human souls and spoke of those who are in Christ as eternally begotten. Because he believed in a basic dualism of soul and body, he held that human souls came into existence independently of and prior to the creation of the material universe containing their physical bodies. This nonbiblical speculation eventually brought Origen into disrepute, but it does not change the fact that he gave to the church the best way to harmonize the biblical terminology of "Father" and "Son" with the doctrine that Christ is God and as God must be eternal like the Father.

It was thus Origen who provided the key that enabled the church subsequently to affirm, at the Council of Nicaea, that the Son is *homoousios to patri*, "of one substance [or essence] with the Father." Indeed, he may even have proposed the key word *homoousios*, for this Greek term occurs in the body of the fragmentary Latin text of Origen's *Commentary on Hebrews*.[23] The term *homoousios* was familiar to the gnostics and would subsequently be utilized by the Neoplatonist Plotinus (205–70) before being taken over by orthodoxy at Nicaea. What distinguished Origen's understanding from that of the Neoplatonists as well as from that of the monarchian patripassians was his insistence that the Son, although of the same substance as the Father, is a distinct *hypostasis* or subsistence. That is to say, a Person.[24]

All of this terminology is difficult, and that for two reasons. First, the doctrine of the Trinity is and will remain a mystery incomprehensible to the human mind. Second, the concept of personhood, which is essential to an understanding of the distinction between the Father, the Son, and the Holy Spirit, was not yet clearly developed. In fact, the Latin expression *persona* was commonly understood to mean "role" or even "actor." It was the theological struggle to understand that the Father, the Son, and the Spirit are real Persons, not merely different roles played by God, that helped the Christian world to understand that a person is real, not just a function or constellation of variable factors. The Western ideas of personhood and individuality were developed against the background of the Christian understanding of the distinctiveness of the Persons of the Trinity. In what we often call the "post-Christian West," as the understanding of the personal nature of God fades from public consciousness, it is becoming more and more difficult to understand and affirm the meaning of human persons.

The concept of distinct Persons (*hypostases*) sharing a common substance or nature (this sharing being known as consubstantiality or *homoousia*) made it possible to formulate the doctrine of the Trinity in a meaningful, noncontradictory way. Difficulties remain, and always will remain, but they arise not from the inadequacy of our terminology but from the nature of the doctrine itself and of the task it seeks to accomplish. Because the doctrine of the Trinity deals with the very nature and inner relationships of the godhead, it will never be understood by human beings in any full sense. It will always remain a mystery, but thanks to Origen, it can at least be expressed in such a way that we can see wherein the mystery lies.

c. Subordination

By asserting the eternal begetting of the Son, Origen countered the assertion that the Son must be later than the Father; with the concept of consubstantiality, he made it possible to conceive of the Son as equal to the Father; indeed, the concept seems to imply absolute equality. Nevertheless, Origen did not entirely throw off the assumptions of earlier Christian thinkers that the Son is subordinate to the Father. Inasmuch as anything that is less than God, no matter how exalted, is not God, it is difficult to reconcile the subordinationistic language of the New Testament and the submission of the Son to the Father with the idea of the full deity of the Son that Origen asserted. The key, of course, is to understand the subordination in what we may call an economic sense, not an ontological one. The Son submits to the will of the Father and executes his plan (*oikonomia*), but he is not therefore inferior in nature to the Father. Origen himself appears to have vacillated somewhat in his formulations on this topic.

The inner life of the Trinity remains inaccessible to the human mind. The concept of ontological equality combined with economic subordination would be explained by theologians in the next century by analogy with the relationship between husband and wife in marriage: they are equal by nature and in honor, but the wife is subordinate to her husband.[25] The fact that this example of marriage was used in the fourth century in the effort to assert

the fundamental equality of the Son to the Father tends to refute charges
that the early church considered women inferior to men, but of course it
cannot explain what remains part of the mystery of the Trinity.

d. The Holy Spirit

From the perspective of later theology, the doctrine of the Trinity appears foundational—so much so that many orthodox thinkers, from those
who produced the so-called Athanasian Creed to the present, contend that
we cannot know God at all if we do not know him as Father, Son, and Holy
Spirit, i.e. as the Holy Trinity. But in all that has been said thus far, it is
evident that the third Person of the Trinity, the Holy Spirit, has hardly been
considered. Origen gives an explanation: this is because many philosophers
have arrived at something resembling the Christian doctrine of the Son of
God, whereas the Holy Spirit is known only from revelation.[26] By saying
this, Origen may appear to be making too great a concession to pagan wisdom, for one of the constant accusations made against early Christian doctrine is that it is more Hellenistic and philosophical than Jewish and biblical.
And Origen seems to lack a very clear conception of the special role and
work of the Holy Spirit. Subsequent classical Christian orthodoxy has
rounded out, so to speak, the doctrine of the Trinity, bringing the Holy
Spirit into full equality with the Father and the Son. It speaks of the Spirit
as sharing fully with the other two Persons in the "external works of God,"
i.e. what God does external to himself in and with the Creation. Origen,
however, ascribed a more limited role to the Holy Spirit: the Spirit works
only in the lives of the saints. For Origen, the Holy Spirit is brought forth
by the Son;[27] Origen does assert that the Spirit is a person and is divine,[28]
but in his discussion of the Spirit he seems to make him quite inferior: all
that exists derives existence from the Father, all that is rational derives rationality from the Word, all that is holy derives holiness from the Spirit.[29]
We must thus say that while Origen has given us the conceptual tool to
understand a Trinity in which the Persons are essentially coequal, he really
develops this coequality only with respect to the Father and the Son. Origen
specifically rejected modalism, but one of the advantages of modalism was
that it rejected all subordination of the Spirit to the Son and of the Son to
the Father. Each Person was fully God in one of his three modes. The first
major task of theology after Origen will be to resist patripassianism and
modalism; the second, to avoid falling into an extreme form of subordinationism, Arianism.

That both Athanasian orthodoxy and Arian heresy, consubstantiality
and subordinationism, will be produced in Alexandria shows the importance
of this center for early Christianity, as well as the importance of Hellenistic

thought generally. Despite the encounter with Gnosticism and its pretensions to a secret gnosis of the mysteries of the unknowable God, Christianity as a whole was unwilling to follow the example of Irenaeus and refrain from speculating about things it could not know. Alexandria provided both intellectual ferment and speculative minds for four more centuries, until the Arab invasions put an end to its eminence in the Christian world.

e. Distinctives of Origen's Christology

Irenaeus was the first great Christian thinker to grapple systematically with the problems created by calling the Son "true God, true man." Tertullian, who came a generation later and who wrote in Latin, was very dependent on Irenaeus. Origen is the second great thinker of Christology. His achievement was the effectuation of a harmony between Hellenistic Logos-speculation and the cosmic Logos-theology of the early Christian apologetes on the one hand and the historical man Jesus of the Gospels on the other. How is it possible to bring the only begotten Son, coeternal with the Father, "into the limits of that man who appeared in Judaea"?[30] In order to do this, Origen turned his attention to something ignored by earlier thinkers: the *soul* of Jesus. For more than three centuries after Origen's time, the question of Jesus' soul would stir the churches. If Jesus the man did not have a human soul, then he was a human body only, not really a man. But if he had a human soul—by which is meant a complete human personality—how could he also have the mind of Christ? Origen tried to answer this question by presenting the human soul of Jesus as the connection between the infinite Logos and the finite, human body.

Origen taught the preexistence of the human soul; this was his way of explaining the apparent arbitrariness of God's election. God's first creative act was the creation of a number of incorporeal spirits, including human souls. As a result of free-will choices made by such souls before birth, turning away from God, they have been given material bodies, to each according to his deserts.[31] This theme only resembles the view of Gnosticism, but is more moral: preexistent souls are assigned their temporal identities on the basis of their moral choices. The concept of the preexistence of the soul will dramatically reappear sixteen centuries later in the doctrine of the Latter-Day Saints (Mormons). On the basis of his doctrine of preexistence, Origen was able to postulate that one particular soul was able to unite itself with the Logos; it was able to enter into a union with the Logos because of its purity and dedication. God created for it a pure, noncorrupt human body, which then was able to encompass the Logos-soul pair. Jesus could suffer and die as a man, but of course the impassible deity was unaffected. After the resurrection, Jesus' humanity is glorified and divinized. Jesus no longer possesses a mere humanity; his human nature has become divine and is, in a sense, consumed in this process of union, but Jesus' soul is eternally preserved in the union with the Logos. Origen sees a similar process of divinization as going on with all the saved after death.

In contrast with Irenaeus, who stressed that the Logos became man, here we have the converse: the man becomes Logos. In contrast with some of his predecessors, Origen maintained the personal nature of the humanity of Jesus. The human personhood of Jesus, not the fact of the incarnation of the Logos, would become the major Christological problem of the coming generations. Origen emphasized the complete humanity of Jesus, who possessed not only a human nature but a human *hypostasis*. The union with the Logos was through the perfect harmony of wills. These thoughts will be recapitulated by the fifth-century Nestorians. But Origen also saw Jesus as ultimately losing his humanity, although not his identity, in the deity of the Logos. This view makes Origen resemble the later Monophysites, opponents of the Nestorians, who liked to claim him as an authority in support of their views.

SELECTED BIBLIOGRAPHY

Barnes, Timothy David. *Tertullian: A Historical and Literary Study.* Oxford: Clarendon, 1971.

Bunsen, Charles Josias. *Hippolytus and His Age.* 2 vols. London: Longman, 1852.

Donaldson, Sir James. *The Apostolical Fathers: A Critical Account of Their Genuine Writings and of Their Doctrines.* Vol. 1 of *A Critical History of Christian Literature and Doctrine: From the Death of the Apostles to the Nicene Council.* London: Macmillan, 1864.

Faye, Eugène de. *Origen and His Work.* New York: Columbia University Press, 1929.

Morgan, James. *The Importance of Tertullian in the Development of Christian Dogma.* London: Kegan Paul, 1928.

Pressense, Edmond de. *Heresy and Christian Doctrine.* London: Hodder & Stoughton, 1873.

7

MONARCHIANISM

The economy of harmony is led back to one; for God is One. It is the
Father who commands, and the Son who obeys, and the Holy Spirit
who gives understanding: the Father who is above all, the Son who is
through all, *and the Holy Spirit who is in all. And we cannot otherwise*
think of one God, but by believing in truth in Father and Son and Holy
Spirit. . . . For it is through this Trinity that the Father is glori-
fied. . . . The whole Scriptures, then, proclaim this truth.

Hippolytus Against the Heresy of Noëtus *14*

There is no doubt that the first heretics were heretical; it is less clear that
they should ever have been thought to be Christian. Simon Magus claimed
to be God; Gnosticism borrowed little more from Christianity than the name
of Christ, which it fitted into a totally non-Christian religious philosophy.
Both the Marcionites and the Montanists had closer and more evident ties
with the nascent Christian church, but their own rival organizations are virtually as old as that of the church itself, and it is hard to say that they fell
away from it. Many early Christians held docetic ideas, which were heretical, but there was never a docetist party or church as such.

It is not until the movement known as monarchianism that we find
those who clearly deserve to be called Christians taking a stand the rest of
the church will plainly identify as an intolerable heresy. The tragedy of
monarchianism lies in the fact that its adherents really were trying to understand Christ correctly. The name "monarchian" is applied to groups that
sought to stress a fundamental biblical and Christian truth, namely, the conviction that God is one, the sole monarch of the universe. The monarchians
rejected the duality or plurality of gods taught by Marcion and the gnostics.
Unfortunately, the term "monarchians" is applied to two quite different
approaches to God's monarchy.

The older variety of monarchianism is designated dynamic monarchianism; it is also called adoptionism. It simply holds that Jesus is a man

95

endowed with a special power from God, and thus in a way adopted as God's Son. Much contemporary Christianity is in essence adoptionistic. Early in the nineteenth century, Friedrich Schleiermacher conceived of Jesus as the man with the most sublime God-consciousness, while Albrecht Ritschl saw him as endowed with the most perfect sense of duty. For the twentieth-century Anglican John A. T. Robinson, Jesus was "the man for others," perfectly transparent to God. Adoptionistic ideas always arise wherever Christians are reluctant to use the language and tools of philosophy to grapple with the apparent conflict between the unity of God and the deity of Christ.

The other variety of monarchianism is called modalistic monarchianism or simply modalism. It resolves the mystery of the Trinity by viewing the three Persons as different modes of the one God; they are not distinct, individual Persons in the sense of orthodoxy. For the adoptionist, Christ is not really God at all, but an adopted man. For the modalist, he is not only God, he is the Father himself. Thus two dramatically different convictions are embraced by the same rather misleading designation, "monarchianism." What they have in common is their conviction that the fundamental unity and oneness of God does not permit a second Person to share the titles of deity.

1. ADOPTIONISM

a. The Beginnings

Undoubtedly, many of the first Christians, if asked to describe the relationship between Jesus and the Father, would have done so in adoptionistic terms. As a distinct heresy, adoptionism did not make its appearance until about the year 190 in Rome, where it was certainly partly a reaction against the gnostic speculation that made of Christ an immaterial aeon. In his *Panarion* (Medicine Chest), a catalogue of heresies put together in the fourth century, Epiphanius claims that adoptionism began in Rome with a man known as Theodotus the Tanner. This first Theodotus began as a Christian but renounced Christ while still living in Byzantium. Then he moved to Rome and began actively to proclaim that Jesus was only *psilos anthropos,* a "mere man," who received the Spirit of God in a special way at his baptism. Although Theodotus professed to hold the Roman rule of faith (now known as the Apostles' Creed), the bishop (or pope) of Rome, Victor (reigned 189–98), excommunicated him. Harnack points out that Theodotus was the first Christian to be branded a heretic despite continuing to profess the rule of faith.[1] His example makes it apparent that the formula of the Apostles' Creed was not explicit enough to ward off such a serious heresy as adoptionism. (Of course, the Creed was used as a confession of faith by candidates for baptism; it was not intended to be the standard for professors of theology.)

Victor's successor as bishop, Zephyrinus (reigned 198–217), found that adoptionism continued to be taught by a certain Aesclypedotus as well as by a second Theodotus, called Theodotus the Money-Changer.[2] These adoptionist monarchians claimed to base their views on Scripture. Much of the New Testament can be read in an adoptionist sense; the number of passages that clearly emphasize the deity and preexistence of Christ are few. But to read the New Testament in an adoptionist way in 210 was to ignore the struggles of the preceding century.

The rise of adoptionism at this date shows that the words of the New Testament themselves are not explicit enough to form an adequate barrier against adoptionism, i.e. thinking of Jesus as a supernaturally endowed, mere human. This development reveals that more explicit formulations, such as those of Nicaea in 325 and of Chalcedon in 451, are necessary. The third-century adoptionists never gained a large following. Their rationalistic, human view of Christ, a kind of proto-Unitarianism, was not strong enough to resist the fires of persecution; Christians had to believe more if they were to face martyrdom. The Christian hoped, in eternal life, to be like Christ (1 John 3:2). Consequently the suggestion that Christ was only a Spirit-adopted man was dreadful for those facing death for his sake; Harnack calls it nihilistic.

Some very early orthodox Christian writings do sound adoptionist, for example, the *Shepherd of Hermas* (ca. 140), but it was more serious to revive adoptionist ideas after Christology had become more explicit. A final representative of adoptionism in Rome was Artemas, three decades after Theodotus the Money-Changer.[3]

In its own day, adoptionism was not a major force within Christianity, but its basic conviction has gained a wide following since the beginning of the nineteenth century. Adolf von Harnack, one of the greatest liberal Christian scholars of any age, himself held an adoptionistic view of Christ. Harnack defended the second- and third-century adoptionists as the true critical thinkers of their day. They used grammatical rather than allegorical exegesis and displayed an interest in logic, mathematics, and the empirical sciences. Harnack admits that they could not stand up to Roman persecution, because they were cool intellectuals, not zealous martyrs. In Harnack's view, the only way to withstand persecution was to be either a Platonist (i.e. a mystic) or an adventist, expecting the prompt return of Christ. The adoptionists were neither; they were analytical Aristotelians, and consequently adoptionism could not survive.[4]

The slogans coined by Irenaeus and Tertullian, "God made man," and "true God and true man," swept adoptionism from the stage. Its basic idea is so appealing, however, that it frequently recurs whenever a rationalistic, antimiraculous interpretation of Scripture comes into fashion. The other variety of monarchianism, modalism, tends to appeal more to Christians who intend to be orthodox but who do not take the trouble to formulate their teachings about the Trinity with sufficient precision to exclude such error.

b. Paul of Samosata

The somewhat primitive adoptionistic views of the two Theodotuses was superseded toward the end of the third century by a more sophisticated view. Its originator was Paul of Samosata (ca. 200–75), bishop of Antioch under Zenobia, Queen of Palmyra. Zenobia temporarily wrested control of Antioch from the Emperor Aurelian (ruled 270–75), who made an abortive attempt to give the empire a unifying religious symbol in the cult of the Invincible Sun. Paul, who also served as Queen Zenobia's treasurer, taught that Jesus was born of a virgin and that the Holy Spirit had been poured out upon him at his baptism. He did call Jesus God, unlike the earlier adoptionists for whom he was a mere man, but by this Paul only meant that through his moral perfection and the miraculous powers granted him at his baptism, Jesus was able to remain in constant union with God. Paul was criticized for these views and finally condemned as a heretic at a local synod in Antioch in 268. Through the protection of Zenobia, however, he was able to hold his episcopal see until the Emperor Aurelian recaptured Antioch in 272. The controversy between orthodoxy and Paul's adoptionism came before the pagan Emperor, for by this time the church, although not yet officially recognized as a legitimate religion, owned enough property to warrant a court decision to dispose of it. Aurelian decided that the property should go to the group that was in harmony with the Roman and Italian bishops, i.e. to the orthodox.

Three successive emperors, Decius (ruled 249–51), Gallus (ruled 251–53), and Valerian (ruled 253–60), had made vigorous and systematic efforts to destroy Christianity, but Valerian's son and successor Gallienus (ruled 260–68) inaugurated a forty-year period of tacit, although not official, toleration. The final great wave of persecution was begun by Diocletian (ruled 284–305) toward the end of his reign. Diocletian reorganized and revitalized the empire and sought to achieve greater unity by suppressing the Christians, but his efforts ended in failure. (In effect, the pagan Aurelian was acting almost like a defender of orthodoxy in removing Paul from his bishopric.)

A sophisticated thinker, Paul apparently influenced later figures who denied the deity of the Son, such as Lucian of Antioch and his pupil Arius. Although his dynamic monarchianism opposed modalism, Paul did have some modalistic ideas, for he spoke of God as having both a Logos (i.e. the Son) and Sophia (Wisdom, i.e. the Holy Spirit), but regarded neither as personal. As an adoptionist, Paul insisted on the true humanity of Jesus and thus strongly opposed docetism. In this period, the principal emphases of orthodox Christology were not yet united in a single party or confession of faith, as they would be at Chalcedon. For the moment, we find one party—such as the adoptionists—emphasizing the humanity of Jesus, and another, the docetic modalists, emphasizing his deity. A satisfactory way of bringing these two truths together was still in the process of being worked out. After Paul was deposed, adoptionism disappeared for five centuries.

2. MODALISM

a. The Beginnings

The word "modalism" is unfamiliar to most Christians, yet it is the most common theological error among people who think themselves orthodox. It is the simplest way to explain the Trinity while preserving the oneness of God; unfortunately, it is incorrect. Adoptionism preserved the unity of the godhead by sacrificing the deity of Christ; modalism, by abandoning the personhood of Christ and the Holy Spirit. Modalism frequently reappears as the result of failure to teach the doctrine of the Trinity clearly. An implicit or naive modalism is sometimes found in modern fundamentalistic circles that insist on the deity of Christ but are unwilling to make the theological effort to formulate a clear doctrine of the Trinity.

Modalism upholds the deity of Christ, but does not see him as a distinct Person vis-à-vis the Father. It holds that God reveals himself under different aspects or modes in different ages—as the Father in Creation and in the giving of the Law, as the Son in Jesus Christ, and as the Holy Spirit after Christ's ascension. Modalism stresses the full deity of Christ and thus does justice to the tremendous impact he made upon his age, and it avoids the suggestion that he is a second God alongside the Father. Unfortunately it abandons the diversity of Persons within the godhead, and thus loses the important concept that Christ is our representative or advocate with the Father.

Logically, modalism makes the events of redemptive history a kind of charade. Not being a distinct person, the Son cannot really represent us to the Father. Modalism must necessarily be docetic and teach that Christ was human in appearance only; the alternative, on the basis of modalistic presuppositions, is that God himself died on the Cross. Since such an idea is considered absurd—except by death-of-God theologians—the normal consequence is the conclusion that while Christ was fully God, he only appeared to be man.

Like adoptionism, modalism has a basis in Scripture. The adoptionists emphasize the Synoptic Gospels and their portrayal of the descent of the Holy Spirit upon Jesus at his baptism. The modalists emphasize the Gospel of John with its statements stressing the oneness of Christ with the Father, for example, "I and my Father are one," and, "He that hath seen me hath seen the Father" (John 10:30, 14:9). Instead of understanding these verses to mean that Christ is a second Person in perfect communion with the Father, they are taken to mean that he and the Father are a single Person, in other words, that he is the Father. The word "one" in the Greek text of John 10:30 is the neuter *hen,* which suggests that the meaning is "one deity, one divine essence," rather than one Person, but this is a rather sophisticated insight. It makes sense only if one can conceive of God as subsisting in distinct Persons, namely, in the Father and the Son (and of course in the Holy Spirit as well). Anyone who has not yet been able to formulate the concept of the Trinity in this explicit way will of course find it simpler and more plausible to understand Christ as saying, "I and the Father are one Person," in other words, as presenting himself as a mode of the Father. If the Son is not a real Person who can stand before the Father and address him, then the later Christian concept of substitutionary satisfaction, which holds that Christ takes our place and pays our debt to the Father, becomes at best a symbol, not a reality. Where modalism prevails, the concept of substitutionary satisfaction, or vicarious atonement, will necessarily be absent, and so modalism is sometimes adopted by those who object to the doctrine of vicarious atonement. More commonly, however, it simply arises as an attempt to reduce the mystery of the Trinity to a more understandable concept, even at the cost of the true humanity of Jesus and the doctrine of substitutionary satisfaction.

The first known modalist was Praxeas. Like several other early heretics, Praxeas was a committed believer. In fact, he was a *confessor*—one who straightforwardly confessed his faith in Christ when haled before a judge—in Asia Minor before traveling to Rome about 190. Both in Asia Minor and in Rome he opposed the Montanists with their concept of new, prophetic revelations. When Praxeas arrived in Rome, Bishop Victor (reigned 189–98) was struggling to put down the adoptionism preached by Theodotus the Tanner, and so his emphasis on the full deity of Christ was welcome. When it was discovered that Praxeas identified Jesus not merely with deity but with the Father and taught that God the Father was born in time, he aroused bitter opposition; Tertullian—who himself later moved into Montanism—wrote his energetic polemic *Against Praxeas* to expose and refute him.

The appearance of modalism in Rome by the last decade of the second century marks the extent of the victory of orthodoxy over Gnosticism, which had been flourishing not many years earlier. Valentinus had been teaching that the Father is so totally above all that is mundane that he is absolutely unknowable and unutterable; Praxeas began to teach not merely that Jesus Christ revealed the Father, but that he actually was the Father. The fact that Gnosticism and adoptionism could not hold their own in the face of orthodoxy, and that orthodoxy itself came under attack from modalism at the opposite end of the theological spectrum, is another evidence of the fact that the early church simply could not deal with the evidence of the New Testament and its own experience of Christ except in terms of acknowledging his deity. It was easier to slip into modalism and confuse Christ with the Father than to say with Gnosticism that he was a mere lesser aeon; or with adoptionism that he was only a man.

Praxeas was followed in Rome by Noëtus, Epigonus, and Cleomenes. Like Praxeas, they taught that the Father himself had suffered and died, and then resurrected himself; they asserted that this is what Scripture itself teaches and that it is the proper way to glorify the Son.[5] Noëtus was evidently motivated by the desire to defend the deity of Christ against the more skeptical views of adoptionism. Even today, many devout Christians who are zealous to defend the doctrine that Christ is fully God against modern, liberal adoptionism fall, like Noëtus, into modalism. Praxeas tried to avoid the problems of patripassianism, of the doctrine that God the Father suffered, by making a distinction between the man Jesus and the Christ, who was the *hypostasis,* or personification, of the Father. Only the man suffered, God did not. Thus the effort to preserve the deity of Christ brings in effect a split in his person; Christ is God, and far more than a merely ''adopted'' man, but Christ adopts the man Jesus and indwells him. When modalism teaches the incarnation of God in Christ, it logically implies patripassianism and even the death of God; if it attempts to say that God did not suffer, and thus to preserve the classical conviction of philosophical theology that God is impassible, then it must make a distinction between God in Christ and the human Jesus and in effect revert to a kind of adoptionism. The struggles of the modalists to do justice to the deity of Christ without falling into patripassianism or a new kind of adoptionism are essentially the results of an effort to understand and make clear what is ultimately a mystery that transcends human understanding, the doctrine of the incarnation.

Later Christian thinkers devised the formula ''communication of attributes'' to express the idea that although Jesus Christ is both fully God and fully man, he is but one person. Because he is one person, and thus a single subject in both the psychological and the grammatical sense, what is said about the person of Christ may logically be said about both God and man. Thus it is both logically sound and theologically correct to say that God was born, suffered, died, and rose again, as long as one does not forget that while the Son is God, God is not only the Son. In the Reformation era,

Luther will develop the idea of the communication of attributes to the point of insisting that the human body of Christ possesses the divine attribute of omnipresence; in the eyes of some of his opponents, Luther's view will compromise the humanity of Christ, although he himself continued to insist that he was defending it. In the effort to avoid this problem, the Zurich Reformer Ulrich Zwingli and John Calvin in Geneva will both so emphasize the distinction between the divine and the human in Christ that they will appear to be in danger of splitting him into two persons.

Both these early adoptionists and modalists as well as the great Reformers all had in common the fact that they earnestly believed in Christ and were trying to help others understand him and believe in him. Nineteenth- and twentieth-century heretics, by comparison, frequently, if not invariably, have given up belief in the Christ of the Bible and propose what sound like similar views and interpretations for quite a different reason, namely, to justify the fact that they do not believe in the Christ of Scripture and of the great creeds and confessions. In other words, while noting that ancient and modern views are frequently quite similar, it is important to recognize that similar language may be used to express very different religious convictions. Praxeas confessed his faith before the authorities and presumably was prepared to give his life for it. Would modern theologians, if challenged to confess their faith in court and give their lives for it, be ready to die for their theology, or would most prefer to explain it away as only a theory or an interpretation? In the absence of persecution, it is impossible to know what others will do. Indeed, even the most orthodox and traditional Christians would be unwise to boast in advance of how they would respond to persecution and the threat of a painful death. Nevertheless, it is fair to say that one senses a tremendous urgency and genuineness in the early heretics that one misses in the more urbane and academic discussions of modern theologians.

b. Sabellianism

Modalism apparently reached its high point early in the third century in the teaching of Sabellius, a little-known figure of Libyan origin who was active in Rome under Bishops (or Popes) Zephyrinus (reigned 198–217) and Callistus I (reigned 217–22). As in the case of many heretics, most of our information about Sabellius consists of descriptions of his doctrine by his orthodox opponents, who were not interested in giving a complete biography. Nevertheless, despite the obscurity of Sabellius as a man, his ideas were so fascinating that they will continue to crop up again and again through the centuries and his name will remain a term of abuse in theological controversies.

Sabellius taught the strict unity of the godhead: "one Person *(hypostasis)*, three names." God is *hyiopator*, Son-Father. The different names, Father, Son, and Spirit, merely describe different forms of revelation; the Son revealed the Father as a ray reveals the sun. Now the Son has returned to heaven, and God reveals himself as the Holy Spirit.[6] The concept that the Trinity subsists in different Persons is lost. Sabellius' view saw the existence of the Son as confined to his earthly work. Consequently he cannot continue to be "an advocate with the Father" (1 John 2:1) or be said to "live forever to make intercession" (Heb. 7:25).

Despite these flaws, Sabellianism seems to have won the adherence of two bishops of Rome, Victor and Zephyrinus, both of whom were involved in bitter struggles with the adoptionists. Zephyrinus' successor, Callistus, repudiated Sabellius, but continued to use rather Sabellian language: the Father, the Son, and the Holy Spirit are *hen kai to auto* ("one and the same"). This is an orthodox formulation if one understands it to mean one and the same God, but Sabellian if the missing word is "person." The Father is the Spirit of God who became flesh in the Virgin's womb. It is the flesh that is to be called the Son. The Father did not suffer himself, but "sympathized" (suffered with) the Son.[7] The entanglement of these three bishops, or early popes, of Rome with Sabellianism has proved a continuing embarrassment to the traditionalist Roman Catholic doctrine of papal infallibility; traditionalist Catholics take refuge in the fact that the details are somewhat obscure and to a large extent supplied by Hippolytus (ca. 170– ca. 236), who was elected by a minority as a counterpope.

The modalism of Sabellius influenced later orthodox formulations in that it insisted on the deity of the Holy Spirit as well as that of the Son, although it did not consider either a distinct Person. By insisting that the Holy Spirit is also God, Sabellianism helped to counteract the tendency to what we may call a kind of ditheism, in other words to see the Son as a kind of secondary divinity beneath the Father and at the same time to look on the Holy Spirit as an impersonal power or influence. What finally defeated Sabellianism was the conviction that Christ really is distinct from the Father, a conviction that naturally results from all those New Testament passages in which we see the Father and the Son dealing with one another as distinct persons. It remained for the Arian controversy a century later to produce a clear explanation of how the Son can be distinct from the Father and yet not different in nature from him.

8

THE GREAT ALTERNATIVE: ARIANISM

If you ask for change, someone philosophizes to you on the Begotten and the Unbegotten. If you ask the price of bread, you are told, "The Father is Greater, and the Son inferior." If you ask, "Is the bath ready?" someone answers, "The Son was created from nothing."

Gregory of Nyssa, On the Deity of the Son and of the Holy Spirit

The defeat of Paul of Samosata represented a victory for a complex theological view over a simpler interpretation of scriptural and credal statements. It meant that Christian doctrine was going to be theological and philosophical and would rely on tools from those disciplines for its understanding and interpretation. Harnack holds that although Gnosticism had not succeeded in Hellenizing Christianity, it scored a delayed victory as doctrine became irrevocably theological in the defeat of Paul of Samosata by pre-Nicene orthodoxy.[1] Where Paul had proclaimed the simple idea of adoption by God, his opponents introduced the concepts of external generation and preexistence.

There are two types of Christians who resist the orthodox view (later to be adopted at Nicaea). Some, like Harnack, are essentially theological liberals and simply do not think that it is correct. They object to it as the result of Hellenization, but it is not so much its Hellenistic pedigree they dislike, but that it presents doctrines they think are false. Many theological conservatives who believe, by contrast, that the Son indeed is fully God also object to the formulas and interpretations of Nicene orthodoxy simply because they are Hellenistic in flavor, make use of philosophical categories and language, and are not simply biblical. By adopting a prejudice against the use of philosophical language and the Hellenistic influence in theology, many Christians who want to be conservative and orthodox deprive themselves of the tools that are necessary to build a stable doctrinal structure and ultimately will fall into some variety of heresy, very likely into one orthodox theology has already rejected.

The adoption of the Nicene Creed in 325 and the Chalcedonian Creed in 451 stabilized the doctrines of the Trinity and Christ for over one thousand years.[2] They made use of Hellenistic categories and thinking to do so. The important question to ask is not whether orthodox theology betrays Hellenistic influence. Nothing else was possible in the cultural climate of the time. The important question is whether this orthodoxy represents a proper and correct interpretation of New Testament Christology or whether it seriously distorts it. The rise and spread of Arianism in the fourth century made it plain that the early rule of faith, the Apostles' Creed, was not sufficiently explicit about the relationship of the Son to the Father. If we are unwilling to accept the Nicene Creed because we find it too Hellenistic, we should not be surprised to fall once again into mistakes of the kind that the newer creed was intended to prevent.

Like both kinds of monarchianism, Arianism originated within the catholic church, among people who wanted to be true to their apostolic heritage. They did not want to discard large parts of it, like Marcion, nor to supplement it with private revelations, like Montanus. Nevertheless, Arianism came to be perceived as one of the most dangerous and pernicious of errors. For a time, however, it was very successful—so successful that its adherents were elevated to the most important bishoprics and it controlled the major part of the church, at least in the East. In the West it was never successful.

Arianism differs from the adoptionism of Paul of Samosata in that while Paul's view was essentially a simple one, Arianism is as abstract and complex as orthodox Christology. Confronted with the idea that the Son is eternally begotten, Paul countered with the simplification "No, Jesus was adopted by the Father at his baptism." Arius, by contrast, denied that the Son is eternally begotten, but admitted him to be first-begotten of the Father and preexistent. This is hardly a simplification of the orthodox position.

Arius and those who followed him were not skeptical or unbelieving, as is certainly the case with many modern thinkers who, like Arius, deny the deity of Christ. Arius not only felt that he could not believe in Christ as eternally begotten, but also that he was compelled to accept him as a supernatural being, although of a somewhat lower order than the Father. This is a way in which Arianism differs from most modern heresies. Moderns who deny the deity of Christ seldom pause in a kind of middle position like that of Arius, but usually drop down to an adoptionist or even lower view of the Saviour. Generalizations are dangerous, but we may say that most ancient heresies were characterized by variant belief; most modern ones, by unbelief, or at least by uncertainty about what to believe. Variant beliefs, strongly held, are common in the modern era, but they are usually held by those who stand beyond the limits of formal Christianity, such as Jehovah's Witnesses.

Arianism has very important implications for one's view of Christ, because it states that he is not fully God. This denial is widespread within modern Christendom, but the resemblance between modern unbelief and early Arianism is not otherwise great, for Arianism has its own supernatural concept of Christ, based on a type of metaphysical speculation that does not appeal to many contemporary Christians. Arianism developed the idea that the Son is a semidivine being created, not begotten, by the Father and having an origin in time, or at least a definite beginning before the creation of the material world. Most modern theology is not at all interested in such speculation and consequently has only its denial of the deity of Christ in common with Arianism. Modern theology is generally skeptical; Arianism denied the full deity of Christ, but did so in the context of a way of thought that was no less credulous than orthodoxy.

The Arian controversy is particularly crucial for orthodoxy for two reasons: first, because it could not have ended otherwise without destroying orthodoxy; and second, because by ending as it did with the establishment of the Nicene, or Niceno-Constantinopolitan, Creed of 325/381, it really created orthodoxy. It did not, of course, create orthodox faith, for that really existed in a more or less clearly defined form from the days of the Apostles. What it did was give the church the first standard by which orthodoxy could be reliably measured. Thus if we may say that Gnosticism gave us a clear monotheism and an explicit doctrine of Creation, and that Marcionism gave us the New Testament canon, we may say that Arianism gave us orthodoxy, or at least trinitarianism.

1. ARIUS, THE LEADER

Arius is one of the first great heretics who has left us with a fairly distinct impression of his personal history and character. He came onto the theological scene together with two great historical events: the rise of monasticism, which began among isolated Christian hermits in Egypt, and the beginning of toleration under Constantine the Great (ruled 306–37, sole Emperor 324–37). Monasticism began in Egypt during the period of relative calm between Gallienus and Diocletian. Christianity was becoming increasingly popular, and in consequence the life of Christians "in the world" was becoming too lax and comfortable to suit many of the more committed believers. Thousands of Egyptian Christians fled to the desert called the Thebais in order to escape the temptations of worldly life, and sometimes to put themselves out of the way of persecution. When persecution resumed under Diocletian, many Christians renounced their faith, only to repent and seek readmission to Christian fellowship when the immediate danger was past. A series of rigorists opposed readmitting the *lapsi,* or defectors, into fellowship, the best known being the Roman presbyter Novatian of Rome, who began a schism in 251, calling for a pure church. His views were opposed by Cyprian of Carthage (ca. 200–58), who favored readmission after a period of probation; Cyprian himself was martyred in the last wave of persecution before Gallienus. A few decades later, Melitus of Lycopolis began a similar rigorist schism in Egypt; as a young monk, Arius was associated with him.

The fact that Arius began as a rigorist in Egypt and spent much time in Alexandria, the home of a theology that stressed the deity of Christ, does not make him a typical Alexandrian. He studied in Antioch under Lucian of Antioch, a theological outsider who maintained a kind of private academy of his own, but who also died for the faith in the last wave of persecution before Constantine legalized the church. Lucian followed in the tradition of Paul of Samosata, emphasizing the humanity and the human will of Jesus. Lucian's view represented an advance over the adoptionist view that Jesus was a mere man supernaturally endowed with the Holy Spirit. He believed that there was a Logos, or personal divine power, created by the Father, that became incarnate in Jesus. Lucian thus sought to integrate the concept of the Logos, by now part and parcel of the church's understanding of Christ, into the monarchian insistence that only the Father is fully and truly God. Thus he saw the Logos as a kind of intermediate, created spiritual being between God and man. Essentially, Lucian taught this idea to Arius, whose rallying cry became the assertion that the Logos, i.e. the Son, is a created being—higher than any other, but different in essence from the Father. Although Lucian and Arius seem to be interested primarily in the nature of Christ, the Arian controversy is called trinitarian, not Christological, because the point at issue was the relationship between the Father and the Son in the Trinity. Arius did not in fact have a true Trinity; the crucial importance of trinitarianism became evident only in the course of the Arian controversy. The later controversies that are called Christological did not deal with the relationship between the Father and the Son within the Trinity, but with the relationship between the deity and humanity of Christ.

a. A Prelude: The Quarrel of the Two Dionysiuses

The Arian controversy divided Christendom for half a century and revealed that government toleration of Christianity did not prevent Christians from practicing intolerance on one another. It is in a way the theological controversy *par excellence.* No sooner had Constantine, the first Christian

Emperor, gained complete control of the empire than he found the church—which he had hoped would help him reunite his vast domain—riven by bitter conflict. The eighteenth-century English historian Edward Gibbon, author of the monumental *Decline and Fall of the Roman Empire*, held Christianity to be a major factor in the decline. For Gibbon the fact that Christians would fight bitterly over "an iota" cast grave doubts on the credibility of their Gospel of redeeming love.

The Arian controversy was the first controversy to be officially decided by an ecumenical council; in fact, it was the cause of the Council of Nicaea, and the Nicene Creed is the church's response to Arianism. Gibbon and others would have us believe that the whole controversy was a dispute over a trifle, simply the *iota* that distinguishes the two Greek words *homoousious*, "of the same substance," and *homoiousios*, "of similar substance." (Actually, the expression *homoiousios* dates from the second stage of the controversy, after Arius was already dead.) Orthodoxy, however, was persuaded that everything that is important depends on excluding the *iota*, on confessing Christ as of the same substance as the Father, not as of like substance. Clearly no major controversy could have developed over a small difference in expression, involving philosophical language not found in Scripture, unless that difference were the symbol of a very fundamental disagreement with a substantial history. The beginning of the disagreement lies in a third-century controversy between two bishops with the same name: Dionysius of Rome and Dionysius of Alexandria.

Rome, we recall, had been the scene of a three-way controversy between adoptionism, orthodoxy, and modalism, during which two bishops of Rome appear to have stood on the wrong side. By virtue of the status of Rome as the capital of the empire, its bishop automatically enjoyed considerable prestige; even before the official recognition of Christianity, the pagan Emperor Aurelian would make affiliation with Rome a criterion for denying the property claims of a rebellious bishop, Paul of Samosata. Such honor seems to have been welcomed by the church at Rome. When some disgruntled believers in Alexandria, the intellectual capital of Christendom, wrote to the Roman Dionysius in 260 asking for a verdict in their controversy with Dionysius of Alexandria, the Roman was happy to oblige.

In Alexandria, Bishop Dionysius faced a considerable problem with Sabellian modalism, which saw the Son and the Father as one and the same Person. To counteract this, he reasserted the teaching of the greatest Alexandrian theologian, the recently deceased Origen, emphasizing that the Son is subordinate to the Father—and if subordinate, then of course evidently a different Person. For reasons that are not clear, Dionysius of Alexandria was showered with titles of honor by his successors: Eusebius called him "the Great."

The brief conflict between Rome and Alexandria is important because of two things it reveals: (1) the direction of Roman theology, and (2) the way in which linguistic difficulties would create misunderstandings between East and West and permit heresy and deviation to be perceived where none existed. In Rome, there was simply a straightforward acceptance of the unity of the godhead without interest in speculation concerning the relationships within the Trinity. Rome felt that Origenistic subordinationism was a kind of tritheism and that the Alexandrian party was separating the Son from the Father, based on philosophy and in deliberate indifference to tradition. Under pressure from his Roman colleague, Dionysius of Alexandria explained himself and accepted all the most important orthodox formulas. The bishop of Rome had rejected the concept that the Persons of the Trinity are divided. The Greek term for "Person" in the Trinity, *hypostasis,* linguistically resembles the Latin *substantia,* which means something very different, namely, "essence" or "nature." To the extent that Greek-speaking Christians spoke about three distinct divine *hypostases* and added that they are divided from one another, they seemed to Latin speakers to be teaching three divine essences. When Latin speakers, on the other hand, spoke of the Son and the Holy Spirit as *personae,* Persons, because of the familiar association of the word *persona* with roles in the theater, this seemed to Greek-speaking Christians to be a reversion to modalism.

It was Origen who contributed the essential concept of the eternal begetting or generation of the Son by the Father, and thus made the doctrine of the coeternality of the three Persons of the Trinity easier to grasp. Another aspect of his Christology influenced Lucian of Antioch, the martyr, and especially his pupil Arius and those who followed him, who denied that the Son is eternally begotten. Origen had indeed strongly emphasized the subordination of the Son to the Father, but Arius went beyond the warrant of Origen in interpreting such a subordination as referring to the being or substance of the Father and the Son: for Arius, the Son might resemble the Father, but if he is subordinate to him, he cannot be of the same substance or nature.

In addition to contributing the crucial concept of the eternal begetting of the Son by the Father, Origen emphasized that the Son is subordinate. Dionysius of Alexandria took Origen's ideas over in a rather wooden fashion without capturing the great scholar's spirit. Origen was vigorously opposed to Sabellian modalism, which destroyed the individuality and personhood of the Son (as well as of the Spirit). Consequently he sought to emphasize the distinction between the Persons of the godhead. He rejected the idea that there is any distinction in nature between the Father and the Son, as would be the case if the Son were created, or even if he were begotten at a point in time, rather than eternally. To avoid making the Son seem identical to the Father, which the identity of their nature might imply, he stressed the distinction in the relationship between them. The Father is *agennetos,* "ingenerate" or "unbegotten," while the Son is *monogenes* or *protogenes,* "only begotten," "first-begotten."

Origen's language is clearly subordinationistic, and Dionysius of Alexandria emphasized the subordination until he was challenged by his namesake in Rome. Then he quickly recalled other terminology from Origen's thought, such as "eternally begotten." Dionysius of Alexandria is also known for disputing John's authorship of Revelation and delaying its recognition as part of the New Testament canon. He objected to the idea of an imminent return of Christ and an earthly millennium and thus foreshadowed the amillennial position that eventually became the accepted view of most of Eastern Orthodoxy and Roman Catholicism.

Origen's admirer Dionysius was succeeded as archbishop of Alexandria by a more practical churchman and more literalistic interpreter of Scripture, Peter (d. 311). Peter attacked Origen's idea of the preexistence of human souls—a curious opinion that would cause Origen to be condemned as heretical by the Emperor Justinian in 543. (Although a kind of Christian Neoplatonist and therefore persuaded that the soul is by nature immortal, Origen taught the resurrection of the body in biblical fashion.)

Although Alexandria was a center of allegorical interpretation, its great interest in the Bible helped to keep the New Testament the ultimate standard of Christian doctrine and to prevent it from being supplanted by churchwritten creeds. Long before the slogan *sola Scriptura* was coined in the Reformation era, Egyptian Christians were treating the Bible as the "perfect rule of faith and practice," as later Protestants would call it.[3] Unfortunately, this interest in the Bible was somewhat undercut by the Alexandrian readiness to resort to allegorical interpretation.

Methodius of Olympus (d. ca. 311) was one of many leaders who died in the last great persecution under Constantine's rival coemperor, Maximinus Daza (ca. 307–13). Although Methodius was not above resorting to allegorical interpretation when he felt that he needed to, he opposed it in general, emphasizing a realistic-literal approach more like that of Irenaeus. Methodius taught that the believer has been cleansed of sin by the blood of Christ, that Christ indwells in him, and the Holy Spirit lives in him, enabling him to lead a good life. The destiny of the Christian is to be raised in a glorified body; his life on earth must be a quest for spiritual perfection. It was natural for him to accept the idea of an earthly millennium in which justice and peace reign on earth.

Although Origen was by no means a gnostic, except in Clement's sense of a knowledgeable believer, he emphasized that salvation comes through knowledge of the truth—a theme at least suggested by Jesus himself (John

8:31–32). Methodius and his followers represent a different, more practical and work-oriented approach. Salvation is the end result of the ongoing transformation of the believer's life by the indwelling Christ. The extreme conclusion that could be drawn from Origen's views is that salvation does not depend on what a believer is or does, but on what he knows. If we replace "knows" with "believes," we have justification by faith alone. Methodius' views can lead to perfectionism and works-righteousness. Although Origen and Martin Luther seem to have little in common, the idea that salvation comes from what one believes is not so different from the assertion that it comes from what one knows, if one understands knowledge, as Origen did, in terms of John 8:31–32.

b. Lucian of Antioch

The great synod at Antioch of about 268, the one that ineffectually condemned the adoptionist bishop of Antioch, Paul of Samosata, affirmed the doctrine of the Logos but explicitly repudiated the term *homoousios,* "consubstantial." Paul's tradition was perpetuated in Antioch by Lucian, who combined a dislike for the allegorical method with a critical interest in Scripture. The school Lucian founded at Antioch remained out of fellowship with the church until a reconciliation occurred shortly before the persecution of 312 in which Lucian was martyred. In Lucian we see the doctrine of the Logos being adapted to suit the chief concern of the adoptionists, the conviction that the Father alone is monarch and that no one like him may stand beside him. Lucian appears to have exercised tremendous influence because of his gifts as a teacher, his exemplary self-discipline, and finally his martyrdom in the last great wave of persecution. This martyrdom came soon after Lucian's formal rapprochement with the church, and eradicated the memory of his long years as a deliberate outsider. Because he was a martyr, it was easy for people to follow his doctrines without suspecting the difficulties inherent in them. In addition to the famous Arius, Eusebius of Nicomedia (d. ca. 342) was among Lucian's pupils.

The central theme of Lucian's Christology that was to stamp it as heretical was his assertion that the Logos was created "out of that which is not." Although Lucian considered the Logos, or Son, to be the highest spiritual being beneath the Father, by stating that the Logos was created, Lucian placed him together with all other created beings in contradistinction to God. Lucian held that the Logos took upon himself a human body, but not a soul; in other words, according to the standards of later orthodoxy, Lucian's Jesus was not only not fully God, he also was not fully man.

For the moment, Lucian's most objectionable doctrine was his view that the Logos is created. However, the idea that the Logos took upon himself only human flesh but not a human soul is also problematic. In the second half of the fourth century, Apollinaris of Laodicea (d. ca. 390) will understand the incarnation as meaning that the Logos took the place of a human soul in Christ. The problem with this view is that a human body indwelt by a spiritual mind, the Logos, is not a true human. In the crucial phrase from John's Gospel, "and the Word was made flesh" (1:14), Lucian and Apollinaris understood "flesh" to mean "physical body," rather than "human nature," as it generally means in the New Testament.

2. THE OUTBREAK OF THE
ARIAN CONTROVERSY

We have few details concerning the life of Arius. We do know that he was very old at the time of his death in 336. Thus when he was ordained presbyter in Alexandria shortly after 311, he was already at a relatively advanced age. The church he entered in Alexandria was still in the reaction against Hellenistic philosophy initiated by Archbishop Peter. Arius was an ascetic and won the respect of the ascetically inclined clergy of Alexandria, but aroused the concern of the new archbishop, Alexander, sometime around 318. Arius presented himself as an opponent of heresies, from Gnosticism to Sabellianism, and soon began to teach explicitly that the Son, far from being another mode of the Father, was of a different nature, a created being. Alexander excommunicated him around 321. Arius had numerous influential friends, including Eusebius of Nicomedia and Eusebius of Caesarea, the noted church historian. Arius persuaded some of them that Alexander's edict of excommunication threatened them as well.

Immediately after his excommunication, Arius began a whirlwind campaign of letter-writing, and Eusebius of Nicomedia also wrote extensively on his behalf. Arius succeeded in gaining the support of several Asian bishops, which made him confident enough to return to Alexandria and begin to teach again without Alexander's approval. About this time, Constantine became sole Emperor. He discovered to his dismay that the church he had adopted was in a huge controversy agitating the entire eastern half of his newly pacified empire. It was an uproar of major proportions; Christians and Christian doctrines became the butt of ridicule in the theater. The first effort of Constantine to deal with the matter was a letter sent jointly to Bishop Alexander and Arius, asking for restraint and concluding: "Give me back my quiet days and carefree nights. Do not let me spend the rest of my days joylessly."[4] It is remarkable that the most powerful man in the world would involve himself in such an ecclesiastical squabble, and even more remarkable that he should express himself so deferentially. It is noteworthy that he addressed both Alexander the bishop and Arius the priest on the same level. The letter was carried by a Spanish bishop, Hosius of Cordova, but Hosius was unable to reconcile the contenders. Hosius came to an understanding with Alexander, who then went to Nicomedia, where he was able to persuade several other bishops of the rightness of his cause. Constantine, annoyed by the rebuff his unprecedented efforts at conciliation had received, decided to adopt a different approach and summoned the first ecumenical council to Nicaea.

The primary point where the difference between Arius and Alexander appears is in the doctrine of the coeternity of the Logos. For Alexander, the Father was never without the Son; for Arius, "there was when he [the Logos] was not." From the records of the dispute, it is apparent that the doctrine of the Holy Spirit—which is, after all, necessary for the doctrine of the Trinity—played virtually no role at this early stage in the controversy. This has sometimes led to the erroneous assumption that theology went through a kind of "binitarian" phase before developing a full trinitarianism. It would be better to say that while trinitarian formulas are found in Scripture and were used from the beginning of the church, their meaning was not really clear until it began to be understood that each of the three members of the Trinity is a Person. This understanding was attained first for the Son, in the course of the Arian controversy. Lucian and Arius stressed that the Son is distinct from the Father. Their orthodox opponents accepted this, but denied that the Son is of a different nature from the Father. Once it was accepted that the Son is a distinct Person of the same nature as the Father, the same formula was immediately used for the Holy Spirit. The development was from an implicit trinitarianism—suggested, but not defined, by the language of Scripture and the liturgy—to an explicit trinitarian theology that sees Father, Son, and Holy Spirit as three distinct Persons, each partaking of the divine nature. The suggestion that Christianity began with a kind of unitarianism and proceeded through "binitarianism" to trinitarianism is false.

What were Arius' motives? His contemporaries charge him with personal vanity and intellectual pride, factors that have played a role in more than one theological controversy. Theologically, he seems to have been tremendously concerned to preserve the monarchy of the Father and to have feared that the orthodox doctrine was making the Son into a second God. This is indeed a legitimate concern. It appears that in Arius it was motivated by an elitist desire for an understanding of God more sophisticated than that of those who simply repeated the orthodox formulas.

Arius' concept of God emphasizes the distinction between the Father and all others, including the Son and the Holy Spirit. When the Bible speaks of the Father "begetting" the Son, Arius calls it a synonym for "creating."

In order to mediate between himself and the world he purposed to create, God created a new spiritual being, called the Wisdom, Image, or Word of God in Scripture. The Son is independent of God and distinct from him; like other rational beings, he could have exercised his free will to disobey God. He is not worthy of divine worship as the Father is, although he is the *ktisma teleion,* the "perfect creature," through whom all other things were made. This Word took upon himself a real human body, but no soul, and could suffer. The Holy Spirit is also a created being like the Son, but less important; the Arian concept of the Trinity was vague.[5]

Neither Arius himself nor any of his early adherents, with the exception of the Sophist Asterius, made an effort to present his views in a systematic fashion. Letters were their chief literary production. To some extent Arianism in its early stage looks like a problem in ecclesiastical politics and church-state relations rather than a heresy. As it turned out, Arius did have a theological position very different from orthodoxy, but the controversy seems to have begun as a power struggle between rival bishops; its theological implications became fully clear only later.

On the other side too most of the early evidence consists of letters—in this case, by Arius' opponent, Bishop Alexander. By his return to Alexandria and his resumption of his activity under the nose of his nominal superior and totally without authorization, Arius resembles another great antagonist of the eternal Sonship of Christ, Michael Servetus (1511–53). Like Arius, Servetus will enter the domain of his chief opponent, John Calvin (1509–64). Arius was not to meet his death by execution at the hands of the orthodox, as Servetus did, but one additional parallel exists. The unhappy conflict with Servetus and Calvin's ruthless way of dealing with him cast a heavy shadow over Reformed Protestantism, one that has not been totally removed even to the present day.[6] Although Arius himself did not suffer execution (he was about to be restored to his full rank when he died in 336), the Arian controversy casts as great a shadow over the beginnings of established catholic orthodoxy as the execution of Servetus does on Calvinism. Prior to the time when Constantine put an end to persecution, Christians had quarreled among themselves, but they had to keep their voices down because of the danger of attracting official notice and further government displeasure. The immediate outbreak of a virulent controversy with personal abuse and maltreatment on both sides just as soon as Constantine removed the threat of persecution was not only a shock to Constantine. It almost makes it appear that theological wrangling is a necessary part of the Christian faith and that the "harmony of the brethren" is an illusion.

As the church expanded, the Scriptures were more widely distributed and an extensive body of commentaries and other theological literature was produced, reflecting many diverse and often conflicting viewpoints. Under Constantine, Christianity became in effect the state religion, although it was not established by law until 380. New members flocked to the churches, and bishops and archbishops became public figures, almost public officials. Because it was growing so rapidly, and because Constantine expected the church to fulfill a public function, that of helping to unify his strife-torn empire, the fierce controversies that wracked the church became a matter for public concern. During the great persecutions, the state often helped to resolve differences among Christians by martyring all those involved in a dispute. Thus Maximinus Daza martyred the orthodox Peter of Alexandria, the pre-Arian Lucian of Antioch, and the outsider Methodius of Olympus. Once Constantine ended the threat of persecution, the full extent of the disunity within the early church became apparent; Arianism was its foremost manifestation.

a. Early Arianism

The theology of Arius seems to be inspired by two different concerns or motifs, one spiritual and moral, the other philosophical or theological. (1) The spiritual-moral motif was Arius' conviction that Christ does not possess deity by nature, but develops into it by virtue of his constant and growing moral unity with God. He is our Saviour in that he presents us with divine truth and furnishes the perfect example of commitment to the good. This view hardly differs from adoptionism; its practical consequence is the imitation of Christ, with the implicit hope that other human beings can attain perfection and partake of divinity even as Christ did. (2) The philosophical-theological motif of Arius' theology is that of the contrast between the One who is utterly transcendent, God, and the world of created things. In order to make Creation possible, God had first to create a spiritual being that could act as a Mediator—as in the Neoplatonic concept of the Logos. Associated with God's Nous ("Mind"), or the world spirit, the Father and the Logos constitute a triad (or a dyad—Arius was not concerned with consistency here). Interestingly, Arius, who considered the Son and the Spirit created beings, was ready to pray to them; Origen, who taught that the Son was eternally begotten of the Father, not made, called for prayer to the Father through the Son.[7] Harnack observes that Arius "is a strict monotheist only with respect to cosmology; as a theologian, he is a polytheist."[8] Indeed, Arius seems to be to the left of Hellenistic Logos-speculation, for he does not even regard the Logos as an emanation of deity, but as a *ktisma,* a "creature," or even "created thing"; yet he would worship him. This created Logos develops into deity. The incarnation is not the self-emptying or humility of the Logos, but the means to his glorification. In this we see not only Arius' affinity with adoptionism as taught by Paul of Samosata but also his humanism.

Arianism must be seen as a doctrinal innovation, coming as it does at a time when traditional doctrines had been fairly well set forth. Although it would take orthodoxy close to three centuries to settle on the definition of consubstantiality, no one had yet ventured to teach what Arius was now proclaiming: that the Logos is radically distinct from the Father, of a different substance. Modalists taught that the Logos is identical to the Father, adoptionists dispensed with the Logos altogether. But to the extent that a Logos was taught at all, no one before Lucian of Antioch and Arius had contended that the Logos is categorically different.

Harnack comments: "Athanasius has exposed the internal difficulties and contradictions [of Arianism], and we can agree with him almost everywhere. A Son who is no Son, a Logos who is no Logos, a monotheism that does not exclude polytheism, two or three essences to be worshipped, although only one is really distinct from that of the creatures, an indefinable being that becomes God only in that it becomes man, and that is neither God nor man, etc. On each individual point, there is apparent clarity, but everything is hollow and formalistic, a childish self-satisfaction in the activity of contentless syllogisms. This was not learned from Origen, who always had realities and goals in mind when he speculated."[9]

The interposition of this created Logos between God and man weakened the possibility of communion with God. Arianism was really a bridge between polytheism and monotheism, but it was neither the worship of the one God of Scripture nor was it true Christianity. It did facilitate the "conversion" of countless pagans during the early decades of the Constantinian era, for it sharply reduced the clash between Christianity, interpreted in an Arian way, and pagan philosophical monotheism.

b. The Council of Nicaea

Constantine at first tried to deal with the conflict between Arius and Alexander by using tact and appealing for sympathy, but the conqueror of the Roman world was not the man to wait long for quarreling divines to heed his entreaty. He had only been sovereign for about ten years when the controversy became so acute that it threatened to destroy the value of Christianity as a source of unity in the empire. According to tradition, 318 bishops, primarily from the East, assembled at government expense in Nicaea, near the newly established capital at Constantinople. Bishops from the Western half of the empire, where Arius had few followers, were a small minority. Harnack supposes that the Emperor failed to summon the Western bishops en masse precisely because he did not wish to give the impression that he was using the influence of the Latin-speaking bishops of the West to put down the more sophisticated theologians of the East.[10] Constantine opened the council with a kind of lay sermon. When the bishops' discussions threatened to degenerate into petty personal squabbles, he silenced them. At first, Constantine seems to have thought that the council would rapidly reach agreement on its own. When it did not, he acted. His power and prestige certainly influenced the rapidity with which the council fathers reached a decision, but the nature of the decision was the result of their own deliberations and political maneuvering.

The Arians, reflecting the self-confidence—or conceit—of Arius himself, came to the conclave expecting victory. They had twenty-eight committed adherents, while the party actively supporting Bishop Alexander included only Marcellus of Ancyra and a handful of other Western bishops. The majority of the uncommitted bishops were poorly educated, rustic clergy: active persecution had ended scarcely a decade earlier, and most of them had lived and worked in obscurity. It is likely that much of the theological debate was over their heads.

The Arians, confident that victory would be theirs, made the great mistake of beginning the council by presenting their own statement of faith, a straightforward document drawn up by Eusebius of Nicomedia. It frankly and flatly denied the deity of Christ, stunning even the least acute of the uncommitted majority. It was roundly rejected. Sensing disaster, the Arians sought to rescue the situation by appealing to Eusebius of Caesarea. This second Eusebius, author of the celebrated *Ecclesiastical History,* was not an Arian, but he found the formulations of Arius easier to accept than those of Alexander, which seemed to him to be pure Sabellianism. Eusebius drew up a creed based on Scripture; it became the blueprint for the Nicene Creed as ultimately adopted. This preliminary creed was quite explicit about Jesus Christ, calling him "the Word of God, God of God, light of light, life of life, the only begotten Son, firstborn of all creation, begotten of the Father before all ages, by whom all things were made."[11] According to Eusebius' own account, the Emperor spoke in favor of his creed and, at the suggestion of Hosius, proposed the addition of the word *homoousios,* "consubstantial." Alexander's party, now in the ascendant, added a number of anathemas explicitly condemning specific Arian positions. (These anathemas were dropped in the revised creed of the Second Ecumenical Council, held in 381.) Faced with this *tour de force,* only two Arian bishops refused to endorse the *homoousian* creed: they were deposed and excommunicated. Arius himself, who was only a presbyter, not a bishop, was also deposed and forbidden to return to Alexandria, where he still had many supporters. The Antiochene party, although it was composed of students of Lucian like Arius himself, abandoned Arius. Constantine ordered the burning of Arius' writings and immediately began to take repressive measures against his supporters. It was the Emperor, not the orthodox bishops, who ordered the repression of the Arian party, but the orthodox welcomed his action. The mutual persecution of Christians by Christians, using the power of the state, had begun.

c. Theological Politics

If we recall that the controversy only began in 321, this resolution, only four years later, appears remarkably swift for a theologians' quarrel, even with imperial assistance. Earlier it was claimed that heresy was the stimulus for the formulation of orthodox theology. Now it will appear evident that declarations of orthodoxy have stimulated the eruption of further heresy. Nicaea decreed, but it did not settle. The Nicene Creed was so sharp and categorical in its language that it created unity among those who opposed it and misgivings among many who accepted it. It was not popular among the admirers of Origen—still the most distinguished name among theologians. They could accept the term *homoousios,* but they were distressed at the lack of any mention of the subordination of the Son to the Father.

The Arians had only modest success in recruiting adherents among Christians, but were able to gather support among pagans and Jews, thus beginning the questionable Christian habit of soliciting theological aid from groups who consider Christian faith false. A modern parallel is offered by the controversy between the Swiss Roman Catholic theologian Hans Küng and the papacy, in which Küng has sought support from non-Catholics and even non-Christians as well as from secular government in maintaining his independent views over against the doctrinal authority of the pope.

Although it was Constantine himself who had proposed the critical term *homoousios* and who named Athanasius as Alexander's successor in Alexandria in 328, the Emperor soon began to listen to Arian sympathizers among the Eastern bishops. In the same year that he appointed Athanasius in Alexandria, Constantine reinstated Eusebius of Nicomedia. He deposed a number of pro-Nicene bishops for various nontheological reasons. In 335, at the prompting of Eusebius of Caesarea, he deposed Athanasius himself— not for dogmatic error, but for treating his subordinates harshly. Athanasius appealed to the old Emperor, but Constantine reaffirmed his removal and exiled him to Trier in 336. No successor was appointed in Alexandria. When Constantine died in 337, the Nicene Creed was official and Arius was dead (of natural causes and at a very advanced age, although his opponents said that he died by the hand of God). The chief advocates of the Nicene Creed, Athanasius, Eustathius of Antioch, and Marcellus of Ancyra, were in exile. The three sons of Constantine allowed them to return, but in the East Constantius made a dramatic turn. Paul of Constantinople, already banished once before, was deposed a second time and his see given to the Arian Eusebius of Nicomedia. When Eusebius of Caesarea, essentially a partisan of the Nicene Creed although not of Athanasius, died about 340 at nearly eighty, he too was succeeded by an Arian. Although Athanasius had returned to Alexandria, rioting drove him out a second time in 339, before Constantius' order for his removal could reach him.

During the middle decades of this century, from 340 to 380, the history of doctrine looks more like the history of court and church intrigues and social unrest. It is a potentially embarrassing fact that the central doctrines hammered out in this period often appear to have been put through by intrigue or mob violence rather than by the common consent of Christendom led by the Holy Spirit. From one perspective, it can be said that the points in dispute were of life-and-death significance for individuals as well as for the church and that zeal and vehemence, if not violence, were justified. There is a vast difference between saying that Jesus Christ is God of one substance with the Father (*homoousios to patri*, the orthodox statement) and saying that he is merely *like* God, of similar substance (*homoiousios*, the most moderate Arian formulation, sometimes called semi-Arian).

The distinction between *homo* ("same") and *homoi* ("similar") may seem trivial, but it was not so subtle that most ordinary Christians failed to grasp what is at stake. If Jesus is of the same substance as the Father, then he is truly God, and it is reasonable to think that he is able to "save . . . to the uttermost" those who come to him (Heb. 7:25). On the other hand, if he is only of similar substance, which was all that even the conservative Arians were willing to concede, then it is not evident that he necessarily possesses the divine power and authority he needs to make an atonement on behalf of the whole human race. The one who believes that Jesus is God can readily accept the idea that he can do for us what we cannot do for ourselves, and believe, in consequence, in justification by faith. The orthodoxy of Nicaea is a necessary foundation for both Roman Catholic and Protestant orthodoxy in subsequent centuries. But if Christ is just another created being, even though he is the firstborn and most exalted of all created beings, then it is more natural to think of him as our teacher and example than as our atoning sacrifice. Rather than simply having faith in him, we are called upon to imitate him. Because it considered Jesus a creature, and attributed our salvation to him, Arianism exalted what a creature can do, and thus incidentally exalted man, especially the highest of men—the Roman Emperor, who had only recently laid aside his claim to be divine.[12] If Christ is God, then he is categorically different from all men, including the Emperor, who is another man just like us. But if Christ is a creature who is like God, this implies that other men, who are also creatures, can likewise resemble God. Thus Arianism, although claiming to be Christian, could endorse a very high spiritual place for the Emperor, even if not deity in the old sense.

The danger Arianism posed for the survival of Christianity lies in the fact that while Christianity is exclusive, Arianism is syncretistic, potentially even polytheistic. By exalting man it threatened to deny that revelation and the church that imparts it are the sole means of access to spiritual truth and the eternal life it brings.

The Arian controversy is closely tied up with the personality of Constantine the Great and his sons, particularly Constantius II, who was sole ruler from 350 to 361 (Constantine II, ruled 337–40; Constans, ruled 337–50; Constantius II, ruled 337–61). Constantine himself had been a pagan and seems to have had a dramatic experience that led to his conversion: before the crucial Battle of the Milvian Bridge in 312, he saw a vision of the monogram for Christ, the ☧ , with the legend "In this sign, conquer." Constantine did conquer, and took the symbol as his standard. We have mentioned his distress at the internal strife that broke out in his new church as soon as he ended the persecutions; we have described how he first sought to reconcile the Arians and the orthodox, and then intervened in the Council of Nicaea. Not only did he secure the victory of what we subsequently know as orthodoxy, but he even gave it the sharp formulation known as the *homoousion* (from the neuter of *homoousios*). However, after he established himself in the East and came to know not only the moderate Eusebius of Caesarea but also the pro-Arian Eusebius of Nicomedia and other pro-Arian clergy, Constantine initiated a series of practical measures designed to restore the fortunes of the Arians. Although capable of violence, even brutality, Constantine became a God-fearing monarch who sought to keep his brutality in check and frequently succeeded.

After his death, his sons continued the policy of favoring the Arians; Constantius, who lived the longest, was a zealous partisan of Arianism. It is not unreasonable to think that the Arian doctrine of a man who became God might have a natural appeal to a powerful monarch who was only one generation removed from the days when the emperors were called divine. Although Arian sympathizers occupied all the important Eastern sees by 340 and the most celebrated defenders of the Nicene position were all in exile, the Arian party faced a difficult problem. The traditionalism that Irenaeus and others saw as the guarantee of truthfulness made it difficult to think of reversing the creed of an ecumenical council. It was not so easy to get rid of the Nicene Creed or the doctrines it promulgates. The writings of Marcellus of Ancyra helped the Arians to do so. Marcellus, one of six Western bishops at Nicaea in 325, was one of the few who had really wanted the *homoousion;* in his later writings, he developed the *homoousian* position in such a way that it really did sound like Sabellian modalism, just as the Arian party had been charging. Marcellus reverted to an older, economic interpretation of the Trinity and denied the existence of distinct *hypostases* in the godhead, which he described as having *hen prosopon,* "one face (mask)." Marcellus taught that the Logos is God's preexistent *dynamis,* "power," which did not really become personal until the incarnation.

Marcellus called only the *incarnate* Christ the Son of God; he did not acknowledge a preincarnate, personal Son. The Logos preexists and is in fact eternal, but is not personal until the incarnation. Thus Marcellus effectively denied the preexistence of Christ. He assumed that Christ's kingdom will end and will be remitted into the hands of God the Father. Marcellus went to Rome when he was deposed at Ancyra in 338, and by wording his views judiciously, persuaded Pope Julius I (reigned 337–52) to accept him as orthodox.[13] Of course he had no difficulty accepting the Roman (Apostles') Creed, which does not address itself specifically to questions such as those raised by the Arians. In any event, Rome had a tradition of tolerance for modalist tendencies since the time of Victor. Athanasius had reservations about Marcellus' views, but he was so interested in affirming the *homoousion* against the Arians that he ignored the need to protect the formula against being interpreted in a modalist sense by his partisan Marcellus.

In the meantime, the party of Eusebius of Nicomedia (now installed as patriarch of Antioch) produced a series of four statements of faith intended to eliminate the most objectionable features of Nicaea. Naturally this led to the charge that the Eusebian party did not really know what they believed.[14] Julius traveled to Antioch to deliberate with the Eusebians, who were eager to reach an understanding they could accept, not least because the Roman party had the support of the vigorous Western Emperor, Constans, while their own supporter Constantius was distracted by a war with the Persians on his eastern border; when Eusebius of Nicomedia died in 342, the conservative Nicene party came to the fore even in the East.

A general council was convened by Constans in Sardica (modern Sofia) on the border between the western and eastern parts of the empire in 343. (It was not subsequently recognized as an ecumenical council.) The Easterners sought to have the expulsion of Athanasius from Alexandria and of Marcellus from Ancyra reaffirmed before the council began—both of these bishops were in attendance. When this demand was rejected, the Eastern bishops withdrew en masse, leaving a purely Western council on the eastern border of the Western empire, presided over by Hosius from Cordova in Spain. The rump council reaffirmed the Nicene Creed (which the Eusebian party also did, at least formally). At this council the confusion between the Greek expression *hypostasis* and the Latin *substantia* clearly wreaked havoc. *Hypostasis* was by now understood by Greek-speakers to mean "concrete realization," i.e. "person": the proper Latin equivalent is *subsistentia*. Unfortunately the Latins confused *hypostasis* with its "false friend" *substantia,* "substance," "essence," or "nature." When they spoke properly of *una substantia* (Greek *ousia*), "one substance (essence)" in the deity, they improperly rendered it into Greek as *mia hypostasis*. To Greeks, this meant one *person* and was pure modalism. Eusebius and his partisans, having walked out of the synod, appealed to their own Eastern Emperor, Constantius. In a new statement of faith, they reaffirmed the Son as the only begotten and called him God of God, but did not use the term *homoousios*.

In the West the tendency to lose the distinctiveness of the Persons was carried further by Photinus, a pupil of Marcellus. He spoke of an *energeia drastike,* an "active energy," of God in Christ. He apparently wanted to safeguard monotheism and the unity of God by dealing only with the fact that Christ does the *work* of God, and not with the question of whether he *is* God. Photinus' ideas remind us of second-century adoptionism and earned him condemnation by two councils at Milan in 345 and 347. Photinus' excess also raised the suspicions of Athanasius concerning Marcellus, who had taught Photinus.

Under pressure from the pro-Nicene Western Emperor Constans and with no support from Constantius, the Eastern bishops subscribed to an *Ekthesis* ("Exposition") couched in basically Western language. They accepted the term *prosopa* for the Persons of the Trinity, despite the fact that its original sense, "face," or even "role," certainly sounded modalistic to them. They were able to evade the use of the Nicene watchword, *homoousios*. Avoiding the obnoxious word itself, they said that the Son is "in all things like [*homoios*] the Father"—also a formulation used by Athanasius. They could not be persuaded to use the obnoxious term *homoousios*.

Constantius, pressed militarily in the East, sought harmony with the Western portion of the empire at all costs, and in 346 allowed his brother's protégé Athanasius to return to Alexandria. This restoration only lasted until Constantius gained unchallenged sole authority after the death of his brother Constans in 350 and his own victory over the usurper Magnentius in 351. He had been frustrated and humiliated by the stubbornness of the Western bishops under his brother's protection. Now he took measures to put them in their place. Athanasius, in the meantime, had continued to rule his diocese harshly; his opponents stirred Constantius up against him, and Constantius forced condemnations of Athanasius through two Western synods, Arles (353) and Milan (355).

Athanasius was deposed but refused to leave until he was physically attacked in a church in 356; then he fled into the desert. Bishops who supported him were sent to the mines. The political victory of the Arian party seemed complete, but this success united the orthodox against them as they themselves had been united by the orthodox victory at Nicaea. Thirty years had passed since Nicaea. There were parallels to the situation before 325, but this time the strategic advantage lay with the temporarily discomfited orthodox party. After the Council of Nicaea, the best thinkers were on the Arian side, except for Athanasius himself and Marcellus of Ancyra. By 356 the intellectually vigorous Arians had passed from the scene. Among the orthodox, Athanasius was still flourishing, and Hilary of Poitiers, a first-rate theologian, was at his side.

d. Radical Arianism

Despite the fact that it was only the support of the Emperor that gave them power, the Arian party did nothing to try to consolidate its position among the mass of believers. These, bishops and people alike, may have been puzzled by the philosophical and theological logic that demanded the use of the term *homoousios*, but they certainly opposed any efforts to diminish the deity and majesty of Christ. Despite this, and the fact that they were reviving proposals spurned by the late Eusebius of Nicomedia, the most widely accepted of the supporters of Arius, Aëtius and Eunomius, took advantage of the protection of Constantius to advocate a radical Arian line. Like Arius himself in 324–25, they appeared to be more interested in telling people what Jesus Christ the Son is *not*, rather than in describing him positively. He was said to *differ* in essence from the Father, to be "unlike" (*anomoios*, rather than *homoios*, "like") the Father, to be a created being, or even thing (the Greek term *ktisma*, "creation," or "created being," is neuter). Even when they admitted that the Son perfectly and truly knows the Father, they minimized the significance of this statement by affirming that other human beings also can come to know him.

The majority of the Easterners repudiated this rationalistic, reductionistic approach—a kind of New England Unitarianism centuries ahead of its time. They were uncomfortable with the term *homoousios*, especially when it was given a modalistic interpretation by Marcellus and Photinus, but they were not prepared to describe Christ as a created thing. The name *homoians* was applied to this party, which balked more at the term *homoousios* than at the claim that the Son has equal dignity with the Father. For political reasons, a number of bishops tried to unite the Arians and the *homoians;* because there was such a difference between them, only an exceptionally vague formula could achieve such an end. Before this could be found, pressed by the triumphant Constantius, the Western bishops met at Sirmium in 357 and produced a pro-Arian statement, forbidding the use of both expressions, *homoousios* and *homoiousios*. This was an open assault on the Nicene Creed, for *homoousios* is its watchword, while *homoiousios* was only a concession made by some moderate Arians to Nicaea, not a battle cry, its prohibition meant little to the Arian party.

The new formula of Sirmium was thus one-sidedly anti-Nicene although it pretended to be impartial. It reaffirmed that the Father is greater than the Son, which is not problematic if it is not understood to imply that he has a different nature. However, Sirmium explicitly rejected the Nicene watchword, "of the same nature." Even though it did not teach a difference in natures, the synod had a pro-Arian impact. The disciples of Aëtius began to fill high posts in the wake of this compromise, which really was an affirmation of radical Arianism.

The compromise of Sirmium, rather like the Dred Scott decision before the American Civil War, went too far and caused the majority of public opinion to react against it. Hardly anyone in the East was a radical, rationalistic Arian like Aëtius. To clarify the troubling situation, Basil of Ancyra persuaded Constantius to take a step backward and approve a formula that was in essence pro-Nicene, even though it did not use the controversial *homoousios,* but substituted the blander *homoiousios* ("of similar nature"). The only difference, the *iota (i),* did not trouble most of the bishops, but Athanasius refused to compromise: it was *Athanasius contra mundum,* "Athanasius against the world." For the moment, the world, willing to compromise and say *homoiousios,* was victorious. The victory of the *homoiousians*—a rather artificial grouping, formed out of a desire for compromise rather than any strong theological impulse—was not less dramatic for being contrived. Basil of Ancyra caused the banishment of Aëtius and a large number of his adherents.

The practice of determining dogma on the basis of whoever had the attention of the court may have begun innocently enough under Constantine, who really did have a theological interest at heart. By 357 doctrines were being imposed or rejected to meet the needs of the fluctuating political tactics of Constantius. Constantius pursued his goal of imposing the *homoiousian* formula on the whole church at a divided synod in 359, held for the West in Rimini, for the East in Seleucia. In the West the Emperor's wishes were disregarded, and the old *homoousian* Nicene formula reaffirmed. The Western delegation sent to Constantinople to secure the approval of Constantius was confined at Nicaea until finally it was coerced into signing a statement (the Declaration of Nicaea) that affirmed only a limited likeness. The Eastern synod in Seleucia was in the hands of the *homoiousians,* but here the opposition did not consist of *homoousians* but of strict Arian Anomoeans, i.e. the followers of Aëtius who insisted that the Son is *unlike* the

Father. The majority's understanding of likeness (like the Father in all things) was quite close to the meaning of the old Nicene Creed. Aëtius was deposed and banned, but the Emperor was unsatisfied with *homoiousian* language and insisted that the Eastern bishops also accept the more liberal language of the Declaration of Nicaea he had forced on the Westerners. Although Aëtius was banned, his friends regained power. We are confronted with the spectacle of a cruel and immoral ruler asserting the right to tell the church what to believe about the nature of Christ. In 361 Constantius II died, leaving the empire to Julian, the last pagan monarch.

3. THE SECOND STAGE OF ARIANISM

By 361, a generation after Nicaea, the victory of the Arians seemed complete. It had been gained almost totally by the favor of the Emperor Constantius. During the struggle, the Nicene party, led by Athanasius, maintained a consistent, almost inflexible commitment to its principle, expressed by the slogan *homoousios*. The more tractable Arians varied their stand as circumstances demanded, now virtually surrendering to the Nicenes, now demanding recognition of the view that the Son is unlike the Father. The accession of Julian showed the internal weakness of the Arian party. Julian, who had abandoned Christianity and returned to paganism, professed to be indifferent to all theological disputes among the Christians, although he appears to have felt more sympathy for the Arians than for the Nicene party. But the Arian party was so lacking in internal strength that it wilted when an Emperor appeared who simply failed to support it as his predecessor had done.

When Julian came to the throne in 361, the Nicene Creed had not been repudiated, but all of its supporters had been banished. Officially, the moderate party, the *homoiousians,* who followed a line developed from Origen's combination of sameness of substance with subordination of function, appeared dominant; but politically the more extreme Arians, favored by Constantius, were rapidly assuming the ascendancy.

Julian (ruled 361–63), known subsequently as "Julian the Apostate," attempted to reinstitute traditional pagan religion. He was the younger son of the half brother of Constantine. After the murder of his father, Julian was brought up in obscurity, first by the moderate Arian Eusebius of Nicomedia and then in schools in Italy and Greece. He was well educated and preferred the pagan heritage to the Christianity he only formally respected. On becoming Emperor, Julian adopted the role of a philosopher, as Marcus Aurelius had, finally coming to oppose Christianity in his twenty-month reign.

Although Julian was hostile to all Christians and, if he favored any group, inclined toward the more philosophical and Hellenistic party, the Arians, his actions sped the triumph of orthodoxy. Professing religious toleration as well as indifference to, or rather contempt for, the doctrinal squabbles of Christians, Julian revoked all exile for religious reasons. This permitted Athanasius and the other pro-Nicene, orthodox leaders to return, if not to power, at least to their old sees. The immediate result, as Julian foresaw and indeed certainly wished, was conflict and confusion among the Christians, but the long-range result was a strengthening of orthodoxy. The supporters of the orthodox position needed to regain much lost ground, politically as well as theologically. Under Constantius, their political support had been eroded. The fact that the pagan Julian was more evenhanded with, or in other words, equally hostile toward, all the quarreling Christian parties, helped the orthodox. The strength of Arianism lay in its political connections. Theologically, the orthodox had to find a way to explain the concept of *homoousia* without falling into modalism.[15] This they did in the years 361–81, between the death of Constantine and the Second Ecumenical Council of Constantinople. These were crucial years for the development of trinitarian doctrine. In these two decades the principles of the full personhood and deity of both the Son and the Holy Spirit were finally definitely and explicitly set forth. Thus the foundation was laid for classical Christology and soteriology, the doctrines of the person and work of Christ.

a. The Synod of Alexandria

As soon as Julian revoked his banishment, Athanasius returned once more to Alexandria. A council was held there in the summer of the same year, 362. It laid the groundwork for the eventual reaffirmation of Nicene orthodoxy at Constantinople in 381. This synod of Alexandria was important as the first to stress the deity and personhood of the Holy Spirit as well as of the Son. It called for the acceptance of the *homoousian* formula without any glosses or footnotes. The synod made no statement concerning whether God should be spoken of as having one *hypostasis* or three and thus avoided the confusion that would have arisen about whether *hypostasis* means "substance" or "person." Although several bishops called for an affirmation that God is one *hypostasis* (which most Easterners would have found modalistic), the synod avoided declaring itself—certainly a prudent concession on the part of the usually precise Athanasius.

Prior to the Council of Nicaea, the chief theological problem had centered on the nature of the Son (and, by implication, of the Holy Spirit). The Son and the Holy Spirit were recognized as distinct from the Father. But if they were distinct, how could they share his nature as God, rather than being created by him? After Nicaea, as the oneness was accepted, the question came to be how they could indeed share the one nature and yet distinctly be three. The encounter with Arius forced the orthodox to emphasize not only the deity but the individuality of the Son and of the Holy Spirit. This left the question as to how the Three can be only one God. Attempts to explain this usually fall into one of two errors: either the unity of nature is emphasized, and modalism results, or the deity of each Person is stressed, in which case the danger is a kind of tritheism.

Modalism often seems like the easiest and most natural way for Christians to digest the mysterious doctrines that the Father is God, the Son God, and the Holy Spirit God, while God is but One. Many attempts, ancient and modern, to explain the Trinity in ordinary language rapidly fall into modalism. Two familiar—and bad—examples are the comparison of the Trinity to water, which can exist as vapor, liquid, or solid; and to a single human, who can be a son, a husband, and a father. The other extreme, a kind of tritheism, is less common. A parallel is found in the modern era in the Mormon concept of the Father, the Son, and the Holy Spirit as three distinct, anthropomorphic divine beings, which is tritheism by orthodox standards.

The orthodox, Nicene expression *homoousios* finally triumphed and has become the standard for right belief. Of course it does not explain the mystery: it simply expresses it. The powerful influence of the moderate Arians coupled with their willingness to compromise were sufficient to guarantee a certain amount of flexibility in interpreting the meaning of *homoousia,* or consubstantiality. In fact, some scholars now allege that the Nicene party won a victory in name only, and that after Constantinople, consubstantiality was really understood in a moderate Arian way. The eighth-century *filioque* controversy represents an attempt by the West to interpret the consubstantiality of the Father and the Son in the strictest way; the refusal of the Eastern church to accept it expressed their fear of an addition that seemed to them to weaken the distinction between the Persons of the Trinity.[16]

b. The Problem of Language

The doctrine of the Trinity is fundamental for the Christian faith, even though the doctrine was not clearly formulated and generally accepted by an ecumenical council until the fourth century. All of the basic Christian convictions about the work of Christ presuppose that he is a distinct Person who can enter into a relationship with the Father. At the same time, Christ must have the attributes of deity with all its power in order to accomplish the gigantic task of reconciliation and redemption.

Although it was necessary for Christianity to *formulate* the doctrine of the Trinity in order to come to grips with its convictions concerning the person and work of Christ, it has proved impossible for Christians actually to *understand* the doctrine or to explain it in any comprehensive way. The doctrine of the Trinity speaks of the inner nature of the transcendent God, a matter that certainly surpasses our human ability to understand and that must be respected as a divine mystery.

Even when people admit that the doctrine of the Trinity is a mystery and must remain a mystery, they are tempted to try to explain it. The statement that there are three Persons, each of whom is God, while God is confessed as One, simply has to be explained to some extent, as otherwise it seems to be self-contradictory and absurd. Christianity has always claimed that its doctrines are consistent with reason although not based upon it.

The safest course for theologians to follow when dealing with the mystery of the Trinity is simply to state it, being careful not to risk getting entangled in explanations. This is what was done at the synod in Alexandria in 362. However, our caution should not prevent us from stating the doctrine fully and understandably enough to make it plain that it is not absurd or self-contradictory, as though one were saying, "Three is one." To fail to do this much is to make the call to faith in Jesus Christ, God's Son, into a summons to blind credulity. This Christians have always refused to do. But to attempt too much more than a straightforward and simple statement is to run the risk of involving oneself in contradictions, absurdities, and errors. Although the two extreme positions, modalism on the one hand and a sort of tritheism on the other, are very ancient, careless or foolhardy teachers continue to fall into them. Even Augustine, in his monumental work *De Trinitate* (On the Trinity), sometimes sounds like a modalist.

What is really at stake in the presentation of the doctrine of the Trinity is the concept of personhood, both in itself and as applied to God. Human beings generally have some kind of a conception of themselves as individuals distinct from their family, tribe, race, and species. At the same time, humans often see this individuality as a defect or weakness and want to be totally identified with a group. To be individual is to be limited, weak, and involved in insoluble conflicts. From this perspective, it is easy to see that the biblical concept of God as personal must appear problematic. Nonbiblical paganism frequently saw the individual gods as personal, but it did not see them as ultimate or transcendent. Hebrew religion places the true God above all such surrogate divinities: he is the "God of gods" (Ps. 136:2). "All the gods of the nations are idols: but the Lord made the heavens" (Ps. 96:5).

Most nonbiblical religions that postulate a single God see him as impersonal and usually as not directly related to the universe. Thus Gnosticism interposed a host of spiritual aeons between the ineffable highest God and the crass, material universe. Biblical religion, by contrast, tells us that it is God himself who made the heavens. To many sophisticated pagans, the Jewish tendency to personalize God seemed shallow and primitive, even if it did possess the charm of permitting us to be made in God's image. If it appeared primitive to think of the Ultimate as personal, i.e. as limited and involved in personal, this-worldly concerns, it seemed both primitive and confused to speak of the deity as tri-personal.

This fundamental problem, the difficult task of conceiving the Infinite One as personal, was made more difficult in that neither of the two languages Christians used to deal with it had a suitable terminology, and in addition the two languages were somewhat at odds with each other. Against this background, it is a triumph of the human mind, or of the Holy Spirit, that the Christian doctrine of the Trinity makes as much sense as it does. The following diagram illustrates the difficulty:

Greek term	Direct Latin equivalent	Meaning of the Greek term	Secondary meaning	Usual Latin term	Meaning of the Latin term	Secondary meaning
ousia	(essentia *)	essence or substance		substantia	essence or substance	
hypostasis	(subsistentia *)	person	substance	persona	person	actor or role
prosopon	(facies *)	face or mask	person	persona		

*These direct Latin equivalents were not generally used in this context.

The Greek term *ousia* is a noun derived from the verb "to be"; the direct Latin equivalent is *essentia*, from *esse*, "to be"; the English equivalents are "essence," from the Latin, and "being," from the Germanic root "be." Unfortunately the usual Latin term used to translate *ousia* is not *essentia*, but *substantia*, from *substo*, "to stand beneath." Thus *consubstantialis* is the Latin translation of *homoousios*. This is the source of numerous difficulties, especially in view of the fact that for decades the Greeks used *ousia* interchangeably with *hypostasis*. *Hypostasis* is derived from *hyphistamai*, "to exist" or "to subsist," and hence has the Latin equivalent *subsistentia*, from the verb *subsisto*. *Subsisto*, which resembles *substo*, from which it is derived, is close to *substo* in meaning, but while *substo* and its derivatives imply the undifferentiated, underlying reality or *substance*, *subsisto* and its derivatives imply a determined, particular reality, not the underlying substance of which that reality partakes. Hence the Greek term *hypostasis*, and to a lesser degree its Latin cognate *subsistentia*, ultimately came to be used to mean what we know as a person: an individual, determined, sentient, *personal* reality that partakes of a general essence: the *hypostasis*, or *subsistentia*, of Mr. Jones is his person, which is his alone; his *ousia,* or *substantia,* which he shares with all other humans, is his human nature.

Unfortunately this already somewhat perplexing situation is made worse by the false friendship between *hypostasis* and *substantia;* in fact, *substantia* is a Latin technical term coined in the imperial period by analogy with the Greek *hypostasis* at a time when *hypostasis* generally was used to mean "underlying substance" rather than "individual, determined reality," i.e. "person." The development of Greek theological language eventually used *hypostasis* in *contradistinction* to *ousia* to designate "individual, personal reality," while the apparently similar Latin word *substantia* was used to *translate* the Greek *ousia* and to mean "underlying reality," i.e. "essence." Latin borrowed the word *persona,* originally "mask," from the Latin legal terminology that distinguishes *persona,* the "person," from *res,* the "thing," to translate *hypostasis.* Unfortunately *persona* has a direct Greek equivalent in *prosopon.* *Prosopon* was used like *persona* to mean a (theatrical) "mask," and also "face," but seldom to mean "person" in the newly developed sense of an individual, sentient representative of a particular reality.

In the effort to make this linguistic tangle intelligible, let us note that when the Greeks described the Trinity as *mia ousia en trisin hypostasesi,* "one substance (essence) in three subsistences (persons)," they could be misunderstood as saying, "one essence in three substances," in other words, three gods. When the Latins, on the other hand, said, *una substantia in tribus personis,* "one substance in three persons," they could be understood as saying one *hypostasis* ("person") in three *roles,* in other words, of teaching Sabellian modalism. As frustrating as this linguistic tangle is to examine at a distance of sixteen centuries, it is hard for us to imagine the indignation and horror provoked among the orthodox by dialogue partners whom they perceived as propounding tritheism or modalism. Nevertheless, we may say in retrospect that the long linguistic confrontation was useful both theologically and psychologically. The distinction between *ousia* and *hypostasis, substantia,* and *persona,* "essence" and "person," had to be clarified in order to permit us even to grasp what is meant by saying that Three—Father, Son, and Holy Spirit—are God, yet God is not three, but One. The effort to gain a clear concept of what is meant by a person as an individual, as applied to the Persons of the Trinity, produced a better understanding of the nature of the human person as something more than a mere temporary constellation of atoms, impulses, and emotions.

Idealistic and postidealistic philosophy, stressing as it does the individuality, freedom, and absolute value of the individual, is a byproduct of the concept of the person produced by trinitarian theology. It may not accept the biblical dictum that man is made by God in his image, but it has accepted a philosophical evaluation of human persons made in the image of the theological understanding of the Persons of God. Our own era is frequently called post-Christian, and consequently it is necessarily posttrinitarian. As the knowledge of the Persons of the holy Trinity fades from the cultural awareness of Western man, his knowledge of the value of individual, human persons fades with it, and man becomes a commodity. Thus in a strange way this most arcane of Christian dogmas, that of the Trinity, and this seemingly petty theologians' quarrel, that over the *iota,* is related to the way in which men and women see themselves and treat one another. A society that has never known Christianity, such as that of pagan Greece, may develop a humanism of its own, but when a society once Christian loses its dogmas, it loses much of its humanity with it.

c. The Revival of Subordinationism

Both the original Arians and the Lucianists who preceded them were concerned to distinguish the Son from the Father, not to confuse them with one another. This is a desire that theology considers legitimate and attempts to meet. The *homoousian* position that triumphed at Nicaea was motivated by the desire to affirm the full deity of Christ while safeguarding monotheism. This deity would be lost if Christ were acknowledged to be a creature; hence, Arianism had to be rejected. But the *homoousian* formula did not safeguard the distinction of the Persons; in fact, it seemed to imperil it. The great Athanasius himself, the foremost advocate of consubstantiality, saw the formula developed by his own ally Marcellus and exaggerated by Marcellus' pupil Photinus in the direction of adoptionism. Thus at Alexandria in 362 Athanasius was willing to forgo the discussion of the number of *hypostases* in the deity as long as the consubstantiality of the Son was accepted. In order to say one *ousia,* three *hypostases,* it is necessary to distinguish between the term *ousia* and *hypostasis,* as otherwise the definition is not merely mysterious but self-contradictory. But how is one to distinguish among the three *hypostases* if each *hypostasis,* or Person, possesses to the full the undivided divine nature? If the Son is consubstantial with the Father and coeternal with him, how does he differ from him?

If each of the Persons of the Trinity is God, then each necessarily possesses the attributes of deity, such as eternity, immutability, and infinity. In what sense, then, can the Persons be said to be distinct from one another, if the attributes they possess are identical? To explain this, theologians coined the term "property," derived from the Latin *proprius* ("proper," i.e. "pertaining to the person or individual"). In theology, a property pertains to one Person alone. In a sense, therefore, we see that the concept of the personal properties of the Father, the Son, and the Holy Spirit is nothing but a conceptual tool to enable us to acknowledge the fundamental fact that they are distinct from one another. When we try to contemplate or conceive of the nature of God, the difference between God as infinite, eternal, and immutable and ourselves and all other creatures as finite, temporal, and mutable makes it impossible for us to conceive distinguishing characteristics within the godhead. Each person is categorically different from us and can basically be described only in terms of negatives (infinite, eternal, unchangeable, etc.) or superlatives (omniscient, omnipotent, all-good, etc.). We cannot make distinctions between the Persons with respect to these attributes, as though one might say that the Father is wiser than the Son, more benevolent, or anything of the sort. The Council of Nicaea affirmed that there is also no distinction with respect to the so-called incommunicable essential attributes, infinity, eternality, and immutability,[17] specifically, that no one may say, "There was when he [the Son] was not." The Son, like the Father, is coeternal. Under such circumstances, how is the Son to be distinguished from the Father? If totally identical in every way, he must *be* the Father, which is modalism. If identical with the Father yet distinct from him, does he not appear as a second Deity alongside the first?

How is it possible to express the distinction between the Persons clearly without destroying the fact that God is one divine substance or being, not three beings? Theology borrows the language of relationships, telling us that the Father begets and sends, while the Son is begotten and the Holy Spirit is sent forth. The human analogies of this language necessarily suggest that the Father, who begets, is prior to the Son, who is begotten. But this analogy is misleading. Origen, who developed the concept of an eternal begetting, suggested the solution. But then we have to admit that the concept of begetting really is inadequate to tell us what the relationship between the Father and the Son is, because the human analogy breaks down when we speak of an eternal begetting. The language is biblical, and it is the best we can have, but it cannot really explain to us a relationship that transcends our ability to comprehend. It does tell us that the Father and the Son are distinct Persons, and this is important. Because the language used to distinguish the Holy Spirit, that of procession or sending forth, is different from that used of the Son, it distinguishes the Holy Spirit from the Son as well as from the Father.

The language of begetting has the disadvantage that it suggests that the Father is prior to the Son. This thought is explicitly condemned by the Nicene Creed, in its earlier version of 325, which condemns all who say, "There was when he [the Son] was not." Augustine overcame this difficulty with his analogy of the sun, which always and constantly produces light and heat. Unfortunately, light and heat are not personal, and the language suggests that the Son and Spirit are mere phenomenal manifestations of one and the same Person, the Father. Augustine's analogies thus tend to depersonalize the Son and the Holy Spirit and can be accepted only with great reservations.[18]

We return thus to the biblical language. It permits us to ascribe the following traditional properties to each of the three Persons: to the Father, ingenerateness; to the Son, begottenness; and to the Holy Spirit, procession. Ultimately this language tells us only that the Father, the Son, and the Holy Spirit are distinct Persons. It also suggests to us part of the meaning of being a person, namely, that one is an individual and not interchangeable with another person: the begetter and the begotten one cannot reverse their roles. Insistence on these personal properties does not really explain the Trinity to us or permit us to understand it, but it does make it clear that in the Trinity we are dealing with three distinctive Persons, not merely with modes or appearances of one and the same Person.

Nicaea clearly affirmed that the distinction between the Father and the Son is not ontological or substantial, inasmuch as both are God. It did not clearly specify wherein that distinctiveness does lie. Inasmuch as it is not ontological, it must be relational, as the language of the Bible continues to assert even when we have stripped "begetting" of its ontological implications. At this point, in order to distinguish the Father, the Son, and the Holy Spirit from one another, the language was allowed to continue to carry its economic implications; that is to say, the Persons of the Trinity were seen to differ in the relationship of commissioner and commissioned, the one sending and the one sent (John 3:16, 14:16). Here, finally, the distinction was allowed to rest; the Son, under *(sub)* the orders of the Father, is clearly *sub*ordinate in the relationship, although not by nature; the same holds true for the Holy Spirit. The second century's naive understanding of the Trinity according to an economic analogy was reaccepted in a somewhat refined form as the only acceptable way to discern personal properties in the three Persons of the Trinity.

d. Norma Normans *and* Norma Normata

The example of the Nicene *homoousion* and its interpretation at the close of the fourth century gives an insight into the fundamental meaning of the Scripture principle, which we may also describe as the distinction between the *norma normans* and the *norma normata*. The *norma normans*, or "norming norm," is the ultimate standard, the standard by which all secondary standards are set. For all Christians, very clearly and explicitly from the time of Irenaeus on, the Holy Scripture itself has been this kind of norm (although the expression *norma normans* itself is of much later origin). Because the Scripture itself is complex on the one hand and lacking in precise theological definitions on the other, it has always been both a theological and a practical pastoral necessity to epitomize the Bible's teachings in credal formulas. These became norms for Christian faith, by which the understanding and interpretation of theologians as well as of candidates for baptism could be measured. Such a creed may be called a *norma normata*, a "normed norm" or "standardized standard." When the naive Christian understanding of basic doctrines was closely scrutinized or even attacked by outsiders or from within the church, it became necessary to reach an explicit consensus concerning whether the naive understanding was actually the correct one. Such an explicit consensus is exemplified in a dramatic way in the ecumenical creeds of Nicaea and Chalcedon. Nevertheless, even a creed is only a structure made up of human terms, and creeds, like the Bible, can be interpreted in more than one way.

If the Bible, because of its size and the variety of its structure, offers many possibilities of divergent interpretations, something similar can be said for the creeds. Because of their brevity—which is a necessary attribute in a test formula—they demand interpretation. We interpret the Scripture by the creeds. But by what standard shall we measure the creeds themselves? The answer, of course, is clearly indicated in the distinction between *normans* and *normata*. Christians naturally turn back to the Scripture itself to test the validity of their standardized standards, the creeds. A creed is *normed*, not *norming*. This statement may sound fine in theory, but how can we be certain that it is in reality the Scripture that norms the creeds, and not the creeds or Reformation confessions of faith that norm our understanding of Scripture? At this point it seems to be necessary to say simply that the proof of the pudding is in the eating. It is here that we have the difference between orthodoxy as G. K. Chesterton praised it, orthodoxy as a positive force enabling us to give to God the right glory that is his due, and orthodoxy in the negative sense in which it becomes a straitjacket for living faith and Christian freedom.

It is impossible to deny that Christianity has developed many examples of Pharisaical dogmatism in doctrinal matters as well as Pharisaical authoritarianism with respect to conduct. Anyone who is familiar with the history and present life of orthodox church bodies and institutions knows that the expression "dead orthodoxy" is not mere rhetorical abuse. The very orthodox formulas that were created to enable Christians to give the right glory to God can become the tools of a deadening formalism; this melancholy process has been repeated frequently in the history of Christianity.

e. The Antiochene-Melitian Schism

Loosely speaking, Alexandria is associated with an emphasis on the divine and the eternal in Christological discussion, and the neighboring patriarchate of Antioch with the human and the historical. From the perspective of later orthodoxy, it would be delightful to be able to say that these two equally valid impulses were constructively united at Chalcedon, but unfortunately it is not that simple. We must also note that Alexandria was not only the birthplace of Athanasian orthodoxy, but also of the Arian heresy; Alexandrian orthodoxy and Arianism have this in common vis-à-vis the Antiochene school: they are not decisively interested in the unity between Christ and humanity. On the other hand, Antioch's theologians were by no means consistent defenders of the complete, historical humanity of Jesus. It was Lucian of Antioch who gave to Arius the decisive impulse for seeing in the Logos, incarnate in Jesus, a spiritual but created being who took the place of a human soul; thus the Christ of Lucian and Arius was not fully human, as the general trend of Antiochene thought would have wished. This residue of Arianism—the idea that the Logos was incarnate in human flesh but not in a man in the full sense of the word—was carried over into Alexandrian orthodoxy after the full victory of the *homoousion* and led ultimately to the conviction that Jesus, after the incarnation, did not possess full and complete humanity. This is the position we shall shortly come to know as monophysitism.

Although a fuller discussion of monophysitism will follow in chapter 11, at this point it is necessary to cast an anticipatory glance. During the phase of theological development we call the trinitarian controversies, what had to be secured was an awareness of the fact that the Son who is incarnate in Jesus Christ is fully divine: "consubstantial with the Father" is the key phrase here. This awareness had to be gained in order to acknowledge in Christ what the Gospel ascribes to him—the power to save all of fallen mankind. But once the deity of Christ came to be acknowledged, the question concerning his full humanity would naturally arise. In accordance with the general philosophical views of the day as well as with the idealistic, otherworldly religious currents of Gnosticism and Neoplatonism, most people found it difficult to associate God himself with a limited, finite, individual human being. It was even more difficult to associate God with a specific man than with human flesh. We have only the one term, "incarnation," which literally means "becoming flesh" (in German, *Fleischwerdung*). The Arian position was that Jesus was the Logos incarnate in a human body— but there was no human soul, i.e. no personality in our sense. Even though the full implications of this line of thought had not yet been grasped by 325, the Nicene Creed, in an almost prophetic way, met the subsequent problem by adding to the usual phrases "and was incarnate by the Holy Spirit of the Virgin Mary, *and was made man."* There is no good English equivalent for this last clause: we might logically say, hominization, but this term is used in quite another sense in biology and anthropology and probably ought not to be introduced at this point. The German equivalent, *Menschwerdung* ("becoming man"), is commonly and correctly used to convey the fuller sense of what is meant by, but not actually expressed in, our English term "incarnation."

During the fifth century, it will become apparent that if Jesus has no human soul and no human personality, he is not fully human. "Incarnation" is easier to conceive than *Menschwerdung,* but only the latter makes the Saviour fully human as well as divine. Orthodoxy, both Roman Catholic and Protestant, has seized upon the full deity of Christ and confesses it boldly, but there is often much confusion about the full humanity, and while never denied in orthodox circles, it is often neglected or even ignored.

The Council of Alexandria, despite the restraint shown even by Athanasius, was unable to effect a full reconciliation between the older *homoousian* party and the newer *homoiousian* group headed by Meletius of Antioch (d. 381); despite the fact that the Antiochene *homoiousians* now accepted the *homoousian* language of Nicaea, the conservatives looked on them as insincere in their conformity, and they in turn looked on the conservatives as tyrannical and as going far beyond the limits set by the Creed of Nicaea. Shortly before his death in battle in 363, the apostate Julian once again sent Athanasius into exile; his successor, the orthodox but otherwise undistinguished Jovian, promptly recalled him. Athanasius, expressing his gratitude to Jovian, found it necessary to warn against those who now accepted the Nicene Creed but gave it a false interpretation. The formula itself was no longer clear enough, despite the fact that it had been adopted in an effort to achieve final clarity. The willingness of a large part of the moderate Arians to accept the *homoousion,* provided a certain flexibility be allowed in interpreting it, led to a temporary rapprochement at a synod in Antioch that same year, in which the more radical Arian, Acacius of Caesarea, agreed with Meletius in reaffirming the Nicene formula. An abrupt political change turned the situation around once again: Jovian's brief reign ended in 364 and he was succeeded by Valens in the East and Valentinian in the West..

Valens immediately decided to lend his authority to the Arian party, and so once again, as under Constantius, Arianism was able to obtain by political means what it could not achieve in church councils. Valens began to discipline and ban not only the representatives of the older Nicene orthodoxy but also those whom some of the orthodox still considered heretical, the moderate *homoiousian* party. The natural result was an even closer alliance between the *homoousians* and the *homoiousians* against the resurgent Arians. Rome remained loyal to Nicaea and furnished the orthodox with a refuge and moral support, but the real scene of the action remained in the East. It was only at this point, after forty years of politically engineered theology, that the controversy began once again to take the form of theological debate rather than political intrigue.

In 370 Basil (330–79) became bishop of Caesarea in Cappadocia; together with his lifelong friend Gregory of Nazianzus (bishop of Constantinople 380–81, d. ca. 390) and his younger brother Gregory, bishop of Nyssa in Cappadocia (d. ca. 395), he was able to throw both the influence of impressive scholarship and the spiritual charisma of exemplary asceticism into the conflict on the side of orthodoxy. (Basil, himself an ascetic, established the great monastic rule of the East). While these theological influences were building, the Western Emperor Valentinian died in 375; his successor, Gratian, was orthodox and as a young man very much under the influence of the first great Latin-speaking church father since Cyprian, Ambrose of Milan (ca. 339–97), the spiritual mentor of Augustine. Valentinian, unlike Valens, had not interfered in church politics; his successor, Gratian, moved decisively to increase the supremacy of the orthodox. The death of Valens at the hands of the Goths—who were, ironically, Arians—in 378 deprived the Arian party in the East of the political support it found so necessary. Gratian elevated a Westerner, Theodosius, to be his coemperor in the East (379–95, sole Emperor 394–95), and this choice spelled the end of Arian influence. Theodosius, who accepted baptism in 380 only after he had become Emperor, immediately issued the edict that in effect made Christianity the state religion of the Roman Empire. The decree specifically refers to the faith he commended to all his subjects as the faith of Bishops Damasus of Rome and Peter of Alexandria, i.e. orthodoxy. The Nicene Creed itself placed the emphasis on the incarnation, passion, resurrection, and Second Coming of Christ, and was thus historical rather than theological in its orientation. In contrast, the decree of Theodosius emphasizes the deity of the Father, Son, and Holy Spirit and the doctrine of the Trinity and does not mention the work of Christ as such. In 381 Theodosius prohibited heretical services in all towns; at the same time, following the example of Constantine, he summoned a general council to meet in the Eastern capital that same year. This Second Ecumenical Council really marks the beginning of ecumenical orthodoxy, for unlike Nicaea, it represented the conclusion rather than the beginning of the conflict with Arianism. Theodosius also took all of the churches out of Arian hands and turned them over to orthodox bishops and priests.

f. The "New" Orthodoxy

The year 381 marks the beginning of a new epoch of Christian history. The Christianization of the Roman Empire and the establishment of Christianity as its official religion are usually associated with Constantine the Great, but it was actually Theodosius I who enacted the necessary legislation. When Constantine abolished the persecution of Christianity and became a Christian himself, Christian doctrine was in a state of flux. The Arian controversy was in its first phase. By the time Theodosius made Christianity the state religion, Arianism had run its course. Consequently what Theodosius established was not simply early catholicism—embracing a moderate diversity of opinion—but an explicit, Nicene orthodoxy. Thus Christianity and orthodoxy were officially established at the same time, in the years 380–81. Prior to Theodosius, the concept of "church" was broader, and despite all the conflicts, Arians could still be considered part of the church. After Theodosius, the church consisted only of the Nicene orthodox; all others were heretics or sectarians.

The question many historians have raised is whether the orthodoxy of 381 was really the old orthodoxy of Nicaea. Harnack, for example, held that during the years between Nicaea and Constantinople the orthodox managed to assert their own watchword, "consubstantial," but at the price of interpreting it in a way that was more compatible with the position of the moderate Arians than with its original Nicene meaning. Harnack and Reinhold Seeberg contend that at Nicaea the expression was meant to convey the fundamental unity of the Father and the Son. For this reason, Nicene orthodoxy was rather close in spirit to modalism. By Constantinople, "consubstantiality" had come to mean the equality of the Persons. In 325 the church was monotheistic, but in a trinitarian way; by 381 the church had become trinitarian first, monotheistic second.

Can it be correct to say that Arianism triumphed in the interpretation of the word *homoousios*, and thus won in practice what it had lost on paper? Not if we recall that the major point of Arianism is that the Son is different in nature from the Father. At Nicaea the emphasis was on the oneness of nature, after Constantinople on the equality of nature. At Constantinople as at Nicaea, it was perfectly clear that Christianity confesses *one* divine substance, not two or three. Thus, despite the difference in emphasis, there was no major difference in meaning. Constantinople was no more tritheistic than Nicaea. The Arians, by their attempts to assert a difference in nature between the Father and the Son, at least helped the orthodox to express the distinction of the Persons clearly enough to forestall a relapse into modalism.

In order to prevent the expression "consubstantial" from being lost to the church during the decades when Arian ideas were in the ascendancy, Athanasius frequently had to stand alone "against the world." Nevertheless, at the moment when he was in the ascendancy again, in Alexandria in 362, he was satisfied with the reaffirmation of consubstantiality, and did not insist on going beyond it to impose the specific interpretation of his Western allies. This quality of absolute firmness under attack but a measure of flexibility in victory is a rare one in leaders, whether ecclesiastical or political.

In addition to the steadfastness of Athanasius, the Nicene party was strengthened by the fact that it was never totally without adherents in the churches of Asia, even when Arianism was in favor with the government and Arians were occupying the important bishoprics of the East. Rome itself never wavered in its commitment to the Nicene language, and this historic firmness is often cited by Roman Catholics in support of their claims for the primacy of the papacy. Compared with Rome, the great Eastern sees were political weather vanes, pointing now one way, now another, as the preferences of the imperial court changed.

g. Semi-Arianism

Between 362 and 381 a short-lived movement known as Semi-Arianism arose. Its adherents accepted the consubstantiality of the Son, and thus appeared to be in harmony with the Nicene Creed. At the same time, they denied the consubstantiality of the Holy Spirit, something the version of 325 does not mention and the final version of 381 only implies. By accepting the consubstantiality of the Son but denying that of the Holy Spirit, Semi-Arianism would have destroyed the orthodox doctrine of the Trinity, which clearly demands belief in three coequal Persons, not two. The facts that Semi-Arianism created only a brief flurry and that the consubstantiality of the Holy Spirit was accepted with little trouble are evidence for the claim that the doctrine of the Trinity did not evolve by stages, but was present in the church in an implicit form from New Testament times. Except for the short-lived Semi-Arian movement, there was no intermediate stage of "binitarianism" in which the deity of the Father and Son were accepted while that of the Holy Spirit was not. As soon as the implications of consubstantiality were recognized in the case of the Son, they were almost immediately seen for the Holy Spirit as well. Trinitarianism was implicit in Christian faith from the beginning; it is only its explicit formulation that took so long to develop.

h. The Second Ecumenical Council

The Holy Spirit was associated with the Father and the Son from the very earliest Christian times because of the well-known baptismal formula ". . . in the name of the Father, and of the Son, and of the Holy Ghost [Spirit]" (Matt. 28:19). But exactly what was meant by the term "Holy Spirit" long remained unclear; it could not really be given a final form until the doctrine of the deity and the distinct personhood of the Son had been properly established. The anthropological question concerning whether man is dichotomous, consisting of body and soul, or trichotomous, consisting of body, soul, and spirit, is difficult to answer with precision on the basis of Scripture, because the several terms are sometimes used synonymously, sometimes in different senses. There is a parallel in the Bible's use of the terms "God," "Father," "Spirit," "Spirit of God," and "Spirit of Christ." Jesus promised to send the Holy Spirit after his departure (John 16:7; cf. Acts 1:8), and also promised to be with his followers always (Matt. 28:20). In professing faith in Father, Son, and Holy Spirit, the early Christians may be said to have simply been confessing their faith in God as Creator, in Christ as Redeemer, and in the ongoing presence of God's Spirit in the church as Witness and Sanctifier, without presupposing any developed explanation of trinitarian doctrine. The ambiguity of biblical language and the theological concepts deriving from it made a clear statement of trinitarian doctrine a practical impossibility in the early centuries. Neither the modalistic nor the Arian interpretations were excluded by second- and third-century definitions.

The language of the New Testament permits the Holy Spirit to be understood as an impersonal force or influence more readily than it does the Son. The attempt to develop an understanding of the Holy Spirit consistent with the trinitarian passages in the New Testament and the orthodox understanding of the Son came to fruition at Constantinople in 381. There were a number of reasons why the personhood of the Spirit took longer to acknowledge than that of the Son: (1) the term *pneuma*, "breath," is neuter in gender and impersonal in its ordinary meaning; (2) the distinctive work of the Holy Spirit, influencing the believer, does not necessarily seem as personal as that of the Father in creating the universe out of nothing or of the Son in redeeming mankind; in addition, those who saw the Spirit as a Person were often heretical, for example the Montanists; (3) many of the early theologians attributed to the Logos, or Word, the revelatory activity later theologians saw as the special, personal work of the Holy Spirit.

Origen made the mistake of looking on the Spirit as created, but he did introduce the idea of an external procession of the Holy Spirit analogous to his idea of the eternal generation of the Son. Tertullian was the first to speak plainly of the Holy Spirit as God and to say that he is of one substance with the Father.

During the first phase of the Arian controversy, little attention was given to the Holy Spirit. Arius' teacher Lucian, according to Arius, described him as the most perfect creature created by the Father through the Son—and thus as subsequent to both Father and Son. The Lucian confessions formulated in Antioch speak vaguely of the Holy Spirit as "the Comforter, Sanctifier, and Perfection of believers"; the orthodox formulations were hardly more precise, speaking of the Spirit as "sent on our behalf by the same Son," which does not particularly suggest that the Spirit is acknowledged as consubstantial with the Father and the Son. Athanasius seems to have become suddenly aware of the problem during the last decade of the reign of Constantius, and immediately adopted a clear position: if the Spirit is consubstantial with the Father and the Son, then it is necessary to worship him; if he is a distinctive, independent Person, then he must share the attributes of the Son, for anything else would disrupt the Trinity and destroy the deity of the Son. As in the case of the redemptive work of the Son—which Athanasius believed the Son could not perform on behalf of creatures if he too was a creature—the Holy Spirit could not himself be only a creature if he was to sanctify and vivify creatures. What Athanasius did not succeed in doing—and what has not really been satisfactorily done since his day—was to clearly distinguish the activity of the Holy Spirit, seen as a distinct Person, from that of the Father and of the Son.

One factor that brought the question of the Holy Spirit more clearly into the foreground in the final phase of the Arian controversy was the attitude of the conservative *homoiousians*. Moved by the excesses of the radical Arians as well as by political and other factors to accommodate themselves to Nicene orthodoxy and thus to accept the consubstantiality of the Son, the *homoiousian* party seemed determined to hold to the Lucian-Arian view that the Spirit, if not the Son, is a created being. In 362 the Synod of Alexandria, which was relatively conciliatory in some respects, affronted the *homoiousian* party by stating that to hold the Holy Spirit to be a creature would split the Trinity and make the profession of adherence to the Nicene Creed hypocritical. The *homoiousians* hesitated to agree: Gregory of Nazianzus, a major theologian of the orthodox party who contributed greatly to the ultimate structure of trinitarian doctrine, bears witness to the confusion that continued to prevail.

Ultimately, the three great Cappadocians, Basil of Caesarea, Gregory of Nazianzus, and Gregory of Nyssa, heeded the warnings of Athanasius and adopted a clear position on the eternality and deity of the Holy Spirit. All three scholars acknowledged that neither Scripture nor the earlier Fathers really gave a clear statement on the question; the ultimate reason for resolv-

ing it in the way orthodoxy did was the analogy with the Son and the necessity of predicating the consubstantiality of the Spirit in order to have an
intelligible doctrine of the Trinity. In order to define personal properties by
which to distinguish him from the Son in his relationship to the Father,
recourse was had to references in John's Gospel to *ekpempsis* ("sending
out") and *ekporeusis* ("procession"), from which theology derives the
rather mysterious "property" of procession. In the last analysis perhaps the
best that one can say concerning these inward works or properties as they
relate to the Holy Spirit is that they are conceptual tools that reaffirm the
commitment of orthodoxy to the deity and distinctive personhood of the
Holy Spirit without in any way explaining or proving them. As an aftermath
to the fourth-century discussion, the Eastern churches continue to reject the
filioque, the later addition to the Nicene Creed, because they see in it a
reduction of the role of the Holy Spirit vis-à-vis the Father and the Son: in
its extreme form, a kind of binitarian, instead of trinitarian, faith.

In contrast to the East, the West rather quickly conceded that the Spirit
is a *persona*—but, at least in the early stages of the discussion, *persona* was
still reminiscent of "role" and not nearly as strong a term as *hypostasis.*
The major changes the Council of Constantinople brought to the Nicene
Creed were two: one judicial, one theological. The series of anathemas of
the Arian position that concluded the creed in its 325 version was
dropped—no doubt a fortunate move if one considers that this creed has
become a prominent part of the liturgy in many churches. The more significant, theological change was the addition of several phrases to define the
Holy Spirit:

> . . . and in the Holy Spirit, the Lord and Giver of Life, who proceeds
> [note continuous present tense!] from the Father, who together with the
> Father and the Son is worshipped and glorified, who spake by the
> prophets.

Even with these additions, the new, Niceno-Constantinopolitan Creed
of 381 seems somewhat vague concerning the Holy Spirit: no explicit mention is made of consubstantiality, nor of "very God of very God," as the
creed so explicitly states about the Son. Of course, what it does affirm is
significant, but only to those who know what the theological code words
mean. The Spirit is called the Lord, a title the religious use of which is
reserved in the biblical tradition for the Deity, i.e. for God himself. The use
of *kyrios,* "Lord," as a title for Jesus in the New Testament is taken by
conservative Christians as ascribing deity to him. The same must be said
when the Holy Spirit is called *Kyrios.* To say that he proceeds from the
Father, rather than that he proceeded at some time in the past, is tantamount

to saying that like the Father he had no beginning. To speak of him as to be worshiped "together with the Father and the Son" is to ascribe personhood as well as equal deity to him. Even so, and even after over twenty years of controversy on the topic, this creed of 381 remains far less explicit about the Holy Spirit than about the Son. Nevertheless, the council of 381 was a milestone in the development of Christian doctrine; from 381, to deny the deity or personhood of the Holy Spirit would stamp one as a heretic just as clearly as to deny the deity or the personhood of the Son. The Emperor Theodosius not only inaugurated Christianity as a state religion, he also inaugurated trinitarian theology, which had only just come to a full and clear expression, as the orthodoxy of the future.

SELECTED BIBLIOGRAPHY

Bethune-Baker, James. *An Introduction to the Early History of Christian Doctrine to the Time of the Council of Chalcedon.* London: Methuen, 1933.

Borchardt, C. F. A. *Hilary of Poitier's Role in the Arian Struggle.* The Hague: Martinus Nijhoff, 1966.

Campenhausen, Hans von. *Ecclesiastical Authority and Spiritual Power in the Church of the First Three Centuries.* London: Black, 1969.

Gregg, Robert C. *Early Arianism—A View of Salvation.* Philadelphia: Fortress Press, 1981.

Gwatkin, Henry Melvill. *Studies of Arianism: Chiefly Referring to the Character and Chronology of the Reaction Which Followed the Council of Nicaea.* Cambridge: Deighton Bellard, 1900.

Jones, A. H. M. *Were Ancient Heresies Disguised Social Movements?* Philadelphia: Fortress Press, 1966.

Knowles, David. *Christian Monasticism.* New York: McGraw-Hill, 1960.

Meijering, E. P. *Orthodoxy and Platonism in Athanasius: Synthesis or Antithesis?* Leiden: Brill, 1974.

Newman, John Henry Cardinal. *The Arians of the Fourth Century.* London: Longmans, 1919.

Nigg, Walter. *Warriors of God: The Great Religious Orders and Their Founders.* New York: Knopf, 1959.

Palanque, J. R. et al. *The Church in the Christian Roman Empire.* New York: Macmillan, 1953.

Patterson, Lloyd George. *God and History in Early Christian Thought.* New York: Seabury, 1967.

Person, Ralph E. *The Mode of Theological Decision Making at the Early Ecumenical Councils: An Inquiry into the Function of Scripture and Tradition at the Councils of Nicaea and Ephesus.* Basel: Friedrich Reinhardt Komissions-Verlag, 1967.

Stevenson, James, ed. *A New Eusebius: Documents Illustrative of the History of the Church to A.D. 337.* London: S.P.C.K., 1968.

Turner, Henry Ernest William. *The Pattern of Christian Truth: A Study in the Relations Between Orthodoxy and Heresy in the Early Church.* London: Mowbray, 1954.

Westbury-Jones, J. *Roman and Christian Imperialism.* Port Washington, N.Y.: Kennikat Press, 1971.

Wishart, Alfred Wesley. *Monks and Monasteries.* Chicago: University Press, 1902.

Wolfson, Harry Austryn. "Philosophical Implications of Arianism and Apollinarianism." *Dumbarton Oaks Papers* 12 (1958): 3-28.

9

THE DOCTRINE
OF THE TRINITY

Thus the connection of the Father in the Son, and of the Son in the Paraclete, produces three coherent Persons, who are yet distinct One from Another. These Three are one essence, not one Person, as it is said, "I and the Father are One," in respect of unity of substance, not singularity of number.

Tertullian Against Praxeas 25

Two heresies within the church, monarchianism and Arianism, were finally put down in a series of decisions that made trinitarianism synonymous with Christianity for over a millennium. It was to be a full two centuries before the church definitively settled on the declaration that the Christian faith necessarily and explicitly means faith in the Trinity. The monarchians, as we have noted, affirmed the oneness of God, but denied that the Son and the Holy Spirit are real Persons, distinct from the Father. The Arians acknowledged the distinctness of the Son (and to an extent of the Spirit) vis-à-vis the Father, but they did not acknowledge him to be fully God. In consequence, the willingness of the Arians to worship the Son and the Holy Spirit even though they were *not* of the substance of the Father led to the charge that Arianism tended to polytheism and thus to paganism.

For centuries the name "Arian" has been detested by the orthodox as the most odious of heresies. This seems remarkable, for the Arians could and did adhere to the Apostles' Creed—unlike the gnostics, for example. But trinitarianism came to be seen as so essential to Christianity that the denial of that crucial word, *homoousios*, was seen as a totally destructive heresy. In fourth-century orthodoxy, the word "Arian" was detested as much as the word "Unitarian," the name of the great modern religious movement that denies the doctrine of the Trinity, came to be hated by orthodox Protestants.

Arianism is incompatible with trinitarianism, and since the fourth century, trinitarian theology has been considered an essential part of the Gospel: "This is the catholic faith, that we worship one God in Trinity and the Trinity in unity, neither confusing the Persons nor dividing the substance."[1] How did such an elaborate concept come to be regarded as an essential implication of the simple Gospel? For nineteenth-century liberal scholars, this type of theological abstraction reflects the influence of Hellenistic thought, specifically of Aristotelianism.[2] It is evident that trinitarian theology required the aid of Hellenistic concepts and categories for its development and expression, but they were the tools by means of which the implications of the New Testament were realized; they were not foreign concepts imposed upon an essentially simple message.

Orthodox trinitarian doctrine is summarized in the definition "One essence [or nature, substance] in three Persons." There is but one God, as the Jewish *Shema* (the prayer "Hear, O Israel . . .") affirms (Deut. 6:4), for there is only one divine essence. This essence subsists in three distinct subjects or Persons. (It would be more contemporary to write, "This essence *exists* . . ." but the older terminology is preferable, because the word "exists" connotes a temporary or localized being. "Subsists" is an unusual word, and alerts the reader to the distinctiveness of this theological concept.) The essence or substance of deity, called the godhead, is not a general category to which each of the Persons belongs, as mankind is a species to which every individual human being belongs. This divine essence is identical with God, and subsists in and only in the three Persons. Humanity is not identical with any particular number of human beings, nor even with all the human beings in existence at this time. The divine Persons are distinct, yet they cannot be separated from the godhead or from one another, as human individuals may be separated from one another. It is apparent that human language is inadequate to do much more than to suggest the nature of the Trinity; it certainly cannot analyze it or explain it.

It is evident that the doctrine of the Trinity is fundamental to the Christian conception of God as personal as well as transcendent. It also has vital implications for the Christian understanding of the nature and destiny of man. Christianity teaches that God is complete in himself. He had no inner need to create in order, as it were, to fulfill himself. Consequently, his decision to create was an act of his free and sovereign will, not a necessary function of his being. In the act of creating, God establishes multiplicity or plurality where before there was only simplicity. However, even before he created, God did not dwell alone and solitary, for the deity was always Three. Thus the decision to create does not destroy an absolute simplicity, for there was always a kind of manyness within the very nature of God.

If one has a concept of the eternal Trinity, one can readily understand that there is at least a measure of multiplicity and variety within ultimate and absolute Reality itself, i.e. within God. This is important for our own idea of human nature and the ultimate destiny of human beings. Those religious views that think of God as absolute and utter Simplicity, without distinction or articulation, are at a loss to find a place for little, individual human selves in the presence of God. They usually conceive of the union or fusion of individual selves in the vast unity of God, where they are absorbed and cease to be individuals. If we conceive of the Trinity as an ongoing, eternal fellowship and communication between distinct Persons, then we can at least begin to understand how the concept of an eternal, personal life for countless created beings such as ourselves does not trouble or disrupt the absolute tranquility of God in eternity. The reason is simple: because God is Three, he is, so to speak, used to communication and conversation, and does not demand absolute silence. Consequently, he does not need to reduce the universe he has made to total stasis and silence. The Christian vision of eternity is not one of being lost in the vastness of God as a drop of water is lost in the ocean, but rather one of receiving a place at the banquet table for the marriage feast of the Lamb.

If trinitarian theology helps the Christian to think in terms of an eternal, personal life, rather than of an impersonal unity with God, it is not surprising that one byproduct of the loss of an explicit trinitarian faith in the modern age is a diminished belief in life after death. Unfortunately, this trinitarian theology that is so vital to Christianity is very hard to formulate in any detail without falling into one pitfall or another, as readers of Augustine's work *De Trinitate* will discover. It is best to limit oneself to saying what God is not according to trinitarian doctrine. Gregory of Nazianzus taught that God is no bare and shabby unity, "as the Jews teach," nor a divided plurality, "as the pagans think." The distinction of the Persons is not a mere question of terminology, for the Persons are real. It is also not one of nature, will, power, eternality, or dignity.[3] It is in fact a *personal* distinction. The Trinity is essentially a communion of Persons from all eternity, not the temporary disruption of a monolithic unity by the begetting of a transient Son or the passing this-worldly intervention of God acting as a Holy Spirit.

1. SOURCES OF TRINITARIANISM

Christians traditionally look on the Bible as a single book: "One Covenant, two Dispensations" is a familiar slogan. Consequently, they look for traces of the Trinity in the Old Testament. Most Christians find the doctrine only suggested there, but for some, it seems to be explicitly taught. The plural form *elohim* is used for "God," seeming to some to imply a plurality of Persons. (*Elohim* is literally translated "gods" and is also used of pagan divinities. Treated as a singular when used of the God of Israel, it may well be what is called the plural of majesty, like the royal we.) Expressions such as the "Word," "Spirit," and "Wisdom" of God as well as the "Angel of the Lord" abound in the Old Testament, and may be understood as referring to divine Persons, although it is difficult to show that this is the writers' intent. Christians often understand the Angel of the Lord, who appears frequently in the Old Testament, as a preincarnation reference to Christ the Son, but this is an inference that pre-Christian Jewish readers did not draw and that post-Christian Jews vigorously deny.

If there are suggestions of the Trinity in the Old Testament, its real sources lie in the New, as well as in the experience of the early Christians. The Old Testament made it plain that God is one. The first Christians were Jews and Jewish proselytes from paganism: the former had grown up as monotheists, while the latter had explicitly repudiated polytheism in favor of Jewish monotheism. There was a movement within early Christianity to repudiate the Old Testament, but Marcion and his sympathizers were rejected and the Old Testament was retained as Christian Scripture. No religion that claims the Old Testament as authoritative can accept any form of polytheism. Yet the New Testament presents Christ, who is not the Father, as God. References to the Holy Spirit as personal and divine are also present, although less numerous and explicit. On a number of occasions the Father, the Son, and the Holy Spirit are mentioned together, as though they were of equal dignity.

In the light of the fact that the doctrines of the deity of Christ and of the Trinity are so central to orthodox Christianity, it may seem strange that explicit references to these concepts are rare in the New Testament. Nevertheless, they are there. Because the New Testament writings were held to be verbally inspired and totally authoritative, even a single reference to Christ as God would have been enough to impel the early church in the direction of trinitarian theology. In addition, of course, the explicit Christological and trinitarian references in Scripture were reinforced by the early church's experience of the presence of Christ and of the Holy Spirit, as the presence of God in their midst.

When it was first examined, the problem of the Trinity was seen in terms of the relationship of the Son to the Father: is he of the same nature, or different? Is he eternally begotten, begotten in time in any sense, or created? The question of the nature of Christ sounds as though it ought to lie in the province called Christology, but actually it is placed in the area of special theology, i.e. the doctrine of God. The relationship between the Father and the Son has to do with the very nature of deity, and is ultimately explained in terms of the doctrine of the Trinity. Only when this relationship has been clearly defined (special theology) does it become possible to address the question of how the human and divine natures are related in Jesus Christ (Christology).

Early in the third century, modalism (or modalistic monarchianism) was proposed as the way to uphold the unity of God while confessing the deity of Christ: Christ, the Son, is a mode or aspect of the Father. As such, he is fully and truly God, but not a distinct Person. Unfortunately, this suggestion makes it hard to see how Jesus can meaningfully pray to the Father if he *is* the Father in another mode. Even more serious, it is impossible to conceive of him as our "advocate with the Father" (1 John 2:1).

It was Tertullian, the first major Latin-speaking theologian, who took the first steps toward resolving this problem and preparing the ground for trinitarian orthodoxy. Tertullian provided the church with several essential terms and concepts. Beginning simply, he first described the Son and the Spirit exclusively in terms of their roles in the plan or "economy" of God. This is called "economic trinitarianism." It emphasizes the unity of God: there is only one divine substance, one divine power, without separation, division, dispersion, or diversity. At the same time, Tertullian emphasized a distribution of functions, a distinction of Persons, a disposition or dispensation of tasks (the Latin *dispensatio* translates the Greek *oikonomia*, "economy"). The deity is one substance, but not a numerical entity: Tertullian says *unum* ("one," neuter), not *unus* ("one," masculine, i.e. personal), following Christ's words in John 10:30.

Tertullian taught his readers to make a distinction between *substantia*, "substance," or "essence," and *persona*, "person." Tertullian's distinction between the Persons of the Trinity in terms of their "economic" functions was natural enough for a man trained as a lawyer, but its full significance was not easily grasped in the East. There the quest was for a philosophical rather than a judicial distinction: the term they chose for "Person" in trinitarian discussion, *hypostasis*, as noted earlier, means "subsistence" but could easily be misunderstood as "substance," with all of the unfortunate consequences to which so fundamental a misunderstanding could lead.[4] Tertullian's work was done a century before the Arian controversy. It furnished the necessary tools to express the deity and personhood of the Son while avoiding confusion between him and the Father.

There were a variety of attempts to explain how the Son could be God, or at the very least called God, and yet not be a second God alongside the Father. (1) The simplest explanation, an idea that constantly recurs, was the modalism of Sabellius: the Son is the Father in another mode or under another aspect. (2) The Son and the Holy Spirit could be seen as specially endowed agents of the Father, as in adoptionism. (3) They can be considered intermediate, created beings, as in Arianism. (4) It was possible to think of them in Neoplatonic terms as emanations descending from the Father to the concrete world.

The spiritual contrast between these variant views and what we now call orthodoxy lay first of all in the goal that each sought to accomplish: the heretical positions had in common a desire to *understand the mystery of God;* the orthodox sought to *preserve the salvation* Christians find in Christ.

Arius began with a theoretical concept, the axiom that only the Father is ingenerate, i.e. never "became." Equating ingenerateness with aseity ("existence in and of himself"), Arius held it to be an essential attribute of God. No one but the Father is *a se,* "of himself"; hence, only the Father is truly and fully God. Athanasius began not with an axiom but with the *experience* of Christ's power to save. Only God has the power to save, therefore Christ must be God. Arius gave a logical answer to a theological question, Athanasius a religious answer to a spiritual one.

The Arian party was not numerically strong, but at various times it received decisive support from the imperial government. Most Eastern Christians, like those in the West, rejected the Arian idea that the Son is a creature, but they were uncertain how to see him in relationship to God. They resisted Marcellus of Ancyra and suspected Athanasius of tending to Marcellus' error, i.e. of failing to see the Son and the Holy Spirit as distinct *hypostases* ("Persons"). When the West continued to hold fast to the doctrine of consubstantiality, the Greeks had to try to understand how the Father, the Son, and the Spirit can be distinct *hypostases,* with each *hypostasis* of the same substance as the Father, without dividing that substance into three distinct Beings. This understanding was attained by the Cappadocian Fathers, Basil of Caesarea (d. ca. 379), his brother Gregory of Nyssa (d. ca. 395), and his friend Gregory of Nazianzus (d. ca. 390).

2. THE CAPPADOCIAN SOLUTION

The Cappadocians made two points: (1) on the one hand, God is *one,* a unity (not a uniformity), who reveals himself as possessing a single will, a single activity, a single glory. Neither the Son nor the Spirit was played off against the Father, as Athanasius and the Westerners feared might happen. (2) On the other hand, this one God is a triad, or trinity, of *hypostases.* Because God acts with a single will toward the created world ("the outward works are undivided"), it is not possible to observe the different Persons in action. Their distinction can only be learned from God's self-disclosure in Scripture. It lies in the internal relationships or properties of the Persons: ingenerateness, begottenness, and procession. This sounds very theoretical.

Reinhold Seeberg puts it caustically: "Thus one arrives at an empty metaphysics or conceptual mythology; the Father begets the Son and causes the Spirit to proceed from himself. In this way the Persons are supposed to be distinguished from one another and also united to one another."[5]

Seeberg was too critical. What the Cappadocians did was to take biblical terminology—"begetting," "proceeding"—and use it to distinguish the Persons. They insisted that the terms have a special meaning in the context of the Trinity and are not to be understood according to their ordinary human analogies. To talk about properties and then say that we cannot know what they mean is exasperating. It may help to remember that the properties *explain nothing;* on the contrary, they are merely conceptual tools or symbols to impress on us that the three Persons are and remain eternally distinct, yet also remain eternally one God.

The so-called properties of the individual Persons are also spoken of as "works," a somewhat puzzling term when we look at each of the properties. The Scripture tells us that God works, and we see evidence of his working all around us: the act of creation is the first of the so-called "outward works" of God, i.e. works that have to do with created realities outside of the deity. Only God's outward works can be known through God's revelation in nature. In addition, there are inward works; these can be known only through special revelation. Inward works are said to "terminate within the godhead." In other words, they represent God's activity or dealing with himself. Some of these inward works, called divine decrees, are shared by all three Persons. The decree to create man and woman appears to be such a shared inward activity: "And God said, Let us make man . . ." (Gen. 1:26). The primary reason for speaking of decrees is to separate God from his creation, to show that his outward works result from a self-generated decision of the divine will, not from any necessity nor as the result of some kind of process involving both God and nature. In the outward works, which we can perceive, we cannot distinguish any particular role for the individual Persons; they act in perfect harmony.[6] The distinctive inward works known as properties, which distinguish the Persons from one another, are basically labels to express the mystery that Three who share one divine Substance are nevertheless distinct from one another.

One may well ask, if the concept is so difficult, how it was ever decided to require an explicit faith in the Trinity for salvation. The answer is that it is not so much that faith in the Trinity was commanded by the church as that such faith is required in order to come to terms with the distinction of Persons in Scripture. John speaks of Jesus as our "advocate with the Father" (1 John 2:1). An advocate must be a different person from the judge.

The doctrine of the Trinity is a theoretical necessity because of the doctrine of the atonement. Apart from the Trinity, which permits Christ to be understood as distinct from the Father and yet as God, we cannot understand how he can represent us to God or make atonement for our sins. If we were not able to believe in the doctrine of the atonement, Christ might be our teacher or example, but he could not be our substitute. The doctrine of the atonement is necessary to permit us to reconcile the biblical emphasis on the wrath of God with the equally biblical emphasis on his mercy. To suggest that God is alternately wrathful and merciful would suggest capriciousness; to suggest that he might merely overlook the sins he so vehemently condemns in Revelation would suggest that he is far from being just. Both of these suggestions are detrimental to a good understanding of the character of God. The doctrine of the substitutionary atonement, in which Christ identifies himself with us and stands in our place before the Father, resolves this problem. It in turn depends on the doctrine of the Trinity.

The fact that the vital doctrine of the atonement depends on the doctrine of the Trinity does not mean that one must understand the teaching of the Cappadocian Fathers in order to understand that one is a sinner or to receive the mercy of God. To suggest this would be to fall into a new variety of Gnosticism, in which salvation would depend on our knowledge. Nevertheless, even if one does not know the doctrine explicitly, one must have at least some experience of the work of each of the Persons in order to be a Christian. One must acknowledge oneself as a sinner before God, and one must come to Jesus as the Saviour. Finally, one must have experienced a measure of the work of the Holy Spirit in order to do these two things.

At least a modicum of an understanding of the Trinity is necessary for the Christian to accept what he experiences and knows of God without resorting to mere fideism (simply believing the words of an authority).[7] God does not require a *sacrificium intellectus*, a "sacrifice of the intellect," as part of faith. Because the sacrifice of the intellect is a violent affront to the integrity of one's soul, it is always dangerous and certainly is a poor way to begin to love God with all one's heart, soul, and mind.

The Christian faith is a complex matter. In order to keep on holding to it once one has begun to appreciate its problematic and paradoxical aspects, it is necessary either simply to suppress one's questions and doubts—not a very happy solution—or to find a noncontradictory way to express basic doctrines. All the major doctrines are interdependent. The doctrine of man as sinner implies the doctrine of man's need of salvation; the doctrine of salvation requires an adequate Saviour, i.e. an adequate Christology. A sound Christology requires a satisfactory concept of God, i.e. a sound special theology—which brings us back to the doctrine of the Trinity.

3. PROBLEMATIC ASPECTS OF TRINITARIAN DOCTRINE

The Cappadocian explanation of the Trinity is based on the concept of the distinctive properties of the Persons. It has been criticized, we noted earlier, on the grounds that it makes the distinction between the Persons merely hypothetical, based on terms such as "ingenerateness," "begottenness," and "procession," which cannot be really meaningful to us. In other words, while the Cappadocians succeeded in devising language that enabled them to distinguish the Father, the Son, and the Holy Spirit from one another as individual Persons without imperiling the oneness of God, the language was so abstract and intangible that it did not really help believers to form a clear picture of what each of the three Persons is like. Additionally, Cappadocian theology stressed the unity of the will of God. If the Son and the Holy Spirit always carry out the will of the Father, it is hard to conceive that they truly have wills of their own, in which case it is hard to see how they can be subjects, i.e. persons, rather than mere objects of the Father's will.

Cappadocian theology reflects an ambiguity that is present in the New Testament itself. At times the expression "God" is used in a way that implies all three Persons of the Trinity, but at other times it is used to mean the Father alone. The word "God" is not used without qualification to refer to the Son or the Holy Spirit. Thus the "will of the Father" is the will of God, and when Jesus speaks of doing the Father's will, he may be said in a sense to be doing his own will as well.[8]

By its abstraction, the Cappadocian theology seems fairly far from the dynamic process by which the Christian community first achieved the conviction of the deity of Christ. It learned to confess Christ as God not so much because of specific claims he made as because of its conviction that no one other than God could do the works Christ did. The first Christians were virtually forced to this conviction, even though their background in Jewish monotheism made them very cautious about ascribing divine honors to anyone other than God himself. In the representative thought of the Cappadocian Fathers, the deity of Christ sounds more like a logical conclusion than a passionate confession. This removes the doctrine of the Trinity from the area of personal encounter, in which believers experienced fellowship with Christ and the Holy Spirit, and makes it the last step in a series of logical deductions. The doctrine of the Trinity was developed in order to explain the divine reality the first Christians experienced, but in the process there is the risk that it will become a mere dogmatic theory totally cut off from living faith.[9]

4. THE PARADOX OF
TRINITARIAN DOCTRINE

The paradox of trinitarian doctrine is this: living faith seems to require it in order to explain the teachings of the New Testament in the light of the facts of Christian experience, but once developed, trinitarianism seems to replace living faith with metaphysical dogmatics. A nontheological faith cannot explain itself, but too theological a faith loses contact with the reason for its existence.

A similar problem will arise when Christians attempt to come to terms with the relationship between the divine and the human in the incarnate Christ. If no effort is made to analyze and explain the relationship, there is great danger that Christ will be understood in a false and defective way—in an adoptionist or a docetic sense, for example. On the other hand, if a serious and conscientious effort is made, the resulting dogmatic explanation may seem far removed from the church's experience of the living Christ. With respect to both trinitarian theology and Christology we may say, something like what Calvin said about predestination: "If anyone with carefree assurance breaks into this place, he will not succeed in satisfying his curiosity and he will enter a labyrinth from which he can find no exit."[10]

Without a coherent doctrine of the Trinity, the New Testament witness to the activity of God in Christ and in the work of the Holy Spirit will tend to force one either into modalism or a kind of tritheism. But if one begins with a doctrine of the Trinity—as a number of orthodox Protestant theologians do—there is the danger that doctrine will take precedence over the New Testament witness and turn living, personal faith into theological metaphysics. It seems apparent that the safest course is to let theological understanding and personal faith go hand in hand. Too much enthusiastic faith without a corresponding degree of theological understanding is almost certain to lead to error, perhaps to serious heresy. Too much doctrine unaccompanied by a living and growing faith is the recipe for dead orthodoxy.

5. FURTHER DEVELOPMENTS

Because the doctrine of the Trinity remains a mystery, we may say that further efforts of Christian thinkers to deal with it do not advance significantly beyond the limits set by the theology of the Cappadocian Fathers. While the East was preoccupied with the Christological issues that arose out of the doctrine of the consubstantiality of the Son with the Father, in the West Augustine made a monumental but only partly successful effort to develop the theology of the Trinity.

a. Augustine and the West

Aurelius Augustine (354–430) is one of the most striking figures of Western civilization. Although he had a Christian mother, Augustine came under Manichaean and Neoplatonic influences as he began what promised to be a brilliant career as a teacher of rhetoric. In his *Confessions,* one of the earliest and most striking examples of an autobiography in world literature, he describes his inner life up to his conversion in 386 and baptism in the following year. In addition to his confessions, Augustine wrote a monumental work of apologetics and philosophy of history, *The City of God,* under the influence of the conquest of Rome by Alaric (410). In *On the Trinity,* Augustine claimed to demonstrate "the true doctrine of the Trinity, according to the authority of the Holy Scriptures." He developed it further than anyone who came before him, and in retrospect seems to have entered Calvin's labyrinth. (Augustine is better known for his views on predestination, which strongly shaped Christianity in western Europe from his day until the present.)

Augustine begins with the conviction that the one God is the Trinity, so that since his time, especially in the West, the Christian faith seems to be saying, "Trinity" first and "God" second. No qualitative distinctions can be made within the Trinity; all three Persons are equal in every way. Augustine goes far toward repudiating the economic subordinationism that had characterized early trinitarian thought. The terminology "Father," "Son," and "Spirit" does not indicate any substantial, qualitative, or quantitative difference between the Persons. They differ from one another only by virtue of the different relationships that exist between them: the Father begets, the Son is begotten, the Spirit proceeds. Augustine goes beyond Origen and the Cappadocians in teaching a kind of complementarity between the Son and the Father: the Father is conditioned by the Son he begets, just as he conditions the Son in begetting him. (This complementarity between the Son and the Father was to be carried further by the Western church in adopting the view that the Holy Spirit proceeds from the Father and the Son, the so-called *filioque* added to the 381 version of the Nicene Creed.) Augustine's concept of the distinctive differences between the Persons has been called "the most delicate and softest line that could be drawn."[11]

In his effort to make the unity of three distinct Persons plausible, Augustine used a great number of illustrations drawn from daily life. Unfortunately, some of them seem to illustrate modalism, rather than a true personal distinction. One of the long-lasting results of his emphasis on the idea of the Trinity was a tendency for the concept of the Trinity to supplant the individual Persons in Western theological thought prior to the Protestant Reformation. God came to be seen primarily as the Trinity, not as the Father, the Son, and the Holy Spirit. These names explained the doctrine. This made the concept of God rather abstract and inaccessible and certainly contributed to the interest in the Virgin Mary and the other saints as intermediaries between Christians and God. In the East, interest was concentrated on the Persons: on the Father, perhaps even more so on the Son, and on the Holy Spirit. The three are confessed as one God, which confession is then explained in terms of the doctrine of the Trinity.

b. The East

The East had no theologian of Augustine's stature in the fifth century. It was three more centuries before the great Eastern theologian John of Damascus (ca. 675–ca. 749) put the finishing touches on the Eastern church's view of the Trinity. John reformulated the heritage of the Cappadocians. His language resembles that of Augustine: God has one substance, one deity, one power, one will, one energy, one origin, one authority, one lordship, and one sovereignty. We know God in three perfect *hypostases* and worship them with a single worship. The major difference between the formulation of John and that of Augustine is that John continues in the Eastern tradition that considers the Father the source of deity. For this reason, the Holy Spirit, to be God, must proceed from the Father alone. (The East continues to this day to reject the Western addition to the Nicene Creed, according to which the Spirit proceeds "from the Father and the Son.") Operating against a background that fully recognized the identity and distinctiveness of the Son and the Spirit, John wanted to make it plain that both the Son and the Spirit are fully God. Hence he emphasized their derivation from the Father, the source of deity. To allow the Spirit to proceed from the Son as well as from the Father, as was already being taught by some Westerners during John's lifetime, could have compromised the deity of the Spirit by clouding his direct origin in the Father.

Augustine worked and taught in the West, where the doctrine of God had frequently tended to be modalistic, or in effect unitarian. For this reason he felt the necessity of demonstrating that the one God is a Trinity. Both of these concerns are necessary to a fully balanced trinitarian theology. During the fifth century, Eastern Christendom did not give much attention to improving its understanding of the Trinity, but moved directly to the issue raised by the orthodox conviction that the Son is fully God. If the Son is fully God, what is the nature of his relationship to humanness in the man Christ Jesus? The deity of the Son became the presupposition for the next great wave of heresies with which Christianity had to contend. The Christological conflicts were upon the church.

SELECTED BIBLIOGRAPHY

Greenslade, Stanley Laurence. *Church and State from Constantine to Theodosius.* London: S.C.M., 1954.

Holmes, Thomas Scott. *The Origin and Development of the Christian Church in Gaul During the First Six Centuries of the Christian Era.* London: Macmillan, 1911.

Jaeger, Werner. *Two Rediscovered Works of Ancient Christian Literature: Gregory of Nyssa and Macarius.* Leiden: Brill, 1954.

Kelly, J. N. D. *Early Christian Doctrines.* San Francisco: Harper & Row, 1978.

Labriolle, Pierre de. *History and Literature of Christianity: From Tertullian to Boëthius.* London: Routledge, 1978.

Ladner, Gerhart B. *The Idea of Reform: Its Impact on Christian Thought and Action in the Age of the Fathers.* Cambridge: Harvard University Press, 1959.

Legreton, Jules. *History of the Dogma of the Trinity from Its Origins to the Council of Nicaea.* London: Burnes, 1939.

Lonergan, Bernard. *The Way to Nicaea: The Dialectical Development of Trinitarian Theology.* London: Darton, Longman & Todd, 1976.

McGiffert, Arthur Cushman. *The West from Tertullian to Erasmus.* Vol. 2 of *A History of Christian Thought.* New York: Scribner, 1933.

Momigliano, Arnaldo. *The Conflict Between Paganism and Christianity in the Fourth Century.* Oxford: Clarendon, 1963.

Newland, G. M. *Hilary of Poitiers: A Study in Theological Method.* Bern: Peter Lang, 1978.

Prestige, George Leonard. *God in Patristic Thought.* London: S.P.C.K., 1952.

————. *St. Basil the Great and Apollinaris of Laodicea.* London: S.P.C.K., 1956.

Rahner, Karl. "Person." In *Sacramentum Mundi: An Encyclopedia of Theology,* edited by Karl Rahner et al., 4:404–419. New York: Herder, 1969.

Stead, Christopher. *Divine Substance.* Oxford: Clarendon, 1977.

Widengren, Geo. *Mani and Manichaeism.* Translated by Charles Kessler. London: Weidenfeld, 1965.

Wolfson, Harry Austryn. *Faith, Trinity, Incarnation.* Vol. 1 of *The Philosophy of the Church Fathers.* Cambridge: Harvard University Press, 1964.

10

CHRISTOLOGY

I thought that all vain talk of all heretics, many as they may be, had been stopped by the Synod which was held at Nicaea. For the Faith there confessed by the Fathers according to the divine Scriptures is enough by itself at once to overthrow all impiety, and to establish the religious belief in Christ.

Athanasius Letter to Epictetus *1*

If we take the word "heresy" in its full ancient sense, then heresy is a very serious thing indeed. The gnostics were heretics: they denied that God is the Creator (as well as repudiating a number of other fundamental truths). The Arians were heretics: they denied that Christ is fully God. In our own day, however, the word "heresy" has become trivialized, and often suggests a bit of detail about which only pedants could take the trouble to quarrel. Terms such as "heresy hunt" and, slightly more respectable, "heresy trial" suggest inquisitorial proceedings and naturally incline one's sympathy to the hunted or accused heretic. Either Gnosticism or Arianism, if triumphant, could have destroyed Christianity as we know it. But as we move into the Christological controversies, we begin to encounter heresies that do not appear so capable of causing fatal injury to Christendom. To keep them in perspective, we must recognize their seriousness without necessarily agreeing with the contending parties of the day that they were as dangerous as Gnosticism and as destructive as Arianism.

The controversies to which we now turn appear to divide Christians from one another, rather than from unbelievers and radical heretics. By the end of the fourth century, it was fully accepted that the Father, the Son, and the Holy Spirit are each God, and that God is one. The deity of Christ was no longer questioned. What was disputed? The way in which the divine Son, the second Person of the Trinity, fully God, could be united with the historical human being, Jesus of Nazareth. How did the Word, which was "in the beginning" (John 1:1) come to be "made flesh" (John 1:14) as the "one mediator between God and men, the man Christ Jesus" (1 Tim. 2:5)? No full answer can be given, because the incarnation, like the Trinity, is a mystery, and will remain so. But the inquisitive human mind insists on trying to answer it.

From the late fourth century until the middle of the fifth century, various solutions were proposed. The more complete they were, the more problems they raised. Finally the Fourth Ecumenical Council, held at Chalcedon in 451, attempted to draw the line and set the limits to speculation on a matter the human mind can never fully comprehend. The Chalcedonian Creed, together with the Nicene Creed, has become the definition and standard for orthodox, trinitarian doctrine. It did not answer all the questions; instead, like the Nicene Creed, it defined certain limits, within which Christians might speculate and differ, outside of which they would be in danger of heresy. Even in its own era, the Chalcedonian Creed was not universally accepted. Two major Christian groups, the Nestorians and the Monophysites, refused to accept it. Unlike the gnostics and the Arians, they still remained firmly within the framework of Nicene orthodoxy.

The Arian controversy began among Christians. When it finally ended, the Arians had either returned to Catholic orthodoxy or simply passed from the scene. The Christological controversies began among Christians, and although they ended with the majority accepting Chalcedon as the standard of orthodoxy, the churches that persisted in rejecting it, while holding to Nicaea, definitely remained Christian, and the Monophysites exist in substantial communities today. When Arian ideas came to be revived by Michael Servetus and other antitrinitarian radicals in the sixteenth century, their proponents insisted on continuing to call themselves Christians, at least for some time, but gradually abandoned the name.

1. CHRISTOLOGY AT THE CLOSE
OF THE FOURTH CENTURY

The solidification of trinitarian doctrine at the close of the fourth century inevitably gave rise to controversy as Christians sought to understand the implications of the incarnation "in fashion as a man" (Phil. 2:8) of the eternal Son of God. Although Jesus Christ was confessed as very God of very God, the impression his followers had of him—and through it, of his Father—was the impression of "the man Christ Jesus." The struggles with docetism and Gnosticism had reaffirmed and strengthened the conviction that Jesus was a real man, not one in appearance only. How could the deity be related to the humanity in a single Person, the "one Lord Jesus" of the Nicene Creed?

From the days of the early church, we see two themes running parallel in the proclamation of Jesus Christ: the eternal, preexistent Son, and the historic, individual man. These two themes do not need to conflict; orthodoxy sets itself the goal of keeping them united. When either one or the other, either the deity or the humanity, is considered in isolation and its implications systematically developed, a one-sided presentation results, eventually leading to a position the orthodox reject as heresy.[1] The earliest attempt to develop the meaning of the deity of Christ as expressed in the Nicene Creed, Apollinarianism, was made in the latter part of the fourth century; its implications virtually denied the humanity of Christ. During the fifth and sixth centuries, greater refinements were introduced, in the positions that will be known as Nestorianism, Eutychianism, monophysitism, monergism, and monothelitism. At the time, the adherents of the Chalcedonian position considered them all heretical, in varying degrees; today we are less certain.

Alexandria, the most sophisticated and theologically the most productive metropolis of early Christianity, gave birth to a number of conflicting views and personalities. Both Arius and Athanasius were active there. On the whole, however, Alexandria is associated with one tendency in Christology, Antioch with its opposite. The church in the West was theologically less fertile, which is one reason why Rome appears more than once as the defender of traditional orthodoxy. The Alexandrian school tried to explain what it means to say that God became man and what happens to the human being God becomes. It soon began to invert its formulation and teach, in effect, that the man becomes God. This was not an adoptionist Christology in which a complete, existing human being is adopted and elevated by God and thus becomes in some sense divine. Instead, it contends that the preexisting Son, always fully God, transformed the humanity of Jesus in assuming it, so that *it,* a humanness, was divinized. Jesus was not a person whom God adopted and exalted to be the Christ, but the Logos, in becoming human, took upon himself a human nature and exalted it to deity.

In contrast to the Cappadocian-Alexandrian tendency, the school of Antioch held firmly to the clear biblical picture of Jesus Christ as a historic, human, individual person. God became incarnate in this person and took *him* on, not *it* (a mere human nature). The tension between the Alexandrian and Antiochene interests was accentuated thanks to the efforts of one man. His intellectual ability is comparable to that of Athanasius and the Cappadocian Fathers, but his name has gone down in obloquy because his views fed into the substance of heresy, rather than orthodoxy. Apollinaris of Laodicaea (d. ca. 390) was a strict adherent of the Nicene *homoousion;* he extolled the deity of Christ, but to his opponents he seemed to be minimizing or destroying his humanity.

Prior to the solidification of trinitarian doctrine, theological interest had centered on the nature of the divine Persons and on the way in which they related to one another in the godhead. The tendency to fragment the godhead into three divine beings was condemned by the orthodox, Athanasian emphasis on the unity of God. Apollinaris began his effort to explain the relationship of God to man in Christ by making an assumption that many think is biblical, even though it is not the only possibility the Bible suggests, namely, that each individual man consists of body *(sarx)*, soul *(psyche)*, and intellect *(nous)*. This is called the trichotomous view of man. Historically Apollinaris may be compared to Arius because like Arius he sought to give a rational explanation of what appeared an insoluble mystery. The simplicity and clarity of his argument rapidly won him adherents, but its apparent threat to the human identity of Jesus mustered the orthodox against him. Theologically, Apollinaris differed from Arius in that he affirmed rather than denied the full deity of Christ and thus never seemed to the faithful to cast doubt upon the ability of Christ to save us from our sins. If Jesus is not fully God—as Arius denied him to be—then ordinary Christians quickly begin to wonder whether he can safely be trusted as having the power to save; if he is not a fully human person, as Apollinaris in effect taught, the danger to salvation is less evident, for full humanity is not necessary to the power of Christ, and hence to the reality of our salvation.

One problem arises, and it is a major one. If Christ is not truly human, how does he help us? If he is less than fully human, it is hard to see how the merit secured by a nonhuman Saviour may justly be applied to human beings. However, this is a somewhat more sophisticated problem than that caused by failure to accept the full deity of Christ. It was perceived as a great problem, and like Arianism it brought contending parties quite literally onto the field, where they not merely verbally but physically assaulted one another. Despite this, Apollinarianism simply was not as capable of destroying Christendom as was the quarrel over the *homoousion*. An Apollinarian theology and church would still be identifiably Christian, albeit defective; an Arian theology and church, at least in their implications, are no longer Christian.

Like Arius, Apollinaris took an acceptable, naive view—in Arius' case, the view that the Son was begotten, in that of Apollinaris, the view that Christ is God—and elaborated it to a point at which it began to threaten another major element of Christian doctrine. Like the Arian controversy, the Christological controversy sparked by Apollinaris began and ended in the East, but was decisively influenced by a clear stand taken by the Western church, particularly by Rome. Apollinaris, unlike Arius, had a firmly established Christological dogma to which he could appeal, that of Nicaea; the Antiochenes, who stressed—correctly, as we believe—the full and complete humanity of Jesus Christ, had no leader of the caliber of Athanasius around whom they could rally. Although Apollinaris was defeated, the Antiochene position was not fully vindicated; its clearest exponent, Nestorius, will ultimately be branded a heretic, and the ultimate solution, although not Apollinarian, will continue to reflect the influence of Apollinaris in a way that far exceeds any ongoing influence of Arius within the main body of orthodoxy.

Apollinaris embodied elements common both to Athanasius and the Antiochenes; Athanasius used many terms and concepts later propounded by Apollinaris; indeed, some of the works of Apollinaris were circulated under the name of Athanasius, thus cloaking them with the latter's impeccably orthodox credentials and to some extent disarming the suspicion they would otherwise have engendered. This was possible because the views of Apollinaris, as we have already indicated, were subtler than those of Arius and it was more difficult to discern why they were objectionable. In Athanasius' *Four Orations Against the Arians,* he speaks of the humanity of Christ more in an instrumental than a personal way. Eusebius of Caesarea spoke of the humanity of Christ as the "human vessel," the "human instrument," and the "temple" of the Logos. However, this language was still paralleled by equivalent language speaking of the Logos uniting himself with a man, not an instrument.

Prior to Nicaea, the position of adoptionism tried to explain the degree to which and the manner in which God gave his power to a man. The developing positions of both Apollinaris and the Antiochene school questioned neither the degree—completely—nor the manner—incarnation, not adoption—and went on to attempt to explain the relationship between God and the man Jesus that incarnation established. The forerunner of the Antiochene position was Eustathius of Antioch (d. ca. 360), who taught that the human Jesus lived in perfect unity with the spiritual Logos. Unlike Apollinaris, who held a trichotomous view of man, dividing him into body, soul, and spirit, Eustathius distinguished only a body and a rational soul, the dichotomous view. The body and soul of Jesus were of the same substance as those of all other human beings. Inasmuch as Eustathius correctly held the divine Logos to be a real person, not a mere spiritual power, to say that Jesus had a rational human soul appeared to give him two personalities, one human and one divine. The understanding of what it means to be a person—an individual with a distinct memory, will, emotion, and a unique personality—was becoming clear only as the doctrine of the Persons of the Trinity came into focus. Consequently, the difficulty caused by postulating two personalities in Christ was not immediately recognized. It was Apollinaris who exposed it and in so doing also attracted attention to his own views and the problems that come from thinking of Jesus as not having a human personality.

2. APOLLINARIS ATTEMPTS TO CLARIFY

Apollinaris rejected the proposition that Jesus possessed a human personality, the idea of Christ as a man united with God; he proposed instead the concept of an incarnate God, of God made flesh. The root of the following developments, including the ultimate monophysite contention that the humanity of Jesus is now divinized, may be expressed by a question: into what kind of flesh can God be made? To suggest that God can be made into weak, passible, sinful, human flesh appears blasphemous. Consequently it seemed necessary to postulate a kind of divine or heavenly flesh of Christ. This concept will become explicit at various times in the course of church history; it will be held by some of the radicals in the Reformation era.[2] Apollinaris would not hear of a distinction between the divine and human in Christ, nor tolerate the suggestion—later to be affirmed by Calvin and Reformed theology generally—that only the human body and soul of Christ were born and suffered. Such a suggestion would lead, he contended, to little more than a man illuminated by God. Jesus is "the God borne by a woman"; there is a *henosis physike,* a "physical (natural) unity," between the divine and the human. Christ is "enfleshed God," "flesh-bearing God"; his flesh is *theïke sarx,* "God-flesh."[3] The incarnation of God appears to have turned into the apotheosis or divinization of the human flesh. We can say of Apollinaris that he held that there were two natures before the incarnation, divine and human, but only one afterward.

Athanasius in his day argued that the Logos had to be fully God, and thus could not have a beginning. Apollinaris argued that Christ himself, in order to be wholly God, had to be immutable *(atreptos)* and thus could not have a human soul, for if so he would have been mutable. Death could have overcome him and he would not have *given* his life in any active sense but only have *been deprived* of it out of necessity as all human beings are. In order to resolve the problem thus created, Apollinaris resorted to the biblical definition of God as Spirit: human flesh needs a spirit to direct and energize it; in Christ, this spirit is not that of a human nous, or "intellect," but the Logos himself. Apollinaris equated the biblical concept of flesh with the Aristotelian view of matter, and the biblical concept of spirit with the Aristotelian view of form. It is the spiritual *form* that animates and gives true character to inert, undifferentiated matter; this is done in all men by the human intellect, or nous, with the sole exception of Jesus Christ, in which the function is performed by the Logos himself. The Logos became flesh, but not a man like ourselves, in that he neither took on nor became a human intellect. Apollinaris' view is the one crudely lampooned by Bishop John A. T. Robinson in *Honest to God,* "God dressed up like a man, like Father Christmas—like a chocolate-coated cookie."[4] What Robinson attributes to traditional Christianity is precisely the view orthodoxy struggled so hard to banish, and finally put down at Chalcedon in 451. Robinson's accusation may have some merit insofar as ordinary believers, if not adequately taught, often do imagine the incarnation in Apollinarian terms; however, this charge cannot fairly be made of orthodoxy, which categorically rejects Apollinarianism.

The view of Jesus Christ as human flesh in union with the divine Logos is subject to the same criticism earlier made of Arianism: instead of a Christ who is both God and man, it confronts us with a remarkable composite figure who is neither God nor man, but a combination. Apollinaris not only used the term *henosis,* "unity," but also *mixis,* "mixture," such as the union of fire and metal in red-hot iron. (His understanding of physics is defective, inasmuch as modern physics does not speak of fire as an element at all.) To us his illustration suggests one element, the metal, being brought to a particular condition, radiance, by the application of heat energy, and points to an impersonal force, rather than to a personal Logos. Nevertheless, it is abundantly evident that Apollinaris thinks of Jesus not as a man with a divinely influenced nature but as possessing "one nature of God the Word made flesh." He explicitly denies that Christ was "a man," for "whoever calls him Who was born of Mary a man, and calls him Who was crucified a man, makes him a man instead of God."[5] Although Apollinaris taught that the flesh of Jesus Christ was deified in consequence of the energizing effect of the Logos, he did not hold that it was preexistent. Christ, like all other humans, was a body of flesh animated and formed by a nous, but with the significant difference that the Nous of Christ was not a human spirit but the divine Logos.

Apollinaris had already begun to teach his Christology by 352, according to Gregory of Nazianzus; but Athanasius took him to task only in 362; ten years later, Apollinaris went to Antioch, where the controversies involving Meletius and Paulinus made it easier for him to establish himself. His own writings and those of his adherents were frequently circulated under the names of other, more orthodox authors, such as Julius of Rome, Gregory the Wonder Worker, and, as indicated earlier, even Athanasius himself. By 377 Basil of Caesarea began to write against him. The task of the orthodox Cappadocians in countering Apollinaris was rendered more difficult by the continuing struggle with the Arians, for Apollinaris strongly supported the very doctrine the Arians denied, that of the *homoousion.* For the first time in two centuries, since the gnostic crisis, orthodoxy was forced to defend not only the full deity but also the full humanity of Christ.

Apollinaris was identified as a heretic before his opponents were able clearly to formulate the precise nature of his heresy. As in the case of orthodoxy's resistance to Arianism, the church sensed that a vital spiritual and religious interest was at stake before it clearly identified the nature of the threat; it rushed to oppose Apollinaris before it was entirely sure why it had to do so. In the case of Arianism, what was at stake was the ability of Jesus Christ, if less than fully God, to save his people. With Apollinaris there was no suggestion that Jesus was less than fully God, but the diminution of his humanity made it less than certain that we are his brethren and consequently his people. It was the religious interest in the humanity of Christ that brought the orthodox into the lists against Apollinaris; the question was whether they would be able to avoid the countercharge of Apollinaris, that they really taught two Christs, one divine and one human.

A man who lacks a human intellect cannot truly be considered a man, as the fundamental element of his humanity, his human mind and the human will associated with it, is plainly lacking. By insisting that Christ's Nous is *atreptos,* "immutable," Apollinaris came into conflict with the Scripture, which speaks of him as growing in knowledge and being at least momentarily in conflict with the will of God (Luke 22:24). The chief flaw in Apollinarianism is the fact that it seems to make the orthodox doctrine of salvation impossible. If Christ is justly to earn the salvation of mankind, he must be a man. This thought anticipates the elaborate doctrine of substitutionary satisfaction to be worked out by Anselm of Canterbury (1033–1109) seven centuries later in *Cur Deus homo* (Why the God-Man?). Christology is necessary for soteriology.[6] The patristic opponents of Apollinaris—for example, Gregory of Nazianzus—had not yet developed the sophisticated treatment of the scholastic Anselm, but Gregory already sensed that if he was to be our substitute for sin, there had to be a basic identity between Jesus Christ and the humanity he was to redeem. For salvation requires that the man Jesus die and be raised for us and then go on to make intercession for us at the right hand of God.[7] It should be apparent that what we need to represent us before God is not mere human flesh, which is not categorically different from that of the animals and which is not the essential element in man; we need a real, complete human being.

It is perplexing that this was not apparent to Apollinaris himself. On the basis of his Aristotelian distinction between form and matter, it is precisely the spiritual-intellectual element, the form, which imparts to the matter of the body its essential nature and makes a human being. He should have seen that Jesus needed a soul to be true man. Gregory of Nazianzus and Gregory of Nyssa both argued that only that which is performed in the human nature of Christ is applicable to our humanity: inasmuch as it was the human *nous* that sinned through the abuse of its freedom, redemption is possible only if the Christ also assumes a human nous so that he can render as a man the obedience the man Adam refused. Salvation is a matter of body and soul. The Redeemer had to possess the power of God in order to free both of these, and he had to bear them both in himself in order to make them free.[8]

The deep concern of these early Fathers with the fact that the soul and the intellect are culpable clearly shows that they did not think that sin was simply a matter of the body and its appetites. To the extent that they extolled asceticism, as they did, it was not because they viewed the body and its appetites as evil per se, but because they believed that only by training the body through ascetic discipline could the rebellious *nous* learn obedience (cf. 1 Cor. 9:26–27). Only as Christ became what we human beings are did he reunite us with God.[9] ''If he had not assumed a human soul, and it were only the deity that won the victory then that which happened would bring us no gain, for what similarity is there between the perfection of the conduct of God and the human soul? . . . He took flesh and soul, and fought by both for both, in that he slew sin in the flesh and diminished its lusts, . . . but the soul he instructed and trained to overcome its passions as well as to bridle the lusts of the flesh.''[10] This is in a sense the counterpart to the earlier argument that Christ had to possess deity in order to have the power to transform us; now the orthodox are concerned to show that he had to be fully human in order that his transforming power actually be transmitted to mankind.

3. ANTICIPATIONS OF CHALCEDON AND ANSELM

If we make two fundamental suppositions: (1) that there are only two or three possibilities to consider in attempting to understand Christ, and that the same ones occur again and again throughout the centuries of Christianity, and (2) that the basic biblical message of sin and salvation naturally expresses itself in what we are coming to call orthodoxy, the achievement of these fourth-century Fathers is impressive. Writing at a time when the intellectual world was still primarily trained to think in terms of Hellenistic philosophy, they produced essentially the same view of the relationship between God and man in Christ that Anselm would articulate seven centuries later and that is still the position of conservative and neoorthodox theology today.

What is at stake here is the concept that the work done in Christ must be done by a human subject, that is, by a real, individual human, not just by human substance. Here again we see the fundamentally personalistic, individualistic, and moral element in biblical religion, and especially in Christianity, coming to the fore.[11] The theological efforts of Apollinaris to explain the mystery of Christ in terms of a divine Logos animating human flesh only led to the formulation and doctrinal solidification of a necessity that Christians had always sensed: that Jesus Christ must be one of us to save us (Heb. 2:17–18). Adolf von Harnack contends that earlier fourth-century Christianity basically naively believed what Apollinaris later carefully formulated, namely, in an *ensarkosis* ("enfleshment") of the deity, with the consequent docetic implication that Jesus Christ was a man in appearance only. Harnack sees in this a recrudescence, or at least a hidden remainder, of earlier Gnosticism. Consequently, Harnack pays tribute to the doctrine of Apollinaris and in effect implies that its rejection was a regressive step for theology: "*This doctrine, measured by the presuppositions and goals of the Greek concept of Christianity as a religion, is perfect.* Apollinaris presents in an unsurpassable way . . . that which at bottom all pious Greeks believed and confessed."[12] Here we see Harnack's systematizing desire to make Christianity a part of a more general class and to make it conform to it, namely, the class of human religions in general. It is against this background and the tendency not merely to misunderstand Christianity but to try to recast it as just another intellectualizing religion that we must understand the protest of Harnack's erstwhile pupil, Karl Barth, that Christianity is not a religion at all.

Harnack believed that the basic promise of early Christianity was to make man divine. To achieve this goal, it was not necessary for Christ to be fully human, for after our divinization we shall no longer be merely human either. Thus Apollinarianism represented a legitimate development, and orthodoxy was in effect its suppression. Seeberg has more correctly perceived that the fundamental promise of the Gospel is not the divinization of man but fellowship with God in eternal life; this fellowship implies a transformation (1 Cor. 15:51; 1 John 3:2). In a sense we may speak of divinization, or apotheosis, but this is a result of our fellowship with God after the resurrection, not the cause of it; the personal fellowship is primary. As we are individual persons who need to be redeemed as persons, not just spirits that need to be freed from bondage to sinful flesh,[13] we need a human redeemer, not one who is merely "God dressed up like a man." Seeberg is correct when he writes, "Thus it is indubitable that in broad circles of the church not only the old formulations concerning 'truly man,' but direct religious sensibility spoke against Apollinaris."[14] Strangely, although Apollinarianism was in full bloom prior to 381, the Council of Constantinople of 381 had nothing to say about it. Basil of Caesarea took up arms against it in 377 and promoted its rejection by Rome that same year. It continued to flourish in the East for a time, until the decree of the Emperor Theodosius I of 388 exiled all Apollinarians.[15]

4. THEOLOGY AT THE CLOSE OF THE FOURTH CENTURY: THE STARTING POINT FOR THE MONOPHYSITE STRUGGLES

The Antiochene school of which we have already spoken set itself apart from that of Alexandria by a greater attention to the biblical texts, by a more consistent, less allegorical, and more literal and grammatical exegesis, and by a hostility to speculation. Its members were more interested in the historic Jesus and in what he did than in theories about the relationship of his natures. They thought in psychological and ethical terms rather than in ontological ones. (Two more modern figures who reflect similar concerns are the British Congregationalist Peter Taylor Forsyth [1848–1921] and the Zurich theologian Emil Brunner [1889–1966].) The Nicene doctrine of the *homoousia* of the Son with the Father required, in Antiochene eyes, the maintenance of a clear distinction between the divine and the human in Christ, and the avoidance of any mixing such as that postulated by Apollinaris. Diodorus of Tarsus (died at about the same time as Apollinaris, ca. 392), Theodore of Mopsuestia (d. ca. 428), and Theodoret of Cyrrhus (d. ca. 458) are the most important representatives of the Antiochene school. Because so few of Diodorus' works have survived it is necessary to refer primarily to those of Theodore of Mopsuestia for our information. Both Diodorus and Theodore were accepted as impeccably orthodox during their own lifetime, but after the deposition of Patriarch Nestorius of Constantinople at the Council of Ephesus in 431, both of them posthumously and undeservedly acquired the reputation of heretics because Nestorius had followed their doctrines.

Presupposing the *homoousia* of the Son and Father, the Antiochenes taught that the Logos took upon himself a human person when Jesus was born of Mary, "a perfect man, [the Logos] constituting his nature of a human soul, intellect, and body."[16] Although it was customary from the New Testament onward to refer to "the man Christ Jesus" (1 Tim. 2:5) or, in patristic language, to "the man of Christ," thus implicitly recognizing his human personhood, it was the Antiochenes who explicitly pointed out that this humanity necessarily implies a human personality. The Antiochenes clearly recognized that Jesus had a human development and experienced human life with its joys and sorrows. Rather than speak of a physical union, a *henosis physike,* as Apollinaris did, Theodore of Mopsuestia speaks of an indwelling *(enoikesis)* of the Son in Jesus Christ, an *enoikesis* that is not that of the divine essence nor of divine energy (which cannot be circumscribed) but of divine benevolence *(eudokia).* At this point the Antiochene view seems in danger of bordering on the adoptionism the doctrine of the *homoousion* was supposed to have definitively overcome; indeed, the Antiochenes spoke of God indwelling the prophets and apostles, as well as all the saints. The Logos indwells the Son of Man, by contrast, in such a way that he imparts to him the fullness of the glory that is his by nature as the consubstantial Son.[17] Jesus Christ possesses a double sonship: the Son of God is Son by nature, the man Jesus Son by grace, but the two are *hen prosopon,* "one person." Here again the linguistic problems that troubled the trinitarian controversy reappear, for while the Greek *prosopon* may mean "person," it normally means "face," and hence Theodore's language suggests a single appearance rather than a single person.

Theodore and his followers were deeply concerned to have the personal history of Jesus understood as a real human history. Although there was never a time when the Logos did not indwell the human Jesus from his conception onward, the Logos did not override or even coerce the human will in Jesus. Thanks to the Logos, Jesus could and did learn moral virtue faster than other men, but he still had to choose to do so, just as others must do. The unity of the person of Christ becomes evident in the unity of will and activity; it is indissoluble, and since the glorification of Jesus it has been made perfect, "making it immutable as to the impulses of the soul, incorruptible and indivisible as to the flesh."[18]

Even as we recognize the zeal to keep the full humanity of Jesus in view, we must acknowledge that this view begins to resemble a kind of possession not by a demon but by the divine Son. The Chalcedonian formula, which the later Monophysites found unacceptable, is already here: two complete natures, one person; but the way in which Theodore develops the concept of the unity of the person is not altogether satisfying. The unity began with the conception of Jesus, but it needed to be fulfilled as the human being freely accepted the working of the indwelling Logos. The language of Theodore very clearly expresses the unity of the person, but with the defect that it sometimes appears that what is called the person of Christ is a kind of hypothetical product of the activity of the two natures, "but, if one looks more closely, on the contrary the *henosis* [unity] is not the product of but the presupposition and basis of the concrete unity of the natures."[19] The thought of the Antiochenes is not so much different from that of Athanasius as it is more developed. Theodore tries to do justice to the full reality of each nature in the context of the essential unity of the person of Christ without falling into the trap of speaking of a mixture or fusion of natures or of the transformation of one into the other. His formulation in *On the Incarnation* anticipates the later Chalcedonian formula almost word for word.[20]

There were three fundamental test questions that appeared in the context of the Christological problem: (1) was God born of Mary; or only a man? (2) did God die on the cross, or only a man? (3) should the human nature of Christ be worshiped? Theodore answered each question clearly and in the affirmative, but always with a qualification, "insofar as the man is united to the Logos." Some such qualification seems to be necessary to avoid monophysitism or docetism, but in the context of later fifth-century disputes it will return to cast unwarranted doubt on the orthodoxy of Theodore and other Antiochenes. The Antiochene position was certainly subtler and more difficult to grasp than the simple proposition of Apollinaris.

No one since the fourth century has called himself an Apollinarian, but the idea of Apollinaris resurfaces wherever there is a combination of orthodox dogmatism and theological naïveté. Much modern twentieth-century conservative Protestantism is implicitly Apollinarian because while it ringingly confesses the deity of Christ, it finds it hard to think that he was really a man. Firmly to assert the deity of Christ is not the same thing as to confess the New Testament faith in him, for in the New Testament he is definitely a man who is revealed to be the Son of God, with all that that implies—not a divine being who reveals himself in human form.

It is customary to see an antagonism between the *homoousion* proclaimed at Nicaea and by Athanasius on the one hand and Antiochene theology on the other. However, to do so is really to assume that *homoousia* necessarily implies Apollinarianism or monophysitism. Indeed this is the supposition of the majority of recent historians of doctrine, most of whom view Nicene orthodoxy with disapproval. The popularized criticism of John A. T. Robinson, noted earlier, assumes in effect that Christian orthodoxy is monophysite at heart. For this reason the condemnation that fell upon the Antiochene school following the excommunication of Nestorius has had serious consequences. Although Chalcedon will in fact accept Antiochene formulations, the personal condemnation and criticisms of Antiochene leaders has made Chalcedon, in retrospect, look like a monophysite victory to all but the Monophysites themselves and has cast orthodoxy in the role of a party concerned only with unknowable divine essence and not at all with practical Christianity, with winning converts to Christ or constructively meeting human social needs.

a. The Two Gregories

The best-known of the three great Cappadocian Fathers, Basil, offers little of distinctive interest in his Christology, but both his friend Gregory of Nazianzus and his younger brother Gregory of Nyssa have much to offer. Gregory of Nazianzus acknowledged two complete natures in Christ, but spoke of a *synapsis* of the two natures: there is a natural unity between God and man in Christ. In consequence, to call Mary the *theotokos* ("God-bearing one") implies too much. Once again the idea that God became man seems in danger of turning into the view that a man becomes God. "His doctrine is typical for many in his time: a monophysitism that does not want to be Monophysite. It was the Christology of the future."[21] Like Gregory of Nazianzus, Gregory of Nyssa emphasized the fact that the Logos took upon himself a complete human nature from the conception of Jesus. More so than his namesake, he attempted to explain the unity of the two natures in Jesus while preserving the specific aspects of his humanity; he does so by making the deity the active principle, the humanity the passive recipient. Gregory of Nazianzus tried to put into words what it can mean to say that deity, i.e. God, has been born and has died on the Cross. To do this, he emphasized that deity has become inseparably united with the human person, Jesus, so that we can correctly say that what Jesus did and experienced deity did and experienced. Gregory of Nyssa, by contrast, has no conception of God suffering.

b. Amphilochius and Epiphanius

The debate between the Apollinarian and Cappadocian views came to a kind of temporary resolution, before the outbreak of the great Christological controversies, in the work of Amphilochius of Iconium. Making a clear distinction between the two natures, divine and human, of Christ, he explicitly affirmed that Christ is *homoousios* with us. He is one Son of two natures, with the natures being neither mixed, changed, nor divided.[22] Unlike the Cappadocians who preceded him, Amphilochius clearly affirmed that Jesus retained his human nature even after his glorification. In his work, then, we have almost reached the final definition that will be decided upon at Chalcedon.

Epiphanius (d. 403) refined the thoughts of Amphilochius. He represents a kind of preliminary consensus at the end of the fourth century, before the attempts to grapple with the mystery of God made man led to a new and fiercer series of Christological conflicts. Like Amphilochius, Epiphanius insisted that Jesus is both God and man by nature—not a deified man or a humanized deity. In the passion of Jesus, the deity did not suffer, as deity is impassible, but because Jesus Christ is one person, we attribute the suffering of the humanity to deity. For this reason, we may properly worship the sufferer on the Cross. The Logos took flesh upon himself in order to be able to suffer with and for us.[23] This argument may not be entirely consistent, but at least it does not dismiss the mystery of the incarnation in the name of God's philosophical attribute of impassibility.

5. THE FIFTH CENTURY

The First Ecumenical Council condemned a man, Arius, but his teaching went on to dominate most of Christendom for another half century. Even after Arianism was put down within the empire, it continued to flourish outside it, among the Goths, due to the fact that the first missionary to the Goths, Ulfilas, was converted as a slave in Constantinople when the city was Arian. The Third Ecumenical Council, held at Ephesus in 431, also condemned a man, Nestorius, and this time the condemnation was more effective. Nestorius, who had been patriarch of Constantinople, was deposed and banished, and those who called themselves his followers were quickly reduced to insignificance within the empire, although outside it Nestorianism spread all the way to China. Arianism, which really was heretical, thus long outlasted the condemnation of Arius; Nestorianism, far less heretical—if indeed in its original version it was heretical at all[24]—was unable to recover from its disaster at Ephesus.

Nestorius, a monk of Antioch, was called to be patriarch of Constantinople during the reign of Theodosius II (ruled 408–50), although he was a supporter of the views of Pelagius against Augustine, which were dominant in the West.[25] Installed at Constantinople, Nestorius found himself embroiled in a rancorous controversy over the use of the term *theotokos* as a title for the Virgin Mary. The term, which means "God-bearing one" (not precisely "Mother of God," as it is frequently translated), originally was descriptive of the man Jesus, born of Mary. In order to assert that he was truly God even when in Mary's womb and during the process of birth, Mary was given the title *theotokos*.

Although it seems illogical to attribute birth to God, who according to most theological definitions has no beginning and cannot experience any process of becoming, if Jesus is fully God, then when Jesus is born, logic requires us to say that God is born and to be willing to call Mary, his mother, the "God-bearing one." This is another consequence of the principle of the communication of attributes *(communicatio idiomatum),* which expresses the conviction that Jesus is both God and man. In later centuries the term *theotokos* will come to be seen as a Mariological term expressive of her personal glory, and will be rejected by many who accept the full deity and preexistence of her Son.

The expression *theotokos* was poorly chosen as a shibboleth to divide the orthodox from heretics, for a number of prominent heretical groups had

no difficulty with it. Arians could use it, although they did not believe that
the Son is of the same substance as the Father, because they did accept him
as a kind of divinity and acknowledged that he was born, suffered, and died.
Apollinarians, with their view that there is only "one incarnate nature of
God the Logos," readily accepted the term. Neither Arians nor Apollinarians were concerned to protect the doctrine of the full humanity and the
human personality of Jesus. The Antiochene school, from which Nestorius
came, sought to maintain the true humanity of Christ. To speak of Mary as
"bearing God" seemed to Nestorius to imply that the One she bore was not
a true man. Nestorius was willing to say that the Christ born of Mary is
God, but did not want to say, "God is born," because to do so implied in
his mind that the One born was not a true man. One must say, "Christ is
born," thus implying, because God and man are one in Christ, that both
God and man are born. To call Mary either "God-bearer" or "man-
bearer," although both are correct in terms of the communication of attributes, appears misleading.

The term *theotokos* originally was intended to affirm the deity of Jesus
Christ, but it gradually came to be a title of honor for Mary. In order to
emphasize the holiness of Christ, it became customary to exalt the holiness
of the one who bore him in her womb. The doctrine of the Virgin Birth
states that Jesus was miraculously conceived by Mary through the power of
the Holy Spirit without any act of sexual intercourse; strictly speaking, it is
a doctrine of virginal conception. Although the New Testament refers to
Jesus as having brothers and sisters, pious tradition began to see these as
collateral relatives or perhaps Joseph's children by an earlier marriage; it
was argued that Mary remained a virgin all her life; finally, it was even
stated that she had delivered Jesus without injury to her virginity, i.e. miraculously, without rupturing the hymen. The tendency to exalt Mary, despite the objections of Protestants and liberal Catholics and reservations of
the Eastern Orthodox, reached high points in Roman Catholicism with the
doctrines of the Immaculate Conception (1854) and the bodily Assumption
(1950).[26] Nestorius observed the beginnings of this development, and
warned against making the Virgin into a goddess.[27]

Nestorius, unlike Arius, was not a theological radical, but rather somewhat of a pedant. Arius fell into error through a desire to be brilliant; Nestorius, in his zeal to be precise and correct at all costs, alienated himself
from the bulk of the church. We have seen that doctrinal extravagances
required the writing of creeds with some rather precise definitions; Nestorius
wanted to be still more precise, and the church would not follow him. Although he criticized the expression *theotokos* as unbiblical, he came to allow
it if used in conjunction with the equally valid expression *anthropotokos,*
"man-bearing one." To omit *anthropotokos* would make it seem as though

Mary had delivered only God, bare of all true humanity. The term he preferred, *Christotokos,* is quite orthodox but was unpopular with those who
emphasized the deity alone and was resented by those devoted to the growing cult of Mary. For the first time, growing popular piety was beginning to
play a role in deciding a major theological issue.

Although the growing devotion to Mary increased the unpopularity of
Nestorius' views, it does not appear to have influenced the definition of
orthodoxy, as—apart from the Christological term *theotokos*—the Chalcedonian Creed of 451 will contain no reference to Mariology. It appears to
have played a great part in arousing popular indignation against the unfortunate Nestorius, whose chief error, in retrospect, appears to have been pedantic exactitude rather than any outright heresy.

Nestorius taught that the two natures of Christ fall together in one *prosopon.* The Greek word is ambiguous: by it, Nestorius apparently meant one
person, which would be quite orthodox, but his opponents understood him
to be saying one *appearance,* and thus to be speaking of only an apparent
unity between the divine and the human in Christ. Nestorius held that the
Logos was indissolubly united with the human personality from the moment
of conception. There was, however, no transformation or mixture of the
natures. Each preserves what is proper to it; hence, one can say only that
the humanity is born, suffers, dies, and was raised; nevertheless, although
there are two natures, there is a single Son. These entirely orthodox views
were first attacked from Alexandria, apparently initially because of ecclesiastical and personal rivalry; here too the problem of Nestorianism seems
to be the first in which personal and regional pride and ambition were decisive—in this case, the desire of Alexandria and its patriarch, Cyril, to attain
the undisputed preeminence in the eastern half of the Roman Empire. This
rivalry had already come to a head under Theophilus, Cyril's uncle and
predecessor in the patriarchate.

a. Cyril of Alexandria

Cyril of Alexandria (d. 444) followed his uncle in principled opposition
to Apollinaris, and acknowledged that Jesus possessed a rational soul;[28] the
Gospels speak plainly of it. He denied that the divine nature was in any way
subject to change or mixture as a consequence of the incarnation. Like the
Antiochenes and in contrast to Apollinaris, he took seriously the Gospel
accounts of Jesus suffering sadness and fear. He acknowledged two perfections *(teleia)* in Christ, human and divine, but avoided the term *physis,*
"nature." As far as the positive presentation of Cyril's position is concerned, it is hard to see any significant difference from that of the Antiochenes as represented by Nestorius. But he attacked them nonetheless, fearing

or claiming to fear that in their interest in preserving the full humanity of Jesus, they let the deity be reduced to a mere appearance or a title. He misunderstood the Antiochenes as holding that the *henosis* of the divine and the human came about only as a relationship between them during the life of Jesus—a momentous misunderstanding Cyril's great influence fastened on the church.

As Cyril understood Nestorius, all of Jesus' saving acts were performed in his human nature only. Hence in Cyril's eyes, they could have no saving power. In addition, Cyril held that God and man must be united in Christ, not merely associated, if our human nature is to participate in the purification and sanctification that association with the Deity, and nothing less, can bring. Only the true God may be worshiped; to suggest that Christ is two Persons (which, be it noted, Nestorius did not do!) would bring a fourth Person into the Trinity itself, the man Jesus. Cyril favored the title *theotokos* and supplemented it with *mater theou*, "mother of God." As a final blow against Nestorius, Cyril charged that his doctrine turned the eucharist into cannibalism.[29] He considered Nestorius' teaching godless, because it makes the historical person and deeds of Christ less than fully divine. Cyril's goal was to keep the Deity among us, as suggested by Christ's title "Emmanuel," so that God might truly and properly be worshiped in worshiping Christ, and so that the eucharistic meal might be a true communion with God, not merely with a man.

Like the heretical Apollinaris and the orthodox Gregory of Nazianzus, Cyril insisted on the unity between God and man in Christ—but in contrast to Apollinaris and with greater clarity than Gregory he insisted that Christ's deity and humanity remain unmixed and unchanged. He acknowledges two natures, but speaks of a *henosis physike*, "natural unity," and introduces the term *henosis kath'hypostasin*, a "unity according to the person": the true unity is "natural" and "hypostatic."[30]

Theodoret objected that Cyril was once again reverting to a *krasis* ("mixture") of the two natures; Cyril vigorously denied this, and claimed that he only wanted to affirm their real unity. In so doing he revived an Apollinarian formula, one incarnate nature of God the Word; if the divine and the human are really united, their union is a true nature, animated by the Logos. Cyril erroneously attributed the formulation to Athanasius, in consequence of the fact, mentioned earlier, that writings of Apollinaris had been circulated under the venerated name of Athanasius. Nevertheless, Cyril insists that both the divine and the human natures remain unchanged, so that in a sense one can say that he implies three natures: one divine, one human, and one of the incarnate Logos. Here apparently Cyril has been willing to strain the meaning of the word "nature": his "one incarnate nature" is not a deified human nature, as in Apollinaris or the later Monophysites, but a theological postulate to underscore the reality of the unity of the unchanged, unmixed divine and human natures in the Person of Christ. Nestorius, by contrast, had strained the concept of the person, calling one person what to others looked like a mere harmonious collaboration between two distinct persons.

The incarnate nature as seen by Cyril was not a real nature in the usual sense, i.e. not a third kind of nature, but later Monophysites understood it to be so. Thus they claimed Cyril as the godfather of their doctrine. Nestorius' incarnate person was a single person, not two as his critics thought, but he could not convince others that it was so. Consequently he has gone down in history as a great heretic although what he actually believed was reaffirmed at Chalcedon. The council of 451 really was far more compatible with the formulations of Nestorius the heretic than with those of Cyril, the doctor of the church. Cyril's "nature" was an emulsion, not a synthesis. It combined immiscible substances, for he used both the Antiochene expression "two perfections" and the Apollinarian phrase "one nature." Cyril's great strength was his concentration on the unity of Christ and his work; from his time on it is appropriate to speak of the Christian conception of God as the *theanthropos,* the *Deus homo,* the God-man.[31]

Cyril stood, or tried to stand, between the Antiochene emphasis on a real duality of unchanged natures and the Apollinarian formulation of the one nature. Perhaps if he had not been misled into attributing the expression *mia physis* to Athanasius, he would not have incorporated it into his system; but even without it, Cyril is more readily capable of being called as a witness for monophysitism than a doctor of the church (the title conferred by the Vatican in 1882!) ought to be. In any event, if the views of Apollinaris and Nestorius have the merit of internal consistency, those of Cyril do not. He can be claimed by both Monophysites and dyophysites. Cyril became a pivotal figure for subsequent developments: his vehement polemics against Nestorius and his followers—despite a great identity in theology—drove them from the orthodox church, while his incorporation of the Antiochene insistence on a unity without confusion or mixture, despite his predilection for monophysite language, acted as a barrier to monophysitism and prevented the Monophysites, despite their appeals to Cyril's teaching, from finding a haven in orthodoxy.

What Cyril could not accomplish with the somewhat muddled formulations of his theology he more successfully pursued by means of political and ecclesiastical diplomacy, appealing to the wife and sister of the Emperor Theodosius II in the East and to Pope Celestine in the West. While Nestorius approached the pope as an equal, Cyril rather obsequiously asked him for direction and instruction. For whatever reason, Celestine turned sharply on Nestorius and rallied to Cyril.

The influence of Rome had been a constant, steadying factor for orthodoxy during the Arian controversy. In the conflict with Nestorius, where the actual theological difference was minimal, Cyril's courting of Rome and Rome's rallying to his cause helped Rome to solidify its claim to a unique authority in the church. At the otherwise undistinguished Council of Ephesus (Third Ecumenical), Nestorius withdrew when his supposed ally John of Antioch failed to arrive; the council then condemned Nestorius. John finally arrived and together with Nestorius and the imperial commissioner convened what they called the true council, and deposed Cyril. The subsequent arrival of the Roman legates permitted a third session to be held, which sustained Cyril. Personal factors influenced the ultimate result: while Cyril intrigued at court, Nestorius ill-advisedly withdrew to a monastery; the Antiochene party abandoned him to his fate, just as the Antiochene adherents of Arius had abandoned him after Nicaea a century earlier.

Following the Council of Ephesus, Cyril was persuaded to agree to a formula of union probably developed by the leading Antiochene, Theodoret of Cyrrhus. It clearly claims Jesus Christ as of one substance with the Father according to the deity and of one substance with us according to the humanity, having a rational soul; a unity of natures is confessed, and the Virgin is called *theotokos*. The formula answers all the concerns of the Antiochene party, but the fact that Nestorius had been condemned and exiled continued to discredit them even though their ideas were being accepted as orthodox. In addition, even this mutually acceptable compromise formula only concealed tensions. The Alexandrian party was preoccupied with the one incarnate nature, and admitted the concept of two natures only in a theoretical sense. The Antiochene party insisted that each nature was full and complete, and although it did confess one incarnate person, Jesus Christ, the idea of two natures constituting a single person seemed to make the idea of the person nothing but a theoretical construction. In the last analysis, neither the Alexandrian nor the Antiochene position fully answers the problems raised by the mystery of the incarnation. Each tried to explain too much, and the only way peace could be restored would be by setting limits beyond which no explanations would be attempted.

b. Theodoret of Cyrrhus

In 437, Cyril demanded that the teachers of Nestorius, Theodore of Mopsuestia and Diodorus of Tarsus, be condemned along with their pupil. Theodoret defended them, and drew upon himself a vehement attack by Cyril's successor in Alexandria, Dioscurus. Theodoret affirmed that the Virgin should be entitled *theotokos* and insisted that the only begotten Son cannot be divided into two persons. But unlike Cyril, he postulated only one nature of Christ, the divine, before the incarnation; the human nature of Christ did not begin to exist until his conception. Theodoret spoke of a physical union, just as Cyril did, but whereas for Cyril the union was the product of two distinct natures joining, for Theodoret the unity of the one person, Christ, provided the basis for the natures to be joined. Theodoret vigorously denied that he divided Christ into two persons, and accepted the claim that the one person of the incarnate Son suffered. Despite this, the Alexandrian party continued to suspect him of seeing Jesus only as a man, and eventually the conflict broke out again with undiminished severity.

c. Latin Writers

Although the controversy raged primarily in the East, three Latin-speaking theologians, Hilary of Poitiers (active ca. 340, d. ca. 367), Ambrose of Milan (ca. 340–97), and Augustine himself (354–430), contributed substantial impulses. Hilary revived the old formula of Tertullian, two natures in one person. He introduced the terms *evacuatio* and *exinanitio* to describe the self-emptying of the Son in his incarnation—but unlike the kenoticists of the modern era, he did not hold that the Son laid aside any of his divine power. To take on a circumscribed, bodily humanity is a demonstration of his omnipotence and would not be possible apart from it. But Hilary so sharply distinguishes the natures with respect to the suffering of Christ that he seems in danger of docetism or Apollinarianism: "Having such a body that could suffer, he suffered, but not as having a nature capable of pain . . . when he accepted drink and food, it is not due to the necessity of the body but out of consent."[32] The philosophical inclination to reject any implication that deity can suffer leads to a situation in which it appears to be only a human body that suffers, but not the Son of God. Ambrose was closer to the older Latin Christology, and simply reaffirmed the old assertions of deity and humanity in one person in a somewhat naive way: "The Lord of majesty is said to be crucified, for the partaker of both natures, that is, of the human and the divine, underwent the passion in the nature of a man."[33] He does not appear to have grappled with the problems being raised at precisely this time by Apollinaris.

Ambrose's disciple Augustine, by contrast, is far more sophisticated. Like Hilary, Augustine seems interested in the philosophical implications of the relationship of the Logos to the created order. Athanasius began with the reality of the redemptive work of Christ in history and worked back from that to the implications of deity; Augustine began with the orthodox doctrine of the deity of the Son, attempted to work out its implications in a speculative way, and then moved from those considerations to a consideration of the implications of the doctrine for our salvation. Although after his conversion from Manichaean dualism he held to the reality of the incarnation in Christ, his doctrine suggests the union of the divine principle with the human rather than a union of two personal natures in one person. Whereas the Greek theologians stressed that Jesus Christ merited our salvation through the suffering he underwent as a man, Augustine saw the suffering as the expression of a salvation already graciously determined by God. At times Augustine sounds Apollinarian as he speaks of Christ as the Person of the Logos, but at others, like the Antiochenes, he sharply distinguishes two natures. Although he did formally accept both natures, Augustine tended to express himself in terms that minimize Jesus' human personhood.

d. Dioscurus of Alexandria

In 444 Dioscurus succeeded Cyril as patriarch in Alexandria. He was not a great theologian like Cyril, but he was far more vigorous and unrelenting in his quest for ecclesiastical power. Unlike Cyril, he thought that he could dispense with the help of Cyril's traditional ally, Rome. When an archimandrite in Constantinople, Eutyches, began to denounce the orthodox party as Nestorian, Dioscurus intervened in the hope of humbling his rival, the patriarch of Constantinople. In 448 Eutyches specifically stated that Jesus had only one nature following the incarnation, although two had been present before it.[34] By saying this, Eutyches went beyond the views of Cyril as well as those of a compromise formulation worked out in the wake of the Third Ecumenical Council. Eutyches was promptly condemned by a synod in Constantinople, but he appealed to the Emperor in the East as well as to Pope Leo I in Rome. The pope, not only a sound theologian but also an adroit ecclesiastical politician, replied in writing, but a hastily convened synod held at Ephesus in 449, the so-called Robber Council, left Leo's communications unread. The triumphant Dioscurus condemned not only Patriarch Flavian of Constantinople but also Pope Leo.

In thus attempting to discredit both the pope and the other patriarch, Dioscurus was showing a lack of political prudence for which no glory borrowed from the illustrious Cyril could compensate. Contrary to what Eutyches had hoped, Leo's *Dogmatic Instruction* continued to teach that Christ possesses two natures after the incarnation. Each nature retains its properties, and the *exinanitio* is not a loss of divine power. Eutyches' position, two natures before the incarnation, one after it, is stamped as godless. Leo asserted the unity of both natures in one person without further defining the unity; he felt uneasy with the position of Nestorius, for Nestorius attempted to explain what he meant by the personal unity, while Leo did not try. The Council of Chalcedon was held in 451 to undo the Robber Council of 449. It set the standard for all later orthodox Christology, but we must unfortunately say that its holy Fathers, apart from the fact that we now call them orthodox, did not behave much more creditably than their "robber" predecessors at Ephesus in 449.

6. THE COUNCIL OF CHALCEDON

Like the Third Ecumenical Council held at Ephesus in 431, which condemned Nestorius, the Council of Ephesus in 449 was held under less than optimal conditions. Decisions were reached not by the unanimous agreement of the participants—the theoretical ideal of a general council—but by virtue of excluding all those who would not agree. The council of 431 had condemned Nestorius. That of 449, under the influence of Eutyches and Dioscurus, reaffirmed and broadened that condemnation. Unfortunately for him, Dioscurus had so overreached himself that the council of 449 was followed almost immediately by a countercouncil, held at Chalcedon in 451. This countercouncil was so successful that it is acclaimed as the Fourth Ecumenical Council. It closes the series of universally accepted church councils. Reacting against the Robber Council and its virulent anti-Nestorianism, the Council of Chalcedon in effect moved back toward a Nestorian position, without, however, rehabilitating Nestorius or his teachings by name. It did this by reaffirming the full, complete humanity of Jesus Christ, after the incarnation as well as before it. The fact that its doctrine has survived and is universally acknowledged as Christian orthodoxy suggests that Chalcedon really did incorporate the spirit of Christianity and represents much more than a mere political triumph of Pope Leo over Patriarch Dioscurus.

Prior to Chalcedon, the name of Nestorius had already been so blackened that he could not be explicitly vindicated or restored to honor. Nevertheless, the position affirmed at Chalcedon now appears to differ very little from that espoused by Nestorius. Dioscurus argued in vain that he held to the doctrine of Athanasius, Gregory, and Cyril (he did not mention Apollinaris!). He clung to the Alexandrian formulation, "one incarnate nature of God the Word." The council fathers were unwilling to heed him, and he was deposed—for disobedience, not heresy. Nestorius' sometime partisan, Theodoret, was reinstated, but at the price of condemning Nestorius, now a very old man in exile.

Leo was represented at Chalcedon by legates. They moved to have his letter to Patriarch Flavian of Constantinople recognized as a binding statement of doctrine.[35] This would in effect have recognized Rome's claim to possess final authority in doctrinal matters. Instead of accepting the legates' motion, the council wrote its own creed, the third and last creed drawn up by an ecumenical council. At the same time, it reaffirmed the creeds of 325 and 381 (accepted at Nicaea and Constantinople, respectively, and now combined into what is usually known as the Nicene Creed). In addition, it expressly prohibited the composition of additional creeds. (For this reason, since Chalcedon such documents are called confessions!) Chalcedon is the second great high-water mark of early Christian theology: it set an imperishable standard for orthodoxy.

Like the Nicene Creed after 325, the Creed of Chalcedon remained a center of controversy for many decades, but it has never been set aside. Even in the twentieth century its classical formulation, "two natures, one person," is the touchstone of Christological orthodoxy.

The Council of Chalcedon was intended as an exercise in unity, but in fact it solved only theoretical theological problems, not practical ecclesiastical ones. Specifically, it did not resolve the problem of the growing alienation of Egyptian Christians from the orthodoxy of Constantinople, where the Emperor and his government resided. The goal of the council was to reestablish harmony between the quarreling Eastern patriarchates and bring Alexandria and Antioch into harmony with Rome, theologically less sophisticated but more reliably orthodox. The arrogance of Patriarch Dioscurus of Alexandria certainly helped turn Pope Leo against him; when Dioscurus was condemned, it was not for his teaching but for the vehemence of his attacks on all those who would not agree with him. The council in effect accepted the position of Nestorius and the moderate Antiochene school.

Chalcedon's condemnation of what it considered the Christological extremes of Nestorianism and monophysitism suppressed those views only within the empire. Nestorianism would enjoy a great expansion into Asia, while the continuing hostility of the Monophysites would facilitate the loss of Egypt to the Moslems. Unlike the Nicene Creed, which erected a barrier against the truly heretical Arians, Chalcedon narrowed the definition of orthodoxy so much that it excluded many who really belonged within it. Nevertheless, because Christological speculation so readily produces heresy, the Creed of Chalcedon is still of great value in setting limits beyond which no attempt should be made to explain the mystery of Christ.

7. THE ORIGINS OF MONOPHYSITISM

Although Apollinaris and his idea that Christ had no human nous, or "mind," were rejected, the concept of one incarnate nature of God the Logos continued to exercise wide appeal. Although the fundamental idea of Nestorius about two distinct natures united in one person was accepted, Nestorius himself remained under condemnation: he and his adherents were accused of teaching two Christs. The condemnation of Nestorius spilled over onto the rest of the essentially orthodox school of Antioch out of which he had come. The creed of the Council of Chalcedon affirmed that each nature is complete; Jesus has a "reasonable soul and body," a complete human nature, and thus is "consubstantial with us" as well as "consubstantial with the Father." These are things Nestorius himself affirmed, and he would have had no difficulty in subscribing to the creed; in fact, as an old man in banishment, he considered that the creed had vindicated him. Cyril of Alexandria had died seven years before the council; he would have been able to sign it only with some mental reservations, while his successor Dioscurus and Eutyches clearly could not accept it at all.[36]

Nestorius had tried to explain the mystery of the incarnation in such a way as to safeguard the full humanity of Jesus Christ and his essential identification with us, but in so doing he seemed to his opponents to compromise the divine majesty of the Son of God. His ideas were fundamentally sound, but the way in which he formulated them and the spirit in which they were put forward sounded pedantic and even skeptical. The Council of Chalcedon affirmed them in their basic principles, and in addition sought to safeguard the deity of Christ by ringing reaffirmations of consubstantiality backed up by a prohibition of further attempts to explain how a man could be God. Although this Antiochene view came to prevail, the pro-Nestorian Antiochene party had committed moral suicide by abandoning Nestorius shortly after his condemnation at Ephesus in 431.

The conviction that Jesus Christ has two complete natures, divine and human, deemed crucial by the Antiochene party, was reaffirmed at Chalcedon. In retrospect, at least to orthodox Christians, the Chalcedonian doctrine of the two natures of Christ seems a necessary conclusion from the New Testament's witness to him. It rallied the majority of Christians around this doctrinal center, leaving a large and enduring group of unsatisfied critics on each wing. On one, the impulse that is more familiar to us in the twentieth century, a kind of skeptical rationalism—today we would call it liberalism— sought to explain the person and work of Jesus in terms of a special calling and spiritual endowment. It acknowledged that God had acted dynamically upon Jesus as well as through him and was willing to speak of his adoption by God, or even of a derivative kind of divinity, without ascribing deity in the full sense to him. This view, which we may term the Christological left, was largely suppressed with the condemnation first of Paul of Samosata, then of Arius and his followers. It is such a natural way to simplify the message concerning Christ and to make it intelligible to the general public that it repeatedly reemerges throughout the history of the church.

On the other wing of the Christological front stood those who were so inspired by the concept of the deity of Christ that such sober and modest language seemed to them to be totally inadequate and even irreverent. They had no appreciation for nice theological distinctions such as that between *theotokos* and *Christotokos;* to reject the one and to insist on the other seemed to them to detract from the glory due to the deity of Christ.

Early in the twentieth century, Reinhold Seeberg spoke of a "widespread contemporary antipathy toward the doctrine of the two natures." This antipathy has not diminished in the many decades that have passed since Seeberg wrote. The Creed of Chalcedon, with its clear affirmations in terms of the essence of God and the essence of man, seems too abstract and static, too ontological—even for many conservative Christians who accept both the deity and humanity of Christ. If contemporary liberal Christianity tends to revert to a kind of adoptionism, contemporary conservative Christians—including evangelicals and fundamentalists as well as traditionalist Roman Catholics—reveal a tendency to drift into a Eutychian or monophysite view, seeing in Christ only his deity and failing to take his humanity as seriously as the Bible and historic orthodoxy require. Thus Chalcedon not only was important for its own day, in setting limits to Christological speculation, but it remains significant for us today, for if we ignore it, nothing is easier than to drift back into the errors it was intended to stop.

Seeberg describes the historic accomplishment of Chalcedon in these terms:

> If it was definitely recognized at Nicaea that God is one, so that whoever says "God" can mean only one and the same God, and not a demigod, and thus that Christ as God is one with the Father, then Chalcedon established the assurance that if Christ is described as a man, then as man he is one with humanity and not a semi-divine human essence. As in Nicaea the mythological concept of a demigod was eliminated from the concept of God, at Chalcedon it was eliminated from our understanding of Jesus the man.[37]

The Creed of Chalcedon became our standard for measuring orthodoxy; where either its affirmation of Christ's deity or of his humanity is rejected, it means that historic orthodoxy has been abandoned. Where its discretion in discussing the mystery of the incarnation is not strictly followed, the speculation that can result often leads, sooner or later, to a loss of the reality the creed affirms. Modern evangelical and fundamentalist Protestants, who incline to disdain Chalcedon and its creed as too philosophical and not couched in strictly biblical language, are not immune to these dangers. The early church had the New Testament and the Apostles' Creed, but these were not explicit enough to prevent problems from arising when people attempted to think through their implications. Those implications are still present today, and thinking them through has become no easier or less problematic for theologians in the twentieth century than it was in the fifth.

A very positive feature of the Chalcedonian Creed is that it did eliminate the concept of a demigod, somehow blending or mingling elements of deity and humanity. Chalcedon leaves us with the incarnation as a mystery, and as such with something that is uncongenial to the analytical and skeptical mentality of the present age, but the concept of a demigod would be an even greater affront to the modern mind. The Creed of Chalcedon is not a theological program, but rather a set of limits; beyond its confines, theology almost invariably will degenerate into skepticism, unbelief, or heresy.

a. *Christology After Chalcedon*

The limits Chalcedon sought to set were not readily accepted everywhere. Most of the Antiochene party, which had already abandoned Nestorius, submitted and accepted it, but some refused and, abandoning the empire where orthodoxy was enforced by law, passed over into Persia. Nestorians carried Christianity far into Asia, and briefly reappeared in the Middle East in the thirteenth century, accompanying the invading Mongol armies. The Alexandrian party was stubborner. The positions of Eutyches and Apollinaris were relinquished and conceded to be wrong, but the Chalcedonian formula, and its advocates, especially Leo of Rome, were attacked as proclaiming a "two-faced idol." The monophysite party could appeal to the authority of the late Cyril. Although he had accepted the Council of Ephesus of 431 and the compromise formula of 433, Cyril had never ceased to speak of the *mia physis,* nevertheless, he was celebrated as thoroughly orthodox.

The fundamental impulse of monophysitism is the insistence that the unity of the divine and the human in Christ is fulfilled in the physical life of Christ and produces *a single nature.* The theory states that the Word becomes flesh, but it works itself out in the human flesh becoming divine. Because they held that Christ's humanity became divine, many, including Cyril and even Gregory of Nazianzus, could be called Monophysites. Here we shall reserve the party name for those who opposed the Council of Chalcedon and the famous letter, or tome, of Leo the Great, i.e. for the time after 451. Opposition to Chalcedon is the real hallmark of the Monophysites; they did not develop a new position. Inasmuch as the empire committed itself and its authority to the implementation of Chalcedon, their resistance led to decades of conflict. It produced a bitter animosity that ultimately resulted in the easy submission of the dissatisfied and alienated monophysite provinces to the surge of Islam.

b. *Varieties of Monophysitism*

The first important Monophysite, Severus, reiterated the traditional statements of orthodoxy and acknowledged two natures in Christ, but went on to assert that in the incarnation a synthesis occurs, producing a single nature or *hypostasis*. Here the identification of *physis* ("nature") with *hypostasis* (in trinitarian discussion, "person") led to confusion. Severus argued that Christ could not have two *hypostases* ("persons"), which was orthodox, but by it, he meant natures, which was not. Severus' views did not substantially differ from those of Cyril. Essentially he was judged a heretic simply because he resisted Chalcedon. What he taught was not heretical, but what he rejected, the Chalcedonian Creed with its doctrine of the two natures, had become the touchstone of orthodoxy. This first variety of monophysitism was nothing more than a quarrelsome variant of orthodoxy. Its representatives were even willing to concede that the soul of Jesus, like our own, could be ignorant of certain matters; they did not demand its deification.

If monophysitism had not gone beyond Severus, it would at most have been schismatic, but not heretical. His successors, Julian of Halicarnassus and Gaianus of Alexandria, pushed the tendency of monophysitism so far as to say that Jesus must have possessed a glorified nature *from the incarnation*, not merely from the resurrection, as most Christians hold; hence his humanity was always *aphthartos*, "indestructible." To the extent that this is a legitimate inference from the original monophysite premise, it produces a docetic Christ, and indeed this party was derided as "aphthartodocetists." Curiously, Julian did not deny the sufferings of Christ, but asserted that miraculously he willed his flesh to suffer, although by nature it was impassible. Human frailties, such as hunger and thirst, sweat and tears, fatigue and fear were foreign to him. Even the less drastic Monophysites who followed Severus insisted that Jesus did not suffer human experiences through his nature, but only according to his will; true humanity thus seems to have been sacrificed, exactly as was the case with Apollinaris.

c. Influence of the Chalcedonian Formula

Chalcedon combined the credal acceptance of the doctrine of Christ's two natures. Unfortunately, Cyril was praised as impeccably orthodox, but he taught one incarnate nature. This created an antinomy that became the task of later Greek theology to attempt to resolve. The monophysite position assumed that a nature is a *hypostasis*, and concluded accordingly that to acknowledge two natures is to acknowledge two *hypostases*, i.e. *two persons*. Leontius of Byzantium (ca. 485–ca. 543) sought to resolve this problem by distinguishing nature from *hypostasis*. The nature is the common ground that possesses all the different attributes that characterize an individual; the *hypostasis* is his individual, concrete existence. It is synonymous with the *prosopon* ("face," "person"). In the case of Jesus Christ, there is but one *hypostasis;* the natures are united according to their essence, but each preserves its distinctiveness (*idiotes*). The human nature is anhypostatic; it is not a particular human *individual* in addition to the divine Logos, but the humanity receives its *hypostasis* ("individuality") only when united with the Logos. The theology of Leontius, despite his efforts to preserve the human nature of Christ, thus seems ultimately to result in a Logos that has in some way taken on an *impersonal* human nature—again suspiciously reminiscent of Apollinaris.

Imperial politics called for peace in the church; Justin I (ruled 518–27) was greatly influenced by his nephew and successor, Justinian I (ruled 527–65), surnamed the Great, who had a vision of reuniting the empire and throwing back the Germanic tribes. It was really Justinian, not Theodosius or Constantine, who made the church a state church and turned heresy into a crime against the state. (The execution of Servetus in Geneva in 1553, as noted earlier, was in accordance with the Justinian Code promulgated one millennium earlier.) Justinian sought to maintain the authority of the Chalcedonian Creed while permitting it to be interpreted in a way that would satisfy the Monophysites. He was willing to acknowledge the ecclesiastical primacy of Rome,[38] but he sought to limit the actual power of the popes.

The theology of Leontius of Byzantium fostered this accommodation with the Monophysites, but one of them, Peter Fullo of Antioch, went too far. He added these striking words: "Holy God, Holy Strong One, Holy Deathless One, who wast crucified for us, have mercy upon us" to the *Trisagion,* or *Sanctus.* This clearly attributed suffering to one of the Trinity, inasmuch as the *Trisagion,* derived from Isaiah 6:3, was understood as a hymn to the Three in One. In the Controversy of the Three Chapters in 544, Theodore of Mopsuestia was posthumously condemned, together with a letter of Ibas of Edessa and some books of Theodoret, despite the fact that Chalcedon had expressly declared Ibas and Theodoret orthodox. Although Western Christians objected to this posthumous condemnation, the popes vacillated, until Pope Vigilius appeared at the Fifth Ecumenical Council, convened at Constantinople in 553. Vigilius protested it and was promptly disavowed by Justinian; soon afterward, he yielded to the council's reaffirmation of the condemnations of 544. The council went further than Leontius in concessions to the Monophysites, reaffirming the hypostatic unity of the natures, the divine nature of the Logos with an anhypostatic human nature.

d. The Monothelite Position

The external unity Justinian enforced pleased no one; his weaker successors could not maintain it. During this period, theological arguments increasingly gave way to imperial pressure and political intrigue. The apparent concession to the Monophysites, the concept of Christ's anhypostatic (or, we might say, impersonal) human nature, gave rise to new discussions concerning the nature of his will: was it divine or human? Was there but one will? Pope Leo and Chalcedon had recognized two wills; but the doctrine was not officially prescribed. Out of this there arose a new compromise position, that which acknowledged two natures but only *hen thelema,* "one will," in Christ (hence: monothelites). This idea clearly made of Christ a truly personal subject, but it reduced his human nature to something impersonal and lifeless: what became of his agony in the Garden of Gethsemane? The argument against it was the view that if a true nature exists, it must possess all the necessary attributes of human nature; this includes a will as well as a soul. In a sense it is puzzling that the concept of an anhypostatic human nature could arise as an alternative to the Apollinarian view of a body without a rational soul, for it seems so similar. An anhypostatic soul seems a contradiction in terms.

If Leontius of Byzantium is understood correctly, in calling Jesus' human nature "anhypostatic" he merely meant to say that it did not exist at all until it existed in the person of the Incarnate Son. It did not preexist, and thus had no independent *hypostasis* of its own, but when it came into existence, it was complete at once. It is risky to attempt to simplify concepts as difficult as this, but the Monophysites appear to have conceived of a moment or an interval when the divine and the human natures existed separately. The human nature was assumed by the Logos at the incarnation, and then ceased to exist as such, but constituted part of the "one incarnate nature." It would be easier to understand this idea if we were able to suppose that the actual incarnation of the Logos took place sometime after the conception of the human Jesus, so that his humanity, or human nature, could have had a real existence on its own prior to the incarnation. However, the Monophysites agree with both the orthodox and the Nestorians in contending that the incarnation and thus the union of the natures began with the very conception of Jesus. Hence the human nature of Jesus seems to be a mere postulate, no longer in existence from the moment of conception and only existing in theory prior to it. The position of the moderating orthodox, that Jesus had an anhypostatic human nature, seems to be saying, in effect, that Jesus had only a potential humanity prior to the actual incarnation, and that at the incarnation the anhypostatic (potential) human nature became hypostatic (individual and actual) by being united with the divine *hypostasis,* the Logos. This view is close to naive reality inasmuch as it says that the human nature did not become hypostatic, in other words, concretely real, until the conception of Jesus, and that after the conception it was altogether real, even though its *hypostasis* is the *hypostasis* of the Logos.

Most modern readers will find it difficult to conceive of what may have been meant by the concept of an anhypostatic human nature and will be hard put to see how the controversy could have assumed such an importance. Its significance lies in the fact that for Christian theology, the great promise of salvation depends on both the deity and humanity of Christ. Unless he is God, he cannot be capable of redeeming humanity, but unless he is also man, there is no reason why the merit of his work should be applied to humanity. The term *hypostasis* was introduced to grapple with the doctrine of the Trinity. In the Trinity, each *hypostasis,* or divine Person, is fully God; deity itself, or the divine nature, is not another Person alongside of the Father, the Son, and the Holy Spirit. To say that there is a human nature, which is full and complete, possessing all the essential human attributes, including a mind, soul, and will, suggests that there is another, a second *hypostasis* or human person alongside the divine *hypostasis* of the Son that was incarnate in Christ. This suggestion seems to divide Christ into two, one of whom is divine but cannot be man, while the other is man and correspondingly cannot be God. The monophysite and monothelite controversies reveal once again the inherent difficulty of saying more than the limits imposed at Chalcedon allow.

The monophysite and monothelite controversies had major political consequences. During the seventh century, first the Persians, then the Arabs took advantage of monophysite resentment of Constantinople to conquer Egypt and Syria, where Monophysites were numerous and restive. The various imperial attempts to restore unity resulted in temporary reconciliation with the Monophysites. They unnecessarily introduced a new problem into the part of Christendom that still maintained its orthodoxy. In general, the orthodox were accustomed to speak of two energies and two wills in Christ, although the expressions "one energy" and "one will" are also found; the commitment of the monophysite party to one energy and one will rather naturally led their opponents to maintain the contrary. Actually the Greek term *energeia* was used by the theologians of the day not in the sense of "power" or "force," but rather of "effect"; in this sense it is easy to postulate more than one *energeia* in Christ. The question of one or two wills was more difficult; especially since there were many "monothelites" who adhered to Chalcedon and repudiated monophysitism but still held to the doctrine of a single will in Christ.

The monothelite understanding of the will of Christ is clearly a refinement of the earlier Antiochene doctrine of Christ's two natures. All Monophysites were monothelites, but many monothelites accepted the doctrine of the two natures. They attempted to explain it on the basis of their understanding of the meaning of the will. Like the other Chalcedonians, they saw the unity of the work of Christ not in a union of his two natures but rather in the unity of his person, and went on to affirm that this personal unity, concretely, means a single will. A double will would destroy the unity of the person. This charge is similar, of course, to the original attacks by Cyril and his partisans on Nestorius, and to the charges of Eutyches and Dioscurus against the compromise formula of 433. Although the Nestorians and the uncompromising Monophysites were lost to the empire, the legitimate theological concerns of both parties continued to make themselves felt among the remaining orthodox. This resulted in a constantly more refined understanding of the natures and person of Christ. According to the monothelite understanding, neither Jesus' human soul nor his human body ever acted other than on the basis of the will of the Logos. The cry of agony in the Garden of Gethsemane (Matt. 26:42) was not the expression of a disharmony between the human and divine wills in Christ, but rather an expression of the fact that the one Christ was truly suffering anxiety and distress in contemplation of his approaching passion.

If this story is not read as an indication of a conflict between two wills in the one Christ, then it confronts us with evidence for the necessity of the trinitarian doctrine that tells us that the Son and the Father are distinct Persons. The apparent temporary disunity between their wills is quite consistent with the orthodox view that they are in fact distinct Persons. If we had to explain Christ's cry of anguish in terms of conflict between a human and a divine will, the analogy would certainly suggest that Christ consisted of two persons.

The monothelite position represents a significant improvement on the somewhat paradoxical Christology of Leontius of Byzantium; its value lies in its interest in Christ as an active subject, that is, as a real person, and not as a kind of theological receptacle in which divine and human elements combine. But unfortunately, even this refinement of the dyophysite position has the weakness that it seems to rob Christ of his human life. The concept of Jesus' human nature as anhypostatic, which was still vague under Leontius, now takes on the concrete sense of meaning that his human nature lacked a will. "The strength of the monothelites lay in their new and deeper understanding of the *hypostasis* and *anhypostasia*, but their weakness in the inability to carry through the perfection of both natures. Conversely, the strength of orthodoxy was its emphasis on this double perfection and its weakness its lifeless conceptions of *hypostasis, anhypostasia,* and *enhypostasia* [the process by which the anhypostatic human nature takes on a proper *hypostasis,* that of the Logos, in the incarnation]."[39] The orthodox continued to accuse the monothelites of denying the natural ability of human nature; what they seem to have meant is only that the human will was never activated independently of the Logos—and this position is hard to oppose without seeming to split the personality of Christ himself.[40]

e. Maximus the Confessor
and Heraclius

The outstanding theologian of the seventh century, Maximus the Confessor (ca. 580–662), was also the strongest opponent of the monothelite position. His theology has set the tone for later developments in Greek thought. The last great Eastern Roman Emperor to rule something like the eastern half of the older empire, Heraclius (ruled 610–41), was comparable to Justinian I in his energy and ability. Unlike Justinian, he was not challenged by a group of Germanic tribes, but first by the revived Persian monarchy, then by the onrush of Islam, which conquered Damascus in 635, Jerusalem and Antioch in 637, and Alexandria in 642. In 638, after the military debacle was already in process, Heraclius made an attempt to stop the self-destructive feuding of the Christians by issuing his *Ekthesis Pisteos*. Acting on the advice of Patriarch Sergius of Constantinople and Pope Honorius (d. 638), Heraclius forbade all discussion of one or two energies; in a letter to Sergius, Pope Honorius affirmed the doctrine of one will, which he held to be self-evident and beyond controversy. This letter of Honorius earned him condemnation on the part of many of his successors, who branded both the monothelite position and Pope Honorius as heretical. (This became the celebrated *Causa Honorii* [Case of Honorius], used as an argument against papal infallibility in 1870. The official Roman Catholic way of dealing with this apparent exception to papal orthodoxy is to say that Honorius was not speaking *ex cathedra* when he wrote to Sergius.)

In the Christological controversy from the days of Nestorius onward, one can observe a shift of the locus of concern. First Apollinaris and his partisans, later Cyril, and finally the Monophysites, were animated by the desire for doctrinal and theological consistency on the basis of the *homoousion* of the Council of Nicaea. This explains their continued appeal to Athanasius, as well as the forgery that attributed works by Apollinaris, including the famous formulation "one incarnate nature," to Athanasius. Nestorius and the Antiochenes, by contrast, were trying to do justice to the historical, human person of Jesus Christ and not allow the substitution of a doctrine of the incarnation for the person of the incarnate Son.

By the time of the monothelite controversy, however, the roles are reversed. Now the consistent advocates of two wills appear to be motivated by dogmatic and theological concerns, while the monothelites are primarily interested in holding to the historic reality of the person of Christ. The dyothelites, generally speaking, take a creed, or rather a credal formulation, the Chalcedonian doctrine of two natures, as their foundation and starting point. Jesus had two perfect and complete natures; to be perfect and complete, his human nature must also have had an energy and will of its own—

theological consistency demands it, regardless of the possible implications for the tangible, concrete person of Jesus Christ. The concern of the monothelites, as we have seen, was to do justice to the experienced reality of the historical Jesus; they insisted on the *homoousion,* i.e. on his consubstantiality with the Father, but that was for them the dogmatic framework, not the experiential foundation. To define two wills and two energies in Jesus would, in their view, make it necessary to see him as a theological formula rather than as a real, historical person.

If one is to take the monothelite position, what becomes of the apparent resistance of Christ to his impending death during the agony at Gethsemane? Monothelites can point to the fact that according to trinitarian doctrine, the Father and the Son are distinct Persons, and hence potentially can have differing wills. To this the defenders of two wills reply that this supposition destroys the unity of the godhead, as it places the Son at odds with the Father. Maximus proposed that Jesus had a free human will, and that it freely expressed itself, but by virtue of its intimate unity with the Logos, it acted immutably and in harmonious accord with him. He reinterpreted Cyril's reference to a single energy as the attempt to underline the intimate accord between the two energies.

Monothelite theology and its "refutation" by Maximus represent the last, presumably final stages in a centuries-long effort to understand what is meant by the unity of deity and humanity in Christ. Originally the personal unity, the *henosis kath'hypostasin,* was expressed by Cyril as a *henosis physike,* "physical (natural) union"; it was the Creed of Chalcedon that required this unity to be defined in terms of an anhypostatic human nature while the effort continued to be made to regard this anhypostatic human nature, in union with the Logos, as a real, human (and divine) person. The divine *hypostasis* of the Logos took into itself the human will as the organ of its activity.

Hardly a decade after the *Ekthesis* of Heraclius, by which time both Syria and Egypt were in the hands of the Arabs, Maximus had succeeded in persuading Pope Martin I (d. 655) to take action against the decree, and against the similar *Typos* of the Emperor Constans II of 648. Constans treated both the pope and Maximus as traitors, and both died in exile. He himself was assassinated in 668. Changing political circumstances—the loss of the monophysite heartlands to Islam—made his successor, Constantine Pogonatus (ruled 668–85), interested in restoring harmony with Rome, in order not to suffer a similar debacle in the West, where he still held extensive possessions. Constantine summoned the Sixth Ecumenical Council to Constantinople in 680–81, the so-called Trullanum. The new pope, Agatho (ca. 577–681), assumed an importance at the Sixth Ecumenical Council similar to that enjoyed by Leo I, through his legates, at Chalcedon. The pope and the Emperor agreed on the doctrine of the two natures, and not only was the monothelite patriarch of Constantinople anathematized, but the late Pope Honorius was posthumously condemned as well. The monothelite position, although repudiated, continued to survive; the Maronite church of Arab-dominated Lebanon remained monothelite until 1182, when it united with Rome under the pressure of the Crusades.

This Sixth Ecumenical Council represented an end to the conflicts. Nicaea and Chalcedon, despite the categorical nature of their pronouncements, had stirred up as much controversy as they resolved, but the Sixth Ecumenical Council finally signaled the end of an era. As Seeberg comments, it was a necessary consequence of the Creed of Chalcedon. The two basic forms of Christology—the Logos becoming flesh (Apollinaris) and the Logos assuming a particular man (Nestorius)—were finally reconciled, certainly not least by the fact that their several adherents had worked the theories, and themselves as well, to mutual exhaustion. Despite the initial successes of the incarnational idea, reflected in the long reign of the "one incarnate nature" formula, after Chalcedon the doctrine of the perfection of both natures was eventually established. Although Chalcedon took place while Nestorius was still alive and repeated his condemnation as a heretic, we see in retrospect that the aged, exiled patriarch was in essence correct when he saw in the Creed of Chalcedon the vindication of his own deepest concerns. The names of Leontius of Byzantium and Maximus the Confessor mark the beginning and the end of the ancient debate on Chalcedon. Leontius suggested a concept, that of an anhypostatic human nature, that at the time seemed to bring him close to the views of Cyril and even to those of the Monophysites. Maximus preserved the terminology of the hypostatic union, but by it he understood something different and more significant—a real unity of divine and human wills in the one *hypostasis* of Jesus Christ. Thanks to centuries of controversy, the church's doctrine of Christ continued—and continues—to acknowledge his perfect and complete humanity. Over and over again through the Christian centuries, tendencies develop to understand Jesus in what we may call a monophysite, Apollinarian, or even a gnostic sense, and to lose his true humanity. Neither Chalcedon nor the Trullanum can prevent this tendency, which seems to reflect a natural impulse of the human religious sense, but they stand as bulwarks against it and as witnesses to the Christian conviction that the Saviour is one of us—the Son of God is the Son of man.

8. CHRISTOLOGICAL CONCLUSIONS

The Council of Chalcedon, the decisions of which were reaffirmed at the Trullanum of 680–81, gave us the formulation of Christological doctrine we now call orthodox. Why did it take over two centuries for debate to cease on a topic, only to leave us with what was already said in 451? The answer surely lies in this: Chalcedon in reality achieved only what its creed claims—discretion—and no more. The creed calls upon Christians to teach "one and the same Son our Lord Jesus Christ—in two natures, inconfusedly, immutably, indivisibly, inseparably . . . not separated or divided into two persons, but one and the same only begotten Son, God, the Word, the Lord Jesus Christ." This was not so much a program as a limit—the program was to teach one and the same Son in two natures; the limit, to do so without confusion, mixture, division, or separation. This teaching was not the background of Chalcedon, but its future. Chalcedon set the goal and the limits for the teaching that was still to come. By the Sixth Ecumenical Council, two hundred and thirty years later, the teaching had been shaped and much progress made. No substantial additional progress has been made to our own day; renewed attempts, such as the kenotic Christology of the nineteenth century or the secular Christology of recent years, must be seen as regressions rather than progress.

The name of Cyril continues in high honor as a teacher of orthodoxy; the Roman Catholic Church conferred the title of doctor of the church on him only in 1882. Nevertheless, the view he espoused, with its implicit monophysitism, was gradually shouldered aside by the dyophysite view that is so close to that of his condemned opponent, Nestorius. In fact, so thoroughly has the dyophysite view established itself as orthodoxy that the term "dyophysite" is strange and unfamiliar to us and needs to be defined. "Monophysite" is more familiar as the designation of a large, if somewhat isolated, branch of Christendom. The ultimate triumph of the insight of Nestorius and Antiochene theology throughout both the Greek- and Latin-speaking branches of Christendom is the recognition that in Jesus Christ we have a unity of the living God and a living man, not just a theanthropic, or divino-human, nature.

Is it proper to say that at Chalcedon politics created theology? There can be no doubt that political factors played a role, and even a very important one. Yet it must be recognized that the content of the New Testament itself, and the formulation and fixation the doctrine of Christ received at Nicaea and Chalcedon, have their own logic, a logic that moved politicians and their policies as well as theologians and their theories.

It would be wrong to see in this development the victory of Latin thought over Greek, or of Roman politics over those of Constantinople and Alexandria. The monophysite doctrines that were eventually rejected did reflect a typically Greek concern, that for the unity of the created with the Creator, of the human with the divine. But the Antiochene-Roman two-natures view that ultimately triumphed also reflected a Greek concern, that for the historic individual and for the person and his human history. There seems to be no way to deal with the trinitarian and incarnational message of the New Testament without making use of the categories and concepts of the Hellenistic civilization in which the New Testament was proclaimed. Contemporary Christians who advocate a kind of de-Hellenization and re-Semitization of Christianity should be aware of the fact that if this is accomplished, it may be at the expense of the doctrines of the Trinity and the incarnation.

SELECTED BIBLIOGRAPHY

Beck, Hans-Georg. *Kirche und Theologische Literatur in Byzantinischen Reich*. Munich: Beck, 1959.

Bouyer, Louis. *The Spirituality of the New Testament and the Fathers*. London: Burns, 1963.

Burkitt, F. C. *The Religion of the Manichees*. Cambridge: University Press, 1925.

Frend, W. H. C. *The Donatist Church: A Movement of Protest in Roman North Africa*. Oxford: Clarendon, 1952.

————. *The Rise of the Monophysite Movement: Chapters in the History of the Church in the Fifth and Sixth Centuries*. Cambridge: University Press, 1972.

Gray, Patrick T. R. *The Defense of Chalcedon in the East (451–553)*. Leiden: Brill, 1979.

Grillmeier, Alois. *Christ in Christian Tradition; from the Apostolic Age to Chalcedon (451)*. New York: Sheed, 1965.

Grillmeier, Alois, and Heinrich Bacht, eds. *Das Konzil von Chalkedon, Geschichte und Gegenwart*. 3 vols. Würzburg: Echter, 1951–54.

Joseph, John. *Nestorians and Their Muslim Neighbors: A Study of Western Influence on Their Relations*. Princeton: University Press, 1961.

Raven, Charles Earle. *Apollinarianism: An Essay on the Christology of the Early Church*. Cambridge: University Press, 1923.

Richards, Jeffrey. *The Popes and the Papacy in the Early Middle Ages, 476–752*. Boston: Routledge, 1979.

Scott, S. Herbert. *The Eastern Churches and the Papacy*. London: Sheed, 1928.

Smith, John Holland, *The Death of Classical Paganism*. New York: Macmillan, 1976.

Vine, Aubrey Russell. *An Approach to Christology*. London: Independent Press, 1948.

————. *The Nestorian Churches.* London: Independent Press, 1937.

Ward, John William Charles. *Doctors and Councils.* London: Faith Press, 1962.

Willis, Geoffrey Grimshaw. *Saint Augustine and the Donatist Controversy.* London: S.P.C.K., 1950.

11

"MINOR" PROBLEMS: ELECTION, FREE WILL, APOSTASY

. . . I refrained from inserting Pelagius' name in my work, wherein I refuted this book of his; for I still thought that I should render a prompter assistance to the truth if I continued to preserve a friendly relation to him, and so to spare his personal feelings, while at the same time I showed no mercy, as I bound not to show it, to the productions of his pen.

Augustine On the Proceedings of Pelagius *47*

The formula for laying the trinitarian and Christological controversies to rest was spelled out at Chalcedon in 451, although it took two more centuries to accomplish this goal. In fact, it was not actually attained until Syria and Egypt, where Nestorianism and monophysitism were strong, were conquered by the Arabs. The theological consensus concerning the doctrines of the Trinity and the person of Christ persisted with few interruptions until the Reformation era. Then, although the leading Protestant Reformers were loyal to Chalcedon, their insistence on Scripture alone unexpectedly took many of their followers away from the trinitarian and Christological orthodoxy to which the leaders still held.

During the period when trinitarian and Christological conflicts were raging, other controversies also arose, two of which merit special attention: the problem of the *lapsi* ("lapsed," i.e. fallen-away Christians) and the question of predestination, or the freedom of the will. The two questions are related inasmuch as a rigorous doctrine of predestination makes lapsing, or falling away, from the faith appear impossible. Because it was brought upon the church by harsh persecution, the problem of lapsed Christians became a serious concern before there was a predestinarian controversy.

1. FALLING AWAY

Orthodox theology teaches that the Fall of man so corrupted human nature that human beings became unable to save themselves, or even to take steps toward receiving salvation, apart from the free, prevenient grace of God. (The term "prevenient" indicates that the grace is given *before* the individual begins to turn to God.) The same term, *lapsus,* designates both the Fall of Adam and Eve and the fault involved when Christians denied Christ rather than face persecution. The terminology indicates that falling away from Christ was seen as a terribly serious matter.

Christianity was exposed to repeated persecutions during the first two centuries of its existence, but one of the most effective was the intensive, systematic, and well-planned persecution of the Emperor Decius (ruled 249–51), the first competent ruler in forty years. Like the "good Emperor" Marcus Aurelius (ruled 161–80), Decius considered the church a threat to the unity of the empire, and was painfully conscious of the fact that the church was gaining strength as the empire was growing weaker.

Decius determined to strike at the church by hunting down its leaders and confiscating its Scriptures, other spiritual writings, and the materials used in worship. Temporarily suspended under Decius' successor Gallus (ruled 251–53), persecution was resumed with full intensity under Valerian (ruled 253–60). During this bloody decade, unnumbered Christians were put to death; others, such as Origen, were not executed but died as a result of the torture to which they were subjected.

In view of the fact that the persecution was swift and ruthless, and that many communities were promptly deprived of their leaders, it is not surprising that large numbers of Christians lapsed. Some actually renounced Christ or sacrificed to the Roman gods. Others, the so-called *libellatici,* bribed officials to give them a *libellus,* "certificate," stating that they had done so, although they actually had not. Once the severe persecution came to an end, many such fallen Christians were filled with remorse and wanted to be restored to the fellowship of the church. Often they appealed to the confessors to intercede for them; confessors were people who had suffered for the faith without being executed. These confessors enjoyed great moral authority, and often seem to have been generous in forgiving the lapsed—perhaps because they had learned the cost of remaining steadfast.

Cyprian (ca. 200–58), bishop of Carthage ca. 248–58, survived the Decian persecution by judicious flight. On his return, he tried to bring some order to the procedure for readmitting those who had lapsed. He curtailed the authority of the confessors to grant easy readmission, but did permit it under certain conditions. This aroused the ire of rigorists who believed that it should never be possible. Novatian, a Roman presbyter who had distinguished himself by opposition to modalism, led a band of followers out of the "lax" church on the ground that mortal sinners simply could not be readmitted (specifically, apostates, murderers, and adulterers).

Novatian, strictly speaking, was a schismatic (one who separates from the catholic church), not a heretic, but in the fifth century legislation of the Christian empire would list him among the heretics. A more serious schism was that begun by Donatus in North Africa in 311, just before Constantine the Great introduced toleration. Donatus denied that the baptism administered by heretics is valid, even if the correct formula was used, and rebaptized all those he encountered whose initial baptism had been performed by a heretic.

In the late twentieth century, where tolerance, indeed virtual indifference toward varying practices such as baptism, is the rule, it may seem odd that a dispute over rebaptism could so stir up the church that Constantine, after allying himself with Christianity, decided to intervene personally. Constantine, as we know, was vitally concerned with unity and harmony in the church, for he expected the church to help him keep his empire together. The question of baptism or rebaptism may seem a minor disciplinary matter compared to the doctrine of consubstantiality, on behalf of which Constantine also intervened. Without a clear doctrine of the deity of the Son—which is what consubstantiality expressed—Christianity could have broken up into various speculative schools.

The practice of baptism, perhaps surprisingly so, was of similar importance for the unity of the church. If the doctrine of Christ be the spiritual foundation of the church, the practice of baptism is the effective means for bringing individuals into it. If one could not be sure of having been incorporated into Christ by baptism, then the mere fact of his consubstantiality with the Father would do one little good. The real question was whether the baptismal ceremony, correctly performed, guaranteed one's incorporation into the church, or whether its effectiveness depended on the spiritual qualities of the ministrant. An alert believer could verify that a baptism was properly performed; what he could hardly know was the spiritual suitability of the ministrant. The majority of the church rejected the position of Donatus, and a series of emperors put pressure on the Donatist church to submit itself to the main body.

Through the centuries, Christians have tended to flock to those perceived as truly spiritual leaders, and if the church as a whole had accepted the idea that the validity of a sacrament depends on the quality of the ministrant, this situation could soon have become uncontrollable.

The problem of persecution and failure to remain loyal to Christ under persecution provided the rigorists with examples of clergy whose conduct seemed to them to render their ministry suspect and in fact worthless. After the persecution of Valerian, the next great wave of affliction broke over the church during the administration of the ruthless and efficient Diocletian (ruled 284–305); Diocletian is famous for his efforts to streamline the governing of the empire and organize its administration as well as the succession to the throne in a stable, reliable way. One task he set himself was to eliminate the church as an obnoxious, antisocial foreign body in his empire: he looked upon Christians as though they were in fact guilty of the antisocial behavior Tertullian had denied in his *Apology* early in the century. Bishop Mensurius of Carthage (d. 311) and his archdeacon, Caecilian, had sought to keep their flock from coming into conflict with the authorities and had tried to discourage those who eagerly sought to be arrested and martyred. After the death of Mensurius, the rigorists objected to the tolerance being shown to those who had lapsed or who had escaped persecution by bribing officials. Donatus of Casae Nigrae, sent by the bishops of Numidia to mediate, sided with the rigorists and appointed a new bishop, Majorinus. At precisely this point, Constantine had defeated and killed Maxentius (312), and his colleague Licinius defeated and killed the last energetic persecutor of the church, Maximinus Daza (313). Licinius promulgated the so-called Constitution, or Edict, of Milan in his name and that of Constantine in 313. Constantine asked the bishop of Rome, Miltiades, to adjudicate the dispute in Carthage. Miltiades decided in favor of Caecilian, who had been consecrated before Majorinus, but Majorinus and above all Donatus would not accept this verdict and created a schism. Essentially the Donatists taught nothing heretical in our sense, but they refused to acknowledge the idea that the sanctity of the church lies in its integrity as an institution; they insisted that it had to lie in the spiritual excellence of its leaders. Despite pressure on the Donatists by both church and state, they survived in North Africa until the advent of Islam. Their strength, however, was broken at the Disputation of Carthage (411), where Augustine himself was their chief adversary, and successfully demanded that the power of the state be used against them. With the biblical slogan *compelle intrare,* "compel them to come in," wrested out of its context in Luke 14:23, Augustine gave ecclesiastical encouragement to the state in its predilection to use its police powers to create a unified church.[1] The imperial government was strongly inclined to do so in any event, with or without ecclesiastical endorsement, but it is a sad reflection on Augustine, the most eminent theologian of the early church in the Latin West, that he not merely approved such repression but actually called for it.

Augustine's zeal to enforce conformity in spiritual matters may seem strange in the light of the fact that he is the most eloquent spokesman in the West, indeed in the whole early church, for the doctrine of predestination. His quarrel with the British monk and advocate of the freedom of the will

Pelagius (active in Rome ca. 400–20), is far more celebrated—and perhaps more justifiable—than his attacks on the Donatists. But in opposing the Pelagian spirit, Augustine was ultimately less successful than in opposing Donatism. There is no real Donatist tradition running through Christian history, but the Pelagian doctrines of the natural goodness of man and the freedom of the human will have arisen time and again in the history of the church. Despite frequent condemnations by councils and individual leaders, the Pelagian spirit apparently cannot be put down; it really seems to prevail, at least on a popular level and in the less drastic form known as Semi-Pelagianism, throughout much popular Roman Catholicism. A more cautious, Protestant approach to the freedom of the will was put forward after Luther's death by his associate Philip Melanchthon (1497–1560), but it is best known in Protestant circles under the name of Arminianism, after the moderate Dutch Reformed scholar Jacob Arminius (1560–1609). Although most of the leading theologians of Protestantism, at least outside of the Wesleyan tradition, profess to follow the views of Calvin rather than those of Arminius, we shall probably not be wrong if we suggest that most modern-day Protestants, including large numbers who belong to Calvinistic, i.e. predestinarian, churches, are consciously or unconsciously more Pelagian than Augustinian, more Arminian than Calvinistic.

2. PREDESTINATION AND PELAGIUS' DOCTRINE OF FREEDOM

Pelagius, a British monk, was active as a Bible teacher in Rome just prior to the conquest of Rome by Alaric in 410—the stunning event that prompted Augustine to write his *magnum opus* defending the role played by Christianity in history, *The City of God* (413–26). Even more so than was the case with those condemned as heretics in the trinitarian and Christological controversies, the details of Pelagius' life and works have been obscured by the hostility of his opponents. After an apparently uncontroversial early career, he was brought to his final views on the nature of man and human freedom about 399; they were expressed in a commentary on Paul's Epistles written in the first decade of the new century. Although he had already become aware, in Rome, of the hostility and opposition of Augustine's adherents, he fled from Rome to Carthage to avoid the armies of Alaric. Unfortunately he encountered far greater theological adversity in Augustine's North Africa than any adversity Alaric might have brought upon him. After a brief encounter with Augustine himself, he moved to Palestine; reportedly he was banished from Jerusalem after 418; after this he disappears from the historical record.

Pelagius appears to have been motivated by practical piety, i.e. by the zeal to lead a perfect Christian life and to encourage others to do so. Although we have not commented on it, the fourth century not only brought the Christianization of the Roman Empire but also the secularization of the Christian church. The monastic movement, which spread rapidly after its beginnings in Egypt early in the fourth century, was one reaction on the part of serious Christians to the lowering of standards as persecution ended and new converts flocked to the church. Pelagius was concerned to show that it was possible to lead a life of moral responsibility, pleasing to God; at the same time, he denounced the pessimistic, otherworldly dualism of the Manichaean movement to which Augustine was once attached and which he never seems entirely to have outgrown. Pelagius denied that Christ stands in opposition to Moses, or the Gospel against the Law. The difference between the Law and the Gospel lies in the content of the commandments. God gave us only commandments we could obey. All sin is voluntary; Pelagius replaced the concept of original sin with that of the bad example Adam gave to his progeny. He did hold that justification occurs through faith alone, without any human merit or works, at baptism. But baptism alone does not enable one to belong to the true church, which must be a fellowship of those who are attaining moral perfection.

Pelagius' cardinal error, in the eyes of his contemporaries and the church since his day, lay in his understanding of the Fall of man. Denying the doctrine of original sin, Pelagius necessarily changed the meaning of the great and controversial sacrament of baptism. In Pelagius' view, grace is given to all to enable them to know and choose the good; in Augustine's view, no one can choose and love the good apart from the grace of God. Pelagius himself, as we have seen, moved away from North Africa and Augustine not long after his arrival there. He left behind him his associate Caelestius, and another partisan, Julian of Eclanum. Julian carried on the battle from 420, and moved into the realm of the Christological discussion as the result of living for a time with Theodore of Mopsuestia. After insisting on the goodness and freedom of the human will, Julian, adopting the Antiochene conviction that Christ had a complete human nature, also said that he could experience not merely temptation but *concupiscentia*, "inordinate desire"; this seems to anticipate Luther's views on the temptations (*Anfechtungen*) of Christ.

The concept of concupiscence plays an important role in Augustine's theology as well as in the concept of man in Western Christendom. Due to the Fall, man's nature is in disharmony with itself and he desires in an inordinate, excessive way those goods God has prepared for him to enjoy in moderation. This is concupiscence; in Augustine's view, sexual union and the begetting of children inevitably involves such inordinate desire; hence we are all conceived in sin, as the Psalmist says (Ps. 51:5). Thus, even as it directs itself toward its legitimate, God-intended objects, man's fallen will now does so in an inordinate, excessive, and therefore sinful way: not only our deeds but our desires are culpable. It is easy to see why Monophysites and monothelites felt it necessary to deny that Jesus had a human will, for the human will was by definition flawed and culpable. Augustine, of course, did not himself draw a monophysite conclusion from his own understanding of the corrupt nature of man's will but, as noted earlier, held to the Western, dyophysite position.

The dangerous aspect of the Pelagian position for Christology lies in the possible implication that without original sin and a naturally corrupt will, man does not need a Saviour so much as a good example; to be a good example, Jesus ought to have been as much like us as possible, as a man who by his nature is incapable of sinning can hardly be an encouragement to other humans as they struggle to resist something of which they know themselves to be quite capable. The danger to our doctrine of God in this controversy lies in the fact that the alternative to Pelagianism seems to be a kind of rigid determinism that would make the unique God the author of all things by his predestinating will, i.e. the author of sin and evil as well as of good.

3. AUGUSTINE AND THE BONDAGE OF THE WILL

Augustine, like the rest of the church, taught that man in his original state was truly free, but he contended that even unfallen man was endued with divine grace and that it was only thanks to this active grace within him that Adam loved God and could subordinate his senses. The Fall deprived him of this grace, permitting evil desire to rule him. The first man may be said *posse non peccare,* "to have been able not to sin," and in consequence, *posse non mori,* "to have been able not to die," but he could never have been said *non posse peccari,* "not to be able to sin," nor *non posse mori,* "not to be able to die." Man was not created good in himself, but morally neutral; the divine grace that enveloped him like a garment made it possible for him to be good.[2] Nevertheless, despite this possibility, Adam perversely and foolishly abused his free will. He rebelled and disobeyed. In consequence, Adam suffered the penalty that his flesh would no longer submit to his intellect.

Pelagius looked on Adam's disobedience as a transitory bad decision that could be reversed; Augustine saw it as a breach of fellowship with disastrous complications. Adam's guilty deed changed his orientation, destroying his original freedom and making it impossible for him to continue to live without continuing to sin. The Fall of Adam transformed human nature into something perverse and defective. Adam's progeny were all conceived by and born to their father in his condition of condemnation, and hence are subject to the same condemnation; in addition to this taint of Adam's sin, they inherit a flawed nature and themselves commit individual, personal sins, for which they themselves are personally responsible. Because all mankind was in Adam when he fell, the whole human race is a *massa damnationis*, a "mass of damnation"; there are no exceptions, not even newborn children. Augustine referred to the baptism of the newborn, which included exorcism, i.e. the driving out of evil powers, as evidence of the church's belief that children are evil from birth.[3] God permitted sin, originally freely chosen by man, to become his master, so that it is no longer possible for him to live except as its slave. Because of this, the entire human race is totally incapable of attaining a moral standard that would merit salvation. Augustine had an essentially pessimistic view of the state, despite his real appreciation for the glories of what we now call classical civilization. The disordered relationship of appetite and will he called concupiscence is not sinful in itself; it is the penalty for sin. Nevertheless, concupiscence is judged as sin by God to the extent that it produces sin; as it inevitably does produce sin, it is always under condemnation.

a. Original Sin

In discussing the doctrine of original sin, we deal with the "Fall of man." Earlier generations had no difficulty understanding that the English word "man," like the Hebrew *adam*, Greek *anthropos*, and German *Mensch*, is generic, referring to both sexes: "Male and female created he them" (Gen. 1:27). Unfortunately in our own day the word "man" is liable to misinterpretation as "adult male," as though Adam and Eve had not both been involved in the Fall. It would be possible to substitute "human" and "humanity" for "man" (the individual) as well as "man" (the race). But to do so might introduce a different kind of misunderstanding, for the expressions "human" and "humanity" often imply a positive value judgment, as in the term "humane," contrasted with "inhuman" or "inhumane." Readers who have borne with terms such as *hypostasis* and *exinanitio* will certainly be able to make the mental adjustment of reminding themselves that the "man" of whom we speak, in discussing sin and the Fall, is *Adam* as God created him / them, male *and* female (both pronouns, "him" and "them," are used in Gen. 1:27).

Just as he did not create anthropology, the doctrine of man, Augustine did not create hamartiology, the doctrine of sin. As a mortal enemy with which to struggle, sin has always been of central importance to the Christian life. The Messiah was given the name "Jesus" because he was to save his people from their *sins* (Matt. 1:21). As a theological concept, it came to be of central importance largely thanks to Augustine. Augustine's understanding of original sin and its effects came to be the foundation for the Western Christian understanding of man as well as for our view of the work of Christ (soteriology). If original sin is understood as radically corrupting in its influence, then sinful man is hopelessly lost and incapable of contributing to his own salvation: "All our righteousnesses are as filthy rags" (Isa. 64:6). If this is the situation—and Augustine understood it to be so—then the work of salvation Christ must perform has to be a completely free work done on man's behalf, with no contribution by man himself, for his corruption has made him incapable of contributing anything. Throughout the history of the church, Augustine's view has appealed to dogmaticians and theologians, and thus has been the formal position of Roman Catholicism, Lutheranism, and Calvinism. Nevertheless, this doctrine has repelled many, not only among the laity, but a substantial number of theologians as well. Pelagianism, like Nestorianism, retains a heretical sound in the ears of most Christians. Nevertheless, the ideas of Pelagius, Augustine's opponent, like those of Nestorius, are frequently held by Christians who would not recognize his name.

Augustine's understanding of original sin is complex—like the phenomenon of sin itself. Adam, through his inordinate desire, fastened concupiscence on all his descendants. Sin thus becomes not merely an offense that brings a penalty, but part of the penalty itself. Concupiscence is the penalty for Adam's first sin, that of *superbia*, "arrogance" or "pride" (cf. 1 John 2:16). Augustine's somewhat imprecise characterization of concupiscence has left many Christians and non-Christians under the false impression that it consists primarily of sexual desire, and that Christians regard all sexual desire as illicit and sexual intercourse as the original sin.

For Augustine, original sin was intellectual or spiritual—although it quickly led to inordinate desire and has made all human sexuality basically excessive and sinful. If God is viewed as sovereign Will, then an act of disregard for this Will destroys the possibility of fellowship with him. No longer able to commune with God, the highest Good, every individual necessarily turns his desires inordinately toward creatures—other human beings and things—in the vain hope that they can satisfy the longing that the absence of God has left in us. Augustine is not referring primarily to sexual desire when he speaks of concupiscence, but to any disordered or exaggerated desire or appetite. Thus he holds that even infants—whose self-centeredness he observed—display concupiscence. In Augustine's day, baptism was increasingly being administered to infants. In order for it to be able to do for infants what it was supposed to do for adults, i.e. forgive their sins, it was necessary to postulate that infants have sin. Inasmuch as infants cannot make meaningful, deliberate choices and thus cannot commit actual sins, Augustine held that the taint of Adam's sin produces in them disordered and misdirected appetites. These are both the penalty for Adam's sin and sinful in themselves. It is out of this mass of sinful humanity that God freely elects some to receive a totally unmerited salvation. From the perspective of the individual, Augustine's view is readily understandable, for every thoughtful Christian is aware that he has done nothing to merit the mercy and favor of God. From the perspective of our human conception of justice, however, it appears atrocious, as Augustine seems to ascribe guilt to those who never had an alternative to becoming sinners.

b. The Freedom of the Will

Augustine and Pelagius differed radically in their view of the human will. Biblically and theologically Augustine's view that the will is in bondage and disordered and cannot freely choose the good is very persuasive. Morally and emotionally it seems dreadful. For this reason, even when most of their theologians teach the bondage of the will, many Western Christians tend to slide back into a kind of Arminian, if not Pelagian, understanding of freedom. Eastern Christendom, by comparison, never accepted Augustine's emphasis on the primacy of the will. Greek Christianity thinks of man more in terms of intellect and reason, and by "will" it often means little more than a particular act of choice, not a basic element of human nature. From the Greek perspective, an individual can and does make depraved choices, but it is hard to conceive of the will itself as depraved, as Augustine did, unless one were also to hold that each of its choices is predetermined and therefore not really a responsible decision at all. Augustine paradoxically held that the depraved will of man is free enough to make responsible choices and thus to incur guilt, but not free enough to make good choices and thus avoid guilt.

Augustine thinks of God primarily in terms of sovereign Will. Those who follow Augustine in the Western Christian tradition, especially Calvinists, emphasize God's act of election, or predestination. Some even place God's decision to predestinate some to salvation and others to damnation as the very first of his decrees, prior to the decision to create man and to allow him to fall. This appears to say that God creates some simply to be damned eternally. It is extremely difficult to make this doctrine of God and his behavior toward man attractive. Augustine, although a strict predestinarian, does not hold this view, called supralapsarian. He holds that God's decrees of election to glory and reprobation to eternal punishment take place after mankind fell and became a "mass of lostness." Because Creation is the expression of the Will of God, in rebelling against God's will man in a sense destroys his own character and makes himself in a sense unreal. No longer participating in the good reality of Creation, man simply is not capable of doing or being good in any real sense, although he still possesses the limited freedom to make choices between certain alternatives. For Augustine and the majority of the Western Christian tradition that follows him, the doctrine of the Fall of man and original sin is crucially necessary for an adequate understanding of man and of God's way of dealing with him. In Augustine's view, God, who knows all things, knew before creating man that man would fall, and resolved to save some from among the fallen,[4] but Augustine did not explicitly teach the supralapsarian view that God purposed from all eternity to damn some and created them to that end.

c. Grace

Inasmuch as the will of man, cut off from God by sin, inevitably directs itself inordinately toward lesser goods and hence constantly aggravates its guilt, Augustine holds that the will must be transformed before man can desire God. Confronted with the same preaching, some are converted, while others fail to respond. Augustine explains this simply by saying that God imparts to some the ability to choose him: he does not make believers out of those who are unwilling, but he makes unwilling hearts willing.[5] "Grace is precisely the irresistible, creative power of God, which becomes active in the human heart as the power of good."[6] Augustine's attempt to defend the concept of willing choice (if not, strictly speaking, of free will) in the context of irresistible grace has long proved problematic for his spiritual descendants, most of whom take refuge either in the doctrine of the freedom of the will or revert to a concept of total predestination in which man's individual choices as well as his will are predetermined.

d. Predestination

In his doctrine of predestination, Augustine explicitly shunned the effort to tone down its apparent harshness by suggesting that God predestines to salvation those who, according to his foreknowledge, will accept the Gospel. The number of the elect is predetermined; it can neither be diminished nor increased.[7] Under normal circumstances, the elect individual is saved by being called through the ministry of the church and by receiving its sacraments and discipline, but Augustine does not exclude the possibility that

God has predestinated to salvation some who will never come into contact with the church. In addition, he acknowledges that there are some who appear outwardly to be pious Christians, but who in reality are not elect and therefore cannot be saved.

In saving some by grace, God exhibits his mercy. By permitting others to fall prey to their justly merited punishment, he exhibits his justice. His choice cannot be questioned by his creatures. Clearly this neat system hinges on the doctrine that after the Fall, all mankind was lost, so that to the extent that God saves any at all, it is an act of unmerited favor. The question why God chooses some while leaving others to pursue their downward course to destruction is hidden in the mystery of his will. From the perspective of those who believe that they are elect, this doctrine is a way of praising the free grace of God, but for those who do not have such confidence, it continues to appear arbitrary and atrocious.

4. THE CONTINUING CONTROVERSY

In the early fifth century, the church as well as the empire was still relatively united. Pelagius and his friend and supporter Caelestius went from North Africa to the East, where Pelagius ran into difficulties with Jerome (ca. 347–420), the translator of the Latin Vulgate Bible. Pelagius appealed to Pope Zosimus in Rome, who temporarily certified his innocence, but the North African clergy continued to attack him, and the Emperor Honorius exiled Pelagius, Caelestius, and their adherents. Pope Zosimus finally acquiesced in condemning Pelagius. The Pelagian cause was taken up by Julian of Eclanum, who lost his diocese for it in 418. Augustine wrote a long, unfinished work against Julian, who responded by calling Augustine unscholarly, irrational, and a Manichaean. Julian wanted the question decided not by ignorant clergy but by the small community of Christian scholars, one of the first recorded examples of an appeal over the heads of the hierarchy to what later would be called the academic community.

Augustine's positions were approved at a large synod in Carthage in 418, and frequently have been reaffirmed by the Western church. He is the most influential Latin theologian prior to Thomas Aquinas, and both the Lutheran and Calvinist reformations are strongly Augustinian in spirit. Nevertheless, the church and many Christians have found it so hard to live with Augustinianism that over the centuries Pelagian and Semi-Pelagian views continue to reappear. Much of Western Christendom is Augustinian-predestinarian in theory, but Semi-Pelagian, free-will in practice. Eastern Christendom, which did not emphasize the fundamental importance of the will, has been spared much of this controversy.

SELECTED BIBLIOGRAPHY

Altaner, Berthold. *Patrology*. Edinburgh: Nelson, 1960.

Chesnut, Roberta C. *Three Monophysite Christologies; Severus of Antioch, Philoxenus of Mabbug and Jacob of Sarug*. Oxford: University Press, 1976.

Freud, W. H. C. *The Rise of the Monophysite Movement*. Cambridge: University Press, 1972.

Gray, Patrick T. R. *The Defense of Chalcedon in the East (451–553)*. Studies in the History of Christian Thought, Vol. 20. Leiden: Brill, 1979.

Luibheid, Colin. "Theodosius II and Heresy." *Journal of Ecclesiastical History* 16 (1965):13–38.

Ottley, Robert L. *The Doctrine of the Incarnation*, Vol. 2. London: Methuen, 1896.

Polman, Andries Derk Rietema. *The Word of God According to St. Augustine*. Grand Rapids, Mich.: Eerdmans, 1961.

Sellers, Robert Victor. *The Council of Chalcedon: A Historical and Doctrinal Survey*. London: S.P.C.K., 1961.

Wallace, David H. "Heilsgeschichte, Kenosis and Chalcedon." In *Oikonomia: Heilsgeschichte als Thema der Theologie*. Hamburg: Herbert Reich, 1967.

12

IMAGES AND HERESY

. . . those who offered adoration to lifeless images allowed the folly of their predecessors to lead them into the same heresies; they either circumscribed in the image that which is uncircumscribable, or they divided the human nature from the divine, correcting one error by another; in avoiding the irrational they fell into the irrational.

Nicephorus Antirrheticus

One of the most striking features of Old Testament religion was its opposition to every form of idolatry. The Jews were not so totally opposed to all forms of pictorial representation as the Moslems were to be, but they resolutely opposed anything resembling image worship. This was also true of the early Christians, certainly prior to Constantine. Opposition to the worship of images was considered by many pagans to be opposition to religion itself, and was one of the reasons why the early Christians were sometimes accused of atheism. Yet somehow between the third century, when the great Alexandrian theologian Origen polemicized against image worship, and the seventh, when Islam broke out, images came to be an indispensable part of much Christian religious life. Exactly when and how this took place and the reasons it became prevalent remain rather obscure; like the transition from adult baptism to infant baptism as the norm of Christian life, it took place without a great deal of debate and discussion, over a period of many decades.

In retrospect, we first become aware of the great place images had come to take in Christian life with the outbreak of a movement intended to banish them, the iconoclastic reformation of the eighth and ninth centuries. Before iconoclasm flashed across the religious stage, the increasing use of images in the church went largely unrecorded. The controversy aroused fierce passions on both sides, and is very well recorded. When it finally ended with the "triumph of Orthodoxy" (the religious use of images), worship and liturgy in the East had taken on the form they preserve today.

Although Constantine the Great and his immediate successors had managed to hold the shaky Roman Empire together, it suffered a terrible shock after its division between Valentinian I (ruled 364–75) in the West and Valens (ruled 364–78) in the East. Although Valens had received the richer and more important eastern part of the empire, he was unable to resist the invading Visigoths and was defeated and killed by them in 378. The Visigoths moved westward and sacked Rome in 410, a tremendous shock to the whole of the Hellenistic world. By 500, the western half of the old empire had been totally lost to the Germanic tribes, relatively few in the total number of their members, who swept into its choicest lands. The Goths were Arians, and their continued dominance in the West would have given Christianity quite a different shape. The conversion of the Franks to Catholic Christianity in 500, followed by the partial reconquest of the West by Justinian I (ruled 527–65), spelled the end of Arianism as a viable alternative expression of the Christian faith.

What Christendom gained with the conversion of the Franks and the decline of the Arian Goths in the West it was on the point of losing in the old heartland of orthodoxy—Syria, Egypt, and North Africa—with the rise of Islam, the youngest of the world's great religions.

For a brief and terrible time, it seemed as though the victorious forces of Islam might sweep both the rest of the Roman Empire and Christianity itself off the face of the earth. Within a few years of Mohammed's death in 632, Islam had conquered Damascus (635), Jerusalem (638), and Alexandria (642). Temporarily checked at Constantinople during a long siege (674–78), the Arabs began a new wave of conquests, subjugating Carthage in 697 and Spain in 711 before finally being thrown back to the Pyrenees by the Frankish King Charles Martel following his great victory at Tours in 732.

For Western Christendom, the victories of Islam had tremendous importance. The definitive loss of Egypt and Syria deprived Christendom of great human resources and shifted its center of gravity toward the northwest. Christianity became a European religion. Deprived of a large part of its constituency, the Eastern patriarchate at Constantinople began to decline vis-à-vis the papacy at Rome. At the same time, the new religion was a vigorous and dangerous adversary for Christianity, nothing like the mélange of degenerate paganism and religious philosophies with which it had successfully contended during its first centuries. The new creed looked down on Christianity as degenerate and polytheistic in rather the same way the Christians had looked down on late paganism. This confident challenge forced Christianity to produce a new generation of scholars and theologians.

1. THE FIRST ICONOCLAST: LEO III

Constantine the Great, who founded Constantinople, might be called the first "Nicene Father" for his role in establishing the doctrine of consubstantiality. Leo III, who saved the city and the Eastern empire, also tried hard to chart a course for the church. He certainly had a tremendous influence on the shaping of Eastern Orthodoxy, but it was by way of reaction to his efforts, not in acceptance of them.

Leo III (reigned 717–41) came to the throne when Constantinople was being besieged for the second time by the Arabs. He found the church as well as the empire in decline, and was convinced that a profound purification was necessary to save them both from the conquering Moslems. The Isaurian dynasty he founded ruled for most of the eighth century (717–802); it repeatedly rescued Constantinople, and with it the Christian East, from the continuing menace of the Arabs and the new threat of the pagan Bulgars. Leo III, even more thoroughly than Justinian, reformed Roman law and attempted to bring it into full harmony with the Christian religion.

When Leo III came to the throne, the Arabs were preparing to deal a death blow to the Eastern empire. On August 15, the Feast of the Assumption, an Arab army encamped before the land walls of Constantinople; the Arab fleet arrived on September 15. The great Arab naval force was repeatedly buffeted by severe storms and wounded by imperial cutters using the newly developed weapon Greek fire. Weakened by epidemics, the Arabs decided to withdraw exactly a year after they had come, again on the day of the Feast of the Assumption. A violent storm virtually destroyed the departing Arab fleet, thanks, the Christians thought, to the intervention of Mary. This might seem to have been a time for rejoicing and consolidation, but Leo felt that the collapse of much of the empire was due to the disgraceful condition of the church, and he began a vigorous and ultimately ill-fated attempt to remedy it.

2. THE USE OF IMAGES

Origen, we noted, opposed the religious use of images by pagans and rejected the arguments of the pagan philosopher Celsus in their favor with the traditional interpretation of the Second Commandment. Prior to the introduction of images in Christian worship, a kind of cult of relics developed. In the New Testament itself, there is the barest suggestion that Paul's clothing was used in ways later applied to the bodily remains and material belongings of the saints (Acts 19:12), called relics.[1]

For a number of centuries, Christians preferred to represent Jesus by a symbolic figure—the Lamb of God or a stylized Good Shepherd—rather than by a portrayal intended to be a likeness. It was not until 692, only a few years before the outbreak of iconoclasm, that a council in Constantinople decreed that Christ should no longer be represented by a lamb, but portrayed "under his human form."[2]

The use of images in worship and the iconoclastic reaction have Christological implications. For the Jews and the early Christians, all attempts to create a likeness of God were prohibited because God has no visible form. Inasmuch as Jesus Christ was a true man, it would have been natural enough to assume that he could be portrayed, but for centuries this was not done. Not only were there no adequate descriptions of him in the New Testament, there was an evident reluctance to attempt to capture the divine, so to speak, by portraying him in painting or sculpture.

Gradually this reluctance faded, and at the beginning of the eighth century we find images in widespread use in the East; in the West, they were less common and for a long time were used as instructional aids rather than in worship. The willingness to portray Christ was based on the conviction that in him, thanks to the union of the divine and the human in a real, flesh-and-blood person, it was in fact possible to create a holy image, or at least an image of the holy One. A number of images were circulated concerning which the claim of miraculous origin was made. While the artist slept, for example, an angel allegedly completed his work. The celebrated Image of Edessa, first mentioned about 600, was supposedly made directly on a towel by the Saviour's face, rather like the mysterious Shroud of Turin that has aroused such interest in recent years. Spurious texts were introduced, purporting to give a precise description of the Saviour and thus enabling painters to create an accurate portrait. Such images, or icons, were generally intended to show the Saviour in his glorified status, not as he appeared on earth to his disciples. The images, especially those supposedly "not made by hands," *acheiropoietai,* soon came to be said to have miraculous powers. When Constantinople was attacked by the Avars in 626, Patriarch Sergius had icons of Mary painted on all the gates of the land walls.

This use of images struck Moslems as pagan and idolatrous; indeed, it rapidly took on forms even modern Orthodox and Roman Catholic writers decry in harsh terms.[3] From the fifth century onward, there are isolated records of scattered protests by church leaders in East and West. In 599 a Bishop Serenus of Marseille, shocked by the cult of images in his diocese, ordered their destruction. Pope Gregory I (reigned 590–604) wrote him that he was correct to prevent their adoration, but should preserve them as "books for the illiterate."[4] It is apparent that in the sixth and seventh centuries the use of images in worship was far from universally accepted. Nevertheless, it was not the subject of heated controversy until the iconoclastic movement broke out.

3. ICONOCLASTIC MEASURES

The first recorded governmental measure taken against images was a decree by Caliph Yazid II in 723 ordering the destruction of all images in churches, temples, and houses. Supposedly he was persuaded to issue this order by a Palestinian Jew who promised that he would enjoy a long life for this pious deed. In fact, the caliph died the following year.[5] The charge is frequently made that hostility to images was fomented by the Jews, who sometimes took advantage of Moslem rule to inconvenience the Christians who for so long had discriminated against them. The Koran does not prohibit all images but only idols. The first caliphs had their palaces decorated with mosaics in the Byzantine style and even used Roman coins; older coins bore the effigy of the Emperor, and from the time of Justinian II (685–95, first reign), that of Christ. It was during this time that the Arabs finally began to reject all images, not merely those used in worship.

Partisans of images, such as Patriarch Nicephoras of Constantinople (reigned 806–15), sought to attribute iconoclasm to Arab influence, spreading from the border regions of the empire to the capital at Constantinople. At first Germanus, patriarch under Leo III, intervened ineffectually on behalf of the use of images, but the local bishops in Asia Minor began to suppress them.[6] The decisive factor, however, was the attitude of the Emperor himself. After 720 Leo replaced the head of Christ on his coins with that of his son and coemperor Constantine V, later with a simple cross. Leo's zeal was increased by a volcanic eruption, which he took as a sign of God's displeasure at idolatrous worship. He himself destroyed an image of Christ traditionally supposed to have been attached to the bronze gate of the imperial palace by Constantine the Great.

By 730 Leo had decided to replace Patriarch Germanus, who was sympathetic to the icons, with his Imperial Chancellor Anastasius. In the meantime, John of Damascus (ca. 675–ca. 749), the most eminent Orthodox theologian since the Cappadocian Fathers, wrote in defense of the icons from his secure refuge in Arab-ruled Palestine.

a. The Iconoclastic Council of 754

The young Constantine was named coemperor by his father in 720, and reigned as sole Emperor from 741 to 775. He appears to have detested icons even more than his father and indeed more than the iconoclastic theologians.

A number of theological arguments were developed by the iconoclasts, chiefly with respect to portrayals of Christ; inasmuch as his human nature cannot be separated from the divine, any attempt to portray him is an attempt to portray God, which is not permissible. A similar difficulty was seen in the attempts to portray the saints who are with God. The representation of Christ was condemned as Nestorian. To replace the icons, the iconoclasts had recourse to the cross and developed a pattern of devotion centered around it.[7] Constantine himself composed a treatise against images, now lost, but extensively cited by Nicephorus in his *Antirrheticus*. In it, he argued that Christ's divine nature cannot be portrayed, but only his human nature. Therefore all portrayals separate the natures and are heretical. The Emperor went further, and used expressions such as a human *prosopon* instead of *hypostasis* and "of two natures" instead of "in two natures." These make him sound close to monophysitism. The Monophysites themselves had not rejected portrayals of Christ although perhaps, on their own terms, they should have done so. One monophysite theologian, Michael the Syrian, called Constantine V orthodox, by which he meant monophysite. At the same time, Constantine refused to call Mary *theotokos* and limited his praise to the expression *Christotokos,* which had been the battle cry of the Nestorians three centuries earlier. It is apparent that despite his "monophysite" argument, Constantine's iconoclasm was not so much the revival of that classic Christological heresy as a kind of Christian primitivism. His position would have caused no problems among Christians prior to the conversion of his first imperial namesake. He apparently rejected the intercession of the saints, a practice unknown among the early Christians; in this too he was primitive as well as modern.

In 754 Constantine held what he called the Seventh Ecumenical Council—a distinction subsequently denied it by Eastern Orthodoxy and Roman Catholicism. Neither the pope nor the three patriarchs of Alexandria, Antioch, and Jerusalem (who were under Arab rule) attended, and the patriarchate of Constantinople was vacant. The council lasted for seven months, apparently because the assembled bishops had to persuade the Emperor not to insist on the promulgation of his views on the nature of Christ and the veneration of Mary. The acts of the council of 754 have all perished, except for its final decision, recorded in the acts of what is now called the Seventh Ecumenical Council, i.e. that of 787, which temporarily restored the use of images. At the same time that it prohibited the veneration, i.e. the religious use of images, the council also forbade their profanation and destruction. From the council and his newly chosen patriarch, also named Constantine, the Emperor secured the right to designate as heretics the adherents of icons, in particular the deposed patriarch Germanus, Bishop George of Cyprus, and the recently deceased John of Damascus.

b. Persecution

Constantine did not immediately begin to treat his opponents, con-demned by his "Seventh Ecumenical Council," as heretics. The external threats to his empire obliged him to try to preserve domestic peace. Inas-much as the monks were almost all fervent iconodules ("image-servants") as the orthodox party was now called, the institution of monasticism itself came into disfavor with the government. In 761 two monks, Peter of Blach-ernae and Andrew the Calybite, were executed, the latter for having called the Emperor a second Julian the Apostate; in this case, of course, Andrew was guilty of the political offense of lese majesty. Some time after this, a general persecution of the most outspoken iconodules began; including the execution—celebrated by the orthodox as a martyrdom—of the saintly her-mit St. Stephen the Younger at the end of 764. The iconoclastic controversy was the first major controversy within the church to be based on something other than a dispute concerning doctrinal fundamentals; the fact that the doctrines in dispute seemed less than fundamental makes it seem all the stranger that in this controversy, for the first time, Christians were executed by a Christian government for religious reasons. The attachment of the monks to the icons provoked humiliations and violent treatment at the hands of the government. In October 767 Patriarch Constantine himself, despite his adherence to the iconoclastic cause, was decapitated. His head was hung up near his former official residence, and the eunuch Nicetas named patri-arch in his place. In addition to the detested images, the iconoclasts also attacked and destroyed treasured relics, including the body of the martyr St. Euphemia, in whose memorial chapel the Creed of Chalcedon had been drawn up in 451. In 770 the military commandant at Ephesus, Michael La-chanodracon, gathered all the monks and nuns he could find and ordered them to marry. Those who refused to marry were blinded and exiled to Cyprus. In addition, Lachanodracon destroyed monasteries and even churches; the hostility of the military of the embattled empire to the monas-tic system as a drain on resources was evident. Constantine expressed his appreciation to this ferocious commander. The Emperor died in 775, after having commended his soul, according to the chronicler Theophanes, to Mary, the *Theotokos* whom he had fought all his life.[8]

The throne passed to his son Leo IV, surnamed the Khazar because of his mother, the baptized Khazar princess Irene. Influenced by his wife, who subsequently played a macabre role in Byzantine history, and who was also named Irene, Leo IV abandoned the repressive policies of his father vis-à-vis the iconodules. Only one incident of brutal repression of iconodules is recorded from his reign, and that—the public whipping of several court of-ficials—was mild indeed compared to the actions of his father, Constantine

V. Leo had his six-year-old son Constantine crowned as coemperor shortly after his own accession to the throne; his own premature death in 780 left the ten-year-old boy sole Emperor. His mother, the energetic and despotic Irene, assumed the regency and shared the throne.

4. THE RETURN OF THE IMAGES

Irene had already moderated the iconoclastic policy of the imperial government during her husband's reign; now that the minority of her son gave her almost unlimited influence on government policy, she moved quickly to put an end to iconoclasm. The iconoclastic patriarch Paul abdicated, and Irene's former secretary, the layman Tarasius, was elected in a popular assembly. The government's first attempt to hold an ecumenical council to restore the veneration of images, in Constantinople in 786, was disrupted by soldiers loyal to the memory and policies of Constantine V. When she recovered control of the situation, Irene replaced the iconoclastic units with more reliable troops from Thrace and reconvened the council, now called the Seventh Ecumenical Council, in Nicaea in 787. The veneration of images was declared orthodox; iconoclasts who recanted were forgiven and continued in fellowship, despite the hostility of radical monks. The council explained that the veneration *(timetike proskynesis)* accorded the images was to be understood as applying to the saint depicted, and not to the image itself; true worship *(latreia)* was reserved for God alone.

When Constantine reached maturity, his power-hungry mother would not step down. In the conflict that arose between them, the ferocious iconoclastic general and favorite of Constantine V, Michael Lachanodracon, took the son's part. Irene was able to stifle the opposition at first, but the Asian troops supported Constantine and he was proclaimed sole ruler in 790. Constantine combined personal cowardice with cruelty, and soon lost the support of his followers. Additionally, he put away his wife of seven years and married his mistress, arousing the strict monastic party against him. His mother was able to thrust him aside and on August 15, 797, Constantine was blinded in the same Purple Chamber in which he had been born less than thirty years earlier.

5. RESURGENT ICONOCLASM

Irene's cruelty eliminated her son as a rival, but did not protect her from the palace revolution that toppled her in favor of Nicephorus I in 802. His energetic rule was ended by his death in battle in 811, to be succeeded by the ineffectual Michael I Rangabe (ruled 811–13). Michael in turn was deposed by another Leo, Leo V, the Armenian (ruled 813–20), who like

Leo III was from Asia Minor and was hostile to the icons. He convened another council, this time in Constantinople in 815, to do away once more with the images. It ordered their destruction, although it did not call them idols. Leo V did not enjoy the popular support of the first two iconoclastic emperors, and was murdered by adherents of Michael the Amorian, who succeeded him as Michael II (ruled 820–29). A moderate iconoclast, Michael did not persecute the devotees of image worship. He took the outstanding iconoclastic scholar John the Grammarian as tutor for his son and successor Theophilus (ruled 829–42), under whom iconoclasm was to enjoy its last, brief flowering. In 837 John the Grammarian was elevated to the patriarchate; an energetic repression of the iconodules began, characterized by severe measures against the monks.

The tremendous number and power of the monks was a burden to the Byzantine economy and military organization, and was deeply resented in this period, when the military pressure on Byzantium from all sides was so severe. But iconoclasm had lost its popular following and the movement ended with the death of Theophilus in 842. He was succeeded by his infant son Michael III (ruled 842–67); under the regency of Theodora, the widow of Theophilus, the government immediately proceeded to restore the images; John the Grammarian was deposed and a synod in March of 843 solemnly reinstituted the veneration of images.

The brief revival of iconoclasm that ended with the pomp and ceremony of the "triumph of orthodoxy" on March 11, 843, produced what we may call Eastern Orthodoxy, the "church of the Seven Councils." From the point of view of the Eastern churches, the Council of Nicaea in 787 was the seventh and last ecumenical council; those Rome has continued to convene and call ecumenical it holds to be regional synods. The coronation of Charlemagne as Roman Emperor in the West (800), followed by the *filioque* controversy and the Photian schism of 867, destroyed the image—or fiction—of a single, ecumenical empire and a single church catholic that had prevailed from the time of Constantine.

SELECTED BIBLIOGRAPHY

Alexander, Paul Julius. *The Patriarch Nicephorus of Constantinople: Ecclesiastical Policy and Image Worship in the Byzantine Empire.* Oxford: Clarendon, 1958.

Barnard, L. W. *The Graeco-Roman and Oriental Background of the Iconoclastic Controversy.* Leiden: Brill, 1974.

Martin, Edward James. *A History of the Iconoclastic Controversy.* London: S.P.C.K., 1930.

Meyendorff, John. *Byzantine Theology; Historical Trends and Doctrinal Themes.* New York: Fordham University Press, 1974.

Pelikan, Jaroslav. *The Spirit of Eastern Christendom (600–1700).* Vol. 2 of *The Christian Tradition.* Chicago: University Press, 1974.

Sheldon-Williams, I. P. "The Pseudo-Dionysius." In *The Cambridge History of Later Greek and Early Medieval Philosophy.* Cambridge: University Press, 1967.

Taylor, Henry Osborn. *The Medieval Mind: A History of the Development of Thought and Emotion in the Middle Ages.* 2 vols. London: Macmillan, 1911.

13

NEW HERESIES,
NEW PROBLEMS

If the procession of the Spirit from the Father is perfect, and it is, because it is a perfect God who proceeds from a perfect God, what then does the procession from the Son add? If it adds something, it is necessary to state what it adds. . . . This theory is absolutely of no usefulness, neither for the Son, nor for anyone . . . there is no way he can gain from it.

Photius Mystagogia

. . . it is of course possible to say that the Holy Spirit proceeds from the Father and the Son, provided that it is understood that the Spirit does not take his very existence from the Son. But this is, of course, the essence of the controversy between the Greek East and the Latin West.

Richard Haugh

Between the great Christological controversies and the Protestant Reformation there was a long period of relative theological peace. The iconoclastic controversy, fierce as it was, really did not affect major doctrines. At about the same time, in another part of Europe that was in direct contact with the Moslems, a new and yet old thesis was put forward: it is known as Spanish adoptionism. Potentially, adoptionism is a very serious deviation, but in this case, it never gained a large enough following to be dangerous. Twice in this era the Western church debated the meaning of the Holy Communion, and as the conflict was resolved, the nature of the church was dramatically affected. Finally predestination, taught by so many of the greatest theologians, and yet so difficult to accept, emerges once again and is once again covered with euphemisms.

After the iconoclastic controversies, the Eastern church never returned to the use of statues in the round, but raised the flat icon to a place of major

219

importance. The West accepted statues as well as flat pictures, but never accorded them the prominence they had in the East. For this reason there was only moderate interest in the iconoclastic controversy that raged in the East.

During the reign of Leo III, Pope Gregory II (reigned 715–31) maintained political loyalty to the Emperor, but refused to accept his iconoclastic regulations. In retaliation, Leo removed Thessalonica, Sicily, and the portion of Italy remaining under his control from papal jurisdiction. This was painful, but not particularly effective, as the advance of the Franks in Italy was rapidly undermining the authority of the Eastern Emperor (whose realm, at this date, authorities call Byzantine, although it still called itself Roman). The greatest symbolic break, however, came when Constantinople was once again under the control of the image worshipers, led by the cruel Empress Irene. Charlemagne (King of the Franks 768–814) was crowned Emperor in Rome on Christmas Day, 800, by Pope Leo III (reigned 795–816). From that date on, two Roman Empires existed—that of the Greek-speaking basileus in Constantinople, and that of the Germanic kaiser of what came to be called the Holy Roman Empire of the German nation. The Byzantine Empire in Constantinople endured until it was finally destroyed by the Turks in 1453. The Holy Roman Empire was ended by Napoleon in 1806, and its last ruler became the Emperor of Austria.

The iconoclastic controversy played a small part in the crowning of the King of the Franks as Roman Emperor, as it helped to push the papacy into throwing off its nominal loyalty to the other Emperor in Constantinople. During the last years of the eighth century, ecclesiastical authority in the West was centered at Rome, but much of the theological activity followed the political power to Aachen, Charlemagne's capital, and to other Frankish towns. The papacy objected to the claims of the Eastern Emperor and the Greek-speaking patriarch of Constantinople to legislate for the Western church. Although Pope Hadrian I (reigned 772–95) did agree to the holding of the Seventh Ecumenical Council in Nicaea in 787, he was pleased to have Charlemagne summon a new one in Frankfort on the Main in 794. Not only did Charlemagne's council place limits on the use of images, it also was forced to take notice of the fact that a number of Western dioceses were using a revised version of the great ecumenical creed of 381. This was the famous addition of the expression *filioque,* "and from the Son," already mentioned earlier.

At a synod of Toledo in 589, King Recared of the Visigoths abandoned Arianism and embraced the catholicism of the Nicene Creed. In order to make it abundantly clear that the Son is coequal with the Father, the *filioque* was added:

. . . and in the Holy Spirit, the Lord and giver of life, who proceeds from the Father *and the Son,* who together with the Father and the Son is worshipped and glorified.

This insertion certainly stresses the consubstantiality of the Son with the Father, but it also seems to place the Holy Spirit in an inferior position, or so Greek-speaking Christians would object. Eventually it became standard throughout the Western church, and was to be adopted by Protestants as well during the Reformation era. Thus the Nicene Creed, instead of uniting Christendom, now exists in two different forms and frequently is a bone of contention. Since the flowering of the ecumenical movement, a number of Western churches have taken to using the Eastern form, at least occasionally. In addition to the theological objection, the East found fault with any addition to an ecumenical creed. Like the "one incarnate nature" formula of Apollinaris, the *filioque* became a fiercely disputed slogan despite the fact that no one on either side of the controversy could satisfactorily explain its implications.

1. THE FILIOQUE:
"AND FROM THE SON"

The addition of the expression *filioque,* "and from the Son," to the Niceno-Constantinopolitan ecumenical creed was seen in the West as the perfectly appropriate final touch to the Nicene doctrine of consubstantiality. Nicaea had authorized the terminology "consubstantial with the Father" to refute beyond all question the Arian contention that the Son is a created being inferior in nature to the Father. The addition of the *filioque* took place in a second round of confrontation on the Arian issue, this time with the Visigoths, who had originally been converted to Christianity when Arianism was in favor at Constantinople. As obscure and difficult to prove theologically as the *filioque* may be, the importance both West and East attached to it reveals how significant the question of the deity of the Son is (and remains). The New Testament is explicit in saying that the Holy Spirit "proceedeth from the Father" (John 15:26). The logic behind the Western addition, "and from the Son" is an inference from statements such as this: "The Holy Ghost, whom the Father will send in my name . . ." (John 14:26) and "God hath sent forth the Spirit of his Son" (Gal. 4:6). It was also seen as a logical consequence of the doctrine of consubstantiality, one that emphasized the full identity of nature between the Father and the Son. Theologians in the East feared that the new definition blurred the distinction between the

Father and the Son and did not show sufficient concern for the deity of the
Holy Spirit.

Political conflicts and ecclesiastical power struggles greatly exacerbated
the tension over the *filioque*. It even appears that the Byzantine Patriarch
Photius seized upon it as a pretext to justify his quarrel with Pope Nicholas
I. Nevertheless, there was theological substance to his objection to it. (As a
matter of fact, some churches in the modern West have become uneasy with
it, and there are signs that some Westerners wish to return to the older
Nicene formula.)

If the Holy Spirit proceeds only from the Father, the Western Church
came to argue, then the Son cannot be said to be truly consubstantial with
him, for the sending forth of the Spirit is an act that pertains to the divine
essence, or substance. Not so, the opponents argued, for spiration-proces-
sion is a *personal* act, one that distinguishes the Persons of the Trinity from
one another and creates the distinctly Christian doctrine of the Trinity, the
Three who are distinctive and individual as Persons and yet are one God.
To attribute the procession to the Son as well as to the Father would destroy
its distinctiveness as a personal act and at the same time diminish or destroy
the distinctiveness of the Son vis-à-vis the Father.

Of course there was no satisfactory way to resolve this problem, inasmuch as both the creed with the *filioque* and the creed without it speak more
explicitly of the Persons of the Trinity than does the Bible itself, on which
they are based. Many centuries later, shortly before the fall of Constantinople, the Greek church was to be pressured into accepting the *filioque,* but its
legates were disavowed on their return to the beleaguered capital.

The question of the *filioque,* we recall, arose in order to make it abundantly clear to the newly converted Arians of Spain that the Son is equal to
the Father. Even so, it failed, for Spain produced a new variety of the old
heresy, adoptionism.

2. SPANISH ADOPTIONISM

Although the *filioque* guaranteed that Spain's Arians had fully returned
to catholic orthodoxy, it could not protect them against the onslaught of
Islam. Smoldering theological conflicts with Constantinople certainly facilitated the Arab conquest of Syria and Egypt. North Africa had been Arian
under the Vandals before Justinian's forces reconquered it, and the Arian
Vandals were neither ethnically nor religiously sympathetic to the rule of
the orthodox Roman Emperor in the East. In Spain, the Visigoths had not
been long restored to orthodoxy when the wave of Islamic conquest overwhelmed them as well.

For three quarters of a century, all of the Spanish peninsula was ruled by Moslems under the Omayyad dynasty in faraway Damascus. When the Abbasids supplanted them in 750, the Omayyads found a refuge at Cordova in Moslem Spain. With some assistance from the Franks, the Christians succeeded in liberating an enclave in the northwestern corner of the peninsula. In the rest of Spain, the bulk of the population remained Christian, but under Moslem rule was cut off from the rest of the Christian world. The Spanish church with its archbishopric at Toledo was virtually autonomous from the time of the Arab conquest.

Pope Hadrian I (reigned 772–95) tried to end this Spanish autonomy as well as to bring to Spain some of the necessary reforms that had been initiated by Boniface in the territories of Charlemagne. There was apparently much that needed reformation in the Spanish church, but Hadrian's legate, Bishop Egila, attempted to do too much at once. In particular, his associate Migetius immediately launched a campaign to reform the morals of the Spanish church. He promptly aroused the opposition of the archbishop of Toledo, Elipandus, who accused Migetius of teaching that the Trinity is composed of three bodily persons, the Father being David, the Son, Jesus, and the Holy Spirit, Paul. It is possible that these charges are exaggerations of something Migetius actually did say, namely, that Jesus is one of the Persons of the Trinity. Such a formulation, like the expressions *theotokos* and "Mother of God," is theologically defensible as a consequence of the communication of characteristics between the divine and human natures in Christ, but it is even more capable of creating vast confusion.

The Spanish Christians whom Migetius sought to influence had retained an affinity for the conservative Latin description of the Incarnate Christ as *assumptus homo*, a "man assumed (taken on) by the Logos." The Mozarabic liturgy used in the Spanish church accordingly spoke of the *adoption* of the concrete human nature by the divine Word. This terminology suggests that in Spain, at the other end of the former Roman Empire, there may have been traces of the discredited emphasis of the Nestorianism of Antioch.

Elipandus produced a confession of faith at Seville in 784. It is perfectly orthodox with respect to the Trinity, but it distinguishes the human nature from the divine in Christ in a way reminiscent of Nestorianism. The son of Mary, taken up by the Word, is not the Son of God by nature, but only by adoption. Elipandus' views immediately caused a vigorous response on the part of two men, Beatus and Etherius, who charged him with heresy. The actual content of Elipandus' Christological views and the question of whether they really constituted adoptionism or simply an imprudent recourse to archaic language can no longer be determined, for his views are available only in the intemperate diatribes of his opponents. They appealed to Pope Hadrian, who seized the opportunity to assert his claim to jurisdiction over Toledo. In an effort to maintain himself against the pope, Elipandus sought allies in the part of Spain under Frankish control, bringing the controversy into the purview of Charlemagne and ultimately of the Council of Frankfort on the Main. His first ally, Bishop Felix of Urgel, was summoned by Charlemagne to Regensburg and there was persuaded to renounce the expression "adoptive son of God." Following this relatively civil treatment, he was transported to Rome, where he was abused by the pope and forced into a humiliating public recantation before making his way back to Arab-ruled territory in Spain.

a. The Theological Issue

As is so often the case in these theological controversies, the conflict seems to have been sparked by a linguistic misunderstanding, or, more specifically, by one party drawing exaggerated implications from a legitimate formulation. The traditional articles of belief refer to the Logos as having assumed a human nature, or "humanity." If the abstract noun "humanity" is rendered in the concrete as "a man"—which the older theological tradition found quite acceptable—then in the incarnation the Word can indeed be said to have assumed a man. The Spanish theologians found in Scripture many references suggesting a double sonship, the eternal sonship of the Logos and the temporal sonship of Jesus, which began with the incarnation. They appealed to one text, supposedly by Jerome (actually by Pacianus of Barcelona), and to another by Isidore of Seville, speaking of "the adoption of flesh by the Word," and "the man adopted by God." To defend their position, the Spanish introduced, probably without knowing their origin, some of the most objectionable formulas of the Christology of Antioch, distinguishing between the Son of God, i.e. the Word, and the son of David—the man.

News of the attitude of the Spanish Christians—whom he hoped eventually to bring under his rule—encouraged Charlemagne to project a Western council to combat their errors as well as to reply to the iconoclastic and countericonoclastic councils of the East. He convened a council in Frankfort on the Main in 794, the first major doctrinal council to be set up on terms prescribed by the bishop of Rome in opposition to a council convened by the Emperor in the East. Hadrian prepared a letter intended for the Spanish bishops, but sent first to the Frankish court. It served as a kind of order of procedure for the Council of Frankfort on the Main when it met.[1] The West was clearly taking its theological direction from Rome. The westward shift of the center of gravity of Christendom placed Constantinople and its intrigues on the periphery; the popes had long been in a position to influence councils in the West, but Frankfort was the first time when their ability to set the agenda for a Western council meant their church-wide leadership.

The Spanish quarrel was resolved as the pope desired; expressions that had been orthodox enough when uttered by Augustine were declared heterodox. The theologian who took up the papal cause and the demand for a terminology more precise than that of Augustine was himself an Augustinian: the court theologian of Charlemagne, the Anglo-Saxon Alcuin (ca. 735–804). Alcuin attempted an approach to Bishop Felix, by now back in Urgel, urging him in diplomatic and polite tones to drop the offensive expression "adoption." Felix replied with a long treatise, accusing his earlier Spanish opponents, Beatus and Etherius, of monophysitism.[2] Unfortunately he designated Jesus Christ as *Deus nuncipativus*, "God by appellation," which rendered his adoptionistic thesis even more objectionable than it had been at first. Felix' tome went to Charlemagne, who submitted it to Alcuin; Alcuin in turn remitted it to three other authorities, Paulinus of Aquilea, Richibod of Trier, and Theodulf of Orléans. In 798 Pope Leo III, who had succeeded Hadrian in 795, held a small council in Rome and condemned the "heresies and blasphemies of Felix." Alcuin's approach was more charitable: summoned to Aachen along with Felix in 800, he was able to persuade Felix to accept an orthodox confession of faith; supposedly, a text of Cyril of Alexandria supplied the final argument. Thus three centuries after his death, the Alexandrian patriarch was still combating Nestorianism. Harnack comments on Alcuin's use of Cyril, "It is interesting to observe how this Anglo-Saxon, Bede's pupil, is entirely dependent on the Greeks in Christology and has here abandoned the Augustinian tradition."[3] Harnack goes on polemically to accuse Alcuin of having wiped out the Gospel accounts of the man Jesus Christ and of destroying his human person. This one-sided "divinization" then led to the second of the minor controversies, because it deflected the interest of believers from the moral and spiritual influence of Christ and from the life of faith and turned it to mystical participation in the deity of Christ via the sacrament of communion, the eucharist. Beatus had introduced the realistic understanding of the eucharist as an argument against adoptionism.

Thus adoptionism was again defeated, but it will reappear as a theological hypothesis again in the eleventh and twelfth centuries. Indeed, from the time of Elipandus on, the church has never been without its adoptionists. In this short-lived Spanish adoptionism there was a significant difference, for it was the consubstantial Son, truly God, who adopted the man; in other words, it was adoptionism on a trinitarian basis. It was more of an offense against Chalcedon than against Nicaea. Modern adoptionism, a widespread view in liberal Christianity, is usually uninterested in the Trinity and represents a reversion to the more familiar third-century variety, in which Jesus was a special man adopted by God.

b. The Aftermath

The unfortunate Felix of Urgel, despite his profession of orthodoxy and the universal esteem in which he was held because of his piety and learning, was not permitted to return to his see. After having been influenced by Archbishop Leidrade of Lyon to accompany him to Charlemagne's capital of Aachen, where Alcuin persuaded him to renounce his adoptionistic formulations, Felix found himself placed permanently under Leidrade's supervision; he had to return with him to Lyons, where he lived until his death in 815. After Felix' death, Leidrade's successor, Agobard, found manuscripts among his papers that persuaded him that the bishop had relapsed into his former errors and that he thought worthy of posthumous refutation. Another partisan and friend of Alcuin, Benedict of Aniane, also produced a refutation of Felix' views.[4]

As metropolitan of Moorish-ruled Toledo, Elipandus did not need to fear either the Roman pope or the Frankish King. His church retained its independence under the Moslems, developed a liturgy of its own, and quite likely persisted in following a number of heretical tendencies. As Spain was reconquered by the Christians, the Inquisition—especially vigorous in its Spanish branch—claimed to have discovered heresies of all kinds among those who had been under Moslem rule. For the time being, however, both Rome and the Franks had to leave the Christians in occupied Spain to be adoptionists if they chose.

Adoptionism raised once again the Christological questions that supposedly were settled at Chalcedon, even though it did so on a small scale. The necessity of having to deal with the heresy of adoptionism spurred theologians among the Germanic Franks to an intense level of activity and thus contributed to what is known as the Carolingian Renaissance.

c. The Filioque in the East

The Council of Toledo not only added the *filioque* to the Nicene Creed but also explicitly required that it be used in the eucharistic liturgy. This practice spread to Frankish-ruled Gaul, but it remained unknown at Rome itself until well into the eighth century. Its spread into all the churches of Latin-speaking Christendom is evidence of the influence of Charlemagne and his Frankish theologians.

The coronation of Charlemagne as Emperor was a shocking challenge to the authority of Constantinople. His political power had been successfully challenged by Germanic invaders, then sharply cut by the Moslems, but the basileus at Constantinople still considered himself the titular ruler of the Christian world. Even before Charlemagne's coronation, the Empress Irene was aware of the challenge he posed to her own majestic claims. The *filioque* question was not yet a matter of great concern to the popes, but in 787 it arose in the context of the Empress's great Seventh Ecumenical Council. Patriarch Tarasius solemnly read the traditional form of the Nicene Creed, which has no reference to the *filioque*. Frankish theologians noted this "error" and criticized it in the *Libri Carolini*. Pope Hadrian supported the Greek usage, but in the meantime Charlemagne attacked the Byzantine possessions in Italy. In an effort to secure Arab help against the Greeks, Charlemagne sent an embassy to Baghdad. Returning, it was accompanied by the abbot of the Latin monastery on the Mount of Olives. On returning to Palestine, Abbot George introduced the *filioque* into the liturgy, and was immediately criticized by the Greek-speaking monks at the nearby monastery of St. Sabbas. Thus a doctrinal argument that later formed the pretext for the schism between Eastern Orthodoxy and Roman Catholicism began as a quarrel about liturgical changes between two groups of monks in Arab-controlled Palestine.

Charlemagne briefly flirted with the thought of marrying the Empress and reuniting the two empires, but nothing came of this proposal, and she was deposed by a coup in 802. In 809 a synod at Aachen ordered the *filioque* to be added to the creed, but the papacy, still mindful of the sensitivities of the Greeks, refused to so do. Half a century later, when the brilliant Eastern Patriarch Photius quarreled with Pope Nicholas I (reigned 858–67), the *filioque* had been added in Rome as well; we are not sure exactly when.

d. Images in the West

It looks almost as though the *filioque* controversy was artificially created by the Franks as part of their claim to be the restored, Christian Roman Empire in the West. Photius picked it up and made it part of his long struggle against the papacy. In addition to challenging the Greeks on this fine theological point, the Franks also objected both to their iconoclasm and then to the way in which they restored the images.

In 787 the Council of Nicaea authorized veneration (the inclination of honor) for images, but denied them *latreia* (*adoratio,* or "worship"). This distinction was lost on the Council of Frankfort, which condemned the "service and adoration" of images allowed at Nicaea. The Western church attempted to follow the maxim laid down by Pope Gregory I almost two centuries earlier: "For this reason pictures are placed in the churches, so that those who are illiterate may read, beholding on the walls, what they cannot read in books."[5] Both Byzantine councils, the iconoclastic council of 754 that condemned images and the iconodule council of 787, were condemned at Frankfort as "infamous" and "inept." For a number of decades Charlemagne and his successors attempted to limit the use of religious images to instruction rather than permit their worship, but ultimately the religious use became general in the West as in the East.

Although the Frankish church may appear to have been progressive in its rejection of image worship, Harnack considered it reactionary because it rejected the adoptionistic proposals of the Spanish. He considered the Christology of the Frankish church to be implicitly monophysite—emphasizing the divine nature of the incarnate Christ. With this idea in the background, the Frankish theologians concluded that Jesus' body also possesses the attributes of deity—such as the ability to be in many places, even on a thousand altars, at one time.[6] The stage was set for the great eucharistic controversies.

3. THE EUCHARISTIC CONTROVERSY

It is very difficult to sort out the tangle of theological controversies that affected the Western church during the eighth and ninth centuries. Adoptionism tended to downgrade the deity of Christ, and it arose on the same soil as the *filioque,* which exalts it. The Western church, which insisted on the *filioque,* at first opposed the realistic theology of images of the East, but subsequently adopted a highly realistic eucharistic theology. The *filioque* position, which won out in the West, was based on Augustinian teaching, but so was the adoptionist position, which was rejected. Augustine's doctrine of predestination was officially reaffirmed, while in practice it tended to be disregarded, but his views were defeated in the eucharistic controversy.

Before the throes of the iconoclastic controversy had subsided in the East, the first great eucharistic controversy broke out in the Frankish West. Both controversies were motivated by the conflict between the popular desire to have something tangible and visible to venerate and the theological conviction that true worship must be spiritual. Both the veneration of icons in the East and the developing eucharistic piety in the West set Christianity off from Islam, which emphasized the transcendence and spirituality of God and rejected Christian forms of piety as gross and idolatrous.

By accepting the veneration of images (only flat icons in the East, statues as well in the West), Christianity may appear to have moved far away from its roots in Jewish monotheism. Christians renumbered the Jewish Decalogue, integrating the prohibition of image worship into the First Commandment instead of giving it a place of its own, as done by Jews and later by Protestant Christians. An even more striking transformation of the form and spirit of Christian worship came with the new eucharistic piety. Both the veneration of images and the new eucharistic piety center the attention of the worshiper on objects that are really present to the senses—images in one case, the eucharistic bread and wine in the other—and seem to draw the attention away from verbal revelation and faith.

According to one French Roman Catholic historian, "The birth, the prolongation, and the occasional bitterness of these quarrels proves that the Occident has emerged from its ancient torpor," and designates the eucharistic controversy as "relatively benign."[7] From a Protestant perspective, the eucharistic controversy is bound to appear as an important stage in the transformation of the Christian faith that ultimately made the Reformation necessary. The controversy was sparked by a Frankish monk, Paschasius Radbertus (d. ca. 860), strongly influenced by Augustine. In 831 he published *On the Body and Blood of the Lord,* the first complete treatment of the eucharist.

The significant feature of Radbertus' book is the fact that he teaches the *corporeal,* or "bodily," presence of Christ during the eucharist. All Christians accepted, in one form or another, the real presence of Christ at his own table, the Lord's Supper, but for centuries no significant effort was made to explain how this is possible. The school of Augustine stressed the real presence of Christ as a mystery. Radbertus sought to explain it in realistic terms: the bread becomes the body, which is then really present.

During the first centuries of Christianity, the communion was a fellowship meal. In order to receive its spiritual blessings, it was necessary for believers to take part, i.e. to receive the bread and wine. It was also spoken of as a sacrifice or as the commemoration of a sacrifice, without further definition. The introduction of the idea of Christ's *bodily* presence made it possible to think of each eucharist as a new sacrifice rather than as a mere commemoration.

In order to be bodily present at thousands of altars, the body of Christ must possess one of the so-called attributes of majesty of God, namely, omnipresence, or ubiquity. To say this is to say that the body of Christ is or has become divine, and this is reminiscent of Apollinaris and the Monophysites: "one incarnate nature." To stress the bodily presence of Christ appears to give believers tangible physical access to him. Where earlier Christians had stressed union with Christ by faith, and by it had meant faith *in him,* the newer view stressed a sacramental union. Faith was still required, but it was not so much the faith of the individual as the faith of the church, which presented Christ to the communicant. The doctrine of the real, corporeal presence of course raised the question whether the body of Christ is there for unbelievers. Can they actually chew him? Is there a *manducatio impiorum,* "devouring by the unbelievers"? Radbertus denied it, but it is implied in his doctrine of the bodily presence, and later became a test of eucharistic orthodoxy.

Radbertus begins his analysis of the sacrament in typical Augustinian fashion: the body of Christ is really present, but only to faith; unbelievers partake of the sacrament—unworthily, of course—but not of Christ and his saving power; for them the sacrament becomes a judgment of damnation. Thus far even John Calvin could follow him. But in addition Radbertus picks up an old element of Greek piety, the conviction that the sacrament nourishes both soul and body for eternal life; it is the so-called medicine of immortality. His Greek precursors, Cyril of Alexandria and John of Damascus, indeed also taught the bodily presence of Christ in the eucharist, but the materialistic implications of this view were mitigated by the fact that they considered Christ's postresurrection body to be spiritual, and left the nature of the miracle of his bodily presence in the eucharist in the realm of mystery. Radbertus for the first time clearly stated that the eucharistic body is the body born of Mary: it becomes present in the eucharist by an act of creation, as he puts it more frequently, of transformation; of the elements of bread and wine, only the appearances remain.

Radbertus explains the persistence of the appearance by saying that a visible transformation is unnecessary and would be offensive. Inconsistently though, like many other writers he also reports incidents in which a lamb appeared or drops of blood were seen at the eucharistic meal. Visible changes could and sometimes did occur. Although the elements really are transformed, only faith can actually eat or feed upon the body of Christ. Radbertus wants to assure his readers that the bodily substance of the Lord is there to nourish them, but he is unwilling to let unbelievers take advantage of it. He then calls the physical appearance of the elements, which is not changed, the symbol of the Christ who is present. With this somewhat abrupt change of direction, Radbertus moved back once again onto Augustinian terrain. The fundamental ambivalence of a position that on the one hand asserts a real transformation while on the other speaks of a symbolic representation was not slow to attract the notice of other theologians. Two reactions were possible: reaffirmation of the symbolic nature of the sacraments, or insistence on the bodily presence of Christ.

Hrabanus Maurus, the "Praeceptor Germaniae," abbot of Fulda (ca. 776–856), took up the first alternative. Apparently referring to Radbertus, although not by name, Hrabanus Maurus denounced the grossly materialistic views of "those who say that the sacrament of the altar is truly the body of Christ"; to receive Christ, he asserted, is to be united with him by faith, to form one body with him. Similar statements will occur later in Calvin and Thomas Cranmer. He seems, in effect, not merely to give up the corporeal presence, on which Radbertus insisted, but also to be in danger of turning the sacrament into nothing but an expression of the communicant's faith.

The battle was also joined by another committed Augustinian, the monk Gottschalk (d. 868). Gottschalk was confined to a monastery at Hautvillers for his radically Augustinian emphasis on predestination, and will receive more attention in a later section. He affirmed that the eucharistic body is really the body and blood of Christ, thus going far beyond Hrabanus' symbolic view, but he denied that the communion in any sense represents a repetition of the sacrifice of Christ. In Paschasius Radbertus, Gottschalk, and Hrabanus Maurus we have an anticipation of the eucharistic controversy of the Reformation era. Radbertus, like the sixteenth-century Catholics, insisted on the bodily presence and mystical sacrifice of Christ at the altar. Gottschalk, like Luther, accepted the bodily presence, but denied that it could be used for any purpose other than that for which it was intended, the communion of the faithful. Hrabanus, like Zwingli, appears to reduce the presence of Christ to nothing but an act of faith.

Radbertus was opposed by a monk from his own monastery of Corbie, Ratramnus. Commissioned by King Charles the Bald to evaluate the work of his abbot, Radbertus, Ratramnus did so in a brief treatise, *On the Body and Blood of Christ.* He opposed Radbertus' miraculous view, in which the eucharistic presence is clearly called a mystery "against nature." He acknowledged that Christ is present, but "in a mystery." At issue was Radbertus' contention that the consecrated elements are identical with the body of Christ born of Mary. Ratramnus denied this, but asserted that believers do receive the body of Christ, for by faith one receives not what one sees, but what one believes. What was distinctive was his insistence on the necessity of faith in order to obtain the benefit of the eucharist. In this, apart from a difference of emphasis, he agreed with Radbertus. Where they differed was in what Ratramnus opposed, namely, the idea that the eucharist involves a nature miracle, in which one substantial reality, that of bread and wine, is transformed into another. Radbertus, and with him the majority party, found the concept of receiving the benefits of Christ's body and blood "by faith" too weak and not tangible enough, and insisted on the nature miracle.

What seems to be at stake here—as again in the eucharistic controversy of the sixteenth century—is confusion among the contenders as to what is meant by "real" and "by faith." Radbertus cannot conceive of a real presence that is not corporeal, i.e. bodily. In order to be really present, Christ must be bodily present, and that in the body that was born of Mary. Inasmuch as the bread and wine continue to look and taste like bread and wine, Radbertus contends that a real but invisible transformation has taken place. Faith is still required, specifically, faith in the assertion that such an invisible transformation has occurred. Ratramnus concentrates his faith not on the change, but on Christ's promise. The Christian must have faith that Christ is really present, and that he can feed on him and be nourished by him, but he does not have to believe in any specific miracle of transformation. The difference between what the two believed takes place was not great, but the difference in the way they explained it was substantial. Ratramnus was a true spiritual descendent of Augustine, and placed primary importance on the faith by which the spiritual realities and benefits were received; Radbertus, although he too began with Augustine, consciously redirected the emphasis of eucharistic doctrine from faith in the words spoken by Christ to faith in a corporeal reality, namely, that of the body of Christ defined as present on the altar. This later became the basis for seeing the Mass as a new sacrifice of Christ. Harnack comments: "The doctrine as Radbertus enunciated it, a Pandora's box of problems for future scholars, was highly understandable to the simple. There is no surer way for a dogma to establish itself than when it possesses these two characteristics."[8]

a. Implications:
The Sacrifice of the Mass

The eucharistic controversy of the ninth century was the opening stage of a development that ultimately resulted in a new understanding of the nature of faith, grace, and the church. The ideas of Radbertus triumphed in part because they were clear and the age demanded assurance concerning the objects of faith. Their success was facilitated by the fact that his opponents were rather vague concerning the drawing of a line between his assertions and theirs. Although Radbertus was chiefly interested in the meaning of the doctrine of the incarnation for the eucharist, and not in the implications of his eucharistic doctrine for the work of Christ, he did lay the intellectual foundation for the view that the Mass is a sacrifice in which Christ is offered anew to his Father. The bodily presence of Christ provided the rationale for a shift in Christian piety from its original basis as founded on the Word and on faith; instead, the religious life came to center on the reality offered in the sacrament.

Neither the teaching of Radbertus nor the text of the eucharistic liturgy prescribes that the Mass be understood as a repetition of the sacrifice of the Saviour on the Cross. The language of the liturgy did permit it, however, and Radbertus' insistence on the bodily presence of Christ on the altar laid the doctrinal foundation for it. The change could hardly have been more significant. To put it crudely, the interest shifted from what Christ does for the believer by his presence to what the priest does with Christ, who is present; from the unseen host at the messianic banquet, Christ becomes the *hostia,* "sacrificial victim." In the early church, the eucharist was the place where believers communed with their Lord in a specially intense way. Only those who believed could discern the body and blood and receive them as spiritual nourishment. When conceived in a very realistic way as the "medicine of immortality," the eucharistic body had to be eaten by the individual to be effective. The new emphasis on the corporeal presence of Christ permitted the church to begin to treat Christ as the victim, rather than as the host, to think of itself as offering him to the Father, rather than as coming to be nourished at his table.

Prior to this controversy in the ninth century, the eucharistic liturgy had come to be celebrated more and more frequently, even when no worshipers were present to take part in the communion. The number of priests was increasing constantly, and each priest was expected to celebrate the eucharistic liturgy daily. This led to the practice of many priests holding the "communion" alone—for themselves only. This clearly lost the concept of an act of communion with fellow believers around the Lord's Table. What remained was communion with Christ himself and with the invisible church. This alone would probably not have justified solitary communion in the eyes of most clergy, but an additional consideration came in that seemed to do so. The communion liturgy places the sacrificial death of Christ not only before the eyes of believers, but also before God's eyes. Gradually, the communion began to be seen not merely as the memorial of a sacrifice but as a new enactment of it, one that earned merit in God's sight. The idea that the communion service is itself a sacrifice resulted from the conviction that Christ was bodily present. His body, once broken on the Cross, is broken again by the hands of the priest in the breaking of the bread and is consumed by the communicants.

b. *The Mass and Penal Theory*

When Christianity was still a minority religion in a pagan world, it exercised a moral supervision over the conduct of its members. Serious sins were dealt with by public confession and penance. When the empire became Christian, the government began to broaden its civil laws to include things considered moral offenses by Christians. Nevertheless, those beyond the reach of the civil law—such as the Emperor Theodosius I—sometimes were publicly confronted and required to repent publicly before being admitted to the communion. But in general the public ministry of the church in dealing with sins fell into disuse.

From the fifth century onward, two important things happened. Roman civil jurisdiction broke down almost everywhere in the West. Consequently, Roman law could not be enforced, and moral offenses, like other conduct prohibited by Roman law, went unpunished. At the same time, the dominant people in the emerging order were generally members of recently converted Germanic tribes. Their sense of personal honor brought a strong aversion to public humiliation. They might have been willing to endure martyrdom for the sake of Christ, but they were very reluctant to endure disgrace before the church—including the people they had conquered—because of moral faults. Religion became more of a private affair. Much was lost in this transition. Where there was no public confession and repentance, there could also be no public absolution, and the repentant sinner was deprived of that assurance that his sins had been pardoned.

The triumph of Augustine's doctrine of the bondage of the will over Pelagius' optimistic moralism left the average Christian facing perfectionist demands with a will inclined to evil. Virtually all sensitive Christians were made painfully aware of how far short they fell of the glory of God. Under such circumstances, the role of the clergy as mediators and advocates with God was expanded. People began to beg the priests not merely to pray for them but actually to do something for them. The new understanding of the bodily presence of Christ in the eucharist gave the priests something of surpassing importance to do: they could sacrifice Christ again for the sins of the faithful. Of course this ability increased the distinction between clergy and laity.

4. THE PROBLEM OF PREDESTINATION

Augustine emphasized the sovereign will of God, and was not too timid to describe it as inflexible and arbitrary. Although predestination—or election, as it is often called—is an important concept in both the Old and the New Testament, Augustine was the first Christian theologian to make it the cornerstone of his approach to theology and the Christian life. Subsequent generations of Christians have tried, with varying success and in various ways, to come to terms with Augustine's doctrine of predestination. Speaking broadly, most of the church through the ages, at least in the West, has been Augustinian in theory, but rather Semi-Pelagian in practice. Augustine looked on his understanding of predestination as the best possible reason for the believer to have confidence about his eternal destiny, but many of his spiritual descendants have found it more a source of dread than of assurance.

The Augustinian concept of predestination has frequently been reaffirmed as the official teaching of both Catholicism and of several branches of Protestantism, but each time it is reasserted, efforts are soon made to qualify it and to make it more compatible with notions of human freedom. In 529, the Council of Orange had officially approved the Augustinian view and had condemned the moderating position known as Semi-Pelagianism as

well as Pelagianism itself. Nevertheless, the concept that man needs to contribute something to his own salvation by his works continued to exist and
to gain adherents. Of course the idea of the eucharist as a meritorious sacrifice contributed to the view that man can earn God's favor.

The importance of the young Frankish church for the spiritual history
of the West is apparent from the fact that the second great ninth-century
conflict was also sparked in a Frankish monastery. Gottschalk, the son of
the Count of Saxony, was entered in the famous monastery at Fulda as a
child in 822. As an adolescent, he protested against this involuntary dedication to the monastic life, and in 829 he was released from his vows. He
continued as a cleric, however, and was ordained a priest shortly before
840. When his forcefully expressed views on predestination got him into
trouble, he was disciplined as a rebellious monk. In 840, Gottschalk made
a pilgrimage to Italy, where his teaching of double predestination (to salvation for some, to damnation for others) aroused the alarm of Bishop Noting
of Verona. Noting wrote to Gottschalk's former abbot at Fulda, Hrabanus
Maurus, who replied with a letter explaining that predestination is based on
divine foreknowledge. This well-intentioned oversimplification of his view
distressed Gottschalk, who carried his doctrine to the mission field—apparently going even to the Bulgars, whom Greeks and Latins were both seeking
to win to Christianity.

Returning to Germany shortly before 848, Gottschalk was summoned
by Hrabanus, now archbishop of Mainz, to give an account of himself.
Gottschalk boldly presented a treatise reaffirming double predestination and
refuting the earlier letter of Hrabanus to Noting. Condemned by the synod,
Gottschalk and the few partisans who rallied to him were publicly whipped
and then relegated to various monasteries to do penance. Gottschalk was
sent to the monastery of Orbais in the archdiocese of Reims. The archbishop, Hincmar (d. 882), appears to have thought that he could lend weight
to his title of primate of all the Frankish lands by dealing in an authoritative
and impressive way with the problem posed by Gottschalk.

Gottschalk, in the meantime, had succeeded in winning the sympathy
of the monks at Orbais. Hincmar summoned him to Reims in 849 and demanded that he burn his own book. When Gottschalk refused, he was
scourged (according to the provision of the Benedictine Rule for disobedient
monks!) until, half dead, he finally submitted. Relegated to another monastery, this time at Hautvillers, he continued to write, and soon his custodians
were deeply influenced by his theology.

Hincmar in the meantime decided to refute Gottschalk's heresy, and
while he did not reduce predestination to foreknowledge, he did insist that
Christ died for all, not only for the elect. Thus he broke with Augustine's

contention, known subsequently as the doctrine of the limited atonement. Several of the same people who had unsuccessfully defended the older Augustinian views on the eucharist now rallied to his doctrine of predestination, and this time they were more successful.

Subject to criticism by Ratramnus of Corbie as well as by the bishops of Troyes and Ferrières, Hincmar tried to defend his cause first by appeals to his monarch, King Charles the Bald, and then by summoning the King's favorite philosopher, John Scotus Erigena (d. ca. 878), to his support. Scotus was more of a linguist than a theologian and attempted to resolve the question by formal syllogisms rather than by appealing to Scripture or the church fathers. His work *On Predestination* brought Hincmar more embarrassment than help by making use of arguments such as this: God, being simple, cannot engage in double predestination. A synod at Valence reaffirmed the Augustinian doctrine of limited atonement, while Hincmar overcame his embarrassment by winning a different controversy with the same opponents, Ratramnus and Gottschalk.

The regular Latin daily office prayed by all priests contained the expression *trina deitas unaque,* "God three-fold and one." Hincmar objected to what he considered the tritheistic implications of calling deity three-fold; Ratramnus and Gottschalk accused him of reverting to Sabellian modalism. Hincmar summoned a synod in his own defense in 860. This local council affirmed the unlimited intent of the atonement and thus vindicated Hincmar's earlier stand. Once again, despite the preponderance of theological opinion in favor of predestination and the Augustinian doctrine of the bondage of the will, it proved impossible to maintain them as the general understanding of the Christian faith. The emerging consensus on the freedom of the will found itself compatible with the idea of a eucharistic sacrifice and man's ability to offer meritorious works to God.

5. CONCLUSION: THE NEW DIRECTION

Both the setting and the subject matter of these ninth-century controversies seem narrow and restricted compared to the great trinitarian and Christological struggles of the earlier centuries, which had set patriarchates against one another and convulsed the whole Roman Empire. These new heresies and controversies, involving adoptionism, the *filioque,* predestination, and the eucharist, were fought out among a small circle of Frankish theologians far from the old centers of religion and culture. The great and controversial universal historian Oswald Spengler sees in this the birth of a new religion, which he labels "Faustian" Christianity, opposed to the earlier, Easter, "Magian" variety.[9] Even if one rejects Spengler's interpretation and believes that Christianity and the church have preserved an essential continuity from the days of the Apostles to the present, it is apparent that their changes have been substantial. Spengler, who has no interest in asserting the authority or truthfulness of Christian doctrine, holds that Christianity underwent a dramatic transformation under the influence of the Germanic, Faustian soul, a transformation that was carried even further by the Reformation. From his perspective, contemporary Roman Catholicism is far from the religion of the Apostles, and Protestantism, whether conservative or liberal, is farther still.

Orthodox Protestants, who seek to claim a legitimate continuity between Reformation Protestantism and the church of the Apostles, are faced with the task of showing that Catholicism changed so much before the Reformation that the Reformation became a necessity. Vis-à-vis Roman Catholicism with its internationalism, humanism, and classical cultural heritage, Protestantism often seems, even to Protestants, to be a narrowly national, Germanic-Scandinavian movement that can hardly claim to represent the universality of the Gospel. If we discover, however, that the direction of Christianity was significantly shifted by Germanic cultural influences *before* the Reformation, then it was natural enough that the corrective also spring primarily from Germanic soil. This indeed appears to be the case. Between the ninth and the thirteenth centuries, Christianity in the West was seriously deflected from its original direction. To a large extent, the German Reformation is perceived as a German protest against the Italian humanism of the Renaissance church. But the major thrust of Luther was doctrinal, not artistic, and the doctrines against which he protested were not the products of Italian artists of the Renaissance, but doctrines of Germanic theologians of the Middle Ages.

It is not difficult to see the continuity in the Orthodox church of the Byzantine East. In fact, before the rise of the ecumenical movement it was common for Protestant polemicists to lampoon it as a fossil. Continuity, despite change, was its strong point. The Cappadocian Fathers of the fourth century would not have felt entirely out of place in Constantinople in the eighth century, or even in the fourteenth. In the Greek church, the theological controversies of the fourth, fifth, and sixth centuries were matters of excited public concern. The wars of the era were largely left to the government and its professional soldiers. In the Latin West of the Middle Ages, theological controversies became a private concern—not least because they were conducted in a learned language not widely understood. They did become the concern of the government, because the government considered the church a department of state, but they could not attract widespread popular attention like the earlier controversies in the East. Prior to Constantine, war had been the government's business, theology that of the church. Constantine made theology public business. Seven centuries later the popes would make war the business of the church.

SELECTED BIBLIOGRAPHY

Akeley, T. C. *Christian Initiation in Spain c. 300–1100.* London: Darton, 1967.

Chenu, Marie Dominique. *Nature, Man, and Society in the Twelfth Century: Essays on New Theological Perspectives in the Latin West.* Chicago: University Press, 1968.

Fahey, John F. *The Eucharistic Teaching of Ratramnus of Corbie.* Mundelein, Ill.: St. Mary of the Lake Seminary, 1951.

Kidd, Beresford James. *The Later Medieval Doctrine of the Eucharistic Sacrifice.* 2d ed. London: S.P.C.K., 1958.

Lietzmann, Hans. *Mass and the Lord's Supper: A Study in the History of the Liturgy with Introduction and Further Inquiry.* Translated by Robert Douglas Richardson. Leiden: Brill, 1979.

Macdonald, Allan John. *Berengar and the Reform of Sacramental Doctrine.* New York: Longmans, 1930.

Moore, R. I. *The Birth of Popular Heresy.* London: Edward Arnold, 1975.

Palmer, Paul F., ed. *Sacraments and Forgiveness: History and Doctrinal Development of Penance, Extreme Unction and Indulgences.* Vol. 2 of *Sources of Christian Theology.* Westminster, Md.: Newman Press, 1959.

Ruseh, William G. *The Later Latin Fathers.* London: Duckworth, 1977.

Ullmann, Walter. *The Origins of the Great Schism: A Study in Fourteenth-Century Ecclesiastical History.* Hamden, Conn.: Archon Books, 1967.

Weltin, Edward George. *The Ancient Popes.* Westminster, Md.: Newman Press, 1964.

14

THE NEW CHURCH AND
THE OLD HERESY:
SCHOLASTICISM,
THE CRUSADES, AND DUALISM

Learn to apprehend something different from what is tasted by the mouth of flesh; to see something different from what is manifested to these fleshly eyes. Learn that God, as a Spirit, is locally everywhere. . . . Consider, then, if anything corporeal can be more sublime than the substance of bread and wine inwardly and efficaciously changed into the Flesh and Blood of Christ . . . believed to be present, and is judged by believers to be nothing else than Christ the Bread of heaven.

Paschasius Radbertus

The predestination controversy unleased by Gottschalk was followed by a period of relative theological calm. Church politics, however, were anything but calm. A final rupture between the Eastern and Western churches took place in 1054 when the pope and the patriarch excommunicated one another. In the East, the Byzantine emperors generally could count on docile obedience from the patriarchs who headed the Greek church. In the West, by contrast, a series of hardy popes battled the German "Roman" emperors and eventually humiliated the Holy Roman Empire. The older monastic orders degenerated, and new orders were formed. In northeastern Europe, the last remaining pagans—Lithuanians and Finns—were converted; efforts to convert the Moslems of North Africa were fruitless. The papacy launched the Crusades, and temporarily recovered the Holy Land. In the process it dealt a fatal wound to the Byzantine Empire and ultimately brought discredit upon itself and upon Christianity generally.

As important as the Crusades were for Christendom, they were not the most important religious events of the Middle Ages. Only the First Crusade (1095–99) was a military success. The Second Crusade (1147–49), inspired by Bernard of Clairvaux (1091–1153), the monk whom Karl Heussi called "the uncrowned ruler of Europe," ended in a debacle, bringing discredit upon Bernard himself and on the church in general.

Bernard is typical of many of the best features of medieval spirituality. A reformer, a mystic, and a scholar, he strongly shaped medieval piety, especially among the religious orders. His influence, together with that of works erroneously ascribed to St. Paul's convert, Dionysius the Areopagite,[1] helped to create a new form of spirituality in the West. Pseudo-Dionysius was popularized in the mysticism of Bernard's contemporary, Hugh of St. Victor (ca. 1097–1141).

The Crusades represent a climax in the secularization of the church. From the time of Constantine onward, the armies of nominally Christian rulers had used Christian emblems and claimed God's protection. Indeed, even today a number of European states, including Britain, the Scandinavian countries, West Germany, Switzerland, and Greece use the cross in flags or other emblems. The church frequently supported and collaborated with military undertakings; the Crusades mark the first time the church itself was the organizing and inspiring force.

Parallel to the turning of the church to the world in the Crusades was the development of a new approach to knowledge: Scholasticism. Running counter to these trends was the rebirth of old heresies: Gnosticism and Marcionite dualism. Spiritual fervor led to the establishment of great new mendicant orders, especially the Dominicans (1216) and the Franciscans (1221–23); it also produced great persecutions, in which the orthodox were no longer the victims but the persecutors.

1. SCHOLASTICISM

After the brilliance of the ninth-century Carolingian Renaissance, decline set in in both the Frankish church and Frankish culture. When the church began to revive, it was no longer thanks to the stimulation provided by a German Emperor, as in Charlemagne's day, but as part of a reform movement in Christianity in which the papacy sought to free itself from all control and supervision by the secular power. While the papacy fought lay investiture—the practice of permitting secular rulers to choose the holders of church offices—a new intellectual life began to flourish in northwestern Europe. Bishop Fulbert of Chartres (d. 1028) founded a theological school and, more important, reintroduced the dialectical method into theology. Fulbert's pupil Berengar of Tours (d. 1088) carried the dialectical method further and might have won fame as an educator had not his ideas on the eucharist brought him condemnation as a heretic.

a. What Is Scholasticism?

In the early church, both East and West, most theology was in the hands of bishops and priests—Irenaeus and Ambrose, Augustine and John Chrysostom, Cyril of Alexandria and the Cappadocian Fathers were all bishops. Tertullian and Origen were not priests, and interestingly enough both of them were reputed heretics—Tertullian rightly so, Origen with less justification. In the Eastern church, both before and after the rupture with Rome in 1054, theology remained largely the province of the hierarchy. In the West it came largely into the hands of a professional academic class. Anselm of Canterbury (1033–1109) was an archbishop; his critic Peter Abelard (1079–1142) was not, and neither were the great names of thirteenth-century theology: Albertus Magnus (ca. 1206–80), Thomas Aquinas (ca. 1225–74), Bonaventure (1221–74), and Duns Scotus (ca. 1265–ca. 1308). The Greek church, with its intellectual leadership in the hands of the hierarchy, remained stable, indeed static. The West, with its developing class of professional, academic theologians, rapidly transformed itself. This transformation was brought about by a new intellectual movement, or rather method, known as Scholasticism. The most important feature of Scholasticism is the importance it attaches to a particular method and what can be done with it. If ancient philosophy relied chiefly on reason, and modern science relies on the experimental method, Scholasticism relied upon ancient authorities.

Scholasticism was to the intellectual life of medieval Christianity what monasticism was to its spiritual life. Although its starting point, its methodology, and its results differ from those of what we call science (i.e. experimental natural science), it is scientific in its own way, and certainly was eager for knowledge (Latin *scientia*), not hostile to it. The fact that the world view of Scholasticism clashes so frequently with that of modern natural science does not mean that Scholasticism was lacking in intellectual honesty or indifferent to truth, but simply that it applied too broadly and self-confidently methods that were useful in certain spheres and totally inadequate in others. (The same criticism, of course, may be applied to scientism, which results from the presumptuous application of the techniques and methods to areas where they do not help us to arrive at truth.) "Thus medieval scholasticism is simply science [i.e. *scientia*, "knowledge"], and to think that it merits a special name in the history of science simply perpetuates an unjustified distrust of it."[2]

Scholasticism was based on biblical and patristic authorities, just as was earlier theology, but it no longer let them speak for themselves. It absolutized them and turned them into building blocks out of which it created a massive edifice of what it supposed to be thoroughly reliable truth. Scholasticism made theology creative in a way it had never been before. Even the most impressive doctrines of early theology—the doctrines of consubstantiality and the two natures of Christ—were essentially attempts to interpret what the early theologians found given in Scripture. The characteristic doctrine of medieval Scholasticism, transubstantiation, was a construction based on two pillars: scriptural teachings and Aristotelian logic. As it drew conclusion after conclusion, it added story after story, and ultimately called forth the Protestant Reformation as a protest against its doctrinal luxuriance.

Earlier theology had tried to see and to understand; to gain a correct *theoria* or vision of spiritual realities. Scholastic theology sought to construct a correct system of knowledge. Assuming that it had a sound foundation, biblical revelation, it used what it took to be a sound method, philosophical logic, to create what it presupposed would be a solid structure of truth. Although Scholasticism plainly differs from natural science and the scientific method, it also differs from their enemy, Gnosticism; it is not interested in secret lore, available only to the gifted and specially initiated, but in solid, reliable truth, capable of being demonstrated to anyone willing to make the necessary intellectual effort to understand it.

Scholasticism is ridiculed for discussing such questions as the number of angels that can dance on the head of a pin. The formulation of the question seems silly, but the issue at stake is a serious one—whether an angel is totally immaterial, or a very finely diffused material reality. Until relatively recent times, natural scientists postulated a similarly "angelic" substance, the ether, diffused throughout the universe, to explain the transmission of light waves through space. The hypothesis of the ether seems absurd today, but it was totally serious when proposed, and there were intelligent reasons for proposing it. The same can be said about the silly-sounding question concerning the angels on the head of a pin.

b. The Eucharistic Controversy and Scholasticism

In the eleventh century, the eucharistic controversy broke out again, this time as a clear contest between authority, and what the Scholastic method could build on authority, and reason, or the questions the Scholastic method could raise taking reason as its point of departure. In the ninth century, the eucharistic controversy had not really been resolved: it had simply worn itself out. The "conservative" view of Paschasius Radbertus—which was really an innovation—had come to prevail, although it had not been made obligatory. Radbertus taught the corporeal presence of Christ in the sacrament. The alternative position, which spoke only of a mysterious presence and emphasized the faith of the recipient, was not so widespread, but it did have impressive support in the Augustinian tradition. Alongside both of these views, which stressed a real presence of Christ, but in different ways, was the concept that the elements were merely symbols, an opinion held by only a very small group.

Although the insistence that the elements were really transformed into the body and blood of Christ is now considered "conservative," it first appeared as an innovation. Its proponents felt that it was necessary not so much because the Scripture demands it as because without it, they could not have the assurance that the sacrament conveys real benefits. Those who opposed this real transformation and the resulting doctrine of the corporeal presence of Christ did so partly for traditional reasons, i.e. because the formulation was a novelty, and partly for rational ones, chiefly arising out of the problems that the doctrine of a physical transformation presents. Although Radbertus' doctrine endeared itself to clergy and laity alike, offering tremendous power to the one and promising magnificent benefits to the other, it also presented a splendid target for rationalist objections.

For a time, it looked as though the claims of theological authority might be forced to submit to the scrutiny of human reason. In the end, authority triumphed over rationalistic criticism, but only by arming itself with equally rationalistic defenses. Thus in a way the eucharistic controversy, in which authority vanquished rational criticism, really was not a triumph of authority or faith at all, as it was won only by making use of reason.

The figure who launched this fateful development was Berengar. He considered it to be self-evident that what the priest places in the believer's mouth during the eucharist is not literal flesh and blood. But he believed that the eucharistic meal really does involve the body and blood of Christ. Where does it place them? It puts them into the believer's understanding. The miracle of the consecration is not that the bread and wine take on a new substance but a new meaning. We cannot physically eat the body of Christ; to speak of such eating really means to appropriate the benefits he earned for us in his body. In Berengar's eyes, this is a *real* eating, but not a physical one. It can be accomplished only by those who believe the words of Christ; he found the idea that an unbeliever could eat the body of Christ in the eucharist absurd. Radbertus really taught two different bodies of Christ, in Berengar's eyes: a real, heavenly body that is seated at the right hand of the Father, and a eucharistic body that is physically broken and eaten during the Mass. Berengar considered his opponents inept, but his sarcasm could not defeat them. He had powerful friends, including Hildebrand, who subsequently became pope as Gregory VII (reigned 1073–85), but at the time, Hildebrand was unable to protect him.

Berengar was condemned twice in the year 1050, first at Rome, then at Vercelli. In 1054, the respected Hildebrand declared himself satisfied with Berengar's orthodoxy, but Berengar was not rehabilitated, and objections to his views continued. He was examined again in 1059, and forced to sign a confession that anticipates the later doctrine of transubstantiation (made official only in 1215): "The bread and wine, after the consecration, . . . are not only a sacrament, but the very body and blood of our Lord Jesus Christ and are sensually, not only as a sacrament but in truth handled and broken by the hands of the priest and crushed by the teeth of the faithful." But hardly had Berengar made this confession than he returned to France and began to proclaim his old views again.

Berengar had apparently persuaded the papacy of the sincerity of his recantation, for the new pope, Alexander II (reigned 1061–73) continued to protect him; he did not suffer the fate of his unfortunate predecessor, Gottschalk. The new count of Anjou, Geoffrey the Bearded, attempted to prevent Berengar from returning to the diocese where he held the rank of archdeacon; Berengar displayed letters from Pope Alexander supporting him; these are now known to be falsifications, perhaps produced by Berengar himself.[3]

In the theological arena, Lanfranc (d. 1089), at that time the abbot of Bec in Normandy (subsequently archbishop of Canterbury), challenged Berengar with his *Book on the Body and Blood of the Lord, Against Berengar* (ca. 1066). This provoked a reply by Berengar, one that thoroughly unmasked his symbolistic understanding and added attacks on the papacy, specifically on the late Popes Leo IX and Nicholas II. Berengar was summoned to appear at a council in Poitiers in 1076; the new pope, Gregory VII (reigned 1073–85), apparently was still relatively well disposed toward him, and Berengar decided to take his case to him at Rome. At another Roman council, in 1079, Berengar once again signed a statement of impeccable eucharistic realism. Following the council, a papal bull anathematized all who should regard Berengar as a heretic, but like the letters of Alexander II, it seems to have been a forgery. In 1080, Berengar declared that his confession was extorted from him and went against his true convictions. Once again he was convoked before a council, once again he retracted, and died not long afterward without causing further trouble—but the views he had defended did not perish with him.

Berengar's eucharistic theory shocked his contemporaries not only because it challenged what had become a major element of Christian piety, the corporeal presence of Christ in the communion, but also because he arrived at it in what seemed an arrogantly rationalistic manner. The failure of his efforts left eucharistic theology more realistic than before. For the first time, it was explicitly stated that even *unbelievers* devour the body of Christ in the eucharist. Eventually, at the Fourth Lateran Council (1215), the realistic position would be made dogmatically binding. By including transubstantiation in its confession of faith, the council placed it on the same level as the doctrines of the Trinity and Christ. This decision would play a great role in the pre-Reformation and Reformation eras, for it made anyone who did not agree with a particular interpretation of the eucharist as much a heretic as an adoptionist or a Unitarian.

2. THE CRUSADES

Gregory VII, who was skillful enough to treat Berengar moderately and prevent the eucharistic controversy from producing martyrs, had other political and disciplinary problems with which to deal. In 1074–75 he conceived the idea of leading an expedition to Constantinople with the joint project of ending the schism of 1054 and helping the Byzantines to reconquer their recently lost Asian dominions. Basil II, called the Bulgar-Slayer, who brought the Eastern empire to its greatest power since the beginning of the Moslem era, had died in 1025, to be succeeded by several weak monarchs; the year 1071 had brought disaster in the East: Romanus IV Diogenes (ruled 1068–71) was defeated and captured by the Turks at Manzikert. The last Byzantine possession in Italy, Bari, was lost to the Normans the same year. Much of Asia Minor, the Eastern empire's heartland, was lost to the Turks.

It remained for Pope Urban II (reigned 1088–99) to organize and launch the great undertaking of the First Crusade. The papacy, still locked in conflict with the German Emperor Henry IV (ruled 1056–1106), effectively took over the Emperor's traditional function of protecting Christians and Christendom. The great monarchs failed to act. While still uncrowned as Emperor, Henry himself was excommunicated in 1080 and, still worse, was crowned by the Antipope Clement III in 1084, thus ruling out the possibility of becoming an ally of Urban. The other powerful monarch of the day, Philip I of France, was also under the ban. The pope had disqualified his own potential champions. The First Crusade became an expedition of the higher feudal nobility, animated by the papacy; it turned the papacy, i.e. the church itself, toward military conquest. Under Alexander II (reigned 1061–73), it had been determined that the lands reconquered from the Moors in Spain would come under papal sovereignty, and Urban II intended to do the same in the Holy Land. The fact that his sudden death in 1099 permitted the victorious Crusaders to establish their own independent states in the Levant does not change the fact that the crusade, as conceived by the pope, was to have been a kind of war of imperialistic expansion for the papacy.

The entire world of Christian feudalism responded to Urban's appeal for a crusade with an enthusiasm that astonished the pope himself. The concept of the Truce of God had been promoted by the church at the end of the tenth century in an effort to end the disastrous warfare that was ruining Western Christendom. It had led to the idea that Christian chivalry was the servant of the church to promote the peace of Christendom, and it assumed that in order to achieve peace and protection of the weak, it might be necessary first to fight.

Before the military crusade was properly organized, a mob of religiously excited peasants led by the charismatic preacher Peter the Hermit had already reached Constantinople. The Emperor Alexius I was only too pleased to have them pass over into Turkish territory, where they were virtually wiped out by the Turks on August 5, 1097. This "people's crusade" spread bad will and hostility among the Greeks it supposedly had come to aid but instead despoiled. It had begun its fatal expedition with a series of massacres of Jews in the German towns of Trier, Cologne, Speyer, Worms, and Mainz, and cast the whole crusading effort in a sorry light.

The story of the Crusades more properly belongs to the history of politics than to that of heresy, but the Crusades must at least be mentioned here because of three of their effects: (1) they manifested and indeed reinforced, at least at first, the power of the papacy as the head of the "Christian world"; (2) they agitated Christians to use force against "unbelievers," including not only Moslems but Jews and heretics and even schismatic Eastern Christians; (3) finally, after initial success, the failure of the Second Crusade and subsequent Crusades undermined the confidence of Christians in the church and its rulers.

3. THE PERENNIAL HERESY
REVIVES: DUALISM

The territories of the Eastern empire that bordered on Arab-conquered lands have already been mentioned as a center of iconoclastic ferment. Although the iconoclasts were fully orthodox in our sense of the word, they did have something in common with another, more serious heresy or family of heresies that originated in the same region. This family is even older than iconoclasm, but it really made its appearance in the Christian *oikumene* rather late, coming fully to the attention of the Eastern church only early in the twelfth century, under the theologically astute and pious Emperor Alexius I Comnenus (ruled 1081–1118).

The same heresy cropped up in western Europe at almost the same time; several "crusades" and the Inquisition were activated against it. What was it? A variety, or rather several varieties, of dualism. One leading historian, Steven Runciman, calls it Manichaeanism,[4] but he makes it clear that this name is essentially a convenience, justifiable in part by its use by Byzantine chronographers. The movement had dualism and often a kind of elitism in common with the gnostics and Marcion as well as with Mani; nevertheless, clear historical connections are hard to trace. The heresy that appears prominently on our stage is that of the Bogomils; in Slavonic, the name "Bogomil" means "beloved of God," and apparently was first the proper name of the heresy's founder, a priest who lived in the reign of the Bulgarian ruler known after his conversion as Czar Peter (ruled 927–69). Later accounts tell us that Bogomil was originally named Jeremiah and renamed himself Bogomil, but this seems implausible. The name "Bogomil," the equivalent of the Greek "Theophilus," was common enough. Although Bogomilism takes its name from him, he did not originate its ideas, which go back to Gnosticism and even beyond, to pre-Christian dualism. The specific predecessors of the Bogomils are the Paulicians, a moderately heretical group that was reconciled to Roman Catholicism in the seventeenth century and that still exists as a so-called Uniate church, in communion with Rome but with its own distinctive rites.

a. The Paulicians

The Paulicians derive their name from the Apostle Paul, and attribute their specific dualistic outlook to Paul. As we recall, the second-century dualist Marcion preserved many of Paul's writings in his abbreviated Bible, because, taken out of context, they are compatible with his dualistic views. Paulicianism appears to have originated in Armenia, a more or less independent principality situated on the Roman-Persian border, which became the Byzantine-Arab border after the Moslem conquest. Frequently Armenia was allied to the Eastern Roman Empire, at times under its sovereignty.

Armenia possesses the distinction of having become the first Christian nation, shortly after 300 and thus prior to the conversion of Constantine, when King Tiridates III accepted the Gospel from St. Gregory the Illuminator. During the fourth century Armenian Christianity was under the influence of the Cappadocian Fathers and was essentially orthodox, but after the Council of Chalcedon in 451 the Armenian church sided with the Egyptians and became monophysite. Apparently it did so largely in order to free itself from the influence of the Emperor in Constantinople, who made use of orthodoxy to enhance his own political power.

At about the same time Gregory the Illuminator brought what would soon be Nicene orthodoxy to Armenia, disciples of Paul of Samosata also brought in adoptionistic influences. In addition, there were apparently numbers of Marcionites in the country, as well as other groups with gnostic and Manichaean ideas. The Orthodox chroniclers disparage these groups, which they designate as "Messalians" (from the Syrian verb for "to pray") or, more abusively, as "Borborites" (from the Greek word for "filth"), but they provide us with very little information about what made them distinctive. Three centuries elapsed between the time when Armenia was converted and the appearance of the recognizably dualistic Paulicians. It is at least conceivable that the Paulicians did descend from the fourth-century Messalians. If this should be true, it would mean that the ancient dualistic heresy survived, at least marginally, alongside the antidualistic theism of orthodox Chalcedonians and Monophysites.

The first comprehensive account of the Paulicians was written much later, about 869, when the Emperor Basil I (867–86) sent Peter Siculus as ambassador to the Paulician principality on his eastern frontier in Asia Minor. In his *History of the Manichaeans, or Paulicians,*[5] Siculus attributes their origin to an otherwise unknown Paul of Samosata (not the adoptionist of the same name). During the reign of Constans II (ruled 641–68), Paulician congregations were found in Byzantine-ruled Armenia. Constans suppressed them, as did one of his successors, Justinian II (Justinian ruled 685–95, when he was ousted in a palace coup; although he was mutilated by having his nose cut off, in order to prevent his return to the throne, he nevertheless did regain it and reigned six more years, 705–11).

Leo III (reigned 717–41), the savior of the empire from the Arabs and the first great iconoclast, was more tolerant of the Paulicians. Nevertheless, the government at Constantinople continued to look on the Paulicians as an unstable factor on its eastern frontier, and one likely to collaborate with the Moslems. The widow of Theophilus, Empress-Regent Theodora (Empress 829–58, became regent on Theophilus' death in 842), forcibly resettled many Paulicians in European Thrace, where she hoped that they would be a bulwark against the orthodox but hostile Bulgars. A second forcible resettlement of Paulicians from Asia Minor to the Balkans took place under the Emperor John I Tzimisces (969–76), the first Byzantine ruler to regain substantial territory from the Arabs in three centuries. The migration of dualistically inclined Paulicians to the Balkans apparently reinforced the nascent Bogomil movement there.

In Thrace, the Paulicians were resettled on the border with the Bulgars, or Bulgarians, a recently Christianized people of Turkish origin. After the

Byzantine missionaries Cyril and Methodius had converted the Slavic Moravians to Eastern Orthodox Christianity, the Bulgarian ruler, Boris, appealed to the Franks to send missionaries to his people. He did not want to be under the ecclesiastical influence of his powerful Byzantine neighbors. The Byzantines themselves sent missionaries as well as an army, and after some hesitation, which contributed to the rivalry between Pope Nicholas I and the Byzantine Patriarch Photius, the Bulgarians accepted Christianity in its Eastern variety. Boris was baptized and took the name "Peter" and the title czar, derived from "Caesar" and the second most exalted title known to the Eastern empire, directly under that of augustus or basileus.

The independent power of the Bulgarians was smashed by the last of the truly powerful Byzantine emperors, Basil II (ruled 975–1025), whose bloody victory over the Bulgarians earned him the title *Bulgaroctonos,* the "Bulgar-Slayer." After Basil's death, the Byzantine throne was occupied by a number of weak rulers, until the empire suffered a disastrous defeat at the hands of the Turks at the Battle of Manzikert (1071). In the same year, the Normans, who had been whittling away at the remnants of Byzantine power in Italy, finally drove the Easterners out of their last bridgehead on the Italian peninsula, Bari, and shortly afterward attacked the Balkan possessions of the empire in Epirus.

The first competent ruler to come to the Byzantine throne after Manzikert was the skillful Alexius I Comnenus (ruled 1081–1118), an astute lay theologian as well as a talented and decisive ruler. Alexius led a contingent of Paulicians against the Normans in Epirus in 1081, where they deserted him before the battle, which he won. On his successful return to Constantinople, he imprisoned both the spiritual and political leaders of the Paulicians. Not only did he send orthodox clergy to convert his Paulician prisoners, he also joined in the effort himself. According to his daughter Anna Comnena, whose *Alexiad* is a remarkable personal document as well as an outstanding history of Alexius' reign, many Paulicians were converted. Two of their leaders, Cusinus and Phulus, were resistant to all efforts at conversion and were kept in prison until they finally died there. According to Anna's account, they were kept in comfortable confinement,[6] which suggests that the orthodox looked on their errors as less dangerous than those of the Bogomils.

b. The Bogomils

During the middle years of his long reign, Alexius had to contend with the Crusaders from the West; ostensibly they were there to aid him, but in fact they represented a great problem for the Byzantine Empire. In the last two years of his reign, Alexius encountered the Bogomil movement, which had gained adherents in Constantinople itself, where they even established a kind of underground church organization with its own bishop. Alexius, pretending to be interested in accepting Bogomilism, invited the Bogomil bishop, Basil, to the palace. While Basil expounded Bogomil doctrines, secretaries hidden behind draperies recorded his words. The Emperor then confronted Basil with the record of his false doctrines and summoned him to renounce them. When Basil refused, he was imprisoned. The Emperor visited him a number of times in prison, pleading with him to be converted, but finally gave up and allowed Basil to be burned to death as decreed by an ecclesiastical synod. The execution of heretics was comparatively infrequent in the Byzantine Empire, and was usually reserved for obstinate leaders, such as the heresiarch Basil. In the West, the Cathars, the spiritual brothers of the Bogomils, would soon discover that persecution and the stake were not to be the fate of leaders only.

Alexius' vigorous grandson, Manuel I Comnenus (1143–80), also found himself confronted with a parallel Bogomil church in Constantinople itself. The Byzantine Patriarch Cosmas Atticus befriended a leading Bogomil monk, Niphon, and was deposed in 1147. During Manuel's reign, Byzantine diplomatic and commercial contacts with western Europe were at a peak, and even Bogomil leaders participated in the interchange. In the year 1167, a synod of Western dualistic heretics was held at St.-Félix-de-Caraman in the South of France. It was presided over by Nicetas, a Bogomil "bishop" recently arrived from Constantinople, thus giving a kind of "episcopal succession" to the dualistic churches in the West. It is difficult to be sure whether dualism in the West was an import from Paulician and Bogomil sources in the East, or arose independently and later made common cause with the Bogomils, but it is apparent that the Western dualists looked on the Bogomils as senior brethren.

c. Characteristics of Bogomilism

The tenets of Bogomilism are essentially dualistic and resemble those of Gnosticism and Manichaeanism, although it is not proved that they derive directly from those much older movements. Bogomilism has a relatively elaborate cosmology, resembling that of Gnosticism, although far less complex. Its relative simplicity made it more understandable to common people. Unlike Gnosticism, which appealed to those who thought themselves a spiritual elite, Bogomilism in the East and the Cathar movement in the West developed and trained an elite from among the ordinary people who were attracted to them. The Bogomil movement appears to have begun as a radical dualism, teaching two eternal principles, evil and good, like Persian Zoroastrianism; later it was modified into a less radical form, which looked

on the dualism it saw in the world as the result of the rebellion of the one
God's eldest son, Satanael. In its final stages, it reverted back to a more
consistently dualistic outlook.

The Bogomils taught that the one supreme God, a totally spiritual
being, had two sons: Satanael, the elder, and Jesus, the younger. The elder
son rebelled and was cast from heaven. In his exile, he created the material
world and man, but was unable to give man life without the help of God.
God gave man life, and man thus was a divided being. Jesus, the Word,
was sent to earth to defeat Satanael, who lost much of his power and was
deprived of the suffix of divinity attached to his name, "-el," becoming
Satan. Satan retained power on earth, but God sent his Holy Spirit to indwell his faithful ones, i.e. the Bogomils. At the end of the age, the Holy
Spirit will ascend to heaven and together with the Word will be reabsorbed
into the Father.

It is apparent that this understanding of God and the world radically
conflicts with orthodox theology. Its doctrine of God is highly dualistic and
like Gnosticism and Marcionism it denies that God is the Creator of the
world. There is no true Trinity; the Word and the Holy Spirit are not really
personal, and in addition there is another power, Satan (Satanael), who is
senior to the Word. Despite these glaring differences, the Bogomils attracted
many ordinary Christians who were not sophisticated enough to see how
different Bogomilism is from what they professed to believe as orthodox
Christians. Many Bogomils, and especially their leaders, exhibited a zeal
and a purity of life that contrasted sharply with the indifference and frivolity
of all too many orthodox ecclesiastics in both East and West. Like the Latter-Day Saints of the modern era, the Bogomils had many doctrines that
flatly contradict those of orthodox Christianity, but their personal lives were
often such that they attracted admirers and converts from the ranks of the
orthodox. Often uninstructed people from an orthodox background failed to
notice the doctrinal incompatibility of Bogomil views with orthodoxy; what
they did notice was Bogomil opposition to familiar features of ordinary
church life, such as baptism and the communion.

According to the first Christian to give a good account of Bogomilism,
Bogomil's contemporary and fellow Bulgarian Cosmas, Bogomil was a
strict dualist.[7] A later account, the *Dogmatic Panoply* of Euthymius Ziga-
benus, was written at the request of the Emperor Alexius I and is supposed
to have been based on the answers the Bogomil bishop, Basil, gave to
Alexius when trying to convert him in the imperial palace.[8] It is Basil's
somewhat modified dualism that is described above, which saw Satan (Satanael) as God's elder son, rather than as a coeternal evil power always
existing alongside of God. After creating Adam, Satanael asked the Father
to give him life, promising that Adam would henceforth serve them both.

Satanael went on to create Eve, had sexual relations with her, and begat Cain. Tempted by Eve, Adam fell from chastity and begat Abel, whom Cain later killed. Satanael was then punished but not defeated. When one human soul appealed to him, God sent his Son, the Word, who entered the Virgin's ear, took flesh from her, and emerged incarnate from the same place. Jesus grew to maturity, appeared to die, then descended into hell, where he bound Satanael and deprived him of his divine title, "-el"; then he returned to the Father. The Christ of Bogomilism is thus docetic, human in appearance only. A real incarnation is excluded, as one would expect from the fact that the Bogomils considered the flesh evil.

Like the Paulicians, the Bogomils detested the cross, for it was the symbol of the Saviour's apparent murder. In this they contrasted sharply with the iconoclasts, for whom the cross was the religious symbol par excellence, taking the place of the multitude of icons favored by the iconodules. The Temple at Jerusalem was once the headquarters of the demons; now, the Bogomils believed, they had their principal center in the Hagia Sophia of Constantinople, Christendom's most splendid church.

Like the gnostics, the Bogomils divided their followers into ordinary believers and the elect, who became qualified as elect by special trials and a distinctive ceremony of initiation. Fantastic claims were made for these elect: each was equal to the Virgin Mary and each could be called the Mother of God, because each was indwelt by the Holy Spirit and gave birth to the Word. The Bogomils limited themselves to one prayer, the Our Father, repeated frequently every day.

According to the tenth-century Bulgarian priest Cosmas, the Bogomils of his day were strict dualists; as we see, those described by Euthymius were less radical. This difference is confirmed in the thirteenth century by Rainerio Sacchoni, an ex-Cathar.[9] To the extent that the radicalism of the Bogomils went beyond the views of the Paulicians, it is possible that the Bogomils drew upon older, occult traditions. The philosopher Michael Psellus (1018–ca.1078) distinguished the little-known Messalians from those he calls Manichaeans (i.e. Paulicians); it is possible that the occult tradition he ascribes to the Messalians goes back to Gnosticism and was passed down to the Bogomils.[10] If so, then this heresy comprises a link with pre-Christian dualism and the more luxuriant ideas of gnostic type that distinguish the Bogomils from the Paulicians. After the temporary conquest of Constantinople by Western armies in 1204, the power of the Byzantine government to keep the Bogomils in check was reduced, and the movement remained strong until the Balkans were conquered by the Turks in the fifteenth century.

After the end of the Comnenus dynasty in 1185, the Bulgarian Empire was revived under the Asen dynasty. As a counterweight to Byzantine influence, the new dynasty negotiated with the papacy, which urged it to suppress the Bogomils. Czar Boris (ruled 1207–18) convened a council at Tirnovo in 1211, which condemned the Bogomils, but Boris was deposed in 1218 by John Asen II (ruled 1218–41). John tolerated the Bogomils, but the movement was wiped out in Bulgaria when the Turks invaded in 1393. It existed farther west, in Bosnia and Dalmatia, where its adherents were called Patarines. When the Turks gained control of the whole peninsula during the fifteenth century, Bogomilism disappeared everywhere. Like the Monophysites eight centuries earlier, the Bogomils proved quite receptive to Islamic proselytization; the bulk of the inhabitants of Bosnia became Moslems.

The Bogomil movement was a challenge to Christian orthodoxy in several ways. Most significant for the common people was the fact that the Bogomils seemed to practice their variety of Christianity more earnestly and sincerely than the majority of the orthodox. Where Christianity could only suggest an answer to the age-old problem of the origin of evil, Bogomil doctrine claimed to explain it. Finally, because too few orthodox Christians were capable of arguing persuasively against the Bogomils, both secular and spiritual authorities used force against them, and what had been the church of the martyrs became the church of the persecutors.

4. THE CATHARS

The most important of all the heretical movements in the Middle Ages was a very complex ferment, primarily dualistic, with direct ties to Bogomilism, known as Catharism. The Cathars were the medieval heretics *per se,* and they deserved that appellation. They should not be confused with another medieval religious group often mistaken for a variety of Catharism because like the Cathars they led a simple and separated life. The Waldensians, or Poor Men of Lyons, were forerunners of Reformation Protestantism, and were neither dualistic nor otherwise heretical in our sense; at the time of the Reformation, they associated themselves with it and became Protestants.

The Cathar movement (from Greek *katharos,* "pure") was both dualistic and elitist. It certainly was stimulated by the dispersion of Bogomils in the West as a result of the attempts of Alexius I to stamp out their heresy. The rapid spread of Cathar doctrines was the crucial factor that caused the papacy to institute the Inquisition. Continuing Cathar success combined with French dynastic politics to produce the so-called Albigensian Crusade (1208–29), terrible wars that ruined the prosperity and culture of the Provence (southern France).

Even before Alexius began to act against the Bogomils in the Eastern

empire, there were outbreaks of fanatical, charismatic, often wildly enthusiastic dualism in the West. A parallel may be seen in the proliferation of
religions and cults related to Hinduism in western Europe and North America today; some are direct imports, others of local origin, but all respond to
a need created by the failure of much Western religion to meet certain deep
human religious needs. Although the modern oriental religious cults are generally monistic rather than dualistic, this modern spiritual current has in
common with the Cathar movement a rejection of the concept of Creation
and of a Creation order and appeals to many by its claim to be able to
explain things more traditional religions cannot.

a. The Beginnings of
Western Manichaeanism

Although the Bogomils stimulated the rise of the Cathar movement in
the West, its rise was too spectacular to be explained by the arrival of a few
Bogomil refugees from the East. If we accept the argument of certain noted
Roman Catholic historians that the West had been free of heresies for
hundreds of years, the sudden flowering of this neo-Manichaeanism appears
quite startling.[11] Even if we recognize that theology was never altogether
tranquil and that adoptionism, iconoclasm, and the eucharistic and predestinarian controversies seriously disturbed the tranquility of Christendom, it is
nevertheless true that nothing in these earlier controversies prepares us for
the violence with which the Cathar movement burst upon the religious
scene.

What distinguished Catharism from traditional Christianity was its radical otherworldliness. During the four centuries since the beginning of
Frankish theology in the West, Christianity had become increasingly worldly
and realistic. The indecisive outcome of the predestination controversy reduced the church's emphasis on the radical sovereignty of the Will of God;
the eucharistic controversy was resolved in the sense of a highly realistic
understanding of the presence of Christ; the conflict between the papacy and
the empire, followed by the enterprise of the Crusades, made the church and
its hierarchy very much a secular power among the other powers.

These changes in theology and spirituality satisfied the religious needs
of some but frustrated those whose sensitivities lay in the direction of a
simpler Bible-centered faith and personal morality. Despite repeated attempts at reform, corruption was rife in the established church; even the
monastic communities were by no means untainted.[12] What the established
church seemed unwilling or unable to provide—enthusiasm, a sense of reli-

gious exaltation, and personal purity—some of the heretics appeared to offer. Although these things did exist in the Catholic Church, which continued to produce men and women of great spiritual power and personal holiness, they were often overshadowed by the widespread corruption of the institution as a whole.

The new dualistic heretical movement dealt with the reality of widespread corruption in two ways: it set an elitist standard for the leaders, the "elect," or "spiritual," members of the community, and the asceticism and self-discipline they displayed made a strong impression on society at large. At the same time, it permitted its rank-and-file adherents to live loosely without being troubled by the guilty conscience such looseness would normally produce among Catholics. Thus it was possible for some to be attracted to the heresy because they were disgusted by the worldliness and corruption they saw in the leaders of the church, while others embraced it because it permitted them a license the church in principle forbade.

During the last quarter of the eleventh century, some of the moral reforms ordered by Gregory VII were beginning to take effect. Of course one of the most sweeping was the prohibition of marriage for priests. Toward the end of the century a Flemish monk named Tanchelm ignited a controversy by denouncing the papal decree that proclaimed that sacraments conferred by married priests were invalid. So many priests were married that such a decree threatened the efficacy of the baptism, communion, and marriage of countless ordinary Christians, who had been told that the validity of the church's sacraments was their guarantee of salvation. Beginning with this inflammatory popular cause, Tanchelm went on to challenge the whole structure of Catholic doctrine and life.

As his second step, Tanchelm condemned the sacraments altogether, beginning with marriage. He put his new views into practice by having affairs with many of the women who accepted his teaching. Like the libertine branch of Gnosticism, he held that the deeds of the flesh cannot affect the purity of the soul. Tanchelm claimed that he was directly inspired by the Holy Spirit and carried out a ceremony in which he "married" the Virgin Mary, recalling the wild claims of the first gnostic, Simon Magus. Imprisoned by the archbishop of Cologne, Tanchelm escaped but shortly afterward was killed by a priest. His followers were numerous in Antwerp around 1125 and are reported elsewhere in northern Germany during the next few decades. The clergy of Liège complained in a letter to the pope in 1144 that these heretics had espoused Manichaean ideas; this is not particularly apparent in Tanchelm, who certainly did not try to behave as the Bogomils expected of the elect, but his contemporary Henry of Lausanne seems to have maintained a higher standard of asceticism, at least for a time, along with dualistic theological ideas.

In this early phase, Tanchelm's heresy was opposed by Bernard of Clairvaux (1091–1153), who at first wanted the heretics to be "taken by arguments, not by arms . . . faith is to be given, not imposed."[13] Bernard soon discovered that although he could inspire kings and knights to "take the cross" and embark on a Crusade, he could not persuade the dualistic heretics to return to the church. By challenging the existing order, in which the church and its institutions were so interwoven with secular institutions, the heretics aroused mob violence and alarmed the secular authorities, who soon began attempting to repress them, ultimately with Bernard's encouragement.

After Tanchelm's murder, a number of other charismatic leaders began preaching a radical spirit-flesh dualism, sometimes setting a remarkable example of asceticism, sometimes allowing free rein to fleshly appetites. Henry the Hermit of Lausanne and Peter of Bruys inflamed hearers throughout the South of France, to the great distress of Bernard as well as of Peter the Venerable, abbot of the great old monastery of Cluny.[14] Peter of Bruys was burned in 1135, and Bernard began a preaching mission against the heresy. When he returned from it in 1145, he felt that he had defeated the errors, but his confidence was misplaced. Henry of Lausanne died at about this time, but his mantle was assumed by Eudes de l'Etoile of Brittany, who changed his name to Aeon and called himself the Judge of the World. Eudes was haled before a council at Reims in 1148 and sentenced to life imprisonment; he died not long afterward.

Despite these apparent setbacks, the dualist view continued to spread. The great council held at St.-Félix-de-Caraman in 1167 was presided over by the recently arrived Bogomil "bishop" of Constantinople, Nicetas, mentioned earlier. The Western dualists thus looked on the Bogomils as their spiritual parents. Nicetas succeeded in persuading the Western heretics to accept a fundamental dualism rather than the modified monarchian dualism of other Bogomils such as Basil. Nicetas ordained a number of bishops: Bernard Raymond for Toulouse, Guiraud Mercier for Carcassonne, Raymond of Casalis for Val d'Aran, and his own disciple Bartholomew of Carcassonne as bishop of Albi, the town from which the movement would derive its name.

The spread of what we now call Albigensianism from the early disorders associated with the name "Tanchelm" around 1115 to the convening of a great council in 1167 rivals that of early Christianity. Of course it is better documented, for the Roman Catholic authorities combated it from the beginning and documented every step of their opposition to it, while the earliest Christian congregations were neither systematically opposed nor even particularly noticed by the authorities of pagan Rome. Why did dualism spread so rapidly? Dualism is a religious idea that is very natural to man, and grows out of the age-old conflict between good and evil. Only with patient effort can Christianity overcome dualistic tendencies within its own fold.

b. Cathar Doctrines

Despite the proliferation of names attached to these dualistic heretics—Bogomils, Publicans (from the Greek *Paulikanoi*, pronounced "pavlikanoi"), Cathars, Albigensians—they seem to manifest a considerable degree of unity in their views, particularly after their council of 1167. The influence of Nicetas apparently resolved the ambivalence between moderate and strict dualism; the stricter variety prevailed. Spiritual beings, imprisoned in base matter, are purified in a cycle of rebirths. The Son is the most perfect of created angels and is specially adopted by the Father; the Holy Spirit is the aeon who is in charge of the celestial spirits who minister to the divine spark in man. Christ only appeared to be man and neither died nor was resurrected. The New Testament is the work of God, the Old that of the Evil One.

Cathar views are thus a mélange of dualistic and gnostic ideas, but we do not know whether they derive from actual contact with dualistic sources or simply reemerged as the products of man's fertile but limited religious fantasy. The Bogomils and the Cathars appear to differ from the earlier Marcionite and Manichaean dualists in their teachings on sexuality, at least for the ordinary believers. Most of the older dualists called for the strictest asceticism—no meat or other animal foods, no wine, and no sexual activity. Marriage was opposed for several reasons. It is an attachment based on the body and its sexual appetites, and it makes it difficult for those who are married to avoid engaging in frequent sexual intercourse. In addition, marriage clearly promotes the bearing of children, which implies bringing new spiritual beings under the domination of fleshly bodies and so helping the cause of Evil. As far as both Bogomils and Cathars are concerned, the testimonies that attribute moral purity to the leaders (the "elect," or "pure"), but license to the generality of followers, are too numerous and unanimous to suppose them all to be hostile fabrications. Because normal heterosexual intercourse is conducive to reproduction, it was discouraged, and various alternative forms of sexual activity encouraged in its place; the vulgar expression "bugger" is a corruption of "Bulgar," the name often given the Bogomils in the West because of their Balkan origin. Although these medieval Manichaeans did permit ordinary believers to live self-indulgent, licentious lives, it was expected that all Cathars would receive the ceremony of the *consolamentum* before death and thus die pure. Because many adherents felt unable to maintain the strict asceticism demanded of the perfect—especially after a long period of licentiousness—many waited until they were at the point of death to receive the *consolamentum;* wealthy Albigenses engaged two companions to be with them at all times, ready to administer the *consolamentum* promptly in case of a sudden danger to life. Others, after receiving the *consolamentum,* immediately began the so-called *endura,* the "fasting unto death."

c. Repression

As distasteful as this resurgence of dualism must appear to orthodox Christians, both in its theory and its practice, it is difficult to consider the means used to oppose it as anything but atrocious. When the Empress-Regent Theodora and later the Emperor John I Tzimisces resettled the Paulicians, they had some substantial political and military reasons for doing so. On the frontier with the Arabs, the Paulicians were unreliable and likely to change sides. Stationed facing the newly converted Christian Bulgarians, they had nothing to gain by abandoning the empire and indeed were likely to lose their land and their homes if they permitted the Bulgarians to overrun them. After Alexius I began severe repression by ordering the execution of the Bogomil Basil, the policy of the government and the church becomes harder to justify;[15] particularly in the Latin West, where in the absence of a strong, centralized government the church itself took up the bloody business of persecution.

The autocrat Alexius I condemned Basil under the old Roman imperial laws, dating back to Justinian I, which treated certain forms of heresy as criminal offenses. In the West, Roman law had been abandoned and only ecclesiastical punishments for heresy existed—for the laity, excommunication, for clergy, confinement in a monastery. When Gottschalk was scourged for refusing to recant, he suffered a monastic penalty, not a secular one. The new Albigensian heresy proved far too powerful to combat with church penalties such as excommunication. Its vigor caused the church to create the Inquisition.

Before heresy was declared a crime, inflamed popular passions had begun to erupt in sporadic acts of violence. These disorders seemed to threaten general anarchy, and both the secular and church authorities began to institute measures to control the heretics, feeling that this was more suitable than efforts to restrain popular indignation and violence against them.[16] These initial acts of repression were outside the law and were both arbitrary and severe. When mercifully disposed preachers found that their efforts at persuasion met with failure, they often resorted to force. "Moderate" penalties such as fines, confiscation of property, and banishment were swiftly superseded by imprisonment, branding, and various forms of capital punishment. This went far beyond what was permitted by canon law at the time. Although the Justinian Code (the *Codex Justinianus*), which was civil law, prescribed the death penalty for adherents of Manichaeanism, the *Decretum*, a collection of Roman Catholic canon law published by Gratian of Bologna in about 1140, called only for fines or exile.

There was no systematic legislation against heresy in the West for the simple reason that heresy had not been a major problem since the Germanic invasions had extinguished the older Roman law, which did legislate against it. In addition, most of those who came under scrutiny as possible heretics were clerics and often monks, and so were subject to ecclesiastical and monastic discipline. It was the combination of the outbreak of controversies and major heresies with an increasing popular sensitivity to religious issues that ultimately made heresies a major problem and led both church and state to take explicit action against it. Although heresy was only an ecclesiastical offense, the close relationship between church and state in medieval society meant that anything that threatened the one disturbed the other as well.

One of the first major figures who challenged church and state to take action against him was Arnold of Brescia, a pupil of Peter Abelard (1079–1142). Arnold led a religious-civil rebellion and effectively ruled Rome 1146–49. When Bishop Manfred of Brescia attempted to enforce church discipline against dissolute clergy, the ascetic Arnold attacked both parties, charging that the wealth of the church was the root of the evil. While the bishop was absent, Arnold raised a rebellion against him and prevented his return. Pope Innocent II (reigned 1130–43) ordered Arnold to leave Italy, which he did, but returned after a brief absence. Expelled from France by King Louis VII on the request of Bernard of Clairvaux, Arnold went to Zurich and Passau before returning to Viterbo in Italy, where he confessed to Pope Eugene III and received absolution. But within a year he began to agitate again. Going to Rome, he aroused the masses and revived for himself the old republican title of "tribune of the people," expelling Pope Eugene. The pope returned with a military force in 1149 but was thrown out again the following year. Finally, in 1154 the new German Emperor, Frederick I Barbarossa (ruled 1152–90), apprehended Arnold and turned him over to the new pope, Hadrian IV (reigned 1154–59), who had him beheaded. Beheading was the penalty for rebellion, a criminal offense against the state, not for heresy.

Although the first half of the twelfth century produced outstanding and charismatic spiritual leaders, such as Bernard of Clairvaux and Hugh of St. Victor, they were unable to make much headway against either the dualistic heretics on the one hand or the political-ecclesiastical rigorists such as Arnold of Brescia on the other. The "faith" of the Age of Faith was by no means a settled and universally accepted norm. Because a number of these medieval heretics did actually agitate against the civil government and actively foment rebellion, at first it was not altogether clear whether the dire penalties they incurred were the punishment for heresy or for sedition. Heresy undermined the social fabric of the Christian monarchies of the day, and many rulers—such as Louis VII of France—truly feared the heretics as revolutionaries. Louis pressed Pope Alexander III (reigned 1159–81) to take decisive action to check the spread of heresy. Alexander complied and a council held in Tours in 1163 issued the first general legislation against heresy produced by the medieval church. The council authorized only imprisonment and confiscation of property as punishments for heretics, although in practice severer penalties, including execution, were already being imposed.[17]

Forcible repression led to violent resistance on the part of many of the Western dualists, for they were not pacifists like the Bogomils. In consequence, the Third Lateran Council (1179) included armed resistance to the authorities among the reasons for anathematizing the dualistic heretics.[18] A papal commission, the forerunner of the dreaded Inquisition, had arrived at Toulouse in the preceding year to ferret out the heretics. Its first victim was a rich bourgeois named Pierre Malan, who claimed to be John the Evangelist. He recanted and was turned over to the secular ruler, the Count of Toulouse, for punishment: his property was confiscated, the house where he met other heretics was destroyed, and he himself was sent to serve the poor in the Holy Land for three years.

In 1184 Pope Lucius III (reigned 1181–85) and the Emperor Frederick I Barbarossa took another step in the organization of the Inquisition, establishing episcopal commissions to control heresy in northern Italy. These commissions were empowered to defrock clerics found guilty of heresy and to "turn them over to the secular authorities." Laymen accused of heresy, if unable to prove their innocence, were likewise handed over to the civil government for punishment. This agreement, dating from 1184, did not prescribe the penalty the state was to impose. The custom of execution by fire appears to date from a slightly later decree issued in Aragon by King Peter II in 1197.

The next major step in the establishment of the Inquisition was taken by Innocent III (reigned 1198–1216) immediately upon ascending to the papacy; he placed the episcopal inquisitorial commissions in southern France under his personal supervision. It was under Innocent III—although not at his behest—that the infamous Fourth Crusade was diverted from the Holy Land to the capture and sack of Constantinople, a grievous wound to the Eastern empire, nearly a millennium old. It never fully recovered, although it survived in a progressively deteriorating condition until 1453. In the West, the same pope launched a "Crusade" against the Cathars, or Albigenses, of southern France in 1208. The Albigensian wars lasted twenty-one years, leaving Provençal culture in ruins and facilitating the rise of France as a strongly centralized nation-state.

In the second century of the Christian Era, most Christians refused to take up arms at all. One millennium later, Christians were not only fighting for the church against "infidels" who had conquered ancient biblical lands, but against other Christians, heretical ones, who asked only to be able to live in peace on their ancestral soil. It took Christianity a thousand years to launch Crusades against non-Christians, and little more than an additional century for it to begin to use them against heretics in its own midst.

5. THE "HERESY" OF POVERTY

No matter how dreadful the use of violence against the dualistic Albigenses was, it must be acknowledged that their heresy is incompatible with Christianity, indeed with biblical religion as such. If they had prevailed, Christianity would have ceased to exist. The fact that so much was at stake helps to explain, although not to justify, the fury with which the medieval church fought against the dualists. At the same time, the fatal nature of the church's conflict with dualism makes it seem strange indeed that the church used similar ferocity in dealing with other dissidents, who really were not heretics at all. These were the preachers of "apostolic poverty," those who contended that Jesus and his disciples owned nothing at all and lived in voluntary, total poverty. Arnold of Brescia, who temporarily unseated a pope, is the most prominent early example of a "heretic" whose major offense was his repudiation of worldly wealth.

Perhaps for medieval popes the crucial factor that caused them to condemn dissidents was really those dissidents' rejection of papal authority; whether they were radically non-Christian, like the dualists, or only excessively simple, like some of the preachers of poverty, the important thing was that they undermined papal authority and with it that of the church that claimed to be the only route to salvation. In any event, both in practice and to some extent in theory Roman Catholicism has frequently failed to make a distinction between heretics whose views would have destroyed the Christian faith and others whose chief offense was the fact that they found formal Christianity inconsistent and hypocritical.

Because the Roman Catholic attack on heresy also hit hard at them, despite their agreement with Catholicism on the affirmations of the great creeds, Protestants too have tended to lose sight of the distinction between heretics properly so called and those branded with the name because they were uncomfortable in a worldly church. From Luther onward, Protestants have been quick to recognize and claim their affinity with many that Rome brands heretical, particularly with the Italian Waldensians and the Bohemian Hussites. Because they deny that "heretics" such as Protestants, Hussites, or Waldensians are dangerous to Christianity, and in fact contend that they are necessary, Protestants tend to overlook the fact that some heretics and the heresies they teach actually threaten the life of the church.

Arnold of Brescia is an example of a charismatic leader who rejected wealth but soon found himself enjoying political power, at least for a short time. A larger and more representative group also taught the "heresy" of poverty, and did so without seeking political power: the Waldensians. They owe their origin, like the slightly later Roman Catholic order the Franciscans, to the conversion of one man to the ideal of poverty.

a. The Waldensians

Waldes, or Waldo (the name "Peter" is attested only relatively late), a well-to-do Lyonnais merchant, experienced a conversion to the ideal of poverty during the course of an economic crisis in 1176. His was not the first, or even the second, of the century's movements against the wealth and luxury of the church. The revolutionary protest of Arnold of Brescia was followed by a number of other movements in Lombardy, in the north of Italy. Between 1164 and 1171 Hugo Speroni, consul in Piacenza, rejected the sacraments, especially baptism, penance, and the eucharist, and sought to replace them with a spiritual communion with the Word; his views are known only from the refutation presented by his fellow student Vacarius (d. ca. 1198). The group Speroni led, the so-called Humiliati, seems to have been a kind of anticipation of the early Quakers, stressing both simplicity of life and intimate, personal fellowship with God through the Word.

Waldo and his followers are better known. As an untrained layman, he was unable to read the Latin Bible, and so asked two clerical friends to translate portions for him. He committed them to memory, and then undertook the task of making the Scriptures available to the public in those "vulgar" translations. (The obsolete expression "vulgar tongue" means "ordinary language," as distinguished from Latin; interestingly, Jerome's Latin translation is called the Vulgate because it was in the ordinary spoken Latin of his day, not in the elegant language of the classics; it was this Vulgate Bible that Waldo had translated into the "vulgar" tongue of southern France.)

After having given away all his possessions, Waldo surrounded himself with a band of men and women who went about preaching the Gospel. Their doctrines were not strange, nor did Waldo intend to innovate. He sought ecclesiastical authorization for this preaching from the Third Lateran Council in 1179 and met with the pope, but Pope Alexander III specifically forbade him to continue. Waldo was undaunted, and soon his followers were widely distributed in southern France and northern Italy; Waldensians seem to have made little progress in adjacent Languedoc, where dualism was already established. Not only were the Waldensians less heretical than the dualists, they were also more moral. Whereas the dualists preached a high morality in theory, but reserved its application to the "pure" and allowed ordinary "believers" to live licentiously, the Waldensians tried to apply to all believers the standards of spirituality hitherto reserved for the religious orders; indeed, unlike the industrious Benedictines, the first Waldensians even rejected manual labor, living from alms. This latter tendency, of course, could not be maintained in any region where Waldensians became numerous. Unlike the dualists, they believed in the deity of Christ and in the Fall of man and retained both penance and the eucharist, although they would accept them only from godly ministrants. They denied the distinctive privileges of the priestly office and allowed any righteous man to pronounce absolution and celebrate the eucharist. In this they clearly anticipate Luther's insistence on the priesthood of all believers. The source and power of their religious conviction lay in their commitment to the authority of Scripture and in their efforts to make it as widely known as possible. Unlike the Cathars, who circulated various legendary versions of biblical texts,[19] the Bibles circulated by the Waldensians were as accurate and reliable as the Vulgate, on which they were based.

b. Further Repression

In March 1180 Waldo appeared at a synod in Lyons before Cardinal Henry of Albano (who had followed Bernard as Abbot of Clairvaux), a vigorous persecutor of the Cathars. Waldo produced a thoroughly orthodox confession and denounced all the errors of the Cathars; what he wanted was nothing more than a kind of lay mendicant order such as that successfully established by Francis of Assisi a generation later. To this the cardinal consented, but conflict soon broke out again. The Waldensians insisted on continuing their lay preaching; women also did it, including converted harlots. Complaints were sent to Rome, and in 1184 Pope Lucius III condemned the Poor Men of Lyons together with the heretical Cathars—despite the fact that Waldo's followers continued to oppose the Cathars very vigorously. Their insistence that a priest must be spiritually worthy to administer the sacraments clashed sharply with the Roman church's insistence on the idea that the holy orders received by all priests were sufficient to make their sacraments valid.

Innocent III was more sensitive than Lucius, and recognized that his predecessor's blanket condemnation of the Poor Men of Lyons and the Humiliati along with the dualist Cathars went too far; he made an effort to reconcile the Humiliati, who were received back into the church as an officially recognized lay fellowship. It was an unusual precedent for a group recently condemned as a heretical sect to be recognized and readmitted. Innocent also succeeded in reconciling large numbers of Waldensians with Rome. In this way he accepted as legitimate the spiritual concerns that had caused the protest of the Waldensians and the Humiliati. The Waldensians of northern Italy, unlike those of southern France, did not disdain manual labor and hence were not dependent on alms. The Italian Waldensians also rejected Waldo's example of leaving his wife; at the same time the Italians were more severe and consistent than the southern French in rejecting the sacramental ministry of unworthy priests. Although none of the Waldensians were as hostile to the established church or nearly as dangerous as the Cathars, they too were persecuted by the Inquisition and would survive only in isolated valleys of Piedmont and Savoy until the Reformation brought them powerful support.

6. PETER ABELARD

The first real flowering of medieval Scholasticism is associated with the names of two men, Peter Abelard (1079–1142) and the somewhat older Anselm of Canterbury (1033–1109). If the movement began earlier, with Fulbert of Chartres (d. 1028) and his pupil Berengar, it was Anselm who carried Scholastic orthodoxy to its greatest development prior to Aquinas; Abelard, in some ways like Berengar, represents the opposite pole of the Scholastic tradition. Under Abelard, the intellect was still in the service of religion, but it began to strain at the bonds dogma and traditionalism imposed, and ultimately ended by shaking the foundations on which it had tried to build. Although Abelard's name has already come up in our discussion as we followed the direction of the Manichaeans of the Middle Ages, and although Arnold of Brescia was his pupil and defended him (Bernard called Arnold Abelard's spear-bearer), Abelard's primary significance lay in his influence on scholarship, not on religious revolution.

As a philosopher and lay theologian prior to 1109, Abelard had shown only disdain for heresy; indeed, throughout his whole life he wanted to be a pious teacher of the church. Only at forty, after his love affair with his pupil Héloïse and his subsequent emasculation at the hands of her enraged uncle, did he become a monk. The priesthood was closed to him because of his mutilation. His thirst for knowledge and his personal vanity made him delight in dialectical argument and in novelty. The heresy with which he will be charged did not result from religious or ascetic motives, as in the case of the Waldensians and the dualists, but from his intellectual curiosity and pride. Abelard had studied with Roscelin, whose views of the Trinity Anselm had found tritheistic and who had had to abjure them in 1092. At the time, Abelard had criticized Roscelin as a "pseudodialectician" and a "pseudo-Christian," but his own first work, which also tried to explain the Trinity, met the same fate at Soissons in 1121; he was not allowed to speak in his own behalf, and had to burn his books with his own hands.[20]

Abelard's error was his conviction that the mystery of the Trinity can be rationally comprehended; he burned his first book (although it later became the basis for his *Christian Theology*), but he did not give up his conviction. He continued to attempt to explain mysteries, and found many admiring pupils; an open conflict did not break out until close to the end of his life when the ubiquitous Bernard took him to task and asked him to give up teaching in ways that were so readily open to misunderstanding.

Abelard seems to have been inclined to comply, but Arnold of Brescia took up his cause and inflamed the conflict. Bernard reacted by excerpting nineteen theses from the works of Abelard and having them condemned as heretical at Sens without granting Abelard a hearing. Abelard appealed to the pope, who heeded Bernard and reaffirmed the decision of Sens; Abelard was condemned to keep silent and spend the rest of his days confined to a monastery. He took sick almost immediately, and was cared for at Cluny, where the Abbot Peter the Venerable succeeded in effecting a reconciliation with Bernard and the reversal of the papal condemnation before Abelard died in 1142. Abelard maintained that his theses that were condemned had been misunderstood, but he did not insist on upholding them. In his last work, *Dialogue Between a Philosopher, a Jew, and a Christian,*[21] Abelard asserted once again his conviction that Christian doctrines can be rationally proved even to Jews and pagans.

In 1140 at Sens, Abelard had tried in vain to rally to his aid Gilbert de La Porrée, the future bishop of Poitiers, calling out: "Tua res agitur!" ("It's your business!") Gilbert declined, but this did not protect him from Bernard's zeal against suspected heresy. Gilbert, although making every effort to be orthodox, was trying too hard to understand the Trinity rationally, in Bernard's view, and creating confusion. He made a distinction between deity, the essence of God, and God himself, the person. To speak of God as a person while saying that deity subsists in the three Persons, Father, Son, and Holy Spirit, seems to suggest a fourth Person, namely, God, alongside the other three. Despite Bernard's eagerness to have him condemned, Gilbert was able to evade conviction as a heretic by correcting some of his formulations.

a. Peter Lombard

If Abelard shaped the mentality of Scholasticism, it was Peter Lombard (d. 1160) who gave it its structure. His most famous work, *Sentences,* is divided into four "books," dealing respectively with God, Creation and the Fall, the incarnation and redemption, and finally the sacraments and eschatology. This structure, which corresponds loosely to that of the ecumenical creeds, has been preserved in most works on dogmatics since his day. He was not universally appreciated: Walter of St. Victor denounced him as one of the "four labyrinths of France," and Abbot Joachim of Floris charged him with making God into a "quaternity," as Bernard had charged Gilbert.

b. Joachim of Floris

Abbot Joachim of Floris (d. ca. 1202), regarded as orthodox during his lifetime, was posthumously condemned by the Fourth Lateran Council in 1215 and is popularly ranked among the great medieval heretics, largely because of the posthumous influence his ideas had on the most radical branch of the new Franciscan order, the so-called spiritual Franciscans. Joachim was certainly orthodox with regard to theology and Christology, but he developed a striking view of history and some remarkable expectations concerning the future; his heresy was historical, or rather eschatological.

Orthodox Christianity has generally divided all history into two periods, marked by the Old and New Testaments, or by Law and Gospel. Although millennial expectancy—the hope that Christ would return to set up a thousand-year kingdom on earth—was prevalent in the early church, the influence of Augustine had caused most traditional Christians to give up the idea of an earthly millennium and to expect the return of Christ to lead immediately to the Last Judgment and the changeless eternal state of heaven. In contrast with this two-period old/new dichotomy, Joachim envisaged a threefold division of history, based on the Persons of the Trinity. The Old Testament era was the Age of the Father, an age of Law; the New Testament period was the Age of the Son, based on the Gospel. The Third Age would be the Age of the Holy Spirit, based on a new covenant and a spiritual, or eternal, Gospel. The Old Testament was the age of civil rule, the New Testament that of the church and the hierarchy; the Third Age would be an age of spiritual government, of a monastic church. Joachim and his followers were obsessed by a sense of the corruption of Christianity and of the oppressiveness of the nominally Christian secular power structures. They expected the church to be reformed by an angelic pope who would abolish all its wealth and display; at the same time they expected the secular order to bring forth an Antichrist. Of course Joachim's ideas were radically critical of the existing church and its hierarchy, and consequently were as odious to the hierarchy as they were attractive to many who sought the church's transformation. They were taken up by one of the new class of spiritual orders that came into being shortly after his death, the Franciscans.

Joachim succeeded in directing the attention of a large segment of Christendom away from the present to the future, from the contemporary church and its claims to a realistic eschatology and the expectation that the Last Days were imminent. His ideas were soon declared heretical and passed from the religious scene, but his periodization of history into three ages continues to fascinate and influence many. The traditional division of world history into antiquity, the Middle Ages, and modernity implies that our present age is the age of fulfillment. G. E. Lessing in the eighteenth century believed that mankind had outgrown both the Law and the Gospel, and had attained a third age of Reason. Russian nationalism considered Moscow the Third Rome, and modern Communist eschatology incorporates some of the old Third Rome mystique. Hitler, in proclaiming his Third Reich, consciously evoked the Holy Roman Empire and the German Empire of Bismarck as its predecessors, but his millennial language reveals that Hitler thought of his Thousand-Year Reich in mystical terms, as far more than a mere restored German Empire. Certainly a part of the fascination Hitler held for Germans, including a surprisingly large number of both liberal and conservative Christians, was due to the fact that consciously or unconsciously he awakened in them expectations of a final, messianic age about to dawn in world history. Moscow and Hitler, of course, are far from anything Joachim would have wished; they correspond more closely to his idea of the Antichrist. Nevertheless, they borrowed his prophetic vision. Although Joachim died before the founding of the Franciscan order, his fame in church history rests on the enthusiasm he inspired among the Franciscans, who saw their founder, Francis, as fulfilling Joachim's hope for an angelic leader.

7. THE NEW ORDERS

The monastery of Cluny, founded in 910, was the starting point for the reform movement that reached its height under Pope Gregory VII (reigned 1073–85). The Cluniac reform movement was based on the strict observance of the Benedictine Rule, and while Cluny exercised a monarchical rule over subsequently established daughter monasteries, it founded no new order. The late eleventh and early twelfth centuries saw the birth of several important new religious orders. Among them, the Cistercians with Bernard of Clairvaux as their most famous member are outstanding, but by no means alone: the Augustinian Canons and the Premonstratensians are the best known among several others. In addition, the twelfth century, as the era of the Crusades, saw the birth of the knightly orders, including the Knights of St. John, the Knights Templars, and, somewhat later, the two German orders, the Knights of the Sword and the Knights of the Cross called the Teutonic Order (combined after 1237). But the most dramatic transformation of monastic life took place with the founding of the mendicant, or begging, orders in the thirteenth century.

The establishment of the mendicant orders represents a continuation within the established church of the impulses that had led to the establishment of the Poor Men of Lyons and the Humiliati. They differed dramatically from the orders that preceded them in their much more radical approach to poverty, a monastic ideal often honored more in the breach than in practice. While earlier monks had sworn a vow of poverty, the vow applied only to individuals, not to the monastery or to the order; a monastery could be wealthy. The new orders rejected all property even for the order. In addition, while the monastic movement had begun in the fourth century as a means to help Christians insure their own salvation away from the temptations of the world, the new movement was directed at the evangelization of the laity and sent its members out into the world, not into the cloister. Although like their predecessors, the Waldensians and the Humiliati, the new orders sharply criticized the clergy and its wealth, unlike them they were supportive of the pope. Because of their poverty and consequent lack of monastic lands and buildings for which to care, the members of the new orders turned out to be dedicated and effective shock troops for the papacy—something that was surely far from the original intention of Francis of Assisi.

Next to Jesus Christ himself, Francis of Assisi (1182–1226) is probably the Christian figure most respected and admired by non-Christians. Militant defenders of orthodoxy, such as Athanasius and Augustine, usually meet with only grudging approval on the part of orthodox Protestants, although Protestantism owes much to them. Francis preached a most un-Protestant piety and his order became an effective instrument of the papacy, but he is always honored. Even non-Christians who are highly critical of the great intellects of Christian history tend to praise Francis, or at the very least not to condemn him. Ironically, his own fame and the development taken by the order he founded would have been hateful to him if he could have foreseen them.

The Waldensians were very similar in spirit to the first Franciscans. They refused to come to terms with the papacy and endured centuries of persecution. The Franciscans did compromise, even before Francis' own early death. Francis lived just long enough to see the beginnings of the transformation that made his order an honored one at the cost of many of

its founder's dearest ideals. Francis and the Franciscan movement were potentially the most explosive phenomenon within Latin Christendom before
Martin Luther. The skill of Pope Honorius III (reigned 1216–27) prevented
an explosion, but the pope's influence also insured that the order would not
become what Francis had hoped.

a. Precursors of Francis of Assisi

Although Francis is the most striking figure of the new movement and
although his order, for centuries, was the most distinctive of the religious
orders, he was not the first to fall in love with the ideal of poverty. We have
already noted that the movement of the Humiliati, akin to the Poor Men of
Lyons, was reconciled to the Roman obedience under Innocent III (reigned
1198–1216). A similar movement had begun in Aragon, under the Waldensian Duran of Huesca; it too was reconciled by Innocent as the Poor Catholics.

In 1204 Bishop Diego (Didacus) of Osma, in Spain, asked Innocent III
to relieve him of his office so that he might go with his assistant Dominic
to evangelize among the Cumans in southern Russia. It was this Bishop
Diego who urged Duran of Huesca to return the Poor Catholics to papal
authority, as he subsequently did, and the farsighted Innocent believed that
he had better use for him closer to home. He sent them to the South of
France, where Bernard of Clairvaux and his Cistercian monks had failed to
check the spread of dualist heresy. Diego died shortly thereafter, leaving his
mission to Dominic, who fulfilled it with amazing success. The idea of a
new order dedicated to preaching may have originated with Pope Innocent
himself; Dominic became its driving force. What began as a mission to the
Cathars of southern France in about 1207 developed into a fast-growing
religious order within a decade. Dominic himself became famous for the
fact that he preached, with skill and enthusiasm, *to* the heretics rather than
against them. His fame and lasting influence result far more from his organizational ability than from his preaching. In 1206 he founded the monastery
of Notre Dame at Prouille, near the Albigensian stronghold of Toulouse,
according to the Rule of the Augustinian Canons. The monastery became
the birthplace of a new order, the Order of Preachers, with its own rule, in
1216. The new Dominican order officially adopted the principle of begging
in 1220.

Dominic had some success at winning Albigenses over to orthodox Catholicism—now increasingly self-consciously *Roman* Catholicism—by the
preaching endeavors he began in 1206, but within two years his peaceful
approach was overshadowed by the first Crusade against heretical Chris-

tians. Catholic horror at the dangerous spread of medieval dualism was fanned by Catholic kings and nobles such as Simon de Montfort, who counted on enriching themselves and expanding their possessions at the expense of the Albigensian heretics. To save himself and his lands, the leading Albigensian nobleman, Raymond VI of Toulouse, accepted Catholicism in June 1209. But his rivals continued to charge him with heresy. He was condemned at Montpellier in 1211 and the Albigensian Crusade began again. It was hardly a propitious time for Dominic's preaching mission.

b. Francis and the Franciscans

The life of Francis of Assisi (1182–1226) is surrounded with so many legends that it is hard to describe it with accuracy. Like Peter Waldo, he came from a well-to-do bourgeois family. As a young man, he set out on military adventures in southern Italy in the hope of becoming a great prince. Taken ill at Spoleto, he had a vision that led him to renounce his wealth, to espouse "Dame Poverty," and to return to Assisi. There, in the chapel of Portiuncula, he heard the voice of the Lord from Matthew 10:7–12; these verses formed the foundation of his conviction that he was called to a life of systematic poverty; shortly afterward, he gathered a few followers with the same zeal. These "little brothers" became the Order of Friars Minor, or Franciscans. In addition to poverty, they set themselves the goal of preaching the Gospel everywhere. Because the Friars, like Waldo's Poor Men, were laymen, they quickly ran into the opposition of the bishops. Francis saw that the only way to overcome it was with the support of the pope, who had already given his enthusiastic support to Dominic. The pope wondered how Francis' friars could gain the theological knowledge needed to preach orthodoxy while maintaining an itinerant, mendicant pattern of life. According to the tradition, it was Innocent who gave Francis oral permission for the Friars to continue their preaching, subject to personal instruction by Francis.

While the Dominicans sought to win back Albigensian heretics, Francis and a number of friars—not yet officially recognized as a religious order—undertook the even more challenging task of preaching to the Moslems. Francis himself went to Egypt in 1219. His missions brought scant results, but did earn Francis the admiration of Cardinal Ugolino (later Pope Gregory IX, reigned 1227–41). Encouraged by Ugolino, Pope Honorius III (reigned 1216–27) recognized the Friars Minor as a distinct order with its own rule in 1223. Francis himself died in 1226, troubled by his fears that the Franciscans were already becoming worldly. He left a testament binding them to keep his original vision, but his benefactor Ugolino, now pope, soon declared that the testament was not binding on his order. The Franciscans remained somewhat distinctive. A small faction, animated by the eschatological visions of Joachim of Floris, tried to preserve Francis' original ideals and were ultimately declared heretical.

c. Joachim and the Spiritual Franciscans

At the beginning of the thirteenth century an entirely new variety of heresy arose. Dualism, as we have already indicated, was not a new idea, but really a very old heresy, in fact a pre-Christian religion. Whether it somehow survived or frequently revived cannot be known with certainty. The movement we shall call the "heresy of poverty," in its various forms, was essentially an attempt to have all Christians, not just a few monks, live according to the "counsels of perfection" found in the Gospels. Traditional monastic spirituality distinguished between the "precepts of the Gospel," which were binding on all Christians, and the "counsels of perfection," including poverty, which could be followed only by the highly committed, i.e. by monks and nuns. The effort to live by the counsels of perfection was simply called "religion" or the "religious life."

This new phenomenon appropriately may be called the Third Heresy; not only because it came as the third of the medieval heretical movements, but because it saw great significance in being third. We have already noted that it divided history into periods in such a way that it claimed to be living in the dawn, or just prior to the dawn, of a new, Third Age, corresponding to the Third Person of the Trinity, the Holy Spirit. The Joachimite movement introduced into Western history both a new awareness of the Holy Spirit and a new and original sense of history.

Each of these three movements—Cathar, Waldensian, and now Joachimite—involved a different Person of the Trinity. The Cathars denied the doctrine of Creation and made of the Father, the Creator God of the Bible, an inferior and unworthy being. In the light of this fundamental duality, the Son and the Holy Spirit played very subordinate roles. The Cathars had no real doctrine of the Trinity. Devotion to the Son, and specifically to the incarnate Son, Jesus Christ, played the major part in stimulating the poverty movement. Of course this was not a denial or diminution of his importance, but rather an attempt to take him and his incarnation seriously. Consequently, it was not a heresy at all. If Jesus Christ is truly man, as orthodox Christology so clearly proclaims, then we human beings must be able to emulate what he did as a man. The Waldensian movement was a protest against the institutionalization and ritualization of the work of Christ that reached its culmination in the medieval emphasis on the sacrifice of the Mass.

The Third Heresy, as we call it, less extreme than the Cathar movement, more so than Waldensianism, was an attempt to come to terms with the reality of the Person and work of the Holy Spirit, the neglected member of the Trinity. Because there had clearly been an age of the Father and of Law—the Old Testament era, in which the Son was altogether unknown, and an age of the Son, the New Testament era with its emphasis on grace— now becoming thoroughly institutionalized in the ministry of the sacraments, for the full recognition of the activity of the Holy Spirit a Third Age had to dawn, in which the Person and work of the Holy Spirit would be paramount. Joachim's "trinitarian" scheme gives us a kind of Christian philosophy of history. It permitted Christians to disapprove of present miseries in the Age of the Son without disapproving of the Son himself, for it presupposed that the present unfulfilled state of Christendom is part of God's plan.

This Third Heresy did represent a reaction to what some saw as an excessive preoccupation with the Son, particularly with his bodily presence in the eucharist. As long as the eucharistic worship of the church had stressed faith, it did not detract from the cardinal thesis of Christianity that union with Christ, the source of our salvation, is by faith engendered by the Holy Spirit, the third Person of the Trinity. But as the eucharist—or more precisely, the Mass—viewed as a sacrifice became ever more central to the Christian's life, the emphasis on the work of the Holy Spirit receded. As the idea grew that the sacrifice of the Mass is of immense value even without the need for those attending to participate in the communion, the role of the Holy Spirit became even less significant.

This particular transformation of the eucharist from a mystical participation in the body and blood of Christ to a repetition of the sacrifice of Christ did not affect the Eastern Orthodox churches, although like Roman Catholicism, Eastern Orthodoxy insists on the real, corporeal presence of Christ in the elements. The Eastern liturgy emphasizes the activity of the Holy Spirit in enabling the believer to participate in the body and blood of Christ. Western developments emphasized the power of the priest to guarantee the corporeal presence of Christ, and then went on to develop theories about what the priest can do with the body of Christ, i.e. offer it anew to God as a mystical sacrifice. This gradual transformation of the eucharist from a participation in to a sacrifice of the body and blood of Christ was dominant in the West by the end of the eleventh century, although transubstantiation, as we have noted, was not officially declared a dogma until 1215.

The same Fourth Lateran Council that promulgated the doctrine of transubstantiation as the official way of understanding what takes place at the consecration of the elements also posthumously condemned the doctrines of the Abbot Joachim together with those of another recently deceased teacher, Amalric of Bena (d. ca. 1206). There appears to have been no direct connection between Joachim in Calabria, at the heel of the Italian boot, and Amalric in Paris, but their concerns are somewhat similar. Joachim, we recall, had accused Peter Lombard of turning the Trinity into a quaternity by treating the deity or divine essence as though it were a fourth Person. Lombard had to be defended against the attacks of Joachim inasmuch as his *Sentences* were being accepted as the standard textbook in Scholastic theology. The council was not able to attack Joachim's three-age view of history directly, inasmuch as he had been commissioned by several popes to write and had submitted his writings for papal approval; the order he founded, the Florensians, was subsequently advised by Honorius III, the same pope who modified the testament of St. Francis, that Joachim was orthodox despite the fact that certain of his doctrines were condemned.

By 1240, approximately four decades after Joachim's death, his admirers among the Franciscans began to circulate a number of prophetic books under his name. In 1254 one of these men, Gerard of Borgio San Donnio, brought out Joachim's three major works under the title of *The Eternal Gospel*. *The Eternal Gospel* contains biting denunciations of the corrupt state of the church and predicts a sweeping transformation under an "angel pope." Needless to say, the ecclesiastical authorities were aroused. Pope Alexander IV (reigned 1254–61) appointed a commission to investigate Joachim's doctrines. It exonerated Joachim and banned only Gerard's introduction to *The Eternal Gospel*. Joachim had thought of himself as fully orthodox and had strengthened his claim to orthodoxy by vigorous attacks on contemporary heretics, not only the dualistic Cathars but also the much milder Waldensians.

Why did Joachim attack the Waldensians, with whom he shared a number of ethical and spiritual ideals? The answer lies in the fact that the Waldensians' reforms would have led to a laïcized Christianity, whereas Joachim dreamed of a totally *monastic* Third Age. Like the Waldensians of his own day and the Protestant Reformers of the sixteenth century, Joachim felt deep disgust at the worldliness of the clergy. But they sought to reform the church by returning it to the simplicity of its origins, while Joachim's hope was to carry it forward to his vision of the Age of the Holy Spirit. In the Age of the Spirit, the new spiritual church would surpass the hierarchical church of the New Testament as that church superseded the synagogue and Temple of the Old.

Joachim's posthumous disciples thought that they saw the Antichrist in the Hohenstaufen Emperor Frederick II (ruled 1215–50), already widely suspect because of his affinity for Islam and his rapport with infidels. Based on Joachim's interpretation of numbers found in the prophecy of Daniel, these Franciscan spirituals expected the full revelation of Frederick as the Antichrist in the year 1260. Unfortunately for this theory, Frederick died unexpectedly in 1250. An effort was made to seek the Antichrist among the surviving members of the Hohenstaufen dynasty, but its last male member, the brilliant young Conradin, was killed in battle in Naples in 1268.

d. Amalric of Bena

Joachim's theory of the three ages of history was orthodox enough to avoid condemnation. Several near contemporaries of his carried the theory to a totally unacceptable extreme. A number of disciples of Amalric of Bena were burned in Paris in 1210 for teaching that God the Father was incarnate in the Old Testament patriarchs, that the Son became incarnate in Mary, and that the Holy Spirit was incarnate in them. Their views were apparently a kind of Neoplatonic pantheism dressed up in Christian terminology, inspired in part by the rediscovery of the work of the ninth-century philosopher John Scotus Erigena. Pantheistic tendencies were also exhibited in the work of David of Dinant, which was also condemned in 1210. David used the works of Aristotle and his Arabic commentators, which had just become known in Latin translations, as the basis for a pantheistic materialism.

These emerging pantheistic tendencies represented a different kind of threat when contrasted with medieval dualism. It was in a sense a more elemental attack on Christian orthodoxy, for the dualists at least accepted the personhood of Christ and the Father, even though they postulated dualistic rivals to them. If the dualists saw Creation as the work of an evil divinity, the pantheists identified it with deity. Neither dualists nor pantheists accepted the sovereign, personal Creator God of the Bible and the creeds. The High Middle Ages are called the Age of Faith. Is it not remarkable that during this period the very nature of God was challenged within Christian and theological circles? Admittedly, the church launched Crusades against the Albigenses and used the Inquisition against the Waldensians in an effort to preserve orthodoxy. Nevertheless, the fact that such categorically anti-Christian thought was now arising from within the bosom of the church itself demonstrates that the emerging doctrinal and intellectual precision of Scholastic theology, far from establishing the faith more fully and making it secure against all doubt, actually opened it to new problems. Although the materialistic-legal-official aspect of the new eucharistic doctrine was to some extent offset by the intense mystical spirituality that accompanied it, this spirituality was largely confined to "religious"—i.e. monastic—circles and did not reach the people in general. The Christian public lived largely by the outward forms.

After the burning of Amalric's writings together with those of a number of his adherents in 1210, Ortlib of Strassburg was condemned because he was willing to listen only to "the Holy Spirit within." His followers were accused of denying Creation and of teaching that the world has always existed. Their teaching corresponds to the philosophy of Aristotle and the Spanish Averroists (after Averroës, or ibn-Rushd, d. 1198). They also denied the resurrection of the dead and the Last Judgment. Little is known about them, but "This is characteristic of the heretical spirituality of the thirteenth century: it flamed up surprisingly here and there, inconstant and with no visible context."[22] The continuing interest in a heretical view of the Holy Spirit is attested by Albertus Magnus (ca. 1206–80), the teacher of Thomas Aquinas (ca. 1225–74), who wrote an analysis of the "heresy of the new spirit" around 1270.

8. THE INQUISITION

a. The Beginnings

The Fourth Lateran Council of 1215 saw the highwater mark of the medieval papacy under Innocent III. Innocent, who had displayed ferocious severity in dealing with the Albigenses but showed comparative mildness vis-à-vis the Humiliati, and who organized the atrocious Fourth Crusade, also sought to reform the morals of the church, but succeeded only in making its differences from ancient catholicism official and permanent. The Fourth Lateran Council established the doctrine of transubstantiation and the sacrament of penance. In addition, the Inquisition, which had begun as a commission of inquiry under Alexander III a generation earlier, now became a permanent part of the church's life. A faith that stressed the power and authority of its officially installed ministry to distribute the body and blood of its Lord seems to have needed an official institution to make certain that its official acts and doctrines were accepted at face value. The Holy Office of the Inquisition was born.

Innocent III pursued the Albigensian heretics vigorously, both with the sword of the Word as preached by Dominic and his Order of Preachers, and with the sword of steel wielded in the protracted and often interrupted Albigensian Crusade (1208–29). But neither remedy was adequate, and dualism survived, along with other heresies. The pope recognized the need for a new organizational structure to identify and root out dangerous heresies. Several earlier popes, including Alexander III, Lucius III, and Gregory VIII, had authorized bishops to proceed against heretics on the basis of rumors alone, without waiting for formal evidence. It was then up to the accused to prove his innocence. This is the beginning of the famous policy of the Inquisition. Basic procedures for the Inquisition were established during the pontificate of Innocent III at the council of 1215. Innocent was succeeded in 1216 by Honorius III. Cardinal Ugolino, adviser and successor to Honorius, befriended Francis of Assisi, but he also strengthened and activated the Inquisition.

The birth of the Inquisition coincided with the Albigensian Crusade and ultimately led to the destruction of Cathar dualism, and incidentally of a once-flourishing Romance culture in the South of France. The severity of crusading commander Simon de Montfort and the inquisitorial excesses undertaken by several bishops at his behest caused several major towns in the South of France to rally to the hero of the Albigensians, Count Raymond VI of Toulouse. But the combined pressure of the Crusades and the Inquisition proved too much. The Albigensians were crushed, Provence ruined, and France became a political unity. King Louis VIII of France demanded title to the lands of the Albigenses as his price for taking part in the Crusade.

The attention of Honorius was called away from the dualist threat in the South of France to the problem of the loss of Jerusalem and the collapsing crusader states in the Near East. Much time was lost in attempting to get action from Emperor Frederick II, the one whom the spiritual Franciscan saw as the coming Antichrist. Eventually Frederick succeeded in recovering Jerusalem, but he did so by making a friendly bargain with the Moslems, rather than waging a holy war—much to the indignation of most of Christendom. Shortly before his death Honorius turned back to his Albigensian Crusade, which faltered again as a result of the sudden death of King Louis VIII of France, Honorius' chief crusader. The Albigensian capital, Toulouse, was finally captured in 1229, early in the pontificate of Honorius' successor, Gregory IX.

Although when he was still a cardinal he was a friend and benefactor of Francis of Assisi, Gregory's actions as pope display little of Francis' spirit. In his constitution published in 1231, *Excommunicamus et Damnamus* (We Excommunicate and Condemn . . .), Gregory established unified procedures for the Inquisition throughout the whole Western church. The ecclesiastical tribunals that tried heretics did not themselves put them to death, but "relinquished them to the secular arm." The secular authorities were obliged to impose the *animadversio debita*, "punishment due," namely, death by burning. Suspects had to perform a year of penance without being proved guilty; if they failed to do so, they were judged to be heretics and punished accordingly. Gregory's constitution denied accused persons the aid of any judge, advocate, or notary and provided for no appeal from any judgment. Even as we deplore the awful severity of these policies, we should note it as evidence for the horror heresy aroused among conscientious churchmen.

The establishment of the Inquisition formalized the long-standing practice of using secular power against erring teachers. What was new about it was that it patently made the church itself the prosecutor, if not the executioner. When a heretic was burned under Alexius I in Constantinople, it was by the authority of the Emperor and to some extent for reasons of state. In a real sense, the Inquisition represented the capitulation of the moral authority of the church in the face of heresy; in Hannah Arendt's famous dictum, "Violence appears where power is in jeopardy." The rationale behind the Inquisition was logical enough as a development of the theological realism and ecclesiastical absolutism of the medieval church: a heretic was far more dangerous than a murderer, for a murderer could only kill the body, but a heretic could destroy both body and soul in hell. Its procedures were so outrageous that they frequently horrified even the none-too-tender secular authorities; the term "mercy" was not in its vocabulary. Hounded by the Inquisition, persecuted dissidents came to see the church of Rome as the "woman drunken with the blood of the saints" (Rev. 17:6). To the extent that the Inquisition was a Roman Catholic phenomenon, it reflects shame on the largest church of Christendom; to the extent that it is a Christian phenomenon, it has done more than any other historical institution to make the Gospel an object of derision in the world at large.

Inquisitorial procedures were faster and more ruthless than those in the secular courts, making the Inquisition a useful tool for tyrants, secular as well as religious. When Frisian and Saxon peasants refused to pay church tithes in 1234, large numbers of them were condemned as heretics and put to death. In the South of France, as we have seen, the Inquisition and a series of Crusades changed the political structure as well as the religious complexion of the territory.

b. Political Heresies

In establishing the Inquisition, the Christian church in the West called on the power of the secular state to help it enforce its claims to spiritual dominion. Theology had become a political theory, or at least a theory with immediate and direct political consequences. To claim that theology has direct secular implications is to open the door to the suggestion that secular and political events have a spiritual significance of their own. The tendency to give a religious interpretation to political events of one's own day runs all through biblical religion, Jewish and Christian alike, into our own day, when Israeli, Soviet, Syrian, and Egyptian moves in the Middle East are interpreted in terms of the prophecies of Daniel or the Revelation of St. John. In the thirteenth century, as we have seen, the Emperor Frederick II was thought to fulfill biblical prophecy concerning the Antichrist. Christians began to cite theological doctrines as the authority for them to overthrow rulers and transform political structures—a thirteenth-century "theology of revolution." Heresy became a political event.

SELECTED BIBLIOGRAPHY

Bainton, Roland H. *Early and Medieval Christianity*. Boston: Beacon Press, 1962.

Coulton, G. G. *Inquisition and Liberty*. Toronto: Heinemann, 1938.

Cumming, G. J., and Derek Baker. *Councils and Assemblies*. Cambridge: University Press, 1971.

Dix, Gregory. *The Shape of the Liturgy*. Westminster: Dacre, 1945.

Döllinger, Ignatius von. *Geschichte der gnostisch-manichäischen Sekten im früheren Mittelalter*. New York: Burt Franklin, n.d.

Garsoïan, Nina G. *The Paulician Heresy*. The Hague: Mouton, 1968.

Gaskoin, C. J. B. *Alcuin: His Life and Work*. New York: Russell & Russell, 1966.

Hahn, Christoph Ulrich. *Geschichte der Ketzer im Mittelalter, besonders im 11. und 13. Jahrhundert*. Stuttgart: Steinkopf, 1850.

―――. *Geschichte der neumanichaeischen Ketzer*. Stuttgart: Steinkopf, 1845.

Kibre, Pearl. *Scholarly Privileges in the Middle Ages: The Rights, Privileges, and Immunities of Scholars and Universities at Bologna, Padua, Paris, and Oxford*. Cambridge, Mass.: Mediaeval Academy of America, 1962.

Landgraf, Artur Michael. *Dogmengeschichte der Frühscholastik*. 8 vols. Regensburg: Friedrich Pustet, 1952.

Lea, Henry Charles. *History of the Inquisition of the Middle Ages*. New York: Russell & Russell, 1955.

Lépicier, Alexis. *Indulgences, Their Origin, Nature and Development*. New York: Benziger, 1928.

Loos, Milan. *Dualist Heresy in the Middle Ages*. Translated by Iris Lewitova. The Hague: Nijhoff, 1974.

Moorman, John. *A History of the Franciscan Order from Its Origins to the Year 1917*. New York: Oxford University Press, 1968.

Oakley, Francis. *The Western Church in the Later Middle Ages*. Ithaca, N.Y.: Cornell University Press, 1979.

Obolensky, Dmitri. *The Bogomils: A Study in Balkan Neo-Manichaeism*. Cambridge: University Press, 1948.

Ozment, Steven. *The Age of Reform, 1250–1550*. New Haven: Yale University Press, 1980.

Pelikan, Jaroslav. *The Growth of Medieval Theology (600–1300)*. Vol. 3 of *The Christian Tradition*. Chicago: University Press, 1978.

Peters, Edward, ed. *Heresy and Authority in Medieval Europe*. Philadelphia: University of Pennsylvania Press, 1980.

Reeves, Marjorie. *Joachim of Fiore and the Prophetic Future*. London: S.C.M., 1976.

Runciman, Steven. *A History of the Crusades*. 2 vols. Cambridge: University Press, 1968.

Russell, Jeffrey Burton. *Dissent and Reform in the Early Middle Ages*. Berkeley: University of California Press, 1965.

Tuberville, Arthur Stanley. *Mediaeval Heresy and the Inquisition*. London: Crosby Lockwood and Son, 1920.

Waddell, Helen Jane. *The Wandering Scholars*. Garden City, N.Y.: Doubleday, 1955.

Williams, Watkin. *St. Bernard of Clairvaux*. Manchester: University Press, 1935.

Wild, Georg. *Bogumilen und Katharer in ihrer Symbolik*. Wiesbaden: Steiner, 1970.

15

THE PIOUS HERETICS

The will to suffer comes of love; the will not to suffer comes of want of love. I much prefer, and it is better and more useful to me, to love God and be sick, rather than to be sound of body and not love God. What God loves is something; what he does not love is nothing.

Meister Eckhart The Book of Divine Love

The heretics whose stories fill these pages were convinced that what the church called orthodoxy was wrong on one or more major points. In the case of dualism, the charge was that the entire presupposition of Christianity, faith in the Father Almighty, Maker of heaven and earth, is mistaken. The church had to fight such heretics in order to survive. As we know, the weapon it chose, from the late twelfth century onward, was the Holy Office of the Inquisition. As the Inquisition raged on, its most striking accomplishments, if we may call them that, benefited French absolutism more than Christian orthodoxy. The Cathars were eventually suppressed—it might be more accurate to say, wiped out. But in the fourteenth century a new wave of heretics appeared. This time they did not challenge orthodox doctrines or seek to replace the church. In fact, like the Poor Men of Lyons, they really should not be called heretics at all, for they only sought to live according to the same Gospel the pope proclaimed and the Inquisition claimed to defend. The first representatives of this new wave were new in a special way: for the first time in the history of the church, a major spiritual movement was carried primarily by women.

1. THE BEGUINES

The Beguine movement began in a simple way. It was the spontaneous expression of the desire of many ordinary women to live lives of dedication to Christ outside the confines and rules of any religious order. After establishing the Friars Minor (men) as the first Franciscan order and encouraging Clara Scifi to establish the second order, the Poor Clares (women), Francis of Assisi also sought to meet the spiritual needs of laymen who could not leave secular life but who wanted to fulfill his ascetic principles. The result was the establishment of the Franciscan Tertiaries, the so-called Third Order of St. Francis. A similar women's movement arose; so many women resolved to live lives of ascetic renunciation that the existing conventual system could not accommodate them. Small groups of women would gather around a spiritual leader, and constitute a kind of informal religious community. There were similar groups of men, smaller and less important, particularly in northern Europe. The men were called Beghards or Lollards.

Groups of women living together in poverty and simplicity but without benefit of any recognized rule or structure of authority began to make their appearance in the Netherlands, the Rhineland, and northern France from about 1250 onward. Although they had nothing in common with the Albigenses, their separatism and asceticism caused them to be suspected of a connection, and from the beginning the Beguines had to struggle against accusations of heresy. The communities they formed lived under the supervision of a local pastor or monastery, but did not take lifelong vows. At first the Beguines were benevolently regarded by the church authorities, but some of them seem to have come under the influence of the pantheistic spirituality of Amalric of Bena. The Roman hierarchy had scant tolerance for women involving themselves in theological issues and disputations. The first two popes to live under the shadow of the French monarchy at Avignon, Clement V (reigned 1305–14) and John XXII (reigned 1316–34), condemned the entire Beguine movement on the grounds that it was under no monastic rule, was bound to no formal obedience, and was encouraging its members to engage in theological disputes concerning the Trinity. Soon Pope John attempted to make a distinction between the small number of actually heretical Beguines and the larger group of innocuously pious women who were merely seeking to live a godly life apart from the world.

The very name "Beguines" is of obscure origin. It first appears in the *Royal Chronicle of Cologne* (1209–11), where it is applied to Albigensians and to followers of Amalric of Bena.[1] Shortly afterward, Jacob of Vitry sought and obtained papal approval to permit small groups of pious women to live together in poverty and chastity without joining an order. These women were apparently orthodox, but somehow the tainted name "Beguines" was attached to them. By 1274 they were attracting hostile attention at a synod in Lyons, where they were accused of trying to deal with theological questions too subtle for untrained laywomen to handle. As they attracted more attention, it became apparent that in general the Beguines were not heretics, and that there was a marked difference between the Beguines of southern Europe and those in the North.

a. Southern Beguines

In Italy, southern France, and the Christian part of Spain, the thirteenth century saw the rise of many small, informal communities of women committed to a simple and godly life. Some of them affiliated with the existing Franciscan Third Order, but many did not. Many of them were influenced by the spiritual ferment in the Franciscan order, particularly by the more radical group known as Franciscan spirituals, or spiritual Franciscans. (By way of distinction, the regular Franciscans were called "conventual.") The spirituals were taken by Abbot Joachim's predictions of a coming Third Age of the Holy Spirit, bringing a spiritual church, and many of them expected this to take place in the year 1260. Spiritual anticipation was high; troops of *flagellantes* wandered through the towns and villages, whipping themselves or one another, and proclaimed the impending end of the age.

In 1260 Gerard Segarelli of Parma founded the Apostolic Brethren in anticipation of the Age of the Spirit. When it failed to materialize, the Apostolic Brethren turned on the existing church, denouncing the wealth and corruption of the clergy and calling for a return to the era of poverty. Like many Reformation and post-Reformation Protestants, they blamed the Emperor Constantine for corrupting Christianity with his legendary donation of wealth and power to a pope of his day, Sylvester I (reigned 314–35).[2] Four of Gerard's Apostolic Brethren were burned at the stake in 1294; Gerard himself was executed in 1300. His mantle was assumed by Fra ("Brother") Dolcino of Novara, who denounced priests, monks, and even begging friars as worldly and fleshly. He rejected the argument of Pope Nicholas III (reigned 1277–80), who said that the friars' houses belonged to him personally, and that they could use them without violating their vow of poverty. This fiction, called the *usus pauper,* did not impress Fra Dolcino. Although his followers supposedly embraced the ideal of apostolic poverty, they became violent and engaged in extensive plunder in northern Lombardy. As a consequence, a "Crusade" was preached against them. Receiving some support from the Ghibelline party, one of the two factions contending for the leadership of the Holy Roman Empire, Dolcino's followers went into hiding to await the advent of the righteous Emperor and the holy pope who would inaugurate a new age. "Fanatical pursuit of poverty had combined with Joachite millennialism to produce the desire for radical upheaval."[3] In 1307 the "crusaders" virtually wiped out the Apostolic Brethren at Novara. One hundred were captured alive, together with their leader. All were executed in brutal fashion. Although burning at the stake, the traditional way to execute heretics, can hardly be considered humane, even more painful tortures were devised for those who were not merely heretics but in addition threatened social upheaval.

One member of the Apostolic Brethren, Bentivenga of Gubbio, escaped before the debacle and attached himself to the Franciscans. At first he gained a reputation for exemplary piety. But soon he organized a group called the "sect of the Spirit of Freedom." Bentivenga taught that the indwelling Spirit of God made all that he and his followers did sinless. They needed no external laws or rules. They were indifferent not only to human suffering, but even to the passion of Christ. The Franciscans had scant tolerance for such antinomian views. Bentivenga and his adherents were condemned to perpetual confinement in a monastery in 1307.

A group of Franciscans, called Fraticelli ("little brothers") was subsequently charged with similar errors,[4] but most of them seem only to have been enthusiastic devotees of "apostolic" poverty. In 1323 Pope John XXII condemned as heresy the contention that Christ and the Apostles had lived in complete poverty without owning any property; this condemnation was too much for the Franciscan Minister General Michael of Cesena, who up till that point had followed the pope, endorsing the cause of the conventual Franciscans and opposing the radically poor spirituals in the order. Deposed and excommunicated, Michael and his fellow Franciscan William of Occam fled to the Holy Roman Emperor, Louis of Bavaria (ruled 1314–47), whom the pope had "suspended" from his throne that same year. Thus the defender of apostolic poverty joined forces with the highest secular sovereign to oppose the temporal power and riches of the pope and the hierarchy. The pope never forgave the rebellious Emperor Louis, but William of Occam's attacks on the papacy took a toll on its prestige.

The southern French and northern Spanish Beguines were involved in the conflict between conventual and spiritual Franciscans because of their desire to be considered part of the Franciscan Third Order. The spiritual Franciscan Peter John Olivi (d. 1298) had a profound influence on them; they compared his writings, especially his commentary on Revelation, to the Gospels themselves. Like Joachim before him, Olivi prophesied a coming age of the Holy Spirit and a spiritual church and called for a strict return to Francis' original views on poverty. He was posthumously repudiated by the order at a general chapter in Marseilles in 1319 and his commentary on Revelation was banned by John XXII in 1326. Although Francis ranks second only to Christ himself in the admiration he enjoyed among Christians of all kinds, within a century of his death, his fundamental views were being condemned by the papacy and his most faithful followers persecuted and killed. For example, four spiritual Franciscans who refused to abandon their ideal of poverty were burned in Marseilles in 1318; three Beguines who were not Franciscans but did share their ideas were executed the following year in Narbonne.

The vehemence with which the papacy, the hierarchy, and even the Franciscan order itself now persecuted the spiritual Franciscans and their followers cannot be explained in terms of heresy and orthodoxy. The spiritual Franciscans were doctrinally orthodox. They proclaimed their obedience to the church and the pope. But they also proclaimed that Jesus and his Apostles had led a life of voluntary, absolute poverty. They were not the first to talk about voluntary poverty or to embrace it for themselves, but by saying that it was Christ's own pattern of life, they cast a deep shadow over his representative here on earth, the pope, who lived in magnificence.

During the period between the accession of Innocent III in 1198 and the death of Boniface VIII in 1303, the papacy had made its most sweeping claims to worldly authority. If the spiritual Franciscans had been ordinary heretics, such as the Waldensians, they might have been less of a threat. But they were Franciscans, and through them the gentle saint seemed to be accusing the papacy. Their combination of social and moral criticism with urgent warnings about the approaching end of the age made them dangerous opponents. The papacy, in its "Babylonian captivity" at Avignon, lacked the moral resources to counter such a challenge effectively, but it still had access to police power, and it did not hesitate to use it. The announcement of the impending end of the present world order necessarily implied that papal authority also was passing away. Whether the spiritual Franciscans could have survived if they had not been persecuted is difficult to say, because the task they set themselves seemed to require superhuman dedication. Apparently the papacy felt that its power and privilege could not survive alongside them.

b. German Beguines and Beghards

The Beguines of southern Europe were associated with the spiritual Franciscans, and although they too were persecuted by the papacy, they seem to have been no more guilty of heresy than the spirituals. The situation of the northern Beguines in Germany and the Low Countries is somewhat different; they were much more radical. They believed more completely in the possibility of achieving sinless perfection on earth, and their zeal to do so involved them in further errors. They began to claim that a human being can be good in himself, because he has been united with God and indeed has become God. In 1308 a German Beguine, Margaret Porete, was condemned for writing a book teaching that the soul can be annihilated by being totally concentrated upon God, after which it is completely free and requires no further moral or spiritual exertion. She continued to spread her views after the condemnation of her book, and was burned in Paris in 1310. In 1307 a synod at Cologne had banned the begging "apostolic Beghards and Beghardesses," who held themselves to be sinless because those who are "led of the Spirit, [ye] are not under the law" (Gal. 5:18). The decrees of Clement V (1311, published in 1317 by John XXII) banning the Beguines explicitly referred to such perfectionism. Nevertheless, the nonheretical Beguines were so numerous that many clergy tried to distinguish them from the heretics in order to defend them; one such was the bishop of Strassburg, John of Dübheim. No sooner had he succeeded in persuading the pope to relax his condemnation, however, than heretical Beguines appeared right in Strassburg, calling themselves the "Sect of the Free Spirit," or the "Brothers and Sisters of Voluntary Poverty." Their ideas sound pantheistic: all that exists is God, and they themselves are divine by nature. Although their view of sin indicates that in theory they could sin without consequences, in fact, like the "perfects" of the Cathars, they seem to have been innocent of immorality and self-indulgence and indeed seem to have led exemplary lives. Unlike the Cathar leaders, they did not wink at immorality among the masses. Bishop John prohibited their books, songs, and doctrines, but seems to have tried to win them back to orthodoxy; there is no record that he persecuted them.

c. German Mysticism

Although the German Beguines were not directly connected with the mysticism that began to flourish in Germany at this time, their ideas clearly had much in common with those of the mystics. A mystic, we recall, may be defined as someone who seeks direct, intimate, personal communion with God. Christianity has always contained an element of mysticism. Christ indwells the believer, and the Holy Spirit bears witness directly within him. During the High Middle Ages, the church doctrine of transubstantiation made the act of personal communion with Christ intensely realistic, even materialistic. On the one hand, the doctrine of the real, bodily presence stimulated many to try to experience in some personal way the communion the doctrine claimed occurs in the eucharist. On the other, the fact that this holiest of sacraments could be celebrated by unworthy priests appeared to many to make a travesty of eucharistic doctrine.

Mysticism tends to do away with the need for intermediaries between the believer and God. The church cannot exist at all without a measure of mysticism, but as soon as mysticism begins to gain ground, it begins to do away with the need for the church's ministers and their services. In the extreme case, the mystic may dispense with the Scripture and even with the Incarnate Christ himself, and seek to relate directly with the uncreated, absolute godhead. Mysticism appears to make the church and institutional religion unnecessary, and thus is a threat to the established church even when it operates within a totally orthodox theology.

The school known as German mysticism had three outstanding representatives: Meister Eckhart (ca. 1260–ca. 1327), John Tauler (ca. 1300–1361), and Henry Suso (ca. 1295–1366). Basically, the German mystics were loyal to the church and its doctrines. Nevertheless, the intense personal piety they promoted seemed to make the institutional church superfluous. Meister Eckhart preached in many congregations frequented by communities of Beguines. Archbishop Henry of Cologne found several suspect points in Eckhart's teaching, chiefly the idea that it is possible to attain a state of sinless perfection and that under the leading of the Spirit one can be perfectly free. Eckhart was a strict ascetic and did not intend his concept of freedom in the Spirit to lead to licentiousness. Formally charged with heresy in 1325, he died before a verdict was handed down and thus was spared the pain of condemnation.

The usual Scholastic interpretation of God's self-description in Exodus 3:14, "I Am That I Am," is that God is being itself: *esse est Deus*. Eckhart also taught that deep within each person there is a "soul spark," the place where God encounters us and comes to dwell. Although he did not deny them or reject them, Eckhart attached less importance to traditional Christian doctrines of sin and forgiveness, of the humanity and the atoning work of Christ, than to his concept of the "birth of God" in the soul and the personal communion with God that results from it. The traditional forms of Catholic piety were quite secondary to the inner spiritual life. Eckhart's views reached Luther through some of the later mystical writers, and also influenced the eccentric Christian mystic Jakob Boehme (1575–1624) as well as non-Christian thinkers such as Immanuel Kant, G. W. F. Hegel, Arthur Schopenhauer, and Friedrich Nietzsche. Eckhart taught that a person does not become good by performing good works. His own prolonged ascetic pattern of life showed him that spiritual exercises in themselves cannot transform the human heart; rather, it is a transformed heart that produces the good works that please God.

Although the goal of Eckhart as well as of the Beguines he influenced was the achievement of a greater and more perfect obedience to Christ by means of a deeper personal relationship with him, the church instinctively feared that any teaching that bypassed its own authority, its sacraments and laws, would certainly lead to moral anarchy. During the Reformation era, Luther's preaching of Christian liberty was quickly appropriated by some as an excuse for antinomianism and licentiousness.

In 1332, five years after Eckhart's death, a Dominican inquisitor, John of Schwenkenfeld, conducted the most thorough recorded interrogation of a number of Beguines. He discovered that new recruits were held to a pattern of strict self-denial and to unpleasant and often dirty manual labor, frequently with no relief even on Sundays and holy days. After a sufficient term of such probation, they were told that they had attained perfection and that no further obedience was required of them. John's efforts to discover evidence of licentious conduct proved futile. He did not uncover any heresy, and no punishment is recorded.[5]

Despite the cruelty of the Inquisition and the unfairness of its procedures, it is apparent that at least some of its examiners were willing to acquit defendants against whom nothing substantial could be proved. Roman Catholic judges in the thirteenth century sometimes found themselves in the same position as pagan judges in imperial Rome when confronted with Christians: they did not like the doctrines the defendant espoused, but it was hard to bring themselves to take violent measures against simple folk whose chief offense seems to have been trying too hard to be good.

Not all testimonies about the Beguines were so innocuous. A male adherent of Beghard, John of Brünn, returned to more traditional Catholicism and became a Dominican monk. After his return, he published some strikingly different charges based on his own experiences as a Beghard. He was a well-to-do, married burgher of Brünn in Bohemia (Brno) when like Peter Waldo and Francis of Assisi he felt called to give up his bourgeois life and embrace a life of poverty. He abandoned his wife and lived with his brother Albert in total, voluntary poverty for twenty years. This brought him to a state of "perfection," in which sin no longer existed for him. After his entry into the Dominican order, John gave a lurid description of his life after having attained "perfection," but claimed that even his licentious behavior was a sincere attempt to find God, not in books but in the "abyss of the Trinity" in his heart.

Another converted heretic, Conrad Kannler, claimed in 1381 that the Holy Spirit had given him the experience of sinless freedom while he was praying in the Cologne cathedral, and even after his return to conventional orthodoxy he continued to assert that such an experience cannot be taught, but must be freely communicated by the Holy Spirit. Kannler stated that for one who had achieved sinless perfection even incest would not be a sin, but this seems to have been a theoretical position only: he added that God would not allow those who were "free in the Spirit" to behave in such a way. Another Beghard, Hans Becker, claimed during interrogation that he had had a similar experience of the Holy Spirit in a church in Mainz, but unlike John of Brünn and Conrad Kannler, Becker predicted the dawn of a new age that would make the present-day church and all of its works into a dead letter, calling the Gospel a "testament of death." Only the inner light of the Holy Spirit is the true "testament of life." Becker was burned in Mainz in 1458.

This strange combination of devotion to poverty and an intense personal spiritual life independent of the traditional ritual and devotion of the church, characteristic of the Beguines and Beghards, was a widespread phenomenon in the fourteenth and fifteenth centuries. It bears witness to the fact that the ordinary Christian life simply failed to meet the spiritual and religious needs of countless Christians.

2. POLITICAL PIETY— POLITICAL HERESY

When Joachim of Floris developed his eschatological reinterpretation of political history, it was in part a reaction to the fact that the papacy had made itself into a secular government and that it claimed to have done so by right. Religious doctrine and political theory became indistinguishable. If those who sought to preserve the ultimate sovereignty of the state—such as the Hohenstaufen Emperor Frederick II—could be called heretics for resisting the political claims of the pope, then it is not surprising that the popes themselves were charged with heresy for making such political claims.[6]

Pope Boniface VIII (reigned 1294–1303), who made the sweeping claim that every human creature had to submit to his authority in order to be saved (*Unam sanctam,* 1302), called cardinals who opposed him heretics and launched a crusade against them. But the pope's battalions were less numerous than those of the King of France. Philip IV sent an adventurer to seize the pope, and although the populace freed him again, Boniface died a few weeks afterward. In order to justify such harsh treatment of the man who claimed to be the Vicar of Christ, Philip initiated posthumous heresy proceedings against him. The next pope, Clement V, although he reigned under Philip's shadow, was able to have the heresy proceedings terminated. However, although Clement was able to salvage a measure of the papacy's honor, he proved himself the willing tool of the King in the most spectacular heresy action of the Middle Ages, one that involved not individuals but a whole religious order—the trial of the Poor Knights of Christ and of the Temple of Solomon.

a. Heretical Chivalry: *The Case of the Knights Templars*

The crusading movement of the twelfth century had created the famous military orders. The Knights Templars were founded about 1128. Their rule was written by Bernard of Clairvaux himself, an auspicious beginning. The second great military order, the Knights of St. John, was set up as a military order in about 1155, but their antecedents go back to a charitable organization founded in the ninth century. After a turbulent history, the Knights of St. John abandoned their military role for a medical one. Both Roman Catholic and Protestant branches still exist today. The youngest of the three great military orders, called the Teutonic Knights *(Deutschritterorden)* or Knights of the Cross (later merged with a smaller German order, the Knights of the Sword), was founded in the Holy Land in 1190, but was expelled before it could accomplish anything there, as a result of the Moslem reconquest of the crusader states. During the Reformation, the grand master accepted Luther's advice and became the Protestant Duke of Prussia. A Catholic branch still exists. The Knights Templars were the most colorful, the richest, and for a time the most powerful of these orders. One major branch of Freemasonry has adopted their name, partly for its romantic associations, partly in protest against the fate that was to befall them. This great military order, formed to protect Christians in the Holy Land, was dramatically and brutally suppressed in the most spectacular police action of the Middle Ages. The reasons were largely political, but the charge was heresy.

The history of the Templars is clouded by charges and countercharges. From the twelfth century onward, the Templars were involved in fratricidal conflicts with the Knights of St. John and with the Christian lords in the Holy Land, conflicts that precipitated the Saracen reconquest. The Knights of St. John stayed in the eastern Mediterranean region, and the Teutonic Knights moved to northeastern Europe. The Templars, by contrast, had no other field of operations; with the loss of the Holy Land, they lost much of their purpose. Their great power and wealth made them appear an attractive prey in the eyes of the reigning Capetian family in France, and also elsewhere. In order to rid himself of the Templars and confiscate their wealth, King Philip the Fair charged them not only with heresy, but with frightful immorality, and particularly with homosexuality. Although the Templars themselves lacked effective propagandists at the time, and although their real adversary was the King of France, not the papacy, the fact that the hated Inquisition was used against them has made them romantic heroes in the eyes of later generations. The Freemasons have adopted the name of their last grand master, Jacques de Molay, as well as some Templar traditions, spreading the charge that the Templars were the innocent victims of papal intrigue and inquisitorial terror. Victims they were, but more of royal French greed than of papal intrigue; Pope Clement V, himself a client of the French King in Avignon, tried for a time to save them. That they were entirely innocent is doubtful. It is unlikely and certainly unproved that they were guilty of the atrocities of which they were accused, but they had few partisans outside their own ranks, and many of the charges were readily believed by outsiders.[7]

As long as the French King was involved in his struggle with Pope Boniface VIII, he solicited the help of the rich and powerful French Templars. When Boniface died and the papacy was relocated in Avignon, Philip felt free to proceed against the order. Why he launched his campaign of extermination against it is uncertain; the historian Henry Charles Lea attributes it to his avarice.[8] An apparently trivial denunciation provided the pretext for the whole matter. In 1304 or 1305 a French adventurer, Esquiu de Floyran of Beziers, appeared at the court of King James II of Aragon with a fantastic story about the "fact" of the Templars—an infamous oath that all those admitted to the order were supposedly required to swear. Esquiu claimed to have shared a prison cell with a Templar while both were under sentence of death. The Templar told him his story, and subsequently Esquiu was released. He made four principal charges: Templars were required to deny the crucified Lord, give an obscene kiss to the one admitting them, and worship an idol; in addition, they were urged to engage in homosexuality to satisfy their sexual appetites.

King James does not seem to have believed Esquiu, but the prospect of being able to dispossess the rich Templars of Aragon was so attractive that he offered the Frenchman a splendid reward if the story could be proved. In 1305 both Pope Clement V and King Philip also learned of the charges. Philip decided to take action against them, but proceeded with such secrecy that the Templars suspected nothing, and even protected him from the mob during a riot in Paris in 1306. The King had quarreled with the grand master, Jacques de Molay, who opposed his project of uniting the two great military orders and making himself grand master of the combined order. Under such circumstances it must have been inconceivable that the King would proceed to exterminate the order he so recently wanted to lead, but this is what happened.

On October 13, 1307, in a lightning police action throughout all of France, virtually all of the Templars were arrested at a single stroke. There was virtually no organized resistance. Contrary to what Philip claimed, the action was not jointly planned with the pope. In order to examine the knights, a new office was created, that of the inquisitor general, given to a Dominican monk, William of Paris. The strict procedures of the Inquisition provided that any confessed heretic who withdrew his confession promptly be turned over to the secular arm as a "relapsed heretic" for his "due punishment"—death by fire. Needless to say, anyone who had been induced—or forced—to confess, even if the confession was extorted by torture, found it extremely hard to repudiate his confession. The ecclesiastical Inquisition knew only two ways of dealing with those suspected of heresy:

first, to obtain a confession and then impose the appropriate ecclesiastical penance; second, to keep the suspect in prison until he should confess or die. The unfortunate Templars were first examined by royal commissions, who obtained such prompt confessions that within less than two weeks King Philip announced that all had confessed.

The imprisoned knights were questioned concerning the major points of Esquiu's denunciation: had they renounced Christ, spat on the Cross, given indecent kisses at their admission to the order, been exhorted to practice homosexuality or actually have practiced it, or worshiped an idol? An astonishingly large number confessed to all of the charges except homosexuality, which was generally denied. Even Grand Master de Molay confessed on October 25 and that same day sent a very curious letter to all members of the order, urging them to disregard their oath of secrecy and tell the truth about all their misdeeds. How such incredible confessions were secured, and so quickly, is difficult to understand. Torture was certainly used without restraint, but not, apparently, on de Molay himself. The inquisitors told the knights, kept in solitary confinement, that their colleagues had all confessed. The speed with which the confessions were obtained is mystifying. It is hard to imagine that even intense torture could have extorted such uniform confessions of guilt from innocent men. Early in 1310 a papal commission of inquiry gave the Templars the impression that they might safely withdraw their confessions and defend their innocence in court. Reassured by this and by the King's promise of safe-conduct, six hundred Templars appeared in Paris to defend the honor of their order before the court. Suddenly, on May 12, 1310, the inquisitor general issued an order to burn at the stake fifty-four knights who had repudiated their confessions, treating them as relapsed heretics. Several smaller groups were burned on succeeding days. The courage of the French branch of the order evaporated entirely. No one could be found to continue to defend the order. In Aragon, by contrast, the Templars adamantly maintained their innocence, denying all charges. The sudden and dramatic collapse of the main body of the Knights Templars in France remained unexplained. The order was abolished the following year at the Council of Vienne.

The mystery of the Templars has never been resolved, nor has an adequate reason been found for the furious rage of King Philip against them. It is virtually inconceivable that the order can have been guilty of the crimes with which it was charged, so inconsistent with its public standards of devotion and self-denial. History records that many Templars, after life imprisonment, revoked their confessions at the point of death. Whatever crimes the Templars may have committed, it is evident that the charges against them were not heresy but idolatry and immorality. It seems more probable that the order could have been involved in a real heresy, such as that of the Marcionites, Montanists, or Monophysites, than that all its members could have been involved in such banal and disgusting perversions of its purpose. The fact that so many of the French Templars confessed with such alacrity, and then subsequently withdrew their confessions, even when faced with death by fire, remains perplexing. In any event, it is evident that the order was not primarily heretical. Its major interest from our perspective lies in the fact that the affair of the Templars enabled the Inquisition to perfect its techniques of dealing with those it accused of heresy.

b. Political Theory as Heresy

If the papacy under Clement V was willing to use the Inquisition to serve the political goals of the King of France, it is not surprising that the next pope, John XXII, made use of it to enforce his own political goals. He used it in Italy against the Franciscan spirituals as well as against the Beguines, and finally brought charges of heresy against the newly elected German Emperor Louis the Bavarian (ruled 1314–47). Louis' "heresy" consisted in not having presented himself for papal approval as Emperor. Once reserved for a doctrinal deviation that threatened the substance of the Christian faith, the term "heresy" had degenerated into meaning disrespect for the newest and most sweeping claims of papal power.

A number of prominent spiritual leaders rallied to the Emperor Louis, including the Franciscan Minister General Michael of Cesena and William of Occam; the most eminent was Marsilius (Marsiglio) of Padua, who together with John of Jandun provided Louis with a new theory of the state in their *Defender of the Peace* (1324). After a long delay, Louis had himself crowned Emperor against the will of the pope, and he and Marsilius were both condemned as heretics. In the meantime, John XXII found himself charged with heresy for teaching soul sleep, the doctrine that the souls of the just sleep until the general resurrection, when they will be awakened for the Last Judgment and will receive eternal life. The Bible itself is not very specific on the point, and many Christians have espoused the idea of soul sleep through the centuries; in any event, the doctrine is not a heresy in our sense. John died in 1334 as a general council was being organized for the purpose of dealing with his "heresy."

How is it possible to take seriously an institution that charged the Holy Roman Emperor, the general of the Franciscan order, the grand master of the Knights Templars, and even the pope himself with heresy? The Inquisition was anything but a joke: its power, its cruelty, and its inexorability frequently surpass even the harsh charges of its critics. Its very existence forms a stain on the history of Christianity that distresses Catholics as well as Protestants. The Inquisition is a liability to all who would present Christianity as a religion of love. From our perspective, its influence was devastating to the Christian concern for doctrinal purity. By calling anything and everything that displeased church authorities "heresy" and persecuting it relentlessly, it makes the legitimate Christian concern for purity of doctrine and the avoidance of heresy look like an ongoing witch-hunt. Thus in the long run it has done more to harm orthodoxy than the herèsies it sought to suppress.

Following the outbreak of the Black Plague, there was an outbreak of wild eschatological enthusiasm in 1349. Bands of penitents wandered through Europe scourging themselves: these Flagellants predicted the imminence of the Last Day and proposed to prepare for its dawn by persecuting the Jews. In the meantime, the papacy, which had continued to lose credibility while in residence at Avignon, was returned to Rome under Pope Urban V (reigned 1362–70), but after the reign of his successor, Gregory XI (reigned 1370–78), two popes were elected, and for over three decades two rival papacies existed, one at Rome, one at Avignon. In 1409 the Council of Pisa deposed both lines and named a new pope, Alexander V (reigned 1409–10), in their place, but neither accepted the judgment, and so Christendom had not two but three popes until the Council of Constance (1414–18), which deposed all three claimants and named Martin V (reigned 1417–31) in their place.

Although the Council of Constance appeared to restore the unity of Western Christendom under a sole pope, it also took a step that foreshadowed the subsequent breakup of Christianity along nationalist lines. Violating a safe-conduct granted by the Emperor Sigismund, the council tried and condemned the Bohemian priest John Hus. He was burned at the stake July 6, 1415. As we shall observe in the next chapter, Hus, like Waldo, was not a heretic in our sense of the word, but—unfortunately for him—he was a direct threat to ecclesiastical authority. Inasmuch as Martin Luther subsequently declared himself a spiritual successor to Hus, and as the fifteenth-century Hussite movement eventually flowed into the sixteenth-century Protestant Reformation, we can call the execution of John Hus at Constance the first action of a general council against a "Protestant." It was also almost the last, for when the Reformation really began in earnest, independent territorial rulers frequently protected Protestants from the full force of Roman Catholic repression.

3. FROM FAITH TO POWER

The early church was a community of faith with little or no political power. The late medieval church was a powerful corporation; it would not be correct to say, "with little or no faith," but it is apparent that the quality of the faith was seriously impaired, so much so that it seemed constantly to need defending by violent repression. After seven centuries of comparative doctrinal calm, the church, particularly in the West, had reached the point of labeling every criticism and challenge heretical. Where no substantial doctrinal issues existed, questions of power, prestige, and property were treated as doctrinal matters.

During the early centuries of Christianity, the faith interacted with Hellenistic culture; indeed, some scholars—such as Adolf von Harnack—contend that Christianity was Hellenized to the degree that it was no longer the religion of the New Testament. We have contended that this interaction with Hellenistic philosophy and culture did not dramatically deform Christianity, and that the faith was clarified and defined by the ecumenical councils, not perverted.

Would Peter and Paul have recognized the Gospel they preached in the Creed of the Council of Chalcedon? Perhaps not, at least not at first sight. Nevertheless, we do contend, with the rest of orthodox Christianity, that Chalcedon is a legitimate and necessary interpretation of the Apostles' doctrines. When we meet the first great Christian theologians—Irenaeus, Tertullian, and Origen—we sense that they would have felt at home in Nicaea, in the Hagia Sophia in Constantinople, and perhaps even in Charlemagne's cathedral in Aachen. We can conceive of Augustine and John Chrysostom being at ease in a service conducted by Bernard of Clairvaux. But for how many centuries can we claim that the sense of continuity was preserved? Bernard may be the last great medieval Catholic with whom the early Fathers would have felt at home. In Bernard's day, decisive changes were already under way. Within three quarters of a century, these changes would turn the medieval church into a new kind of institution. Augustine, and perhaps even John Chrysostom, might have found himself more in harmony with the Reformer Martin Luther than with the great Scholastic Thomas Aquinas (1225–74), who lived only a century after Bernard. What separated Thomas from Bernard was the doctrine of transubstantiation.

The promulgation of the doctrine of transubstantiation in the year 1215 began the transformation of the church from a community of faith to a custodian of sacraments. When Paul speaks of Christians as "stewards of the mysteries of God" (1 Cor. 4:1), he has *doctrinal* mysteries in mind. He thought of the sacraments only secondarily if at all in this context. As we have seen, what the church was seeking in enunciating the doctrine of transubstantiation was a way to assure the faithful that their spiritual needs were completely met in the ministry of the church. An unfortunate byproduct of this legitimate concern was the growing feeling that the church has custody over the very body of Christ and hence over salvation. Gradually it came to perceive heresy not so much as a challenge to the truth of Christian doctrine as an attack on its stewardship and on the power that that stewardship brought with it.

The real spiritual authority accumulated in twelve centuries of efforts to preserve the "faith once delivered" was quickly dissipated when those efforts came to be concentrated on preserving the church's own claims. Exactly two centuries after the Fourth Lateran Council, John Hus, a Bohemian priest, was burned at Constance. Hus was not a heretic in the classical sense. He was neither an Arian nor a Cathar. All that he asked was that the church return to its own eucharistic practice of earlier centuries. Why was this perceived as a deadly threat? Because the church, in espousing transubstantiation, had committed itself to one interpretation of its role, an interpretation that could tolerate no challenges.

It is true that the Western church, growing increasingly *Roman* Catholic with the centuries, remained strong enough to survive two challenges: the first by John Wyclif, the second by the man he inspired, John Hus. It defeated them, but they represented the harbingers of a movement that Catholicism could resist, but not crush: the Protestant Reformation.

SELECTED BIBLIOGRAPHY

Cowdrey, H. E. J. *The Cluniacs and the Gregorian Reform.* Oxford: University Press, 1970.

Elliott-Binns, Leonard. *The History of the Decline and Fall of the Medieval Papacy.* Hamden, Conn.: Archon Books, 1967.

Greenway, George W. *Arnold of Brescia.* Cambridge: University Press, 1931.

Hyma, Albert. *The Brethren of the Common Life.* Grand Rapids, Mich.: Eerdmans, 1950.

Leff, Gordon. *Heresy in the Middle Ages.* 2 vols. New York: Barnes & Noble, 1967.

McDonnell, Ernest W. *The Beguines and Beghards in Medieval Culture: With Special Emphasis on the Belgian Scene.* New Brunswick, N.J.: Rutgers University Press, 1954.

Russell, Jeffrey B. *Religious Dissent in the Middle Ages.* New York: Wiley, 1971.

Spitz, Lewis W. *The Religious Renaissance of the German Humanists.* Cambridge: Harvard University Press, 1963.

16

THE PROTESTANT REFORMATION

Therefore, Christians should stand to the death for maintaining Christ's gospel and true understanding thereof, gotten by holy life and great study, and not set their faith or trust in sinful prelates and their clerks, nor their understanding of holy writ. For with their worldly life, full of pride . . . they are unable to perceive the truth of holy writ, and high pureness of God.

John Wyclif Antichrist's Labour to Destroy Holy Writ *3*

Despite bitter and at times bloody conflicts, heretical movements never succeeded in undermining the unity of the Christian faith during its first fifteen centuries. This is true despite the potentially destructive and seductive nature of many of the heretical views that were propagated, from Arianism to dualism. During the fifteenth century, a relatively minor "heretical" challenge, the demand to be allowed to distribute the wine as well as the bread of the eucharist to the people, caused a major schism, creating a Czech separatism that has persisted to the present day. In the sixteenth century, Martin Luther protested against indulgences—a traditional accretion that had been formally authorized less than half a century earlier—and spoke, in Pauline and Augustinian fashion, of justification by faith. These apparently minor variations from the Catholic norm were explosive. The external unity of Christendom was shattered to such an extent that it has not yet recovered.

Christianity has never been the same since the Reformation. This much is evident at first sight. The indulgence controversy sparked by Luther was potentially no more fundamental then iconoclasm; indeed, it seems less so. But it created a new confession, in fact, a new approach to Christianity, in a way iconoclasm could not. What was there about the Protestant Reformation that made it permanent while other attempts at reform, such as iconoclasm, vanished without leaving a trace?

From the Protestant perspective, it is tempting to contend that Protestantism has survived because it represents the legitimate expression of the Christian Gospel and is indeed, in Paul's words, "the power of God unto salvation." From a historical and sociological perspective, it is evident that the rise of Protestantism coincided with the rise of linguistic separatism and nation-states in Europe—although it was precisely the heartland of Protestantism, Germany, that did not become a united nation until 1871, three and a quarter centuries after Luther. The beginnings of modern science, with its impact on the old, authority-based scholarship of the church, also contributed to the permanence of the breakup of Christian unity.

If one is to contend that the Reformation recovered a necessary element of the Gospel, it is necessary to argue that medieval Catholicism had lost it. And indeed this is precisely what seems to have been the case. Prior to the thirteenth century, heretical movements represented an exaggeration or an amputation of particular elements of the historic Christian faith. They were eccentric, while the church as a whole—whatever its faults—remained closer to the center. Consequently, the heretical movements were sooner or later sloughed off and Christendom remained more or less unified. But after the thirteenth century—with the definition of transubstantiation, the absolutist claims of the papacy, and the creation of the Inquisition—it was the medieval church itself that had moved away from the center. Its tremendous size, universality, and institutional strength enabled it to survive and even to grow, despite the damage wrought by Protestantism, but it no longer occupied the center; Reformation Protestantism—despite its particularity, nationalism, and frequent doctrinal one-sidedness—could credibly claim to have recovered vital elements of the Gospel and thus to be more in accord with the New Testament and its message than Catholicism.

The degree to which the medieval church had moved out of the main channel of Christian faith and spirituality is shown by the fact that a moderate, limited reformist demand, such as that made first by Hus and later by Luther, could lead to permanent divisions. The fatigue of the "Second Age" of the church had become overwhelming, and if the Reformation did not produce the spiritual church, the community of monks envisaged by Joachim of Floris, it definitely did introduce a new principle. Fidelity to the Scripture as the Word of God—something the church has always extolled but not always manifested—came to take precedence over institutional unity and continuity.

The eucharistic controversies may not have appeared to be as significant in the story of Christianity as other conflicts—the Albigensian movement or the iconoclastic controversy, to mention only two. Nevertheless, the way in which they were resolved—the doctrine of transubstantiation with all that it implied for priestly and papal authority, for the sacrificial office of the church, and for the way of Christian life—created such a fundamental transformation within the church that it made the Reformation inevitable. If Berengar of Tours had been tolerated, the view of Luther would not have seemed so extreme.

The Protestant Reformation did not burst unheralded on the church. Two major figures preceded it, whom we may look upon as the last of the medieval "heretics" or the first of the modern Reformers: the Englishman John Wyclif (ca. 1330–84) and the Czech John Hus (ca. 1369–1415).

1. WYCLIF, HUS, AND THE HUSSITES

When King Philip IV of France coveted the possessions of the Templars, the pope helped him to destroy them and in the process enhanced his own power by developing the Inquisition. When Edward III of England (ruled 1327–77), only a few years later, decided that he needed revenues from church lands and properties to carry on his Hundred Years' War with France, he turned against the power of the pope, and in John Wyclif he found an advocate to support him. Wyclif advocated the supreme authority of the Bible (*On the Truth of Holy Scripture,* 1378), defended the right of the king to deal with ecclesiastical abuses and confiscate church property (*On the Office of the King,* 1379), and finally named Christ as the sole head of the church and the pope as the Antichrist (*On the Power of the Pope,* 1379). Wyclif alarmed Edward's successor, Richard II (ruled 1377–99), and was sent back to his parish at Lutterworth, but his ideas found a hearing far away in Prague.

a. John Hus

Jerome of Prague had studied in Oxford with Wyclif and had brought Wyclif's books back to Bohemia with him. From Jerome, the young scholar John Hus learned of Wyclif's criticism of transubstantiation; this became the basis of his own teaching. Hus's popularity gained him many rivals. Inasmuch as Wyclif had already been condemned as a heretic, Hus's use of Wyclif's writings gave German teachers in bilingual Prague the excuse to attack their more popular Czech counterpart in 1403. In the meantime Hus had become an extremely popular preacher. He took part in the reorganization of the University of Prague in 1409; in it, the Czechs were given preeminence over the hitherto dominant Germans. The Germans withdrew to Leipzig, where they founded the first German university.

The archbishop of Prague, Sbinko von Hasenburg, who previously had supported Hus and had made him a preacher of the synod in 1403, took offense at Hus's charges of simony and secured a papal bull condemning him from Pope Alexander V, the pope chosen by the Council of Pisa to replace the rival popes of Rome and Avignon. Forced to leave Prague in 1412, Hus took refuge in southern Bohemia, where he wrote numerous tracts in Czech as well as in Latin. He appealed to the authority of Christ against the papal ban, and expected to be exonerated at the reforming Council of Constance, summoned in 1414. Given a safe-conduct by the German Emperor Sigismund (ruled 1410–37), he presented himself in Constance, where he was immediately imprisoned. The council posthumously condemned Wyclif as a heretic in May 1415; in England, his body was exhumed and burned. Hus himself was condemned after a three-day hearing in the presence of Sigismund, who did not honor his promise of safe-conduct. Hus was burned at the stake on July 6, 1415, despite Sigismund's ineffectual efforts to spare him. His colleague Jerome of Prague managed to escape from Constance, but was caught and taken back, and was burned the following year.

This judicial murder made John Hus a national hero and gave rise to a mass movement out of which a new church grew. By contrast, Wyclif had ended his life in peace and comparative obscurity at Lutterworth. Nevertheless the Bohemian martyr was less of an innovator in theological matters than the Oxford master. Hus really sought nothing more radical than a return to the older eucharistic practice of allowing the people to communicate ''in both kinds.'' The abandonment of this traditional practice by the Roman church was a result of the new doctrine of transubstantiation and of the changing understanding of the meaning of the eucharistic meal it reflected. Because Christ was bodily present in the bread, and of course alive, it was contended that his blood must also be present; hence there was no need to take communion in both kinds. The commandment of Christ, ''Drink ye all of it'' (Matt. 26:27), did not apply to the laity, as it was addressed to the Apostles, all of whom were priests and bishops. The possibility that wine might be spilled and thus lead to a sacrilege was greater than the danger of dropping bread. In addition, the new emphasis on the Mass as a meritorious sacrifice naturally reduced the need for individuals actually to receive the communion in order to benefit from the Mass.

The psychological pressure caused by the new emphasis on Christ's corporeal presence was so great that many believers were afraid to take communion at all for fear of being involved in sacrilege. Consequently they had to be ordered to receive the communion as a duty. Hus wanted to restore the ancient eucharistic meal to its original importance and make Christians once again look on it as a wonderful privilege, not as a dangerous duty. The fact that he could be opposed, condemned, and burned for teaching something that had been normative for thirteen centuries and that was still the normal practice in the Eastern churches shows the pivotal importance to the church of the new approach to the eucharist resulting from the doctrine of transubstantiation.

Hus's attitude toward the eucharist provided the legal pretext for his condemnation and fiery death. It was his enormous zeal for the purity of the church, inspired by Wyclif, and the consequent ferocity of his attacks on the clergy that caused them to deal with him as a deadly menace, for he was threatening the whole structure of priestly authority. He contended that no one not elected by God, and most assuredly no mortal sinner, could be a true priest, even though his official acts might be valid. Hus appealed to all "true Christians" to shun services conducted by sinful, worldly clergy. To make matters worse, he was an ethnic Bohemian preaching in Czech to a Bohemian majority populace in German-dominated Prague. His charges, his personality, and his nationality combined to make him totally unacceptable to the higher clergy, who were either Germans or Germanified Bohemians. The fact that it was another German, the Emperor Sigismund, who broke his word to Hus and permitted him to be burned, made Hus into a Czech national hero and created the first reformed national church. The first outbreak of national religious sentiment on such a scale since the monophysite controversy, the Hussite movement united the Slavic Bohemians, Moravians, and even the Poles against the dominant Germans. The Germans, who represented the empire, saw themselves as the trustees of papal authority.

The Bohemians rebelled en masse against the decisions of the council, demanding freedom of preaching and the right to take communion in both kinds. In 1419 there was the first defenestration in Prague, when seven town councillors were thrown out of the windows of the town hall to their deaths. King Wenceslaus IV of Bohemia, Emperor Sigismund's older brother, died soon afterward. Sigismund, in order to secure the Bohemian crown for himself, led a "Crusade" against the nationalistic Hussites the following year. For eleven more years the German monarch tried in vain to subjugate the Czechs. The Hussites split into two groups but always stood together against the German Catholics. The free preaching of the Gospel and the chalice at communion for the laity were their minimum demands; ultimately, the Council of Basel (1431–49) had to accept them in order to bring the moderate majority of the Hussites back into the Roman fold. Insistence on frequent communion had been a demand of Bohemian reformers prior to Hus; while he himself did not insist on the cup for the laity (although he was condemned at Constance for so doing), communion in both kinds symbolized an attack on clerical privilege and was demanded for social as well as for spiritual reasons.

Many Hussites combined their zeal for the purity of the church and the simplicity of the clergy with eschatological visions of the imminent return of Christ. The more radical Hussites took Mark 13:14 literally and fled to two mountains, renamed Horeb (in northern Bohemia) and Tábor (between Prague and České Budějovice). From them, the two radical groups derived their names, the Horebites and the more prominent Taborites. The Taborite leader, John Žižka, effectively organized the Hussites to resist the crusading armies. Žižka destroyed a still more radical group of "Adamites"—perhaps Beghards—in a battle at Tabor in 1421. The moderate, episcopally organized Hussites, or Utraquists, aided by many of the nobility, defeated the radical Taborites in 1434. Their principal demands were granted by the Council of Basel. Bohemia was able to keep a kind of national "reformed" church. It remained under Rome, relatively independent but not strikingly different in doctrine, until the Counter-Reformation. Then the full authority of Rome was restored.

b. Joan of Arc and Savonarola: Political Heretics

The conflict between the German Emperor and the pope on the one side and the Bohemian Hussites on the other was marked by a strong element of politics; the fate of Joan of Arc was entirely political. Joan sparked the national revival that enabled the French to free themselves of the English presence in France. She was condemned as a heretic in Rouen (for hearing "voices") and upon her "relapse"—which was the donning of male attire—she was burned at the stake in 1431. The verdict of heresy against her was revoked in 1455, and in 1920 she was declared a saint by the same Roman Catholic Church whose inquisitors had burned her. Her trial and condemnation were clearly politically motivated and Joan has no real place in the story of heresy.

The last great prophet of "apostolic simplicity" was the Dominican monk Girolamo Savonarola (1452–98). A zealous opponent of the decadent, self-indulgent life of the Renaissance nobility and clergy in Florence, Savonarola helped expel the ruling de' Medici family from the city in 1494, after which he became the town's ruler. Like Arnold of Brescia before him, Savonarola began with a moralistic criticism of clerical corruption and went on to become a kind of popular democratic revolutionary, but he was a man of greater and more overwhelming spirituality than Arnold. His political influence was a by-product of his fiery eschatological proclamation of the impending judgment of God. Inspired by the Joachimite vision of things to come, his proclamation of the millennial significance of contemporary political events aroused the multitudes, while his distinctive spirituality led to the conversion of no less a figure than Michelangelo.

Savonarola's religious convictions and his political influence brought him into conflict with the infamous Spanish Pope Alexander VI (Rodrigo Borgia, 1492–1503), whose personal values and life were the opposite of all Savonarola considered sacred. He disregarded Alexander's excommunication until he was overthrown and imprisoned in 1497. Under torture, he made a number of confessions that he subsequently withdrew, which caused him to be burned as a relapsed heretic in 1498. In 1558 his sermons and books were pronounced orthodox, and he too may ultimately be canonized by the Roman church. Savonarola's "heresy," like Joan's, was essentially that of mounting effective political opposition to those with political power—the English invaders in Joan's case, the pope in that of Savonarola.

On the eve of the Reformation, there was a final heresy trial involving doctrines rather than political criticism: that of an Augustinian monk, John of Wesel. In 1479 the Inquisition at Mainz forced John to abjure a number of "heresies" involving original sin, indulgences, fasting, and the immaculate conception of Mary; his case became a cause célèbre for the early humanists. Forty-one years later another Augustinian, Martin Luther, would be tried in absentia in Rome and condemned. His territorial lord, Duke Frederick of Saxony, protected him and he was kept out of the hands of Rome and the Inquisition. The national sentiment that had not been strong enough to protect John Hus in 1415 or Savonarola in 1498 was adequate to shield Luther in 1520.

2. HERESY AND THE REFORMATION

For almost one thousand years, the church as a whole enjoyed immunity from major heresies within its own body. The revival of Manichaean dualism among the Bogomils in the East and the Cathars in the West was a serious threat, because it combined spiritual fervor with effective criticisms of ecclesiastical corruption. But neither group was *within* the church. Instead, each rapidly created its own counterchurch structure; neither movement found a haven within the church itself. Bogomils and Cathars were real heretics. Their doctrine separated them from the fundamentals of the Christian faith, as defined by the creeds. Many other movements the church of the time regarded as heretical—the Waldensians, the spiritual Franciscans, and the Beguines—appear in retrospect to have remained basically orthodox. They sought a purer and more apostolic Christianity than that which the church actually practiced, but not new doctrines. One after another, they were cited and condemned as heretics, sometimes on very flimsy pretexts, paid the penalty, and passed from the scene. The church emerged from the conflicts apparently unchallenged, at least in its structure.

During the course of the fourteenth and fifteenth centuries, it is apparent that the charge of heresy became a tool for the maintenance of ecclesiastical or political power rather than for the preservation of pure doctrine. If as notorious a sinner as the Borgia Pope Alexander VI can condemn an ascetic Dominican friar, Savonarola, as a heretic, it is evident that the concept of heresy has lost its old meaning. Because real heresy had become rare within the church, the charge of heresy was bandied about. It came to be considered frivolous. Unfortunately, those who are unable to take heresy seriously will find it difficult to preserve orthodoxy. To preserve the truth, it is necessary to be willing to condemn and repudiate doctrines that contradict it. Unfortunately, nothing in the history of the church has done more to tarnish the name of "orthodoxy" and to make the term "heretic" into a badge of honor than the excesses of church authorities in stamping all those who criticize them, for whatever reason, heretics.

This sweeping oversimplification makes the necessary defense of the truth against heresy seem cruel, vicious, and oppressive as well as intellectually dishonest. Edward Gibbon ridiculed fourth-century Christians for fighting over the *iota* that separated Arianism from orthodoxy. But the orthodox had to fight against the *iota,* for if it had been inserted, Christianity would have ceased to exist in the form in which we know it. Compared with the Arians, the heretics of the thirteenth century posed no such threat to the substance of the faith. If the Poor Men of Lyons, the Beguines, Wyclif, or Hus had had their way, Christianity would have changed somewhat, but it would not have been mutilated theologically. The faith of the Waldensians was still Christian, even if their organization was no longer Catholic. Perhaps if Catholicism had tolerated them, it would not have had to face the challenge of the Protestant Reformation. But because it had trivialized heresy, and had persecuted every critic as a heretic, it was unable to recognize what Luther was doing. In his case, the charge of heresy was no longer fatal.

At the beginning, Luther's concerns had nothing to do with heresy in our sense. At first Luther vigorously objected to being classed with Hus, as John Eck (1486–1543) argued in the Leipzig Disputation. Of course Luther, still quite a Catholic loyalist at heart in 1519, assumed at first that Hus— whose works he had never read—was really heretical. But when he read them, he found that he agreed with them. It was indulgences, not transubstantiation, that first aroused Luther's criticism. But the sweeping changes in the church resulting from the doctrine of transubstantiation were the factor that made Luther's revolt inevitable. The Catholic concern for an assured understanding of the sacraments ultimately led to Luther, whose work appears to have destroyed the possibility that Christians can ever again be in general agreement on matters of faith. Luther wanted to introduce no new teaching, but rather to purge the church of heresies it had accumulated over the centuries. The results of his work were to cause something that had not yet happened within the church, despite all the turmoil that preceded him: heresy became institutionalized within the church. Prior to the Reformation, heresy had forced its adherents to the fringes. After Luther, heresy became part of Christianity, if not part of the Christian faith.

Luther was not in fact a real heretic in our sense, any more than Hus. But the church of his day perceived him as such, and it could not get rid of him. Since then the church, despite splitting into various branches, has found it increasingly difficult to eliminate genuine heresy. Luther was concerned to find room within Catholicism for the truths he had rediscovered. But because Catholicism could not or would not accept them, its unity was shattered, and now there seems to be a place within Christendom for virtually any and every heresy—or, more precisely, heresy as a concept has ceased to exist.

At first the Reformers hesitated to call Catholicism itself a heresy: they wanted to reform the church, not ruin it. In the last analysis, however, they were really charging it with heresy, saying that the church itself was guilty of a deviation in doctrine that destroyed the unity of Christianity. Nevertheless, the "deviations" discovered by Luther and Zwingli—such as the hawking of indulgences and dietary rules for Lent—seem trivial by comparison with earlier problems such as Christology and predestination. The place Catholicism gave to such minor rules and practices did indeed reflect a fundamental transformation of the nature of the church and its message from a company of believers to an institution administering grace. This transformation is symbolized in the change from the Lord's Supper as communion into the Mass as mystic sacrifice. Even so, it remained and still remains difficult for the minority, Protestants, to call the majority, Roman Catholics, heretical and to brand Catholicism a heresy. For some reason, Protestants found it easier to call the pope the Antichrist than a heretic. "Orthodoxy" had come to mean "majority" and "heresy," "minority."

The Renaissance had presupposed rather than questioned traditional Christianity. Nevertheless, it did represent a different way of thinking about man and consequently about his relationship with God. Writers such as Petrarch and Lorenzo Valla were devout men concerned with understanding the essential nature of Christianity and grace. Their direct spiritual descendants, Desiderius Erasmus and Luther's friend John Staupitz, sympathized with and to some extent sparked the efforts of Luther, Zwingli, and even John Laski. The rapid spread of Luther's Ninety-five Theses was the result of the humanists' advance preparation of the intellectual world. Erasmus finally rejected Luther, but without him and the other humanists, Luther's efforts might have ended like those of Hus.

In his major monograph on medieval heresy, Herbert Grundmann contends that the condemnation of Luther in 1520 brought the history of medieval heresy to an end.[1] In a purely formal sense, this is true. Grundmann suggests that because Lutheranism became orthodoxy in Saxony and elsewhere in Germany, the unity of the medieval church was shattered, and a condemnation for heresy had real significance only where political power supported the condemning body, namely, the Roman church and its Inquisition. One can agree with Grundmann that the history of heresy in the medieval sense is over without accepting his suggestion that the loss of political support for orthodoxy was the major reason. *Landeskirchen*, "national churches," had existed before Elector Frederick the Wise protected Luther. The first Germanic churches were Arian national churches, and over the centuries there were a number of ethnic groups whose faith differed as much from orthodoxy as did Lutheranism.

Although their Roman Catholic opponents charged them with heresy—and they often accused one another as well—the Protestants were the first great innovators in Christian history to whom the title "heretic" has not stuck. The reason for this is simple: the Protestants were not really the great innovators. They did bring change, but it was in the wake of changes already wrought under the aegis of papal authority; their own goal was a return to the fundamentals. If Luther had been a contemporary of Bernard of Clairvaux, he would probably have fared better at Bernard's hands than did Abelard; even Calvin might have been able to live with the severe abbot of Clairvaux. By accepting the dramatic innovation of transubstantiation without noticing it, Catholicism lost the ability to brand defections from its own position as heretical.

a. Justification by Faith

Luther's great spiritual discovery—dating from his famous "Tower Experience" of 1512[2]—was nothing less than what he called the Gospel, the message that "a man is justified by faith *alone*, apart from the works of the Law" (Rom. 3:28). The word "alone" is not in the original, as Luther knew; he claimed that it was necessary to add it in German to give his translation the full force of the original. The concept of justification by faith is by no means new with Luther. Indeed, the ecumenically minded Roman Catholic scholar Hans Küng has in effect contended that Luther's doctrine really was fully and satisfactorily Catholic, but of course Küng himself has been rebuked by the pope.[3]

Justification by faith is a concept that is quite consistent with the teachings of the Apostle Paul—in whose writings Luther rediscovered it—and indeed with the whole emphasis of the early church on the finished work of Christ. If the redemptive work of Christ is finished, if no further sacrifice is needed, then very logically the sinner's condition before God does not depend on what the sinner himself can do today, but on his relationship to what Christ has done. This relationship is established by faith, and thus faith is sufficient for salvation.

From the early Middle Ages onward, the doctrine of the merits of Christ's work underwent a decisive change: with the doctrine of his bodily presence, through the miracle of transubstantiation, the Mass became a real sacrifice, a new and absolutely necessary supplement to the original sacrifice. It was not justification by faith that was the innovation and therefore the heresy; transubstantiation was the innovation that made the orthodoxy of the past into the heresy of the present. It made the promise of justification by faith alone appear fraudulent.

b. The Priesthood of All Believers

Early Christianity emphasized the role of Jesus Christ as the great High Priest, and in addition spoke of all Christians as members of a royal priesthood. With his advocacy of justification by faith, Luther believed that he could dispense with the concepts of the priestly office developed by Catholicism and required by the doctrine of transubstantiation. This was a far more radical attack on the priesthood as Catholicism understood it than anything that had been said within the confines of the church in centuries. Prior to Luther, the clergy had been charged with corrupt living, excessive claims to authority, and a host of other offenses. Luther charged them with irrelevance.

In both the Old Testament and the New, the priesthood is important. The role of a priest is twofold: he offers sacrifices to God and he mediates between God and man. During much of the Old Testament period, the importance of the priesthood was checked by the greater importance of the Prophets. In the New Testament, as we have noted, Jesus himself is the supreme, indeed the only true Priest.

Apart from Jesus Christ, the great High Priest, and the "royal priesthood," to which all Christians belong, the early church had little to say about priests. The first congregations had "bishops" or "overseers," "elders," and "deacons." Neither the Greek or Latin terms for "priest" were used of Christian ministers (except, of course, for Jesus himself). Paul emphasized Jesus Christ as the "one mediator between God and men" (1 Tim. 2:5). It was Christ himself who made a perfect, once-for-all offering (Heb. 9:26–28), after which further offerings are redundant. The office and the role of human priests within Christianity came to be increasingly important as the centuries passed: transubstantiation made it essential. Unfortunately, many of the same priests whose ministry was declared to be essential lived such corrupt lives that their flocks could not accept them as authentic. Indeed, from the record, one gains the impression that during the Middle Ages, priests whose lives corresponded to the dignity of their office were rare.[4] Even the religious congregations of monks and nuns were sometimes no better, despite the fact that they were founded with the highest ideals and the greatest zeal.

Neither repeated attempts at reform nor the foundation of new orders seems to have been able to restore monasticism to the level of purity and moral fervor that characterized the beginnings of the monastic movements. The charges brought by the early reformers—frequently themselves members of religious orders—claiming that the clergy, including the orders, were corrupt, created the fear that the sacraments, so essential for personal salvation, were not being validly administered.

In theory the doctrine of transubstantiation could have provided Christians with great assurance. They could attend Mass in the confidence that each Mass represented a meritorious sacrifice to God. According to Roman Catholic teaching, the sacraments are effective *ex opere operato,* "from (by virtue of) the work performed." In theory the virtue or spirituality of the ministering clergy is irrelevant to the efficacy of the sacrament. In practice, however, decadent clergy lost the trust of the people, and particularly of those most concerned about their personal salvation. When wandering preachers living lives of "apostolic poverty," charged that a self-indulgent, affluent priest simply could not administer God's holiest gifts, many believed them. The reverence that people felt for those who had the power to change bread and wine into the very body and blood of Christ turned to rage when people felt that they were being deceived and that their eternal salvation was in jeopardy.

The Protestant Reformation dramatically changed the idea of the priesthood. By emphasizing the unique, once-for-all sacrifice of Christ at Calvary, the Reformers stressed Jesus himself as the incomparable High Priest. By reaffirming the New Testament designation of all believers as priests, the sharp distinction between ordained clergy and laity was toned down, if not abolished. In fact, neither the Lutherans nor the Reformed ever really succeeded in implementing this principle. They relied on magisterial authority, i.e. on the government, to reform the church; this led to the need to provide an official church structure to collaborate with the state. The Anabaptists, on the other hand, refused to collaborate with secular governments. They could and did come closer to realizing Luther's principle of the priesthood of all believers than was possible for Lutheran and Calvinist state churches. Established Protestantism soon created a new hierarchy of academics and professors, but it has never really replaced the sacrificing priesthood, operating with official powers, with anything comparable.

c. Sola Scriptura

The principle that Scripture alone has the final authority in matters of faith and morals is an old one in Christendom, one that has never really been repudiated, not even by the Roman church. As articulated by Luther and the other Reformers it had a tremendous impact on the existing structure of spiritual authority. Combined with the concept of the priesthood of all believers, it gave to the ordinary Christian an authority and confidence that had revolutionary impact. An academically trained clergy could never develop autocratic power such as that wielded by the Roman Catholic hierarchy. As long as any ordinary believer could have access to the sacred text, no priest could lord it over him. The Reformation necessarily brought a new emphasis on literacy and on making education available to all, so that all might read the Bible and judge its meaning for themselves. At least some of the problems that the Catholics predicted would be caused by "private interpretation" immediately made their appearance. Rival interpretations of Scripture began to arise alongside Luther's. Within four years of posting the Ninety-five Theses, Luther had to face the challenge of radicals in his own camp, who charged that he was failing to carry the Reformation as far as his own principles required. He rejected them brusquely, but not so much by force of scriptural arguments, as his own principle of *sola Scriptura* would have required, but simply by imposing the strength of his own charismatic authority. From this point on, the course of the Lutheran Reformation was charted not solely on the basis of what Scripture could be shown to require, but also partly on the basis of what Luther was willing to permit.

d. Protestantism and Heresy

Are the central doctrines of Protestantism, i.e. justification by faith, the priesthood of all believers, and the authority of Scripture alone, heretical? In the sense of the councils of Nicaea and Chalcedon, they are not; in the sense of the Council of Vienne, which condemned the concept of apostolic poverty as heretical, they certainly are. Grundmann is right: the history of heresy effectively ends with Luther. But it was not because in Luther and his successors heresy was victorious—even though Catholicism certainly looked on them as vicious heretics. It is because of the fact that Luther's success—and that of other Reformers as well—destroyed the catholicity of Western Christendom and replaced it with the principle of the territorial church. When what is orthodox in one jurisdiction is heretical across the border, then "heresy" and "orthodoxy" have lost their original meaning. When the heresy and orthodoxy of major doctrines is decided on the basis of local power politics, the concepts have lost their value for distinguishing between truth and falsehood.

In recent decades, another explanation has been offered: Protestantism put an end to the old questions of heresy and orthodoxy because Protestantism is not a specific set of convictions that can be analyzed in terms of heresy and orthodoxy, but is simply the principle of continual self-criticism and constant doctrinal development. Protestantism is progress, in doctrine as well as in society. This view, advocated in our century by Ernst Troeltsch and Paul Tillich, clearly represents the abandonment of the idea that there was ever a "faith once delivered to the saints," which it is the saints' duty to preserve intact. Protestantism, by this definition, would not be a set of heretical doctrines but the principle of heresy itself. Of course Troeltsch and Tillich did not mean to imply that Protestantism is an evil, but rather that fixity of doctrines is an evil from which Protestantism continually delivers us by constantly reforming its own doctrines once it has finished with those of Catholicism.

To the lover of the Middle Ages, Protestantism appears responsible for the breakup of Christian Europe, and thus evil. To the lover of modernity, even to the secularist, Protestantism appears to be a force for progress, and thus good, even if it retains an unnecessary amount of dogmatism on its own. To appreciate the positive contribution of the Protestant Reformation, it is necessary to reject both of these suggestions. Protestantism institutionalized neither heresy nor progress.

With regard to the charge that it established heretical doctrines as the recognized religion of formerly Catholic regions, Protestantism must reply that it simply recovered the truth, and that unfortunately only some of the Christian nations were willing to accept it. It was never the intention of the Reformers to fragment Christendom doctrinally, but this was the inevitable result of their partial success. With regard to the claim made by some that the "Protestant principle" is a principle of continual self-criticism and ongoing doctrinal change, we must reply that there is an orthodox Protestantism that is committed to keeping the "faith once delivered," whose highest goal is fidelity, not progress.

The spirit of the Reformation was not "progressive" but rather "reactionary." It sought to return to its sources, to the Bible, and to turn away from the erroneous doctrinal advances of medieval Catholicism. In many ways, the spirit of the first Reformers resembles that of twentieth-century fundamentalists: it was a desire for "that old-time religion," for simplicity and solidity.

If Protestantism were essentially a form of protest and of progress, it would be senseless to compare it to ancient standards, such as the creeds of Nicaea and Chalcedon. But Reformation Protestantism claimed to be nothing more than the straightforward, simple, and correct interpretation of ancient Scripture. The fourth- and fifth-century creeds make essentially the same claim, a claim most Protestants have accepted in endorsing the creeds.

Consequently, it makes sense to compare Protestant doctrines with the creeds.

If we accept the creeds of Nicaea and Chalcedon as the adequate tests for orthodoxy, and if Protestantism accepts them and conforms to them, then Protestantism must be accepted as orthodox. Indifference to the creeds or rejection of them—common among Protestants today—does not make contemporary Protestants "more Protestant," but rather less so. The *raison d'être* of orthodox Protestantism is not a claim to be more progressive than Roman Catholicism, but rather the contrary: more ancient, closer to the historic Christian faith, than Catholicism. In order to justify its existence as a separate expression of Christian faith, Protestantism has to claim that it is not heresy, but rather a necessary correction of heresy. Thus—despite the reluctance of Protestants to label Roman Catholicism "heresy"—in effect that is what their very existence implies. Only if Catholicism represents an intolerable falling away from the "faith once delivered" can the splitting of the church by the Reformers be condoned.

e. Roman Catholicism and Heresy

In our sense of the word "heresy," Reformation Protestantism is not heretical. Its characteristic differences with Roman Catholicism do not touch the Nicene and Chalcedonian foundations of orthodoxy. They are not "fundamental" differences in the strictest sense, in that they do not deal with the doctrines of the Trinity and Christ. By the same token, Roman Catholicism cannot be heretical in our sense, because it too holds the ancient standards. Yet Catholicism and Protestantism accuse each other of heresy, often implicitly denying to one another the possibility of salvation. In order to make sense of this, we are really going to have to introduce a category of heresy that is not really heretical in the sense we have used thus far, and yet is sufficiently serious to justify both the Reformation and the continuing separation of the Christian confessions that has followed it.

The strongest accusation that can be made against Roman Catholicism from this perspective is not that it is heretical in structure, but that it is heretical in effect, in that it effectively undercuts its own formal adherence to the major Christological stands of its official creeds. In other words, Reformation Protestantism acknowledges that Catholicism possesses the fundamental articles of the faith, but claims that it so overlays them with extraneous and sometimes false doctrines that the foundations are no longer accessible to the majority of Catholic believers. We assert, for example, that the Catholic interpretation of the real presence of Christ in the eucharist in the precise terms of transubstantiation effectively changed the meaning of the very fundamental doctrine of the incarnation, even though Catholicism formally insists that it proclaims the incarnation.[5] (Today, of course, the situation has changed again. Post–Vatican II Roman Catholicism differs in some significant ways from that of the anti-Protestant Council of Trent. Our concern here is with the Catholicism against which the Reformers protested, and our claim is that even though it remained formally orthodox in our sense, in practice it had moved so far from orthodoxy that the Reformation, painful as it was, was both necessary and unavoidable.)

3. MARTIN LUTHER

The church historian Walther Koehler calls Martin Luther "the great, inexhaustible stimulator," and continues, "strictly speaking, 'heretics' no longer exist, if the final decision lies with the conscience."[6] Where the conscience of the individual believer is the supreme judge, the concept of heresy becomes meaningless, as heresy presupposes an objective, external standard by which to measure beliefs. Prior to 1517, Christianity was perceived as a unity. It is true that the Greek-speaking Eastern church (together with its Slavonic-speaking siblings) was split off from the Latin-speaking Western church by the mutual excommunications of pope and patriarch in 1054. But despite this, Christendom was still perceived as a unity, as "the church." Although it was not Luther's intention to found a new church, but simply to purify the old one, from the time of the Reformation there were new churches—first the Lutheran, then the Reformed, and finally the Anglican. From its beginning, the Reformation created new churches as no other movement had succeeded in doing. The first hundred years after the Reformation produced more volumes of dogmatic theology than the Middle Ages in East and West combined—a dubious accomplishment not due solely to the invention of printing. Christendom was still a recognizable entity, but the visible unity of the church was shattered.[7]

a. Ad Fontes!: *"To the Sources!"*

From its earliest days, the Christian church has professed to hold the Scripture as its primary and final authority and as the bearer of divinely revealed truth. In both East and West the Bible never ceased to be the formal authority, but in practice tradition and ecclesiastical authority became increasingly important. The Reformation emphasis on Scripture alone dramatically altered the self-awareness of Christianity. To some—the Protestants—it seemed a return to the old foundations, to others, a new building on an entirely new groundwork. The Reformation of the sixteenth century effectively challenged the claim of Roman Catholicism to be the church. Others had accused Catholicism or the papacy of being the Antichrist, as the Reformers also did more than once, but no one else was able to set up rival institutions whose claims appeared as impressive as Rome's.

The cry *Ad fontes!* implied that the Catholic Church had failed or proved false in its self-appointed task as the steward of the mysteries of God. If it had succeeded in accurately transmitting the heritage entrusted to it, there would have been no need to return to the sources. The Reformers' appeal—actually raised by the humanists just before the onset of the Reformation—called on Christians to return the church to its beginnings and make a fresh start. No greater indictment of the Catholic theory of tradition and development could be imagined. Inasmuch as Catholicism essentially claimed to be the religion once delivered to the saints, for humanists and Reformers to point out the tremendous changes between the early centuries and the sixteenth was terribly damaging.

b. The Pattern of Church History

Both the Renaissance and the Reformation, although for different reasons, looked on the Catholic "Age of Faith" as a period of decline. Joachim of Floris taught his followers to look forward to a Third Age with a new, spiritual church, one that would fulfill what had only been promised in the earlier ages. Protestantism, by contrast, did not present itself as a new and different Third Age, but as a return to authenticity. Luther wanted to purge the medieval church of all that was inconsistent with the true Gospel. It was certainly not his intention to create a "Lutheranism" patterned on his own ideas and personality. For this reason he called his church "evangelical," but the term "Lutheran" soon came into use, to set Luther's followers off from the other main branch of the Continental Reformation, the Reformed. This Reformed branch of Protestantism, initiated by Ulrich Zwingli in Zurich but more decisively influenced by John Calvin of Geneva, insisted on calling itself Reformed to stress its intention of reshaping the church to make it conform once again to its original, ancient pattern.

In retrospect it is apparent that the early Protestants made two mistakes in their attempt to recover the distinctives of early Christianity. First, they were wrong and anachronistic in thinking that the first congregations were patterned on Scripture, because of course those congregations were older than much of the New Testament. Ideally, those early congregations were in conformity with Scripture, but strictly speaking, they were not constructed with Scripture as their blueprint. Second, the Reformers were mistaken in thinking that they had succeeded in creating congregations that really resembled those of the early church, although it is possible to argue that Protestant worship was closer in spirit to that of the early church than was the liturgy of medieval Catholicism. Nevertheless, despite these important qualifications, Protestantism still continues to insist that it recovered a

New Testament Christianity that was submerged and virtually lost in Roman Catholicism. Otherwise neither the Reformation nor modern Protestantism could have any legitimate *raison d'être*.

The traditional Catholic view of world history divided time into two parts: before and after Christ. The history of the church itself was a continuity, with no dramatic transformations or developments between Pentecost and the return of Christ. Since Augustine, Roman Catholicism has been essentially amillennial; in other words, it does not look forward to an earthly reign of Christ, but expects his return to be immediately followed by the Last Judgment and the translation of all the saved to heaven. The church, in its present form, thus represents as nearly perfect an institution as possible in the present world. Joachim of Floris, we recall, viewed the period in which he lived, at the turn of the twelfth and thirteenth centuries, as the period of decline of the Second Age, and looked to a new, Third Age of eschatological fulfillment. Protestantism did not look for a radical transformation such as Joachim envisaged with his idea of a spiritual church, but rather for a return to the purity of the early church, but like Joachim it postulated a serious decline in the Catholicism of its day.

Early Protestants, unlike some of the radicals, were not willing to suppose that God had completely forsaken the church or left himself altogether without witnesses. They saw a continuity between the early church and their own day in the isolated but recurrent witness of some of the mystics and some of the groups Catholicism condemned as heretical: the Waldensians and the Hussites, both of which groups quickly rallied to the Reformation when it began.

More important for Luther and Calvin than this thread of continuity they saw in some of the peripheral movements of the medieval church was the continuity they believed existed by means of conformity to the Scripture. Back in the second Christian century, Irenaeus of Lyons had stressed the apostolic heritage and presented the united church, represented by all its bishops in harmony, as the guarantor of apostolicity. Apostolicity remained of crucial importance for the Reformers, but they did not see it guaranteed by the continuity of the hierarchy, for they considered that both popes and councils had erred. They found apostolicity in conformity with the writings of the Apostles, not with the traditions of their successors, the bishops. Tradition continued to play a role in Protestantism, both the traditions of the church fathers and the new, rapidly developing traditions of Protestant Scholasticism.

c. *Luther's Doctrine of God*

The doctrine of transubstantiation gave the believing Roman Catholic the confidence that in the sacrament of the altar he could "have" God incarnate, Jesus Christ, present with him in bodily form. This doctrine, as we have seen, took the focus of Catholic faith away from the Word of God and brought it to bear upon a liturgical event and upon the sacramental body and blood of Christ. Luther took the focus away from the sacrament and the priesthood and centered it once again on the Word of God and on faith. Because we have God's word in Scripture, Luther could say, "Habemus Deum," "We have God."[8] His understanding of God was rooted in his personal experience of justification, not in any metaphysical analysis; he warned against "speculations about the mere majesty of God."[9]

Luther's doctrine of God remained thoroughly traditional in what it affirmed, but broke with the Scholastic understanding of the knowability and understandability of God. For Luther, as for the German mystics, God is *Deus absconditus*, the "hidden God," inaccessible to human reason. For Luther as for Augustine before him, God was primarily sovereign, inscrutable Will. He combined a strong emphasis on God's providence and predestination with a lively interest in Satan and his power in a way that remains paradoxical. Although God is sovereign and works even in Satan and in ungodly men,[10] yet Satan is independent enough to carry on a full-scale rebellion against God, even to the degree of establishing false churches, such as those of Thomas Münzer and Ulrich Zwingli.

By emphasizing the sole authority of Scripture and downgrading the works of the church fathers and the decisions of ecumenical councils, Luther created a problem for his followers. On the one hand, Lutherans wanted to affirm traditional theology with respect to the doctrines of the Trinity and Christ, but on the other those doctrines are not explicit in Scripture. They are the product of the theology of the church fathers and the councils. Among Luther's disciples and successors, Philipp Melanchthon showed the greatest willingness to take over the theological heritage of the early church intact. Other Lutherans, more radical—or perhaps more faithful to Luther's own example—sought to develop all their doctrine from the pages of Scripture itself, with little or no recourse to the church fathers and the theological tradition. This produced two significant results. Lutheran theologians wrote, one after another, extensive works of systematic theology, purporting to draw them exclusively from Scripture. Lutheran theologians produced as many complete works of dogmatics in a few years as the early and medieval church had produced over the course of centuries. At the same time, this expansive production resulted in a vast, solid, and relatively consistent Lutheran theological tradition; for several centuries much Lutheran orthodox theology consisted largely of repetition of and reaction to earlier writings in the Lutheran tradition. Despite Luther's own disdain for theological tradition, his Lutheran successors quickly developed a very impressive theological tradition of their own. Modern orthodox Lutheran theology bears as strong a Scholastic stamp—limited to the "fathers" of Lutheranism—as does traditional Catholic theology.[11]

d. Christology

Luther's Christology was as majestic as that of any of his Roman Catholic predecessors; more majestic, in fact, because, as we shall see, it tended to monophysitism, the deification of the human nature of Christ. A high Christology was an existential as well as a logical necessity for Luther as a consequence of his radical view of the Fall, sin, and the resulting depravity of man and the bondage of the human will. Luther's radical understanding of sin and the Fall was grounded experientially as well as theologically. The story of his own struggle with sin and his inability to bend his will to obedience even to a gracious God until God gave him the crucial insight into justification by faith is very well known. It has become as much a part of the Lutheran theological and devotional tradition as the conversion of Paul on the road to Damascus.

In Luther's view, sin has corrupted every aspect of man's being, even or especially his reason, which has consequently become "the devil's bride." Since man's reason is corrupt and his will is bound, salvation must come to him as a totally free gift of God; there is nothing he can do to merit it or even to prepare himself for it. Following Augustine and anticipating the slightly later work of John Calvin, Luther taught a thoroughgoing predestinarianism that amounts to a virtual determinism. As was the case with Augustine, Gottschalk, and other predestinarians in the Roman Catholic tradition, Luther's strict view proved very difficult for his followers to keep, and Lutherans beginning with Philipp Melanchthon have modified it to varying degrees, allowing a greater place for the exercise of the human will.

Luther's concept of the servitude of the human will had implications for his Christology. Although he formally accepted the doctrine of Christ's two natures as defined by the Council of Chalcedon, his radical suspicion of the reason and will of man made him inclined to downgrade the humanity of Christ and emphasize his deity, at least by implication. Nevertheless, his Christology was so orthodox that his Roman Catholic opponents found nothing in it to criticize.

Unlike those theologians who looked on Scripture as a compendium of theological truths, from which doctrine could be extracted, Luther approached it with the desperate existential need to find a gracious, favorable God. He was concerned first of all with its tropological, or moral, sense, i.e. its application to the believer to give him salvation and assurance.[12] Luther's early spiritual development involved a protracted struggle with *Anfechtung* (usually translated "temptation," but with a very strong flavor of spiritual aggression). For Luther one of the most important features about the incarnate Christ was that he too endured *Anfechtung,* both in the desert after his baptism and in Gethsemane before his trial and crucifixion.

Traditional Roman Catholic piety stressed the sufferings of Christ as a model for contemplation. The familiar Good Friday hymn "O Sacred Head, Sore Wounded" goes back to Bernard of Clairvaux and is typical of meditation on the physical suffering Christ endured for our sakes. Nevertheless, despite its anguish, this suffering was seen as a victory: Jesus vanquished Satan and overcame the world precisely through the Cross. The impression is given that Jesus sovereignly endured humiliation and suffering in the flesh while retaining spiritual self-control and mastery, summed up in his prayer "Father, forgive them; for they know not what they do" (Luke 23:34).

Luther carried his concept of Christ's incarnation and true humanity further still, and emphasized his conviction that Christ suffered terrible spiritual and psychological agony, i.e. *Anfechtung,* just as we do. Although Luther denied that Jesus had ever sinned, he contended that at Calvary Jesus felt the weight of our sin and was conscious of being abandoned by God.[13] For Luther it was important to know that Christ had suffered the feeling of being accursed and forsaken just as Luther did. "We must wrap Christ, and recognize him wrapped in sins, death, and all pain just as in flesh and blood."[14] "If I deny Christ as a sinner, then I deny the crucified one."[15] For Luther the Cross was hardly a victory: it was the greatest possible humiliation. Luther did his utmost to make the full humanity of Christ apparent to his hearers and readers. He emphasized the naturalness of Mary's delivery, and also that she not only suckled Jesus but had to change his diapers and wash his bottom. These references are less heroic than the typical medieval meditations on Christ's agony, but they are certainly legitimate implications of the orthodox teaching of the incarnation.

Luther's emphasis on the humanity of Jesus provided part of the inspiration for the human "historical Jesus" of nineteenth-century liberal scholarship, but Luther was far from looking upon Jesus as primarily or exclusively a man. Indeed, Luther identified Jesus so fully with God that he seems in danger of falling into patripassianism: Jesus is "Lord of Sabaoth and there is no other God," "the Lord of Hosts," "the Creator of all." By placing the deity and the humanity in sharp juxtaposition, Luther preserved the paradoxical element of the doctrine of the incarnation: Jesus is at one and the same time "the most just of all and the most sinful, the most glorious and the most despairing."[16] In like manner, the believer, in Christ, is *simul justus ac peccator,* "at the same time justified and a sinner." Nevertheless, despite all his emphasis on the humanity of Christ, his understanding of what Jesus could and did do for us was such that it seemed to require that this humanity be deified. In other words, Luther presented part of his position in a way that is reminiscent of Apollinaris and the Monophysites. This became clear in his attitude toward his first great controversy with another important Reformation leader, the eucharistic conflict with Zwingli.

e. The New Eucharistic Controversy

The eucharistic controversies of the Middle Ages centered on the question of the *bodily* presence of Christ in the eucharist. All the contending parties believed Christ to be present and held that believers received his body and his blood. What was in dispute was how the body and blood are present and how they are received. The solution, involving the concept of transubstantiation, was the doctrine of the bodily presence of Christ, whose body is physically consumed by communicants, both by those who truly believe and by those who participate unworthily or in unbelief. From time to time during the Middle Ages and again at the outset of the Reformation, teachers arose who contended that the body and blood of Christ are present only to faith, and only as symbols. In general, however, the great majority of Christians believed in the *real* presence of Christ, even when they could not agree as to the manner of his presence. It is important to note that those who denied the transubstantiation of the elements did not, in general, dispute the real presence of Christ. Those who affirmed transubstantiation did so because they could not conceive of Christ as really present unless present in the substance of his body and blood. Those who accepted a spiritual presence as thoroughly *real* did not see the need for postulating a miracle of transubstantiation.

Although Walther Koehler calls him "the great stimulator," Luther's mentality was essentially conservative. His original intention was to reject and change only what was necessary. Unfortunately, during Luther's brief "protective custody" at the Wartburg during several months in 1521–22, Andreas Bodenstein of Karlstadt (usually called simply Karlstadt, 1480–1541) had tried to push the cause of the Protestant Reformation along faster in Wittenberg. After Luther's return, Karlstadt was isolated and forced to lead an itinerant existence for a number of years, during which he produced five tracts on the eucharist (1524), denying the real presence of Christ. Jesus' word "this" in "This is my body" (Mark 14:22), according to Karlstadt, referred to his physical body, to which he pointed as he spoke. Luther reacted with vehemence in December of that same year, and Karlstadt temporarily submitted in 1525.

Karlstadt, however, was not the only one to doubt the bodily presence of Christ in the eucharist. The far more influential Ulrich Zwingli, who had begun to reform the church in Zurich independently of Luther's example, interpreted the "is" of the words of institution to mean "signifies." Zwingli argued that inasmuch as the physical body of Christ is seated at the right hand of the Father in heaven, it cannot be present at all the altars of the world when communion is being celebrated. Hence the "is" must mean "signifies." Luther rejected transubstantiation as a Scholastic fiction, but took the "is" with strict literalness, and taught that the body of Christ became present together with the elements at the institution of the eucharist.

In order to refute Zwingli's rationalist objection, Luther argued from the deity of Christ and the traditional doctrine of the communication of attributes. If Jesus is fully God, then the attributes of his deity can also be attributed to his humanity, in this case to his body. Deity possesses the attributes of omnipresence, or ubiquity, the ability to be everywhere at once. Because of the communication of attributes, Jesus' humanity must also possess the characteristic of ubiquity; thus his body too is ubiquitous, or omnipresent.[17] Since Christ is "an undivided person [and] with God, where God is [i.e. everywhere], he must be."[18] Koehler comments: "Strictly analyzed, Luther has not had the humanity partake of the attributes of deity, but rather had the humanity taken up into the personal unity, so that no true humanity remains."[19] Thus in his effort to defend the real, bodily presence of Christ in the sacrament, Luther inclined dangerously to monophysitism, the doctrine that after the incarnation Christ possesses only one incarnate divine nature. Luther also carried his understanding of the communication of attributes in another direction, and argued that what is said of the humanity of Christ must also be said of deity: "I believe thus that not only the human nature but the divine or the true God as well suffered for us and died . . . thus, it is rightly said, the death of God."[20] This terminology is reminiscent of patripassianism or Sabellian modalism, and furnished a point of departure for Lutherans participating in the short-lived death-of-God movement of the 1960s.

The doctrine of transubstantiation—not that of the real presence—transformed the nature of Catholic devotion and spiritual life. It did not create the doctrinal and ethical problems the Reformation sought to resolve, but once it had been made into binding dogma in 1215, it made their gradual and peaceful resolution impossible. Transubstantiation was a theological formula intended to preserve the essential doctrine of the *real* presence of Christ, but it created unanticipated problems by appearing to give the priests and the church transcendent, miraculous powers. Luther, like his conservative Roman Catholic predecessors, was convinced that it was essential to preserve the doctrine of the real presence. Those who challenged him went further than Ratramnus or Berengar of Tours, for they wanted to reduce the eucharist to a mere symbol or memorial. In fighting to defend the doctrine of the real presence, Luther, like his Catholic predecessors, had recourse to a theological explanation that in retrospect seems to have produced more problems than it resolved.

In the Marburg Colloquy of 1529, Luther and Zwingli were able to agree on fourteen of fifteen points at issue, but separated on the fifteenth. Luther wanted to insist that the word *est,* "is," of Mark 14:22 means what it says: the bread *is* the body of Christ. Zwingli interpreted it as *significat,* "represents." Luther told the shocked Swiss Reformer, "Ye have a different spirit than we."[21] Zwingli was concerned that nothing be done to spiritualize the true humanity of Christ; his identity with us, as a real, flesh-and-blood human being (on which Luther himself insisted when discussing the incarnation), had to be preserved, even in glory. If Jesus is seated at the right hand of the Father in heaven, then his physical body—which is by its very nature of limited dimensions—cannot be present at communion services on earth.

In his effort to assure the reality of the presence of Christ with us, Luther was persuaded that it had to be bodily to be real; hence, the body had to be there at the communion. Inasmuch as the body is plainly *not* there to any human sense, and in view of the fact that the normal understanding of "body" is that of something that can be perceived by the senses, it was necessary for Luther to modify his definition of "body" in order to be able to claim that the body is present when the communion is observed. Unfortunately, a ubiquitous body is unlike anything we know, and it is hard to believe that it should be called a body at all. Luther explained that Christ was ubiquitous even when on earth, and went on to say that in a sense believers are ubiquitous too: "Not only was Christ in heaven while he walked on earth, but the Apostles too, and all of us as well, who are mortals here on earth, insofar as we believe in Christ."[22]

In order to safeguard the doctrine of the real presence, Luther seems to be teaching a kind of double reality: the physical reality, of which we are all aware, and another reality according to which Christ is always in heaven and those who believe in him are always there with him. There is nothing very strange in teaching a twofold reality, physical and spiritual; this is consistent with the New Testament world view. What is distinctive in Luther is his insistence on calling this second reality physical, or bodily, as well as the first. If "body" is no longer what we normally mean it to be, then to say that Christ is human and has a real body will no longer be as unambiguous as it would otherwise seem.

The implications of Luther's eucharistic doctrine for Christology are monophysite or docetic: on the one hand, if Christ's body is ubiquitous, then it is hard to conceive of it as a *human* body, and then it is difficult to imagine what can remain of his human nature. On the other hand, if Christ is really with us in the eucharist, although his body seems to be absent, it is easy to spring to the conclusion that when the body seemed to be with us, or seemed to be human, it was only an appearance.

Luther himself firmly resisted all tendencies to abandon the realism of the Chalcedonian doctrine of the two natures of Christ, but his attempt to explain the real presence contains implications that could undermine it if allowed to run their full course. The Creed of Chalcedon specifically *limited* speculation. This limitation is exasperating but necessary, if the doctrine of the two natures in one person is not to produce logical absurdities. Luther himself respected the limits, despite his penchant for paradox. But in the century after Luther, the attempt of several orthodox Lutherans to apply the attributes of deity in a thoroughgoing way to the man Christ Jesus will result in a Christological position that seems virtually to do away with his true humanity.

The eucharistic controversy between Luther and Zwingli reveals how difficult it is even for dedicated and well-intentioned Christian teachers to explain and interpret a fundamental Christian doctrine, such as that of the incarnation, without creating more problems than they resolve. The New Testament message confronts believers with a number of formidable mysteries and at the same time calls upon them to use their minds in the effort to proclaim and interpret them. There is a point in the proclamation of the mystery where human understanding reaches its limit. To stop too soon in the effort to understand and to interpret leaves the believer facing a contradiction or an absurdity; to go too far often leads him into a logical impossibility. One of the greatest challenges to the Christian witness is to explain as much as can be explained, and thus not to leave believers in ignorance where clarification is possible, but to stop when the limits of understanding have been reached, and thus not trespass on the mystery of God: "The secret things belong unto the Lord our God" (Deut. 29:29). Luther, like many other great theologians, respected the limits. Like the followers of other leaders, some of his followers, in seeking to be faithful to his insights and to continue building on his foundations, plunged themselves into problems that cannot be resolved. One reaction to the full and complete application of the attributes of deity to the man Jesus Christ was the turning of the coin and the application of the attributes of humanity to God, so that in our own century it has been said—in quite a different sense from Luther's meaning—God is dead.

f. The Communication of Attributes

As we recall, the expression "communication of attributes" is a technical theological term to express the implications of the two natures of Christ united in one person. It means that because of the unity of the person, what is attributed to the deity may be attributed to the humanity and vice versa. During the middle of the sixteenth century, the deity of Christ was denied by a number of radicals of various sorts. The second and third generation of Protestant theologians found it necessary to expound the doctrine more rigorously than the first. A paramount example is Martin Chemnitz (1522–86); he attempted to systematize and clarify Luther's understanding of the communication.

In Luther's view, the divine nature fully permeates the human nature in Christ as the soul permeates the body. Luther did not assert, as Apollinaris had done, that the divine nature or the Logos *is* the soul of Christ. On the contrary, he asserted that Christ has a human soul, indeed that he has a human psychological life and suffered real *Anfechtung*. But how many of the attributes of deity can in any real sense be shared by a human being without totally destroying his humanity? Chemnitz divided the *idiomata*, "personal characteristics (attributes)" of God, into three *genera* or classes: the *genus idiomaticum*, including the so-called positive or communicable attributes such as mercy, justice, love, and truth. The second *genus*, called *apotelesmaticum*, involves the purpose or work of redemption, which also belongs to both natures, the human and the divine. The third category, the *genus majestaticum*, involves the problematic attributes that normally would be said to pertain to deity alone: the incommunicable attributes of majesty such as infinity, eternity, and immutability. The attribute of ubiquity belongs to the *genus majestaticum*. Can the humanity of Christ partake of the attributes of majesty and remain human? Luther and his followers unequivocally asserted that it can; it is this assertion that makes Lutheran theology sometimes sound monophysite, despite its formal adherence to the teachings of the Council of Chalcedon.

Logically, Chemnitz should have considered a fourth *genus*, a *genus tapeinoticum*, that of the attributes of humility, for logic would say that deity also participates in the humble attributes of Christ's human nature. This theme was not developed at the time, no doubt because to ascribe human attributes to God would threaten to destroy his deity. In our own day, it has been taken to its ultimate conclusion in the proclamation of the death of God. Instead of dealing extensively with Christ's human nature, Lutheran orthodoxy preferred to concentrate on his status of humiliation.

g. Christ's Two Statuses

A distinction was made between Christ in the *status humiliationis*, in the "status (condition) of humiliation," and Christ in the *status exaltationis*, in the "status of exaltation (glorification)." In both conditions the concept of the communication of attributes causes logical problems. What became of the attributes of deity during the humiliation? Jesus himself states that he is not omniscient (Mark 13:32), a text that remains a challenge to orthodox Christology. In Philippians 2:5–8, Paul speaks of Jesus as emptying himself; what is the real significance of this emptying, or *kenosis*, for the deity of Christ? If it is simply that Jesus did not use his divine power or allow it to be seen, but held it back, as Luther says,[23] then it is hard to say that he was truly man or that he was for a time forsaken by God and standing before the abyss, as Luther strongly emphasized.

The suggestion that Christ merely concealed and did not use the divine powers he fully possessed is called a *krypsis,* "concealment," rather than a *kenosis* and does not seem to come to terms with Philippians 2:7 and the other New Testament texts that speak of Jesus' humanity and its limitations. During the seventeenth century, the orthodox Lutheran theologians of the University of Tübingen, led for example by Theodore Thummius (d. 1630), interpreted the concept of the genus of majesty in the sense of *krypsis* rather than *kenosis,* teaching that Christ from the moment of his conception was seated at the right hand of the majesty on high, and that he constantly exercised his entire majesty while on earth, even at the moment of his death. Walther Koehler comments: "How Luther's wonderful idea of the Hidden God has been trivialized!"[24] The incarnation appears to have become only playacting. These "cryptic" theologians were opposed by the "kenotic" Lutherans at the University of Giessen, led by Balthasar Mentzer (d. 1627): they taught that although Jesus Christ received the full title to the attributes of deity at the moment of his conception, with rare exceptions he refrained from exercising them. Specifically, he did not exercise them in "cryptic" fashion. If the Tübingen position seems to make the humanity of Jesus nothing more than a gigantic As If—God looking and acting as if he were a man, but all the while secretly exercising his sovereignty over the universe, the Giessen position at least permits the postulate of a human Jesus. Orthodox Lutheranism essentially followed the Tübingen school; Article VIII of the Lutheran Formula of Concord (1577) understood the self-emptying in terms of mere concealment. All Lutherans were agreed that the glorified Christ, after his resurrection and ascension, does possess the attributes of majesty, and hence can be and is ubiquitous, everywhere, in a sense in which this was not at all true of Jesus during his earthly ministry. It was this concept of ubiquity, to which Luther had resorted to support his view of the bodily presence of Christ in the eucharist, that then led to his irreconcilable break with Zwingli.

4. ZWINGLI AND CALVIN

a. *Ulrich Zwingli*

Ulrich or Huldreich ("rich in favor") Zwingli (1484–1531) was only seven weeks younger than Luther and came to his own reformed convictions prior to Luther's posting of the Ninety-five Theses. He knew Erasmus (ca.

1466–1536) in Basel and was strongly influenced by his humanism, although the Zwinglian branch of the Reformation ultimately moved further away from the Catholic piety Erasmus continued to practice than Luther ever did. Zwingli emphasized the fact that he was not decisively influenced by Luther; indeed, at first he intended only an Erasmian purification of Christianity, not a Lutheran reformation. Luther's reforming activities were sparked by a religious abuse, specifically by the selling of indulgences. Luther denounced this traffic as a false and deceptive hope that kept troubled sinners from trusting in Christ alone and thus from being saved.

Zwingli had been a chaplain with Swiss mercenary troops in Italian campaigns, including the disastrous defeat of the Swiss by Francis I of France at Marignano (Melegnano) in 1515. His first impulse was an attempt to put an end to the recruiting of Swiss soldiers as foreign mercenaries, a practice tied to papal privileges. In 1520 he gave up a papal pension he had been receiving for facilitating such recruitment on behalf of the pope. Zwingli's first reformation tract was published in 1522, *On the Choice and Freedom of Foods,* and was a response to an attempt by the bishop of Constance to enforce abstinence from meat during Lent, a more trivial quarrel than indulgences. His protest unintentionally led to an iconoclastic uproar in Zurich in the fall of 1523, a year after Karlstadt had deliberately unleashed iconoclasm in Wittenberg. Zwingli's reforming efforts required the direct participation of the Zurich town council, inasmuch as Zurich was a republic, not a feudal principality. Zwingli's close ties to the Zurich government and its policies led him to promote the death penalty for some early Anabaptists in 1525,[25] and his advocacy of using military measures to promote the Reformation in central Switzerland led to his death in battle in 1531.

Unlike Luther, who spent his spiritually decisive years in a monastery and as a professor of theology, Zwingli was a man of the world—a priest, but also a soldier, a humanist, and a politician. Unlike Luther, who feared and detested human reason, Zwingli was a rationalist, very much in the spirit of Erasmus. Not only Scripture but also human reason is a norm by which faith and piety can be reformed. He strongly emphasized predestination, and went beyond Luther and even further than Calvin, several years later, would go, in contending that God had intended sin in order to manifest his own glory. Zwingli saw the great men of pagan antiquity as predestined to salvation. He did not think the fall to have been as radical as Luther held it. In consequence he had a more positive attitude toward worldly government than Luther,[26] and was more willing than Luther to participate in it; ultimately he met his death in a battle provoked when Zurich tried to induce the Roman Catholic cantons of central Switzerland to accept the Reformation by establishing a blockade (the Battle of Kappel, October 11, 1531).

Zwingli had begun to rationalize the concept of the Lord's Supper as early as 1523, when he encountered the views of the Dutchman Cornelius Henrixs Hoen, who interpreted the "is" of Mark 14:22 as "signifies." Zwingli persuaded the Basel and Strassburg reformers Johannes Oecolampadius (1482–1531) and Martin Bucer (1491–1551) to follow him in accepting a symbolic understanding of the presence of Christ. Johann Bugenhagen (1485–1558), Luther's colleague in Wittenberg, attacked Zwingli, who replied in 1527; Luther took up his pen against Zwingli in a tract, "That these words of Christ 'This is my Body' still stand firm against the Fanatics" (April 1527). Zwingli replied and Luther countered with his "Confession of the Lord's Supper" (March 1528).

Luther's sensitivity to efforts to change the doctrine of the real presence into a symbolic presence had certainly been heightened because of the fact that this was one of the positions favored by the eccentric Karlstadt, who had tried to take over the direction of the Reformation in Wittenberg while Luther was in seclusion in Wartburg Castle. In addition to his own convictions of the cruciality of the real presence, Luther was very wary of anything he considered an attempt to change the direction of the Reformation he had launched. The fact that Zwingli pointedly claimed to have rediscovered the meaning of the Gospel independently of Luther did not, of course, make Luther more sympathetic.

Despite Luther's harsh verdict on Zwingli, it must be acknowledged that the Zurich Reformer was as loyal to the ecumenical creeds as Luther. Zwingli fully accepted the deity of Christ; indeed, he contended that this doctrine was necessary for our salvation. Nevertheless, unlike Luther he saw Christ's redemptive work largely in his overcoming of the obstacles to our salvation; then, by his example and his preaching, Christ taught saving doctrine and morals.[27] For Luther the most important aspect of the humanity of Christ was the fact that it identifies us with him; echoes of Irenaeus are plainly heard. For Zwingli, Jesus' humanity has more of a psychological than an ontological significance: Jesus will naturally be sympathetic to us because he is our brother and knows and shares our human weaknesses (Heb. 2:12–13, 4:15–16). Because of his humanity, Jesus is not so much our archetype or exemplar, as Luther put it, but rather our moral example to be observed and imitated. Like many medieval writers, Zwingli emphasized Christ's example. Medieval writers such as Bernard had emphasized Christ's sufferings, while Zwingli emphasized his obedience and his teaching, but both thus stressed the accomplishments of Christ whether in endurance or obedience. Luther, by contrast, emphasized his temptations and doubts—something that played a very small part in Zwingli's thought. For Zwingli, Jesus was never the victim of serious temptation to sin; Jesus appears as a hero, "mild," "friendly," "deathless," and "sweet-smelling."[28]

Zwingli too accepted the doctrine of communication of attributes, but he changed its significance. He could not conceive of the creature, i.e. the humanity, as sharing in any fundamental attributes of the Creator. Zwingli speaks of Christ as conceived *in* the Virgin Mary, but not *out* of her flesh, so that he in effect rejected the anti-Nestorian, Chalcedonian formulation *theotokos,* the "God-bearing one." Only the human being was born, and only the human experienced the dereliction of the Cross. Although in 1523 he still spoke of Christ as "omnipresent, for he is the eternal God,"[29] once he became involved in the eucharistic dispute, he followed Aristotelian logic in asserting that the finite cannot become infinite. "Omnipresence can pertain to the deity alone and may in no way be communicated to the human nature. His body even after the resurrection cannot in any way be ubiquitous like the deity; according to the divine nature, he is everywhere."[30] The evident consequence of this analysis is a splitting of the unity of the person of Jesus Christ into two. "If there is a threat of Monophysitism with Luther, in which one nature is absorbed by the other, with Zwingli there is that of Nestorianism, in which the two natures fall apart from one another, although neither the one nor the other threat was intended."[31]

Zwingli interpreted the communication of attributes as *alloiosis,* or "equivalency," the substitution of one term for another; thanks to the unity of the person of Christ, each of the two natures united in his person may be spoken of in terms of the other; it is not a true communication, but rather a verbal predication. Luther condemned this interpretation as the work of the devil and his grandmother,[32] but Zwingli's logic found attentive listeners; even Melanchthon began to "zwingle" after the encounter with Zwingli at Marburg. Melanchthon modified Luther's view of the agony in the garden as Jesus' resistance to the Father, and saw in it only the trembling of the human nature, which was being taxed beyond its endurance.[33] Like Zwingli, Melanchthon interpreted the temptation of Jesus as self-deception on Satan's part. Jesus could not really be tempted, but Satan deluded himself into thinking that it might be possible.

On a more frivolous note—although it was meant quite seriously—Luther's supporter Johann Brenz attempted a novel refutation of Zwingli's insistence that the body of Christ is physically present at the right hand of God in heaven. Brenz computed the distance between the earth and heaven by means of his own, and arrived at the distance of 16,338,562 German miles. Given the speed of Jesus' ascent from the Mount of Olives, as Brenz estimated it, Brenz concluded that the body of Jesus could not yet have reached heaven by the sixteenth century.[34]

b. Calvin

John Calvin (1509–64) has not given his name to any church, unlike
Luther, Menno Simons, and Kaspar Schwenkfeld. Nevertheless, Calvin's
thought has had a much more thoroughgoing and pervasive influence on
Protestantism than that of Luther. Without Luther, Protestantism could
hardly have begun; without Calvin, it could hardly have survived. Calvin
was twenty-six years younger than Luther and Zwingli. Because his church
is also called Reformed, there is a tendency to think of Calvin as closer to
Zwingli than to Luther. This is only partly true. Calvin has much in common with both Luther and Zwingli, and in many ways he differs from them
both. On the question of the eucharist, he definitely affirmed the real presence of Christ, rejecting any mere symbolic or memorial interpretation. He
did not accept the Lutheran explanation of the manner of Christ's presence,
and rejected the concept of ubiquity, which he felt made Jesus' humanity
nothing but an appearance. Like Zwingli, he taught that Christ has kept his
human body, glorified but still limited in its dimensions, and that it will
remain in heaven until the Second Coming.[35] Nevertheless, Calvin affirms
that Christ is truly presented to us in the sacrament, just as though he were
there, to be seen and touched.[36] Thus he asserts the reality of Christ's presence, but does not seek to explain it.[37]

5. THE RADICALS AND SPIRITUALISTS

The story of the Protestant Reformation is usually told as the history of
the Lutherans and the Reformed, and perhaps of the Anglicans—those
churches that obtained the protection and help of their governments and that
could count on government support for their reforms. George H. Williams
has coined the expression "magisterial Reformation" to distinguish them
from another group, which he calls the "radical Reformation."[38] Many radicals differed both from Catholicism and from the magisterial Reformers, all
of whom held essentially to Chalcedonian orthodoxy. To the degree that
orthodox Protestants emphasized the communication of attributes, they
found themselves involved in the familiar and difficult problem of trying to
explain how the deity and the humanity can be united in a single person.
Although the various radical groups differed from one another, all of them
rejected the authority of the councils and their creeds. The Chalcedonian
Creed was erected as a barrier to Christological speculation that could result
in heresy; by turning away from its use, the radicals left themselves open to
speculation and many of them soon revived ancient heresies.

Among the diverse trends of the radical Reformation two are worthy of
our attention here: radical discipleship and radical spirituality, sometimes

appearing separately, sometimes together. Like the Franciscans, Waldensians, and Beguines, who wanted to live out the Christian faith in consistent discipleship, a number of the radical groups of the Reformation era were much more interested in reforming the Christian life than in doctrine, and consequently remained doctrinally more or less orthodox. In general, however, the desire for a more radical standard of discipleship was associated with a dualistic dichotomy between the spiritual and the carnal or the secular. A common characteristic of these spiritualistic radicals was the feeling that what is truly spiritual cannot be confined to the "flesh"—neither to a written, printed text, as in the case of the Word of God, nor to a human body, as in the case of Christ, the living Word. This immediately brought them into conflict with the Catholic and Protestant theology that accepted the Creed of Chalcedon.

Abandoning the distinctive two-natures formula of Chalcedon, the radicals were free to deal with the implications either of humanity or of deity without having to worry about the other. A smaller number reverted to an Arian or adoptionistic view of Christ, and the first stirrings of the modern heresy of Unitarianism began. A larger group emphasized the deity of Christ's being to such an extent that the humanity seemed to disappear; in this they had much in common with the early Monophysites, although they usually lacked their theological sophistication.

As we know, the Chalcedonian Creed emphasizes that Jesus was a real man, "consubstantial with us according to the humanity," and as such implies that he had a human life story; Chalcedonian Christians have traditionally shown far more interest in the doctrine of Christ than in his human history. *Although the validity of writing a life of the historical Jesus is clearly implicit in the two-natures doctrine of the Creed of Chalcedon, in fact Christians only became interested in writing it when they no longer believed the essential points of the creed.*

By dividing the deity and the humanity from one another, free rein is also given to the imagination to deal with Christ not as a historic, human person but rather as a cosmic spiritual or idealistic principle. At one end of the radical spectrum stood people such as Laelius and Faustus Socinus, to whom the origins of modern Unitarianism can be traced; they were interested in Jesus the man. At the other extreme we have the cosmic speculations of Sebastian Franck (1499–ca. 1543) and other natural philosophers. The largest group of radicals, called collectively Anabaptists, did not go to either of these extremes. They took the historicity of Jesus with the utmost seriousness, and at the same time stressed his deity. Because they had difficulty thinking of the deity being involved with sinful human nature, and yet wanted to do justice to Jesus as a man, they conceived of him as a different kind of man, a divinized man, rather like the ancient Monophysites. In order to do so, they developed a novel concept, that of the celestial, or heavenly, flesh of Christ.

a. The Heavenly Flesh

A number of the radicals, including not only Thomas Münzer (ca. 1489–1525) and Melchior Hoffmann (ca. 1495–ca.1543) but also Kaspar Schwenkfeld (1489–1561) and Menno Simons (1496–1561), both of whom founded churches that exist today (the Schwenkfelder Church and the Mennonite Church), advocated the concept of a heavenly flesh of Christ in order to spare the deity contact with our sinful human flesh. Menno spoke of Jesus as born "in" Mary's body, but not of it: as a ray of light passes through a glass of water and is refracted by it but does not take on substance from it, so the heavenly flesh of Jesus passed through Mary's body without taking anything from it. According to Melchior Hoffmann, the Word "became" flesh, and did not take flesh from Mary. To have done so would have made him part of Adam's sinful race, an intolerable thought (although precisely the point of orthodox Christology and the orthodox doctrine of Christ's vicarious atonement!). Schwenkfeld too denied any communication of attributes: from his conception onward, Christ had a glorified or deified flesh, not human flesh.

To what extent was this heavenly-flesh concept a byproduct of the Reformation movement itself? George Williams sees it as a consequence of the Reformers' attempt to hold to the doctrine of Chalcedon while rejecting the widely held Roman Catholic teaching concerning the Immaculate Conception of Mary (namely, that Mary was conceived by the natural sexual union of her parents, but that from her conception she was miraculously preserved from the taint of original sin to which all other human beings are subject). The radicals argued, like the Roman Catholics, that if Jesus was born of a mother tainted with sin, he could not himself have been sinless. The Catholic solution was the doctrine of Mary's Immaculate Conception and perpetual sinlessness; the radicals' solution was to explain that while Jesus was begotten and carried in Mary's womb, he was not born of her; he did not derive his flesh from her. Williams sees the sudden appearance of the concept of heavenly flesh as a consequence of the medieval concept that the heavenly food of the eucharist really is the flesh of Christ. If it really is his flesh, it is evidently quite different from ours. This suggests that the "flesh" the Word became has always been of a different nature and not really like our own.

A Strassburg radical, Clement Ziegler, wrote that the Son had a body born of the Father within the Trinity before the foundation of the world was laid: "If the splendor of the first [heavenly] body were not there in the second body of Christ, which he took upon himself from the Virgin Mary, the fleshly body of Christ would have been mortal and would not have been resurrected. . . . Why therefore do we not take the body of Christ according to its divinity instead of according to the humanity of the flesh?"[39] Melchior Hoffmann denied that Jesus had a human body at all, like the second-century gnostic Valentinus, who taught that Christ brought his body with him from heaven. Christ took nothing from Mary, but passed through her "as water through a pipe." The medieval theory that pearls were formed by dew descending from heaven and crystallizing in the oyster was applied by Hoffmann to the birth of Christ.

Unlike Hoffmann, Kaspar Schwenkfeld formally held to two natures in Christ, but he held even Christ's human nature to be "begotten, not made." Because the humanity of Christ is noncreaturely, the believer who enters into communion with him also begins to take on a different, noncreaturely nature. It is apparent that much of this speculation is an effort to overcome the duality between Creator and creation, between Spirit and flesh, that troubled the gnostics and other dualists. The fundamental biblical dichotomy between Creation and Fall, between the will of God and man's sinful rebellion, takes on a secondary role.

The most influential of those who taught the doctrine of the heavenly flesh, and the one whose name is most likely to be recognized today, was Menno Simons (1496–1561). Menno has earned an honorable place in Christian history by his leadership in gathering the shattered and dispersed Anabaptists following the disastrous end of the Anabaptist "Kingdom of God" at Münster in 1534–35. Not only were the Anabaptist leaders and many of their followers in the ill-fated kingdom tortured and killed, but the aversion their excesses aroused was applied to all of the many varieties of religious radicals and led to hostility and persecution throughout Germany and the Low Countries. Menno succeeded in rallying a large number of the Anabaptists, in winning them away from the extreme, eschatologically colored fantasies of the Münsterites, and in instituting a system of congregational discipline that rapidly won the respect of the more traditional Christians. Menno retained the distinctive view of the heavenly flesh he had learned from Melchior Hoffmann:

> For Christ Jesus, as to his origin, is no earthly man, that is, a fruit of the flesh and blood of Adam. He is a heavenly fruit or man. For his beginning or origin is of the Father [John 16:28], like unto the first Adam, sin excepted.[40]

Here Menno seems to be proposing a spiritual, noncreated origin for Adam as well as for Christ.

Because of his conviction that the communion is a participation in this heavenly flesh, Menno instituted a rigorous policy of congregational discipline; excommunication became a matter of the utmost seriousness and severity for his followers. In this respect, one may say that the Mennonites only put into practice something that ought to have been implicit in the Roman Catholic doctrine of the eucharist as well. Because Catholicism and magisterial Protestantism were essentially national churches to which whole populations belonged, it proved all but impossible for them to exercise congregational discipline in an effective way. Mennonite congregations consisted primarily of committed, adult converts who were ready to face persecution, and who thus willingly submitted to a discipline the mass of Roman Catholics and nominal Protestants would have rejected. Although the name is not usually applied to them, Menno and his followers represent a Reformation-era revival of monophysitism.[41]

The heritage of Menno Simons is perpetuated and honored in Mennonite communities scattered throughout North America, and existing to a lesser extent in Europe, the Soviet Union, and South America. A different fate awaited one of the most brilliant and eccentric advocates of a heavenly-flesh doctrine, the Spanish physician Michael Servetus (1511–53). Servetus has gone down in church and secular history as a martyr to Calvinistic intolerance; his execution in Geneva represents a stain that Reformed Protestantism has never quite been able to efface.

As a young man, Servetus propounded the distinctive views that ultimately led him to the stake: his *On the Errors of the Trinity* appeared in 1531. He held God to be one Person only; this God was the literal, natural father of Jesus Christ, who was therefore God's natural Son. The body of Christ is the body of the godhead . . . divine and of the substance of deity.[42] According to Servetus, when the Word became flesh, he brought his flesh down with him from heaven. Although Servetus denied the deity and preexistence of Christ, he too was evidently trying to grapple with Christ's overwhelming majesty; he was unable to conceive of him as a mere man, even as one adopted by God, but had to postulate a direct, natural relationship with God. Servetus was condemned to death in Geneva for his denial of the Trinity. Calvin's colleague Guillaume Farel accompanied him to the stake at Champel, persistently imploring him to recant and be spared (an option not offered to the victims of the Inquisition). Servetus remained adamant, and even reaffirmed his theological conviction in his dying words at the stake, "O Jesus, Son of the eternal God, have mercy on me!"[43]

b. Christ in Us

The proponents of the heavenly-flesh doctrine were trying to explain the incredible impact of a single historical figure, Jesus of Nazareth, and could do so only by seeing him as a divine Visitor from heaven, thus minimizing his humanity and his consubstantiality with us. We may call this a kind of divine realism. Rather like the Roman Catholic doctrine of transubstantiation, it insists that the divine substance is, or at least was, present among us in bodily, physical form. The age was not lacking in efforts to give a more spiritual interpretation to Christ, to explain him not in terms of a historic manifestation of divinity, but of a spiritual presence in the believer. Instead of speaking of heavenly flesh—flesh that looks and feels like ours, but has a different origin, they gave Jesus a spiritual body. This spiritual Christ-body indwelt his physical body, and likewise can indwell the believer. The Lutheran pastor Valentine Weigel (1533–88), the Dominican Giordano Bruno (b. 1548, executed by the Inquisition at Rome, 1600), and the shoemaker-mystic Jakob Boehme (1575–1624) all spoke of a mystic communion with the spiritual Christ that made the church, its doctrines, and its sacraments irrelevant. Natural philosophers such as Agrippa von Nettesheim (ca. 1486–1535) and Theophrastus Bombastus von Hohenheim, known as Paracelsus (ca. 1493–1541), had prepared the way for these views with their Platonic speculation. A more recent exponent of similar views is the English Quaker Robert Barclay (1648–90). Such a spiritualizing view eliminates many of the conceptual problems associated with the doctrine of the incarnation, but it fails to do justice to the existential reality of human beings as creatures consisting of a body-soul unity, not as essentially spiritual souls temporarily inhabiting physical bodies.

c. The Historical, Human Jesus: Laelius and Faustus Socinus

The advocates of the heavenly flesh believed that Jesus was a real, historical figure, and resorted to their distinctive view of his divine origin to explain his person and work. Other writers, who emphasized his spiritual indwelling, had no need to concern themselves with the nature of his human flesh. The Reformation era also witnessed the rise of a third idea, one that saw Jesus as primarily a man like ourselves, only with an unusual degree of religious insight resulting from a particular endowment or adoption by God. These last thinkers are the direct progenitors of modern Unitarianism as well as of modern Protestant and Catholic liberalism.

Although it frequently produced heretics, Italy was no haven for them; the vast majority of nonconformists of Italian origin found it possible to survive only by fleeing the vicinity of the pope and his Inquisition. Among the many classed as heretics by the Roman church, some were distinctly heretical even by our more exacting definition. Two of the most influential were an uncle and nephew, Laelius and Faustus Socinus (1525–62 and

1539–1604), whose quest for freedom of thought led them from Italy first to Rhaetia (modern Graubünden, Switzerland), and then to Poland. In Poland Faustus took advantage of that nation's unique religious tolerance to lay the foundations of modern Unitarianism.

In contrast with the doctrines of Hoffmann, Menno, and Schwenkfeld, these Italian thinkers emphasized not the grandeur of Christ's humanity, but its normalcy. Although Servetus had denied the preexistence of Christ, he acknowledged his divinity as the natural Son of God and died with a prayer to Jesus on his lips. The Socini were far more rationalistic and critical. Jesus was a true man—otherwise he would not have been able to die—and as man he could not have been God. Of course this is precisely the argument Paul faced when he wrote, "Christ crucified . . . unto the Greeks foolishness" (1 Cor. 1:23). The reversion to this line of argument makes it look as though the theological struggles of the first five centuries of Christianity were all for naught. This collapse of centuries of laborious theological work within less than half a century of the outbreak of the Reformation is alarming to those of us who believe that the Reformation was a necessary corrective to the doctrinal as well as moral failings of medieval Christianity. It gives substance to the traditional Catholic charge that the Reformation principles of Scripture alone and private interpretation open the floodgates to theological chaos. It is also possible, and in fact to some extent it is even evident, that much of this rationalistic skepticism, criticism, and unbelief was active in pre-Reformation Catholicism. Luther's successful defiance of Rome and the Inquisition released the pressure seal that had kept skepticism confined, and permitted it to boil over, but Luther did not create it; it had been brewing for centuries.

d. The End of Constantinian Christianity

It has become increasingly fashionable in recent years to speak of the "end of the Constantinian era." Constantine the Great was the man who established the close tie between the Christian church and the secular government that dominated Christendom for so many years, and which still exists in a residual form in the state churches of several European nations. To say that his era has ended means that the church has definitely been severed from the state, and that the state has become secular. (It would not be correct to suggest that the tie between the state and *religion* began with Constantine, because the pagan Roman Empire, like virtually every other ancient society, had a religious ethos of its own.)

Although Constantine is usually remembered for the steps he took toward making Christianity the established religion of the Roman Empire, it would not be wrong to consider him the one who inaugurated the centuries of trinitarian orthodoxy. It was he who proposed and perhaps even imposed the expression *homoousios* at the Council of Nicaea in 325, and it was he who provided government aid to the orthodox and exerted government pressure against nonconformists. The Reformation was not the end of the state-church era; in fact, Lutheranism, Calvinism, and Anglicanism all developed distinctive forms of the state church. But perhaps we can see in the Reformation era the end of trinitarianism as the unquestioned conviction of Christians.

At a number of points the suggestion has been made that the Roman Catholic doctrine of transubstantiation, formalized in 1215, so rigidly committed the church and theology to an eccentric position that the ensuing tensions made Luther's Reformation inevitable. Interestingly enough, it was the eucharistic controversy—still consisting of reactions to both Catholic transubstantiation and the modified Lutheran understanding of the real, bodily presence of Christ—that sparked the first massive outbreaks of antitrinitarianism.

e. Polish Antitrinitarians

The symbolic understanding of the eucharist adopted by Zwingli and fought by Luther had originated with a Dutchman, Cornelius Hoen. There was very little religious freedom in the Netherlands in the early years of the Reformation. Some of the Dutch dissidents—called "sacramentarians" for their symbolic understanding of the eucharist—emigrated and found refuge in Prussia in the years 1527–31. (Prussia at this time consisted of two parts, West Prussia, which was part of the Kingdom of Poland, and East Prussia, formerly the territory of the Teutonic Order, now an autonomous duchy under the former grand master, Albert of Brandenberg. The duchy was a fief of the Polish King.)

In the sixteenth century, the Kingdom of Poland and the associated Grand Duchy of Lithuania was the largest state in Europe, embracing a variety of different languages and several confessions. There were Poles, Lithuanians, Germans, White Russians, Ukrainians, and even Armenians; there were Roman Catholics, Eastern Orthodox, and many Jews. When the Reformation came to Poland, it came in all its variety. The first to appear were Lutherans in Poland's German-speaking lands, followed by Calvinists in the Polish-speaking heartland. Shortly thereafter, radicals of various kinds appeared in Little Poland and the Grand Duchy of Lithuania, attracted by an attitude of religious tolerance unparalleled in Europe.

Lutheranism in Poland remained largely confined to the King's German-speaking subjects and vassals in the two Prussias and in Silesia. The Poles themselves inclined more to Calvinism, which had an outstanding advocate in the nobleman John Łaski (Johannes a Lasco, 1499–1560), a pupil of Erasmus and a friend of Thomas Cranmer. Unfortunately for Łaski's efforts to create a stable, united Protestant church in Poland, the large number of radical Italian Protestants who had taken refuge in the country soon succeeded in splitting the Reformed church into an orthodox, trinitarian "major" and an antitrinitarian "minor" branch. Soon the so-called Minor Church came to be called Socinian after the men whose teaching so strongly shaped it; Socinianism is the direct ancestor of modern Unitarianism.

In addition to the Italian influence in southern Poland, native Polish radicals found a refuge at the court of the Grand Hetman, or Viceroy, of Lithuania in Vilnius. He invited Martin Czechowic (b. 1532) and the nobleman Simon Budny (1533–84) to the duchy, where Budny eventually produced a kind of neo-Judaism and briefly hoped to create a kind of ecumenical monotheism. A third Pole, Peter Gonesius (Goniadz), had been influenced while a student at Padua and Tübingen by Matteo Gribaldi (1506–62). Gribaldi began as a Calvinist, but attacked Calvin for his execution of Servetus, whom Gribaldi had courageously visited in prison in Geneva. While at Tübingen Gribaldi developed the view that the Trinity consists of three distinct gods, with the Father as the monarch. He soon lost his post, but not before having influenced Gonesius, who also became an advocate of believer's baptism by immersion.

Another Italian Calvinist refugee, Francesco Stancari (1501–74), settled in Pinczow, near the old Polish capital of Cracow, in 1559. He promptly created an uproar about what he considered Arianism or tritheism and attacked the irenic Philipp Melanchthon, greatly admired by the Polish Protestants, calling him the Arius of the North.[44] The Polish Calvinists retorted by charging Stancari with modalism. The intemperate Stancari claimed to be the only non-Arian in Poland and announced that one hundred Luthers, two hundred Melanchthons, three hundred Heinrich Bullingers, four hundred Peter Martyrs, and five hundred Calvins all ground together with mortar and pestle would not produce an ounce of true theology.[45] Stancari was so provocative that the usually peaceable Łaski threw a Bible at him at the Synod of Pinczow in 1559. Death soon overtook Łaski, and the task of dealing with Stancari fell to another.

The task was taken up by an Italian-born court physician, Giorgio Blandrata (ca. 1515–ca. 1588). Blandrata made the fateful suggestion that the best way to deal with Stancari was to abandon the philosophical language of technical theology and return to the simple language of the Bible and the Apostles' Creed. In view of the fact that the technical theological language had been introduced in the fourth and fifth centuries precisely because the phrases of the Bible and the creed were not explicit enough to prevent heresy, it is not surprising that Blandrata's proposal facilitated its reappearance.

Although classical theology is certainly not without problems, historically it is almost always the case that to appeal to the Bible alone, disdaining the tools of theology, leads to the reemergence of ancient heresies. In the wake of Blandrata's suggestion, Poland fell first into a kind of tritheism, then moved into Unitarianism.

f. Tritheism and Polytheism

In Geneva, Calvin maintained a lively interest in the theological problems of the Reformed church in Poland—doubtless properly so, as to a large extent they were produced by errant Calvinists. When he learned that Blandrata had converted the first Protestant pastor in Cracow, Gregory Paul, to his ideas of biblical simplicity, Calvin commented, "In order to avoid the absurdity of Stancari [he] falls into the more fetid error of tritheism."[46] Stanislas Sarnicki, a Calvinist who had lost his church as a result of Stancari's attacks, tried to reestablish himself in Cracow by exposing Paul as a tritheist. Stancari tried to defend his view that the Son is a lesser, distinct deity, different from the Father, by resorting to the original language of the Constantinopolitan Creed of 381, which specifies that the Holy Spirit proceeds from the Father and does not mention the Son.

Farther east, in the grand duchy, Czechowic and Budny were teaching a similar variety of tritheism; most of the inhabitants of the grand duchy were Eastern Orthodox who had never accepted the Western *filioque* addition to the creed. In 1565 the Protestant Grand Hetman Nicholas Radziwiłł, who had protected the antitrinitarians, died and was succeeded by his Catholic son. The son was prepared to tolerate trinitarian Protestantism but not antitrinitarianism. At a debate in Piotrków Trybunalski that same year, the orthodox Calvinists became convinced of the futility of discussing theology with the antitrinitarians and walked out on them. The antitrinitarians formed the so-called Minor Church; at first it included tritheists who prayed to Christ as well as unitarians who did not, but soon, under the influence of Faustus Socinus, it would be distinctly unitarian.

In the meantime, Stancari had moved to the autonomous principality of Transylvania on the Polish-Hungarian-Turkish frontier, a Hungarian-speaking region that had received a substantial contingent of German settlers, the Siebenberger Saxons, in the Middle Ages. Stancari encountered Ferenc Dávid, who had briefly been a Lutheran but then became superintendent of the Reformed church in the principality; Dávid began to preach against the doctrine of the Trinity. Blandrata was now also in Transylvania, and together with Dávid he appeared at a synod in Alba Iulia in April 1556, appealing for a return to strict biblical language. They acknowledged the equality of the three Persons, but refused to acknowledge that they shared a

common divine substance, for that, in their minds, would create a "quaternity" consisting of the Father, the Son, the Holy Spirit, and Deity itself.
Within a year they dropped the concept of the equality of the Persons and
became explicitly unitarian.

In 1567 Blandrata made common cause with Dávid in publishing the
latter's *On the False and True Unity of God the Father, Son, and Holy
Ghost*. This tract claimed that doing away with the doctrine of the Trinity
would bring the Reformation to true fulfillment. The culmination would
come with the personal return of Christ, which they predicted for 1570. This
expectation of Christ's imminent return makes it apparent that these early
Unitarians were no skeptics. They were not antitrinitarians because they
were unwilling to accept miraculous or mysterious doctrines, but because
they believed the doctrine of the Trinity false. Dávid succeeded in persuading the monarch, John II Sigismund, to extend toleration to the Unitarians.

Wishing to counter antitrinitarianism, Peter Melius, a Calvinist superintendent in Turkish-controlled Hungary, invited the Unitarians to meet him
in a debate there in 1568, then agreed to meet them in Alba Iulia instead.
The trinitarian Calvinists did poorly. Melius resorted to claiming a direct
personal revelation in the hope of improving his cause: "During the night,"
he announced, "the Lord revealed to me who he is and how he is [God's]
true and proper Son." The King observed wryly, "Pastor Peter, if last night
you were instructed as to who the Son of God is, what, I ask, were you
preaching before?"[47] The discomfited Calvinists went back to the Turkish-
controlled part of Hungary, and the King established Unitarianism (not yet
called by that name) as the state religion in Transylvania. Thus it was that
the denomination most Americans associate with the urbane civility of Boston actually once was the established church in that obscure corner of Europe best known in America as the home of the legendary Count Dracula.

g. Unitarianism

This Transylvanian church, which we have called "unitarian" although
the term was not yet in use, began to exert an influence back in Poland-
Lithuania. Stancari and Blandrata originally went to Transylvania from Poland-Lithuania; now the influence was flowing in the other direction. For a
number of years, both Transylvania and Poland-Lithuania were centers of a
religious tolerance unknown elsewhere. The last two monarchs of the Jagel-
lonian royal house of Poland, King John II Sigismund of Transylvania and
Sigismund II Augustus of Poland, both supporters of religious toleration,
died in 1572. Both were succeeded by a tolerant Catholic, Stephen Báthory
(Bátory). Báthory was first elected King in Transylvania in 1572, then King
of Poland and Grand Duke of Lithuania in 1575, after Henry of Valois,
Sigismund's successor, left Poland to become King of France.

One of the most radical varieties of theology was fostered in Lithuania by Simon Budny. In 1574 he published a so-called critical edition of the New Testament, eliminating many of the texts used to establish the doctrine of the Trinity as "later interpolations." He allied himself with the colorful Greek refugee Jacob Paleologus—who claimed descent from the Byzantine imperial family—in developing a curious view in which Semitic ancestry and Christian faith could each contribute to an individual's justification.[48] Paleologus had already produced a tract, *On the Three Nations* (1572), in which he argued that Jews, Christians, and "Christian Turks" will all be saved. "Christian Turks" are Moslems who inhabit formerly Christian lands and are the descendants of Christians. Paleologus subsequently had the poor judgment to leave Poland, which was tolerant, for Bohemia, which was not. He was arrested there, sent to Rome, tried, and executed in 1581.

The most important of the radicals in Poland was Faustus Socinus, who arrived there in 1579. He created a clear and coherent unitarian theology in the Minor Church, centered in Rakov. At first he was refused admission to the church because he refused to pray to Christ and denied his substitutionary satisfaction. Both of these doctrines were still held in the Minor Church, but ultimately his views prevailed, and Polish antitrinitarianism became clearly unitarian and Socinian. When Poland gave up its policy of toleration a century later, its Socinians fled to Holland. Curiously, it was these Socinians who introduced the Dutch Mennonites to the practice of baptism by immersion, a practice they had learned from Peter Gonesius. Until this time, the Mennonites had performed adult baptism by pouring, not immersion. From the Dutch, English refugees adopted it. Ultimately, despite its Socinian heritage, it was adopted by North American and English Baptists. Thus by a strange accident of history, a practice that is well attested in the New Testament, baptism by immersion, was transmitted to the trinitarian Baptists thanks to the radically antitrinitarian Polish Socinians.

SELECTED BIBLIOGRAPHY

Bainton, Roland, ed. *Concerning Heretics, Attributed to Sebastian Castellio.* New York: Columbia University Press, 1935.

Blanke, Fritz. *Brothers in Christ.* Scottdale, Penn.: Herald Press, 1961.

Hildebrandt, Franz. *Melanchthon: Alien or Ally?* Cambridge: University Press, 1946.

Hillerbrand, Hans J. *The Protestant Reformation.* New York: Macmillan, 1968.

Huizinga, Johan. *Erasmus and the Age of Reformation.* New York: Harper, 1957.

Kot, Stanisłas. *Socinianism in Poland: The Social and Political Ideas of the Polish Antitrinitarians in the Sixteenth and Seventeenth Centuries.* Translated by Earle Morse Wilbur. Boston: Beacon Press, 1957.

Lortz, Joseph. *The Reformation in Germany*. 2 vols. New York: Herder, 1968.

McNeill, John T. *The History and Character of Calvinism*. New York: Oxford, 1962.

Tavard, George Henri. *Holy Writ or Holy Church: The Crisis of the Protestant Reformation*. New York: Harper, 1960.

Walton, Robert C. *Zwingli's Theocracy*. Toronto: University Press, 1967.

Williams, George Huntston. *The Polish Brethren: Documentation of the History and Thought of Unitarianism in the Polish-Lithuanian Commonwealth and in the Diaspora, 1601–1685*. Chico, Calif.: Scholars Press, 1980.

17

THE AGE OF ORTHODOXY

All these errors, and the errors like to these, and also those which depend on these and follow from them, we reject and condemn, as being false and heretical, and as being inconsistent with the Word of God, with the three approved Symbols, the Augsburg Confession, with the Apology of the same, the Schmalkald Articles, and the Catechisms of Luther; which errors also all the godly, high and low alike, ought to beware of and avoid, unless they wish to hazard their own eternal salvation.

Formula of Concord
"Of Other Heresies and Sects," Art. II

The Protestant Reformation began with tremendous enthusiasm and hope as the attempt to bring Christianity back to its true foundations in biblical faith. It soon gave way to an ecclesiastical and doctrinal chaos so great that Protestants must now ask themselves whether the concept of heresy any longer means anything. Where there is no consensus on orthodoxy, nothing can be heretical. The first Protestants demanded spiritual liberty (although most of them soon narrowed the concept to mean liberty only for their interpretation of the Gospel). But where such liberty really existed in the form of true toleration—as in Transylvania and in Poland-Lithuania—the results were disastrous in terms of Protestant orthodoxy. A kind of Unitarianism became the established religion in Transylvania, while in Poland-Lithuania the various quarreling Protestants engendered so much strife and confusion that almost the whole nation gladly threw itself back into the arms of the Catholic Counter-Reformation. As a practical matter, Protestantism, despite its profession of commitment to private interpretation and Christian liberty, survived and grew only where it received not only a large measure of government support but where there was also at least a degree of government regulation of heresy and dissent.[1]

From the perspective of an orthodox or evangelical Protestant looking at the history of Protestantism and trying to envisage its future in the "Christian" West, the present situation of Protestantism is perplexing and its future developments difficult to predict. The original stronghold of Protestantism was in the Germanic countries of western Europe; it was established by law, protected, and to a large extent funded, by local or national governments, and the training of its ministry was provided by the state. To a large extent this situation still prevails in Britain, the Netherlands, the Scandinavian countries, Switzerland, and West Germany. Despite varying degrees of official establishment and frequently heavy financial support from the state, official Protestantism is spiritually feeble all over western Europe. Often the tiny, non-state-supported free churches and independent congregations have more worshipers and certainly more active participants than the nominally much larger established churches. In North America, and particularly in the United States, there is not only no government support of religion, but one must actually speak of increasing governmental hostility to religion since World War II. Nevertheless, it is in the United States and Canada that Protestantism—both the traditional churches that correspond to the European state churches, and the newer evangelical and fundamentalist fellowships—is still vigorous and flourishing. Most recent developments show that for the first time in history, nonestablished Protestants, evangelicals and particularly Pentecostals, now make up the majority of Protestant Christianity.[2]

Protestantism relied heavily on government support for its start; yet where it receives government support today, it is perilously feeble. Conservative Protestants in the United States are divided between those who would like a return to some kind of official or quasi-official collaboration between church and state,[3] and those who seek what might almost be called an adversary relationship with the state, including some who go so far as to suggest that the church ought to welcome taxation by the state. Organized Protestantism is almost totally "liberal" in western Europe,[4] and also visibly enfeebled, while in the United States, where it receives no government support, it is vigorous but virtually chaotic. It may be helpful to review the way in which sixteenth- and early seventeenth-century European Protestantism tried to deal with the chaos that so rapidly developed within its ranks. We shall turn to the salient features of late sixteenth- and early seventeenth-century Protestant theology and church life, to the rise of Protestant orthodoxy and Scholasticism.

European Protestantism was divided into three or four main families. The lines of division and the distinctions between them are often vague and somewhat arbitrary, but it is convenient to group the early Protestants into two main "magisterial" branches and to divide the radicals into two groups. The magisterial Reformation falls into Lutheran and Reformed (or Calvinist) branches; it would be possible to call Anglicanism a third branch, but inasmuch as it was theologically influenced by the Calvinist Reformation, especially at the beginning, and was rather different from Lutheranism, we may place the early Anglicans among the Reformed, at least prior to the nineteenth century.[5] The radical Reformation involved a tremendous variety of doctrinal and disciplinary positions, but it makes sense to subdivide it into those groups that were radical in their life-style and discipleship, but conservative in their doctrine—such as the Mennonites and Baptists—and those who embraced antitrinitarianism or other marked heresies.

Lutheranism and Calvinism represent the two main theological traditions in early Protestantism. Calvinism, as we have noted, claimed to be a more thorough and consistently biblical reformation than Lutheranism. As a matter of historical fact, Calvinism has been more fissiparous than Lutheranism, has produced more splits, often over apparently insignificant differences. At the same time, during the sixteenth and seventeenth centuries, Calvinism also spawned varieties of theological liberalism, including Unitarianism; Lutherans, by contrast, were not immune to vagaries of faith and practice, but during the first two Protestant centuries, Lutheranism produced much less heresy in our sense than Calvinism.

The Reformation claims as its reason for existence that it is far more faithful to the biblical message and historic Christianity than traditional Roman Catholicism, and it can advance powerful arguments to support this claim. Nevertheless, the Reformation quickly produced far more doctrinal chaos than the church had experienced since the second century, when it had to contend with Gnosticism, Marcionism, and Montanism all at the same time. Calvinism sought to reform the church more thoroughly and in a more consistent way than it thought Luther had. Yet out of Calvin's rigor and consistency somehow came antitrinitarianism, the Minor Church of Poland with its curious expressions of both tritheism and Unitarianism.

The question that all this must raise is whether orthodoxy can be maintained and heresy avoided except at the price either of rigid thought control at one extreme or the acceptance of doctrinal chaos at the other. The desire to enforce orthodoxy at all costs produced the Inquisition; the zeal to attain a higher standard of orthodoxy regardless of how many fellow Christians were prepared to follow, in a context of religious tolerance, led to the theological Tower of Babel that arose in sixteenth-century Poland. Although Lutheranism was not altogether lacking in inquisitorial tendencies and procedures, on the whole Lutheranism sought to preserve orthodoxy by means of a consensus arrived at through persuasion. Sometimes the language was harsh and the tactics were rude, but in retrospect the doctrinal accomplishments of early Lutheranism in producing a unified, orthodox tradition are indeed impressive.

1. LUTHERAN ORTHODOXY

At the very beginning of the Reformation, the strong personality and tremendous energy of Luther himself was able to suppress centrifugal trends, so that one has the impression that the succession from Luther to Lutheran orthodoxy was relatively tranquil. This impression is somewhat misleading, because from almost the very moment Luther began his work of Reformation, he had to contend with dissent within his own ranks.

a. Early Controversies

After having been likened by the pope to a wild boar trampling the church's vineyard, Luther suddenly found himself facing a similar "boar" in Wittenberg. While he was enjoying his ten months' seclusion in Wartburg Castle, working on his epoch-making German translation of the Bible, one of his colleagues in Wittenberg thought that in Luther's absence more needed to be done to advance the cause of the Reformation. Andreas Bodenstein of Karlstadt (ca. 1480–1541), whom we recently met in connection with the eucharistic controversy, made a series of demands in Wittenberg, intended to correct certain abuses that he felt Luther had not yet touched, especially monastic celibacy and the continuing celebration of the Mass in the old Catholic way. Between Christmas 1521 and Epiphany 1522, Karlstadt introduced evangelical communion services in Wittenberg, while the German congregation of Augustinian monks—Luther's order—met in Wittenberg and voted its own dissolution. An outbreak of image smashing followed in February, shortly before Luther's return. On March 6 Luther began to take matters into his own hands, brought Karlstadt to heel, and reduced the innovations in the Mass to a minimum. At about the same time Wittenberg was visited by the "Zwickau prophets," followers of the revolutionary priest turned Lutheran pastor, in nearby Zwickau, Thomas Münzer.

Münzer's story is associated with the Peasants' War of 1524–25. Münzer is an enigmatic figure who aroused Luther's ire not only by his strange ideas (among them, the conviction that each believer must pass through the psychological experience of hell in order to attain mystic tranquility), but also by vehement personal attacks. He joined the peasant rebellion, was captured by the feudal forces under Philip of Hesse, and beheaded in 1525. Luther was especially fierce in his denunciation of anyone he thought to be turning the Reformation to political ends. In the long run, however, a greater challenge to Lutheran unity developed from within his own camp among those who were influenced by the logic and biblical arguments of Zwingli and Calvin.

Philipp Melanchthon (1497–1560), a more systematic thinker than Luther, had already produced the first Lutheran dogmatics, his *Loci communes* (Commonplaces), while Luther was in the Wartburg. Melanchthon was favorably impressed by Zwingli's reasoning, and in 1540 was willing to accept the slightly altered Augsburg Confession, the so-called *Augustana variata,* which Calvin also accepted. The irenic and conciliatory Melanchthon was willing to make concessions both to the Reformed and to Roman Catholics and was more in the tradition of Erasmus than was Luther. Not a strict predestinarian like Luther, Melanchthon was suspected of advocating synergism—the doctrine that the human will actively cooperates with the will of God in preparing for and accepting God's grace. The fact that Luther's closest friend and personal disciple seemed, even while Luther was still alive, to be drifting away from some of the great Reformer's basic convictions alarmed younger Lutherans who feared that the Gospel was being compromised by Melanchthon's concessions.

b. The True-Born Lutherans

The Istrian Matthias Flacius (or Vlačić) Illyricus (1520–75), who had been a pupil of Luther's during the Reformer's last years, became the leader of a movement intended to preserve Luther's doctrines in pristine purity. This strict Lutheran party is called the *Gnesiolutheraner,* which we may render as "true-born Lutherans," and opposed Melanchthon's disciples, dubbed Philippists. Their influence emanated from the newly founded Academy of Jena, which became a university in 1577. Philippists and true-born Lutherans found themselves on the same side in the first antinomian controversy, brought on by the assertion of John Agricola that, contrary to Luther, the Old Testament Law should not be preached at all, not even in an "evangelical" sense as an incentive to repentance. Agricola's views were rejected by Luther and Melanchthon, but like Semi-Pelagianism in other quarters, what was officially rejected has nevertheless largely come to prevail among modern Lutherans.

The first Christological controversy among the Lutherans was opened by Andreas Osiander (1498–1552), who sided with Luther against Zwingli in the eucharistic colloquy at Marburg in 1529. Roman Catholicism had taught a progressive justification, beginning with faith and baptism, but augmented by good works. Luther, Melanchthon, and the orthodox Lutheran tradition emphasized that justification is instantaneous and *forensic:* the believer is instantly pronounced innocent before the court (*in foro*) of divine justice. His subsequent life of faith and obedience brings him sanctification; he already possesses justification. Osiander opposed this emphasis on a purely forensic righteousness with the doctrine that the divine Christ, dwelling in the believer, not merely permits him to be declared righteous but actually makes him righteous. Osiander thus recaptured elements of the older mystical and eucharistic tradition in which the believer, by feeding upon Christ in faith and through the sacrament, is progressively transformed and becomes more and more like Christ. Although Melanchthon and the Philippists insisted on forensic justification, they also insisted on the necessity for believers to engage in good works, provoking the true-born Lutheran Nikolaus von Amsdorf to counter with the assertion that good works are actually an obstacle to salvation.

Calvin's understanding of the eucharist had originally been close to Luther's, but in 1549 the Genevan Reformer reached an understanding with the German-speaking Swiss churches of Zwinglian sentiments and his relationship to the Lutherans was clouded. Melanchthon's sympathy for Calvin provoked the zealous Lutheran Joachim Westphal to attack them both in 1552. A full-fledged controversy broke out between the Lutherans and the Reformed in 1552, and Melanchthon's efforts to be conciliatory earned him the accusation of being a crypto-Calvinist, a charge that was hurled at him again and again until his death. On predestination, however, which many regard as the central distinctive of Calvinism, Melanchthon was far from Calvin. His pupil John Pfeffinger of Leipzig went so far as to teach that the human will cooperates with divine grace in conversion, and was immediately denounced by Flacius and Amsdorf. In the process of combating Pfeffinger, Flacius made an assertion with serious implications: he claimed that since the Fall, sin belongs to the *substantia*, or "essential nature," of man.

The sweeping Christological implications of Flacius' view are apparent. If man is by nature a sinner, then in the incarnation either Jesus became a sinner or did not truly assume a human nature. Flacius argued in a monophysite way and was declared heretical in the Weimar Colloquium of 1560. If sin belongs to the very nature of man, then Christ cannot be consubstantial with us, as the Chalcedonian Creed affirms, unless sin also belongs to *his* nature, which the creed denies. The fear that Christ cannot be fully human and yet free of sin has led many conservative Protestants to sound as though they were Monophysites or even docetists, not taking the humanity of Christ seriously. Conversely, other Protestants have been led by the same logic to conclude that because he was truly and fully human, Jesus must also have suffered from ignorance and have been involved in sin. The mistake lies in thinking that the Fall has so altered human nature that sin is now an essential component of humanity, so that no one and nothing can be human without thereby partaking in error and even in sin.

Melanchthon died on April 19, 1560, and thus was released from the constant quarreling of his fellow theologians. In addition to his efforts—

largely unsuccessful at the time—to introduce a measure of irenicism and compromise into relationships both with Roman Catholics and the Reformed, Melanchthon also bequeathed a high standard of humanistic and scientific interest to Lutheran theology. Luther's personal example and influence, if strictly followed, would have tended to keep Lutheranism more limited in its outlook—confined more narrowly to the Bible, to such traditionalism as Luther retained, and to Luther's own work—in a word, more Lutheran. Melanchthon helped to make Lutheranism more academic, and thereby to create the typically Protestant situation in which spiritual leadership is not in the hands of priests or pastors but of professors, with all that that has implied.

c. Lutheran Fundamentals:
The Formula of Concord

Reformed theology displays in a lesser degree some of the internationalism of the Roman Catholicism out of which it sprang. The first of the Reformed, Zwingli, was a German-speaking Swiss, the most celebrated, Calvin, a Frenchman; the lands most productive of Reformed thought were England, Scotland, and the Netherlands. The Lutheran Reformation, by contrast, was far more exclusively German. Scandinavia, where Lutheranism had total success, is not Germany, but even Scandinavia was closely tied to German Lutheran influences, far more so, for example, than the Netherlands or Scotland to Geneva. One of the advantages of this greater cultural homogeneity of Lutheranism was the fact that it was able to develop a unified confessional tradition. In the 1560s and 1570s, however, in the aftermath of the eucharistic and synergistic controversies, it appeared for a time as though Lutheranism would dissolve into contending factions.

In 1557, imperial officials organized the Colloquy of Worms, the last attempt on the part of the Holy Roman Empire to reconcile Catholics and Protestants. The most notable result of this colloquy was the fact that the Catholics became aware of the seriousness of the divisions within Lutheranism. The Lutheran princes of Germany sought to arrive at a consensus, but were frustrated by the bellicose Flacians of ducal Saxony. In 1559 the Palatinate became Reformed, increasing the apprehension of the true-born Lutherans that Melanchthon's supporters were secret Calvinists. At the Diet of Naumburg in 1561, the Lutheran princes attempted to achieve a compromise, but the opposition of the strict Lutherans to the altered Augsburg Confession, the *Augustana Variata*, was too vehement. Resolution did not come until a new duke of Saxony, John Frederick, removed Flacius and other leading strict Lutherans from their positions, while across the border in Electoral Saxony, the Philippists were suffering a similar fate. Although Elector Augustus sympathized with the Philippists, when his physician, Kaspar Peucer, Melanchthon's son-in-law, tried to slip Calvin's doctrine of the eucharist into the Saxon liturgy, the Elector stepped in, prohibited the changes, and imprisoned those who had supported them. With the removal of the leading controversialists, the way was cleared for the adoption of the Formula of Concord in 1577.

The impulse to the Formula of Concord came from Jacob Andreä, chancellor of the University of Tübingen, supported by Dukes Ulrich of Württemberg and Julius of Brunswick as well as by Julius' Lutheran theologians Martin Chemnitz (1522–86) and Nicholas Selnecker. Together with other southern and western German theologians they drew up the Formula of Concord. On June 25, 1580, exactly fifty years after the presentation of the *Confessio Augustana*, the Book of Concord was published in Dresden, containing the three ancient creeds—the Nicene, Apostles', and Athanasian—the *Confessio Augustana*, together with its Apology (or explanation), the Schmalkald Articles, Melanchthon's *Treatise on the Power and Primacy of the Pope*, Luther's Small and Large Catechisms, and the Formula of Concord. It was signed by eighty-six imperial estates and over eight thousand Lutheran theologians and represented, despite the resistance of a few, a real solidification of Lutheranism. Crypto-Calvinism did raise its standard once again in Electoral Saxony, under a favorably inclined prince, Christian I (ruled 1586–91), but on his death his chancellor, Nicholas Crell, who had furthered the cause of Calvinism, was arrested, tried, and finally executed in 1601—one of the rare cases of a Protestant authority executing another magisterial Protestant for a confessional deviation.

d. Orthodox Theology

The Formula of Concord of 1577 was drafted exactly sixty years after Luther posted his Ninety-five Theses and thirty-one years after his death. There were very few theologians still active who had come under his direct influence. It had taken Latin Christianity in the West about one thousand years to produce the systematic approach to theology known as Scholasticism. Lutheranism had begun to produce its own variety of Scholasticism only a few decades after Luther. This accomplishment reveals the extent to which Lutheranism really took over and utilized much of the spirit of traditional Catholic theology, notwithstanding its continuing vigorous polemical activity against Rome. This is reminiscent of the way in which early Christianity took over many elements of traditional Jewish theology and concepts of worship, despite its confrontation with Judaism. Orthodox Lutheranism soon became characterized by formalism and a very conservative attitude toward its own rapidly developing theological tradition. Eight thousand Lutheran theologians all working at the same time are certainly capable of rapidly producing an impressive bulk of theological tradition.

In theory, orthodox Lutheran theology is based directly on the exegesis of the Bible, but in practice it is apparent that Lutheran theologians soon began to build on and develop the tradition of their immediate predecessors and sometimes of their contemporaries. Only their conviction that the Bible is verbally inspired and absolutely trustworthy can explain their self-confidence in erecting immense and theoretical doctrinal structures with such astonishing rapidity and facility. Lutheran theology soon committed itself to an explicit doctrine of verbal inspiration. This doctrine is implicit in Luther, although he did not always treat the Bible as though he fully subscribed to it. The doctrine of verbal inspiration became the indispensable theoretical foundation for all subsequent developments in Lutheranism.

After recording a certain dismay at the way in which the principle of *sola Scriptura* opened the door to theological chaos in the sixteenth century, it is only fair to note that the Lutherans, the Protestants who held to it most strictly, were also the ones who produced the greatest theological stability. It is evident that under the right circumstances, and perhaps with the necessary aid of some very strong and charismatic leaders, the principle of *sola Scriptura* may lead to stability and doctrinal unity. Although the orthodox Lutherans did not follow the lead of Philipp Melanchthon in explicitly making use of church tradition, they did develop a traditionalistic attitude, which expressed itself in a century of doctrinal stability, from Martin Chemnitz to David Hollaz (1648–1713). The doctrine of biblical infallibility need not produce the confusion we have observed, for example, among the Protestants of Poland.

Lutherans tended to treat the Bible as a handbook of divine revelation, paying little attention to the history of the Jews and the church and even less to the idea of the development of doctrines within the Bible itself. Later Reformed theology developed the idea of the covenant and became interested in the redemptive process in history *(Heilsgeschichte)*, but for the first Protestants, especially the Lutherans, it was a sacred text. Not only the words and letters, but even the vowel points of the Hebrew text, added by editors centuries after the originals were written, were supposed to be divinely inspired. The first to express this view was the ill-fated Flacius, who carried it over to his understanding of Christ and thus became a kind of Monophysite. Essentially he believed that if the Bible is God's Book at all, it must be his down to the last vowel point: "God spoke the holy letters or their doctrine to the human race."[6] The Philippists had no quarrel with him on this point, for they too needed a totally reliable Scripture with which to confront the Roman pontiff and his centuries of theological tradition. The dean of orthodox Lutheran theology, Johann Gerhard (1582–1637), adopted Flacius' view of verbal inspiration in his *Loci Theologici,* the *magnum opus* of orthodoxy.

Another very important orthodox Lutheran was Martin Chemnitz (1522–86), who earned fame with his *Examination of the Council of Trent.* The Council of Trent, which met in three long sessions—1545–47, 1551–52, and 1562–63—represented the attempt of Roman Catholicism to reform itself and defeat the Reformation. It adopted a potentially devastating tactic against the Protestants, the argument that the Bible is obscure. Whereas early Catholic controversialists such as John Eck had argued against the Lutherans from Scripture, thus implicitly accepting it as their final authority, by the time of Trent the Catholics had decided to stress the insufficiency, obscurity, and uncertainty of Scripture and emphasize the necessity of tradition and the papal teaching office. Chemnitz regularly referred to the Bible with the complete expression *scriptura divinitus inspirata,* "divinely inspired Scripture." He makes it clear that in his opinion even those things Jesus said orally in the presence of his disciples were not simply recalled, but instead were subsequently verbally dictated to them by the Holy Spirit. As the expression of early Christian doctrines and their defense clearly took shape under the influence of the encounter with heretics and heathens, so orthodox Lutheranism was shaped by the need to define, authenticate, and defend itself not merely against the Catholics but also against Calvinists, enthusiasts, Socinians, and even Philippists.

Chemnitz expresses no precise ideas concerning the nature of the process of inspiration. It was crucial, in Chemnitz's view, that the presupposition of the inspiration of Scripture—which was also accepted by the Catholics—be shown to include the concepts of its clarity and sufficiency. Aegidius Hunnius succeeded Chemnitz as the chief spokesman of orthodoxy; he considered the divine inspiration of Scripture so self-evident that no justification was required: "Holy Scripture, dictated by God," and, "God speaking to us in Holy Scripture," are one and the same.[7] The most important of these early orthodox Lutherans was Johann Gerhard, whose position is a model for Lutheran orthodoxy from his own day to the present. In his *Locus de Scriptura* (1602), the words of Holy Scripture are called the very words of the Holy Spirit. If the Scripture is *theopneustos,* "God-breathed," then the biblical writers are mere amanuenses or secretaries.[8] Gerhard held the precise text of the Bible to be the express work and design of the Holy Spirit—a position that inevitably caused difficulties in the eighteenth century, as scholars became increasingly aware of problems and variations in textual transmission. He explicitly extended this divine act of inspiration to the vowel points of the Masoretic text of the Old Testament, for the vowel points are essential to the complete sense of the text, and if they were not inspired, then the whole Scripture could not be called *theopneustos*.[9] Needless to say, this position is sufficient to cause Gerhard's entire view of Scripture to be written off by countless modern theologians as completely untenable. Those, such as the present writer, who wish to maintain something essentially like Gerhard's doctrine of verbal inspiration must find a way to separate his principle from the logically neat but critically absurd attachment to the Hebrew vowel points.

e. Contrasts with Calvinism?

Orthodox, or high, Lutheranism as it developed at the end of the sixteenth century is characterized by its detailed, precise, and very strict definition of the verbal inspiration of Scripture—extending, as we have seen, to the Hebrew vowel points. Calvin, a generation younger than Luther, was more precise than Luther in expressing his convictions about the implications of biblical authority, but not nearly as explicit as the great dogmatic theologians of Lutheran orthodoxy. However, it would be misleading to suppose that Luther himself had a moderate view of biblical authority, that Calvin was stronger on this point, and that the orthodox Lutherans were the most dogmatic of all. In point of fact there is no substantial difference between any of them.

In recent decades the doctrine of biblical inerrancy has been attributed primarily to nineteenth-century American Calvinists. It was the early orthodox Lutherans—Flacius, Chemnitz, and Gerhard—who worked out in the fullest possible way the implications of their understanding of inspiration. Emphasis on inerrancy is at least as Lutheran as it is Calvinistic. But it was primarily the English-speaking Presbyterians, i.e. Reformed theologians at Princeton Theological Seminary—Charles and A. A. Hodge and Benjamin B. Warfield—who expressed the doctrines of plenary inspiration and biblical inerrancy in the form they take in present-day controversies. In our own day, some Lutheran theologians are fond of citing Luther's most tempestuous criticisms and detractions of parts of Scripture as evidence that he did not believe in inerrancy. The later orthodox Lutherans, who so explicitly did so believe, may then be dismissed as more Scholastic than Lutheran. The impression is given that biblical inerrancy is a late, contrived, primarily Aristotelian and Scholastic doctrine that may be Calvinistic but cannot be genuinely Lutheran. This is misleading. Where early Lutherans and Calvinists differed was not with regard to the authority of Scripture or its inerrancy, but with respect to the role of the Holy Spirit in making that authority known and convincing to the Christian, the so-called internal testimony.

Like the Lutherans, the Calvinists presupposed that divine inspiration necessarily implies verbal inspiration. Calvin frequently spoke of divine dictation. Jerome Zanchi (1516–90), a professor at Heidelberg, the intellectual center of German Calvinism, worked out a doctrine of verbal inspiration that paralleled the views of his orthodox Lutheran contemporaries while demonstrating a greater awareness of the way in which the text developed historically. Zanchi was concerned to set precise limits for the authoritative canon of the Bible; this was the first time since the fourth century that the traditional canon had been questioned or had to be justified. The traditional canon is precisely that, a traditional collection of books ultimately accepted and acknowledged to be authoritative by the consent of the whole church. Inasmuch as both Reformed and Lutheran theology denied the authority of tradition, it was necessary to attempt to show internal reasons—i.e. biblical reasons—why the canon of Scripture contains all the books it contains and no others. Zanchi's argument does leave a certain role for human testimony and tradition, although Zanchi, like Calvin, asserts that the final, convincing evidence is simply the testimony of the Holy Spirit.[10]

The Lutherans, following Article V of the Augsburg Confession, had a different understanding of the internal testimony of the Holy Spirit. It does not authenticate the validity of the claims of Scripture for the believer; instead, its essential function is psychological rather than epistemological: it gives the believer peace of mind. Surprisingly, the orthodox Lutheran Gerhard charges the Calvinists—usually perceived as dour—with being enthusiasts, like the fanatics, Anabaptists, and Schwenkfelders.[11] Gerhard claims that the Calvinistic view of predestination forces them to seek something beyond the plain testimony of Scripture itself, namely, an internal testimony of the Spirit, for salvation—for if Scripture itself had the power to convince those who hear it that it is God's Word, it could convince everyone, not just the elect. Gerhard believes that all who sincerely try to understand the Scripture can perceive it as God's Word; the elect accept it and are converted, while the others harden their hearts and refuse to accept it; they resist and reject God's grace. The Calvinists, who believe that grace is irresistible, must logically hold that if an individual has not accepted the Scripture, it is because he did not receive the special grace that is necessary to do so. This quarrel between Gerhard's view of universal grace and the ability of man to reject it and the Reformed view of particular grace and its irresistibility is still carried on by conservative Lutherans and Calvinists today.

f. Protestant Traditionalism

The Reformation began with the slogan "To the sources!" and sought to deal a fatal blow to the place of church tradition in shaping faith and life. But tradition cannot be eliminated as a force in the life of the church except at the cost of continuity; if all tradition is rejected, the church will be in constant, disruptive change. Despite their efforts not to be influenced by the authority of tradition, each of the major Reformation churches soon found itself both borrowing from the past and building up a traditionalism of its own. When he came into conflict with Zwingli and his allies on the question of the eucharist, Luther first pointed to tradition to bolster his argument that the undivided church supported his views. But when Melanchthon called on traditional authorities to undergird his own slightly different interpretation, Luther flatly stated that he would sooner reject all the ancient writers and all their testimonies rather than change his own conviction, based on Scripture.

In doing away with the authority of churches and councils to interpret Scripture, Luther relied on his concept of the clarity or perspicacity of Scripture. But when the Anabaptists and other radicals discovered Scripture to be teaching things the Lutherans found detestable, Lutherans learned the usefulness of tradition to help them confirm their own ostensibly clear and self-evident interpretations of Scripture. In addition, by repeating and building on one another's interpretations and arguments, Lutherans soon created their own distinctive dogmatic tradition and consulted one another's opinions just as readily as medieval theologians had consulted those of their patristic predecessors. Melanchthon, a humanist and somewhat of a universalist, had more of a sense of history than Luther, and promoted wide reading in early Christian literature. Melanchthon's willingness to respect tradition as an authority received an additional impulse when he confronted the most serious of all attacks on traditional belief, antitrinitarianism.

g. Antitrinitarianism

Luther was roused to his greatest indignation by the peasants' use of his teachings to justify their rebellion. Melanchthon reacted most strongly to the strictly theological provocation of antitrinitarianism put forward by John Campanus (1500–75) in Wittenberg in 1529. Campanus began by challenging Luther's doctrine of the bodily presence of Christ in the Lord's Supper, just as Zwingli and some others were doing. Campanus not only saw the concept of the body of Christ in the Supper as allegorical: he went on to speak of the Persons of the Trinity in the same way. Melanchthon was so disturbed that at one point he urged that such blasphemy be punished by death.[12] Melanchthon's suggestion was not followed, but the fact that it was made at all by so irenic a man shows the degree of horror that antitrinitarian views aroused. Eager as they had been to shake off the shackles of Roman authority, the first Lutherans were terribly afraid of losing all doctrinal coherence. This sentiment is reflected in the strong commitment to the Nicene Creed that begins the *Confessio Augustana,* or Augsburg Confession, of

1530. The *Augustana* criticizes most of those whose teachings it rejects in genteel tones. Even the Anabaptists are condemned objectively, because of their teachings. The "Samosatans," as Melanchthon calls the antitrinitarians, are bitterly denounced as blasphemers of the Word and of the Holy Spirit.[13]

A decade after his encounter with Campanus, Melanchthon's attention was attracted by the most celebrated of all early antitrinitarians, Michael Servetus himself (1511–53). Melanchthon undertook to refute the dangerous ideas of Servetus, but found himself somewhat at a loss if he was forced to argue from the Bible alone. By 1539, when he wrote *On the Church and the Authority of the Word of God,* Melanchthon revealed a growing willingness to accept the authoritative value of the testimonies of the ancient church, particularly as an aid to understanding some of the more difficult passages of Scripture. Among the members of the first generation of Lutherans, Melanchthon was the most willing to give weight to ecclesiastical tradition. This earned him the hostility of many of those who thought that he was turning away from the path of loyalty to Luther. It indicates that Melanchthon had recognized the fact that led to the first ecumenical creeds: the words of Scripture alone, without theological interpretation, do not in themselves offer a barrier to antitrinitarian views.

h. Polemics

The publication of the Book of Concord in 1580 brought an end to efforts such as Melanchthon's to tie Lutheranism to the older ecclesiastical tradition. It did this not by asserting a strict and unembellished biblicism, but by showing that in the six decades since the Diet of Worms, Lutheranism had produced a substantial theological tradition of its own and did not need to draw heavily from the Catholic tradition. One of the reasons why Lutheranism could be so productive was the immense number of professional theologians the Reformation had created. Because of the emphasis on university training, language study, and the humanities, in effect every Lutheran pastor was a professional theologian. Eight thousand "theologians" signed the Formula of Concord in 1577. Statistics are lacking, but it must have taken the early church centuries to produce the number Lutheranism brought forth in sixty years.

So many theologians interpreting and reinterpreting the Scripture, Luther, and one another not only produced a lot of theology, but also considerable conflict. The seventeenth century became a century of theological polemics. Given the number of theologians teaching, writing, and publishing, and the natural desire to earn respect and perhaps a measure of fame for one's "contribution," the temptation to innovate rather than simply restate old truths must have been great. Under the circumstances, it is surprising that Lutheran theology, during the first two centuries, remained as constant and as internally consistent as it did. Theologian after theologian produced large works of dogmatics, each drawn in theory from the Bible alone without dependence on earlier writers. Although the Lutheran theologians managed to display a substantial degree of agreement with one another, it may well have been because as a group they were largely aiming their shafts at Catholics and Calvinists, rather than at each other. Thus in a curious way books that were intended as polemical protests against the traditionalism of Catholicism themselves came to constitute the tradition of Lutheranism.

Although Melanchthon's irenic and compromising spirit was rejected in the sixteenth century, it revived again in the seventeenth, particularly in the early kind of ecumenical movement known as syncretism or irenicism.[14] "Its revival in the seventeenth century was ultimately fateful for the Lutheran character of German Protestantism," writes Otto Ritschl; "without it, there would still be no Protestant Union today." Ritschl refers to the Lutheran-Calvinist union imposed by the governments of several German Protestant states from 1817 onward, which produced what one leading scholar called the "Calvinization of Lutheranism."[15]

2. ORTHODOX CALVINISM

Like Lutheranism, Calvinism also soon developed a kind of orthodoxy and scholastic tradition of its own, but it was never as unified and homogeneous as Lutheranism. Although Lutheranism really began with one man, Martin Luther, Calvinism, or the Reformed movement, began with a number of leaders in a number of different centers. Lutheranism was able to settle its early internal controversies more or less definitively; the Philippists and Gnesio-Lutherans have long since passed from the scene. The first great internal controversy of the Calvinists, by contrast, that on the relationship between predestination and the freedom of the will, has never subsided, and the descendants of the early contenders are carrying the battle on today. As we compare the two movements, we may take as symbolic of each a word it brought into the center of theological interest: in the case of the Lutherans, that word is "Gospel," in the case of the Calvinists, "covenant."

a. The Covenant

For Lutherans, the Gospel has two parts, the Law and the Gospel; to speak of the Gospel is to evoke the polarity between Law and Gospel. For Calvinists, the covenant has two dispensations, the old and the new; the word itself evokes their unity and essential similarity. Calvinism is the most

Jewish branch of Christianity, and as such was the first to develop an interest in the Jews and their institutions. Prior to the development of the idea of the covenant as Federal Theology *(Bundestheologie)* by the Low German Calvinist Johannes Coccejus (Koch, 1603–69), Christians had tended to look on the whole Bible as a kind of compendium or codex of Christian doctrine and law. Covenant theology brought with it a realization that God does not merely utter words of revelation, but works in and through real human history. The Old Testament took on a life and value of its own, and was no longer seen merely as a handbook of doctrines. The idea of continuity had already been stressed by Zwingli, the first of the Reformed school, and was further developed by Calvin. The concept of the covenant led to the idea of *Heilsgeschichte* (history of salvation or redemptive history). Coccejus introduced the concept of divine *abrogationes,* adjustments to the covenant that became necessary in human history as a consequence of the Fall of man and other human actions and decisions; this insight has been elaborated by nineteenth- and twentieth-century theologians into the theological school of dispensationalism, which makes sharp distinctions between the various ways in which God administers the universe and offers man his salvation in succeeding dispensations.

b. The Doctrine of God

The antitrinitarianism and early Unitarianism of Transylvania and Poland sprang from Calvinist roots. What was Calvinism's vision of God that could give rise, in a matter of decades, to such a great break with orthodox theology? In contrast to Luther, Calvin was not only more systematic but had a more unified view of the world and God's ways of dealing with it and us. He emphasized not only the continuity between the Old Testament and the New, but also that between the natural knowledge of God and the saving knowledge that comes through revelation. Calvin taught that natural man is both hampered by his finitude and blinded by sin, so that he can at best dimly appreciate the testimonies God has given us of himself through the nature he has created; nevertheless, in principle he asserted the essential unity of knowledge and the fact that revelation will correspond to nature when both are properly understood.

The characteristic feature of Calvin's doctrine of God is his emphasis on God's providence, his sovereign and all-seeing activity in the ordering of the universe. God's Will expresses itself in a series of decrees, which may be conceived as particular expressions or determinations of his Will. For strict Calvinists of the old school, God reveals himself primarily as Will; in the covenant theological tradition, the acts of God's Will are seen as decisions to express his fundamental being, which is characterized by love. Both traditions emphasize the sovereignty of God and the doctrine that all that exists and occurs does so because of his Will. From this perspective, Reformed theology is the opposite of ancient dualism; far from being a separate principle, powerful and independent of God or the good, evil appears as subordinate to God and dependent on him, to the extent that it appears that he is its Creator and that it exists according to his Will. The more one emphasizes the sovereignty of God and predestination—especially double predestination, which foreordains some to damnation as well as others to salvation—the more God appears responsible for the existence of evil.

Traditional Scholastic theology attempted to resolve the problem of evil by asserting two things: first, that evil is not itself created, but is a deficiency in a created good; second, that while God foresees the fact that his creatures will sin and permits them to do so, he does not will that they do so, but wills that they abstain from sin. Calvin rejects this argument as a subterfuge and does not shrink from the implication that God willed the fall of the first man.[16] For Calvin himself, the doctrine of predestination is more in the nature of a conclusion drawn from his fundamental conviction concerning the sovereignty of God than the starting point for his theology. Later Calvinists made predestination their point of departure, and conceived the sovereignty of God in terms even more absolute and forbidding than the austere vision of Calvin.

Against the background of his understanding of God as sovereign Providence, Calvin clearly emphasizes his conviction that Scripture itself teaches that God is one in three Persons. He defends the use of nonbiblical terms such as *hypostasis* and ''Person.'' Thus he takes a stand against arguments such as those to be raised by Blandrata and other antitrinitarians that would banish philosophical language from theology and places himself in conscious continuity with the theology of the patristic age.[17] The doctrine of the Trinity guarantees the deity of Christ. Christ is God made man, possessing two natures, both of which preserve their distinctive properties. He accepts the concept of the communication of attributes, but does not see it as extending to the *genus of majesty* (he does not himself use this term). Thus the body of Christ does not possess the attribute of omnipresence, or ubiquity; hence Calvin does not teach the bodily presence of Christ in the eucharist, although he does affirm Christ's real presence. The Westminster Confession puts Calvin's conviction rather succinctly: ''The body and blood of Christ being then, not corporally in, with, or under the bread and wine, yet as really, but spiritually present to the faith of believers.''[18]

The Lutherans look on this Calvinist denial of the bodily presence of Christ as a repudiation not merely of his real presence but of his ability to be present, i.e. of his deity. They accused the Calvinists of severing Christ's human nature from the divine, and thus of reviving Nestorianism. When

Calvin brought the divine and the human together by teaching that Christ mediates for us in his deity as well as in his humanity, the argumentative Italian Calvinist Stancari charged that this made the Son inferior to the Father, calling Calvin a subordinationist and an Arian. If the Lutheran emphasis on the communication of attributes smacks of monophysitism, Calvin's position does sound Nestorian. Nevertheless, Calvin, like Luther, consistently reaffirmed his adherence to the traditional trinitarian and Christological statements of Nicaea and Chalcedon. His Nestorianism remains only an implication of his strict distinction between the deity and humanity of Christ. It is possible to extrapolate from Calvin's teachings and to accuse him of a Nestorian tendency to separate the human Jesus from the divine Christ, but Calvin resolutely refused to make such a connection. Indeed, such an extrapolation from orthodox principles is precisely what the Creed of Chalcedon is intended to prevent, and it or something like it is almost always made when the creed with its warnings is allowed to fall into disuse.

c. Arminius and the Freedom of the Will

During the sixteenth century, Lutheranism had its synergistic controversy concerning the ability of the human will to cooperate with divine grace in conversion. Similar questions agitated the Reformed camp, where they produced the major "heresy" within Calvinism, Arminianism. Inasmuch as it is the theology of Calvin rather than that of Luther that has predominated in the shaping of English-speaking Protestantism, the Calvinist-Arminian controversy continues until the present day among and sometimes within many English-speaking Protestant denominations.

Jacob Arminius (1560–1609) was once the pupil of Théodore de Bèze (Beza, 1519–1605), Calvin's successor in Geneva. During his long period at the head of the Genevan church, Bèze developed Calvin's doctrine of predestination to its logical extreme, producing the doctrine that is called supralapsarian or Hypercalvinist. In addition to making Calvin's doctrine of predestination even more radical, Bèze also lifted it from the secondary place it occupies with both Calvin and Augustine and made it his point of departure. Supralapsarianism is the conviction that the first of the divine decrees or purposes was the decree to predestinate—to elect some to eternal bliss and to condemn others to eternal damnation. The decrees to create man and to permit him to Fall follow the decree of predestination. In other words, some human beings are created for the express purpose of receiving eternal life, others for the express purpose of being damned forever. This decree of predestination is said to stand "above," i.e. before, the Fall (supra lapsum).

For Bèze, Creation and the Fall were the means chosen by God to implement his determination to predestine some to blessedness, others to eternal misery. Supralapsarianism implies that God is responsible for the Fall. Bèze and most of his followers nevertheless insisted that Adam possessed a free will, and thus that the Creator is not responsible for sin and evil, but this insistence appears to be inconsistent with the basic supralapsarian scheme. Supralapsarianism presents a radical alternative to dualism: evil exists through the will of God and in the service of his highest purpose, which is to glorify himself. Through the free grace shown to elect sinners, God displays his mercy; through the just condemnation of the reprobate for the sins they willingly committed, he exhibits his justice.

Among the most consistent of the supralapsarians was Franciscus Gomarus of Leyden (1563–1641). He went so far as to say that Christ was elected by the Father to be our Mediator and Redeemer only to carry out God's determination to predestinate some to salvation. In other words, the Christian's standing with God does not depend primarily on his relationship with Christ, but on God's decree. Because God has decreed the Christian's salvation, he provides Christ to be his Mediator and Redeemer. Although it could not fully explain it, traditional theology thought of God forgiving us for Christ's sake, because Christ has become a human like ourselves and has taken the burden of our sin upon him. The attention of the believer is concentrated on historical, this-worldly events and realities: on the incarnation, the crucifixion, and the resurrection. This concentration was carried still further by Roman Catholic doctrine, which stressed the real, corporeal presence of Christ in the eucharist and the renewal of his one bloody sacrifice in the repeated, unbloody sacrifice of the Mass. Supralapsarian theology removes the attention of the believer from the historical person of Christ and his work, and centers it on the eternal decree of God, cold and intellectual, before all time. Although Bèze's supralapsarianism was formally orthodox and accepted the Chalcedonian Creed, this side of orthodoxy is not really integral to the supralapsarian vision. Everything depends on God's decree to predestinate, not on the person and work of the Redeemer. Although his deity is still formally confessed, it has become peripheral. This is doubtless one reason why orthodox Calvinists show a higher degree of susceptibility to Unitarianism, with its reductionist view of Christ, than their orthodox counterparts among the Lutherans.

Traditional Calvinism attempts to maintain that God bears no responsibility for man's sin by making a distinction between inner necessity and external compulsion. Man is under an inner necessity to sin, but there is no external compulsion; he chooses to sin by an exercise of his will, and thus he sins willingly and deliberately, although of necessity. While Arminius acknowledged that it is possible to make such a distinction, he held that it was not adequate to relieve God of the responsibility for the sin of his creatures. The only way to do this, Arminius contended, was to deny that man sins out of necessity.

Arminius also had to contend with John Macorrius (1588–1644), who went beyond Bèze and Gomarus by plainly stating that God decrees that man sin. Macorrius, Bèze, and Gomarus were all compelled by the logic of their view of the sovereignty of God to disregard biblical statements concerning human freedom. If all things occur according to God's sovereign will, then those who are lost are lost by his will, and logically God must will that they sin in order to deserve the punishment he intends to impose. Assigned the task of defending Bèze's supralapsarian position against the criticism of the humanist Dirck Volckerts Coornhert, Arminius came to the conclusion that Bèze's views were wrong, and proposed an alternative. The first of God's decrees was not to predestinate, but to create; the second, to permit his creatures to fall; the third, to provide a means of grace; the fourth decree was to predestinate some to salvation. God predestinates those who, by his divine foreknowledge, he knows will repent and accept his grace. Arminius was not a synergist insofar as he did not regard man's acceptance of grace as in any sense a work, a cooperation with God. His views were immediately attacked. His early death in 1609 spared him the experience of seeing them suppressed by the Synod of Dordt (1618–19).

Unfortunately for Arminius' reputation, his views were defended after his death by the slightly younger Konrad Vorst (1569–1622), who had not known him personally. Vorst was in contact with Socinians, and his rationalistic commitment to the freedom of the will was accompanied by a rationalistic minimizing of the deity of Christ. Another supporter of Arminius' views, the celebrated jurist Hugo Grotius (1583–1645), opposed Faustus Socinus' views, but this very opposition shows that they were present in Reformed circles. It was not long before another admirer of Arminius, Stephen Curcellaeus (1586–1659), began, in typical Socinian fashion, to attack the traditional trinitarian terminology—terms such as *trinitas, persona,* and *hypostasis*—and to defend the right of Socinians to be called Christians.

The first Arminian to produce a dogmatic theology, Philip of Limborch (1633–1712), reaffirmed the eternal deity of the Son and the Holy Spirit and thus moved Arminianism away from the teachings of Socinus. Nevertheless, in their quest for tolerance for their views, the Arminians also pleaded for the Socinians, i.e. for Unitarians, and frequently showed openness to their views on the Trinity and the deity of Christ. The fact that their adversaries on the question of the freedom of the will sometimes made common cause with the Unitarians reinforced the strict Calvinists in their conviction that to falter on the doctrine of predestination was but the first step on the road to unitarian apostasy. Predestination for Calvinists thus became somewhat of a litmus test for orthodoxy, as the doctrine of consubstantiation was for the Lutherans.

3. CHRISTOLOGICAL CONTROVERSY AGAIN

While the Arminians were challenging the Calvinistic doctrine of predestination and gradually developing an affinity with the antitrinitarian Socinians, the orthodox Lutherans divided on a Christological issue. Having followed Luther's interpretation of the communication of attributes to affirm that Jesus Christ possessed the attributes of majesty in his humanity, some zealous Lutherans went on to express views even more reminiscent of monophysitism. If Christ possessed the attributes of deity even as a man, it is apparent that in his status of humility, he emptied himself of them, appearing as a man among men. This self-emptying (Latin *exinanitio,* Greek *kenosis*) now came under scrutiny. One school of theologians, centered at Tübingen, the citadel of conservative Lutheranism, insisted that Christ retained all his divine authority while incarnate on earth and that he continued to exercise it, although in a hidden or cryptic manner. Matthew Hafenreffer (d. 1620), Luke Osiander the Younger (d. 1638), and Theodore Thummius (d. 1630) vigorously advocated this view. Its flaws seem apparent: if Christ retained and exercised all his divine power and authority while here on earth, but did so invisibly and secretly, it is hard to conceive that he really became man, for the human condition is characterized by limitations and weakness, not by invisible, omnipotent powers.

A conflicting interpretation was propounded by Balthasar Mentzer (d. 1627) of the University of Giessen. Mentzer contended that Christ had voluntarily laid aside his divine powers and had not used them during his earthly life. The Tübingen position not only seems to place the true humanity of Christ in doubt, but also reduces the value of his personal presence— on earth and at the Lord's Supper—by teaching that he was and is always omnipresent. Like Bèze's supralapsarianism, the Tübingen position was an effort to draw out the logical implications of an orthodox doctrine; it did not meet with the approval of most Lutherans. Stigmatized as "extraorthodox," it was nevertheless tolerated and not regarded as a disruptive heresy, despite the fact that it seems to have rather monophysite implications.[19] A pastor in Rostock, Jakob Lütkemann (d. 1655) carried the concept of self-emptying further than the Giessen school and contended that Christ surrendered his deity at the moment of death in order to be able to die. For this clearly Nestorian proposition he was deprived of his pastorate.

4. THE TRANSITION TO PIETISM

While the thousands of professional theologians the Reformation had produced disputed about the concepts of *kenosis* and *krypsis,* at least some of them felt that the spiritual life of the ordinary believer was being neglected. What influence does the deity of Christ have on the believer in his daily life? In *Four Books on True Christianity*,[20] John Arndt (1555–1621), a physician as well as a theologian, attempted to work out the implications of the doctrine that Christ indwells the believer. He produced a new and controversial introspective mysticism akin to that expounded earlier by Kaspar Schwenkfeld. Heinrich Rathmann of Danzig (d. 1628) asserted that it is the indwelling Christ who communicates spiritual truth, not the Bible words themselves. This was a step closer to the Reformed idea that the Word cannot communicate its truth to the hearer without the internal testimony of the Holy Spirit, and undercuts the orthodox Lutheran insistence that the Word itself *is* a means of grace. A better-known and more eccentric figure than Rathmann and Arndt was Jakob Boehme (1575–1624), whose mysticism influenced the Romantic movement as well as non-Christian philosophers such as Friedrich von Schelling and Hegel. Within Lutheranism, there is a direct line between Arndt's "practical Christianity" with its preoccupation with the indwelling Christ and the next major development in Protestant spirituality, Pietism.

SELECTED BIBLIOGRAPHY

Conrad, Bergendoff. *The Church of the Lutheran Reformation: A History of Lutheranism*. St. Louis: Concordia, 1967.

Drummond, Andrew Landale. *German Protestantism Since Luther*. London: Epworth, 1951.

Franks, Robert S. *The Work of Christ: A Historical Study of Christian Doctrine*. New York: Nelson, 1962.

Klug, E. F. *From Luther to Chemnitz: On Scripture and the Word*. Grand Rapids, Mich.: Eerdmans, 1971.

Leonard, Emile G. *A History of Protestantism: The Establishment*. London: Nelson, 1967.

Leube, Hans. *Kalvinismus und Luthertum im Zeitalter der Orthodoxie*. Leipzig, 1928.

Preus, Robert. *The Inspiration of Scripture: A Study of the Theology of the Seventeenth Century Lutheran Dogmaticians*. St. Louis: Concordia, 1957.

Raitt, Jill, ed. *Shapers of Religious Traditions in Germany, Switzerland and Poland, 1560–1600*. New Haven: Yale University Press, 1981.

Reu, Johann Michael. *In the Interest of Lutheran Unity: Two Lectures: Unionism and What Is Scripture and How Can We Become Certain of Its Divine Origin*. Columbus, Ohio: Lutheran Book, 1940.

18

PIETISM AND HERESY

Even as the Jews were not to let it suffice them to have escaped from Babylon, but were to desire to restore again the house of the Lord and the beauty of its worship, so we may not be satisfied with the knowledge that we have left Babylon, but we must be careful to correct imperfections which still prevail.

I have never been of the opinion, and am not so now, that the Reformation of Luther was brought to completion as one might hope.

Philipp Jakob Spener

The most important theological phenomenon between the Protestant Reformation and theological liberalism is the movement known as Pietism. The first stirrings occurred among Calvinists in the Netherlands and northern Germany, and similar impulses appeared among Roman Catholics, but Pietism is really identified with Lutheranism. Lutheranism produced the rigid Scholastic orthodoxy to which Pietism was a reaction, and the three great leaders of Pietism were Lutherans. The history of Pietism follows the lives of the three great Germans, Philipp Jakob Spener, August Hermann Francke, and Nikolaus Ludwig von Zinzendorf, and continues with the founders of Methodism, John and Charles Wesley. When we look at the theological and spiritual concerns of Pietism, however, we see that they were important not only to those called Pietists but to virtually all serious Christians since the Reformation, and indeed before it as well. If we look at Pietism as an intellectual or sociological movement, we find astonishing similarities to the spirit of the age against which it fought, i.e. the Enlightenment. Karl Barth, a conservative but deeply suspicious of Pietism, went so far as to call it the religious side of the Enlightenment[1]—and detested it with surprising heartiness.

Pietism, like Protestantism, is complex. Sometimes its impact appears to be the opposite of what its leaders desired. Pietism and the movements that descend from it—including much of evangelicalism, Protestant foreign missions, and the modern evangelism exemplified by Billy Graham—remain the most vigorous spiritual force within contemporary Christianity. In some places, such as in Germany, where Pietism was born, the movement seems defensive and withdrawn from the world of the twentieth century. In North America, by contrast, Pietism, its descendants, and its allies are taking the offensive against secularism in movements such as the Moral Majority and the International Council on Biblical Inerrancy.

The historical beginnings of Pietism lie in the orthodox Protestantism of the late sixteenth and seventeenth centuries. Its spiritual beginnings lie in the hearts of those who seek to be "doers of the Word, and not hearers only." During the period of Protestant orthodoxy, which was also the period of bloody and brutal religious wars, creeds and confessions, the standards of orthodoxy, were becoming longer and longer. By the middle of the seventeenth century, wrangling dogmaticians had defined the "fundamentals" of saving faith in such detail that hardly anyone but a specialist could hope to know them all. Christianity desperately needed to be simplified, clarified, and intensified.

In the first half of the sixteenth century, Luther tried to reform public morals in Wittenberg and Calvin did the same, a bit more systematically, in Geneva. In this, they had the support of the state as well as the enthusiasm of a large part of the population behind them. By the end of the century, however, it began to look as though the Reformation had foundered. Once again, with notable but rare exceptions, the aristocracy was as self-indulgent and the common people as debased as they had been before the Reformation began.

Pietism began with a series of spontaneous efforts to get people to take the evangelical faith seriously and live it as though they believed it. An important forerunner of the Pietist movement was John Arndt, whose best-known work is entitled *Four Books on True Christianity*. Arndt was a kind of a mystic; far more important to him than doctrine was a personal relationship with Christ. As far as the first Pietists—and especially Spener, considered the founder of the movement—were concerned, they were not innovators at all, but the legitimate heirs of Martin Luther. Soon Pietism did develop some very distinctive emphases, which distinguished it from ordinary Lutheran orthodoxy. The most important was its doctrine of the new birth and its insistence on the importance of consciously experiencing conversion. The ideas were by no means new: Jesus himself taught the new birth (John 3:3). The Pietists' insistence on taking them seriously was new.

Pietism was intensely personal. It began by trying to get individuals to take their official religious commitments as deeply binding, personal obligations. Incidentally, by so doing it made them better members of society, and soon came to the attention of secular government as a useful tool of civic education. Thus before long it found itself favored by rulers, some of whom, like Constantine, may have been personally converted, but who incidentally or primarily were looking for something to make responsible citizens out of their subjects. Pietism never became a church, and certainly not an established church, but it soon began to develop many of the problems that typified establishment. Instead of stressing personal Christianity, at a certain point much of Pietism began to cultivate the Christian personality, and soon found itself more Romantic than Christian. In trying to show that the true faith changes lives, segments of Pietism began to stress "life, not doctrine," and ended by forgetting about doctrine altogether.

The positive features of Pietism are many. Several of the most commendable—and socially valuable—aspects of Protestantism were pioneered and developed not by the great Reformers but by their Pietistic descendants. From Bible printing and distribution at home to foreign missions abroad, from orphanages and elementary schools to hospitals and homes for the handicapped and aged, the Pietists did all they could to fulfill the commandments, evangelize, and care for those in distress and want. On the negative side, the individualism Pietism shared with the Enlightenment helped to destroy the sense of the church as a community. By its indifference to specific doctrines, Pietism helped to undermine the idea that the Christian faith is a valid system of truth, not merely an emotional or sentimental attitude toward life.

Curiously, in practice Pietism was often more hostile to the church as an institution than to government. The typical arrangement within European Protestantism was that of an established, or government-supported, church. Although the Pietists did not disrupt this arrangement, they tended to bypass it, because they preferred to work with little groups of highly committed believers rather than with an officially established institution. Pietists in North America readily found themselves at home with the separation of church and state. In both Europe and North America Pietism often established a close working relationship with favorably disposed rulers, but was not particularly concerned with constitutional and legal structures. It is partly because of the highly Pietistic and revivalistic nature of much American Protestantism that in the United States, where conservative Protestantism is stronger than anywhere else in the world, government and law are highly secular.

Pietism developed and changed in the course of its long history. (Although hardly anyone calls himself a Pietist today, most independent Protestant churches and many small Protestant denominations are essentially Pietistic in spirit.) When Pietism underwent a renaissance in the nineteenth century, it became more individualistic and less intellectual in outlook. It is this nineteenth-century Pietism that is the direct ancestor of most conservative Protestantism in Europe and North America today. At the outset, Pietism shared the doctrinal convictions of orthodoxy, but it came to place an ever larger emphasis on life rather than doctrine.

In its early stages, Pietism was a movement intended to give conviction and fervor to existing Protestant communities; in other words, it revived churches, rather than individuals, although it began with individuals. At first it opposed the deadness of "dead orthodoxy," while retaining the orthodoxy. Later, it came increasingly to oppose, if not orthodoxy itself, at least the attitude of concern for right doctrine out of which orthodox theology grows. Slogans such as "life, not doctrine" and "faith, not facts" may be used by people who hold orthodox doctrines and who believe that faith does correspond to facts, but they may also be used by those who disdain both doctrine and historical facts.

In the modern situation, the subjective and individualistic aspects of Pietism make the Christianity it teaches look like another form of psychological self-help rather than a coherent structure of truth. Its theology can no longer be the queen of the sciences, not even in name. Of course, it must be acknowledged that a Pietism that has replaced personal Christianity with the "Christian" personality is no longer the Pietism of Spener, Francke, and Zinzendorf, and that it is no fairer to blame Spener for individualism than to blame Luther for higher criticism.

1. SYNCRETISM AND PIETISM

In modern usage, "syncretism" refers to a mixing of religions. This is something no one committed to the truth of Christianity can accept. In the sixteenth and seventeenth centuries, however, the word had a positive sense, rather like our modern expression "ecumenical." Like our expression "ecumenical," it was loathed by many of, if not all, the defenders of orthodoxy as an inducement to *carte blanche* for doctrinal deviation and as an abandonment of the fundamentals of the faith. A syncretistic, or union, movement followed closely upon the interconfessional polemics of the sixteenth century, but it did not put an end to them. They continued with vigor. "Syncretism" and its advocates had one thing in common with orthodoxy and its polemicists. Both the syncretists and the polemicists were trying to establish and define the *fundamentals of the faith,* the polemicists in order to defend them against the assaults of heretics, the syncretists in order to use them as a basis for agreement with those who differed from one another only on secondary matters.

The movement that is called syncretism or irenicism had some eminently practical reasons for its existence: during the sixteenth century, all of eastern Europe appeared to be threatened by the Turks, who had captured Constantinople in 1453 and largely liquidated the Christian position in the East; the Turkish conquest of the Balkans, which was already well under way by then, seemed to be expanding irresistibly into central Europe. Both Protestants and Catholics alike had good reason to try to find a basis for mutual cooperation against the power of the Islamic Turks.

The progress of the Calvinistic movement within the German (or Holy Roman) Empire was dramatically checked by the Peace of Augsburg of September 25, 1555. This treaty guaranteed toleration to the new Lutheran churches, but it excluded the Calvinists (as well as radical Christians). The Lutheran Formula of Concord of 1577 broke all ecclesiastical connections with the Reformed churches. From 1580 onward the Reformed in Germany were exposed to repressive measures while the Lutherans were protected. The Calvinists frequently and urgently appealed to the Lutherans to make common cause with them against Rome and the Counter-Reformation, but these appeals fell on deaf ears; the Lutherans were content with their own status until the outbreak of the Thirty Years' War in 1618. The war began with a series of major victories by the Catholics. These led to the infamous Edict of Restitution of March 6, 1629. For the first time, the Lutherans as well as the Reformed faced forcible re-Catholicization. Then, almost too late, the Lutherans of Germany realized that the suppression of the Reformed was but a step away from the abolition of their own once-secure Lutheran position. Help for the Protestants came with the intervention of the Lutheran Swedes under King Gustavus Vasa. Protestantism was not destroyed, but it had lost much through the failure of Lutherans and Calvinists to find a way to make common cause against Rome.

Despite the fact that Lutherans recognized the Reformed as fellow Protestants, they frequently followed the slogan "Better the Pope than Calvin." Their logic was based on the conviction that when Lutheranism was at peace with Rome, the Catholics were willing to leave them undisturbed in their faith, whereas the Calvinists always sought peace with the Lutherans as a preliminary to Calvinistic efforts to undermine the distinctiveness of Lutheranism and make Calvinists of them all. For this reason Lutherans were wary of compromise with Calvinists. This widespread Lutheran fear of the influence of Calvinism may seem odd in view of the fact that it was the Catholic Counter-Reformation rather than Calvinism that used both persuasion and force to make serious inroads into Lutheran territories. This suspicion of the Calvinists reveals the fact that Lutheranism as a movement is less radical than Calvinism. It appeared to some to be too hesistant in carrying out the implications of its own evangelical principles.

Before the Reformation was ten years old, Luther had had to take a strong stand against people whom he considered theological and political radicals, i.e. against Karlstadt and his "fanatics" and against Thomas Münzer and the peasants' rebellion. After having preached Christian liberty, Luther suddenly called for a hardening of ecclesiastical discipline. To many, this seemed arbitrary and inconsistent, particularly as it was exercised not within the congregation by committed Christians but on a territorial basis by the secular authorities. Luther thus made a conscious change from his early commitment to a church composed only of true believers; the secular prince became an "emergency bishop," using his political power at Luther's behest to channel and constrain the spiritual impulses of reformation. Even Luther's friend and closest coworker, Melanchthon, felt this inconsistency and was repeatedly drawn toward the Reformed position as a more consistent carrying out of Luther's first evangelical impulses.

Unlike Luther, Melanchthon did not immediately put Zwingli and the South Germans in a class with the "fanatics," Karlstadt and the prophets of Zwickau. He appreciated their view of the sacraments and their approach to the disciplines of the Christian life. Consequently, he tried to establish a better, more catholic consensus concerning the substance of the Christian faith than appeared to be emerging on the basis of Luther's somewhat arbitrary biblicism. Melanchthon's traditionalism brought him closer to Erasmus, humanism, and potentially even Roman Catholicism, and his support for a measure of freedom of the will placed him at odds with the emphatically predestinarian Calvinists. Nevertheless, as we have seen, Melanchthon was considered by many to be a crypto-Calvinist and ultimately his partisans were outmaneuvered by the "true-born" Lutherans.

2. POLEMICS

Early in the Reformation era, religious debates and dialogues were intended to arrive at unity or reunion between the contending parties. Unfortunately, this was seldom, if ever, their result. By the mid-sixteenth century, particularly after the Council of Trent, theological dialogue and colloquy had degenerated almost everywhere into vehement and often highly offensive polemics. One's own theological position became both the presupposition and the foreordained conclusion of any debate; the only purpose of the "disputation" was to demonstrate, at least to the satisfaction of one's partisans, the correctness of one's own theological position. Inasmuch as the contending parties almost invariably agreed on the authority of Scripture and generally accepted the same rules of logic, in theory the possibility should have existed for one side to persuade the other by reasoned biblical arguments; in practice, however, this does not ever seem to have happened.

Despite their apparent fruitlessness, the polemics of the era of orthodoxy served in a sense to unite all the quarreling confessions. The fact that each struggled so hard to show that it possessed the truth indicates that all were convinced that there is an absolute truth to the Christian faith and that it can be known and accepted by human beings. Polemics molded theology because the way in which one's opponents attack one influences one's own position. Because it is necessary to defend precisely the positions the opponent is attacking, in a way one's theological rivals, not the inner logic of one's own beliefs, can come to set the agenda for the development of one's doctrinal position. This was evidently what happened in the case of the creeds of the early church: their content was determined by the challenges of Gnosticism, docetism, Arianism, and other heresies. Christian theology, we noted, was thus to a large extent the stepchild of Christian heresy.

In the Reformation era, by contrast, what separated the Lutherans from Zwingli's party at Marburg in 1529 was far less than the iota that separated the orthodox from the Semi-Arians in the fourth century. The difference between Luther and Zwingli on the Lord's Supper was far less substantial than that between the eternal generation and the creation of the Logos, but it became the point of departure for a whole confessional tradition. The differences among the Protestants set the theological agenda in the sixteenth century as the differences between orthodox and Arians had set it in the fourth. Because the differences were often petty, the confessions they produced also may seem petty and overly precise when contrasted with the great creeds of the early church. The spiritualizers' challenge to the early Lutherans led to the characteristic Lutheran concept of the Word and the sacraments as means of grace. Later, attacks on the Calvinistic doctrine of predestination caused it to assume an even greater importance within Calvinism than it had had for Calvin himself.

a. Justification:
Forensic or Transforming?

The polemics of sixteenth- and seventeenth-century Protestantism tended to push Reformation and party insights and slogans to their logical and sometimes absurd extremes. The concept that justification is "by faith alone, apart from the works of the Law," was shared by all the magisterial Reformers, but the Calvinists—like many radical Reformers and the later Pietists—appeared to water it down in practice by stressing good works and the disciplines of the Christian life. It would have been logical for Lutherans to go on from a discussion of justification by faith to speak of the effects of such justification in the believer's life, thus avoiding the mistake of understanding justification as merely forensic—an entry in the register of the heavenly court—with no tangible results in the believer himself.

Constant pressure on the Lutherans from the Anabaptists and to some extent from the Reformed to emphasize works kept the Lutherans from making the logical distinction between "works-righteousness" and the "works of the righteous." In the heat of the controversy, confessional Lutheranism sometimes became ensconced in a commitment to "faith alone" that amounted to hostility to good works and a godly life and seemed to turn Christianity into theory only, with no discernible practical implications. From the early days of the Reformation onward, Lutherans were embroiled in controversies within Lutheranism and across confessional lines in an effort to come to terms with the practical implications of justification without reverting to an insistence on the necessity of good works for salvation.

b. The Theology of Controversy: Protestant Scholasticism

Although the early disputations were intended to reconcile the contending parties, the goal of later polemics was rather to protect one's own adherents from falling into heresy. Theological formulations came to be developed to meet the needs of the polemical situation, not primarily to edify and instruct Christians. The result was a theology that was far more suited to the debating hall than to the sanctuary.

Polemical disputes, whether carried on in oral proceedings or by the publication of "tracts"—many of which attained the size of large volumes—almost never led to a verdict, let alone a true consensus. Consequently, most disputations were followed by a series of analyses and commentaries trying to demonstrate that one's own side had really won. Inasmuch as there was no better way to demonstrate this after a colloquy than there had been during it, many, if not all, of the polemicists resorted to *ad hominem* arguments coupled with bitter personal denunciations of their opponents.

An effort to pass from polemics for the sake of self-justification to a sober analysis and criticism that could lead to better understanding and potentially even to agreement is demonstrated by the response of Martin Chemnitz to the Roman Catholics' Counter-Reformation Council of Trent (1545–63). When the council was first convened, there was at least some hope that it would reach a positive accommodation with the Reformation. As it turned out, however, the council massively rejected and condemned the Reformation and each of its distinctive doctrines. It then imposed a greater doctrinal and disciplinary rigidity on Catholicism than had prevailed before the Reformation. Chemnitz produced the first measured and comprehensive Protestant reply, his *Examination of the Council of Trent,* between 1565 and 1573. The Roman Catholic Cardinal Robert Bellarmine replied on an equally high level with his *Disputations Concerning the Controversies of the Christian Faith* (1581–92).

Each skillful attack required a careful and impressive rebuttal. Leading Protestants were forced to study Roman Catholic Scholasticism in order to face its arguments. This led them to appreciate it and ultimately to imitate it, producing a kind of Protestant Scholasticism. (A century later Philipp Jakob Spener, the first great Pietist, believed that Scholasticism had so ruined Luther's Reformation that a major rescue operation was necessary.)

c. The Quest for the Fundamentals

Although the opposing parties usually expected one another to end up in hell, the close examination of one another's arguments and methods sometimes led to mutual appreciation. Since only a small number of the articles of belief were in dispute, the polemics made people aware of the large number of tenets all held in common. This then raised the question of whether the points in dispute were truly fundamental, for if not, then to split Christendom because of them was fratricidal. The magisterial Reformation agreed with the Roman Catholics on all those things the early councils had said were the substance of the Christian faith. No one could ignore the fact that at least some of the points in dispute between Catholics and Protestants, or between Lutherans and the Reformed, were trivial. If some were trivial, which ones were so fundamental that it was worth splitting the church, fighting, and perhaps even dying to protect them? The ongoing polemics of the century and a half following Luther's Ninety-five Theses forced Protestants and Catholics alike to try to define what they considered fundamentals. For the Catholics this was more natural than for the Protestants. Protestant emphasis on plenary, verbal inspiration made every statement of Scripture the Word of God, and Catholics promptly told them that therefore everything in the Bible must be held as equally important and equally fundamental. The Reformed slipped out of this trap more promptly than the Lutherans, who for a long time resisted the impulse to define some things as fundamental, others as secondary.

The effort to settle upon certain articles as the fundamentals of Christianity had positive and negative results. The positive results included helping believers to penetrate the noise and confusion of the polemical encounters and concentrate their attention on the essential teachings of their faith. In addition, defining a limited number of articles as fundamental gave the churches a more secure basis for excluding divisive teachers and their opinions. A negative effect was the creation of the impression that all of the nonfundamental articles—which included much of what the theologians had been quarreling about—were superfluous or even trivial.

There were three approaches to determining the fundamentals. The traditionalists simply took over the articles inherited from the Apostles' Creed and the great ecumenical creeds of the early centuries. Of course the Roman Catholic controversialists favored this approach; in addition, it was also used by Melanchthon and the Philippists. What is called the "liberal" approach—promoted by Jacobus Acontius—would actually be fundamentalistic in modern terminology, for Acontius wanted to limit the articles of faith to those things Scripture expressly requires. Most of the Lutherans were in what we may call the "positivist" group: taking Scripture as their starting point, they used reason and logic to build up a positive doctrinal structure. Their goal was a coherent body of dogmatics. They felt that the position of Acontius would lead to the loss of doctrinal substance; this is another way of saying that the Bible itself does not explicitly specify many doctrines that must be believed. Both the traditionalists and the positivists went beyond the explicit warrant of Scripture in building up their system of fundamentals; they did so because they felt that a comprehensive system of truth and logical consistency required it. Of course this is precisely what the early church fathers had done. It shows that, strictly speaking, the Reformation principle of *sola Scriptura* is not sufficient to produce a full-fledged dogmatic system. Whenever reformers seek to limit themselves narrowly to what Scripture explicitly requires, they wind up with a minimal system. Thus the radically scriptural principle of Acontius often leads to the pruning away of traditional doctrines that characterized later Protestant liberalism.

In his polemics against the Council of Trent, Chemnitz criticized the Catholic view of tradition as a source of revelation; nevertheless, he himself developed an approach analogous to it, contending that those scriptural doctrines that have been more fully developed and more clearly expounded in the course of church history are more important to the solid foundation of the Christian faith.[2] Thus even for the leading opponent of Trent with its traditionalism, tradition continued to play a role. The challenge that faced the traditionalist Lutherans was that of being able to appropriate what they considered the necessary elements in Christian tradition without succumbing to the arguments drawn by Catholicism from tradition in order to support its own claims.

3. IRENICS, OR "SYNCRETISM"

The seventeenth century was not only the century of bitter wars of religion, but also the century of irenicism (which, as we have seen, was often called "syncretism," a term that has taken on another, less positive meaning in our own day). The several branches of Protestants and the Roman Catholics with them would not have been able to engage in colloquia and disputations if they had not had a great deal in common. In the midst of bitter controversy, the adversaries could not fail to notice this fact. As they disputed with one another, the Protestants could not help being drawn together by the oppressive threat of a resurgent Roman Catholicism, backed by imperial power. Catholics and Protestants alike could not fail to recognize that they had much in common when faced with the threat of Turkish invasion or skeptical unbelief. During the late sixteenth and early seventeenth centuries, a number of theologians hopefully brought out works called *irenica* (from the Greek *eirene*, "peace"). Some of these works sought to reconcile Protestants with Roman Catholics, others Lutherans with Reformed, and a few endeavored to bring about an understanding between trinitarian Protestants and Socinians. Inasmuch as the Socinians had left the framework of Nicene Christianity, it appears that Reformation-era irenics, like modern ecumenicism, was sometimes willing to blur important differences in the effort to achieve at least a measure of apparent unity.

a. The Vincentian Canon

The goal of these irenic efforts was called syncretism. Our modern use of the word should not confuse us. In the seventeenth century, it did not signify a *pastiche* of different religions, but rather an alliance of essentially like-minded believers against unbelief. Erasmus, Zwingli, Melanchthon, Bucer, and Calvin all use the term to mean holding together against a common foe.

The Strassburg Reformer Martin Bucer had made attempts at achieving an irenic syncretism in the opening years of the Reformation. John Łaski made a similar effort among the divided and embattled Protestants of Poland. The moderate Roman Catholics Georg Witzel (1501–73) and George Cassander (1513–66) proposed a kind of irenic Catholicism to Emperor Maximilian II (ruled 1564–76). Cassander paraphrased the fifth-century canon of Vincent of Lérins, "We must hold to that which has been believed everywhere, at all times, and by everyone," and argued in favor of a "universal consensus of antiquity," reaching back to the years of imperially recognized Catholicism between the reign of the Emperor Constantine and the pontificate of Pope Gregory I.[3] Cassander assumed—with some justification—that the Protestants looked on the church of the early centuries as essentially sound and were willing to accept what it taught.

At the beginning of the sixteenth century, the deposed Roman Catholic archbishop of Spoleto, Marco Antonio de Dominis, also sought to reunite Protestants and Roman Catholics along Vincentian lines. He converted to Anglicanism in 1617 but returned to Roman Catholicism in 1622. Notwithstanding this return, he died in a Roman prison in 1624 and was posthumously condemned by the Inquisition. He conceived of the one true church as being composed of Eastern Orthodox, Roman Catholics, and orthodox Protestants. The only true and obligatory articles of faith are those contained in Scripture or else authoritatively transmitted by the early church in documentary form, not orally, as coming from the Apostles themselves. All other articles are superficial and should be rejected by all the churches.

From the nature of Roman Catholic traditionalism, it is apparent that the irenic solution of de Dominis would have changed Catholicism more than Protestantism. In 1631, another Roman Catholic, Kaspar Scioppius, attempted to bring about an understanding between Catholics and Protestants on the article of justification by faith, arguing that Luther's principle of *sola fide* was acceptable to the Roman church inasmuch as by it Luther meant not "mere" faith but the whole life of faith, which includes hope and love. Scioppius' well-intentioned efforts overlooked the fact that Protestants refused to accept his explanation of what is meant by *sola fide*. The Lutheran Nicholas Hunnius described it as a "tricky concealment of the established error, using honeyed and false words in order to get behind simple people and take them captive."[4] These few Catholic efforts lacked official backing and met with no real response on the part of Protestants. More important than any Protestant reaction to tentative Catholic overtures was the fact that the most important German Lutheran state, Electoral Saxony, preferred to make common cause with the Hapsburgs and thus effectively support the Counter-Reformation. The defection of Electoral Saxony from support of Protestant solidarity gravely weakened Protestantism, despite the fact that there was no open political rupture between the Lutheran and the Reformed estates before the outbreak of the Thirty Years' War. At the time, Lutheran controversialists were accusing the Calvinists of Mohammedanism, and the Calvinists charging the Lutherans with being carnivorous in their doctrine of the Lord's Supper. In 1602 the orthodox Lutheran Polycarp Leyser charged the Calvinists with sympathy for the "eastern Antichrist," Islam.[5] Thus orthodox Lutherans sought theological justification for the political decision of Lutheran Electoral Saxony to support the Hapsburgs at the expense of Protestant interests. Of course, as long as their own safety seemed to be guaranteed by the Peace of Augsburg, the Lutherans had no particular interest in making common cause with the Calvinists.

Accordingly, it was the Calvinists who made the first serious efforts on the Protestant side to achieve a measure of interconfessional unity. The first appeal was made by the *Irenicum* of Franz Junius of Heidelberg, published in Geneva in 1613, but it was too general and contained too little theological substance to impress the Lutherans. In the Palatinate, the most important Calvinistic principality of Germany, a more serious effort was made in 1606, the *True-Hearted Admonition of the Palatine Churches to All Other*

Evangelical Churches in Germany.[6] The Palatine Christians pointed out, correctly, that the papacy had never accepted the Peace of Augsburg, and that when the Catholics had regained power in Aachen and Fulda, they forgot their tolerance and expelled the "protected" Lutherans as well as the unprotected Calvinists. They attempted to persuade the Lutherans that their Reformed view of the eucharist was not sufficiently different from the Lutheran to warrant refusal to stand together against Rome. In 1615 David Pareus published another *Irenicum,* arguing that Lutherans and Calvinists are agreed on all essential fundamental doctrines as well as in most of the articles of theology and therefore could and should unite against Rome; he proposed convening a general synod for the purpose. He was vigorously opposed by Leonhard Hütter of Wittenberg; Hütter rejected Pareus' distinction between fundamental doctrines and theological articles. For Hütter, the whole Bible was fundamental.

An encounter did take place a few years after Pareus' *Irenicum,* between the Reformed court chaplain Paul Steinius of Kassel and the Lutheran theologian Balthasar Mentzer, whom we have already met as the protagonist of a moderate Christology against the "ultraorthodox" of Tübingen. Steinius preached a "peace sermon" in Kassel on June 22, 1618, to which Mentzer replied the following year with his *Well-Intentioned Reminder.* Mentzer denied that the two groups shared the same foundation of faith, but acknowledged a unity nevertheless, and called for "mutual service . . . and upright love."[7] Compared to the bitter denunciation with which Hütter had replied to Pareus, the exchange between Mentzer and Steinius was relatively cordial, although neither side compromised its position. Hütter had died in 1616, and by the outbreak of the Thirty Years' War Lutherans and Calvinists were treating each other with relative courtesy. Unfortunately for the hopes of the Reformed party in Germany for an accommodation with the more powerful Lutherans, the Arminian controversy reawakened Lutheran apprehensions the irenicists had tried to allay. Observing the rigor with which the orthodox predestinarian Calvinists suppressed the Arminians, despite the fact that the Arminians were closer to them on most doctrinal matters than the Lutherans, led the orthodox Lutherans to fear that if they tolerated the Reformed in their territories and churches, the Reformed would soon try to take over. This reveals a surprising lack of self-confidence on the part of the orthodox Lutherans, one that perhaps stems from a subconscious awareness of the fact that Luther and his followers, after launching the Reformation, had rather abruptly checked its progress. Confronted by all kinds of radicals, Luther and his followers felt that they had taken the Reformation far enough, and that no one should be allowed to carry it further. For the Reformed, of course, as for the radicals and later for the Pietists, this seemed to be a halfway measure.

These efforts at unity on the eve of the the Thirty Years' War were doomed by the apprehension of the Lutherans and the hidden ambitions of the Calvinists. Nevertheless, many Calvinists were shocked at the way the Lutherans were prepared to allow the Catholics a free hand against Calvinism provided their own rights were spared. In the destructive but often indecisive fighting that characterized the early years of the war, the fact that the Protestants could not unite enabled the Catholic party to gain a series of victories, culminating in a major defeat for the German and Bohemian Protestants in 1629. On the basis of the ascendancy thus gained, the German imperial government immediately published the so-called Edict of Restitution, reestablishing Roman Catholicism as the official religion in all Protestant territories, without regard for whether they were Reformed or Lutheran. Germany's Lutherans suddenly realized the danger they had brought on themselves by failing to stand together with the numerically smaller Reformed group.

The eventual survival of Protestantism in Germany was secured only by timely military intervention, first by the Lutheran Swedes, then by Catholic France, which was more interested in weakening the Hapsburgs than in reestablishing Catholicism in Germany. Nevertheless, the Lutheran and Reformed theologians did make an effort to come to an agreement, holding a colloquy in Leipzig in 1631. Agreement was reached on a broad range of issues, but controversy continued over the presence of Christ in the eucharist and, with less vigor, over whether a person, once elect, can fall from grace.[8] Unfortunately for the optimism that the Leipzig Colloquy generated, the cause of reunion was promptly taken up by a well-meaning but inept Scottish Presbyterian, John Durie. Durie spent four decades working for reunion, traveling all over Germany. Unfortunately, he aroused more suspicion than trust. He met with some encouragement among the Swedish Lutherans, but the Germans were almost entirely unresponsive.

b. Socinian Influences

Irenicism began with efforts by Christologically orthodox Calvinists to persuade the Lutherans to make common cause with them. Soon the Socinians—who by now had become distinctly unitarian—joined in, more in the effort to gain tolerance and support from the orthodox Protestants than with any expectation of forming a united front against the Roman Catholics. A first effort was made by the remarkable Jacobus Acontius, the same man who proposed limiting the fundamental articles to statements definitely required by Scripture. Acontius may have studied under Melanchthon in Wittenberg; he spent the final years of his life in London during the reign of Queen Elizabeth I, where he attended the Strangers' Church, which had once been headed by John Łaski.

Because Acontius believed that only those doctrines explicitly required by Scripture constituted the fundamentals of truly Christian faith, he accepted all the major Protestant confessions as orthodox and urged that all Protestants work together. He accepted the teachings of the Apostles' Creed, but charged that it did not distinguish true believers from the followers of Satan, inasmuch as it was also used by the papacy. Acontius drew up a creed of his own, in which he omitted the Nicene doctrine of consubstantiality. It is not clear whether he actually rejected it or merely considered it impossible to prove from Scripture, but his reductionist approach resembles that later adopted by the Socinians. George Williams considers Acontius a forerunner of Deism rather than a Unitarian.[9]

The major doctrinal statement of the Polish-based Socinians is the famous Racovian Catechism of 1605, which Valentine Schmalz completed after the death of Faustus Socinus. Schmalz dedicated a German translation to the University of Wittenberg in 1608 and a Latin version to King James I of England, the patron of the Authorized (King James) Version of the Bible, in 1609. (King James denounced the gift as a book of Satan.) Like Acontius, the Socinians reduced the number of necessary articles of faith to a minimum. This reduction seemed perfectly reasonable to them inasmuch as their primary emphasis was on an enlightened understanding and a moral life, not on articles to be believed. The major significance of the Socinians to the question of syncretism lies in their complex relationship to the Reformed and the Lutherans. Because they considered themselves Christians and wanted to be recognized and accepted as such, they sought to minimize the importance of their differences with more orthodox Protestants. This they did very simply by denying the importance of any articles on which they differed. The Protestants, and especially the Reformed, were concerned to show that they were not Socinians, and consequently had to emphasize the essential importance of precisely those articles. In the same way, the Lutherans found it possible to respond to Socinian reductionism only by reemphasizing the fundamental articles of faith.

As long as the Socinians were centered in Poland and the country maintained its policy of religious tolerance, they could simplify and rewrite creeds and confessions as they wished. When they became active in the Netherlands, however, the Socinians proved an embarrassment to the Arminians. Like the Socinians, the Arminians felt that their survival in the Netherlands depended on their being able to persuade the dominant Calvinists that they were theologically and Christologically orthodox and that they ought to enjoy toleration; unlike the Socinians, they really were orthodox, at least at the beginning. The Arminians were in the awkward position of espousing complete religious toleration for all Protestant Christians on the one hand while trying to prove that the Socinians were not Christian on the other. Like the Socinians, the Arminians were more indifferent to creeds and confessional statements than were either the Calvinists or the Lutherans, for they stressed how one lived rather than what one believed.

Arminians and Socinians combined in trying to secure toleration from the majority rather than attaining unity on the basis of a consensus on fundamentals, which would have been difficult for them in any case. The modern ecumenical movement has set minimal doctrinal standards for membership (the Unitarians, for example, are not admitted), like the Lutheran and Reformed irenicists, but in practice it behaves rather as the Socinians would have wished and is more interested in practical matters, such as development, than in doctrine.

c. Arminian Efforts

In the German Palatinate, the Reformed Church called for a general synod to bring all Protestants together. At almost the same time, Jacob Arminius made the same appeal in the Netherlands (1605). Unlike the Germans, however, Arminius included the proviso that the majority (i.e. the orthodox Reformed of the Netherlands) ought not to be permitted to impose its views on the minority, to which his followers belonged. The famous legal scholar Hugo Grotius (1583–1645), the founder of the discipline of international law, joined in the appeal to unity made by the moderate German Catholic George Cassander.[10] Grotius' attitude was typical of Arminian irenicism: on the one hand, he specifically reaffirmed disputed doctrines such as the Virgin Birth and the Second Coming; on the other, he emphasized that it is the commands and promises of Christ that form the basis of salvation, not the doctrines of the Trinity or of the two natures of Christ, which were not required articles of faith until the time of Constantine. Grotius, like the more radical Anabaptists, considered the establishment of Christianity an evil.

After Grotius, another Arminian, Stephen Curcellaeus, declared that it was a serious error to require belief in every doctrine that can be proved from Scripture: only those teachings Scripture itself declares to be necessary for salvation, and the conclusions that are correctly drawn from them, may be required of Christians. Among the doctrines he considered necessary Curcellaeus named the doctrine that the Bible is the Word of God, the doctrine of God and his attributes, of Creation, of God's providential government of the world (but not including predestination!), and of his intention to judge men, made in his image, rewarding the virtuous and punishing the evil. On the other hand, it was not necessary to believe that God subsists in three coequal divine Persons; in fact, it cannot be argued from the Bible. It is necessary to believe that Jesus Christ is a true man, conceived of the Holy Spirit and born of the Virgin Mary, and also that he is the Son of God and is himself God, although subordinate to the Father. The way in which the two natures are united cannot be determined, and Nestorius cannot be condemned for his rejection of the unbiblical expression *theotokos*, "Mother of God."[11] Curcellaeus had a detailed understanding of the three offices of Christ as Prophet, Priest, and King, and of his vicarious sacrifices through which Christians are reconciled with God.

After setting these moderate requirements, Curcellaeus weakened them by calling for mutual tolerance among those who could not agree. Philip of Limborch, the great systematic theologian of early Arminianism, went further than Curcellaeus in making doctrinal requirements a function of the authority of the church, rather than a deduction from an infallible Bible. For him heresy was a disciplinary concept related to church authority rather than a theological concept depending upon biblical truth. Philip broke with the accepted view of both Catholics and most Protestants, namely, that the civil government has the duty to enforce right doctrine, and made the enforcement of doctrine purely a matter of church discipline. He thus became the architect of the modern doctrine of religious tolerance, which at least originally was not based on indifference to questions of right doctrine, but on the conviction that such questions lie outside the province of secular government. He saw heresy as a threat to the church, to be opposed by the church, but not as a threat to the social order.

Like the more radical Socinians, the Arminians emphasized life rather than faith. They did not agree with the Lutherans and the Reformed that faith, in the sense of sincerely believed right doctrine, provides the motivation for holy living. Later Arminians began to look on salvation as a reward for a Christian life, although this idea would have been as odious to Arminius himself as to Calvin. The Socinians were less attached to doctrinal specifics than even the Arminians; from the beginning, they taught that salvation is achieved by a godly and moral life.

This Arminian willingness to reduce the number of necessary doctrines to a minimum and emphasize the moral life as a means of attaining harmony among different Christian groups was not at all like what their Lutheran contemporaries wanted. The Lutherans wanted the necessary doctrinal requirements to be absolutely clear and settled, so that it would be evident that all Christians stand in the same place vis-à-vis the unbelieving world. In contrast, the trinitarian Arminians, like the unitarian Socinians, downgraded doctrine and emphasized morals. Their goal was to embrace as many people as possible in their efforts to create a Christian community with which Christ would be pleased. Although the Arminians and the Socinians differed significantly on theology and Christology, their practical emphasis on personal and public morality and the task of building a Christian community paved the way for extensive contacts in the future.

4. THE FUNDAMENTALS

As a practical matter, the Arminians and Socinians sought to facilitate cooperation among the differing confessions by cutting down on the number of doctrines they held to be fundamental. Both the Lutherans and the Roman Catholics, by contrast, sought to define enough articles as fundamental to justify their own existence as independent churches. Lutherans, Roman Catholics, and Reformed Christians, unlike the Arminians, were not seeking a lowest common denominator, a doctrinal minimum all would accept, but sought rather to establish as many doctrines as possible in common so that disputed points would be reduced to a minimum. Given this difference, it is apparent that what the orthodox Protestants and the Roman Catholics hoped to accomplish by "syncretism" was quite different from the goals of the Arminians and Socinians: the more orthodox parties sought a mutually acceptable agreement, the more liberal mutual toleration.

Acontius' approach to the question of fundamental doctrines has the merit of simplicity. By contrast, although both Lutherans and Reformed claimed that they operated on the principle of *sola Scriptura*, in practice they tended to take over the heritage of the ecumenical creeds and the first councils, and then to try to show that this traditional faith was in fact altogether Scriptural. It is easier to take the received doctrines of the creeds and attempt to show that they are consistent with Scripture than it is to begin with the Scripture and re-create the creeds. Like the Lutherans and the Reformed, and unlike the Arminians and the Socinians, the Roman Catholics had an elaborate structure of doctrines they considered fundamental, but in practice they tended to adopt a somewhat more Arminian policy and stress the obedience and good works of the pious life more than the exercise of doctrinal faith.

a. Lutheran Considerations

The single-minded Lutheran concentration on justification by faith and the Lutherans' comparative disregard for obedience and good works created problems for them in their disputes with the Catholics. It naturally came to be of tremendous importance to define precisely what does belong to saving faith and what does not, as by implication an incorrect or incomplete faith could imperil one's salvation. The Roman Catholics were not slow to put the finger on this tender spot. In the Religious Colloquium of Regensburg in 1601, the Jesuit Adam Tanner told his Lutheran counterparts that their Scripture principle required them to take everything Scripture teaches as an article of faith, and the fact that they rejected the Catholic concept of implicit faith meant that Lutherans had to know all Scripture teaches in order to be able to believe it explicitly.

The orthodox Lutheran Aegidius Hunnius accepted the proposition that all Scripture must be believed, but then proposed to make a distinction between things to be believed—i.e. all Scripture teaches—and things that are to be considered *articles of faith*. Thus the Bible teaches that Judah committed incest with his daughter-in-law Tamar (Gen. 38:1–26), and this story is true and must be believed, but it is not an article of faith. Tanner proposed instead that it is the task of the church as a whole to know and believe everything Scripture teaches, down to the details, but that this task need not be fulfilled by every Christian. All the individual has to do is to assent to the truth of the body of doctrine held in trust by the church. Thus for the Roman Catholic, faith was primarily a matter of accepting the teaching authority of the church and conceding, in advance, that all the church teaches is true. For the Lutheran, faith involves one's personal trust in God, not merely acceptance of certain articles plus the acknowledgment that whatever the Roman Catholic Church teaches besides must be true. Nevertheless, as a practical matter it is impossible for anyone to know all Scripture teaches, and hence it is impossible for anyone to have explicit faith in every scriptural assertion. Consequently, in practice the Lutheran, like the Catholic, must be willing to state that some articles belong to the substance of the faith and therefore must be known and explicitly believed, while others are secondary. The difficulty for Hunnius and the other orthodox Lutherans came in trying to show scriptural justification for settling on certain traditional articles—most of them also stressed by Catholics as well as by Calvinists—and reducing the rest to a secondary place.

In 1608 the Socinians of Poland had dedicated the German translation of their Racovian Catechism to the University of Wittenberg. The faculty of theology produced a series of replies, the most thorough being that of Balthasar Meisner in 1623. Meisner objected to the Socinians' tendency to call important questions mere matters of individual opinion and decision;[12] inasmuch as he and other Lutherans felt called to defend as fundamental several doctrines brushed aside by the Socinians, the Socinians were to some extent setting the agenda for the Lutherans. Like the Roman Catholics at Regensburg in 1601, in theory Meisner called for the acceptance of everything that is taught in the Bible. However, he held that it is not necessary to know all the historical material in the Bible in order to be saved.

Both the Roman Catholics and the orthodox Lutherans agreed in principle that it is not necessary to know the entire content of the Bible to be saved, and both required Christians to acknowledge, in principle, the truth of everything Scripture teaches, whether they know a particular scriptural teaching or not. Because they denied the concept of justification by faith alone, Catholics were willing to settle for an implicit faith in teachings one does not know explicitly, but Lutherans found implicit faith to be a contradiction of the very idea of faith. However, inasmuch as it is a practical impossibility for the ordinary Christian to know everything the Bible teaches, the Lutherans had to set forth a limited and manageable number of fundamentals that have to be believed in order for one to have saving faith. This is precisely what Gerhard did. It is also what the Socinians did, but they did it as a matter of convenience, because they did not believe in justification by faith at all. Unfortunately, because Meisner followed the policy of defending as fundamental whatever traditional articles the Socinians attacked, rather than trying to determine them on the basis of explicit biblical principles, his set of fundamental principles is not systematic and comprehensive.

Meisner's successor in the effort to set forth the fundamentals of Lutheranism was Nicholas Hunnius (1585–1643), who as a sixteen-year-old had accompanied his father to the Regensburg Colloquy. Even before Meisner produced his reply, Hunnius wrote an *Examination of the Errors of the Photinians* (1618). This abusive name for the Socinians was derived from that of the ninth-century Greek patriarch Photius, who had quarreled with Pope Nicholas I over the *filioque* added to the Nicene Creed. It is a strange way to designate the Socinians, for Patriarch Photius was orthodox, despite his differences with Pope Nicholas, while the Socinians rejected the basic orthodox creeds. Hunnius went on to write a *Diaskepsis* (Examination) of the fundamental differences between the Lutherans and the Calvinists.[13] Actually the *Diaskepsis* stresses the points of agreement between the two major Protestant confessions and criticizes the Roman Catholics and the Socinians.

Unfortunately for Hunnius' hopes for Lutheran-Calvinistic cooperation, the Dutch Calvinist Synod of Dordt (1618–19) took vigorous action to repress the Arminians, giving Hunnius the impression that it was not possible to collaborate with Calvinists unless one was willing to grant them every disputed point. Consequently, he turned against projects for reunion. His last major work, written in 1641, opposed the efforts of John Durie to unify the German Lutherans and Calvinists in the desperate situation of the Thirty Years' War. Durie, a Scottish Presbyterian, believed that he was called to reconcile the quarreling Protestants, and traveled incessantly about Germany in his effort to do so. Nicholas Hunnius, who had at first been willing to describe a few doctrines as fundamental and others as nonessential, eventually reverted to the view held by his father Aegidius, namely, that Christians must give assent to everything Scripture teaches, not merely to fundamentals. The work of Andreas Sennert in 1666 shows how much anti-Calvinistic sentiments were influencing Lutheranism. Sennert defined thirty-three articles of faith, of which he called only the first three fundamental. They were articles that distinguished the Lutherans from the Reformed: the universal grace and mercy of God, the universal merit of Jesus Christ, and the universal calling by the Word.[14] The classic tenets of the ancient creeds, which the Lutherans shared with the Calvinists, as well as the doctrine of justification, which they also had in common, he reduced to secondary importance.

b. Calvinist Responses

Gisbert Voet (1588–1676), the outstanding Calvinist Scholastic of the Netherlands, wrote *On Fundamental Articles and Errors* in 1637. In it he espoused the position put forward by the Jesuit Tanner at Regensburg in 1601, stating that all the articles of faith—i.e. everything the Bible teaches—are fundamental and necessary for salvation. In general, this has been the theoretical position of the Reformed party as well as of many later biblicists who are not bound to a specific confessional tradition. In practice, however, the Reformed, like the Catholics and the Lutherans, do emphasize certain fundamentals.

In 1661, the Reformed professor of theology Sebastian Curtius of Marburg made a distinction between the foundation of knowledge and the foundation of faith. For faith, only those articles that relate directly to salvation in Christ are to be considered fundamental and thus necessary. The foundation of knowledge is the Scripture, and no one can be saved who rejects the foundation, but it is not necessary that one's explicit faith extend to everything contained in Scripture.[15] In Reformed Zurich, Johann Heinrich Heidegger opposed the Catholic challenge to prescribe the number of articles necessary for salvation, and reasserted that because Scripture is perfect, all it contains must be believed explicitly. In practice, he relented and admitted that not everything need be known explicitly. Roman Catholics continued to exploit this ambiguity in the Protestant understanding of saving faith.

5. THE PIETIST IMPULSE

Georg Calixtus (1586–1656), professor of theology at the newly founded University of Helmstedt (closed down by the Napoleonic Wars), developed a mediating theology seeking an understanding with the Calvinists; like Melanchthon and the Philippists before him, Calixtus was somewhat of a traditionalist and sought to show that Lutheranism was essentially in harmony with what the early church had believed. By so doing, he weakened some of the distinctives of Lutheranism, winning praise from some Roman Catholics and hostility from the defenders of Lutheran orthodoxy such as Johann Gerhard and the prolific systematic theologian Abraham Calov (1612–86). Like John Łaski, Calixtus has found admirers among modern ecumenists.[16] The Helmstedt theologians were interested in the natural sciences and mathematics as well as theology; some of their interests were carried further by the great mathematician Gottfried Wilhelm von Leibniz (1646–1716), who also attempted to promote the syncretistic cause by theological dialogue.

a. Reform Orthodoxy:
A Step Toward Pietism

The efforts of dogmaticians such as Gerhard and Calov produced impressive structures of orthodox theology, while at the same time the Helmstedters and others extended their offers of fellowship to Catholics and Calvinists, but all of this theological activity did little to meet the spiritual needs of ordinary people. Building on the impulses of Johann Arndt's "practical Christianity," a school of Lutheranism arose that tried to combine orthodox dogmatics with practical popular religion. Called reform orthodoxy, it forms a kind of bridge to Lutheran Pietism.

The first important step taken by reform orthodoxy in the direction that led to Pietism was the effort to implement Luther's concept of the priesthood of all believers. In practice, Protestantism was as heavily dominated by professors and pastors as Catholicism was by bishops and priests. Luther retained the principle of individual confession to the minister (*Ohrenbeichte*). Whatever its positive features, individual confession tended to set the pastor off from his people. During and immediately after the Thirty Years' War, three Lutherans, Johann Matthias Meyfart (1590–1642), John Quistorp (1584–1648), and Theophilus Grossgebauer (1627–61), attempted to bring Lutheranism closer to the people.

The idea of the priesthood of all believers also had democratic implications for society. Johann Valentin Andreä (1586–1654), influenced by the Utopias of the English Catholic Thomas More (1478–1535) and the Dominican Tomasso Campanella (1568–1639), proposed creating a kind of Christian republic, a "Christopolis," called a little "colony of the Jerusalem built by Arndt."[17] This brief flash of democratic social ideas among Lutherans— who otherwise were quite committed to princely authority—was based on the idea that those fit to exercise spiritual authority in the priesthood of all believers are also fit to assume civil responsibilities as well. The Calvinists, by contrast, wanted to limit the authority of rulers because of Calvin's emphasis on the depravity of man.

Reform orthodoxy was a great attempt by Lutherans to produce perceptible results in society based on the evangelical doctrines Luther had succeeded in establishing in many German states. Luther briefly toyed with the idea of an *ecclesiola in ecclesia*, a little church of personally committed Christians within the bigger church of formal Christians, but he soon adapted himself to the idea of a *Landeskirche,* or "territorial (established) church." Instead of devoting themselves to helping their parishioners understand and apply the Gospel principles Luther had rediscovered, many Lutheran theologians expended most of their energy in quarrels with representatives of other confessions as well as with one another. The new Protestant emphasis on academic erudition removed the pastors and their controversies as far from the people and their concerns as the priests had ever been. As early as 1580, Lutheranism was plainly exhibiting symptoms of "dead orthodoxy."

Not only was the church failing to transform society, but the Thirty Years' War gave many the feeling that society itself was collapsing. Inspired by the brief success of the English Puritans, reform orthodoxy thought that it could transform German society by getting Christians to practice their religion consistently. In 1661 Grossgebauer published his appeal, the *Watchman's Voice from Ruined Zion.*[18] The movement's emphasis on the individual and his personal life marks a transition to the motifs of Lutheran Pietism.

b. Church Music

Martin Luther introduced meaningful hymns sung in the language of the people as one of the fundamental aspects of Reformation worship. The first phase of the Reformation took the universal church out of the center of attention and replaced it with the local congregation; this second wave of Reformation, if we may call it that, redirected attention from the congregation to the individual believer. Christians began to sing "I" rather than "we." The hymn, originally emphasized by Luther in the effort to enable all the people to participate in worship and experience a sense of unity, came to be the expression of the individual in his quest for God; in its extreme form, it became the vehicle for an individualistic preoccupation with the self.

c. Jakob Boehme

Individualism in religion often takes the form of mysticism. Both orthodoxy and Pietism were influenced by a man whose religious contribution defies classification, Jakob Boehme (1575–1624). His mysticism provides a link between the Reformation with its concern for doctrine and the nineteenth-century Romantic movement, which largely abandoned doctrine for sentiment. Under the impression that he was inspired by the Holy Spirit, Boehme broke with the Reformation standard of historical-grammatical interpretation of Scripture and began to look on the Cross and other specific Christian concepts and symbols as universals: the Cross was not important as history, but as the "conjunction of opposites," a view reminiscent of Gnosticism. In 1613 a heresy trial ordered Boehme to keep silent, but disciples continued to flock to him; Boehme saw himself as a catalyst for the final apocalyptic conflict between Christ and Satan.

A biography of Boehme was written by Abraham von Franckenberg (1593–1652), celebrating him as a great prophet and spiritual leader. Franckenberg, a Protestant, introduced another Protestant, Johannes Scheffler (1624–77), to Boehme's works. Scheffler thought that mysticism such as Boehme's could bridge the doctrinal barriers between the confessions. When orthodox Lutherans protested, Scheffler abandoned Lutheranism and became a Catholic, writing under the pen name "Angelus Silesius." Scheffler's disciple Quirinus Kuhlmann (1651–89) proclaimed Boehme the last prophet and the bearer of the Eternal Gospel; for this heresy, he was burned by the Catholic authorities. Kuhlmann was briefly associated with Gottfried Arnold (1666–1714), author of the massive *Impartial History of the Church and of Heretics* (1699–1700). He too saw mysticism as the solution to the fragmentation of the church.

6. PIETISM AND ORTHODOXY

Syncretism had failed to reach its goal of attaining a Christian consensus; as a compromise movement, it could not cope with the fervent commitment of so many orthodox Lutherans, Calvinists, and Roman Catholics. The only way to bring them together was not by persuading them to agree on a kind of least-common-denominator confession, but by giving them something that inspired them more than orthodox doctrines. Reform orthodoxy, without abandoning correct doctrines, had turned its attention to practical Christianity; Jakob Boehme and some of the other mystics seemed ready to abandon the distinctives of the various orthodox traditions altogether. In the latter part of the seventeenth century a new movement arose, one that would affect the future of Protestantism and through it of European civilization as much as the Reformation and the Enlightenment. For many, the new movement, known as Pietism, represented the revitalization of Christianity; for some, including the movement's founder, Philipp Jakob Spener, it represented the fulfillment of what the Reformation had promised. For others, including the modern neoorthodox theologian Karl Barth (1886–1968), it represents the abandonment of the church and orthodox doctrine and is one of the most divisive forces within Christendom. Like Karl Barth, Francis A. Schaeffer (b. 1912) considers Pietism religious individualism and sentimentality carried to a dangerous extreme, although Schaeffer is more positive than Barth in evaluating its accomplishments.[19]

From our perspective, Pietism continued what the Reformation had begun in making the concept of heresy virtually irrelevant. The Reformation in effect legitimatized and officially established permanent divisions within Christianity, something often in evidence but never accepted before the sixteenth century. When one denomination's orthodoxy is another's heresy, the concept of heresy as an objective deviation from a generally accepted Christian consensus becomes unworkable. Pietism made religion so much a personal matter that questions about doctrine often degenerated into mere questions of personal opinion. The original Pietists were in fact orthodox, as many Pietists have been through the succeeding years, but they directed the attention of Christians away from orthodoxy and heresy to piety and personal discipline.

a. Pietism: A Historical Problem

The Reformers saw themselves as recovering the authentic faith of the New Testament, and to a lesser degree of the early church. The magisterial Reformers such as Luther, Zwingli, Calvin, and Archbishop Thomas Cranmer (1489–1556), despite their principle of *sola Scriptura,* took over the Christian tradition in varying degrees and resisted the efforts of the "fanatics" to re-create the primitive church of the first century. The result, of course, was the reappearance of an orthodox theology and a highly structured church life, one that failed to meet some of the spiritual needs and desires that had led to the beginning of the Reformation in the first place.

A century and a half after Luther posted his theses, it was no longer merely the radicals who felt that his Reformation had ended in halfway measures before it had been fully achieved. Those who felt called upon to resume the work of Reformation believed that they were continuing what Luther began. Just as Luther had postulated that the true faith of the first Christians had been obscured by layers of nonbiblical tradition and Scholastic theology, so they felt that Luther's initiatives has been submerged in a new Scholasticism. The classic historian of Pietism Albrecht Ritschl analyzes it differently, and sees Pietism not as the fulfillment of the Reformation but as a renewal of the impulse of medieval mysticism.[20]

Which view is correct? Is Pietism a fulfillment of Lutheranism or a return to mysticism? The question is complicated by the fact that Luther himself was drawn to the mystics, who seemed to him to be more authentic examples of Christian faith and life than the Scholastic theologians and philosophers of the Middle Ages. It is probably correct to say that to the extent that Luther represented individualism in religion and opposed the formal and collective religion of traditional Catholicism, Pietism continued in the path he pioneered. To the extent that he represented a new orthodoxy and institutionalized forms, Pietism represented a revolt and immediately came under attack from Luther's orthodox followers.

b. *Principles of Pietism*

The practical Christianity of Arndt, reform orthodoxy, and mysticism all contributed to the origins of Pietism. Each of these currents sought to develop the practical implications of formally held faith, the Christian life, or the so-called *praxis pietatis,* "practice of piety," which became the fundamental concern of Pietism. Reform orthodoxy, as we recall, had made the effort to reform all of "Christian" society in a way that if successful would have produced utopian results. Pietism gave up this endeavor, and concentrated on what we call the principle of the *ecclesiola in ecclesia,* the "little church within the church." Luther himself had had inclinations to establish the *ecclesiola* principle as part of his work of Reformation, but he soon determined to follow the opposite principle of a territorial church.

The Pietist movement thus did achieve at least one of the goals Luther once envisaged: the creation of a spiritually active, deeply committed, restricted fellowship of true and obedient believers within the fold of the more prosaic, conventional, and frequently indifferent territorial church. But inasmuch as Pietism only put into practice on a limited scale what orthodox Protestantism in theory expected from all church members, i.e. from the whole population of a "Christian" state, its very existence was an affront to the orthodox ministry. If the church were effective, there would be no place for conventicles of the serious-minded; to undertake to form them, no matter how tactfully the project is presented, is always an affront to established orthodoxy.

c. *The Beginnings*

In a sense all serious Christianity must be in a measure Pietistic, and so it is difficult to speak of the beginnings of Pietism. The expression came into use with Philipp Spener and August Hermann Francke, late in the seventeenth century, but elements we now recognize as Pietistic had begun to appear several decades earlier, in the Reformed churches of the Netherlands. Gisbert Voet (1588–1676), called the "Dutch pope" because of his widely recognized spiritual authority, gathered a small group of Christians seeking to conform their lives to the laws of God; they were encouraged in "precision," which became an important concern of later Pietists and anticipates the approach of the Methodists.

Jean de Labadie (1610–74), a French Jesuit who embraced the Reformed faith and sought refuge in Geneva for a time, attempted to found a congregation there consisting only of members whose lives gave evidence that they were predestinated to salvation. Later, in Holland, he became the pastor of a French-speaking congregation in Middelburg, which he eventually led to separate from the established, Reformed church. The congregation he established continued in existence in German East Frisia for a number of decades after his death; it practiced a limited and voluntary Christian communism.

Labadie was rather a legalist, and a kind of "voluntary" or supposedly spontaneous attention to law is a characteristic feature of both early and modern Pietism. A more mystical approach was represented by the Dutch ministers William and Gerhard Teelinck; like the more legalistic Labadie, they urged separation from the hypocrisy and indifference of the established church, although formally they remained within it. This Netherlandish precursor to German Pietism was motivated by the typically Calvinist interest in having the life of the congregation match its profession of faith; where it differed from Calvin was in abandoning the effort to secure such conformity from all the members of a territorial church, and in trying to achieve it on a more limited scale in a separatist congregation. "Precisionism" and "puritanism" are terms used to describe the efforts of Voet and the other Dutch separatists.

Between the beginnings of the Dutch conventicle movement and the birth of true Pietism in Germany lies the terrible devastation of the Thirty Years' War. For some, it was the war itself that furnished the decisive impulse to transform reform orthodoxy into Pietism. A new edition of Arndt's *True Christianity* was published by Philipp Jakob Spener (1635–1705) in 1675, the signal for the beginning of the new movement. Spener's feeling that he was building on the heritage of reform orthodoxy is indicated by his wish that Johann Valentin Andreä could be brought back to life.

d. Philipp Jakob Spener

Although a number of currents and impulses that resemble those of Pietism had been active in northern European Protestantism for decades, the movement properly so called originated with Spener. As a student of theology, Spener studied both Luther and the literature of English Puritanism. He visited Basel, Geneva, and Lyons, and came to know Jean de Labadie and his conventicle movement. In 1663 Spener was called to Strassburg, in 1666 to Frankfurt. He gathered small groups of zealous young people around him in what came to be called *collegia pietatis*, "colleges of piety." He wrote a preface to his new edition of Arndt's *True Christianity;* this preface proved so popular that it was soon published separately as *Pia Desideria* (Pious Desires), with the subtitle "Hearty Desire for a God-Pleasing Improvement of the True Evangelical Churches Together with Some Simple Christian Proposals to That End." Abraham Calov, the most eminent orthodox Lutheran dogmatician of the day, welcomed Spener's *Pious Desires*.

Spener made six specific proposals, most of which would appeal to any serious-minded Christian pastor: first, he called for serious and intensive personal Bible study; second, for putting the ideal of the priesthood of all believers into practice; third, for attention to the duties of brotherly love; fourth, for an end to theological polemics; fifth, for a reformation of theological education; and sixth, for sermons intended to build up the hearers rather than display the learning of the preacher. This essay became the manifesto of the Pietists.

Spener wanted his little colleges of piety to remain within the church, but some of his friends began to separate from it. Spener, by contrast, repeatedly assured church and civil authorities that his program was not separatistic. In 1686 Elector John George III of Saxony called Spener to Dresden as court chaplain, the most prestigious post in German Lutheranism. When tension with the Lutheran Elector developed, Spener turned to the Reformed Duke of Brandenburg, who gave him a similar appointment in Berlin. Spener's willingness to move from Lutheran Dresden to Calvinist Berlin revealed that confessional distinctives were not of primary importance to him. Soon afterward, the new Saxon elector, Augustus the Strong, accepted Catholicism in order to become King of Poland. The Prussian ruling house became patrons of the Pietists until the reign of the skeptical King Frederick the Great (ruled 1740–86), the friend of Voltaire.

Spener thought he knew exactly where he belonged in the history of the church, which he divided into three-hundred-year eras. The first, golden age ended with Constantine and the Council of Nicaea in 325. Then came the age of imperial patronage, followed by Scholasticism. The fourth, beginning with the rise of mysticism, brought relief from the decadence and corruption of the medieval papacy and Scholastic theology. The fifth period, beginning with Luther, was a great improvement, but Luther's Reformation extended to doctrine only, not to life. Spener took on the task of reforming life to correspond to Luther's reformation of doctrine. The rise of Protestant Scholasticism had stopped the Reformation; Spener and his allies were determined to start it moving again. His view of the Roman church and the papacy was as critical as Luther's: the pope, in his eyes, was putting himself in Christ's place and deserved the title of Antichrist. Rome's greatest failure was the promotion of reason and philosophy instead of knowledge of the Scripture.

Spener admired Luther and considered his teaching correct, but not carried through to a proper conclusion. Due to Luther's failure to reform Christian life, a new Scholasticism arose. Theology flourished at the universities, but children were not taught the catechism. Luther's successors had virtually abandoned his concept of the priesthood of all believers. While the most faithful of Luther's successors wrangled constantly with one another and with non-Lutherans in polemical disputations, Spener and his Pietists abandoned polemics to concentrate on practical, social needs. As a result they gained the appreciation of the secular world, where the more orthodox theologians had harvested antagonism.

The first Pietists believed with all their heart, but because they did not quarrel about doctrines, their conduct led others to think that doctrine is less important than orthodoxy has always claimed. By making religion increasingly individualistic and by being relatively unconcerned about doctrine, the Pietists helped to make the old distinction between orthodoxy and heresy seem artificial and irrelevant to those who came after them.

e. Spener's Successors: Francke and Zinzendorf

Spener and his friends generated tremendous energy, as great as that which marked the beginning of the Reformation or the founding of the mendicant orders in the Middle Ages. They founded institutions for orphans and the aged; they established schools and published prolifically; they engaged in personal evangelism and foreign missions. In fact, the Protestant missionary movement is the product of Pietism. Protestantism began as a zeal for truth, and for decades seemed to leave good works, or at least the doctrine of good works, entirely to the papacy. It was Pietism that gave works back to Protestantism, and in the long run permitted the rise of a nondogmatic Christianity that sometimes seems incapable of answering the simplest doctrinal questions.

Spener's two successors, August Hermann Francke (1663–1727) and Count Nikolaus Ludwig von Zinzendorf (1700–60), each made a distinctive contribution. In addition, Zinzendorf had a very important influence on the Wesleys, and thus indirectly Pietism gave rise to the Methodist movement in the Anglo-Saxon world. Francke was to Pietism what Paul was to Christianity—not its founder, but certainly the one who gave it its distinctive character. His distinctive contribution was his emphasis on the experience of conversion and the new birth. In 1689 Francke began holding *collegia biblica,* "Bible seminars"; although he himself did not make a particular kind of conversion experience the criterion for one's salvation, many of his followers did jump to this conclusion. The orthodox theologians of Leipzig protested against Francke's activities, but he was immediately offered a professorship at the newly founded University of Halle, which became the citadel of Pietism for several decades. His friend and coworker, the Freiherr von Canstein, founded the Halle Bible Society in 1710. Within seven years, the new society had distributed 80,000 complete Bibles and 100,000 New

Testaments, compared to only 20,000 Bibles printed in all of Germany between 1534 and 1626.[21] Like Spener, Francke was theologically orthodox,
but his concentration on Christian experience and the new birth tended to
put doctrinal issues into the background.

Count von Zinzendorf came from a noble family that had been forced
out of Austria as a consequence of the Counter-Reformation there. His father was acquainted with Spener and sent the son to Francke's school for
sons of the aristocracy in Halle, where he was converted at fifteen. On the
family estates at Oberlausitz in Saxony, Zinzendorf provided a refuge for
German-speaking Protestants from Hapsburg Bohemia and Moravia. The
colony was located on a little hill, the Hutberg, and changed its name to
Herrnhut ("Lord's protection").

Zinzendorf wanted to make religion enjoyable, and in fact succeeded
in making Pietism emotional and sentimental, concentrating on Jesus' sufferings, wounds, and blood as our source of assurance. Much contemporary
Protestant hymnody is directly or indirectly influenced by Zinzendorf, although similar themes have been present in Christian piety from its beginnings. In Zinzendorf a transition seems to have been reached. The reform
orthodox movement, hymn-writer Paul Gerhardt, and Spener had all emphasized the individual and his response to the Christian message in an effort
to make certain that the objective theological doctrines produced a tangible
result in the believer. By Zinzendorf's time, sentimentality seems to become
more important than the objective truth on which it was originally based.
The first great modern theological liberal, Friedrich Schleiermacher (1768–
1834), who came from a Pietist background, would essentially replace doctrine with sentiment altogether.

Zinzendorf stressed the individual's personal experience of communion
with Christ as the basis for a true unity among believers. His small community at Herrnhut developed an astonishing missionary movement and for
over a century was the dominant force in German Protestant missions. Despite the fact that the Pietists were outdoing the more conventional Lutherans in areas of endeavor where the Lutherans should have been strong, orthodoxy tended to look on Pietism not as an ally but as a menace.

f. The Conflict with Orthodoxy

The first conflicts between orthodox Lutherans and Pietists resulted
from the tendency of the Pietists to form separate conventicles and disdain
association with the established church. By 1695 Pietists had established
little cells all over Germany, and orthodox theologians were beginning to
find fault with Spener. In 1695 alone fifteen different attacks on him were
published. The most substantial criticism of Pietism was published by a
Wittenberg professor, Valentin Ernst Löscher (1673–1749), after Spener's

death.[22] Pietism made the most of the favor it found at the Prussian court and the Prussian University of Halle. Francke himself wanted to reform society through the church, and while he made use of all the available spiritual means at his disposal, he also welcomed the government assistance provided by the King of Prussia. In 1729 King Frederick William I issued an order that all candidates for ministerial posts in Prussia had to study for two years at Halle. In 1723 pressure from the Pietists had caused the removal of one of Germany's leading philosophers, Christian von Wolff (1679–1754), from his chair at the university. The skeptical monarch Frederick II restored Wolff to his chair immediately upon succeeding to the throne in 1740.

g. Problems of Pietism

Pietism was not a heresy in any sense of the word, but by stressing personal experience and religious sentiment, it removed many of the obstacles to heresy. Löscher criticized Pietism for valuing piety above truth. Orthodox Lutheranism promised the believer assurance on the basis of the infallible Word of God; Pietism encouraged the believer to seek a subjective assurance through spiritual exercises, which sometimes degenerated into a new kind of legalism. Pietism, especially from the time of Francke onward, tended toward perfectionism—the doctrine that the true believer can and indeed must avoid all sin in the present life. Löscher accused the Pietists of abandoning Luther for the pre-Reformation mystics and Reformation-era spiritualists.

Pietism essentially sought to make Christian believers active, happy, and effective by helping them to a more intense experience of conversion and fellowship with God. It began by presupposing the truth of Protestant orthodoxy, but because it stressed life rather than truth, its adherents gradually lost sight of the doctrinal basis underlying the pious life. Stressing the necessity of individual religious experience, it lost objective criteria for authenticating the validity of such experience. Its reluctance to engage in theological controversy and polemics was certainly refreshing after a century and a half of acrimonious quarrels, but this reluctance did carry with it the half-hidden suggestion that dogmas were not worth defending. The dangers of this approach were exhibited in the life and work of Gottfried Arnold (1666–1714), who stood in a mediating position between Pietism and spiritualistic mysticism.

Arnold had studied theology in orthodox Lutheran Wittenberg, but became discouraged with orthodoxy. He became acquainted with Spener, who helped him obtain a history professorship in Giessen. There he wrote his controversial *Impartial History of the Church and of Heretics,* in which he presented heretics through the ages as the real Christians. His unfavorable opinion of the institutional church influenced historians of the Enlightenment era to look on the history of the church as the history of the decline of an ideal. In 1700, a year after the *Impartial History*, Arnold published *The Secret of the Divine Sophia*, in which he proposed to lead "understanding readers" into a true knowledge of the love of the invisible deity by exposing them to the great mystics in whom the life of the Spirit was exhibited. Arnold followed the speculations of Jakob Boehme in thinking of the true human as an androgynous man-woman, destined for betrothal to the heavenly Wisdom. Needless to say, such flights of fancy did nothing to calm the apprehensions of the orthodox.

h. Biblicism

Pietism began during the last decades of the great age of Protestant theological orthodoxy and continued strong into the period of the Enlightenment. It saw itself as a faithful continuation of the Reformation, but its individualism overrode its orthodoxy and brought it close to the spirit of the Enlightenment. Although the God-centeredness and spiritual fervor of Pietism were certainly opposed to the humanism and cool rationality of the Enlightenment, Pietism made no great effort to defend the truth of orthodox doctrines against the skepticism of the Enlightenment and thus permitted its own foundations to be sapped. Nevertheless, two aspects of Pietism strengthened the Christian community to resist skepticism even though they did not meet its challenges head on: biblicism and millennialism.

The Duchy of Württemberg with its theological faculty at Tübingen was a center of what we have called Lutheran ultraorthodoxy in the mid-seventeenth century. Toward the end of the century, as Pietism penetrated Württemberg, Andreas Hofstetter (1637–1720), a friend of Spener, secured a declaration from the Württemberg Consistory clearing the movement of all suspicion of heresy. Pietism was cultivated by the regular church pastors, and never became as separatistic in Württemberg as it had been in Saxony.

The most important Württemberg Pietist was Johann Albrecht Bengel (1687–1752). Bengel actively promoted Bible study among the laity and a high degree of interest in the Scripture, rather than in mere doctrine, among theologians. In addition, Bengel promoted millennial expectancy. Both biblicism and millennialism helped the church to resist the propaganda of the Enlightenment, biblicism by promoting a good knowledge of the Scripture itself, millennialism by undercutting the humanistic self-satisfaction of the Enlightenment. Bengel opposed the efforts of Zinzendorf to portray his own brand of separatistic Herrnhut Pietism as the legitimate continuation of Luther's Reformation, and proposed instead the Württemberg model of church-centered Pietism. His influence is still felt in southwestern Germany, where

Pietism continues strong in the established church to the present day. His commitment to conservative biblical scholarship has been honored by the establishment of a conservative foundation for theological studies at the University of Tübingen in 1967, the Albrecht-Bengel-Haus.

i. The Legacy of Pietism

If it had not been for Spener and those who followed him and attempted to carry out his *Pious Desires,* European Protestantism might have completely degenerated into nothing but acrimonious theological factionalism. One of the great accomplishments of Pietism was to rescue Protestantism from the dominance of the academic profession and to make faith, devotion, and knowledge of the Bible accessible to ordinary people. Its emphasis on personal Christianity made the Christian life an experiential reality, not merely a theological postulate. Its emphasis on the priesthood of all believers and the necessity for faith to be active in love tapped tremendous reservoirs of spiritual energy and accomplished enduring achievements in the areas of Christian education, social work, and home and foreign missions. As a consequence of the Enlightenment and religious skepticism, the older Protestant orthodoxy would virtually cease to exist. Where conservative, biblical impulses in Protestantism have survived, it has almost always been in a Pietistic setting, so that modern conservative Protestantism is very largely Pietistic in origin.

At the same time, Pietism is partly responsible for the religious individualism that has permitted Protestantism to become theologically and ethically highly pluralistic. Its emphasis on deeds rather than creeds has permitted modern Protestantism to degenerate into a kind of spiritually illiterate moralism. Interest in the truth of theological doctrines has been left largely to the strong conservatives, now often labeled fundamentalists. In a theological climate in which no doctrine can be labeled heresy, no teacher a heretic, the proclamation and defense of biblical and theological truth has become a curiosity. Without Pietism, Protestantism might never have survived the eighteenth century, but with Pietism, it may ultimately cease to be Protestantism.

SELECTED BIBLIOGRAPHY

Chadwick, Henry, ed. *Lessing's Theological Writings: Selections in Translation with an Introductory Essay.* London: Adam & Charles Black, 1956.

Deeter, Allen C. "An Historical and Theological Introduction to Philipp Jakob Spener's Pia Desideria: A Study in Early German Pietism." Princeton: University Press, 1963.

Horst, Hermann. *Ketzer in Deutschland*. Cologne: Kipenheuer und Witsch, 1978.

Jameson, J. Franklin, ed. *Persecution and Liberty*. New York: Century, 1931.

Knox, R. A. *Enthusiasm: A Chapter in the History of Religion, with Special Reference to the 17th and 18th Centuries*. New York: Oxford, 1950.

Miller, Samuel J. T. "Molanus, Lutheran Irenicist (1633–1722)." *Church History* 22 (September 1953): 197–218.

Roessle, Julius. *Von Bengel bis Blaumhardt: Gestalten und Bilder aus der Geschichte des Schwäbischen Pietismus*. Metzingen: Franz, 1960.

Scharlemann, Robert. "Theology in Church and University: The Post-Reformation Development." *Church History* 33 (March 1964): 23–33.

Towlson, Clifford W. *Moravian and Methodist: Relationships and Influences in the 18th Century*. London: Epworth, 1957.

Walgrave, Jan Hendrik. *Unfolding Revelation: The Nature of Doctrinal Development*. Philadelphia: Westminster Press, 1972.

Wallmann, Johannes. *Philipp Jakob Spener und die Anfänge des Pietismus*. Tübingen: Mohr, 1970.

19

THE HERESY
OF ENLIGHTENMENT

The Religion of religions cannot collect material enough for its pure interest in all things human. As nothing is more irreligious than to demand general uniformity in mankind, so nothing is more unchristian than to seek uniformity in religion.

Friedrich Schleiermacher
On Religion: Speeches to Its Cultured Despisers

The Protestant Reformation was dominated by German thinking and German theology. Outside the Holy Roman Empire (which at that time included German-speaking Switzerland as well as the Low Countries), Protestantism enjoyed great and lasting success only in largely Germanic lands—in Scandinavia and Britain, for example, although not in Celtic Ireland. Compared to the Reformation, the Enlightenment was a more truly European phenomenon, embracing the Latin countries as well as the Germanic ones. There was a significant difference between the impact of the Enlightenment in Germany and Britain on the one hand and in France and Italy on the other. In the Latin countries, the "Age of Reason" was decidedly antireligious. In Germany, and to a lesser extent in England as well, the Enlightenment came to terms with established religion. It transformed it rather than attacking it: the result was liberal Protestantism.

It was the Age of the Enlightenment—which stressed, not for the last time, the idea that man had "come of age"—that first conceived the idea of progress and that no longer identified Protestantism with doctrinal truth but with doctrinal "progress." During this era, liberal and radical theology virtually came to dominate the churches and spiritual life throughout the German-speaking states. Strong bastions of conservative conviction survived, but they were cut off both from the German universities and from most international contact and influence. During and after this period, many conservative Protestants left Germany and Scandinavia for North America, creating centers of traditional Protestantism in the New World but weakening conservatism in their home churches.

To call the religion of the Enlightenment liberalism always arouses criticism. Strictly speaking, what we know as liberal Christianity began during the eighteenth century and continued unchecked until World War I. The war rudely shattered many optimistic illusions about man and his future, and was followed by a revival of interest in orthodox doctrines and a distrust in man's potential for good. Neoorthodoxy was a reaction to liberalism and rationalism, and is strikingly different from old Protestant liberalism, but it is also often called liberal by Protestant conservatives. Neoorthodoxy in turn has been superseded by existentialist interpretation and other modern theologies that consider themselves neither neoorthodox nor liberal, but that are also often dubbed liberal by old-line conservatives. Neoorthodoxy, like traditional Protestantism, to a large extent acknowledges the orthodox creeds, which the liberal movements do not, but neoorthodoxy does not recognize the absolute authority and plenary inspiration of Scripture. To some extent this justifies lumping it together with existentialist theology and old-fashioned liberalism as "liberal," but to do so creates misunderstandings.

Liberalism, contrasted with orthodox Protestantism, is clearly heretical, for it repudiates the central tenets of the orthodox confessions. Neoorthodoxy in general reaffirms them, although sometimes in a sense that is more reminiscent of Gnosticism or Neoplatonism than of Christian orthodoxy. Nevertheless, neoorthodoxy usually cannot be distinguished from orthodoxy or called heretical on the basis of the traditional creeds, which it accepts. Within conservative Protestantism, there is a desire to lump neoorthodoxy together with liberalism and modern theology because they all accept biblical criticism and deny the older concepts of the inspiration and authority of Scripture.

All the movements we have mentioned—from liberalism through neoorthodoxy to existentialistic interpretation and other forms of modern theology—were pioneered and developed, if not exclusively produced, in Germany. As theology has come to be seen as an academic science, German theology has been the most self-consciously scientific. This has led to a tendency to ignore or at least to undervalue the achievements of Protestant theologians from other countries. Even the great Karl Barth, in his *Protestant Theology in the Nineteenth Century*,[1] does not consider any theologians other than German or Swiss. Although he himself was Reformed, Barth totally ignored the monumental theological accomplishments of American Reformed theologians, not to mention those of the German-speaking theologians of the Lutheran Church–Missouri Synod, or, closer to his Basel home, of such outstanding Dutch writers as Abraham Kuyper (1837–1920).

1. THE RELIGIOUS ENLIGHTENMENT

Because of the secular perspective of most of the study of intellectual history in the United States, the Enlightenment is seen largely as a secular movement centered in France. The influence of Enlightenment rationalism was soon felt in British North America, and was a major factor in the War of Independence and the establishment of the United States. It should not be overlooked, however, that the indirect influence of the Enlightenment on American life through the transformation of Protestant theology is at least as great and certainly is longer-lasting, continuing as it does to the present day.

Although he was not one of its early pioneers, the critical Königsberg philosopher Immanuel Kant (1724–1804) provides us with the best definition of the Enlightenment, one particularly appropriate for the understanding of its influence on Christian thought, especially German Protestant thought. "Enlightenment," he writes, "is the emergence of man from his self-inflicted immaturity. Immaturity is the inability to use one's reason without making use of the guidance of another."[2] Inasmuch as Christianity is by its very nature a religion of divine revelation, one that presupposes that human reason needs guidance and in fact is guided by God's revelation, it is apparent that Kant's principle is totally incompatible with Christianity as it has been understood. Despite this evident conflict, many Protestants and not a few Roman Catholics have entertained the illusion that it is possible to have an "enlightened" Christianity that extols reason but does not altogether dispense with revelation. Kant himself did not shrink back from this step: one of his programmatic writings is entitled *Religion Within the Limits of Reason Alone* (1793); it brought a clash with the Prussian government. Liberal Protestantism has typically tried to accept the Enlightenment without doing away with revelation, and in the process has often reduced revelation to the expression of religious sensitivity and spiritual exaltation on the part of a people, as in Herder, or of individuals, as in Schleiermacher.

Kant's perception of the ages of faith and the dominance of Christianity as ages of immaturity is reflected in the views of Gotthold Ephraim Lessing (1729–81) in *The Education of the Human Race* (1780). Just as the New Testament represented a higher and fuller revelation of the nature and purposes of God than the Old, so too, Lessing was convinced, the Age of Reason represented a divinely ordained advance to maturity and was superior to even the tutelage of the New Testament.

Pietism had perceived itself as the legitimate continuation of the Reformation, particularly of Luther's impulse toward the personalization of religion. By dispensing with the formal structures of the church and church government and the traditional emphasis on dogma and theology, Pietism prepared the way for the day in which an increasing number of religious leaders would abandon the external guidance of Scripture and orthodox doctrine as the Pietists themselves had abandoned the external structure of ecclesiastical institutions. Looking on Luther's Reformation not as primarily the personal appropriation of traditional religious values, but rather as a liberation from traditional views, the men of the Enlightenment could also claim in a sense to be fulfilling what Luther began. During the period of the Enlightenment, its foremost representatives clashed fiercely both with Protestant orthodoxy and Pietism; consequently, it did not occur to the first rationalists to claim Luther as an example. More recently, as noted earlier, this claim has been made for them by those who see the fundamental principle of Protestantism as progress.

In *The Education of the Human Race,* Lessing imitated Joachim of Floris in dividing all history into three revelatory stages, but for Lessing the ultimate stage was not that of the Holy Spirit, but that of the human spirit.

a. Negative Factors

Although the men of the Enlightenment saw themselves as pioneers and breakers of new ground, in some respects the movement was an expression of exhaustion, the exhaustion of traditional Christianity, particularly of Protestantism, after more than two centuries of unremitting polemics and, at times, religious warfare. The original assumption of the Reformation was that the whole church ultimately could and would be reformed. But two centuries of polemics had not only failed to bring Protestantism and Catholicism into harmony, they had also left apparently irreconcilable disagreements within Protestantism. Where Protestant orthodoxy was able to preserve its authority—often thanks only to government favor—it seldom proved capable of creating a wholesome moral and spiritual reformation in the life of the people. The dichotomy between the high claims of orthodoxy and the pitiable achievements it produced caused widespread disillusionment with religion. The Pietists, as we have seen, represented the most significant effort to remedy the situation by interiorizing the faith and attempting to cultivate spiritual fruit in the piety and conduct of all who would allow themselves to be led by them. Pietism remained a minority movement, however, and despite its long involvement with the intellectual life of two major universities, its major strength was never among the intellectuals.

Many of the more intellectual Christians hoped and worked for interconfessional reunion. Gottfried Wilhelm von Leibniz (1646–1716) and

Bishop Jacques Bénigne Bossuet (1627–1704) of Meaux are two of the outstanding examples. Of course reunion could be achieved only at the cost of some of the confessional distinctives for the sake of which disputations had been held, diatribes written, and, not infrequently, blood shed; the fact that reunion was so earnestly sought reveals a weakening of the doctrinal convictions that had produced division.

Although orthodoxy showed signs of fatigue and thus facilitated the rise of the Enlightenment, superstition was by no means extinct. (Indeed, the advance of modern science and technology in the twentieth century has by no means banned superstition, witchcraft, and the occult from modern society.) Toward the close of the seventeenth century, belief in the prevalence of witchcraft was widespread, and countless unfortunates were burned or drowned because of charges of necromancy. In Amsterdam, the otherwise orthodox pastor Balthasar Bekker lost his pulpit for attacking beliefs in magic and the occult and explaining demon possession naturalistically in *The Enchanted World*. The book was immediately translated into several languages. Christian Thomasius (1655–1728) of Leipzig University, the first professor to lecture in German there rather than the traditional Latin, was called to the University of Halle, the stronghold of Pietism, in 1694. Like Bekker, he attacked belief in witches and demons as superstition. Although belief in witchcraft is part of no orthodox confession, the skepticism that derided witchcraft could also be directed against other doctrines more integral to Christianity.

b. Positive Factors

The prevalence of superstition made popular religion an easy target for skeptical intellectuals, while orthodoxy was too lethargic to rise to its own defense, or even to distinguish itself from superstition. In addition to these negative factors, which weakened orthodox Protestantism, there were some positive reasons for the rise of liberalism. It is a mistake to look on liberal Protestantism as the product of nothing more than skepticism or unwillingness to believe. It had at its roots a number of religious impulses orthodoxy neglected or ignored.[3] For example, the need to learn how to live together with members of other confessions was a legitimate need, especially in Europe. Boundaries between territories were frequently boundaries between confessions, and sometimes the territories were small and the boundaries close together. A territory often changed its religion when it changed rulers. All these factors impelled Protestants to seek a common basis for agreement, rather than stiffly maintaining inherited orthodoxies. Unfortunately, the virtue of toleration that these conditions fostered can become a vice if it instills the idea that because religious convictions vary among decent people, religious truth is a matter of personal taste.[4]

The Netherlands had to struggle for decades to escape from the religious repression of Spanish rule; for a time the Dutch Calvinists were noted for their strictness and severity, but during the middle of the seventeenth century the Netherlands introduced the toleration Poland-Lithuania was abandoning. René Descartes (1596–1650), Benedict (Baruch) Spinoza (1632–77), and Pierre Bayle (1647–1706) all enjoyed its benefits. Although he believed in God, Descartes created a philosophical world view indifferent to revelation and religion; Spinoza, a Jew, denied the reality of a personal God and belief in individual immortality. Although he was expelled from the synagogue, Spinoza's criticism of traditional theism, i.e. of belief in a personal God, became widely known and contributed to the decay of Christian doctrinal positions. The Dutch Arminians fought for tolerance, first for themselves, then for the unitarian Socinians, leading, incidentally, to an increasingly broad conception of the meaning of the word "Christian."

The voyages of exploration, European colonization of the New World, and the rise of modern science all contributed to the spread of the Enlightenment by broadening the horizons of men and women and creating the impression that the old Christian world view, which was narrow by definition, was also limited, arbitrary, and inadequate. The relationship between Christianity and the rise of natural science has been examined by many scientists, historians, and philosophers;[5] Christian doctrine, especially the doctrine of Creation, furnished an indispensable presupposition for the rise of experimental science. Experimental science, once established, gave man an increasing confidence in his own ability to understand the universe. In this respect, the impact of the sciences was greater among the nonscientists, for the most eminent scientists were often men of faith.

2. THE RELIGION OF
THE ENLIGHTENMENT

Christianity is characterized by particularity. The Jews are a particular people, with a peculiar history. Jesus Christ appeared, lived, died, and rose again under a particular set of historical circumstances, and in a particular place. The religion of the Enlightenment was characterized by the zeal for the universal; only what is universally applicable and understandable can be considered as having absolute validity. The Englishman Edward Herbert of Cherbury (1583–1648) limited the concept of true religion to that which is universally recognized by all rational minds and which can therefore be considered universally binding. He defined five basic principles: (1) there is a God; (2) God must be worshiped; (3) the chief parts of worship are virtue and piety (not orthodoxy!); (4) man is bound to repent of sin and despise it;

(5) virtue will be rewarded and vice punished both in the present world and in the hereafter. Herbert accordingly advocated mutual tolerance for all religions. Thomas Hobbes (1588–1679), a few years younger, went beyond Herbert in attacking Christianity and wanted the state to place considerable restrictions on religion. John Locke (1632–1704), one of the founders of modern democratic thought in the Anglo-Saxon world, continued to accept the principal Christian dogmas, including the inspiration of Scripture and belief in miracles, which Hobbes had denied. An outstanding advocate of tolerance, Locke specifically excluded from it both atheists and Roman Catholics. Locke defended traditional religion in *The Reasonableness of Christianity* (1695), but he weakened the absolute claims of biblical revelation by stressing its harmony with natural reason.

The generation that came after Locke was unwilling to follow him in continuing to accept scriptural revelation as its standard, even in his rather attenuated sense. The English Deists, or freethinkers, were religious, but their religion was "natural religion," independent of supernatural revelation. "Irrational" doctrines such as the Trinity and the incarnation were rigorously excluded and morality rather than dogma was stressed. The New Testament itself was reinterpreted or disregarded in order to interpret Jesus as a prophet of this natural religion. The dogmas of both Christianity and non-Christian religions were exposed to a critical analysis that was both harsh and unrelenting, if not necessarily sound.

An Irishman, John Toland (1670–1722), wrote *Christianity Not Mysterious* (1696), and Matthew Tindal (1656–1733) produced the *magnum opus* of English Deism, *Christianity as Old as the Creation* (1730), in an effort to remake Christianity into a kind of naturalistic religious philosophy. Under such circumstances it is not surprising that the historical reliability of the Bible was called into question by many thinkers, including Anthony Collins (1676–1729), Thomas Woolston (1669–1773), and Thomas Morgan (d. 1743). In 1747–48 Peter Annet and Conyers Middleton disputed the reliability of the miracle stories in the Bible, Annet on the basis of Spinoza's monism. The major opposition to the natural religion and skepticism of Deism came not from orthodoxy, but from the revival movement initiated by John Wesley (1703–91) which had close ties to German Pietism. Thus in a way the nondogmatic religion of the heart, Pietism, became the chief obstacle to the triumph of Deism, the nondogmatic religion of the mind. Pietism and the Wesleyan movement did nothing to secure the doctrinal foundations of Protestant orthodoxy, but largely contented themselves with the quest for revival, conversion, and personal holiness.

Caustic, often inaccurate criticism of the influence of Christianity in history characterized Edward Gibbon's monumental work *The Decline and Fall of the Roman Empire* (1776–88). The Scotsman David Hume (1711–

76), in *The Natural History of Religion* (1755), challenged the Deistic conviction that monotheism is natural, and argued that primitive religion was founded on fear and was polytheistic.

The skeptical thinking that was produced in such quantity in Britain was at first more widely read and accepted on the Continent than in Britain itself. In France, Roman Catholicism had been able to maintain its power by persecuting the Protestants in alliance with the monarchical absolutism of the *ancien régime*. Charles de Montesquieu (1689–1755), who devised the concept of checks and balances put into practice in the United States Constitution, helped popularize Deistic ideas in France, but the best-known critic of religion of the French Enlightenment is François Marie Arouet de Voltaire (1694–1778). Voltaire popularized English natural theology in France and gave the French Enlightenment its sharply anti-Christian tone. Voltaire considered belief in the existence of God a practical necessity, but unlike the English Deists and Immanuel Kant he denied the immortality of the soul and thus promoted materialism. He was also a zealous advocate of toleration.

Julien Offray de La Mettrie (1709–51) declared sensual pleasure to be the dominant theme of morals, preparing the way for hedonism and utilitarianism; his *L'Homme machine* (Man, a Machine, 1748) propagated a materialistic understanding of man, as did Baron Paul Henri Dietrich d'Holbach (1723–89) in his *System of Nature* (1770); Holbach considered religious faith an illusion. A different note was sounded by Geneva-born Jean-Jacques Rousseau (1712–78), who turned away from rational analysis to stress the primacy of feeling. His "Profession of Faith of a Vicar of Savoy," contained in *Émile: Or, Education* (1762), is a plea for natural religion based on sentiment, rather than on reason and common sense. In this respect Rousseau was a forerunner of the Romantic movement.

3. THE ENLIGHTENMENT
AND GERMAN PROTESTANTISM

The ideas of the Enlightenment made slower progress in Germany than in France and England, due in part to the persistence of the strength of orthodox Protestantism. Pietism emphasized personal devotion and opposed skepticism and religious indifference, but its stress on the individual and his religious feelings helped to pave the way for the pronounced individualism of the Enlightenment. Christian von Wolff (1679–1754), who ran into difficulties with the Pietists at Halle, argued that there is a middle ground between the pure truths of revelation and those of reason where reason can be used in support of revelation. Both the orthodox Lutherans and the Pietists correctly perceived that where religious truth can be supported by reason, it can also be attacked. Theology, the queen of the sciences, was about to face a revolution. It was the beginning of the secularization of education.

a. The Secularization of Education

Thanks to their influence with Frederick William I, the King of Prussia, the Pietists were able to keep representatives of the Enlightenment from securing professorships during a number of decades, until the accession of Frederick II in 1740. Frederick recalled Wolff to Halle and established religious tolerance throughout Prussia. He even permitted the Jesuit order to remain active in the country when it was banned by Pope Clement XIV in 1773. Although Germany at this time was divided into a number of independent states, several of which were Roman Catholic and theologically conservative, education at the university level was rapidly secularized in the Protestant lands. The rapid development of increasingly secular philosophical schools—rational, critical, idealistic, and Romantic—exercised a marked influence on theology in part because theology continued to be regarded as one of the "sciences." The tools of reason Christian von Wolff and John Locke had used to defend many traditional Christian doctrines and values could also be used to criticize and challenge them, and this took place with growing frequency and vigor. Popular educators such as Christoph Friedrich Nicolai (1733–1811), publisher of the *Allgemeine deutsche Bibliothek* (General German Library, a popular encyclopedia), and the Jewish philosopher Moses Mendelssohn (1729–86, grandfather of the famous composer), proclaimed an idealism that was religious and moral but indifferent or hostile to orthodox Christian doctrine. The fact that many theologians had in effect compromised by stressing the moral aspect of Christianity and downgrading its specific doctrinal content made it difficult to resist the appeal of those who continued to uphold the principles of Christian morality while growing increasingly critical of its doctrines. The fact that Christianity was established and the churches thus financially secure combined with the German insistence on a highly academic preparation for the clergy; the result was a church that continued to preserve traditional forms staffed by clergy who were rapidly becoming indifferent to the content that underlay them.

b. The Religion of the Enlightenment

In France the Enlightenment was largely hostile to religion and forced Catholicism into a defensive attitude, which enabled Catholicism to preserve its doctrinal distinctives for a century; theological modernism did not become a substantial problem within Catholicism until near the end of the

nineteenth century. In Germany representatives of the Enlightenment continued to accept the idea of God, immortality, and revelation and thus did not
appear as hostile or as dangerous to Christianity as their counterparts in
France. The growing academic sophistication of Protestant theologians as
they reached out into other disciplines—into philosophy, philology, and history—tended to make traditional dogmatics appear less important. Johann
Lorenz von Mosheim (1693–1755) wrote extensively on the early history of
Christianity (*Commentary on Christian Matters Before Constantine*, 1753),
making extensive use of primary sources and beginning to examine the textual tradition of Scripture in a critical way. The orthodox theologian Johann
Georg Walch (1693–1775), an opponent of Pietism, also began to examine
the development of doctrine. In Leipzig, Johann August Ernesti (1707–81)
began critical examination of the texts and traditions of the New Testament
while Johann David Michaelis (1717–91) did the same thing for the Old in
Göttingen.

From 1750 on, a new theology, called "neology," developed in

Christian von Wolff had been banished from Halle from 1723 to 1740,
but his influence was perpetuated by Siegmund Jakob Baumgarten (1706–
57), the teacher of Immanuel Kant. Baumgarten attempted an elaborate rational defense of orthodoxy, and in effect challenged his pupil to take the
opposite position, namely, that the natural world cannot tell us anything at
all about the supernatural and therefore all of the traditional proofs of the
existence of God are invalid. The defense of the faith was largely left to the
Pietists, who concentrated on life rather than on doctrine. In consequence,
"theology" and "theological science" in Germany became increasingly
critical, liberal, and skeptical, and those who held to traditional convictions
expressed them in practical living without trying to defend them with scholarly arguments. This is one of the sources of the antischolarly, antiacademic
attitude of much conservative Protestantism. As a number of scholars expressed critical and liberal views, many conservatives simply abandoned the
academic field to them and retreated to the parish, foreign missions, and
various types of social work. The fact that in Germany the Pietists continued
to enjoy a substantial measure of government favor well into the nineteenth
century appears to have helped to lull them to the fact that the foundations
of their religious life were being undermined by the success of liberalism in
winning control of university education.

From 1750 on, a new theology, called "neology," developed in
Germany's Protestant faculties of theology. The philosopher Christian Für-
chtegott Gellert (1715–69) at Leipzig represented a conservative, supernat-
uralistic position, but the New Testament scholar Johann Salomo Semler
(1725–91) at Halle subjected the canon of the New Testament to rationalistic,
antisupernaturalistic criticism and maintained that the traditional canon is the
result of the triumph of the Roman influence in early church politics rather

than of any particular guidance by the Holy Spirit. Thus the University of Halle dramatically shifted from being a bastion of Pietistic conservatism to being a center of radical criticism of the foundations of Pietism as well as of orthodoxy.

The theologians of the Reformation and their polemical successors had thoroughly battered the Roman Catholic view of the authority of the church and tradition and had placed all of their confidence in the authority of the written texts of Scripture. Now Semler and a host of imitators began to argue that Scripture itself was the product of church tradition, and indeed was not even the result of a harmonious consensus, as Irenaeus had claimed, but of the triumph of one particular ecclesiastic party over the others. The fact that this party was the Roman of course further compromised it in Protestant eyes; old prejudices and hostilities combined with liberal criticism to make the received canon of Scripture appear to be the accidental product of historical circumstances. Semler was an intellectual elitist and approved teaching traditional, orthodox doctrines to the common people; thus he endorsed the Edict on Religion of 1788, in which the Prussian state required that all pastors conform to orthodox doctrines in their preaching. For himself and other "mature intellectuals" he reserved the right to divergent private opinions. Needless to say, this policy of mental reservation increased the distrust by the Pietists and other conservatives of university theologians and helped to lead to the alienation between academic theology and the religion of the common people.

Wolff, who had been generally sympathetic to orthodoxy but who had honestly applied his philosophical tools to it, had been forced from Halle by suspicious Pietists. The next generation of Pietists appeared satisfied by the outward conformity of Semler, who was far more dangerous. For the next few decades, educational and church officials remained conservative, orthodox, or Pietistic in many German states, but permitted the growth of liberal theology at the universities under their control as long as the theologians took the precaution of expressing a measure of outward conformity to traditional doctrines. Karl Friedrich Bahrdt (1741–92), briefly Semler's colleague at Halle, was imprudent enough to deny the concept of supernatural revelation altogether and ended his life as an innkeeper.

In Hamburg Hermann Samuel Reimarus (1694–1768), a high school (*Gymnasium*) professor, preserved the appearance of conformity by publishing a number of papers in the style of Christian von Wolff while actually holding a totally heretical view of Christ. This became known only after his radical papers were published as *Fragments of an Unknown* in the years 1774–77 by the influential dramatist and critic Lessing. Reimarus went far beyond the incipient Unitarianism of Servetus and the Socinians, who preserved a great measure of respect for Jesus Christ while denying that he is coeternal with the Father. Reimarus held that Jesus was a failed political Messiah and that Christianity is a fraud perpetuated by the disciples, who stole his body and proclaimed to the credulous that he was risen from the dead. Reimarus' views were based far more on his own skeptical and anti-supernaturalistic prejudices than on any new critical findings concerning the reliability of the New Testament documents. The orthodox theology of the day did not possess the critical and historical sophistication to counter Reimarus' assertions in a scholarly way, and resorted to dogmatic condemnations. Lessing was opposed by the orthodox chief pastor of Hamburg, Johann Melchior Goeze (1717–86), who also made the mistake of challenging "worldly" drama and the highly successful romance *The Sorrows of Young Werther*, by Germany's greatest literary figure, Johann Wolfgang von Goethe (1749–1832). Lessing turned the drama to propagandistic use in his parable *Nathan the Wise* (1779), in which, like the sixteenth-century radical Jacob Paleologus, he argued that each of the three great monotheistic religions is equally divine in origin. The difference between Lessing and Paleologus lies in the fact that Paleologus, a somewhat inconsistent mystic and enthusiast, undoubtedly believed that God really had inspired all three religions, while Lessing wanted them all reduced to the level of possibly edifying superstitions, among which he seems to have valued Christianity least.

The skill of Lessing on the one hand and the heavy-handed dogmatism of his opponents on the other helped to make orthodoxy appear narrow and increasingly unattractive. To the extent that orthodox figures such as Luther remained popular Protestant heroes, they were eulogized more as rebels and Romantic heroes than as men of faith with very definite doctrinal convictions.

Although for a time no university theologian descended to the level of Reimarus and presented the Apostles as religious charlatans, opposition to the miraculous and a naturalistic reinterpretation of most biblical miracles became commonplace. Another Halle professor, J. A. L. Wegscheider (1771–1849), produced the *Institutes of Dogmatic Theology* in 1815; by 1844 it had reached its eighth edition. The remarkable popularity of long and erudite works of theology in Germany testifies not only to the high degree of scholarship that characterized that country's numerous Protestant clergy, but also to the residual hold that orthodox doctrines had on large numbers of people. It took extensive evidence and persuasive arguments to persuade people to reject them. The fact that the defenders of the orthodox position did not reply with equally substantial works but took refuge in reaffirmations of dogmatic and Pietistic convictions gradually undermined their position and left liberalism almost totally unchallenged in the universities. Wegscheider's *Institutes* retained the structure of orthodox dogmatics, but excised everything that seemed to him to be contrary to sound common sense, including revelation and miracles. The most plausible reason for continuing to hold to major orthodox ideas while rejecting the divine revelation from which they are derived and the credibility of the miracles that had served as evidence for them lies in the tremendous hold that Christianity had on European culture, which it had been shaping for fifteen hundred years. This was, of course, a mere traditionalism and a much weaker variety of it than that found in Roman Catholicism, and it was doomed to fade with time, except where it was reinforced and reinvigorated by the fires of revival.

Christianity retained its emotional hold on the masses. Most people still had deeply felt religious needs that could not be met by the speculations of rationalistic or idealistic philosophy. German Pietism as well as its numerically stronger Anglo-Saxon offshoot, the Wesleyan movement, addressed the spiritual needs and moral concerns of millions, but did little or nothing to stop the liberal drift of the academically and philosophically trained minority. The first and most impressive effort to do so was made by a man with a Moravian background and education and a Pietist heart, who felt that the spiritual and religious values of Christianity could be defended only by reestablishing them on an entirely different basis from that of scriptural revelation and traditional theological arguments: Friedrich D. E. Schleiermacher.

4. IDEALISM:
RELIGIOUS SUBJECTIVITY

The eighteenth century had taught most intellectuals to think of human reason as sovereign and self-reliant. Far too many eighteenth-century Christians had gone along with this idea. Many who remained persuaded that man is not sovereign and must rely on God rather than on himself and his reason simply turned their back on intellectual and academic pursuits. Because the great majority of people in every age are neither intellectually nor academically rigorous, revivalists and evangelists found that they could reach and win millions without bothering to confront and refute the skepticism and debunking of traditional doctrines in which the liberals were so proficient. Among those who did attempt to come to terms with Enlightenment thought, most chose the path of compromise and alliance with moderate rationalists such as Wolff and Locke. This latter group, never very influential among the mass of Christians at large, was skillfully humiliated by the critical philosophy of Kant. Protestant Germany was willing to believe, but it needed a better reason for believing than the mere self-assured proclamation of so many Pietists. The excesses of the French Revolution had shaken the confidence of the intellectuals as well as of the masses in the rule of reason, but traditional orthodoxy and its dogmatic structure were in terrible disrepair.

Schleiermacher tried to revive Christianity not by refuting the rationalistic arguments of his detractors—with many of which he agreed—but by shifting the focus of the discussion to an area where he felt that Christianity could successfully reassert itself and where rationalistic criticism could no longer harm it—to the realm of the human spirit, its sentiments, ideals, and taste.

Traditional Christianity has always been first of all an objective religion. In contrast to Gnosticism and other varieties of religious philosophy, it teaches that the world is objectively real, the handiwork of a personal Creator. It presents God as acting in real, space-time history and as speaking human words in propositional revelation. It teaches that God became incarnate in one, historic human being, Jesus of Nazareth, and that the cosmic triumph of good over evil took place at a precise point in human, secular history, "under Pontius Pilate." It looks forward to a definite, if not precisely predictable, end to history with the personal return of Christ. In Roman Catholicism, the objectivity of Christianity was carried to the point of the doctrine of the transformation of bread and wine into the body and blood of Christ during the sacrament of the altar. Protestantism broke with such sacramental realism but also preserved an intense commitment to objectivity with its doctrine of verbal revelation, extending in its extreme form to the inspiration of the vowel points of the Masoretic text of the Hebrew Old Testament. Christianity has never been without a subjective side, frequently developed to an intense degree by mystics, charismatics, and enthusiasts, but always based on an objective foundation.

Protestantism with its principle of private interpretation and the direct accountability of the individual to God rather than a mediate accountability to and through the church is more open to subjectivism than is traditional Catholicism. Traditional accounts of Luther's spiritual struggles often stress their intensely personal nature. Nevertheless, Luther remained firmly rooted to the objectivity of God's revelation in Scripture; his concept of the clarity of Scripture was directed not only against Roman claims that interpretation by church authority is vital, but also against the "fanatics" who held that the Word requires a mystical illumination by the Holy Spirit to be understood.

The rationalism of the Enlightenment criticized Christianity as accidental and arbitrary, based on historical incidents rather than on universal reason. This criticism bit deeply into popular confidence in the authority of Christianity, especially because it was not adequately opposed by the orthodox. At the same time its emphasis on the human mind and its ability to reason promoted a brash individualism. When confidence in the ability of reason to discover universal truths waned, self-centered individualism remained. In literature and the arts, this led to Romanticism, in philosophy to idealism, in religion to the kind of Christian Romanticism developed by Schleiermacher.

Not long after the more radical of the Protestant neologians began to challenge the historical truth of the Bible, other Protestants began to try to rehabilitate it by exalting it as sublimely inspired spiritual art. After initial steps by the Prussian Johann Georg Hamann (1730–88) and the Swiss Johann Kaspar Lavater (1741–1801), the most influential effort was made by another Prussian, Johann Gottfried von Herder (1744–1803). Herder extolled the beauty and authority of the Bible as the product of the religious genius of the Jewish people in *The Spirit of Hebrew Poetry* (1782–83). In a strange way, this extolling of the Bible as the product of inspired Jewish seers and poets may have contributed to anti-Semitism in the nineteenth and twentieth centuries; intellectuals who rejected the authority of the Old Testament began to resent the Jews as the perpetrators of a gigantic hoax on Gentile, especially Aryan, civilization. Herder envisaged Christianity as contributing, together with classical antiquity, to a new religion of humanity. The relativizing of Scripture to a mere cultural or artistic phenomenon, no matter how "inspired" in merely human terms, naturally renders the fierce controversy between orthodoxy and heresy irrelevant, or at least no more significant than conflicts in literature or art.

As noted earlier, the critical philosophy of Immanuel Kant dealt a severe blow to traditional orthodoxy, particularly to the extent that it depended on reason and evidence from nature rather than on revelation alone. After having presented his powerful attacks on the traditional proofs of the existence of God in the *Critique of Pure Reason* (1781), Kant presented belief in God and personal immortality, as well as in the freedom of the will, as "necessary postulates of practical reason" in the *Critique of Practical Reason* (1788). For Kant, reflection on ethics inevitably leads man to religion, but religion consists essentially of "the recognition of our duties as divine commandments," in other words, of the recognition that man has absolute and necessary duties and obligations, not mere social conventions. Religious doctrine becomes irrelevant except as it directly relates to ethical obligations. Indeed, to the extent that a religious doctrine—such as that of the atonement—tells us that we cannot and need not fulfill all the stipulations of divine Law, but that Christ has fulfilled them in our place, such a doctrine is contrary to the ethical imperative and in Kant's sense is irreligious.

While Goethe was extolling the autonomy of the Romantic, egotistical intellectual in *Faust* and proclaiming that ceaseless striving in itself earns salvation, his younger contemporary Johann Gottlieb Fichte (1762–1814) proclaimed the absoluteness of the self. God is not a being in himself, but only the moral order of the world. For this Fichte was dismissed from his professorship in Jena (Saxony) but received another in Berlin. Friedrich Wilhelm Joseph von Schelling (1775–1854) developed a speculative, pantheistic philosophy of religion. His praise of the Absolute was taken by many of his contemporaries as praise for the God of Christianity, as was the idealism of

G. W. F. Hegel (1770–1831). All of these poets and philosophers did much to rehabilitate the concept of religion in the eyes of the intellectual world, but the "religion" for which they were winning back intellectual respectability was no longer Christianity but a nebulous cosmic spirituality without a definite creed or doctrines. The man who collected many of these impulses and brought them to bear on Christianity was Schleiermacher, the most influential figure in Protestant theology since the Reformation. From the perspective of orthodoxy, Schleiermacher was a great heretic, a kind of an adoptionist, whose Christ was the supreme incarnation of human sensitivity to God, not of the preexistent Word.

Schleiermacher so changed the conditions of theological discourse that since his time most sophisticated Protestants have dropped the word "heresy" from their vocabulary; it is only a small minority of dogmatically determined Protestants, orthodox or fundamentalistic, who still feel comfortable with it.

5. THE RELIGIOUS ROMANTIC:
SCHLEIERMACHER

In 1799 revolutionary France was triumphant over monarchist Germany and Reason seemed to have beaten down Religion, both orthodoxy and Pietism. An anonymous manifesto was published that year: *On Religion: Speeches to Its Cultured Despisers.* It tried to win back the lost ground by restating Protestant religion in terms of the prevailing sentiments of the day, primarily of aesthetics: religion is "perspective and feeling," a "sense and taste for the Infinite." As such it is unique and independent of metaphysics and morality; it can do something neither of these can, appeal to the religious imagination. The rising Romantic movement disdained the cold rationality of the Enlightenment and exalted the singular, the individual, the heroic. Schleiermacher, the author, responded to this taste by extolling Jesus as one of the "greatest heroes of religion," divine in the sense that he represented the highest possible level of religious consciousness. The great American conservative theologian Augustus Hopkins Strong (1836–1921) praised Schleiermacher for having "freed Christianity from the coils of rationalism,"[6] but he did so only to mire it in sentimentality.

Schleiermacher wanted to reform theological education, and his programmatic *Brief Outline of the Study of Theology* (1811) was highly influential. In his *magnum opus, The Christian Faith* (1821–22; 2d ed., 1831), he retained much of the terminology of orthodoxy, reworking it in the light of his emphasis on the importance of the religious consciousness. Jesus Christ is "distinguished from all others by the constant power of his God-consciousness, which was a real being of God in him.''[7] Jesus brings those who believe in him into the power of his own God-consciousness. Thus they are ''saved'' and experience eternity now; the concept of an afterlife in heaven becomes superfluous, like the traditional articles of orthodox confessions.

All Protestant theology after Schleiermacher has been influenced by him. He never repudiated his Pietistic heritage, and many Pietists were unperceptive enough to welcome his support for ''religion.'' Many of his disciples were more conservative than he, and modified their own positions to bring them closer to orthodoxy, but after more than a century and a half, it is Schleiermacher's influence, not theirs, that remains.

6. THE FRAGMENTATION OF THEOLOGY

Prior to the Protestant Reformation, the major split within Christendom was between Roman Catholicism and Eastern Orthodoxy. The numerous dualistic movements were banished completely into the realm of heresy, and the churches descended from monophysitism were largely isolated from the rest of Christendom by Islam. The tension between Eastern Orthodoxy and Roman Catholicism was high, exacerbated by the Turkish conquest of Constantinople in 1204 as well as by the failure of the Latin West to aid the restored Eastern Roman Empire during its final struggle with the Turks. Nevertheless, East and West were still perceived as one church, separated into two parts by schism, not by heresy.

The Reformation created the perception that there were three or four churches—in addition to Roman Catholicism, there was Lutheranism, the Reformed churches, and Anglicanism. In addition, of course, there were the numerous radical groups, some of which were orthodox in their doctrines of God and Christ, and several of which were distinctly heretical. Nevertheless, despite this disunity and the polemics that made it so apparent, there was still a kind of consensus among the major churches of the Reformation and Roman Catholicism; Eastern Orthodoxy as well, although not in active touch with the Western churches, also shared it. Each of the major churches accepted the great ecumenical creeds, the Apostles', Nicene, and Chalcedonian symbols, and was persuaded that the doctrine they express is both true and necessary. They differed among themselves about *what else* might be required, but there was no doubt among them that at least the doctrines of the ecumenical creeds were required. In the seventeenth century, polemicists and ''syncretists'' alike were persuaded of the truth of orthodoxy and considered it foundational for Christian faith and life, even while quarreling over certain tenets and interpretations. After Schleiermacher, this could no longer be said. Orthodox Christians remained in all denominations, and perhaps the prevailing sentiment of the majority of nominal Christians was the assumption that orthodox doctrines are true, but Christian theology lost its bearings and not only no longer gave the old answers but frequently failed to ask the old questions at all.

If it had not been for Schleiermacher, it is possible that the antisupernaturalists such as Reimarus and the radically skeptical philosophers such as Kant would have destroyed Christianity as the fundamental assumption of Western society. Thanks to Schleiermacher, Christianity survived within Protestant Europe, but what survived was a religion of sentiment called Christianity; it was no longer the Christianity of the New Testament or the ecumenical creeds.

If what Schleiermacher taught was indeed the Christian faith and the discipline he practiced was truly theology, then the old distinction between orthodoxy and heresy is at best irrelevant, at worst meaningless. Fortunately for the more orthodox-minded who followed him, Schleiermacher was not the only nineteenth-century theologian of note. Conservative Reformed theology found a new focus in the Netherlands, especially under Abraham Kuyper (1837–1920); in the United States, conservative Reformed theology flourished at Princeton Theological Seminary, particularly under Archibald Alexander (1772–1851), Charles Hodge (1797–1878), A. A. Hodge (1823–86), and Benjamin B. Warfield (1851–1921). There was a reinvigoration of orthodox Lutheranism on the European Continent, and especially under the emigré German C. F. W. Walther (1811–87), the outstanding early leader of the Lutheran Church–Missouri Synod. Anglicanism underwent a liturgical and theological revival in the Oxford movement, which ended with the conversion of a number of prominent Anglicans to Roman Catholicism. Despite all of these theological developments, the vitality of Christianity in the nineteenth century depended not so much on them as on the revival movements that swept across Europe and North America.

7. THE NEW TÜBINGEN SCHOOL

At one time the University of Tübingen was the center of an ultraorthodox Lutheranism; it was a stronghold of Pietism, which was more church-oriented in Württemberg than elsewhere in Germany. Under Gottlob Christian Storr (1746–1805), Tübingen theology was conspicuously orthodox; it was this stiff orthodox Lutheranism that the philosophers Schelling and Hegel studied when they began their careers as students of theology, and it was against it that they rebelled. But it was likewise Tübingen that nurtured the nineteenth century's most spectacular theological radical, David Friedrich Strauss (1808–74), an instructor there from 1832 until he was dismissed for his heretical views in 1839.

At its peak, Tübingen orthodoxy was ably represented by Johann Albrecht Bengel (1687–1752), who combined massive and tireless scholarship and considerable critical acumen with a vigorous commitment to the Pietistic conviction that the Bible is a unity with the Holy Spirit as its author, and is internally consistent and totally reliable. The historian Emanuel Hirsch comments thus on Bengel's achievement: "It is a very consistent carrying through of Pietistic presuppositions, in which nothing can be altered without everything collapsing."[8] Bengel found a valiant imitator in Storr, who challenged both Kant and Semler as well as a number of lesser opponents of orthodoxy. His last courageously orthodox successor in Tübingen was Johann C. F. Steudel (1779–1837), who helped to banish the notorious Strauss, but who lost his credibility as a result of his intemperate and dogmatic posture. Although they opposed Kant's critical skepticism and disputed its results, Storr, Steudel, and their allies accepted Kant's axiom that human reason is incapable of reaching any theoretical conclusions concerning the supernatural. Rather than argue for the faith on rational grounds and thus expose it and themselves to rational attacks, these defenders of orthodoxy sought to rest faith entirely on biblical assertions accepted on faith.

Under the withering attacks of the Age of Reason and the critical philosophers it produced, generation after generation of Christians seeking to preserve their orthodoxy declined to meet the critics on their own ground and retreated to a different kind of defense, claiming to base their faith on something that cannot be scrutinized and refuted. For Schleiermacher, it was man's aesthetic sense; for these last representatives of Tübingen orthodoxy, it was the simple authority of Scripture. A theologian from the latter part of the nineteenth century, Albrecht Ritschl (1822–89), saw faith primarily as an ethical matter, not subject to historical criticism. Karl Barth (1886–1968) will gain notoriety as what contemporary Anglican theologian Eric Mascall calls an "extreme revelationist," because he will hold that the only possible source of the knowledge of God is via the direct address of God's Word; God speaks to us in Scripture, but his word is not subject to critical scrutiny or disproof and neither need nor can be proved.

More important in the life of the church than the theses of the theologians were the sermons of the evangelists. Wherever the orthodox faith was listless and ineffectual, either because it had grown stiff and cold through many decades of formalistic dogmatism, because it had been withered by rationalistic criticism, or for any other reason, there was the possibility that a revival would break out and ignite Christians to fresh enthusiasm. From the perspective of theology, or orthodoxy and the heresies that challenged it, the revival movements tended to presuppose orthodoxy and to brush classical and innovative heresy aside, but without refuting it or even really addressing the concerns out of which it arose. The succeeding revivals of orthodoxy were more emotional than intellectual, and faded again as the emotions that had carried them cooled. From Pietism onward, no revival to the present day has had the long-term impact of earlier reform movements. One revival has had to follow on the heels of another with increasing rapidity. Thus, despite the zeal and industry exhibited at Tübingen, for example, orthodox Protestantism in Germany was unable to preserve a solid intellectual foundation for the faith it sought to defend. Orthodoxy came to depend on periodic revivals for its very survival. And now we must ask whether what survived through a succession of revivals was still orthodoxy. Augustine would have recognized Luther's message, and Luther would have recognized Spener's, but would any of them have recognized Schleiermacher's? And whose example is really the pattern for more recent evangelists and their revivals? There is little doubt whom they would like to emulate; in the following chapter, we shall ask to what extent they succeed in their endeavors.

SELECTED BIBLIOGRAPHY

Aner, Karl. *Die Theologie der Lessingzeit*. Hildesheim: Georg Olms, 1964.

Chadwick, Owen. *The Secularization of the European Mind in the Nineteenth Century*. Cambridge: University Press, 1975.

Cockshut, A. O. J. *Religious Controversies of the Nineteenth Century: Selected Documents*. Lincoln: University of Nebraska Press, 1966.

Cragg, Gerald Robertson. *From Puritanism to the Age of Reason: A Study of Changes in Religious Thought Within the Church of England 1660 to 1700*. Cambridge: University Press, 1950.

Creed, John Martin, and John Sandwith Boyssmith. *Religious Thought in the Eighteenth Century: Illustrated from Writers of the Period*. Cambridge: University Press, 1934.

Dickens, Arthur Geoffrey. *The German Nation and Martin Luther*. New York: Harper & Row, 1974.

Garvie, Alfred E. *The Ritschlian Theology: Critical and Constructive*. Edinburgh: T. & T. Clark, 1902.

Goldmann, Lucien. *The Philosophy of the Enlightenment: The Christian Burgess and the Enlightenment*. Translated by Henry Maas. Cambridge: M.I.T. Press, 1968.

Harris, Horton. *David Friedrich Strauss and His Theology*. Cambridge: University Press, 1973.

————. *The Tübingen School*. London: Oxford, 1975.

Livingston, James C. *Modern Christian Thought from the Enlightenment to Vatican II*. New York: Macmillan, 1971.

Mackintosh, Hugh Ross. *Types of Modern Theology: Schleiermacher to Barth*. New York: Scribner, 1958.

Niebuhr, Richard R. *Schleiermacher on Christ and Religion*. New York: Scribner, 1964.

Patrick, Denzil G. M. *Pascal and Kierkegaard*. London: Lutterworth, 1947.

Reardon, Bernhard M. G., ed., *Liberal Protestantism*. London: Adam & Charles Black, 1968.

Tatlow, Tissington. *The Story of the Student Christian Movement of Great Britain and Ireland*. London: S.C.M., 1933.

Weinel, Heinrich. *Jesus in the Nineteenth Century and After*. Edinburgh: T & T Clark, 1914.

20

THE ORTHODOXY OF REVIVAL: A REVIVAL OF ORTHODOXY?

I could not help exposing the impiety of these letter-learned teachers who say we are not now to receive the Holy Ghost and who count the doctrine of the new birth, enthusiasm. . . . Every day do I see the necessity of speaking out more and more. God knows my heart, that I do not speak out of resentment. I heartily wish all the Lord's servants were prophets; I wish the Church of England was the joy of the whole earth. But I cannot see her sinking into papistical ignorance and refined Deism, and not open my mouth against those who, by their sensual, luke-warm lives and unscriptural, superficial doctrines, thus cause her to err. O Lord, send out, we beseech Thee, Thy light and Thy truth.

George Whitefield Journals

For over a thousand years after the Council of Chalcedon, the major doctrinal controversies within Christendom all took place among contenders who were all orthodox in the sense of Nicaea and Chalcedon. Both iconoclasts and iconodules, both predestinarians and advocates of free will, both advocates of a bodily presence in the eucharist and their opponents subscribed to the doctrines of the Trinity, the consubstantiality of the Son, and the two natures of Christ. There were those such as the Albigenses who were non-Chalcedonians, but they were essentially totally beyond the fringe of Christianity. It does not make much sense to accuse a dualist of not accepting the Chalcedonian doctrine of the two natures of Christ when he does not even agree with the fundamental biblical assertion that God is the Creator.

The great magisterial Reformers all accepted the ecumenical creeds, and the majority of those in the radical Reformation, even though they might not have made use of the creeds, accepted their tenets. The doctrine of the heavenly flesh of Christ, with its monophysite implications, which was held by Menno Simons, and others, might seem to require the repudiation of Chalcedon, but the Mennonites usually did not pursue the issue to that point.

During the thousand years after Chalcedon, heretics who rejected Nicaea and Chalcedon either voluntarily left the church or were put out of it— sometimes, alas, by violent means such as the stake. Within two hundred and fifty years of the Protestant Reformation, however, the situation had changed dramatically. The Socinians, whose movement began in the sixteenth century and flourished in the seventeenth, wanted to be considered Christians, but had to resign themselves to being judged heretics by Catholics and Protestants alike. They denied essential Christian doctrines, and were forced outside the boundaries of Christianity. By the eighteenth century, daring spirits were being equally negative, but doing so *within the church*. H. S. Reimarus and J. S. Semler changed the basic rules of theological controversy, for they denied doctrines such as the deity of Christ and deliberately remained within the church while doing so. It is true that Reimarus' radical works were published after his death, and that Semler made a point of demonstrating his conformity with the church in various ways, but within a few decades, such prudent dissimulation was no longer necessary.

During the nineteenth century, the formal structure of Protestantism remained orthodox, but its intellectuals and scholars largely repudiated orthodoxy. In Protestant lands, the church had virtually become a department of the government. Doctrinal disputes came to be handled as bureaucratic problems. The principle of the state (territorial) church meant that all ordinary citizens within a given territory belonged to the same church. Even in the United States, with the constitutional principle of the separation of church and state, a kind of generalized Protestantism was considered the national religion until the second half of the nineteenth century.

Despite the formal orthodoxy, or, better said, traditionalism, of most Protestant churches in the nineteenth century, dissenters found for the first time that they could disown basic Christian doctrines and still remain within the church, sometimes even retaining high church or academic posts. For over a century, Roman Catholicism was able to restrain similar developments within its own fold; its dissenters were reduced to silence, or had to leave. Not until the second half of the twentieth century would Catholicism have to endure a situation in which prominent figures in the church and theology could doubt or even deny traditional doctrines with impunity.

By the nineteenth century Protestantism had virtually become synonymous with the culture of northern Europe and North America. When religiously committed leaders attempted to revive or reinvigorate the church, they expected to influence all of society and addressed themselves to the society in general. Unfortunately for the church, or at least for orthodoxy, society was in rapid change during the nineteenth century. To the extent that Christianity was identified with Christendom, i.e. with the society around it, it was swept along by those changes, and the transformation that could be accomplished by revival within Christianity became more and more limited.

After the conversion of Constantine, Christianity came to dominate Western culture. Movements that influenced the church and faith also deeply influenced the culture. The Protestant Reformation was the next-to-last such spiritual movement that deeply marked the culture; Pietism was, up to the present, the last. The Reformers, like the Eastern Orthodox and Western, or Latin, Catholics before them, took it for granted that they should influence their society and culture through two means: through the transformation of individuals and by changing social and political structures. To a very large extent, they succeeded, although their success was always far less complete than their leaders had hoped. The Pietists expected to transform society by transforming individuals, and to a large extent they were able to do so. The Sunday school movement, Bible distribution, foreign missions, and even the abolition of slavery in the British Empire and the United States owe much, if not everything, to the efforts of committed, Pietistic individuals.

During the latter part of the eighteenth century and to an increasing extent during the nineteenth, Christianity became more individualistic. Attempts to reform the church centered on individuals and their personal spiritual lives, not on society. It is true that Christianity continued to exert a strong force within society, but it increasingly exhausted itself in winning—and sometimes losing—single-issue campaigns, such as the abolition of slavery and prohibition. The ability of Christianity to permeate and gradually to remake society was being lost, even though the number of Christians in society was reaching hitherto unattained heights. Although it was winning the battle for individual hearts in millions of cases throughout Christendom, Christianity was no longer winning the battle for the mind, neither for the mind of society nor for the minds of individuals. Lives were changed, churches were transformed, some major legislative changes were introduced, but the foundations of doctrine were not consolidated. The Christian world and life view was gradually lost and Christianity became, for the first time since Constantine, primarily a private religion. For many years, even for several decades, as revival succeeded revival in Europe and America, the extent of this change was not fully apparent.

The impulses that produced Pietism led to two centuries of revival; indeed, the revival movement is still going on, although in an attenuated form, in the worldwide ministry of evangelists such as Billy Graham. Nevertheless, despite the fact that virtually all of the revivalists and evangelists were or are personally orthodox, for the most part they changed hearts, not minds, and revived sentiments, not doctrine. Revivalism in the nineteenth and twentieth centuries was a cure for coldness of heart, not for skepticism.

1. JOHN WESLEY AND THE METHODISTS

Pietism on the European Continent had a strong Lutheran flavor and flourished in as well as alongside the churches and the university theological faculties. In Britain and North America the situation was different. Despite the fact that England and Scotland both had established churches, making the raising up of independent congregations difficult, Pietism in Britain largely existed outside the established churches of England and Scotland. In North America, where there were no longer any established churches in the English sense by the nineteenth century, Pietism also established its own denominations. The best known and most important of these was Methodism.

a. The Beginnings

The Methodist movement—not originally meant to be a distinct denomination—grew directly out of the impact of Count von Zinzendorf and the two brothers John and Charles Wesley (1703–91 and 1707–88, respectively). Zinzendorf and his Herrnhuters worked on a small scale, founding little Moravian communities here and there. It was at one such community, in London, that John Wesley heard Pietistic Bible teaching (based on a commentary by Luther) and found his heart "strangely warmed." In view of the future development of Methodism, which is commonly considered Arminian in its view of grace, it is interesting to note that Wesley's own conversion was stimulated by Luther, mediated through Zinzendorf.

The Lutheran Pietists were the most sentimental of the Lutherans, and Zinzendorf and his Moravians were the most sentimental of the Pietists. They combined action with their sentiment, and it is their activism rather than, or at least more than, their sentiment that they passed on to Wesleyanism, a movement that far outgrew its original Pietistic beginnings. Wesleyan Methodism, like Pietism, tends to make life central and doctrine secondary. This was a desirable and even necessary corrective in situations where orthodoxy means no more than repeating correct formulas with little or no spiritual life. But in a situation where the formulas are by and large no longer correct, or even known at all, emphasis on enthusiasm and its effects rather than on doctrine and its implications is very problematic indeed for a religion claiming to originate in revealed truth.

The founders of Methodism, John Wesley and his younger brother Charles, received strong impulses from Zinzendorf and the Moravian Brethren of Herrnhut. John Wesley spent two weeks at Herrnhut in the summer of 1738, following the Wesleys' conversion in a Moravian fellowship in London earlier that year. For a time the Wesleys collaborated with the equally enthusiastic George Whitefield (1714–70), one of the most effective preachers and evangelists ever to use the English language. Whitefield, unlike John Wesley, believed in predestination; they quarreled on this point as early as 1741, and the predestinarians ultimately left the Wesleyan movement.

The movement Whitefield and the Wesleys initiated produced immediate and tangible results in areas where Anglicanism had been inactive or ineffectual: in foreign missions, in Bible distribution, and in launching a movement against slavery. Their movement was the beginning in English-speaking lands of the variety of Protestantism known as evangelicalism. The evangelical movement is remarkable for the fact that while it stressed certain basic doctrines and called for personal conversions, it had an immediate and marked impact on all of society. The social impact of early evangelicalism has been largely forgotten by the movement's modern heirs; their opposition to the "social Gospel" of liberal Protestantism has rendered them far less activistic than their eighteenth- and nineteenth-century forebears.[1]

b. Revival in North America

The direct influence of Wesley and the Wesleyan revival led to the establishment of strong and flourishing Methodist churches in North America, where they rapidly became a very prominent part of the Protestant church scene. Even more important than the role played by Methodism as such is the role of the revival impulse: revivalism is as characteristic of North American religious life in the eighteenth and nineteenth centuries as polemicism was of German Protestantism in the seventeenth, and its influence has by no means disappeared even in the twentieth. Revivals and revivalism became the chief defense of the orthodox and the pious against liberalism and unbelief. The question that we must ask is whether it offered an adequate defense against heresy. Is revival orthodox? Or is it really concerned at all about the problem of the conflict between heresy and orthodoxy? The revivalists were not at all indifferent to doctrinal questions; indeed, they usually subscribed to an orthodox variety of Protestantism. But their zeal was for revival, not for the reformation of doctrine and theology. Consequently the religion that resulted from their efforts was often quite different from classical Protestant orthodoxy.

The dominant religious tradition of the North American colonies of Britian was Calvinism. It took on a particularly characteristic form in New England, where a Puritan Congregationalism was the established religion in several colonies. In Massachusetts the parish was a governmental as well as an ecclesiastical unit. In order to join the church in the fullest sense, to "own" or take the covenant upon himself, a believer had to be able to testify to his own conversion. Inasmuch as many otherwise solid citizens could not or would not give such testimony, but could not reasonably be excluded from the life of the community, the concept of the "halfway covenant" grew up for those who were willing to accept the ministry and discipline of the church without being able to claim an individual conversion experience. Although the logic of the traditional understanding of the Lord's Supper requires that participation in the communion be reserved for converted Christians, Solomon Stoddard (1643–1729), pastor in Northampton, considered the communion a means of conversion and encouraged the "unconverted" (in the sense of those who lacked an individual experience of conversion) to participate in it.

Stoddard's grandson, Jonathan Edwards (1703–58), was also his successor as pastor at Northampton from 1727 to 1750, when Edwards was deposed, afterward becoming president of Princeton College. A rigorist, Edwards rejected the idea of the halfway covenant and would administer baptism and serve the communion only to converted believers (and to their children, in the case of baptism). He is best known for his preaching of hell and damnation; his sermon "Sinners in the Hands of an Angry God" has become part of American folklore. Theologically, however, Edwards is significant as the originator of what is called the New England theology, which is the result of combining a predestinarian Calvinism with an urgent call to repentance and conversion. In *A Careful and Strict Inquiry into the Modern Prevailing Notions of That Freedom of the Will* (1754) Edwards reformulated traditional predestinarian doctrine with the emphasis that grace imparts to man the will to love God in freedom.

Edwards was followed by his friend and pupil Samuel Hopkins (1721–1803), one of the first theologians to speak of dogmatics as a system: his *System of Doctrines Contained in Divine Revelation* was published in 1793. Hopkins introduced the idea of "mediate imputation." As applied to the fall of man, "mediate imputation" means that the guilt of Adam's sin is not directly imputed to all his descendants (the classical doctrine of original sin). Instead, they inherit Adam's flawed and sinful disposition, and become individually guilty as they carry out their sinful propensity. The Christological significance of this doctrine lies in its parallel application to the work of Christ. Like the guilt of Adam, the righteousness of Christ is not directly imputed to us: we must appropriate it in conversion. The interest of theology was pointed away from the doctrines of the person and work of Christ to the psychology of conversion, a shift that was consistent with the interest of the age in the individual and his personal liberty. American theology, both within the Reformed tradition and outside of it, became more anthropocentric. At first this new interest did not imply any deviation in the area of Christological doctrine, but it gradually paved the way for the more adoptionist Christology that typifies liberal Christianity in the United States.

Orthodox Protestant theology traditionally emphasizes the doctrine of the Trinity and teaches the deity of Christ as the incarnation of the Son, the second Person of the Trinity. The great Christological controversies of the early church as well as the eucharistic and kenotic controversies of the sixteenth and seventeenth centuries were attempts to answer questions concerning what it means to say that God has become a specific, individual, historical human being, Jesus Christ. Most revivalistic religion readily assumed the deity of Christ, and asked what it meant to be saved and how conversion can be produced.

2. REVIVAL ON THE EUROPEAN CONTINENT

The same winds of revival swept over the European Continent, particularly over Germany and Switzerland. However, because Protestantism was so much more solidly established on the Continent than in the United States, and because theological education was in the hands of the publicly supported university faculties of theology, the waves of revival did not mold the church in Europe as they did in the United States. In Germany, religious liberalism was tied closely to patriotism and the nationalistic movement that helped free Germany from Napoleon. Although a large minority of Germans remained Roman Catholic, Germany tended to be identified with Protestantism and Protestantism with progress, i.e. with liberal thought and idealistic philosophy. The dynamic role played by religious radicals and even by atheists in the German nationalist movement gave them immediate recognition as patriots and made it harder for the more orthodox and more pious to criticize them for their theology.

J. G. Fichte, the philosopher of Absolute Being who had been forced to leave the university at Jena (Saxony) in 1799 in the so-called Atheists' Controversy, won sympathy for his patriotic tracts combining religion and philosophy with the politics of the day; one of them is entitled *Instruction in the Blessed Life* (1806). Schleiermacher, whose father was an army chaplain, had to leave the University of Halle when the French closed it in 1806; from Berlin he inflamed his congregation to patriotic fervor in a series of rousing anti-French sermons. Patriotism was not limited to the liberals: E. M. Arndt (1769–1860), Karl Theodor Körner (1791–1813), and Max von Schenkendorf (1783–1817) were conservatives who also took up the nationalistic cause. Typically, these orthodox Christian patriots stressed the fatherhood of God, his justice, and his providential ordering of the universe, rather than Christ and his reconciliation. After the liberation of Germany from Napoleon in 1814, two main conservative directions appeared within German Protestantism: one a self-consciously Lutheran renewal of orthodoxy, the other a revival movement similar to those in Britain and North America.

a. Lutheran Renewal

Although the influence of Calvin is more widely diffused among Protestants of various nationalities and cultures, the personality of Martin Luther has left a more distinct stamp on his followers. In academic theology, the rationalism of the eighteenth century remained dominant, but the traditional supernaturalism of the Pietist movement survived alongside it. Neither liberalism nor Pietism was interested in the doctrinal differences between Lutheranism and Calvinism. After the defeat of Napoleon, Prussia became the largest and strongest German state and incorporated a number of smaller, formerly independent states together with their various state churches, some Lutheran, some Reformed. Prussia's King Frederick William III was upright and pious, but theologically naive; in his zeal to bring together the Christians under his rule, he mandated a Union of Lutheran and Reformed churches in Prussia on September 27, 1817—only weeks short of the three-hundredth anniversary of Luther's posting of the Ninety-five Theses. The new Union met with considerable public approval, but its validity was challenged only four weeks later by Klaus Harms (1778–1855), a former disciple of Schleiermacher turned orthodox Lutheran. On October 31, Harms published a new set of Ninety-five Theses in Kiel, calling for a return to the traditional faith of the Lutheran confessions. His appeal combined a desire for orthodoxy with a Romantic, nationalistic idealization of Luther as an authentic German hero. The Germanocentric Lutheran orthodoxy of Harms failed to gain control of the state churches in Germany, but it has survived in a vigorous transplant in North America, the Lutheran Church–Missouri Synod. Despite some important points of agreement by contrast with liberal theology, this orthodox Lutheranism was hostile to revivalistic Pietism; the great architect of conservative Lutheranism in North America, C. F. W. Walther, tells of his own conversion as a struggle to liberate himself from the bondage of Pietistic legalism.[2]

b. Erweckung

"In the years after 1817, the turn to the simple faith and the pious customs of the fathers became more and more widespread and decisive. The general conditions of the day—the French rule, the national liberation move-

ment and the subsequent national disillusionment, the tricentennial of the
Reformation, political reaction and economic depression, the Romantic
mood, the religiously deepened supernaturalism, and a few outstanding leaders, such as Schleiermacher, all worked in the same direction."[3] Karl Heussi's description of the bewildering complex of factors leading up to the nineteenth century *Erweckung*, "awakening," in Germany leaves the reader
wondering what kind of a movement it can have been. One thing that is
missing is the recovery of a solid basis of biblical authority; the movement
flourished alongside of Lutheran orthodoxy, but did little either to revive
orthodoxy or to draw strength from it. The fatal dichotomy between orthodox theory and Pietist practice that was only a tendency with Francke and
Zinzendorf became a reality in the nineteenth-century *Erweckung*.

In the nineteenth century, for the first time in the long history of the
church, widespread spiritual revival took place unaccompanied by a revival
of orthodox theology. The contrast with the Reformation and early Pietism
is considerable: both Lutheranism and Calvinism were largely university-
centered, and Pietism had its center for decades at the University of Halle.
In the North American colonies, revival leaders such as Jonathan Edwards
and Timothy Dwight were educators, presidents respectively of Princeton
and Yale. But by the time of the nineteenth-century *Erweckung* the university connection was broken, especially where the churches were state-sup-
ported and theology was taught in public universities.

Neither supernaturalism nor a strong commitment to the Bible as the
Word of God faded, but rather the effort to defend them within the intellectual community in academic terms. The new revivals rejected the naturalistic
religion of Deism as well as the skepticism of the Enlightenment, but did
not refute them. The challenge that man's mind had raised was answered by
an appeal to his heart. The modern mentality that had undermined faith was
countered with an equally modern sentimentality, rather than with a renewal
of the Christian mentality. Although the language of this newer revival
movement was very similar to that of early Pietism, its mentality was different: it was more sentimental, less scholarly. Scholarship may have
seemed dry and perhaps irrelevant at times to Spener and Francke, but they
did not consider it dangerous; the modern Pietistic movement looked on it
from the beginning as an adversary. This antipathy was only partly justified,
for while the universities were often hostile to faith, most of the great figures
of Reformation and post-Reformation Protestantism were men of scholarship. Modern revivalism and evangelicalism, by contrast, does have its
scholars and its educators, but by and large they are insignificant figures
compared to the great evangelists such as Dwight L. Moody, Billy Sunday,
and—in our own day—Billy Graham.

The new Pietism overwhelmed skepticism with sentiment but did not answer it. While it presupposed a foundation of historic orthodoxy, the new movement did nothing to repair the tremendous damage that had been done to orthodoxy by a century and more of rationalism and skepticism. Consequently the modern revival movement totally lacks an intellectual foundation. It has produced no Irenaeus or Augustine, no Bernard or Aquinas, no Luther, Calvin, or Melanchthon. There were some great scholars among nineteenth-century orthodox Lutherans and Calvinists—the names of Ernst Wilhelm Hengstenberg (1802–69) in Berlin and Charles Hodge (1797–1878) in Princeton being two of the most prominent. But their learning, impressive though it was, was rejected by their liberal academic colleagues on the one hand and largely ignored by the modern Pietists on the other; there was very little integration of learning and spiritual life.

c. The Influence of Romanticism

The Romantic movement that sprang up all over Europe at the end of the eighteenth century has been characterized by T. E. Hulme as "spilt religion." It rejected the cold rationalism of the Age of Reason in favor of a rebirth of *enthusiasm*—including, but not confined to, religion. The mood of the Romantics, however secular and impious they may have been, was compatible with the warmth and emotional fervor of the religious awakenings, but not compatible with the dogmatic rigor of orthodoxy.

The new Pietism shared with Romanticism a common hostility to the academic education of the day, often resorting to simple denunciation rather than venturing to challenge the rationalists on their own terms. Thus Gottfried Menken (1768–1831) denounced the reigning Kantian critical philosophy of his day as blasphemous and anti-Christian. Menken's contemporary Schleiermacher warned the orthodox that their dogmatic intransigence would serve the cause of unbelief: "This blockade, the complete starvation of all science . . . will raise the flag of unbelief, compelled by you, because you have so isolated yourselves. Is the knot of history to be untied in such a way that Christianity will be left with barbarism, and scholarship with unbelief?"[4] Although Menken rejected rationalism and liberalism and was one of the early leaders of the revival, he considered conformity to the confessions "servile" and criticized the Heidelberg Catechism for its emphasis on the wrath of God. In other words, while objecting to the critical subjectivism of the liberals, he did not oppose it with objective standards but rather with a pious subjectivity. He emphasized the concept of the devil and his agents, the demons, as well as some very precise ideas concerning the Last Day.

Sixteenth-century Lutheran theologians had been reluctant to accept the idea that all biblical doctrines are fundamental, although their Roman Catholic opponents argued that this is a logical implication of the doctrine of biblical inerrancy. Menken, who was indifferent to the confessions that set forth fundamentals and emphasized a number of doctrines that, while found in Scripture, appear less central, went so far as to call the Bible "Light of Light," a phrase that the Nicene Creed ascribes to God the Son.[5] Such lavish praise for the Bible gave a measure of credibility to the charges that Pietism was bibliolatry, Bible worship. Like Schleiermacher, Menken was a Prussian patriot, and identified Christian humility with obedience to the King.

The new Pietist biblicism broke more drastically with the tradition of classical theology than had been the case with the *sola Scriptura* principle of Luther. Luther's Reformation was theological, and Spener's early Pietism criticized it for neglecting the Christian life. Spener and Francke stressed the life but without opposing theology; the modern Pietist movement is antitheological. Its attention to details rather than structure permitted it to construct a new method in eschatology. Unlike Joachim of Floris, who divided history into grand, sweeping periods, modern Pietism likes to construct a detailed timetable and discern the correspondence between the figures of prophecy and contemporaneous events. Old Testament prophecies take on a new importance. "For Menken, Old Testament religion takes precedence over the Gospel. . . . All the threads that bind Christian thought to the education and thought of the Indo-Germanic peoples, be they Greeks, Romans, or modern Europeans, are severed. An alien, Oriental religion remains."[6] For the first time, modern Pietism made Christianity seem alien to the culture it had shaped. Modern Pietism made both Hellenistic and Latin culture—which had so strongly influenced classical theology—appear to have no legitimate contribution to make, and thus effectively discredited much of the theological tradition of Christianity without actually attacking it.

Like the New England theology, Menken's Pietism abandoned the traditional emphasis on the doctrine of original sin as the imputation of Adam's guilt to his descendants, and taught only that all human beings inherit the tendency to sin. Inasmuch as sin became less radical in its effects, a less radical salvation was required, and Christology underwent a certain modification. Menken interpreted the concept of self-emptying, or *kenosis*, in the Epistle to the Philippians in terms of a complete laying aside by Christ of his divine attributes. This produced a more complete identification with us, but appeared to forfeit part of the orthodox Chalcedonian doctrine of Christ's two natures. Menken and his fellow Pietists had no intention of detracting from the deity of Christ, but their indifference to the historic formula of Chalcedon, worked out after so many decades of conflict, left them open to the same exaggerations and errors Chalcedon was intended to prevent. As the Romantics had valued creativity, the Pietists prized spontaneity, and at times confused new ways of expressing old truths with new ideas no longer compatible with old truths.

Menken's kenotic ideas were carried further by Gottfried Thomasius (1802–75), who developed the modern Lutheran kenotic theory in two major works, *Contributions to Church Christology* (1845) and *The Person and Work of Christ* (1852). Thomasius taught that the divine Logos laid aside all of the attributes of deity incompatible with humanity, especially his omnipotence, ubiquity, and omniscience. This view was developed by the Danish Lutheran Bishop Hans Martensen (1808–84). Martensen saw in this new kenotic theology a key to the understanding of the mystery of the incarnation. Unfortunately his idea of a God who transforms himself into a man affects the immutability of deity and divides the Trinity, creating more problems than it solves. Although they were Lutherans, Thomasius and Martensen moved in a direction opposite to that of Luther's Christology. Luther had stressed the communication of the attributes of deity to Christ in his humanity; the new kenotic theory appears to apply to deity the limitations of humanity. Rather than stressing that God became incarnate in one man, Jesus Christ, with all of the conceptual problems such a doctrine brings, this new view suggested a kind of dialectical humanization of God; its ultimate consequence is the "death of God" theology of Thomas J. J. Altizer. In Berlin and Rostock, the orthodox Lutherans Hengstenberg and Friedrich Adolf Philippi (1809–92) stressed Lutheran confessionalism and the orthodoxy of the seventeenth century, but their impact was far less than that of Martensen's redoubtable Danish adversary, Søren Kierkegaard (1813–55).

d. Kierkegaard

In the Denmark of Kierkegaard's day, the tie between nation and church was even more strongly developed than in patriotic Prussia. Nikolai F. S. Grundtvig (1783–1872), who after a varied career became a bishop in the Lutheran church of Denmark, was an enthusiastic admirer of Norse mythology, and wanted to turn the Lutheran state church into a kind of Norse Christianity. Grundtvig was a Romantic and a traditionalist; following P. C. Kierkegaard, Søren's brother, he attributed the Apostles' Creed to Jesus himself; he supposed him to have taught it to the Apostles after his resurrection. Søren opposed Grundtvig's complacent identification of Christianity with popular Danish culture, and sought to achieve a new authenticity by taking its doctrines with radical seriousness.

In retrospect, Kierkegaard has become the best-known theological figure of the early nineteenth century, but he was virtually unknown outside Denmark in his own day. From one perspective, Kierkegaard was radically opposed to the accommodation of Christianity to culture advocated by

Schleiermacher and Grundtvig. Where they had sought to make Christianity at home in their culture, Kierkegaard sought to expose the radical clash between Christianity and humanism. Nevertheless, with his radical subjectivism, Kierkegaard had little use for confessions and creeds. Like Schleiermacher, he was indifferent to the doctrine of the Trinity, which he never mentions. In recent decades he has become a Danish national hero even to conservative Danish Lutherans, who claim that he presupposed orthodox doctrines and merely sought to take them with intense seriousness. The more prevalent impression is that Kierkegaard was more concerned about the intensity and seriousness of the individual Christian than about the orthodoxy or truth of his doctrines. In any event it is evident that Kierkegaard did not think it necessary to stress the objective truth of historic Christian doctrines. Like Schleiermacher, Kierkegaard succeeded in making Christianity once again interesting to people who had found it unattractive, but he failed to communicate to them an interest in its objective doctrinal content or its truth.

3. THE QUESTION OF ORTHODOXY

The revival movement in both Europe and North America became the foremost expression of conservative Protestantism in the nineteenth century; in North America, it is still a vital force even today. From almost every perspective, it appears more vigorous and more impressive, and perhaps also more appealing, than the more traditional Protestant orthodoxies that have also survived into our day.

The early Pietist movement, although intended as an antidote to dead orthodoxy, was itself fairly orthodox; it sought to revive orthodoxy, not to provide an alternative to it. The modern Pietist movement had to struggle not with dead orthodoxy but with liberalism and Romanticism; it did so not by defending its own terrain, but by attacking them on theirs. It attacked the rationality of liberalism with a new religion of feeling, and, adopting much of the Romantic mood, sought to Christianize it by directing its hero worship to the person of Jesus Christ. It sought to be modern and relevant, and to show that Christianity is not the mere cultivation of antiquities. It sought to be national and patriotic, and in so doing it lost sight of the universality of the Gospel. It was never its intention to lose touch with historic orthodoxy, but it thought that it could do without the creeds and confessions that had been the cause of earlier religious wars. By so doing, it gave up too much of what those treaties had been intended to secure. In consequence, we must say that while modern revivalists can be and often are personally orthodox, orthodoxy is not a concern of revivalists or a major characteristic of the modern revival, i.e. evangelical, movement. It refuses to be liberal, but it is not theological enough to be orthodox.

SELECTED BIBLIOGRAPHY

Baker, Derek. *Schism, Heresy and Religious Protest*. Cambridge: University Press, 1972.

Casserley, Julian Victor Langmead. *The Retreat from Christianity in the Modern World*. New York: Longmans, 1952.

Emerson, Roger L. "Heresy, the Social Order, and English Deism." *Church History* 37 (December 1968): 389–403.

Glick, G. Wayne. "Nineteenth Century Theological and Cultural Influences on Adolf Harnack." *Church History* 28 (June 1959): 157–82.

Groff, Warren F., and Donald E. Miller. *The Shaping of Modern Christian Thought*. Cleveland: World, 1968.

Groh, John E. *Nineteenth Century German Protestantism: The Church as Social Model*. Washington, D.C.: University Press of America, 1982.

Hasenhüttl, Gotthold, and Josef Nolte. *Formen kirchlicher Ketzerbewältigung*. Düsseldorf: Patmos, 1976.

Krumm, John M. *Modern Heresies*. Greenwich, Conn.: Seabury, 1961.

Mackintosh, Hugh Ross. *Types of Modern Theology*. New York: Scribner, 1958.

Opie, John, ed. *Jonathan Edwards and the Enlightenment*. Lexington, Mass.: D. C. Heath, 1969.

Rahner, Karl. *On Heresy*. New York: Herder, 1964.

Reardon, Bernard M. G. *Liberal Protestantism*. Stanford: University Press, 1968.

Schultz, Hans Jürgen. *Tendenzen der Theologie im 20. Jahrhundert: Eine Geschichte in Porträts*. Stuttgart: Kreuz, 1966.

Zahrnt, Heinze. *The Question of God: Protestant Theology in the Twentieth Century*. Translated by R. A. Wilson. New York: Harcourt, Brace & World, 1969.

21

THE RESURGENCE AND RELAPSE OF ORTHODOXY

Hypotheses are nets: only he who casts them makes a catch.

Novalis

The creed of the Council of Chalcedon inaugurated the age of orthodox Christology in 451. Not everyone agreed with Chalcedon's characteristic formulation of the mystery of Christ, expressed in terms of full deity, full humanity, and a single person. But for fifteen centuries the formula of Chalcedon defined the limits of Christological concern. Of course, there was orthodoxy in the sense defined by the Chalcedonian Creed before Chalcedon. The thesis of this work is the contention that faith in Jesus Christ as true God and true man, one person, has always been the decisive characteristic of the community of faith he established.

It took the early church four centuries to arrive at its definitive formulation of Christological doctrine. That formulation has lasted well; its fifteen-hundredth anniversary was celebrated in 1951. The 1980s are far too close to 1951 to write a definitive opinion of that celebration. Yet it is beginning to look as though that tremendous anniversary—which marked an epochal triumph of a complex creed that had stood the test of fifteen centuries—must be seen as a commemoration rather than a celebration.[1] The year 451 marked the beginning of defined orthodoxy, with respect to the doctrine of Christ, within Christendom. The year 1951 may someday be seen as marking its end.

Orthodoxy has not vanished. Indeed, it can be said that there are more truly orthodox Christian believers in the world today than at any time since the Apostles began to preach. For fifteen hundred years the Chalcedonian Creed was the standard for Christian teaching about the person of the Lord.

Not only did it provide the standard, but with its limiting terms, it set the boundaries for Christological discussion and controversy. In the Reformation era, when some of the more radical thinkers deviated from the principles of Chalcedon, they were rapidly expelled from the Christian community. Today, only three decades after the sesquimillennial celebrations, the standard appears to be forgotten. Not only is Chalcedon no longer the touchstone; teaching and discussion about Christ hardly even fits into the framework erected at Chalcedon.

For those who seek to be and remain fully orthodox, evangelical, and catholic, the loss of the Chalcedonian Creed as a standard may not be a disaster, but it causes tremendous disorientation. It involves a transformation the magnitude of which cannot be ignored. This goes beyond anything that has happened so far in the history of Christianity with its constant interplay of heresy and orthodoxy. The great historians of the faith may contend, from their various viewpoints, that the development of early catholic, medieval, or Reformation theology represented a distortion of the New Testament message. The conflict of orthodoxy with the Enlightenment and the varieties of liberalism it engendered was long and fierce, and is not yet entirely past. But the eclipse of Chalcedon—whether it is permanent or only transitory— is more ominous than anything that has happened so far.

Historians of Christianity and its relationship to society often claim that Constantine created Christian Europe, or Christendom, but that now we are in the post-Constantinian era. In theology, we have to say that we now seem to have entered a post-Chalcedonian era. The transformation this development portends is greater than anything that has yet happened within Christianity. It can be compared only to the transition within biblical monotheism itself, from the unitary monotheism of Israel to the trinitarianism of the Council of Chalcedon. The difference is symbolized by the transition from the prayer *Shema Yisroel*, of Deuteronomy 6:4 ("Hear, O Israel: The Lord our God is one Lord . . ."), to the confession of the Athanasian Creed, "We worship one God in Trinity, and Trinity in unity."

Was the transition from the personal monotheism of Israel to the tripersonal theism of Nicaea a legitimate development of Old Testament revelation? Christians affirm that it is, holding that Nicaea represents a fuller unfolding, not a distortion, of the self-disclosure of the God of Israel. Indeed, the trinitarianism of Nicaea and the Christological definitions of Chalcedon are seen as the valid and necessary interpretation of the claims of Jesus Christ in the context of the Old Testament witness to the God who is One. Without Nicaea and Chalcedon, it would not have been possible to maintain that Christianity is a biblical religion, the legitimate daughter of Old Testament Judaism. Today the clarity and necessity of Chalcedon, if not refuted or disproved, has been widely forgotten and ignored. Christianity took four centuries to formulate its witness to the deity and humanity of Christ in the context of the one God of Abraham, Isaac, and Jacob in such a way that it preserved a coherent approach to the unity of truth. It has taken fifteen centuries more to forget Chalcedon again; as it loses touch with Chalcedon, the Christian world is in the process of losing its coherence. It is in fact losing the conviction that there is any final truth about the one who said, "I am the way, the truth, and the life" (John 14:6).

1. AT THE GATES OF HELL

Can Christianity long continue to exist without heresy to spur it? The threat of post-Chalcedonian theology is not that it teaches new heresies—those orthodoxy can resist—but that it is in the process not merely of abolishing the concept of heresy, but of forgetting that such a thing was important, or even that it ever existed. If they place reliance on the words of the Bible, Christians can confidently continue to affirm their trust in Christ's promise for his church: "The gates of hell shall not prevail against it" (Matt. 16:18).

At many times during the nearly two thousand years since Christ made his promise to Peter, the church has seemed close to being overwhelmed by those "gates of hell." Gnosticism and Arianism, despite their Christian vestments, represented something fundamentally different; if either of them had triumphed, Christianity as we know it would have ceased to exist. Other challenges were severe, and the conflicts they aroused fierce, sometimes bloody. But the Nestorians and the Monophysites, had either's cause triumphed, would not have destroyed Christianity. Nor would the iconoclasts, or the Lollards, or the Lutherans, the Romanists of Trent, or even the Mennonites. Protestant liberalism was more dangerous; the great Presbyterian controversialist J. G. Machen was correct when he called it "another religion." But even the Protestant liberalism of the nineteenth and twentieth centuries had this in common with orthodoxy: it was fighting about the same things. Its convictions were different, radically different, but it was concerned to explain the same question, even if it ended by explaining it away: how the man Jesus of Nazareth came to be confessed as "true God and true man." Post-Chalcedonian theology, for the first time, is no longer concerned. It may be difficult to persuade, or refute, a passionate opponent, but one can at least argue with him. When he forgets what he wanted to argue about, no dispute is possible.

If the second half of the nineteenth century saw orthodoxy in retreat before liberalism, both within Catholicism and among Protestants, the first decades of the twentieth century shattered the élan of liberalism more thoroughly than all the arguments of all the orthodox. Liberalism had set aside the perfections of Christ for the perfectability of man and the perpetuality of progress; World War I destroyed them both. Protestantism and Catholicism both began to react against liberalism before World War I. Pope Leo XIII (reigned 1878–1903) had decreed the subordination of critical religious science to the authority of St. Thomas early in his reign (bull *Aeterni Patris,* 1879). Pius X (reigned 1903–14) condemned the errors of modernist Catholicism decisively in 1907 (in the so-called Syllabus of Errors, the bull *Lamentabili*). In Protestant circles, "fundamentalism" had its birth in North America early in the century, but the real strength of Protestant traditionalism was expressed not by the contentions of the fundamentalists, but by the spread of revivalism and the international missionary movement. The strong theological reaction within Protestantism immediately followed the European disaster of World War I. It seemed for a moment—indeed, for two or three decades—as though orthodoxy would undergo a full-scale resurgence.

2. THE RESURGENCE OF
ORTHODOX THEOLOGY

During most of the history of Christianity, doctrine, piety, and ethics have gone hand in hand. The great theologians were frequently, if not always, the great preachers. The greatest intellectual luminaries of Catholicism, such as Thomas Aquinas and Bonaventure, if not always preachers themselves, nevertheless came from the preaching and mendicant orders: Aquinas was a Dominican (O.P., i.e. Order of Preachers), Bonaventura a Franciscan. The architects of Protestant theology, Luther and Calvin, spent more time and energy preaching than in any other activity. Even today, over four centuries after his death, there remain voluminous unedited manuscript transcripts of sermons Calvin preached so industriously in Geneva. Some, if not all, of the great nineteenth-century revivalists were theologically productive. By the twentieth century, revivalism seemed largely cut off from theological productivity, sometimes even from theological literacy. Some, if not many, of our own century's theological leaders have maintained an active preaching career, but the great majority are better known for initiating controversies than for conversions. At no time in the history of the church has there been a greater tendency for the heart and head to be separated. The most recent revival of piety and evangelism coincided with a notable resurgence of orthodoxy, but the two were not integrally related. Perhaps the failure of Chalcedonian orthodoxy so soon after its great jubilee of 1951 is to be attributed to this fatal separation.

The four-hundredth anniversary of the beginning of the Protestant Reformation occurred in 1917, during the fourth and final winter of the Great War. There was little time or energy in the great Protestant nations—Germany, Britain, and the United States—to celebrate Luther and his achievement; indeed, only the Germans were truly enthusiastic about him, for Lutheranism appeared far too Germanic to suit the taste of the warring British and Americans. (In the United States, much Lutheran theology and church life was carried on in German, as well as in the Scandinavian languages, until the hostilities engendered by World War I abruptly checked this.)

In defeated Germany, after the war, there was a kind of Luther renaissance, sparked by the Berlin church historian Karl Holl (1866–1926). Fifteen years younger than the celebrated Adolf von Harnack (1851–1930), Holl represented a theological generation that was no longer satisfied with the liberalism of nineteenth- and early twentieth-century Protestant culture. Holl and a group of younger scholars who followed him, such as Paul Althaus (1888–1966) and Werner Elert (1885–1954), revived as much as they could of Luther's faith without, however, rebuilding the foundations liberalism had sapped. Adolf Schlatter (1852–1938), a contemporary and adversary of Harnack, was the outstanding biblical scholar among the conservatives. His Tübingen colleague Karl Heim (1874–1958), a worthy descendant of Württemberg Pietism, reaffirmed the unique validity of the Christian faith and vigorously challenged the secularistic presuppositions of contemporary physical science. Heim, one of the few German university theologians who was willing to identify with popular piety, evangelism, and even the evangelistic German student movement Studentenmission in Deutschland suffered an eclipse under Nazism; his work began to enjoy a revival in the 1970s. Althaus, Elert, Schlatter, and Heim essentially reaffirmed an orthodox, Chalcedonian Christology, but all accepted, to varying degrees, the methodology, if not the antitheistic presuppositions, of liberal biblical scholarship. Thus they did not rediscover a sufficiently firm foundation to undergird their attempted reconstructions of orthodoxy. Like the so-called neoorthodox theologians, they were self-consciously Protestant, in fact even Lutheran, and opposed any sacrifice of Protestant distinctives for the sake of making common cause with Roman Catholics.

It was two Swiss Calvinists, rather than German Lutherans, who made the most striking effort to shift the helm of Protestant theology and chart a new course for the ark of the church. The movement they inaugurated, called variously "theology of the Word," "theology of crisis," and "dialectical theology," is now best known under the name "neoorthodoxy." Each of these designations tells us something important about the movement. As a self-conscious "theology of the Word," it sought to recover the use of the Bible as God's authoritative Word of direct command to us, rather than as our source book for the study of religion. This Word places man and all his proud work and wisdom under divine judgment, and hence in "crisis"—a conclusion that imposed itself on European religion as it emerged from the carnage and rubble of war. It called itself "dialectical" in that it stressed the antithesis between God and the world, between divine revelation "perpendicularly from above," and man's conceited and often misled quest for knowledge. This new theology was not dialectical in the sense of Hegel, for whom the clash of thesis and antithesis resulted in synthesis, a fresh stage in the ascent to ultimate truth. It was instead dialectical in the sense of Kierkegaard, an unresolved, paradoxical tension in which the divine is in constant confrontation with the temporal and worldly, challenging it, judging it, condemning it, and us with it, and yet offering salvation to us in accord with "the foolishness of God [which] is wiser than men" (1 Cor. 1:25).

Protestant neoorthodoxy represents a change from traditional Protestant conservatism in that it appears to have had its roots in the Christian social conscience of thinkers such as Hermann Kutter (1863–1931) and Leonard Ragaz (1868–1948). Traditional Protestant orthodoxy tended to ignore the concerns of the social reformers and meliorists and to stick to the preaching of revival and the teaching of familiar dogma. Personal compassion and charity were by no means foreign to orthodox Protestants, but where social legislation was concerned, they generally preferred to preserve the status quo. Consequently, they were little affected by the failure of social reformers to achieve significant improvements in the human condition. Neoorthodox theologians, coming out of liberal Protestantism and deeply persuaded that the Gospel ought to bring social progress as well as salvation, were profoundly marked by its catastrophic failure to do so. War, inflation, and worldwide depression starkly revealed the failure of man's pretensions to political and economic wisdom and justice, and cast a deep shadow on the claim that "scientific theology" could produce a more perfect religion than the simple preaching of the Word.

Nineteenth-century theology with its interest in history and comparative religion and its naive assumption that all of life is characterized by evolutionary progress naturally regarded early thought—and hence early doctrine—as primitive and imperfect. The claim of creedal and confessional affirmations to be true was not so much rejected as simply pushed aside as out-of-date and irrelevant. Perhaps the most brilliant in a series of outstanding figures, Adolf Harnack committed the disqualifying spiritual blunder of welcoming World War I and endorsing the imperial policies of Kaiser Wilhelm II. Any historical relevancy that led to such practical consequences branded itself as highly suspect. Harnack, knighted by the kaiser in 1914 (and von Harnack thereafter), never quite regained his ability to impress his contemporaries as a man whose unquestioned learning gave him true spiritual and moral authority.

Against this background—the collapse of what Barbara Tuchman called the "proud tower"—a new movement arose, profoundly distrustful of historicism and relativism, committed to reestablishing the fundamental doctrines of orthodox Christianity. Its chief representatives were Karl Barth (1886–1968) and Emil Brunner (1889–1966). They rediscovered the exclusiveness of theology and the Bible's claim to unquestioned authority, rejecting culture and philosophy as sources of religious knowledge and spiritual values. As their thought developed, Barth and Brunner came to disagree about the total rejection of natural revelation, for Brunner accepted it to a degree.

The neoorthodoxy of Barth and of Brunner was church-centered, in contrast with liberalism, which was preoccupied with the academic world, and also in contrast with Pietism with its emphasis on the individual and his religious experience. Thus, although neoorthodoxy sought to reaffirm traditional doctrines, it did not seek to ally itself with those who had never forsaken them, who were chiefly to be found among the heirs of Pietism. It brought a new and more radically biblical understanding of human sin and its effects. Consequently it required a more radical and more theological understanding of the person of Christ, the Saviour from sin. Indeed, Barth made Christology the central preoccupation of his great unfinished work, *Church Dogmatics* (1932–62), so much so that his approach has been criticized as "Christomonism."

Barth emphasized that the central content of the New Testament is the redemptive work of Christ, not the doctrine of his two natures, but went on to stress that it is necessary to understand who Christ is in order to be able to comprehend what he accomplished for us. In this respect, Barth deliberately swam against the current of recent and contemporary theology, which on the whole believes that it is sufficient to speak of the work of Christ—however understood—and devote little attention to questions of "ontology," of who he is and of what his nature(s) may be. Barth deliberately stated the mystery of Christ in the language of Chalcedon, which he considered not merely suitable but virtually necessary in order to do justice to the biblical message.[2] Barth explicitly committed himself to the three great affirmations of Chalcedon: to the full deity of Christ, to the full humanity of Christ, and to the unity of his person. He went still further, affirming not only the doctrine of the Virgin Birth of Christ but even the anti-Nestorian slogan that calls Mary the *theotokos,* "God-bearing one," as well as its paraphrase in the term "Mother of God."[3] It is hardly possible to conceive of a more vigorous reaffirmation of Chalcedon. Barth does betray a Reformed rather than a Lutheran understanding of the mystery with respect to the communication of attributes. Thus he retains the famous "extra Calvinisticum" of seventeenth-century Lutheran-Calvinist polemics. The humanity of Christ was fully taken into the Logos, but the Logos is not fully embraced by the humanity: something remains, an "extra." The Word continues to exist outside (*extra*) the human flesh of Jesus. Thus, despite his affirmation of the *theotokos*, Barth perpetuates the typical Calvinist tendency, in Christological matters, to lean in the direction of Nestorius rather than that of the Monophysites. Nevertheless, both in word and in spirit Barth remained distinctly and deliberately Chalcedonian, the last Protestant theologian of his stature to do so without reservation.

Brunner also began with a clear reaffirmation of Chalcedonian theology, but unlike Barth, in later life he began to slip away from it. In his early work, *The Mediator* (1927), Brunner affirmed, in order, the deity and humanity of Christ and the unity of his person.[4] Even in *The Mediator*, however, Brunner showed a certain uneasiness with the language of Chalcedon. He feared that the patristic understanding of the communication of Christ's attributes between the divine and the human natures could give the "fatal" impression of a mixing of those attributes—even though the creed itself expressly prohibits such a mixing. Shortly after the publication of *The Mediator*, Brunner took the theme of the reality of salvation as encounter as a leitmotif for his theology. This caused him to reorient his approach to Christology; while he never denied the doctrinal concern of Chalcedon—clarity concerning the two natures of Christ—he came to consider it "superfluous." Consequently his *Dogmatics* (1946–60) reveals a loss of Christological substance. The discussion of the two natures of Christ is brought in as an explanation or interpretation of his saving work, not as the foundation for it. Brunner's turning away from orthodox concerns—although not, he claimed, from orthodox doctrines—may already be said to mark the beginning of a relapse of neoorthodoxy into the liberal uncertainties from which it had appeared ready to escape. What appears as only a tendency in Brunner will become the characteristic feature of the thought of Rudolf Bultmann (1886–1976), the only theological figure of the interwar period whose influence continued to grow and expand after the sesquimillennial of Chalcedon.

Thus three men, born within three years of one another (two in 1886, one in 1889), rapidly carried theology through a succession of viewpoints it had taken the early church centuries to develop and affirm (or reject). But before turning to the individual who brought his followers all the way back from the Christology of Chalcedon to a primitive form of adoptionism, Bultmann, we must look at the efforts of some of his other contemporaries to maintain traditional orthodoxy.

3. THE NEW SHAPE OF EVANGELICALISM

Martin Luther favored the name "evangelical" as the designation for churches that acknowledge the primacy of justification by faith. The word came to be adopted, in Europe, as the generic label for Protestants of all varieties. In the English-speaking countries it has a more restricted significance, for it refers to a particular type of Protestantism, also called "conservative," "orthodox," or sometimes "fundamentalist," characterized by conservative doctrine, an emphasis on individual conversion and piety, and frequently an attitude of separation from the "world." Evangelical Protestants clearly have roots in German Pietism as well as in British nonconformity. Their number also includes representatives of an undiluted Protestant orthodoxy.

From the close perspective forced upon us by the fact that these most recent developments are contemporary with us, it is difficult to assess their importance or long-range impact, as it was possible to do for pre-twentieth-century heretics and doctrines. We can discern the influence of David Friedrich Strauss in the nineteenth century far more clearly than that of Bishop John A. T. Robinson (b. 1919) or evangelist Billy Graham (b. 1918) in our own. Our vision is obscured by the fact that the secular world and much of the established church tends to celebrate only the more "critical," in other words, less orthodox, theologians, and to treat them as though only they were leaving a mark on history. Among evangelicals, it is the evangelists and controversial social activists such as Billy Graham and Jerry Falwell who become media celebrities and even household words. Evangelicalism may produce a theological mind second to none in our century—something that may be said about Carl F. H. Henry (b. 1912), but his name is far less familiar to the Christian world, and certainly to the general public, than those of scandalous but less substantial innovators such as Harvey A. Cox (b. 1929) and Thomas J. J. Altizer (b. 1927).

In his massive treatment of recent Christian history, *Protestant Theology in the Nineteenth Century,*[5] Karl Barth, the modern defender of Chalcedonian orthodoxy, did not even mention his orthodox Presbyterian predecessor, Charles Hodge (1797–1878), whose *Systematic Theology* remains a standard work for conservative Protestants a century after its publication. Bishop Charles Gore (1853–1932), Anglican defender of Chalcedon and author of *The Incarnation of the Son of God* (1891) as well as editor of *Lux Mundi* (1889), also went unmentioned by Barth, whether from deliberate judgment or out of ignorance. The thoroughly conservative American Presbyterian theologian Francis A. Schaeffer (b. 1912) had written voluminously on theological issues such as biblical inspiration, the doctrine of God, and the doctrine of Christ, but was allowed to remain in relative obscurity outside his own circle until he began to take controversial stands on social and political issues. It would be comforting to think that from the perspective of a later century, Charles Hodge will loom larger than David Friedrich Strauss, Charles Gore will loom larger than Albrecht Ritschl, and Carl Henry will loom larger than Harvey Cox. This will happen only if the degree and kind of orthodoxy they represent again comes to occupy the center of the theological stage; for the present, it has been pushed to the periphery.

Within popular evangelicalism, it may appear that the jubilee year of 1951 was just the beginning of a real revitalization. The city-wide evangelistic "crusades" of William F. ("Billy") Graham began in the United States in the late 1940s, and within a few years had spread to virtually every corner of the non-Communist world. The name of Billy Graham, unlike that of his friend and mentor Carl Henry, has become a household word throughout Christendom. Graham, like another evangelical, William R. Bright (b. 1921), founder of a lay evangelistic movement called Campus Crusade, has always been orthodox in our Chalcedonian sense, but his primary concern is not right doctrine but individual conversion.

At the point of the jubilee of Chalcedon, dynamic leaders such as Graham and Bright were poised to begin leading an advance of Christianity into the final decades of this millennium. Because they were successful, they attracted the attention of the general public, which regarded them and others like them as a vanguard of the resurgence of a kind of traditional Christianity, looking on them with gratitude or apprehension as individual sentiments demanded. At the same time, because they were not theological or doctrinal—although they were sometimes derided as dogmatic because of the firmness with which they hold their convictions—such leaders have been capable of reviving individuals and revitalizing congregations, but not of exercising any significant effect on theology itself. Thus conservative Protestantism, in the final decades of our twentieth century, is in the paradoxical position of being stronger than ever before in terms of numbers, but not in terms of theological influence. This must be said in spite of the increasing role played by orthodox Protestants in theological education, usually in newly established theological seminaries.

While the great historic seminaries and university faculties of theology dwindle and languish, or devote themselves increasingly to the study of comparative religion and related fields, new institutions with a strongly conservative commitment are flourishing, sometimes attracting far more students than their older and more prestigious sister schools. In Britain, and especially in the United States, orthodox theology is vigorous and aggressive both in newly established schools as well as in some older centers where liberalism has long prevailed. Even in Basel, Switzerland, the home of Karl

Barth, the university's faculty of theology, with five centuries of theological tradition, now graduates far fewer new ministers each year than its privately funded, belligerently conservative new neighbor, a "free theological academy" in adjacent Riehen. France with its tiny Protestant population now has two university-level faculties of orthodox Protestant theology, alongside the more famous—and liberal—faculties at Paris and Strasbourg.

Despite the evidence of the continuing vigor of traditional theology, the conservative and traditionalist movements still represent only a small part of the total ecclesiastical and theological establishment of Protestantism. Within that establishment, it is necessary to say not only that the traditional canons of conservative conviction, such as the Christology of Chalcedon, are not accepted; we must frankly acknowledge that throughout much of the Christian world they are no longer even consulted. This is particularly true of the man whose work—in scope and in size far inferior to that of Karl Barth—has set the direction for most theology since the 1950s, Rudolf Bultmann.

4. BULTMANN: THE REORIENTATION OF CHRISTIANITY

Although Rudolf Bultmann is a contemporary of Barth and Brunner, his influence was not deeply felt in the theological world until the 1950s, when that of Barth and Brunner was already beginning to wane. One of the signs that appeared to indicate a consolidation and strengthening of Christianity in the twentieth century was the establishment of the World Council of Churches in 1948, as the union of two early organizations, the Faith and Order Movement and the Life and Work Movement. A major motive for the establishment of the World Council was the widespread desire to present a united testimony to the non-Christian world in order to evangelize it more effectively. The council's confession was very simple: it required members only to "acknowledge Jesus Christ as God and Saviour." In the early church, such a formulation would have laid its advocates open to charges of monophysitism. In the twentieth century, however, true Monophysites are rare. The evident point of the confession was to insist on the deity of Jesus Christ even before asserting his saving work. From this perspective, the confession, although brief, does echo the traditional faith of orthodoxy through the centuries.

In 1951, Bultmann was invited by a group of liberal Swiss theologians to examine the confession of the World Council in the light of the New Testament. First, Bultmann pointed out that the World Council's terse formula did not reflect the conviction of the ancient church that Jesus Christ is true God *and* true man. From this allusion to the Chalcedonian doctrine of the two natures, he went on to condemn not the World Council but the council of 451 for first taking notice of the problem created by calling Christ both God and man, and then proceeding to resolve it in a way that is "totally impossible for our thought."[6] As early as 1926, Bultmann had claimed that we can know virtually nothing of the actual life and teaching of Jesus. In his eyes, the Christian faith represents the teaching of the early church, not that of Jesus. Despite this agnosticism with respect to the real Jesus, Bultmann did believe that Jesus had a decisive significance for us today, because his work was "eschatological" in nature. What this means, however, has little to do with the traditional understanding of the return of Christ and the Last Things. Jesus' eschatological work consists in making the meaning of our individual existences clear to us in radical honesty. Bultmann believed that the goal of Jesus and his early disciples was only to bring men to a new, authentic self-understanding. Unfortunately—or so it would seem—they expressed this concern in "mythological" language, which was natural for them but is unintelligible to us.

Bultmann gave new meanings to the terms "myth" and "mythological." Mythological language is language that speaks of that which is transcendent, for example of God, in terms of this world. Such language, Bultmann held, is necessarily totally meaningless to modern man. Modern man is compelled by his modern science to look on the world as a self-contained, closed whole, into which no supernatural power can intrude. If one adopts this definition of mythology (which is not the usual sense of the term in literature and comparative religious studies), then it is apparent that the entire Gospel, indeed the whole Bible, from cover to cover, is mythological. Nothing could be more mythological than the language of the Chalcedonian Creed. For Bultmann, the New Testament statements about the person of Christ are really to be understood as attempts to express the significance of his work. They only appear to be making objective statements about Jesus.

The efforts of the early church, culminating in the Chalcedonian Creed, to define the person and the nature(s) of Christ in an objective way involve a progressive distortion of the intention of the New Testament accounts. The early church applied titles of deity to Christ "in order to express how the world and man are placed in a new situation by the appearance of Jesus and thus are called to make a decision for or against God, or for or against the world."[7] It seems far simpler and a great deal more realistic to say that the early church applied such titles to Christ because it was convinced of his deity by the wonder of his resurrection. Inasmuch as Bultmann believed that the accounts of the resurrection itself were created rather than experienced by the first followers of Christ, in his eyes that cannot prove anything about Jesus but only reflect what his followers experienced in their association with him.

From the perspective of our study, Bultmann's view hardly deserves to be called a heresy. Most, if not all, of the great heresies were attempts to explain, to come to terms with the sweeping implications of the birth, life, death, and resurrection of Jesus. The events themselves were seen as real, if totally unique, occurrences that had to be explained. One set of explanations, found by Christians to be most adequate, we now designate as orthodoxy; the others, differing from it, are heresies. For Bultmann the events vary from the extremely improbable to the altogether inconceivable. They are not realities that need to be explained, either in orthodox or heretical terms, but rather they are themselves explanations. What they "explain," or rather attest, is how much Jesus meant to his disciples.

If we were to attempt to place Bultmann's views into the category of a familiar heresy, we might call him an adoptionist, for he was convinced that Jesus was a mere man. But even this weak term would say too much, for the adoptionist who thinks that Jesus was only a man nevertheless conceives of a real, personal God and some objective event when that God adopted Jesus. Bultmann is unwilling to say anything about a personal God, and certainly unwilling to discuss such a God intervening in any objective way in the real world. Such a discussion would clearly be mythological, and as such incomprehensible and unacceptable to contemporary man. With Bultmann, then, theology and Christology have not merely moved beyond orthodoxy, they have moved beyond heresy. Even heresy was a doctrine *about Christ,* albeit a wrong one. Bultmann's presentation is not a doctrine *about* anyone or anything: it is instead an urgent appeal to human beings to understand themselves in a new way, on the basis of an encounter with an amazing story, a very interesting one, but one that never actually "happened" in any usual meaning of the word.

With this approach, "theology" as we know it virtually ceases to exist. For the nineteenth-century materialist Ludwig Feuerbach (1804–72), all theological statements were really anthropological statements in disguise. Bultmann fulfilled Feuerbach's analysis. For him theology ceases to be about God; it certainly has nothing to do with a Christ who is true God and true man. Instead it is about human beings and how they can attain a new understanding of the meaning of individual *Existenz.* Attempts to grapple with Bultmann theologically are very difficult. In fact, to the extent that one meets with him on his chosen terrain, they are doomed to failure. That which traditional theology and Christology would extol and defend, namely, the objective reality of God and of the divine and human Christ, simply cannot be discussed within Bultmann's frame of reference.

In his denial of the truth of various New Testament and credal statements about Jesus, Bultmann introduces nothing that is new by comparison with the skeptics of an earlier age. What is new is his conviction, in the light of his skepticism and disbelief, that the story of Jesus remains of crucial significance for contemporary man, and that his own variety of disbelief is the key to that significance. In one way, Bultmann and his ideas can be likened to Gnosticism. Like the gnostics, he believes that nothing is as it seems, as common sense would have us see it, but requires a totally new interpretation in the light of a key, a secret comprehension known to the gnostics alone. Like the teachings of Gnosticism, what Bultmann says corresponds very little to the New Testament story, other than to use its terminology. Like Gnosticism, Bultmann's thought is fanciful and fascinating, and of course terribly frustrating. In itself it might not appear to be of great importance to the history of Christian faith, for it really has rather little to do with that faith as most of us understand it. Bultmann's direct influence today is declining. Theology—and particularly New Testament studies, Bultmann's specialty—has gone beyond him and his original denials and imaginative proposals. But everyone and everything that follows Bultmann, in the sense of depending on him, shares with his work the fact that it no longer has anything to do with theology. The year 1951, the fifteen-hundredth anniversary of Chalcedon, saw the publication of the first of the immense jubilee volumes of Grillmeier and Bacht. If they were representative of the direction theology was to take after 1951, our story would be quite different. Bultmann's little address on the World Council's confession was delivered in 1951. It has proved symbolic. It may be said to signal the passage of theology, if not of the faith of Christians, into the post-Chalcedonian era. In 1954, in the concluding volume of the jubilee series, the Roman Catholic theologian Rudolf Schnackenburg described Bultmann's theology and evaluated its correctness; as a rather traditional Roman Catholic, Schnackenburg finds Bultmann's presuppositions false and his conclusions absurd.[8] In 1954, there were very few Roman Catholics who would have taken Bultmann's part against Schnackenburg. Today, less than thirty years later, even Roman Catholic theology seems to be moving in Bultmann's suggested paths. It is his essay, not the great jubilee volumes, that has been the signpost for much subsequent Catholicism. Most of this development took place after the jubilee, and thus falls beyond the limits we have set ourselves. It is too close for analysis (and in many ways too different from all that went before it). Nevertheless, we must observe that Bultmann, although a "Protestant," might well find himself more at home in the Catholicism of the 1980s, at least at the university level, than Schnackenburg, although a Jesuit.

5. POSTJUBILEE CATHOLICISM

While Protestantism and Eastern Orthodoxy were drawing together, ultimately establishing the World Council of Churches, in order to give an impression of unity to the non-Christian world, Roman Catholicism apparently maintained an unbroken sense of confidence in its unique authority and its right to stand for all Christianity. On January 6, 1928 (January 6 being the day on which Eastern Orthodoxy celebrates the coming of Christ), Pope Pius XI, in the bull *Mortalium animos,* prohibited Catholic participation in ecumenical enterprises and called upon all non-Catholic Christians to submit to Rome as the only possible way to attain unity. On November 1, 1950, his successor, Pius XII, declared the doctrine of the bodily assumption of the Virgin Mary into heaven to be an obligatory article of faith. Even the Christologically orthodox Protestants who reaffirmed Chalcedon, going so far as to accept the term *theotokos,* nevertheless fiercely opposed the glori-fication of Mary herself. Thus the pope's action seemed a particularly dra-matic way of turning his back on the World Council's overtures toward unity. Indeed, the papal bull *Munificentissimus Deus* even alienated the Eastern Orthodox; although they had long celebrated the Feast of the As-sumption, they refused to accept it as a dogma because it was not officially declared to be such by any one of the first seven ecumenical councils. Dur-ing the immediate postwar years, Roman Catholicism seemed vigorous, self-confident, and on the advance.

After a period in which general councils—regarded as ecumenical by the papacy—were frequent in the West, the outbreak of the Protestant Ref-ormation appears to have made them rare. The work of the Counter-Refor-mation was inaugurated by the interrupted and long-protracted Council of Trent (1545–63). It was three centuries before another general council was convened, the Vatican Council of 1869–70. As Trent had taken a strong stand against the Reformation, the First Vatican Council massively reaf-firmed papal supremacy, even to the point of decreeing the dogma of papal infallibility.

The Council of Trent opposed Protestantism, but like Protestantism it presupposed the authority and infallibility of the Bible. It held that the Bible is not altogether clear or sufficient, as the Protestants claimed, and in addi-tion the council was persuaded that Protestants misinterpreted it, but in prin-ciple its authority was reaffirmed. At the time of the Council of Trent, there were no significant challenges to the principle of biblical infallibility within the Christian world. The Catholics added the authority of the church and tradition, but did not question the status of Scripture. If Catholicism were to have diminished the authority of Scripture in order to defer to biblical and historical criticism, 1869–70 would have been an appropriate time to do so. Within Protestant circles, skeptical liberalism was in full flower and orthodoxy in retreat. It is true that liberalism continued to advance into the twentieth century and beyond, with its most recent initiative being the exis-tentialist interpretation of Bultmann and his school. However, from the twentieth century onward, Protestant liberalism has been challenged on its own territory by a number of developments that have tended to rehabilitate the authority of the Bible as well as to discredit a number of naive liberal assumptions about its unreliability. In view of the fact that Roman Catholicism survived the challenges of the nineteenth century and was maintaining and even reinforcing its own distinctive position in 1950—by which time conservative and neoorthodox Protestants had broken the force of the liberal onslaught—it would have been natural to expect it to enter the 1980s still intact. Instead, the reaffirmations of the early postwar era seem to have been a kind of last hurrah, a sort of Pickett's Charge of the papacy, just prior to the beginning of disasters.

Pius XII, in many respects a true successor of Pius IX—the pope of Vatican I and papal infallibility—died in 1958, to be succeeded by the brief but pivotal reign of John XXIII (1958–63). John XXIII, in an effort to bring the church up to date (*aggiornamento*) without losing doctrinal or spiritual substance, convened the Second Vatican Council, 1962–65. John authorized liturgical reforms, and the Vatican Council took ample advantage of the opportunity. The Latin Mass, standardized at the Council of Trent and fully reflecting the crucial Roman Catholic doctrine of transubstantiation, was translated into all of the vernacular languages of the world, generally obscuring the doctrine of transubstantiation in the process. Bible reading and Bible study were encouraged, and fellowship with Protestants sought: the fact of separation was not denied, but those separated were called brothers. In the hands of many Roman Catholics, the new openness to Scripture has produced a kind of evangelical variety of Catholicism, bringing them closer to conservative Protestants. Together with conservative Protestants, these "evangelical" Catholics emphasize many of the fundamental doctrines of orthodox Christianity, including even the Reformation distinctives of justification by faith and the authority of Scripture. At the same time, the new Catholic approach has opened the gates of Catholicism's intellectual citadels to critical and even radically skeptical biblical scholarship. Catholicism became infatuated with some of the most naive "discoveries" of nineteenth-century Protestant criticism. Rudolf Schnackenburg's suspicion and rejection of Bultmann and his approach does not characterize the Catholicism of the 1960s and beyond. Quite the contrary: Roman Catholic theologians accommodated themselves to Protestant heresies, both old and new, with astonishing rapidity. Soon they were duplicating and even going beyond many of the vagaries of liberal and radical Protestants. The Jesuit order, founded in 1540 as a kind of papal shock troop against the Protestant Reformation, ceased to be a stronghold of obedience and conservatism. Jesuit scholars produced the great jubilee volumes commemorating Chalcedon, but Pierre Teilhard de Chardin (1881–1955) was also a Jesuit. Teilhard enjoyed tremendous popularity in the years immediately following his death. He was hailed as the man who was supposedly translating Catholic doctrine into modern thought, and particularly into the evolutionary frame of reference of modern biological science. In Teilhard's view, Christ became the Omega Point of all evolution; he was persuaded that he had overcome the evolutionary challenge to Christian faith by seeing evolution not as directing itself toward an ever-increasing, planless diversity, but as being directed by God in an ascent toward an ever-increasing concentration in Christ, its final point, so that ultimately "God may be all in all" (1 Cor. 15:28).[9] If Bultmann destroyed the theological dimension in Christ, Teilhard in effect abandoned his historicity. He did not of course deny the historical Jesus and the incarnation, but his historical person and work of atonement became incidental to his cosmic role as the ultimate point of evolutionary progress. After several years of great popular attention, Teilhard's views lost popularity. In general, they had little impact on Catholic dogmaticians, theologians, and Bible scholars. They are significant because their popularity reveals the extent to which the theological imagination of the modern Catholic world has been cut loose from the standards of orthodoxy, not merely in the area of exclusively Roman doctrines such as papal infallibility, but in the area of such fundamental concepts as that of the deity and humanity of Jesus Christ.

In the last years of Teilhard's life, other Roman Catholic theologians, such as Karl Rahner (b. 1904), Hans Küng (b. 1928) and, most recently, Eduard Schillebeeckx (b. 1914), began to make a name for themselves in theology. At first it appeared that they were going to take Roman Catholicism in a more biblical direction, and thus to make it more evangelical (in Luther's sense). It soon became apparent, however, that they were cutting Catholicism loose from its biblical and traditional moorings. Küng first gained attention by defending the Protestant view of justification by faith—as restated by Barth—as legitimate and compatible with Catholicism. More recently he has attacked not merely the doctrine of papal infallibility, which in its present form dates only from 1870, but also the traditional theological concerns of orthodox Christology. Like Brunner and Bultmann, he is interested less in who Christ is than in what he does. Schillebeeckx, whose *Christ, the Experience of Jesus as Lord* is the most ambitious new Roman Catholic investigation into Christology, in essence dispenses with the old categories of Chalcedonian orthodoxy. Roman Catholic theology, no less than Protestant, is moving so far from the questions and concerns that shaped the ecumenical creeds that it is hard to use them to categorize it as orthodox or heretical. It may soon be necessary to say of mainstream Roman Catholic theology that it, like most Protestantism, is neither orthodox nor heretical, but another religion.

EPILOGUE:
SIGNS OF HIS COMING?

And when the thousand years are expired, Satan shall be loosed out of his prison.

Revelation 20:7

The orthodox doctrine of the person and natures of Jesus Christ is one on which there has been a very large degree of agreement throughout the Christian world for more than fifteen centuries. The doctrine of the return of Christ, called eschatology or the doctrine of the Last Things, by contrast, is one on which Christians have never come to substantial agreement. Orthodox believers all recognize that the Scripture teaches and the creeds affirm that Christ shall "come again to judge the living and the dead." But the time of his coming, and the signs that are to precede it, have been interpreted in several different ways. Through the centuries, there have been any number of premature alarms.

There was a wave of eschatological expectation as the year 1000 approached: the calendar seemed to be showing the end of the thousand years of Revelation 20. This expectation was disappointed, but it arose again in the years 1200 and 1260, which coincided with computations based on eschatological prophecies in Daniel. Over and over again Christians have allowed themselves to be persuaded, sometimes by rather implausible arguments, that the "signs of his coming" were fulfilled and that the return of Christ was imminent. During the 1970s, the detailed eschatological calculations of a layman, Hal Lindsey, sold millions of copies to Christians and non-Christians alike, even to Moslems.

Jesus spoke frequently of his return. The Apostles present it as a blessed hope, one of the chief comforts of believers in trouble and persecution. Indeed, the theory has been put forward that the Apostles, or even

447

Jesus himself, expected an immediate return shortly after the ascension and that early Christian theology was developed in an attempt to explain and to deal with the "delayed parousia," or Second Coming. Skeptics had already appeared in the first century, ridiculing the Christians' expectations and scoffing: "All things continue as they were from the beginning of the creation" (2 Pet. 3:4). Paul warned against messianic hysteria and told believers that Christ's return will occur only after there has been a "great apostasy," presided over by the "man of sin" (2 Thess. 2:3).

Through the Christian centuries, believers have sought to identify the "man of sin" in order to be able to predict the time of the Second Coming. Many figures, ranging from Roman emperors to contemporary religious and political leaders, have been suggested, but so far no one has been convincing. The "great apostasy" has also been identified with various movements of heresy and unbelief, but apparently falsely so, if eschatological prophecy is reliable, for Christ has not yet returned.

Political events too have been urged as the fulfillment of some of the prerequisites laid down by Scripture for the return of Christ. There are many prophecies about the return of the Jews to their homeland. Frequently, it was expected that these events would be inaugurated by the Messiah himself, but it was also held that they would precede his return. At just about the time we have proposed for the end of the Chalcedonian era in theology, the fifteen-hundredth jubilee of 1951, the Jews finally did return to political power in the Holy Land. The state of Israel was established in 1948. Even more recently, in 1967, the Jewish people gained full possession of Jerusalem in the Six-Day War. One prophecy of Jesus, unrealized for 1897 years, seems to have been fulfilled: "Jerusalem shall be trodden down of the Gentiles, until the times of the Gentiles be fulfilled" (Luke 21:24).

Between 1948, when Israel was established, and 1967, when Jerusalem was recaptured, the "times of the Gentiles" were brought to an end—at least for the present—in the Holy Land. Nineteen forty-eight was the year that the World Council of Churches was founded, with world evangelization as part of its goal. By 1967 the World Council's Commission on Church and Society was redirecting the energies of the council, and through it of much of Christendom, in the name of "liberation theology," toward political revolution. The jubilee of Chalcedon was enthusiastically celebrated in 1951. In 1963 Bishop John A. T. Robinson published *Honest to God*, a *succès de scandale*, popularizing in the English-speaking world the non-theistic Christology of Bultmann. Indeed, Robinson's book, in translation, also publicized it in Germany, for it was far easier to read and understand than Bultmann's original presentation. By 1965 the American Baptist Harvey Cox had made publishing history with *The Secular City;* American admirers of Tillich and Bultmann such as Thomas J. J. Altizer and Paul van Buren were promoting their "theology" of the "death of God." The "death of God" fad was short-lived, but theology has not recovered. Van Buren himself was a doctoral student under Karl Barth, and wrote his dissertation on a very traditional topic: Calvin's doctrine of the atonement. By the mid-1960s he was following Bultmann and Dietrich Bonhoeffer (1906–45), promoting *The Secular Meaning of the Gospel.* In the nineteen years in which modern Israel was consolidating its control of its ancient territories, including Jerusalem, orthodoxy was not merely losing control in Christian theology; theology itself appears to have lost its mind.

After Bultmann, Altizer, and Cox it may be necessary to say that the "times of the Gentiles" are at an end in theology as well. Greek and Latin theologians created orthodoxy, and for fifteen hundred years their creation was considered not merely acceptable, but vitally necessary. Karl Barth was the last theologian of world significance to make this assertion with force. The passing of the Chalcedonian era—if indeed it is past—coincides with a repudiation of the "Greek" as well as the "Latin" influence in theology and with an appeal for a self-conscious kind of Semitization (albeit one that has hardly more to do with the historic faith of Israel than with that of Gentile Christianity).

"Salvation is of the Jews" (John 4:22), but theology and Christology, in our sense, are of the Greeks. The Christology of Chalcedon stands and falls with the contention that this "Greekness" is legitimate. Indeed, the historical Christian conviction that "this man," Jesus Christ, is able to "save . . . to the uttermost" (Heb. 7:24–25) because of who he is depends on this legitimacy. To repudiate the "Greek" interest in ontology, i.e. in who Christ *is,* signals not merely the end of the Chalcedonian era but—as far as theology is concerned—the end of the "times of the Gentiles."

Does the reconquest of Jerusalem by the new state of Israel have immediate bearing on the end of the present age? Is it a sign of the imminent return of Christ? Christians have been warned by Jesus himself to be cautious about trying to discover the time of his return, yet he also advised them to "watch." It is in the light of this admonition that we must consider the apparent collapse of Chalcedonian theology. Is this also a sign? Can it be the beginning of the "falling away" foretold by Paul? Again, caution is in order. The correct answer will be evident only when the predicted final events actually take place; it cannot be determined by speculation.

The geographical city of Jerusalem had already endured many shocks before the Six-Day War transferred it into Jewish hands once again in 1967. The historical doctrine of Chalcedon had also already endured many shocks before "existentialist interpretation" and the "death of God." It too may survive to endure many more. When the calendar stood at one thousand years since the birth of Christ, hundreds of thousands of Christians took it for a sign of the end, but it was not. Neither were the calendar dates 1200 and 1260. But Jerusalem is more important in the timetable of history than calendar dates. And so is Chalcedon.

NOTES

Chapter II

[1] Leon Poliakov, *The Aryan Myth: A History of Racist and Nationalist Ideas in Europe*, tr. Edmund Howard (New York: Basic Books, 1974).

[2] Adolf Harnack, *Lehrbuch der Dogmengeschichte*, 4th ed. (Tübingen: Mohr, 1909), I, 19. Harnack (1851–1930) was knighted by the last German kaiser in 1914 and became von Harnack.

[3] Gotthold Ephraim Lessing, *Über den Beweis des Geistes und der Kraft* (On the Demonstration of the Spirit and of Power, 1777). See the monographs by L. P. Wessel and Henry O. Chadwick, noted in the selected bibliography, for Lessing's theology.

[4] The claim that Christianity is not a religion was popularized by Karl Barth (1886–1968). Barth was reacting to the "history of religions" school of thought that made Christianity only one example among many of man's search for God. If religion is defined as man's search for God, Barth argued, then Christianity is not a religion, because it is God's search for man. This is an important truth to remember, but it cannot be denied that, from a sociological perspective, Christianity is indeed a religion and has many external resemblances to other religions.

[5] Seneca-Paul correspondence: see Jan Nicolaas Svenster, *Paul and Seneca* (Leiden: Brill, 1961).

[6] Gaius Valerius Catullus, *Lesbia of Catullus*, tr. Michael Rutherford (Albany, N.Y.: Carnal Press, 1972).

[7] Harnack, *Dogmengeschichte*, I, 12.

[8] The personal commitment and pattern of life of contemporary religious groups orthodox Christianity calls deeply heretical, such as Mormonism and the Jehovah's Witnesses, frequently shame the orthodox churches. The missionary zeal of both Mormons and Witnesses, for example, is precisely what one ought to be able to expect from orthodox Christians if they really believe in the truth of the doctrines to which their credal and confessional positions formally commit them.

Chapter III

[1] The creed, usually called the Nicene Creed, was substantially drawn up at the Council of Nicaea in 325, but an extended passage concerning the Holy Spirit, the church, and the world to come was added at Constantinople in 381. The proper name of our present creed is "Niceno-Constantinopolitan," but this cumbersome term is seldom used.

[2] This summary is adapted from that of Adolf Harnack, *Lehrbuch der Dogmengeschichte*, 4th ed. (Tübingen: Mohr, 1909), I, 88.

[3] In recent decades, both liberal and conservative New Testament scholars have come to acknowledge the Jewish nature of John's Gospel and to understand his anti-Jewish remarks as referring not to the Jewish people, to which John and Jesus both belonged, but to the Jewish religious establishment.

451

Chapter IV

¹ Christian legalism must begin with the assumption that Christ has paid the debt for human sin. Hence, it is not particularly prone to an antitrinitarian or adoptionist theology. However, to the extent that it does see man as earning, at least to an extent, his salvation, it does not strongly require that Christ pay the price for our sin; consequently, it is not so crucial that he possess full deity, nor that the Son and the Father be distinct Persons, one of whom makes propitiation to the other. Consequently, legalism does frequently have ties with a unitarian theology and an adoptionist view of Jesus Christ as a saintly man, adopted by God and filled with the Holy Spirit.
² Strictly speaking, process theology, derived from the thought of philosopher Alfred North Whitehead (1861–1947), prefers to be called panentheism, not pantheism, and seeks to preserve the concept of God as personal, which pantheism denies. Nevertheless, the similarities between process theology, or panentheism, and pantheism are substantial.
³ Christianity shows a certain ambivalence toward the world. The most familiar verse in the whole Bible, John 3:16, tells us that God loved the world, but 1 John 2:15 warns us not to love the world. From a Christian perspective, the world as God's handiwork cannot be evil in itself. It is precisely because God created it so wonderful that it can exert a seductive influence on man, even in its flawed and fallen state, and can induce him to idolize and worship it.
⁴ The Greek word *gnosis* comes from the Greek verb meaning "to know" and is the ordinary expression for "knowledge." For this reason Irenaeus refuses to allow his opponents undisputed title to the word. As used in his day and since, however, *gnosis* generally refers to an esoteric, secret lore that purports to explain everyday reality in a way quite different from the commonsense understanding, and hence to oppose mere material reality. For this reason Eric Voegelin applies the term "gnostic" to some modern political movements. In the New Testament, the common word for knowledge is *epignosis*, which differs from "gnosis" in that it is not based on speculation and arcane lore, but on concrete, personal experience. Unfortunately, one major Christian teacher, Clement of Alexandria (d. ca. 215), principal of the first Christian "seminary" there, took the terms "gnosis" and "gnostic" in their literal sense and called the mature Christian the true gnostic. Clement's terminology was not widely accepted, however, and the term "gnostic" generally remains a term of reproach.
⁵ The *Didache*, or *The Teaching of the Twelve Apostles*, mentioned by Eusebius of Caesarea though there is no certainty as to its date, origin, or author. Although a critical reaction against its significance took place in the earlier part of this century, its place as a valuable composition of the earliest of Apostolic Fathers texts is secure. The *Instructions of the Apostles* (its original title) is a compilation of regulations standardized for use in early Christian congregations (early second century and following), possibly originating from the church of Antioch in Syria. Chapters 1–6 utilize a Jewish form of instruction, "the two ways," and are concerned with ethical matters for catechumens (candidates for Christian baptism). Chapters 7–15 are concerned with baptism, the eucharist, prayer, fasting, how to treat itinerant ministers, and the appointment of elders and deacons. Chapter 16 concentrates on the signs of Christ's Second Coming.
⁶ Tertullian, *On the Prescription of Heretics* 7. Cf. idem, *Apologetics* 46.
⁷ We may almost say that the development of the body of doctrine preceded the arrival of the complete New Testament, for while the different books of the New Testament were written before or near the end of the first century and the Apostles' Creed dates from no earlier than 125, the first documentary evidence for the existence of a fairly complete New Testament canon, the Muratorian Fragment, dates from ca. 200, and the canonicity of some books of the New Testament remained controversial until into the fourth century, by which time many substantial doctrinal works had been written.
⁸ Outstanding among recent treatments of gnosis and the whole gnostic movement is the work of the Jewish scholar Hans Jonas, at one time a pupil of Rudolf Bultmann and a sharp critic of Bultmann's intrusion of what Jonas calls pagan ideas into the world of the

New Testament. Cf. Hans Jonas, *The Gnostic Religion: The Message of the Alien God and the Beginnings of Christianity* (Boston: Beacon Press, 1958).

[9] Eric Voegelin, *Science, Religion and Politics: Two Essays* (Chicago: Regnery, 1968).

[10] Arthur Drews (1865–1935), an atheistic philosopher at the University of Karlsruhe, wrote a caustic attack on the historicity of Jesus, *Die Christusmythe* (Jena: E. Diederichs, 1910–11), as well as similar attempts to discredit the New Testament accounts of Mary and Peter. In many respects the work of Drews represented the optimistic, self-confident, even arrogant humanism that preceded World War I. After the war, pessimism and an atmosphere of crisis pervaded Protestantism; Karl Barth is its best-known representative. Although more recent radical scholarship continues to doubt the historicity of the resurrection as well as other specific events and sayings recorded in Scripture, the historicity of Jesus Christ himself is no longer questioned by scholars with any claim to objectivity.

[11] G. E. Lessing, *Über den Beweis des Geistes und der Kraft* (1777).

[12] Rome thought of itself as eternal; while educated Roman subjects knew that their empire was not the first in the history of the world, it seemed to them to represent a kind of natural culmination of all that had gone before. When Persia conquered Egypt and Babylon, when Alexander conquered Persia, when Rome took over Alexander's heritage, the ancient world and its civilization were not shaken. But when Rome itself went from crisis to crisis and could find no satisfying answers to its problems, even though the ultimate collapse was not yet imminent, forebodings arose that gave rise to questions of cosmic, not merely personal, scope.

[13] One of the striking features of the history of the New Testament text is that the gnostic movement did not produce cleverly altered versions of the canonical Gospels, although such would have been extremely valuable to it. Why this did not happen is impossible to say. Conservative Christians are inclined to see in it an example of God's providential care in preserving the Scripture in an authentic, reliable form. It is possible that the Synoptic Gospels and even the Gospel of John were well enough known by the time Gnosticism began seriously to challenge the church, from 125 onward, so that an emendation of the text in a gnostic way would not have been credible.

[14] Origen, *Contra Celsum* (Against Celsus) 2.12.

[15] Franz Overbeck (*Studien zur Geschichte der alten Kirche* [Schloss-Chemnitz: Schmeitzner, 1875], 184) and Harnack seem to have a vague and elusive idea of the relationship between Gnosticism and worldliness, or secularity. For Overbeck "worldliness" seems to involve accepting the evils of the world without seeking to change them according to Gospel principles; Gnosticism certainly promoted this, but contemporary usage would call it otherworldliness. As a matter of historical record, Harnack was "worldly" in Overbeck's sense (and hence somewhat gnostic), as he endorsed Kaiser William II and his aims in World War I in bellicose terms, apparently untroubled by Jesus' words "Blessed are the peacemakers" (Matt. 5:9). Karl Barth (1886–1968) was disillusioned by Harnack's "worldliness" in this respect; this was part of the impetus that led Barth to reject Harnack's type of liberalism and inaugurate an otherworldly Christianity that is now known as neoorthodoxy.

[16] Adolf Harnack, *Lehrbuch der Dogmengeschichte*, 4th ed. (Tübingen: Mohr, 1909), I, 250, 254. Harnack gives the gnostics credit for being the first Christian dogmaticians. They intended to present Christianity as the absolute and final religion, and for this reason they opposed all other religions, including Judaism. But for these gnostics, Christianity was really identical in content with their exotic religious philosophy; all they sought in accepting Christ and his teaching was to gain a revelation to authenticate their philosophy—as so many heretics have done since them. Harnack comments, "Thus they [the gnostics] are the Christians who tried to conquer Christianity for Hellenistic culture and the culture for Christianity in a rapid advance. In so doing, they surrendered the Old Testament in order to facilitate the conclusion of an alliance between the two powers and to achieve the possibility of asserting the absoluteness of Christianity" (250–51). Curiously, Harnack and many of his liberal theological colleagues were themselves in the forefront of the modern effort to discredit the Old Testament and turn the New into reli-

gious philosophy. (Cf. Harnack, *What Is Christianity?* tr. Thomas Bailey Saunders [New York: Harper, 1957].) This modern theological anti-Semitism furnished, in a strange way, part of the impetus to modern racism. Cf. Léon Poliakov, *The Aryan Myth: A History of Racist and Nationalistic Ideas in Europe,* tr. Edmund Howard (New York: Basic Books, 1974).

[17] Harnack, *Dogmengeschichte,* I, 252f.

[18] Eusebius, *Ecclesiastical History* 4.22.5–7. Cf. Hegesippus, *Seven Jewish Heresies.*

[19] Justin Martyr, *First Apology* 26.

[20] Although Gnosticism postulated a kind of ultimate spiritual reality as the origin of all things, its doctrine of emanations descending and degenerating until some became so base that they could form the material world created a situation in which the material is estranged *by nature* from the spiritual. According to the Christian doctrine of Creation and the Fall, God himself created the material world good; its estrangement is not the fault of a base nature, but rather the consequence of the voluntary rebellion of man, and is thus moral, not ontological.

[21] It is not a coincidence that the rejection of the authority of the Old Testament as reliable divine revelation during the nineteenth century was followed by an impact of German idealistic philosophy on theology that resembles the impact of Hellenistic thought in the gnostic period. The Old Testament, tied to the material creation and to human history, is a major bulwark against the ever-present tendency to turn historic Christianity into a religious philosophy.

[22] Philip Schaff, *The Creeds of Christendom with a History and Critical Notes,* 4th ed. (Grand Rapids, Mich.: Baker, 1966), II, 11–12.

[23] See Willi Marxsen, *The Resurrection of Jesus of Nazareth,* tr. Margaret Kohl (Philadelphia: Fortress Press, 1970).

[24] Reinhold Seeberg, *Lehrbuch der Dogmengeschichte,* 2d ed. (Leipzig: Diechert, 1908), II, 222f.

[25] In a provocative book, *Christian Counseling and the Occult* (Grand Rapids, Mich.: Kregel, 1965), Kurt Koch observes that where the Gospel was diffused, even though by no means all the population personally accepted it, occult beliefs and practices virtually vanished. As faith in the Gospel has receded, those beliefs have swept back in to take its place.

[26] Although it is common to speak of the doctrine of the divinity of Christ, because the term "divinity" is often used loosely and does not necessarily imply full deity, the expression "deity of Christ" is preferable to designate the orthodox doctrine.

[27] Opposition to the God of Israel is a characteristic of most systems that emphasize religious speculation about the cosmic order, precisely because the God of Israel both creates the cosmos and acts in real human history. His sovereignty and the detailed clarity with which he reveals at least part of his will to individual human beings is a hindrance to free flights of speculative fantasy. The New Testament is easier to integrate into cosmological speculation than the Old, provided it is cut off and taken in isolation from the Old, which it presupposes.

[28] See Irenaeus, *Against Heresies* 3.3.4.

[29] Seeberg, *Dogmengeschichte,* I, 228.

[30] From our perspective, Gnosticism seems altogether incompatible with historic Christianity. When we recognize how many twentieth-century Christians are fascinated by modern speculation—such as that of Paul Tillich and Teilhard de Chardin—without recognizing its incompatibility with biblical faith, we can better understand the susceptibility of second-century believers. With regard to another modern theologian, Rudolf Bultmann, it was his former pupil Hans Jonas, a great authority on Gnosticism, who called his thought "profoundly pagan." Jonas, a Jew, saw what many Christians have not yet realized.

[31] Irenaeus, *Against Heresies* 1.24.1–2.

[32] Gnosticism betrays a formal similarity to two modern offshoots of Christianity: to Christian Science, which like Gnosticism has a highly dualistic world view, and to Mormonism, which is not dualistic, but which like Gnosticism has a complex doctrine of divine, spiritual, and angelic realities. The rise of these two modern movements shows

that the impulses that created Gnosticism were not confined to the Hellenistic period alone.
[33] Irenaeus, *Against Heresies* 1.11.
[34] Seeberg, *Dogmengeschichte*, I, 235.
[35] Two of the most celebrated problems of Christianity involve the origin of evil and the question of predestination versus free will. Christianity holds that God made all that exists, yet is not responsible for the existence of evil, and likewise that God predestines to salvation, yet is not responsible for the damnation of those who are lost. Rather than call these assertions "paradoxes" or "contradictions," some theologians prefer to use less objectionable terms such as "antinomies," but the problems remain.
[36] Harnack and others looked on Christian theology as the Hellenization of Christianity in response to Gnosticism, a cure that for them was hardly preferable to the disease; in fact, one feels that they rather admire the gnostics for the cosmic dimensions of their system. At the same time, thinkers such as Harnack and Paul Tillich can be charged with making their version of Christianity into a new kind of Gnosticism in which speculative theories once again are substituted for historic faith.
[37] Tertullian, *Against Marcion* 4.6. Orthodox Lutheranism sometimes elevates the contrast between Law and Gospel to a degree reminiscent of Marcion, although its fidelity to the entire Old and New Testament canon preserves it from falling into Marcionism. An example of this Lutheran approach is offered by C. F. W. Walther, patriarch of the Lutheran Church–Missouri Synod, in *Law and Gospel* (St. Louis: Concordia, n.d.).
[38] One consequence of Marcion's rejection of the Old Testament was hostility to the Jews. Both Roman Catholicism and Lutheranism, which are more critical of Old Testament Law than the Reformed tradition, are also more inclined to anti-Semitism. The rejection of the authenticity and authority of the Old Testament by nineteenth-century liberalism was followed by virulent anti-Semitism, especially in Germany. Léon Poliakov (*The Aryan Myth*) sees a causal connection.
[39] Tertullian, *On the Prescription of Heretics* 30; idem, *Against Marcion* 1.28.
[40] Seeberg, *Dogmengeschichte*, I, 250.
[41] Karl Heussi, *Kompendium der Kirchengeschichte*, 12th ed. (Tübingen: Mohr, 1956), 48. Seeberg, *Dogmengeschichte*, I, 253f.
[42] Marcion and Montanus each emphasized a valid principle of Christian faith. Marcion believed that the Scripture should be taken as fully authoritative in its literal sense, but his problem was that he eliminated most of what ought to be recognized as Scripture, and thus came up with a truncated canon. Montanus believed in the guidance of the Holy Spirit, but felt that new, direct revelation could so amplify what is revealed in Scripture that it constitutes a major change. In other words, whereas Marcion amputated parts of the canon, Montanus expanded it.
[43] Epiphanius, *History of the Church* 48.4.
[44] The expression "magisterial Reformation" was introduced by George H. Williams to designate those Protestants, such as Luther, Zwingli, and Calvin, who enrolled the civil magistrates as their allies and agents for the reformation of the church.

Chapter V

[1] The Muratorian Canon is named for Lodovico Antonio Muratori (d. 1750), who discovered it in a library in Milan. It contains most of the New Testament, omitting 1 and 2 Peter, James, 3 John, and perhaps Hebrews. Although the Muratorian Canon dates from the late second or early third century, the present New Testament canon was not acknowledged everywhere until the fourth century.
[2] Johann Salomo Semler (1725–91), *Abhandlung von freier Untersuchung des Canons* (Halle: C. H. Hemmerde, 1776).
[3] *The Teaching of the Twelve Apostles* 4.1. Adolf Harnack, *Lehrbuch der Dogmengeschichte*, 4th ed. (Tübingen: Mohr, 1909), I, 372.
[4] Rudolf Bultmann (1884–1976), an outstanding German New Testament scholar, reduced what can be reliably known about Jesus and his message to a bare minimum. His method

is known as demythologization and his school of interpretation is called existentialist theology. See his *Jesus Christ and Mythology* (New York: Scribner: 1958).

Chapter VI

[1] Adolf Harnack, *Lehrbuch der Dogmengeschichte*, 4th ed. (Tübingen: Mohr, 1909), I, 409.

[2] Irenaeus, *Against Heresies* 2.1.1.

[3] Ibid. 2.28.1; 28.3.9; 28.2.4; 28.3.2.

[4] Ibid. 2.23.3; 5.13.3.

[5] Tertullian, *On the Soul* 41.16; idem, *On the Flesh of Christ* 16.

[6] Irenaeus, *Against Heresies* 4.12.2; 4.12.5; 4.13.1; 4.15.1; 4.15.5. Here we observe a periodization of history into epochs or dispensations. For Irenaeus, we are in the final or at least the penultimate dispensation: the Third Covenant is valid until the return of Christ. Cf. Reinhold Seeberg, *Lehrbuch der Dogmengeschichte*, 2d ed. (Leipzig: Diechert, 1908), I, 290.

[7] In the light of the frequent appeal to tradition in the early church, we should remind ourselves that *paradosis*, or *traditio*, fundamentally meant a faithful handing over of those precious goods Christ had entrusted to his disciples, including first of all the Scripture. The concept of tradition as an additional source of religious knowledge, supplementing or even surpassing Scripture, is gnostic, not early Christian.

[8] Irenaeus, *Against Heresies* 2.28.3.

[9] Ibid. 3.5.1.

[10] When the expression "God" is used in the first three centuries, it usually refers specifically to God the Father, not to the godhead or to the concept of the Trinity, which had not yet been explicitly formulated. Irenaeus, *Against Heresies* 2.28.5.

[11] Harnack, *Dogmengeschichte*, I, 583: a striking testimony to the true catholicity of our first "systematic theologian."

[12] The allegation that the Logos had an origin in time, or even "before time," i.e. that "there was, when he [the Logos] was not," became a rallying cry of the Arians and was condemned at Nicaea in 325—a century and a half after Irenaeus.

[13] Irenaeus, *Against Heresies* 2.12.2; 2.13.2; 2.13.8; 2.28.4–9; 2.29.3.

[14] Ibid. 2.30.9. Cf. ibid. 3.18.1.

[15] Ibid. 2.30.9.

[16] Harnack, *Dogmengeschichte*, I, 586 n.

[17] Irenaeus, *Against Heresies* 3.9.3.

[18] Irenaeus carried his concepts of recapitulation and the identification of Jesus with us so far that he contended that Jesus experienced all stages of human life, including old age. *Against Heresies* 2.22.

[19] For some, the expression "death of God" was rhetorical hyperbole to emphasize the fact that modern secular man has forgotten God; for others, such as Thomas J. J. Altizer, it was patripassianism taken to its extreme: God became so fully identified with man that he died in Jesus, and consequently no longer exists.

[20] Leviticus 21:20 was interpreted as prohibiting the ordination of a castrated man as an elder (*presbyteros*); Origen was ordained in Palestine, about 230, and was excommunicated by Bishop Demetrius of Alexandria.

[21] Origen, *On Romans* 1.1; idem, *De principiis* 1.2.8. Origen makes Christ the embodiment of all of the various ideas that gnostics and others postulated as mediators between the simplicity of God and the multiplicity of the universe, but for Origen Christ was not a mere postulate: he was incarnate in history.

[22] Origen, *De principiis* 1.

[23] Origen, *Commentary on Hebrews. Fragments* (ed. Lommatzsch) 24.359. Cited in Seeberg, *Dogmengeschichte*, I, 415.

[24] Monarchians (from Gk. *monos*, "one," and *archon*, "ruler"), that there is only one divine Person and will, that of the Father. The Son may be an adopted, chosen man

(dynamic monarchianism or adoptionism) or he may be thought of as merely a mode or manifestation of the Father (modalism, hence, patripassianism). Adoptionism in one form or another is a recurring heresy; it appeals to the optimistic view of man: with a little help (adoption), a man can be Christ. Modalism constantly reappears among conservative Christians who accept the deity of Christ, often because they need it to resolve the conceptual difficulty posed by the doctrine of the Trinity.

[25] Gregory of Nazianzus, *Fifth Theological Oration* 2, in Jacques-Paul Migne, *Patrologia Graeca* (Collection of the Greek Fathers), XXXVI.
[26] Origen, *De principiis* 1.3.1–4.
[27] Origen, *On John* 2.10.15.
[28] Ibid. 13.36.231f.
[29] Origen, *De principiis* 1.3.8.
[30] Ibid. 2.6.2.
[31] Ibid. 2.9.6; 3.5.4; 2.1.1–4.

Chapter VII

[1] Eusebius, *Ecclesiastical History* 5.28.6. Cf. Adolf Harnack, *Lehrbuch der Dogmengeschichte*, 4th ed. (Tübingen: Mohr, 1909), I, 709.
[2] Hippolytus, *Refutation of All Heresies* 7.36.
[3] Eusebius, *Ecclesiastical History* 5.28.3.
[4] Harnack, *Dogmengeschichte*, I, 711f.
[5] Hippolytus, *Against Noëtus* 3.
[6] Epiphanius, *Histories* 62.1.
[7] Hippolytus, *Refutation of All Heresies* 9.12.

Chapter VIII

[1] Adolf Harnack, *Lehrbuch der Dogmengeschichte*, 4th ed. (Tübingen: Mohr, 1909), I, 730.
[2] The present form of the Nicene Creed dates from the Council of Constantinople in 381, which dropped a number of anathemas aimed at Arianism and added the final section, beginning with the words "the Lord and giver of life."
[3] Cf. the classic work by Theodor Zahn, *Grundriss der Geschichte des neutestamentlichen Kanons*, 2d ed. (Leipzig: Deichert, 1904), 7ff., as well as John K. S. Reid, *The Authority of Scripture: A Study of the Reformation and Post-Reformation Understanding of the Bible* (New York: Harper, 1957).
[4] Eusebius of Caesarea, *Life of Constantine* 2.72.
[5] The Arians may in fact have meant by the Trinity: God (before the Son was begotten), the Father (thereafter), and the Son. Cf. Athanasius, *On the Synods* 15.
[6] Servetus challenged the authority of Calvin at a time when it was already somewhat in question by going to Geneva despite Calvin's explicit warnings to him not to do so. When identified and charged in Geneva, he brought countercharges against Calvin. He was sentenced under provisions of Roman civil law dating from the era of the Emperor Justinian (ruled 527–65), not for ecclesiastical offenses. Calvin actively sought his execution; after his condemnation, Calvin sought to have the legal penalty, burning, modified to a more merciful form of execution, but the town council, apparently angry at Calvin as well as at Servetus, insisted on applying the full rigor of the law.
[7] Origen, *Against Celsus* 8.13; ibid. 8.26.
[8] Harnack, *Dogmengeschichte*, II, 220.
[9] Ibid., II, 222.
[10] Ibid., II, 227 n.
[11] Theodoret, *History of the Church* 1.2.

[12] The word "humanism" has become a term of abuse among conservative Protestants in America, who associate it with the militant, antireligious secularism of the two *Humanist Manifestoes*. Originally, humanism was a movement with a high veneration for classical culture and the artistic achievements of humanity, and it included many Christians, most notably Erasmus of Rotterdam (ca. 1466–1536).

[13] The date at which one ought to begin calling the bishops of Rome popes is fairly arbitrary. Roman Catholic tradition calls Peter the first pope. The term "pope" is used for village priests in the East, and most scholars see the papacy as a relatively late institution. We shall call the bishops of Rome popes from the Council of Nicaea (325) onward.

[14] The formulas are presented and discussed in Harnack, *Dogmengeschichte*, II, 244–45.

[15] Harnack claims that the *homoousian* party won a hollow victory, and that in order to win they had to accept the subordinationist interpretation of the Trinity favored by the moderate *homoiousians*. What he is really saying is that the *homoousian*, or orthodox, party was originally modalistic and gave up its modalism to reconcile the subordinationists. In any event, the final understanding of *homoousios* accepted the idea that the Son is subordinate to the Father in the divine economy. Harnack, *Dogmengeschichte*, II, 260–64.

[16] In 589 at the Third Council of Toledo, the Arian King Recared of the Visigoths accepted Catholic orthodoxy. At this council, the term *filioque*, "and from the Son," was added to the Latin text of the Nicene Creed to make the statement about the Holy Spirit read, "who proceeds from the *Father and the Son*." This addition remained controversial in the West for two centuries, and Eastern Orthodoxy has never accepted it.

[17] The so-called incommunicable, or absolute, attributes are qualities that cannot be communicated to, i.e. shared with, creatures; they are absolute attributes, in that they either are possessed absolutely or not at all. The communicable, or relative, attributes, such as power, goodness, and love, can be shared with creatures; we may exhibit them to a relative degree, whereas God exhibits them to a superlative degree.

[18] Augustine, *On the Trinity* 11.8.13.

Chapter IX

[1] The Athanasian Creed is called the *Quicumque Vult* ("whosoever will") because it begins with the words "Whosoever will be saved . . ." Of undetermined origin, it is widely used in Western Christendom but has never been recognized as an ecumenical creed by Eastern Orthodoxy. It is probably no earlier than 450 but some ascribe it to Ambrose of Milan (ca. 340–97); it is noteworthy because it gives us a very clear statement of the Western understanding of the doctrine of the Trinity, particularly as promulgated by Ambrose's more famous pupil, Augustine.

[2] Adolf Harnack, *Lehrbuch der Dogmengeschichte*, 4th ed. (Tübingen: Mohr, 1909), II, 295.

[3] Ibid., II, 296.

[4] The same difficulty will cause problems in understanding the person and natures of Christ in the fifth century; for even if one admits that one divine nature may subsist in three Persons, how is it possible to believe that in Jesus Christ there are two full and complete natures, one divine, one human, yet only one person?

[5] Reinhold Seeberg, *Lehrbuch der Dogmengeschichte*, 2d ed. (Leipzig: Diechert, 1908), II, 137.

[6] Like almost every other attempt to make a simple statement about God, this simple-sounding statement must unfortunately be qualified. Christ's redemptive work involves both advocacy and propitiation vis-à-vis the Father (1 John 2:1–2). The fact that Christ bore our condemnation (Isa. 53:5) and called himself forsaken by God (Matt. 27:46) suggests that there was at least a momentary division between the Persons of the godhead. Matthew 27:46, the famous cry of dereliction, remains problematic despite all our careful efforts: "My God, my God, why hast thou forsaken me?"

[7] The term "fideism," from Latin *fides,* "faith," refers to the attitude that merely accepts doctrines as true because they are pronounced by the accepted authority whether that authority be the church, a leader, or the Bible itself.

[8] Eastern Orthodox opposition to the *filioque,* or double procession, of the Holy Spirit (from the Son as well as from the Father) has in mind this difference between the Father as ingenerate and the Son as the divine, begotten intermediary in Creation between the Father and the creatures. If the Spirit is thought to derive from the Son, not from the Father alone, this would appear to reduce him to the level of a creature.

[9] Seeberg, *Dogmengeschichte,* II, 138f.

[10] Calvin, *Institutes* 3.21.1.

[11] Seeberg, *Dogmengeschichte,* II, 147.

Chapter X

[1] Athanasius, *Fourth Oration Against the Arians* 34–36.

[2] See below, Chapter 16; George H. Williams, *The Radical Reformation* (Philadelphia: Westminster Press, 1962), Chapter 11.

[3] Apollinaris, *Fragments* (ed. Lietzmann) 70, 108, 109, 113. The expression "God-flesh" is awkward, but "divine flesh" does not convey the full sense of the original.

[4] John A. T. Robinson, *Honest to God* (Philadelphia: Westminster Press, 1965), 66, 69.

[5] Apollinaris, *On the Faith of the Incarnation* 9.

[6] Christology is the doctrine of the person of Christ; its classical formulation is the classical Chalcedonian doctrine of the two natures of Christ. Soteriology is the doctrine of the work of Christ; it tells us that he is our substitute, making vicarious atonement for our sins.

[7] Gregory of Nazianzus, *Orations* 30.14.

[8] Reinhold Seeberg, *Lehrbuch der Dogmengeschichte,* 2d ed. (Leipzig: Diechert, 1908), II, 170.

[9] Gregory of Nyssa, *Against the Eunomians* 2.10.

[10] Theodore of Mopsuestia, *On the Incarnation* 15.3.

[11] The modern concept of the person as an individual grew up as a result of the effort to explain how the Three, the Father, the Son, and the Holy Spirit, can each be God with all that that means. If this concept of individuality is cut off from the concept of the unity of nature, or in our case of the essential unity of mankind, the concept of community and collectivity is lost and one can understand neither the Fall of man in Adam nor man's redemption in Christ.

[12] Adolf Harnack, *Lehrbuch der Dogmengeschichte,* 4th ed. (Tübingen: Mohr, 1909), II, 330. On the one hand, Harnack deplores the "Hellenization" of Christianity that produced early orthodoxy theology, but on the other hand he objects to the "reactionary" efforts of the orthodox to oppose the critical, intellectual, Hellenistic Apollinaris.

[13] The reader should bear in mind that although the New Testament uses the word "flesh" to refer to the whole of fallen man's human nature, here it is used in its more Platonic or gnostic sense of man's physical body and its appetites.

[14] Seeberg, *Dogmengeschichte,* II, 171, 171 n.

[15] *Codex Theodosianus* 16.5.

[16] Theodore of Mopsuestia, *Exposition of the Faith,* in Jacques-Paul Migne, *Patrologia Graeca* (Collection of the Greek Fathers, hereafter referred to as *P.G.*), LXVI, 328.

[17] Idem, *On the Incarnation* 7, in Migne, *P.G.,* LXVI, 296.

[18] Idem, *Catechism,* in Migne, *P.G.,* LXVI, 326; idem, *On the Incarnation* 14, in Migne, *P.G.,* LXVI, 308; idem, *Against Apollinaris* 3.16, in Migne, *P.G.,* LXVI, 317.

[19] Reinhold Seeberg, *Lehrbuch der Dogmengeschichte,* 3d ed. (Erlangen and Leipzig: Diechert, 1920–30), II, 192.

[20] Theodore of Mopsuestia, *On the Incarnation, P.G.,* LXVI, 291–92.

[21] Seeberg, *Dogmengeschichte* (3d ed.), II, 201.

[22] Amphilocus of Iconium, Fragment 22, in Migne, *P.G.,* XXXIX, 117.

[23] Harnack, *Dogmengeschichte*, II, 358, n. 3.

[24] Milton V. Anastos, "Nestorius Was Orthodox," *Dumbarton Oaks Papers* 16 (1962): 119–40.

[25] The conflict between Augustine and Pelagius is discussed in Chapter 11.

[26] The doctrine of the Immaculate Conception of Mary asserts that she was miraculously preserved from the taint of original sin, but not that she herself was virgin-born.

[27] Friedrich Loofs, *Nestoriana. Die Fragmente des Nestorius* (Halle: Niemeyer, 1905), 353.

[28] In recent decades, Eastern Orthodox Christians have once again come to accept Cyril's monophysite-sounding language.

[29] Cyril of Alexandria, *Against Nestorius* 4.5, in Migne, *P.G.*, LXXVI, 192.

[30] Idem, *Explication* 7, in Migne, *P.G.*, LXXVI, 300; idem, *Against Nestorius* 1, in Migne, *P.G.*, LXXVI, 17.

[31] Although the term "God-man" is well established in our theological tradition, it seems preferable to say "God and man" and thus avoid the monophysite implications of "God-man."

[32] Hilary of Poitiers, *On the Trinity* 10.24.

[33] Ambrose, *On the Faith* 2.7.58.

[34] Johannes Domenicus Mansi, *Sanctorum conciliorum et decretorum collectio nova* (hereafter referred to as *Decretals*) 7.744 (Lucca: J. Salani, 1748–52); *Decretals* 7.741.

[35] Leo the Great, *The Tome of Leo*, in *Epistles* 28.

[36] Seeberg, *Dogmengeschichte*, II, 246.

[37] Ibid., II, 247.

[38] Justinian, *Codex Justinianus*, Novel 131.2.

[39] Seeberg, *Dogmengeschichte*, II, 269.

[40] Adolf von Harnack claims that the monothelite position represents only the attempt of the government at Constantinople to conciliate the Monophysites and to prevent them from abandoning the empire. Nevertheless, there is a genuine theological problem at stake: how can we conceive of Jesus Christ as possessing two complete, distinct natures without losing him as a real, historical person to whom we can relate? Harnack, *Dogmengeschichte*, II, 426f.

Chapter XI

[1] It is not only Christian rulers who take an interest in church unity. Non-Christian and atheistic states such as Japan during World War II and the Soviet Union today have encouraged or even forced various Christian denominations to unite.

[2] Augustine, *The City of God* 14.27.

[3] Augustine, *On the Grace of Christ and Original Sin* 17.19ff.

[4] Augustine, *On Predestination* 10.19.

[5] Augustine, *Unfinished Work Against Julian* 2.157.

[6] Reinhold Seeberg, *Lehrbuch der Dogmengeschichte*, 2d ed. (Leipzig: Diechert, 1908), II, 466.

[7] Augustine, *On Reproof and Grace* 13.39.

Chapter XII

[1] *Martyrdom of Polycarp* 18.

[2] Johannes Domenicus Mansi, *Sanctorum concilorium et decretorum collectio nova* (hereafter referred to as *Decretals*) 11.977–80 (Lucca: J. Salani, 1748–52).

[3] Louis Bréhier and René Aigrain, *Grégroire le Grand, les états barbares et la conquête arabe*, in Augustin Fliche and Victor Martin, eds., *Histoire de l'Église depuis les origines jusqu'a nos jours* (n.p.: Bloud & Gay, 1937), V, 444f.

[4] *Regesta* 9.208; 10.10.

[5] Mansi, *Decretals* 13.44; also 197ff.

[6] Nicephorus, *Antirrheticus* 3.

[7] Although modern Protestantism is not directly related to the iconoclastic movement, most non-Lutheran, non-Anglican Protestants also reject the crucifix in favor of a simple cross. Unlike the early iconoclasts, however, most modern Protestants make ample use of imaginative, often sentimental portraits of Christ.

[8] Theophanes, *Chronicle*, at Anno 6267.

Chapter XIII

[1] Émile Amann, *L'Époque carolingienne*, in Augustin Fliche and Victor Martin, eds., *Histoire de l'Église depuis les origines jusqu'a nos jours* (n.p.: Bloud & Gay, 1937), VI, 141. Mansi assumed that Hadrian's letter was written in response to the council.

[2] Alcuin, *Seven Books Against Felix* 4, in Jacques-Paul Migne, *Patrologia Latina* (Collection of the Latin Fathers, hereafter referred to as *P.L.*), CI.

[3] Adolf Harnack, *Lehrbuch der Dogmengeschichte*, 4th ed. (Tübingen: Mohr, 1909), III, 286f.

[4] Agobard, *Tract Against Felix*, in Migne, *P.L.*, CIV, 49–70; Benedict of Aniane, *Dispute Against Relician Impiety*, in Migne, *P.L.*, CIII, 1399–1411.

[5] Gregory the Great, *Letters* 3.3.

[6] Harnack, *Dogmengeschichte*, III, 300ff.

[7] Émile Amann, *L'Époque carolingienne*, in Fliche and Martin, *Histoire de l'Église*, VI, 315.

[8] Harnack, *Dogmengeschichte*, III, 320.

[9] Oswald Spengler, *The Decline of the West*, tr. Charles Francis Atkinson (New York: Knopf; 1962), I, XXX.

Chapter XIV

[1] Dionysius the Areopagite, Paul's Athenian convert (Acts 17:34), is the ostensible author of four extremely influential tracts, *On the Heavenly Hierarchy, On the Ecclesiastical Hierarchy, On the Divine Names,* and *On Mystical Theology,* presumably written in Syria around 500. From the ninth century, in Latin translation, the works of the false Dionysius had a profound impact in the West.

[2] Adolf Harnack, *Lehrbuch der Dogmengeschichte*, 4th ed. (Tübingen: Mohr, 1909), III, 355.

[3] Christian Erdmann, "Gregor VII und Berengar von Tours," in *Quellen und Forschungen aus Italienischen Archiven und Bibliotheken* 28 (1937–38): 48–74.

[4] Steven Runciman, *The Medieval Manichee. A Study of the Christian Dualist Heresy* (Cambridge: University Press, 1947).

[5] In Jacques-Paul Migne, *Patrologia Graeca* (Collection of the Greek Fathers, hereafter referred to as *P.G.*), CIV, 1240–1349.

[6] Anna Comnena, *The Alexiad of the Princess Anna Comnena, Being the History of the Reign of Her Father, Alexius I, Emperor of the Romans, 1081–1118 A.D.*, tr. Elizabeth A. S. Davies (London: Routledge, 1928), 14.8–9.383–9.

[7] Cosmas, *Slovo Kozmyi Presbitera*, ed. Mikhail G. Popruzhenko (St. Petersburg: n.p., 1907), 2837. Cited in Runciman, *Medieval Manichee*, 73.

[8] Anna Comnena, *Alexiad* 11.9.

[9] Rainerio Sacchoni, *Summa de Catharis et Leonistis*. Cited in Runciman, *Medieval Manichee*, 81.

[10] Michael Psellus, *On the Operation of the Demons*, in Migne, *P.G.*, CXXII, 824f. Cf. Runciman, *Medieval Manichee*, 90.

[11] Cf. Augustin Fliche, Raymonde Foreville, and Jean Rousset, *Du premier Concile de Latran à l'avènement d'Innocent III (1123–1198)*, in Augustin Fliche and Victor Martin,

Histoire de l'Église depuis les origines jusqu'a nos jours (n.p.: Bloud & Gay, 1937), IX, 19.

[12] See G. G. Coulton, *Five Centuries of Religion*, 4 vols. (New York: Farrar, Strauss & Giroux, 1979).

[13] Bernard of Clairvaux, *Sermons on the Canticle of Canticles*, 2 vols. (Dublin: Browne and Nolan, 1920).

[14] Peter the Venerable, *Tractate Against the Petrobrusians*, in Migne, *Patrologia Latina* (Collection of the Latin Fathers, hereafter referred to as *P.L.*), CLXXXIX, 719–850. See Fliche et al., *Du premier Concile de Latran*, in *Histoire de l'Église*, IX, 97.

[15] As atrocious as this persecution of heretics was, it should be noted that in general heretics could escape it by recanting. Thus it resembles the ancient Roman persecution of Christians more than the modern Nazi persecution of Jews or that of political dissidents by Communists. Conversion to Christianity did not protect a Jew from the Nazis. While Communists frequently require "self-accusation," as the medieval Christians required repentance, after the self-accusation the "criminal" is usually punished anyway.

[16] Fliche et al., *Du premier Concile de Latran*, in *Histoire de l'Église*, IX, Part 2, 344.

[17] Johannes Domenicus Mansi, *Sanctorum concilorium et decretorum collectio nova* (hereafter referred to as *Decretals*) 21.1177 (Lucca: J. Salani, 1748–52).

[18] Mansi, *Decretals* 22.476–78.

[19] Runciman, *Medieval Manichee*, 167.

[20] Long lost, Peter Abelard's *Tractate on the Divine Unity and Trinity* was found and published for the first time by Remigius Stölzle in 1891.

[21] In Migne, *P.L.*, CLXXVIII, 1161–82.

[22] Herbert Grundmann, *Ketzergeschichte des Mittelalters*, in Kurt Dietrich Schmidt and Ernst Wolf, eds., *Die Kirche in ihrer Geschichte* (Göttingen: Vandenhoeck und Ruprecht, 1963), C-45.

Chapter XV

[1] *Chronica regia Coloniensis*, ed. Georg Waitz, 1880, 185ff., 229ff., 233f. Cited in Herbert Grundmann, *Ketzergeschichte des Mittelalters*, in Kurt Dietrich Schmidt and Ernst Wolf, eds., *Die Kirche in ihrer Geschichte* (Göttingen: Vandenhoeck und Ruprecht, 1963), G-48.

[2] The so-called Donation of Constantine is a fictitious grant by the Emperor Constantine of wealth and political authority to his contemporary Sylvester, bishop of Rome. It was exposed as a forgery by Lorenzo Valla in the fifteenth century. Prior to that it was frequently cited as a basis for the worldly power of the papacy.

[3] Grundmann, *Ketzergeschichte*, G-50.

[4] Decima L. Dovie, *The Nature and the Effects of the Heresy of the Fraticelli* (Manchester: University Press, 1932).

[5] John of Schwenkenfeld's report was published in Bolesław Ulanowski, ed., *Scripta rerum Polonicarum* (n.p. 1898), XIII, 239–55.

[6] Ernst Benz, *Ecclesia spiritualis: Kirchenidee und Geschichtstheologie der Franziskanischen Reformation* (Stuttgart: Kohlhammer, 1934), is the classical work on the movement sparked by Joachim of Floris.

[7] The basic documentation may be found in Georges Lizenard, ed., *Le Dossier de l'affaire des Templiers* (Paris: Belles Lettres, 1964).

[8] Henry Charles Lea, *History of the Inquisition of the Middle Ages*, 3 vols. (New York: Russell & Russell, 1958), III, 325–34.

Chapter XVI

[1] Herbert Grundmann, *Ketzergeschichte des Mittelalters*, in Kurt Dietrich Schmidt and Ernst Wolf, eds., *Die Kirche in ihrer Geschichte* (Göttingen: Vandenhoeck und Ruprecht, 1963), IV, G-66.

[2] The precise date is sometime between 1511 and 1513.

[3] Hans Küng, *Justification: The Doctrine of Karl Barth and a Catholic Reflection*, tr. Thomas Collins, Edmund E. Tolk, and David Granskou (New York: Nelson, 1964).

[4] George Gorden Coulton, *Five Centuries of Religion*, 4 vols. (New York: Farrar, Strauss & Giroux, 1979).

[5] Transubstantiation (like the later Lutheran doctrine of consubstantiation) clearly presupposes that the body of Christ possesses the divine attribute of ubiquity, or omnipresence. If Christ's physical (human) body can be omnipresent, then there is a strong suggestion that the body, and with it Christ's humanity, has been deified; in other words, transubstantiation can have monophysite implications.

[6] Walther Koehler, *Dogmengeschichte als Geschichte des christlichen Selbstewusstseins. Das Zeitalter der Reformation* (Zurich: Niehaus, 1951), 77f.

[7] Several of the earlier church controversies and heresies must have appeared at the time as though they would create new churches. However, in the course of time, the Arians returned to orthodoxy or went over to Islam, Nestorians and most Monophysites found themselves outside the borders of the Roman Empire and were lost to view, and Bogomils and Albigenses were excluded from Christianity altogether. Protestantism is the movement that has created a plurality of churches, all claiming to venerate the Lord who promised to build only one.

[8] Martin Luther, *Commentary on Romans;* idem, *Weimarer Ausgabe* (hereafter referred to as *WA*), LVI, 51.

[9] Luther, *WA*, V, 562. Cf. ibid., XXXIX, 390.

[10] Ibid. XVIII, 709.

[11] The best example of this is offered by the great dogmaticians of the Lutheran Church–Missouri Synod in the United States, especially by Francis Pieper and John Theodore Mueller.

[12] Koehler, *Dogmengeschichte*, II, 207. Cf. Luther, *WA*, III, 335.

[13] Luther, *WA*, XXVII, 109.

[14] Ibid., IX, pt.1, 434.

[15] Ibid., V, 602.

[16] Ibid., III, 226.

[17] For a full discussion, see Walther Koehler, *Zum Abendmahlsstreite zwischen Luther und Zwingli* (Weimar: H. Böhlaus, 1917); see also Hermann Sasse, *This Is My Body: Luther's Contention for the Real Presence in the Sacrament of the Altar*. Adelaide: Lutheran Publishing House, 1977.

[18] Luther, *WA*, XXVI, 255f.

[19] Koehler, *Dogmengeschichte*, II, 217.

[20] Luther, *WA*, L, 590.

[21] Actually spoken to Bucer in reference to the view of the Swiss church contingent on the last day of the Marburg Colloquy; Zwingli was present. Sasse, *This Is My Body*, 213–14.

[22] Luther, *WA*, XXVI, 345.

[23] Ibid., XLV, 240.

[24] Koehler, *Dogmengeschichte*, II, 223.

[25] George H. Williams, *The Radical Reformation* (Philadelphia: Westminster Press, 1962), 144ff.

[26] See Robert Clifford Walton, *Zwingli's Theocracy* (Toronto: University Press, 1967).

[27] Ulrich Zwingli, *Werke*, in *Corpus Reformatorum* (hereafter referred to as *CR*), ed. Karl G. Bretschneider and Heinrich E. Bindell (Leipzig: M. Heinsius, 1834ff.), IV, 221. Cf. Koehler, *Dogmengeschichte*, II, 224.

[28] Zwingli, *Werke*, *CR*, I, 356, 350, 352; ibid., IV, 458.

[29] Ibid., II, 127.

[30] Ibid., VIII, 639.

[31] Koehler, *Dogmengeschichte*, II, 226f.

[32] Luther, *WA*, XXVI, 321ff.

[33] Philipp Melanchthon, *Werke*, *CR*, XXI, 629.

[34] Koehler, *Dogmengeschichte*, II, 228f.

[35] Calvin, *Institutes of the Christian Religion* 2.16.7.

[36] Ibid. 4.17.1.

[37] Ibid. 4.17.3.

[38] The classical work on the topic, which created the now-accepted designations "magisterial" and "radical," is George H. Williams, *The Radical Reformation* (see footnote 25 above).

[39] Manfred Krebs and Jean Rott, eds., *Elsass, I: Stadt Strassburg 1522–1532*, in *Quellen zur Geschichte der Wiedertäufer, VII, Quellen und Forschungen zur Reformationsgeschichte* (Gütersloh: Mohn, 1959), XXVI.

[40] Menno Simons, *Complete Writings*, ed. Harold S. Bender (Scottsdale, Pa.: Mennonite, 1956), 863.

[41] As we apply the name of a classical heresy, monophysitism, to an existing Christian group, the Mennonites, we should note once again that monophysitism is consistent with the Apostles' and Nicene creeds, and that Monophysites and Mennonites, unlike Arians and Unitarians, should certainly be classified as Christians.

[42] Michael Servetus, *The Two Treatises of Servetus on the Trinity: On the Errors of the Trinity*, ed. Earl Morse Wilbur (Cambridge: Harvard University Press, 1932), 200 (= I, 9).

[43] Williams, *Radical Reformation*, 614. Cf. Roland H. Bainton, *Hunted Heretic: The Life and Death of Michael Servetus 1511–1553* (Boston: Beacon Press, 1960), 212.

[44] Letter of December 4, 1650, in Theodor Wotschke, ed., *Briefwechsel der Schweizer mit den Polen* (Leipzig: n.p., 1908), no. 268.

[45] Williams, *Radical Reformation*, 660.

[46] Calvin, *Brief Admonition to the Polish Brethren* (January 16, 1563), in Calvin, *Opera, CR*, IX, 633f; Wotschke, *Briefwechsel*, no. 226.

[47] Theodor Wotschke, "Zur Geschichte des Antitrinitarismus," *Archiv für Reformationsgeschichte* 23 (1926): 95f.

[48] Williams, *Radical Reformation*, 740.

Chapter XVII

[1] Although the first Protestants were to some extent persecuted, most of the great leaders, such as Luther, Zwingli, Calvin, and Bucer, were able to preach and teach with virtual impunity. Zwingli lost his life in a battle provoked by his own political measures. Among the magisterial Reformers, the only martyrs were under the repression of Bloody Mary in England. Many Anabaptist leaders as well as large numbers of their followers suffered martyrdom.

[2] Cf. David B. Barrett, ed., *World Christian Encyclopedia* (New York: Oxford, 1982).

[3] This is the position advocated by the Moral Majority, but also by more sophisticated thinkers such as Francis A. Schaeffer.

[4] Strictly speaking, the expression "liberal" in theology is applied only to "classical nineteenth-century liberalism," while newer movements, such as neoorthodoxy, existentialist theology, and process theology, eschew the name "liberal." All of these movements are subject to the fundamental criticisms of J. Gresham Machen in *Christianity and Liberalism* (Grand Rapids, Mich.: Eerdmans, 1956).

[5] The very earliest steps toward "reformation" in England, taken on orders from King Henry VIII, simply involved rebellion against the pope. Under King Edward VI and again under Queen Elizabeth I the English Reformation was strongly influenced by Reformed thinkers, including the exiles Peter Martyr Vermigli and John Łaski (or a Lasco). Later Anglicanism developed "Catholic" tendencies that have obscured its Reformed heritage, except among the evangelical Anglicans. The Low Church tradition includes both evangelical and liberal branches.

[6] Matthias Flacius Illyricus, *Clavis Scripturae sacrae.*

[7] Aegidius Hunnius, *Prima controversia generalis Roberti Bellarmini . . . examinata et refutata*, in Hunnius, *Opera Latina* (Frankfort on the Main: Porssius, 1606–9), II, 232.

[8] Although most modern conservative Protestants repudiate any "mechanical dictation" of Scripture, and affirm that in the process of inspiration, the Holy Spirit did not suppress the individuality of the human authors, orthodox Protestants frequently do use expressions such as "dictation" and "secretary." It is important to remember that ancient and medieval secretaries contributed more to the final version of their texts than do modern secretaries typing from a Dictaphone.

[9] Johann Gerhard, *Loci theologici* (Stuttgart: Cotta, 1610), II, 272.

[10] Jerome Zanchi, *De sacra Scriptura tractatus integer*, in *Opera theologica* (Geneva, 1619), VIII, 322f.

[11] Gerhard, *Loci theologici*, VI, 130b.

[12] Philipp Melanchthon, *Epistolae*, in *Corpus Reformatorum*, ed. Karl G. Bretschneider and Heinrich Bindell (Leipzig: M. Heinsius, 1834ff.), II, 33f. Cf. George H. Williams, *The Radical Reformation* (Philadelphia: Westminster Press, 1962), 272f.

[13] *Confessio Augustana*, in Philip Schaff, *The Creeds of Christendom with a History and Critical Notes*, 4th ed. (Grand Rapids, Mich.: Baker, 1966), III.

[14] In seventeenth-century usage, the expression "syncretism" does not refer to the mixing of religions but rather to interconfessional rapprochement.

[15] Otto Ritschl, *Dogmengeschichte*, I, 403.

[16] Calvin, *Institutes* 1.18.2; 2.4.3.

[17] Ibid. 1.13.5–6.

[18] *Westminster Confession* (1646), Article XXIX, Section VII.

[19] Ritschl, *Dogmengeschichte*, IV, 187.

[20] Johann Arndt, *De vero Christianismo libri 4* (Lüneburg: Stern, 1625).

Chapter XVIII

[1] Karl Barth, *Protestant Theology in the Nineteenth Century* (Valley Forge: Judson, 1973).

[2] Martin Chemnitz, *Loci theologici*, ed. P. Leyser (Frankfort and Wittenberg: Schumacher, 1653), 15. Cited in Otto Ritschl, *Dogmengeschichte des Protestantismus* (Leipzig: J. C. Hinrich, 1908–27), IV, 253.

[3] George Cassander, *De articulis religionis inter Catholicos et Protestantes . . .* , in Cassander, *Opera Omnia* (Paris: Drouart, 1616), 895.

[4] Kaspar Schoppe (Caspar or Gaspar Scioppius), *Consultatio de causis et modis* (Augsburg: Apergerus, 1631), fol. Es; Nicholas Hunnius, *Consultatio oder Wohlmeinendes Bedencken* (Lübeck, 1667), 306f.

[5] Polycarp Leyser, *Ob und warumb man lieber mit den Papisten . . .* Cited in Ritschl, *Dogmengeschichte*, IV, 251.

[6] Printed in Melchior Goldast, *Politische reichshandel; das ist allerhand gemeine acten . . .* (Frankfort: J. Bringern, 1614), 894ff.

[7] Balthasar Mentzer, *Wolgemeinte Erinnerung von der concione irenica oder Friedenspredigt . . .* (Giessen: Hampelius, 1619), 44f.

[8] Ritschl, *Dogmengeschichte*, IV, 259.

[9] George H. Williams, *The Radical Reformation* (Philadelphia: Westminster Press, 1962), 783f.

[10] Hugo Grotius, *Annotata ad consultationem Cassandri*, in his *Opera theologica* (Basel: E. and J. R. Thurnisius, 1732), IV, 615ff.

[11] Stephen Curcellaeus, *Opera Theologica* (Amsterdam: Elsevirius, 1675). Cited in Ritschl, *Dogmengeschichte*, IV, 285f.

[12] Balthasar Meisner, *Brevis consideratio theologiae Photinianae* (Wittenberg: Heyden, 1623), 635. Cited in Ritschl, *Dogmengeschichte*, IV, 303.

[13] Nicholas Hunnius, *Diaskepsis theologica de fundamentali dissensu doctrinae Evangelicae-Lutheranae et Calvinianae seu Reformatae* (Wittenberg: Helwigius, 1626).

[14] Andreas Sennert, *De articulis fidei fundamentalibus exercitatio theologica* (Wittenberg: J. Röhner, 1666), 17.

[15] In recent American Protestant history, those who insist on inerrancy are the "fundamentalists"; they stress a limited number of "fundamentals," one of which, the inerrancy of Scripture, is precisely the doctrine that logically ought to make everything the Bible asserts equally fundamental. In practice no one believes this or lives by it, but it is difficult to settle on a biblical principle for treating parts of the Bible as less fundamental than others.

[16] H. Schlüsser, George Calixt, Theologie und Kirchenpolitik. Eine Studie zur Ökumenizität des Luthertums (N.p., n.d.).

[17] Hans Leube, "Das Erbe Martin Luthers und die geganwartige theologische Forschung," in Robert Jelke, ed., Festschrift für D. Ludwig Ihmels (Leipzig: Dörffling & Franke, 1928), 140.

[18] Gottlieb Grossgebauer, Wächterstimme aus dem verwüsteten Zion (Frankfort on the Main, 1661).

[19] Karl Barth, Protestant Theology in the Nineteenth Century (Valley Forge: Judson, 1973). See also Francis A. Schaeffer, The Christian Manifesto (New York: Crossroads, 1982).

[20] Albrecht Ritschl, Geschichte des Pietismus (Bonn: A. Marcus, 1880–86), I.

[21] Kantzenbach, Friedrich Wilhelm, Orthdoxie und Pietismus (Gütersloh: Gütersloher Verlagshaus, 1966), 157.

[22] Valentin Ernst Löscher, Vollständiger Timotheus Verinus (N.p., 1718–22).

Chapter XIX

[1] Karl Barth, Protestant Theology in the Nineteenth Century (Valley Forge: Judson, 1973).

[2] Immanuel Kant, Was ist Aufklärung? (1784).

[3] Walter Nigg's Geschichte des religiösen Liberalismus. Entstehung—Blütezeit—Ausklang (Zurich and Leipzig: Niehan, 1937) is an excellent positive evaluation of liberalism.

[4] "A classic treatment on toleration is Wilbur Kitchener Jordan's The Development of Religious Toleration in England from the Convention of the Long Parliament to the Restoration. 1640–1660: the Revolutionary Experiments and Dominant Religious Thought (Cambridge: Harvard University Press, 1938).

[5] Alfred North Whitehead (1861–1947) is the most celebrated advocate of the view that natural science originated in Christian faith. Cf. esp. Stanley L. Jaki, The Road of Science and the Ways to God (Chicago: University of Chicago Press, 1978).

[6] Systematic Theology (Rochester: Andrews,1886), 8.

[7] Der christliche Glaube (Halle an der Saale: Hendel, 1921), 34.

[8] Geschichte der neueren evangelischen Theologie (Gütersloh: Mohn, 1949–54), V, 98.

Chapter XX

[1] Twentieth-century evangelicals have largely failed to emulate the social concern of their evangelical forebears. This failure has been given a name and excoriated by David O. Moberg in his critical appraisal, The Great Reversal: Evangelism and Social Concern (Philadelphia: Lippincott, 1977).

[2] C. F. W. Walther, Law and Gospel (St. Louis: Concordia, n.d.; originally published in German, Concordia, 1893).

[3] Karl Heussi, Kompendium der Kirchengeschichte (Tübingen: Mohr, 1960), par. 117h, 465.

[4] Friedrich Schleiermacher, "Second Letter to Lücke," in Werke zur Theologie, II, 614. Cited in Hirsch, Geschichte der evangelischen Theologie, II, 91.

[5] Gottfried Menken, "To the Bible," in Schriften (Bremen: Heyse, 1858), VII, 334.

[6] Hirsch, Geschichte, V, 98.

Chapter XXI

[1] The monumental work commemorating the Council of 451 is *Das Konzil von Chalkedon, Geschichte und Gegenwart,* ed. Alois Grillmeier and Heinrich Bacht, 3 vol. (Würzburg: Echter, 1951–54).

[2] Karl Barth, *Church Dogmatics,* ed. G. W. Bromiley and T. F. Torrance (Edinburgh: Clark, 1936–77), I/2, 126.

[3] Ibid., I/2, 138.

[4] Emil Brunner, *The Mediator,* trans. Olive Wyon (London: Lutterworth, 1934), 322–27.

[5] Karl Barth, *Protestant Theology in the Nineteenth Century* (Valley Forge, Judson, 1973).

[6] Rudolf Bultmann, "Das christologische Bekenntnis des Ökumenischen Rates," in *Evangelische Theologie* 11 (1951–52): 10.

[7] Ibid., 9.

[8] Rudolf Schnackenburg, "Der Abstand der christologischen Aussagen des Neuen Testaments vom chalkedonischen Bekenntnis nach der Deutung Rudolf Bultmanns," in *Das Konzil von Chalkedon,* III, 675–93.

[9] Pierre Teilhard de Chardin, *Le Phénomène humain* (Paris: Seuil, 1955), 327.

INDEX

Primary references are given in **boldface**; incidental references appear in brackets ( ).
Occurrences found in the footnotes are *italicized*.
The words *heresy* and *orthodoxy* have been indexed selectively.
Books or other writings are located under the authors' names.

469

Critical issues

Page 204, 367, 368